U0358499

福建历史文化外译丛书

总主编 葛桂录

岳峰 章琳 主编

Fuzhou's Cangshan District: Past and Present at the Crosspoint of China-Western Cultures

汉英双语

上册

文化仓山的前世今生

上海交通大学出版社
SHANGHAI JIAO TONG UNIVERSITY PRESS

图书在版编目（CIP）数据

　文化仓山的前世今生：上下册：汉、英/岳峰，
章琳主编. —上海：上海交通大学出版社，2025.1
（福建历史文化外译丛书/葛桂录总主编）. —ISBN
978 - 7 - 313 - 31617 - 2

　Ⅰ. K297.14

　中国国家版本馆 CIP 数据核字第 2024X58P31 号

文化仓山的前世今生（上下册）（汉英双语）
WENHUA CANGSHAN DE QIANSHI JINSHENG（SHANGXIA CE）（HANYING SHUANGYU）

主　　编：岳　峰　章　琳	
出版发行：上海交通大学出版社	地　　址：上海市番禺路 951 号
邮政编码：200030	电　　话：021 - 64071208
印　　制：上海文浩包装科技有限公司	经　　销：全国新华书店
开　　本：787mm×1092mm　1/16	印　　张：47.75
字　　数：1093 千字	
版　　次：2025 年 1 月第 1 版	印　　次：2025 年 1 月第 1 次印刷
书　　号：ISBN 978 - 7 - 313 - 31617 - 2	电子书号：ISBN 978 - 7 - 88941 - 683 - 2
定　　价（上下册）：368.00 元	

《文化仓山的前世今生》编委会

总 主 编：葛桂录

主　　编：岳　峰　章　琳

编 委 会：李亦仁　倪美飞　林鲁文　林金水
　　　　　戴显群　王绍祥　岳　峰　池志海

撰　　写：洪　梅　李巧兰　林丽玲　廖秋玲　赖黎群
　　　　　林　斌　陈　琳　黄丹青　李秀香　徐勤良
　　　　　陈榕烽

图片提供：池志海、各章主题机构与本书作者

中共福州市仓山区委宣传部策划

序

文化仓山：近现代中外文明互鉴的巨舰

葛桂录

福州西北环山，东南向海，闽江、乌龙江自西而东注入台湾海峡。闽江与乌龙江的离而复合形成了一座南北窄、东西长的岛屿，总面积 112.8 平方千米，曰南台岛，这是一座冲积而成的船舰型巨岛。两江南北夹持，旧时上游山民将木材谷物等顺流浮下，就囤积在水涘。因为盐仓聚集于此，仓前山的地名由此而来。仓，自然是闽货；山，应该就是这临江而仁的烟台山。偶然从市场的渔人口中得知，他们把闽江、乌龙江唤作大水。是的，这穿城而过的大水，赋予福州生生不息的脉动与心跳，感知世情潮汐的翻来覆去。

人称福州乃有福之州。福见山水，福在文化，尤其是福在素有"琼花玉岛"美誉之称的文化仓山。高空俯瞰，文化仓山所处的南台岛像一艘巨舰，承载着千年榕城的繁盛文脉，散发着百年中外文化交流互鉴的底蕴，气象斐然。这里曾涌现出"近代中国开眼看世界"的几位杰出人物：林则徐、严几道、陈季同、林琴南。林则徐主持编译《四洲志》，让中国人第一次了解了世界历史地理的信息，震动了中国知识界，原来天朝之外还有如此美妙的新世界。"精通西学第一人"的严复，提出"信达雅"的翻译理念，翻译《天演论》等诸多西方学术名著，成为近代中国开启民智的一代宗师。马尾船政学堂毕业生陈季同，在中国首次提出"世界文学"观念，他在法国巴黎高等师范学校的演讲，让罗曼·罗兰激赏，极大地塑造了欧洲人心目中的中国正面形象。林纾翻译的 150多部外国文学作品，最早让中国人知道了一批世界著名文学家，改变了现代中国文学的版图。"林译小说"作为一种文化符号，是中国人开眼看世界的窗口。这些引领近代中国走向世界的先驱，一百多年以前，就生活在我们的周围，或者说我们有幸踏进了他们的历史烟尘之中。尤其是烟台山历史文化风貌区作为福州最早中西交汇、文化交融的开放窗口，曾经见证了近代中外文明碰撞的初期场景，留下了丰富的历史遗韵与人文底蕴。一百多年之前，域外世界文明已经来到了福州仓山。

仓山文化在福州本土文化中独树一帜，带有典型的异域文化特质，这点与官宦云集的鼓楼区和商贾文化突出的台江区大有不同。穿行于老仓山的寻常巷陌，随处可见欧式花园洋房，造型各异的医院、学校和教堂，新奇气派的西餐馆与电影院，甚至还有国内少见的跑马场。有着两千多年悠久历史的福州恰恰在相对偏远的南台岛上呈现出完全不一样的欧美风情。中国传统文化的熏陶、淳朴民风的沐浴、当地原有的海洋文化与名人文化的渗透，再加上欧美文化的浸润，可谓是古之源融聚今之流，形成"有福之州"独特的文化景观，彰显出了不同的气质与风貌。

在近现代中外文化交往史上，中西医结合、中外教育相融、中外宗教信仰交汇、中外出版互通，构成其文化交互影响的四大板块，成就了中外文化相处与文明互鉴之道，也铸就了文化仓山的前世今生。

本书充分运用耶鲁大学所藏关于近代福州文化仓山的第一手档案资料，在福建地方文化史专家的指导下，撰成一部完整体现近现代中西文化交汇中的仓山文化地图。从塔亭医院到福州市第二医院、从马高爱医院到福建医科大学附属协和医院的前世今生，可见在晚清民国时期西学人文启蒙新流的背景下，开辟了仓山近代医疗卫生空间，引发中西医大辩论，最后达成中西汇通的思想，形成传统中医与现代医学双峰对峙的局面。从毓英女校到福州第十六中学、从三一学校到福州外国语学校、从英华学校到福建师大附中、从私立华南女子文理学院到福建华南女子职业技术学院、从福建协和大学到福建师范大学，从仓山地区各级各类学校的前世今生，可见中西文化教育交流的行行足迹，某种程度上激发且促进了西学东渐，进而引发中西文化的多维度多层面碰撞。从福音精舍到福建神学院的前世今生，可见牧师们面对现实，采用文化协商和调适策略，入乡随俗，穿戴当地服装，学习研究福州方言，甚至还能达到和本地人流利对话的程度。仓山出版业同样不可忽视。福州曾是中国南方重要的寺院刻书中心，延续这样的文化传统，加之近代以来巨大的出版需求以及传教士们带来的世界上较先进的出版技术和理念，促进仓山成为福建近代出版业的发源地，进而改变了福州甚至中国的社会历史面貌：识字群体的扩大，西方科学与技术的引入，革命思想的传播，无不受益于出版业的发展。由上可见，作为中外文化多维碰撞的荟萃之地，文化仓山的前世今生承载着多少梦想与希望。

走进一座城市，延续它的城市记忆，体验它所蕴涵的历史文化的深度。踏入一片区域，展现它的时代潮流，感受它所飘荡的潮范与烟火气。作为福州城市新地标的"闽江之心"，就是历史文化风貌与现代都市时尚的交响，更是文化仓山今生新的绽放。特别是重新焕发生机的烟台山历史文化街区，那么多充满温情的故事，唤醒着蒙尘的历史记忆：宁静的巷弄或街角，看似平凡的日常风景，却隐藏许多创意、设计、美学的生活元素，呈示出烟台山新旧交融的人文风情，让人徜徉其中而心旷神怡，如同面对丰盛的审美飨宴，也随时随地触发对过往岁月的遐思。那些富于艺术感的巧心思扮靓历史的容颜，搭建汇通当下与往昔的精神津梁，引领着文化仓山的光明未来。

Preface

Fuzhou's Cangshan District:
A Hub of Cultural Exchanges Since the Mid-1800s

GE Guilu

Fuzhou, conventional Foochow, cradled by mountains in the northwest and embraced by the sea in the southeast, is traversed by the Minjiang River coursing eastward before merging into the Taiwan Strait. The Minjiang River, together with its branch, the Wulong River, has deposited sediments over time, giving rise to Nantai Island—a 112. 8-square-kilometer ship-shaped landmass, which is currently known as Cangshan. The term "Cang" symbolizes storage, while "Shan" refers to Yantai Mountain standing alongside the river. In ancient times, mountain dwellers would float timber and grains downstream, storing them by the river. Over time, the government established salt storage at Yantai Mountain, contributing to the name Cangshan. For thousands of years, Cangshan has been nurtured by the two "Great Waters" as the local fishermen call the Minjiang River and the Wulong River. They serve as the very cradle of the city and allow us to perceive the ebb and flow of history.

Fuzhou is also aptly named the "city of blessings" in Chinese. It is truly blessed with not only natural beauty but also cultural profundity, with Cangshan standing out as an embodiment of its rich cultural heritage. Throughout its history, Fuzhou has cultivated eminent figures like Lin Zexu(1785 – 1850), Yan Fu(1854 – 1921), Chen Jitong(1851 – 1907), and Lin Shu(1852 – 1924), who played pivotal roles in enlightening modern China. Lin Zexu oversaw the compilation and translation of Hugh Murray's *An Encyclopedia of Geography* (1834) into *Si zhou zhi*, providing the Chinese people with their initial glimpse into world history and geography. Yan Fu, acclaimed as a "trailblazer of Western learning", introduced the tripartite translation principles of "faithfulness, expressiveness, and elegance", and translated a number of Western academic classics, including *Evolution and Ethics* (1893) by T. H. Huxley. Chen Jitong, a graduate of the Mawei Naval Academy (Fuzhou), pioneered the concept of "world literature" in China. His speech at École Normale Supérieure in Paris greatly impressed Romain Rolland (1866 – 1944), contributing to a positive image of China in the international arena. Lin Shu expanded the horizons of Chinese readers and revolutionized modern Chinese literature by translating over 150 world-renowned foreign literary works. All these pioneers just lived, about a century ago, in the very places we now call home; we are fortunate to walk into their historical footsteps. In this context, Yantai Mountain in Cangshan, holds a special place in history as it encapsulates the early encounters with foreign civilizations that profoundly shaped the cultural landscape of Fuzhou.

In contrast to the official-gathering Gulou District and the merchant-driven Taijiang District, Cangshan District exudes a distinct air of exoticism. A leisurely stroll down the streets in Cangshan will unveils a diverse array of European-style houses, hospitals, schools, and churches. Trendy restaurants, cinemas, and even a rare sight in China—a racecourse—can also be found. This spectacle is the outcome of the fusion of traditional Chinese culture with local customs, the influence of celebrities, maritime culture and Western elements.

In cultural exchanges between China and the West during modern times, four major areas take center stage: medicine, education, religious beliefs, and publications. Together, they exemplify the reciprocal learning that occurs between diverse cultures. Cangshan, in this regard, contributes to this narrative.

Based on Yale University archives and insights from local cultural historians, this book offers an overview of Cangshan's cultural landscape, highlighting the impact of cultural fusion during modern times. The evolution of medical care during the Late Qing Period and the convergence of Chinese and Western medicine can be observed through the transformation of institutions, such as the former Takding Hospital, now known as Fuzhou Second Hospital, and the former Magaw Memorial Hospital, which has become the present Fujian Medical University Union Hospital together with the former Foochow Missionary Hospital. By examining a range of educational institutions, such as the former girls' boarding school Uk Ing, now known as Fuzhou No. 16 Junior High School, the former Trinity College Foochow, which is currently Fuzhou Foreign Languages School, the former Anglo-Chinese College, now the Affiliated High School of Fujian Normal University, and the former Hwa Nan High School, currently Fujian Hwa Nan Women's Voc-Tech College, along with the transformation of Fujian Christian University into Fujian Normal University, we gain insights into how the Chinese educational system encountered, clashed, and incorporated Western educational ideologies. The case of the former Gospel Hall and the present Fujian Theological Seminary exemplifies how pastors adapted to local culture by embracing Chinese traditional attire and learning the Fuzhou dialect. Furthermore, the publishing industry deserves equal attention. Inheriting from Fuzhou's temple publishing legacy, Cangshan emerged as Fujian's publishing hub, fueled by increasing demand and advanced techniques brought by missionaries. This thriving industry facilitated expanded literacy, the introduction of Western science and technology, and the dissemination of revolutionary ideas. Ultimately, Cangshan symbolizes the aspirations that emerge from the intersection of Chinese and foreign cultures, making it a captivating case study of cultural fusion and development.

To grasp the essence of a city, one must delve into its ancient roots, immerse in its vibrant present, and witness the unfolding of its ever-evolving tapestry. Like a celestial bridge spanning time, the restored Yantai Mountain Historical and Cultural District beckons, bridging the past and present, paving the way for a future where cultural exchanges bloom in full splendor.

目　录

CONTENTS

CHAPTER
ONE

从塔亭医院到福州市第二医院①

From Takding Hospital to Fuzhou Second Hospital

第一章 福

---

① 本章图片除标注来源的以外，均由福州市第二医院提供。

千年榕城，百年仓山。作为福州近代最早接触西方文化的地块，仓山承载了百年前开放通商的浮浮沉沉，一如烟台山上蜿蜒曲径的巷道，耐人寻味。在游人如织的打卡点，和斑驳建筑打个招呼，在石厝银杏树前留个影，或是驻足凝神感受展馆里浓郁的人文气息，一个世纪前的"西风东渐"即刻生动再现，如 VR 在手，令人难以忘怀。

在仓山还有一种更让人难以割舍的风景：透过今生看前世。这类风景历史厚重，却不显山露水；历尽沧桑，仍紧跟时代步伐；改颜换貌，亦能坚守初心。位于仓山区上藤路上有着百年历史的福州市第二医院①就隐藏着这样一道独特风景。这家现代三甲市级医院的前身——塔亭医院，给当时陷于困顿的人们带来了崭新的诊疗体验和知识空间，成为晚清民国时期中国社会人文启蒙的一个缩影。如今，史海钩沉，我们探寻其如烟往事，往者不可谏，来者尤可追。

∷ 福州市第二医院
∷ Fuzhou Second Hospital

---

① 福州市第二医院：2023 年 6 月 19 日，由福州市第二医院牵头，整合福州神经精神病防治院、福州市妇幼保健院，成立"一院三区"的福州市第二总医院。本章讲述福州市第二医院历史。

Cangshan, a district in the south of Fuzhou, is much better known for its once standing at the forefront of the earliest encounter with Western civilizations that were thrust upon a city of more than two thousand years in the 1840s. Its century-old panorama of being opened up as a district in one of the first treaty ports is a trajectory no less winding than the paths in Yantai Mountain where today's tourists swarm to have a VR experience, as it were, in various restored scenic spots: a "Hello" to ancient buildings, a snapshot of the storied ginko tree before St. John's Church, or a gaze from the attentive listener in exhibition halls, and these are visits impressive enough to bring back those old days when the East met the West more than a century ago.

Yet an even more inviting landscape that should never be missed in Cangshan District is the richness of its past that has long been buried in some of its present institutions. Despite a history long enough to declare itself as a past glory, each of these organizations projects itself more as a new development that keeps up with the times; their ups and downs in history have left traces of change on their modern look, yet the unchanged melody is the original commitment they have delivered in constant flux. Fuzhou Second Hospital[1], a Grade-A medical establishment located at Shangteng Road, is such a time-honored place worthy of a historical exploration, as its predecessor, Takding Hospital, once a new public place that brought different clinical experiences and knowledge of Western medicine to people who were stuck in tight corners, was arguably recognized as the epitome of social enlightenment that took place in the late Qing Dynasty and the Republic of China. Now a dip into its history is a chance to have its old stories unfurl before us with the hope that the continuity of history is always under our care.

福州市第二医院前身：塔亭医院（20 世纪 50 年代初）（来源：池志海）
The predecessor of Fuzhou Second Hospital: Takding Hospital in the early 1950s (Source: Chi Zhihai)

---

[1] Fuzhou Second Hospital took the initiative and the lead to merge the other two hospitals—Fuzhou Psychiatric Hospital and Fuzhou Maternal and Child Health Hospital—to form Fuzhou Second General Hospital on June 19, 2023. This chapter concerns the history of Fuzhou Second Hospital.

历史沿革

叙事塔亭路

　　福州市第二医院位于上藤路 47 号，是仓山区市属公立医院，也是省内唯一一家中西医结合三甲医院，更是福建地区骨科最有名的医院，每天来此寻医问药者不计其数。但是人们或许并不知道眼前这个地方已历经百多年风云，其前世是当地人津津乐道的"第一西医院——塔亭医院"。

　　之所以叫塔亭医院，很可能与塔亭路有关。旧时烟台山亦称藤山，这座小山的坡道富有诗意，弯弯曲曲，忽陡忽平，一不留神曲径通幽处又豁然开朗，驻足细品，道上满满的历史意境。塔亭路所在区域旧时亦称时升里，是垂直于主干道上藤路上的一条小道，西向与麦园路和梅坞路相通，东向直通塔亭医院。民国时期，烟台山的主要街道下渡街被改为上藤路、中藤路、下藤路（孟丰敏，2016：265），当时医院所在位置是中藤路 29 号。现在的上藤路范围应该与从前有所不同。对于晚清时期的洋人来说，往返于中洲岛和烟台山的路与位于梅坞路顶的塔亭路，近在咫尺。

．医院西大门处门坊基部的浮雕是当年延寿塔浮
．雕围栏。（2022）
．Stone reliefs once circling the foundation of the
．Longevity Pagoda now set in the memorial
．gateway at the West Gate of the Hospital.
．(2022)

　　关于塔亭路的由来，没有确切记载，不过，据民国时期出版的《藤山志》所记："塔亭，在延寿塔旁，为远行者休憩之所，今则亭废而名仍存"。而从《雁峰延寿塔序》"藤山雁峰之耸一塔，挺然立于顺懿庙前，相传为唐末陈三娘所造……"的记载来看，雁峰即指梅坞顶到上藤路之间的小山包，塔亭路因此也称雁塔境。当年，孝女陈三娘为双亲益寿延年，建造了"延寿塔"，原塔七层，呈八角形，塔旁有"延寿亭"，供人休息。一塔一亭，简称"塔亭"。民国十四年（1925 年）因道路修建拆移该塔。据说移塔时，人们发现塔里有千余枚古币，其中有隋唐宋时期的铜币。"文革"时期，该塔再遭损毁，仅留存两层。后人曾在今娘奶庙（即顺懿庙）斜对面的小吃店里发现几块延寿塔的浮雕围栏。如今这几块朴实古雅的石雕静静地嵌在医院西大门入口处的牌坊基部，任凭人们感叹岁月蹉跎。

● Trace of History

Tating Road

Located at No. 47 Shangteng Road is a medical institution that has enjoyed a good name in its different historical times: Fuzhou Second Hospital. Now a municipal public hospital in Cangshan District and the only certified Grade-A hospital in Fujian Province to have traditional Chinese medicine (TCM) and Western medicine well integrated into its clinical practice, the hospital is best-known for its orthopedics treatment that brings relief to numerous patients each day, but visitors coming here for medical care may not be aware of the past fame this century-old place once had—it was locally reputed as the first Western hospital, also named as Takding Hospital.

Takding Hospital was most likely named after Tating Road, a path among many in Yantai Mountain, then known as Tengshan, where visitors today take delights in aesthetic discoveries when up or down the hilly lanes that sometimes lead to a hidden view or a sudden reminder of history. Standing vertically across Shangteng Road, Tating Road runs eastward from the intersection of Maiyuan Road and Meiwu Road in the west down through into the hospital. The main road in Tating block (or known as Shishengli in the old documents) was Xiadu (or Foochow Romanized A Do) Street, which was divided into three sections in the upper, middle and lower areas respectively named as Shangteng Road, Zhongteng Road and Xiateng Road in the period of the Republic of China. No. 29 Zhongteng Road, for example, was the address of the hospital at that time, and this discrepancy from today's address tells the passage of time. For foreigners who arrived in the late Qing Dynasty, Tating Road was easily accessible when they traveled between Zhongzhou Island and Yantai Mountain.

There is no definite record of the origin of Tating (Foochow Romanized "Takding") Road, but evidence shows that "Takding" comes from a pagoda ("ta") and a pavilion ("ting") built around long ago. According to *Tengshan Annals* published in the Republic of China, "Takding Pavilion, erected close to the Longevity Pagoda as a place of rest for travelers, no longer exists but its name remains. " Another document about the Longevity Pagoda suggests that the Pagoda standing before a temple on Yanfeng—the hillock between the hilltop of Meiwu Road and Shangteng Road— was constructed by Lady the Third, or *chensanniang*, in the late Tang Dynasty to wish her parents long life. Indeed, some copper coins from the Sui and Tang dynasties together with thousands of other ancient coins were discovered in the pagoda when it had to be displaced to the roadside for the road construction in 1925. This seven-story octagonal pagoda was unfortunately destroyed with only two floors left during the Cultural Revolution. Nobody knows when exactly the pagoda vanished from the area, but some of its exquisite ornamental stone relief fence that was once around the foundation was found in recent years in a local restaurant close to the temple. Now these stone reliefs are perfectly set into the base of the memorial gateway in the West Gate of the hospital, drawing passers-by to stand and stare.

医院西大门处，正对着的就是当年和延寿塔紧挨着的顺懿庙，即塔亭临水陈太后祖庙，庙里供奉着备受福州当地人尊崇的妇幼保护神——临水夫人陈靖姑。传说唐朝时期出生于下渡的陈靖姑修得道家闾山正法，为民施法祈雨，脱胎殉身，死后升仙显灵，成为保胎佑童女神。仓山地区古时水灾瘟疫不断，祖庙自然寄托了民众驱邪避瘟的心愿。民国时期，该庙曾作为救火会场所，当时救火会多以寺庙为会址。如今，祖庙里信众不断，延寿塔却踪迹难觅。不过，一塔一亭一庙，寄托着人们美好的祈愿，世代传承，早已成为塔亭叙事的魅力要素。

100 多年前，这片巷弄又如磁石一般吸引着福州开埠后的各种新元素。这里曾经金融气息浓郁，是有名的银行街，有 1867 年首家在福州设立分行的外资银行——汇丰银行，还有演绎旧时钱庄与现代银行纠葛的台湾银行。这里毗邻本地人开在梅坞顶、人气十足的福州第一家西餐厅——快活林，还有大胆创新、顺应时代、走国际路线的兰记脱胎漆器店。1866 年，英国圣公会在这里建起了基督教明道堂；1887 年，一家西式医院也迁到这里，取名塔亭医院。伴随着传教意图，塔亭医院也带来了近代西方医学知识。当地人益寿延年之求，妇孺卫生健康之愿，从此多了具体实在的科学护佑。

塔亭路和上藤路（2022）
View of Tating Road and Shangteng Road（2022）

医院西门（曾经的正门）与陈太后祖庙相对（2022）
The West Gate, once the main entrance of the hospital, opposite Ancestral Temple of Tating Linshui Empress Chen（2022）

Opposite the West Gate stands Ancestral Temple of Tating Linshui Empress Chen, also known as Shunyi Temple, dedicated to Chen Jinggu (or Lady Linshui meaning Lady at the Water's Edge) who was born in Xiadu in the Tang Dynasty and said to use Daoist power she learned from the Lüshan School to help people in need, and in one attempt to sacrifice herself and her fetus to pray for rain for the local people. The temple was built in memory of her who was believed to become an even more powerful deity after her death to protect women and children. Plagued by endless floods and pestilence in the old days, local people also went to this temple to seek comfort and make wishes; in the Republic of China, it served as a station of local fire brigade, rendering locals physical protection of life and property. Today the temple stands not just as a place for worship goers, but a cultural reminder of the special landscape comprised of a pagoda, a pavilion and a temple that has, for generations, long expressed people's lifelong quest for blessings and thus has become part and parcel of Takding narrative with its enduring charm.

Narrow and short as it looks today, Tating Road was a magnet attracting new elements that came along with the opening of Fuzhou as a treaty port more than a century ago. Nicknamed as "Street of Banks", it had HSBC, the first foreign bank in Fuzhou that opened its branch here in 1867, and Bank of Taiwan Ltd., a modern bank that had special relationships with the old-style local bank called *qianzhuang*. At its west end connecting Meiwu Road was the first Western restaurant in Fuzhou, which was popular and known as *kuaihuolin,* or Happy Woods as its Chinese name suggests. And another renowned local company, Lang Kee Bodiless Lacquerware, was also located here to internationalize its products. In 1866, the Church of England had its church, Mingdao Church (the Anglican Church) established here. In 1887, Takding Hospital, the forerunner of Western hospitals in Fuzhou, began its medical services here—although with missionary intention, it turned out to be an additional protective force, thanks to the modern medical knowledge it introduced, to meet, in a more concrete and scientific way, people's wish for longevity, and health care for women and children in particular.

塔亭路上的明道堂(2022)
Mingdao Church (the Anglican Church) at Tating Road (2022)

塔亭路靠近上藤路的部分(2022)
Tating Road close to Shangteng Road (2022)

医院名称由来

历史上，围绕着塔亭医院出现过不少名字，但随着时光流逝，这些名字及其背后的故事多已湮没在岁月长河中。据院史记载，塔亭医院最早可追溯到 1848 年，当时英国皇家海军和英国领事馆在南台中洲岛联合筹办医院，为外籍侨民和英国军人服务。1842 年，福州成为五口通商口岸之一，后来烟台山所在区域划定为外国人居住区，而中洲岛附近有许多泊船码头，故名"海港医院"。当时外国侨民并不多。由于外国人不受欢迎，第一任英国驻福州领事只好姗姗来迟，1844 年抵榕时，他只身一人。至 1847 年，仅 7 个外国人到过福州，大部分是领事馆的工作人员，且更换频繁。三年后，人数增至 10 人，多为传教士（廖乐柏，2010：153）。1851 年年底，传教士及家属总计 27 名，不过这个数字容易让人误解，实际情况是，到 1853 年，近一半病故或离榕，仅剩 15 人（Carlson，1974：11）。

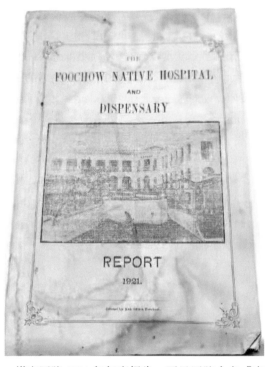

塔亭医院 1921 年年度报告，可见医院全名〔来源：上海医药博物馆（集团）〕
The official name, Foochow Native Hospital and Dispensary, clearly seen on the cover the 1921 Medical Report〔Source: Shanghai Pharmaceutical Museum（Group）〕

初来乍到，水土不服、环境差异，加上卫生状况恶劣，引发了外侨一系列身体不适。数据表明，其中 1850 年外侨社区死亡率特别高。当年传教士们与千里之外家人的往来书信中，有的详细记载着令人唏嘘的最后时日，有人感叹"传教士们被逼向永恒之地"，丧偶的传教士甚至写信请求教会支援，生死问题困扰着留守的传教士，为西侨民提供医疗服务遂为必要之举。不过这种考虑最终一直到 1861 年闽海关新关的成立，才在海关医务官一职上得以正式兑现。这样看来，1848 年的海港医院就显得弥足珍贵了。

当年海港医院的具体位置和建筑形态已无法考证，但可以想见，这是一家规模十分有限的混合临床诊所。1853 年福州茶道开通，福州一跃成为世界有名的贸易港，随着贸易量加大，外籍人数持续增加。到 1857 年，福州侨民达到 57 人，仅次于上海、广州，名列第三，因此为外侨诊疗的压力也随之增加。与此同时，福州城内和郊区已出现若干教会医院和药房。如 1850 年，大英教会下属安立甘会（以下统称圣公会）首先开启福州城的西医诊所服务，之后，美部会创办"圣教医院"等。虽然教会诊所主要面向中国人，但外侨的健康保障显然多了选择。

Different Names

Stories about how Takding Hospital got its different names in history must be interesting, especially when exact records of such account are scarce. According to the Hospital's archives, Takding Hospital dates back to 1848 when the British Royal Navy and the British Consulate jointly ran a hospital named Port Hospital at Zhongzhou Island for foreigners and the British army men that resided in Fuzhou. Yet before 1848, there did not seem to be enough foreigners to necessitate a hospital. For example, no foreign officers came when Fuzhou was announced to be a treaty port in 1842 and later Yantai Mountain was designated as foreigners' living area, and it was not until 1844 that the first British Consul arrived, alone. Up to 1847, seven foreigners had ever been to Fuzhou, most of whom were staff of the Consulate in high turnover. Three years later, there were ten foreigners and most were missionaries. By the end of 1851, twenty-seven missionaries and their families were here, but that could be quite a misleading figure, because in 1853 only fifteen remained in Fuzhou with the rest dead or leaving.

Maladaptation to local conditions and terrible hygiene problems caused new comers' physical disorders and statistics showed that the death rate in the Foreign Community in 1850 was particularly high. Some missionaries' correspondence with their families from afar recorded their last saddening days; some lamented about missionaries being driven to eternity and some widowed missionaries even wrote letters to the church to request for a wife. Troubled by the matter of life and death, foreigners felt it a must to have a hospital, but this consideration was not officially finalized until 1861 when the New Customs was established and had its medical officers to take on the health care of foreigners. Port Hospital that was open in 1848 was, therefore, quite significant.

Important as it was, Port Hospital, with no document left to tell its exact location and architectural style, was assumed to be a clinical dispensary too small to meet the demand of the growing Foreign Community as the result of the prosperous foreign trade since Fuzhou opened its tea route in 1853 and became a world-famous trading port. Foreigners in 1857, for example, increased to fifty-seven just behind Shanghai and Guangzhou and the Hospital had, ever since then, been put under extra pressure. Fortunately, there appeared at the same time a few missionary hospitals and dispensaries that began their medical services targeting local people in the city and on the suburbs, the first of which within the city was a Western dispensary run by the Church Missionary Society (CMS) in 1850 and later another by American Board. These medical places became an alternative to foreigners' health care.

同当时通商口岸时期各家洋行一样，医院作为机构也有中英文两个名称。此时，这家医院出现在外国公司名录上的英文名是 Foochow Native Hospital and Dispensary，这种机构的正式名称主要用于正式文件，如《1921 年医院年度报告》。有趣的是，塔亭医院这一英文起名和大多数同时期西方教会医院名称有所不同。当时不少教会医院使用 Memorial 字样，以纪念人或事件。如差不多同时期设在仓山的马高爱医院，英文名为 Magaw Memorial Hospital，据说是为了纪念医院捐资者——巴尔的摩一位女信徒。又如南平市第一医院前身口士吡哩医院的英文名 Alden Speare Memorial Hospital，也是纪念捐款人。不过，后人回顾塔亭医院历史时，也可细细感受下"本地医馆"一词呈现的精妙预见性：扎根本土，惠及当地，前世今生，不离不弃。

当然，当时人们看不到历史演化进程中"本地"一词的风情，塔亭医院的英文名在当时看来，似乎显得太过冗长且毫无特色，因此常常被人忽略。在当年外国传教士的回忆录中，塔亭医院更多被称作"社团医院"，这一称呼既体现了西侨民的归属感，也揭示了塔亭医院主要财政来源之一：福州西侨社团。在一篇题为《在榕幸福日》的文章中，作者写道："会议已经结束，她们将奔赴全省各地；伊达将留在福州的社团医院……"1904 年商行名录显示，伊达正是塔亭医院（即福州地方医院及医馆）的护士。而在《胡氏姐妹》中的一张手绘福州地图上，塔亭医院的位置上清楚地写着"社团医院"。

按照塔亭医院的正式英文名，译成"福州地方医馆及药房"并无不妥，但无论当地人还是外国人，都对"塔亭"一词情有独钟。医院在 1952 年由福州市总工会接办时曾改名为"福州市工人医院"，后由福州市人民政府接办，于 1954 年改为"福州市立第二医院"，1956 年又正式改为"福州市第二医院"。改名前，医院正门上显示的正是中文名"塔亭医院"，而最早的塔亭大楼的立面高处则写着"闽省塔亭医院"。这些称呼似乎反映了当地人的塔亭情结，或许也表达了外国人入乡随俗的态度，当然也不失为文化差异自我和解的表白。正如当年大名鼎鼎的怡和洋行，耳熟能详的正是"怡和"，粤语发音，与中文相似，其英文名 Jardine，Matheson & Co.，Ltd 反倒让人有距离感。根据"塔亭"的中文发音，英文文献可见"Tak Ding"和"Tah Ding"两种拼写。如一篇 1939 年发表在华南女院新闻摘要的校友部分的新闻，提到印尼爪哇校友为缓解福州地区当时的痢疾疫情捐赠奎宁时写道："……给华南女院的 8 000 片药片已寄出，同样数量的奎宁送给福州协和医院和由安立甘会开在福州的塔亭医院。"

塔亭医院于 1951 年由私立医院改为公立医院——福州工人医院剪彩仪式

The ribbon cutting ceremony on the occasion of Takding Hospital being transformed from a private to a public medical institution named Fuzhou Workers Hospital in 1951

Like most foreign companies in the period of treaty ports, the hospital also had both Chinese and English names. Its English name Foochow Native Hospital and Dispensary easily found in the Directory of Hong List was normally used in official documents such as the *1921 Medical Report*. Interestingly, the English name of the hospital had no "Memorial" included as most missionary hospitals did. Another hospital in Cangshan in the same period, for example, was named Magaw Memorial Hospital to memorize a female benefactor in Baltimore. So was Alden Speare Memorial Hospital, now Nanping First Hospital. What its English name did include, however, when viewed in hindsight, was some visionary element in "native hospital", words that seem magical enough to play fortunetelling games about the hospital's longstanding commitment to the local residents, foreign or native.

Legacy as such, of course, should be taken as the result of historical development and therefore was unlikely to be understood at that time. In effect, this English name appeared too long and characterless to be preferred. The hospital was, in some memoirs by foreign missionaries, often referred to, as a "community hospital", a better name to suggest foreign patients' sense of belonging to, and an important financial source from, the Foreign Community. One article titled *Happy Days in Foochow* reads "... the meeting is over and they are heading for different areas of the province; Ida is to stay at the community hospital, ..." Ida turned out to be the nurse of this hospital in the 1904 Hong List. Likewise, in a handmade map in the book *the Woolf Sisters*, the hospital site was marked precisely as "Community Hospital".

The hospital's Chinese name could have been anything from the literal translation of its official English name, but people, be a native or a foreigner, used to favor "Takding Hospital". The Chinese characters of "Takding Hospital" remained at the hospital entrance before the hospital was renamed Fuzhou Workers Hospital when Fuzhou Municipal General Trade Union took it over in 1952, and later when under Fuzhou Municipal Government it was renamed Fuzhou Second Municipal Hospital and again Fuzhou Second Hospital respectively in 1954 and 1956. In some old photos, its Chinese name suggesting Fujian Provincial Takding Hospital was conspicuous high on façade of the central building. Possibly inspired by the particular Takding complex, the name "Takding Hospital" was a successful adaptation to the local customs and a good example of reconciliation in cultural differences. This is also true of Jardine, Matheson & Co., Ltd, a foreign company much better known as Ewo, the Cantonese pronunciation of its Chinese name "*yihe*". Based on its Chinese sound, "Takding" was found in historical documents to have two spellings: "Tak Ding" and "Tah Ding". One periodical publication in 1939 about the news in Hwa Nan College, for example, recording the quinine sent from its alumnae in Java to the college to ease the prevalence of malaria in Foochow reads: "...8,000 tablets are on their way for Hwa Nan, and like quantities also as their gift to Foochow Christian Union Hospital and Tah Ding, the Anglican Hospital in Foochow."

虽然我们无法得知当时西方人因何采纳了"塔亭"一词，但用"亭"来指医院，却是西方人所理解和欣赏的。"亭"者，停也，人所集也，在中国汉字中可以指凉亭，是供人们户外休息用的建筑物。颇为有趣的是，英文中"pavilion"经常用来指医院的建筑，当年传教士建的福州保福山医院（今吉祥山）的手术楼正面外墙依稀可见 E. Y. Smith Operating Pavilion 字样。事实上，"pavilion"是 19—20 世纪英美医院主要建筑风格的用词。这一称为"亭式布局"的建筑源于 18 世纪的法国，与当时流行病病因学如瘴气理论相适应，主要通过合理空间分配和隔离，改善医院内部环境，特别是通风状况，有效降低病人死亡率。英国护士南丁格尔是这一建筑方案的先行者，在她的成功实践和推动下，19 世纪中叶英国医院开始引入"亭式病房区"，即一定容量的病房区建筑上各自独立。这种医院建筑模式很快流行起来，直到 20 世纪。1886 年当位于中洲岛的西式医馆遭遇火灾，考虑搬迁新址时，几位有着医学背景的英国人是否在此处一塔一亭的风情中，看到了心中医院的理想之地？通风、和谐、延年益寿、健康福祉，就这样在中国的凉亭和西方的医院之间碰撞共鸣。

医院肇始与性质

1866 年，这是目前比较统一的塔亭医院起始年代。由于"海港医院"许多重要情况已无考，称其为肇始颇有牵强之嫌。从医院创办缘起和宗旨来看，海港医院的服务范围和对象十分有限，与后来的塔亭医院有着明显区别。根据市二医院档案，创办于 1866 年的塔亭医院的创办宗旨有如下表述："英国侨民为求利便外侨及其雇佣人员的疾病治疗，并利及当地人民的西法医治的需要，方捐资创办本院，以便利中外人士求得西法治病为宗旨。"这与塔亭医院后来的行医实践吻合。虽然不能排除海港医院为当地人提供医疗便利的可能，但从承办方、人员、规模等方面考量，为当地人服务不符合海港医院应有之义。事实上，旨在使当地人皈依基督教的医务传教，19 世纪 50 年代前 6 年经温敦成功实践后，一度归于沉寂，一直到 19 世纪 70 年代才又开启新局，因此海港医院与医务传教没有天然联系。

Although the specific reason why foreigners adopted "Takding" was unknown, the association of a pavilion with a hospital was something they could well appreciate. A "pavilion" in Chinese is a stop where people gather, or rather, an outdoor roofed structure for rest. In English, "pavilion" is often used to mean hospital buildings. For example, one building in Foochow Ponasang Hospital (around today's Jixiangshan Hill) built by missionaries was named E. Y. Smith Operating Pavilion. Indeed, "pavilion" was a key term in the 19th and 20th centuries to indicate the construction style of British and American hospitals, most of which followed a "pavilion plan" that originated in France in the 18th century as the result of the popular miasmic theory. The plan, strongly advocated and practiced by the British nurse Florence Nightingale, came into style from the mid-19th century to the 20th century because of its proper partition and separation and the improved ventilation within the hospital that effectively reduced the death rate. In 1886 when Foochow Native Hospital needed a new site after it was burned down in a fire at Zhongzhou Island, did foreigners with medical background happen to find at Tating Road such a suitable place where a pagoda and a pavilion stood to bring ventilation, peace, longevity and well-being, something a western hospital was looking for?

Inception and Nature

The beginning year of the hospital that has so far been agreed upon was 1866. The history of its alleged predecessor, Port Hospital, is often mentioned but not officially included simply because of the lack of strong evidence of documents, for that matter. Given the initial goal, Port Hospital must have offered services, probably in most cases, exclusive to foreigners, which was different from Takding Hospital. According to the archives in the Hospital, Takding Hospital, financed by the Foreign Community, was established in 1866 " to facilitate the medical services for foreign residents and the employees they hired, and also to meet the local demand of Western medicine", which proved to be in agreement with its actual practice. Service from Port Hospital to local people was not impossible, but it should never be assumed as its business considering the original aim and its capacity in staff and facilities. Indeed, medical services dedicated to converting the locals were under missionaries' charge, and evidence shows that after Welton's successful medical attempts in the first six years of the 1850s, missionary medical activities faded to silence until the 1870s, suggesting that Port Hospital had no root in missionary service.

不仅如此，原承办方英国皇家海军和英国领事馆很可能针对 19 世纪五六十年代出现的新情况审时度势了一番，认为侨民的卫生健康任务不应该再由自己包揽。与此同时，三大教会之美部会、美以美会和英国圣公会自 1847 年起先后派遣传教士进入福州传教，其中具有医学知识和医务实践的传教士除了走街串巷医务传教，西侨民的健康保障自然也落在他们的肩上。传教士们在经历了 9 年传教无人皈依的尴尬局面后，终于在50 年代看到了一线曙光，于是更多传教士来到福州。医务传教背后通常有国外宗教团体或民间慈善机构给予财政和人员的支持，因此传教士在当地开办医院有资金和人员优势。与此相反，英国领事馆，这个通商口岸时期以保障英国侨民，特别是英国商人利益为己任的机构，刚刚从开埠前期频频受挫的沮丧中走出，考虑到 50 年代刚见起色的茶叶贸易，以及 1861 年伴随着刚刚攫取的海关实际控制权摆在眼前的利益，很可能意识到使馆已无精力也无必要继续承办医院。最终，1866 年 2 月医院交由福州西侨社团和英国安立甘会接办，更名为"福州地方医馆及药房"。

　　当医院交由西侨社团和安立甘会接办，其有别于一般的教会医院，更多地表现为官商合办的私立医院。首先，它承袭了原"海港医院"的业务，仍然是西侨民心中的医院。据市二院档案记载，"塔亭医院初创，是由西侨团体集资建成，经费也受其补贴"。之后，西侨社团长期保持对塔亭医院的全部补贴。历史上，西侨团体曾是保福山医院（1870—1889）的重要资助方。资料显示，民国时期，洋行是医院很重要的捐资方。事实上，塔亭医院长期以来都由西侨团体组成的董事会主持院务，董事会成员常常包括实力雄厚的洋商。如裕昌洋行老板就曾任医院董事会的秘书和财务官。从档案中有关沿革部分可见，"1866 年英侨先租用民房，设备简陋，只有床位 6 张。1868 年以大洋 2 636元购得中洲傍江空地计 6 方丈建筑新院舍，增加医疗使用器械和设备"。后来塔亭医院还设有外国人专属的产房和病房，医院的年度报告则有西侨民住院人数统计。此时，福州地方医馆及药房是西侨团体非常重要的健康保障。

中洲岛（1912 年以前）上标有"药房""药局"字样的建筑若干（来源：池志海）
Zhongzhou Island before 1912 where names of "Dispensary" or "Pharmacy" can be seen on some buildings (Source: Chi Zhihai)

In addition, the British Royal Navy and the British Consulate, the co-initiators of Port Hospital, might have sized up the situation of the 1850s and 1860s and decided not to take full responsibility for the health care of the Foreign Community. For one thing, more missionaries came to Fuzhou when the success of first local convert in the late 1850s removed the embarrassment they suffered in the nine years of futile efforts. With medical background in education and practice, these missionaries, although busy with medical services to the locals in disguise of their conversion intention, became understandably the ones foreign residents would depend on for health care. Strongly supported by foreign religious communities or non-governmental charities, missionary hospitals had, in terms of funds and staff, the edge on the British Consulate that was established in the treaty ports mainly as an organization to safeguard the interest of the British merchants. For another, the British Consulate, now more tempted by the tea trade that began to pick up in the 1850s and the lucrative business from the New Customs that was under their control, came to realize that it was no longer necessary to invest in Port Hospital which was, therefore, later in February, 1866 handed over to Fuzhou Foreign Community and CMC and renamed as Foochow Native Hospital and Dispensary.

The handover made the Hospital different from most missionary hospitals: It became a private hospital jointly run by government officials and business people. On the one hand, its original business from Port Hospital to serve the foreign residents remained unchanged, as can be seen in the archives that read "Takding Hospital based its beginning on the funds raised by and the expenditures subsidized by the Foreign Community". The Community, once an important financial support to Ponasang Hospital (1870 – 1889), kept a longstanding financial support to cover all the subsidies, and foreign hongs turned out to be a very important source of this contribution in the Republic of China. Besides, the board of the hospital comprised members, often the deep pockets, from the community. The owner of Odell & Co. , for example, was once Secretary and Treasurer of the board. The archives show that the hospital largely depended on the effort of the foreign residents who "first rented a local house in 1866 to make a simple hospital with only six beds, and later in 1868 built a new hospital furnished with more medical equipment on a waterfront area bought at 2, 636 *yuan* covering approximately 67 square meters at Zhongzhou Island". It is no surprising that later there was one ward and one operating room exclusive only to the foreign patients and the hospital's annual report would specify the number of European patients treated in wards, as it had been recognized as their own hospital that was certain to ensure their health.

另外，塔亭医院一直保持着与官方的联系。如前所述，医务传教温敦于 1856 年离开福州，1870 年柯为良重新开展业务，这 14 年间福州的三大教会没有传教医生。这段时间关注西侨民健康的除了海港医院和福州本地医馆，还有 1861 年成立的闽海关新关。闽海关设有医务部，部里的工作人员属于海关内班人员，他们不仅为闽海关职员提供医疗服务，还参与福州西侨团体居住地的医务实践。如老资格海关官员连尼既是海关医务官员，又被委以塔亭医院主要负责人一职。1921 年出版的该医院年度报告显示，医院的董事会成员中主要人物有使馆领事菲利普斯和海关专员乐善。与此同时，塔亭医院除了与其他教会医院有联系，更是保持了与船政医疗系统、英国海军、领事馆等官方机构间的密切联系。

基于此，早期的塔亭医院很可能并不像多数教会医院那样，一开始就充满了皈依基督的气氛，一如武汉汉口医院的办院宗旨那般开宗明义，"医治病患，以彰显基督之爱"。尽管如此，塔亭医院在接下来的发展中，尤其是医院 1887 年迁往塔亭路后，与教会关系密切，医院作风与教会医院相同，成为当地人眼中的教会医院。医院后来也事实上成为英国圣公会在福州南台的医务机关（周典恩，2010：87）。在福州，圣公会是早期创办教会医院最多的教会，其中塔亭医院是福州地区该教会主要医院之一。据档案记载，和西侨团体一样，安立甘会也长期为塔亭医院提供全部补贴，1887 年医院开始接受安立甘女差会的资助，同时由女差会派遣的师姑管理。尽管初期官商私立性质明显，教会不参与医院院务，但医院的运行与教会密切相关，如医护人员都出身教会，医院里设有灵修室等。由于教会医院早期行医施药对象多为社会弱势群体，塔亭医院因此带有浓重的人道主义色彩。

塔亭医院自成立以来，历经晚清、民国，及至中华人民共和国，一路走来，始终留驻仓山，当地人亲切地称之为"第一西医院"，当属实至名归。在近代晚清中国社会出现的教会和医学的特殊关系中，塔亭医院的出现为福州仓山开辟了新的近代医疗空间，促进了当地医疗卫生近代化进程，成为晚清民国时期西学人文启蒙的一股新流。

塔亭医院旧照，可见大楼中间"闽省塔亭医院"字样

An old photo of Takding Hospital with its Chinese name—Min Provincial Takding Hospital on the façade of the building

On the other hand, Takding Hospital was in constant contact with the official organizations. The New Customs under foreign control set up in 1861 was a case in point. With a medical department, the New Customs had staff ranked as in-door surgeons responsible for the health care of its employees, but this medical office also worked with Port Hospital and Foochow Native Hospital and Dispensary especially during a lapse of fourteen years from Welton's departure in 1856 to Osgood's resumption in 1870 when no doctors from the three missions were available. The Customs' official, Thomas Rennie, for instance, was a medical officer, but assigned to be in charge of Takding Hospital as its superintendent. According to the medical report of Takding Hospital in 1921, the board of the Hospital had members like H. Philips, a consul, and P. Walsham, a Customs commissioner. Apart from missionary hospitals, the Hospital interacted also with the medical department of Foochow Shipyard, the British Navy and the British Council, etc.

Admittedly, Takding Hospital at its early stage was not driven by any evangelical purposes as were missionary hospitals such as the one in Hankou, Wuhan, that declared "to have patients treated by the love of Jesus". The Hospital, nevertheless, since its relocation in 1887 to Tating Road, had developed a close relationship with the church, making itself recognized by locals as a missionary hospital and accepted both as a medical office and one of the main hospitals in Nantai by Church Mission Society (CMS), the church that established the most missionary hospitals in the early times. Like the Foreign Community, CMS also gave full support of the subsidies that started in 1887 specifically by Church of England Zenana Missionary Society (CEZMS), a mission agency that provided not only funds but also nurses to supervise the management. As a private institution, the hospital at its initial stage only included officers and merchants as the members of the board, but its operations by and large were imprinted with religious considerations, as it was evidenced by its medical personnel that had a Christian background, and a chapel that had a particularly designated place in the hospital. Furthermore, the Hospital's free services to the underprivileged especially at the early stage like most missionary hospitals made it invested with humanitarian characteristics.

Takding Hospital, since its beginning all the way through the late Qing Dynasty and the Republic of China to the People's Republic of China, has never abandoned Cangshan, and because of this persistence, it has been hailed as "the first Western hospital". This well-deserved reputation also came from the significant contributions the hospital had made to the breaking of the new ground for alternative clinical space, and to the acceleration of the modernization process of local hygiene and health care, when the interwined relations between the church and the medical sciences in the early modern Chinese society made the emerging hospital a place to meet the new wave of Western humanistic enlightenment.

● 发展和贡献

自 1866 年医院肇始到 1952 年由中华人民共和国接收，塔亭医院在近一个世纪的岁月里，行走在晚清民国的飘摇风雨中，冲在抗日战争救亡的硝烟弹雨中，与时代互动，护佑一方民众，启迪科学卫生知识，同时培养了一批近代医护人员，为福州地区西医发展奠定了基础。

互动良好的合作

19 世纪晚清闭关锁国，危机四伏，却是西方商人和传教士的向往之地。鸦片战争后，商人和传教士一起来了，传教士谴责鸦片贩子，却不得不与他们打交道。这是两类很不一样的洋人，到了陆地，他们自然形成了两个群体，据说通商口岸的当地人很容易就可以区分他们。不过，在福州，传教士和商人关系融洽，相互依存，共同发展，塔亭医院正是在两者融合关系中得以发展。

1850 年 5 月，英国传教士温敦乘坐开往福州的帆船，憧憬着开辟医务传教。15 年前伯驾在广州的成功实践让他满怀信心。近代医院制度源于欧洲，设立医院成为中世纪欧洲传教手段之一。文艺复兴后，现代医院初具雏形，传教士开始利用医院进行慈善事业或到其他大洲开展传教工作。温敦就是许许多多希望通过世俗行医，借以"疗体"达到"疗灵"的医学传教士中的一员。不过让他没想到的是，在福州的 6 年，也是他见证传教颗粒无收的"最黑暗"时刻，有时他不得不为传教同胞开出啤酒、红酒当药方，帮他们渡过沮丧时刻。所幸，他在福州的传教医务可以带来些安慰。尽管初期医务传教屡屡受挫，但在他的坚持下，1850—1856 年间年均诊疗达 2 000～3 000人次，他最终赢得当地人信任，成为官方许可入城居住的第一个传教士，也是第一个在福州展开医务传教的人。而派遣温敦的正是日后长期支持塔亭医院的安立甘会，二者的合作成为塔亭医院教会色彩的浓墨一笔。

● Development and Contributions

Throughout a history of nearly one hundred years from its inception in 1866 to the takeover by the People's Republic of China in 1952, Takding Hospital, in all its interactions with the times—going through thick and thin in the late Qing Dynasty and the Republic of China, and its standing up to the Japanese aggressors, for example—proved to be an important contributor in local life protection, enlightenment of new medical sciences and cultivation of western medical personnel, all making for the foundation laid for the development of western medicine in early modern Fuzhou.

Supporting Parties

China in the late Qing Dynasty with a door closed to the outside world, although beset with crisis, was an enchanting destination to both Western merchants and missionaries who came together immediately after the Opium Wars. Unable to see eye to eye in the opium trade, these early Western comers were alleged to split into two groups that people at the treaty ports could easily tell apart. Missionaries and merchants in Fuzhou, however, got along and formed a special bond of interdependence upon each other. It was in this rapport that Takding Hospital developed.

One day in May 1850, a ship sailing for Fuzhou carried a British missionary, Welton, who looked confident at the thought of building in Fuzhou a medical mission that had already proven successful fifteen years before in a hospital in Guangzhou by Peter Parker. Early modern hospitals that originated in Europe as an institution were recognized in the Middle Ages as an important means to missionary work, and later after the Renaissance they developed into a more recent prototype that prompted missionaries to start using hospitals to practice charity or to travel to other continents for evangelism through medical service. Welton was one of these missionaries who expected to "heal souls" in their secular attempt to "heal bodies", and his six-year stay in Fuzhou was a good example of mixed feelings. In those darkest years when missionaries were thrown into great depression due to their fruitless conversion, Welton could do nothing but prescribe beer and wine to cheer his fellows up. His tireless efforts in medical services brought something of a silver lining, though. Without giving in to the frustration that troubled him at the outset, Welton made a record of average annual treatment up to 2,000~3,000 people during 1850 – 1856, which credited him with trust from the locals and the officials, and the government permission into the city as the first foreign medical missionary. The church that sent Welton to Fuzhou was none other than CMS, a mission that would later give Takding Hospital its long-term support, and this collaboration between the two highlighted the element of church in Takding Hospital.

安立甘会是大英教会成立于1799年的英国海外传道会，即英国圣公会差会（简称"英国圣公会"），其英文名称历史上有一定变化，国内使用的中文译名亦有所不同。1912年英国圣公会与其他在中国的安立甘会合并，改称"中华圣公会"（简称"圣公会"）。该会虽然稍晚于美部会和美以美会进入福州，却是最早开展医务传教实践和派遣医生来福建最多的教会。不过大英教会早期并不看好福州的传教事业。据说，1854年，维多利亚主教反对温敦在福州的医务实践。1859年，急于求成的主教甚至赞成放弃在福州的传教事业（Ellsworth，1974：62-65）。当时，美国教会也考虑中断在华传教。这和英国人在福州头十年通商开埠毫无进展，打算放弃福州港的心情如出一辙。事实上，圣公会后来在福州发展顺利，该会一些著名人物参与了福州地区近代文教医药卫生事业的发展，客观上促进了福州近代化的演变。

　　英国圣公会女差会，简称"女差会"或"女部"，同样在塔亭医院有着举足轻重的地位和作用。该差会1880年成立，最初为在印度传教而设，其中"Zenana"指代印度妇女。差会于1884年派遣传教士前往中国，首站即往福建，传教中心很快辐射福州及周边地区，1912年女差会加入中华圣公会。该女差会为医院提供津贴，但更为重要的是，它为塔亭医院提供不可或缺的医务护理人员。师姑们以院为家，其言行举止深深烙着教会印记，但她们言传身教带出了一批早期护理人员。20世纪20年代以前，塔亭医院一直仅有一名医生负责，医院日常运作很大部分依靠安立甘会派来的师姑们，如今年过七旬、八旬的老塔亭人记忆深处仍然留有师姑们的身影。

　　一直以来，塔亭医院的实际所有人是西侨团体，其董事会成员包括使馆官员和西侨位高权重的人物，圣公会不参与塔亭医院的院务管理，但抗日战争期间，医院受到圣公会福建教区的保护，双方结下了战友般深厚情谊。抗日战争结束后，西侨团体在1947年聘请福建教区为医院产业管理委员会委员之一，紧接着又请该教区医务部接受医院院务管理权。1950年，西侨团体迫于时局撤出中国前，把塔亭医院的产权移交给了福建教区。医院由中华人民共和国接收时，塔亭医院董事长一职由牧师王德熙担任，董事会成员包括医务界、教育界、商界等各方人士。塔亭医院在时代变迁中即将完成新的互动。

新政府1951年接收塔亭医院之前，医院的董事会成员
Members of Board of Directors in 1951 just before the takeover by the new government

CMS, short for the Church Mission Society, a name that changed in 1812 from the Society for Missions to Africa and the East founded by the Church of England in London in 1799, has different translated Chinese names in use, and in 1912 it joined other Anglican churches to form the Anglican-episcopal Church in China. Although a bit later than the other two missions into Fuzhou, CMC sent the most doctors to Fujian and was the earliest to begin medical mission. Its missionary cause in Fuzhou in the early days was, nonetheless, never favored by the Church of England, as is evidenced by the attitude of Bishop Victoria who in 1854 expressed strong disapproval and in 1859 agreed to abandon it because of no fruitful prospect in sight. A similar letdown permeated the American mission. Like the same old story in which the British almost gave up Fuzhou after their futile attempts in commerce in the first ten years, CMC stayed and ended up with some well-known figures who played a part in the evolution of local education and medical sciences and, in effect, pushed forward the process of modernization in Fuzhou.

CEAMS, short for the Church of England Zenana Missionary Society, was another mission no less important than CMC. Founded in 1880 initially for the spread of Christianity in India, as the Indian term "Zenana" used to stand for women may suggest, CEZMS began sending in 1884 missionaries to Fujian, their first main focus of expansion in China, Fuzhou and its neighboring areas being the first stations. Like CMC, it joined the Anglican-episcopal Church in China in 1921. Its support to the Hospital was not only subsidies, but, more importantly, also the nursing personnel often referred to as "shigu" or Home Sister. Designated by CEZMS as resident staff, these missionary females performed their duties with impressively missionary demeanor, but worthy of note is their irreplaceable role in cultivating early nursing talents who learned from the hands-on experiences under the instructions of these sisters. With only one foreign doctor taking responsibility before the 1920s, Takding Hospital had its daily operations under the actual charge of these resident sisters whose legacy still lives on vividly in the memory of some old Takding folks who are now in their seventies or eighties.

As the actual proprietor of Takding Hospital for quite a long time, the Foochow Foreign Community was in full charge of the hospital's administration through the hospital's board of directors that was comprised of officials in the consulates and men of consequence from the Community. That right of administration of the hospital was entrusted to the Fukien Church, a church under the Anglican-episcopal church in China, shortly after it was invited in 1947 to be the committee member of the Hospital's Property Management Committee, as a result of a special bond forged between the two parties during the War of Resistance Against Japanese Aggression when the hospital was well protected by the Church. In 1950, the hospital's ownership was transferred to the Church by the Community who was leaving China. Later right before the new takeover by the Chinese government, Takding Hospital had a new board now made up of members that included doctors, educators and businessmen, etc. and chaired by Bishop Wang Dexi, ready for another round of interaction in the new historical era.

作为地方医馆，塔亭医院信守为西侨和本地居民服务的承诺，医院的发展因此备受多方关注。1886 年医院遭遇一场重大变故，但这次意外却弥足珍贵。现在看来，它开启了医院发展的新时机，也记录下了人们关注的目光。光绪 12 年（1886 年）5 月 23 日，中洲岛发生一场大火，这场大火烧毁了福州医馆，却留下了塔亭医院在中洲岛的记录，见证了塔亭医院在人们心中的地位。清末《点石斋画报》于 1886 年 7 月 17 日出版的题为《医局成灾》的新闻画上有如下文字，其中可见医院"济世"口碑和部分设备状况：

> 闽省南台中洲，有美医（美医之说有误，编者按）设立济世医局，已历多年。凡华人之抱痒垂危和缓束手者，皆得到局乞医，著手成春，屡著奇效。日前厨房失慎，遽兆焚如，十万病魔，一齐惊退。当有数十西人，冒火冲烟，舍命救护，先将病房中男妇老幼，剑负而逃，然后汲水浇灌，灭此狂焰。所有贵重物件，悉付祖龙氏。最可惜者，有一显微镜，大可数百倍，购时出价五百金，至此亦遭火劫云。

无独有偶，这场大火在 1887 年海关的《医务报告》中也有提及。根据这份报告，当时位于中洲岛的福州地方医馆紧挨附近民居，医院拥挤，入口狭窄，颇有火灾隐患。大火之后，医院迁至新址及至建设，备受各方厚爱，"择新址空地，保新楼之敞，地方官员，西侨团体，本地商贾，咸来相助"。很快，新大楼在塔亭路上落成，除了男病房，医院新增了一间女病房，由海关商务部资助所建，为纪念不久前去世的英国外交官夏巴礼。档案显示，这次新楼耗资 2 900 大洋。翌年 4 月，新楼门诊部完工，6 月住院部开始接待病人，床位 10 余张。曾多年担任塔亭医院院长的连尼，此刻作为海关官员记录这个焕然一新的医院时，心中涌动着感激与自豪。他在报告中总结道："越来越多的西侨人士和本地民众来新医院看病，看来医院很受欢迎。"

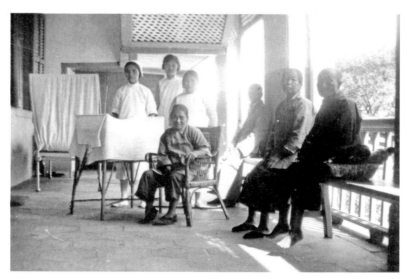

：塔亭医院病患与护理人员
：Patients and nursing personnel in Takding Hospital

As a native dispensary, Takding Hospital kept committed to its medical services to both Westerners and locals, and in turn, received attention from many sides. A disaster that occurred in 1886 proved to be a disguised blessing as it gave a record of concern from people as well as a new start for the hospital. It was this big fire at Zhongzhou Island on 23 May 1886 that destroyed the hospital while leaving the evidence of its existence and fame. Below is an explanation to a news illustration titled *Fire Disaster in a Dispensary* published on 7 July 1886 in *Dianshizhai Pictorial*.

Situated at Zhongzhou Island, Nantai of Min Province was a Western voluntary hospital that had helped people in need for years. Local Chinese that were sick or dying with no other way out would come here for treatments that were allegedly believed to produce magical results. Recently a kitchen nearby caught fire and in no time the raging flames engulfed the hospital, so much so that they seemed to also frighten all the monsters of disease away. As quickly as they could, a dozen Westerners risked their lives to run straight into the burning hospital to help the patients out, men or women, and for the young, they carried, before they put out the fire with water. Alas! All valuables were burned down to ashes and the biggest shame was the ruin of a microscope with a magnifying power up to several hundred times that was purchased for five hundred dollars.

That conflagration, coincidentally, was mentioned in the Customs Medical Report of 1887 that also tells what the hospital was like before and after the blaze. A crowded hospital with a narrow entrance that had "constant dread of a fire arising in native property" was the picture of the Native Dispensary when it was located at Zhongzhou Island. After it was burned down, according to the report, the hospital was able to "procure a more open site, and erect thereon a more substantial and commodious building" that cost a total of 2,900 dollars, thanks to "the combined generosity of native officials, foreign residents, and native merchants". Completed in April 1887 at Tating Road was the department for outpatients, and two months later the new hospital was ready to receive inpatients who would be accommodated in a ten-bed building that had a woman's ward added "through the aid of members of the Chamber of Commerce" in memory of the late Sir Harry Parkes. Full of gratitude and pride, Thomas Rennie, the Customs medical doctor who was also assigned to take charge of the hospital for some years, wrote at the end of the report, "From the increasing numbers of both classes of patients, the new hospital seems to be highly appreciated."

发展壮大

仅病床 6 张，病人不多，这就是 1866 年医院在中洲岛开业时的情况。至 1882 年，医院住院病人达 498 人，门诊 2 480 人。迁到塔亭路后，医院保持平稳发展势头。1880—1900 年间，医院共计诊治 13 546 名住院病人和 97 285 名门诊患者。1921 年记录可诊治的疾病达 200 多种，涉及内外科共 20 大类。同年，塔亭医院开办了护士学校，很快有了自己的助产士和护士，与医院的发展相适应。1921—1922 年间，福州有 9 家私立医院可以接收住院病人，但仅有两家有能力接收 20 个以上病人住院治疗，塔亭医院正是其中一家。1921 年，医院住院人数达到 1 469 人，门诊达 3 654 人。另一家是 1919 年在仓山郑家楼成立的日本医院，该院后来迁址他处，抗日战争后停办。

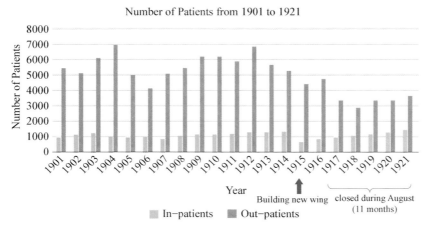

塔亭医院 20 世纪前 20 年的诊疗数量〔来源：上海医药博物馆（集团）〕
Statistics about patients in Takding Hospital in the first two decades of the 20th century [Source: Shanghai Pharmaceutical Museum (Group)]

20 世纪 20 年代，全国范围的反基督教运动和北伐战争（1926—1927）引发的高涨的民族主义情绪冲击着教会医院。江西、安徽和福建的教会医院遭受重大打击，许多教会医院因此关闭。紧急关头，福建教区主教恒约翰大力推进教会中国化，塔亭医院也顺势而为，对自身医疗事业进行本土化的积极调整。医院开始聘用医学院校毕业生。其中毕业于山东齐鲁大学医学院的王灼祖是塔亭医院首位学院制西医，另一位是毕业于上海圣约翰大学的陈颂磐。一直以来靠一名洋人医生主导的局面正悄然发生改变。而在这之前，林叨安作为塔亭医院的第一位华人医生，已在塔亭医院服务多年。他常年追随外国传教医生，主要以助手的身份参与医务实践，代表了第一批西医体系下华人医生的成长模式。

Growth

Six beds for a small number of patients were the recorded facilities at the beginning days of the Native Hospital in 1866, but in 1882 the inpatients and outpatients grew to 498 and 2,408 respectively. After its relocation to Tating Road, the hospital kept a steady growth both in visits and stays, say, a total number of 13,546 inpatients and 97,285 outpatients from 1880 to 1900, and in 1921, over 200 diseases classified into twenty types were treated. To meet the growth, a new nursing school was set up in 1921 that before long produced its own midwives and nurses. Of all the nine private hospitals that could receive inpatients in 1921 – 1922, Takding Hospital was one of the only two that could take in more than twenty, with 1,469 inpatients and 3,654 outpatients in 1921, the other being a Japanese Hospital founded in 1919 at Zhengjia Building in Cangshan and later displaced elsewhere until its end after the War of Resistance Against Japanese Aggression.

The 1920s was a period of vicissitudes when many missionary hospitals in Fujian, Jiangxi and Anhui were forced to shut down in the surge of outpouring nationalism triggered by the Anti-Christianity Movement and the Northern Expedition (1926 – 1927). To survive such a precarious situation, Takding Hospital started to localize its staff as a positive response to the Chinization of Western churches, a movement greatly pushed forward by John Hind, Bishop of Fukien Diocese. Chinese doctors with formal medical education began to work in Takding Hospital. The first was Wang Zhuozu, a graduate of Cheeloo University in Shandong, and then Chen Songpan, of St. John's University in Shanghai. Before them, Lin Dao'an, the first Chinese doctor of this hospital, had worked for many years but only as an assistant to Western missionary doctors, representing the earliest Chinese doctors of Western medicine that learnt from medical practice. Now with new Chinese doctors who could work independently, a change to the longstanding system—one foreign doctor in charge—was taking place unawares.

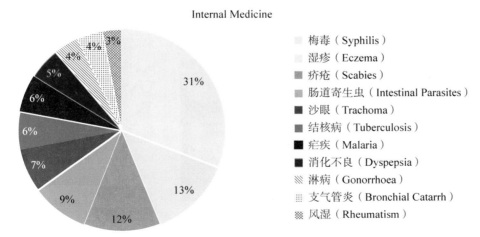

Internal Medicine

- 梅毒（Syphilis）
- 湿疹（Eczema）
- 疥疮（Scabies）
- 肠道寄生虫（Intestinal Parasites）
- 沙眼（Trachoma）
- 结核病（Tuberculosis）
- 疟疾（Malaria）
- 消化不良（Dyspepsia）
- 淋病（Gonorrhoea）
- 支气管炎（Bronchial Catarrh）
- 风湿（Rheumatism）

: 塔亭医院 1921 年内科疾病诊疗情况图［来源：上海医药博物馆（集团）］
: Diseases treated in Takding Hospital in 1921 [Source: Shanghai Pharmaceutical Museum (Group)]

20 世纪 30 年代，大量西方卫生知识传入中国，学校毕业的医学生和护士不断加入塔亭医院，华人开始参与科室负责和管理工作，他们的作用得以彰显。20 世纪 20 年代，陈颂磐初来医院时，院长戴满和护士长俞和平都是外籍。1934 年陈宗磐任外科主管医师，产科工作也交由塔亭护校第一届毕业的助产士包罗以负责。由于外科的重要性，对于西医院而言，这一任命非同寻常。与此同时，医院科室也有新的发展。陈颂磐 20 世纪 20 年代入职后曾对医院的内科、儿外、妇外等进行了意义重大的分科定型，到 20 世纪 30 年代医院已有包括内科、外科、妇科、化验室、药房、供应室、营养室等科室部门，手术室扩建，建立了早晚查房制度。同一时期医院开始规范门诊收费。各科室出现了具体分工负责人。1937 年，医院新建化验室，一台显微镜查四大常规。抗日战争期间，陈宗磐从英国院长黄约翰手中接过手术室负责人职责，开始主持外科工作，手术室迅速发展，增设六间特护室。此外，可以现配粉剂、片剂、针剂等在医院建立初期就扮演着很重要作用的药房也交由俞世壁负责，西药房很快更新迭代成药库。翁文基负责日常事务工作。一时间，医院出现中国医务人员忙碌的身影。

1944 年，中国医生陈颂磐担任院长，中国医生开始全面主持医院工作，其间郑淑玉、薛德英、黄腓力、方景光、陈尚娟、何祖焕、刘涓等医生陆续加入，医院规模不断扩大，医疗服务不断拓新。抗日战争胜利后，医院发现小儿传染病发病率和死亡率高，特别是麻疹、结核病等感染性疾病猖獗。为解决这一问题，医院把儿科从内科分出来，成立独立科室，院长陈颂磐亲自主诊，名闻全市。1946 年，医院在妇产科设 23 个床位，实行独立值班制，一时为人称颂。医院还增设一个社会服务部，由专人负责，重点调查、审批、办理减免军烈属、城镇居民以及农民就医中无法缴纳的医疗费用，经查实属困难者分文不取，减免的费用由院方日常收入冲转。

塔亭医院药房（来源：陈美爱）
The dispensary of Takding Hospital (Source: Chen Meiai)

In the 1930s, encouraged by the greater support to the Western medical science in China, more Chinese graduates from medical and nursing schools joined Takding Hospital, some of whom began to take the leading role. Unlike the previous decade when foreign personnel played dominant roles such as Moorhead as the Superintendent and Irene Walters as the Nursing Supervisor, Chinese medical workers now began to assume important responsibilities. For example, Chen Zongpan served as a surgeon in 1934, which was quite significant as surgery was inseparable to the business in Western hospitals, and later during the War of Resistance Against Japanese Aggression, as a surgeon-in-charge who took over the leadership of the operation room from John Webster, the then acting superintendent. Chen Songpan was an even more important Chinese doctor who brought great changes to the hospital infrastructures and operation. On the heels of his crucial division of the basic departments of internal medicine, pediatrics and gynecological surgery that began in the 1920s, Chen Songpan established in the 1930s a wider range of departments such as internal medicine, surgery, gynecology, laboratory, pharmacy, nutrition, supply-room, etc., each of which was put under the charge of designated personnel. Bao Luoyi, for instance, was in charge of obstetrics department, Yu Shibi, for the dispensary, and Weng Wenji, for daily affairs. Meanwhile, there were new practices such as morning and evening ward rounds for inpatients and charging scheme for outpatients. Updated infrastructures included a new laboratory set up in 1937 with a microscope for the routine test, six new rooms as the extension of the operation room for special care, and a dispensary with greater capacity to produce medicine in the form of powder, tablets and injection, which would soon grow into a drug storehouse. Now the organized Chinese staff were distinctly better recognized.

The designation of Chen Songpan as director in 1944 marked the beginning of Chinese people to take charge of the hospital management. During this period, more Chinese doctors such as Xue Deying, Huang Feili, Fang Jingguang, Chen Shangjuan, He Zuhuan, Liu Juan, etc., joined in, pushing medical services in this period to new heights and gaining more recognition from the public. For example, in response to the post-war high incidence and death rate of pediatric infectious diseases, measles and tuberculosis in particular, pediatrics became an independent department out of the internal medicine department with Chen Songpan as the attending physician. Similarly, department of obstetrics and gynecology adopted a duty system of its own for all the twenty-three beds it provided. The prestige the hospital enjoyed also came from the deduction of medical expenses supported by the Social Service Department. After the investigation, examination and approval done by the specially assigned personnel, such patients as family members of revolutionary martyrs and servicemen, urban citizens and countryside farmers who, if proven in real difficulty, were likely to have services free of charge. The charge that had been written off would be covered by the hospital revenues.

在新的历史条件下，西侨团体趋于萎缩，原先的经费来源出现较大变化，业务收入开始成为经费来源的一个重要部分。20 世纪 50 年代，医院始设会计、出纳，负责登账，取代之前总管财政收支的总务长。当时，医院每月出一份总收支报告，送给德商禅臣会计审核。随着医院业务量增大，1946 年医院靠业务收入建起了护士学校楼。1948 年，医院接受"中国国际救济委员会"所拨经费和部分业务收入，建成一栋门诊大楼。1949 年，医院病床已达 160 张（林恩燕，2016），其门诊量、住院、初诊、复诊数量在当时福建教区圣公会所办医院中居首位（周典恩，2004）。

20 世纪 50 年代，医院改制成公立医院之前，塔亭医院的行政设置（1951 年统计）已趋于完整。具体职位包括院长，副院长及校长，医务主任，外科主任，产科主任，主治医师，总务主任，会计，事务，统计，出纳，登记，药库管理，社会服务部及教育、消毒室主任，饮食房主任，药房主任，药剂士等。当时，全院有 123 人，包括主治医师 9 人，护士 29 人，另外还有事务人员、化验员、助产士、调剂员、教员和工友。经过近百年的发展，此时的塔亭医院已经在各方帮助和自身努力下，从缺人手、少设施，发展成科室设备齐全的名副其实的当地大医院，医务人员正等待着新政府的指引，继续在新的历史时期造福一方百姓。

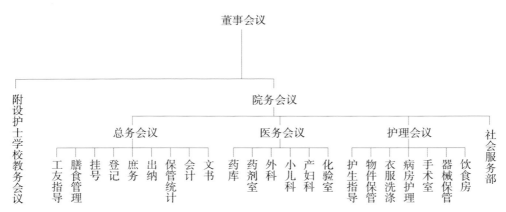

：塔亭医院组织系统表（1951）
：A chart of organizational structure in Takding Hospital in 1951

Meanwhile, the funding sources now largely relied on the hospital service revenues rather than on the shrinking subscription from the Foreign Community in the new historical times. The increasing business income necessitated the particular position for finance personnel. For example, in the 1950s, the hospital began to have the cashier and the accountant to replace the previous director of General Service Office who had duties of keeping account, being responsible for the monthly report of the financial revenue and expenditure that was to be submitted to the accountant in Siemssen & Co. for auditing. The growing service revenue was such that it gave the full financial support to the erection of the nursing school building in 1946, and in 1948 partial funds for the construction of an outpatient building, more substantial funds of which was from the appropriation from International Relief Committee of China. With a capacity of 160 beds in 1949, Takding Hospital ranked first among the hospitals run by the Anglican Church of Fukien in terms of visits, initial or return, by outpatients and inpatients.

Before its transformation into a public hospital in the 1950s, Takding Hospital had developed a complete organizational structure in which Board of Directors governed the executive committee comprised of four sections—General Affairs Committee, Medical Committee, Nursing Committee and Social Service Department—that concerned positions such as Director, Deputy Director, School Principal, Director of Medical Affairs, Surgeon-in-Charge, Obstetrician-in-Charge, Attending Physician, Director of General Service, Accountant, clerk, statistician, cashier, registrar, pharmacist, and personnel in charge of drug storehouse, social service and education department, sterilizing room, canteen and pharmacy. Among 123 employees were nine attending physicians, twenty-nine nurses and a certain number of clerks, laboratory technicians, midwives, coordinators, teachers and workers. With great support from various parties, Takding Hospital had worked so hard in the past decades that it turned the original small dispensary short of staff and facilities into a big local hospital worthy of its reputation as an important institution, and that it gained enough momentum for another round of adjustment under the new government's guidance for the continuity of its everlasting commitment to the care of local residents.

塔亭医院婴儿房（来源：陈美爱）
Infant wards in Takding Hospital
(Source: Chen Meiai)

护佑生命，救死扶伤

在近百年行医历史中，塔亭医院用心护佑当地侨民和居民健康福祉，传播近代医学卫生知识，点点滴滴，常为人传颂。晚清时期《点石斋画报》（2014：229）曾记载了塔亭医院时任外科医生亚当为眼疾患者诊疗的经过：

乃福州时升里塔亭衕地方，有济世馆……凡疑难杂症，医治获痊者，姑勿暇论。所奇者，有乡人王玉山，素业手艺，双目失明业已九年。一日至该馆求治。经西医亚丹先生为之诊治，曰：目珠似薤子，一重又一重，共三十二重，今子目有翳，在第四重，宜用刀割之，药水敷之，去其蔽障，则目自明矣；惟不可割至第五重，盖第五重系最要之枢，幸是处尚无翳耳。如法治之，旬余，目果复明。于是该处瞽人闻而求治者，踵趾相接……

西医最早来华医务传教时发现当时眼疾求诊人满为患，传教士伯驾 1835 年在广州开的全国首家西医院，正是以治疗眼疾为主的眼科医院。在福建，当地人流传着一种说法："耳不治不聋，眼不治不瞎。"当时，民间剃头理发的地方，除了为客人掏耳朵，还帮客人刮眼睑，这种风俗无疑成为当地眼疾问题严重的原因之一。据记载，福建省 20 世纪 20 年代求诊最多的是眼疾，尤其是沙眼。西医亚当为当地人行医的时间应该是 19 世纪八九十年代，这说明眼疾在晚清民国时期的福州相当普遍，这与"当时中国人沙眼和白内障最为普遍"的描述相符合（何小莲，2006：59）。虽然民国时期仓山地区中医眼科享有盛名，一些祖传中药制剂在治疗白内障、青光眼等眼疾上疗效独到，但中西医各有所长，当时西医提供的医疗对于底层老百姓来说更易理解也更易接受，因此，西医就此扎下了根。

	眼疾名称	Names of Eye Disorders
1	颗粒性结膜炎/沙眼	Trachoma
2	匐行性角膜溃疡	Ulcer of Cornea
3	睑内翻	Entropion
4	结膜炎	Conjunctivitis，Simple
5	白内障	Cataract
6	翼状胬肉	Pterygium
7	虹膜炎	Iritis
8	全眼炎	Panopthalmitis
9	睑缘炎	Blepharitis
10	前房积脓	Hypopeon

塔亭医院 1921 年诊疗量排名前十的眼疾〔来源：上海医药博物馆（集团）〕
The first ten eye disorders treated in 1921 in Takding Hospital〔Source: Shanghai Pharmaceutical Museum (Group)〕

Guardian of Life and Health

In Takding Hospital's century-old narrative of practicing medicines, what has never been undersung was its image as a protector of both foreign and native residents' health and life, and the positive part it played in the spread of early modern medical knowledge. This dual role was well presented in a caption to the illustration in *Dianshizhai Pictorial* of the late Qing Dynasty which recorded how Thomas Beat Adam, the surgeon of Takding Hospital, treated his patient who suffered from eye disorders.

Standing at Takding Road in Shishengli Community in Foochow was a Western voluntary hospital for people in need...Stories about its magical treatment in complicated medial cases are too many to tell, but the following is surely an amazing one. A countryman named Wang Yushan was a handicraftsman who had been blind for nine years. When one day he came to the hospital for help, he was received by Dr. Adam who explained to him that human eyes were like onions with altogether thirty-two layers and that the problem with his eyes was corneal opacity that happened in the fourth and could be cured through surgery and eyedrops to have the leukoma removed. According to Adam, Wang was lucky because his problem was not in the fifth layer, the most crucial area that should avoid any touch of an ophthalmic scalpel. Treated as such for more than ten days, Wang finally regained his lost eyesight. Since then more local blind people came...

Patients with eye problems constituted the greatest overcrowding in the Western medical service, as was observed by the early missionary doctors, one of whom, Peter Parker for that reason set up the first western-style hospital in China, initially opened in Guangzhou as "Eye Infirmary" in 1835. A similar prevalence of eye diseases also happened in Fujian where one of its local customs at the barber's was to give its clients, in addition to a haircut, a service to have their ears picked and their eyelids scraped, a practice presumably for the sake of sanitation as well as a treatment but in effect resulting in more serious diseases especially in eyes, as is suggested in a local saying to the effect that one stood to lose his hearing or eyesight if one had his ears or eyes treated as such. Documents in the 1920s showed that most patients in Fujian came to hospitals for the treatment of their eye disorders, trachoma in particular, and that fit the description of the nationwide problems of trachoma and cataract. For all the good reputation Cangshan had enjoyed since the Republic of China, of using traditional Chinese medicine that had passed on through generations to ease eye discomfort such as cataract and glaucoma to certain curative effect, the medical aid from Western hospitals, like the one Dr. Adam gave in the 1880s and 1890s, was more easily appreciated, accessible and thus more acceptable, especially to the people at the grassroots level. Out of the grassroots, as it were, grew the root of Western hospitals.

为了实践"人道主义，救死扶伤"精神，医院医务人员秉承医德，如今院史上记载着对后人仍意义深远的医德四句话："重病者先急救，后收钱；病人骂不还口，病人打不还手；对危急病人，医务人员没有上下班界限；医务人员口中不述病人的不治之症，要组织会诊。"历史上的塔亭医院有着一套严格的制度，规约医务人员，以确保病患获得良好的就医体验。

和今天资金雄厚的私立医院不同，塔亭医院的经费并不宽裕。医院1921的年度报告记录了详细的收支情况，并提及"开销激增"而"捐款减少"。但即便如此，早期它和大多数教会医院一样，实行免费行医施药。医院创办初期，当地人对西医持怀疑观望态度，门诊不收费便有一定吸引力，而住院时间不论长短一律收银元五角，护理和伙食费自理。20世纪30年代，医院开始收取门诊和住院费，病房每周收费一次，其中的费用包括病床位费、药费、饮食费以及三大常规化验费，打针及特种化验另外收费。但周一、周三下午仍然免费诊病，对于贫穷病人实施免费施诊施药。不仅如此，医院也为普通民众免费注射疫苗，如接种水痘，同时宣传公共卫生，担负着鼠疫、霍乱、天花等时疫防治工作。通过施医赠药，塔亭医院为当地民众解除疾患，向当地社区普及近代科学卫生知识，成为福州近代化进程演变过程中一支不可忽视的力量。

：塔亭医院改制前收费表（1951）
：A table of hospital charge before its transformation（1951）

让塔亭医院声名远播的还有一些发生在抗日战争时期的故事，这些故事近年来由一批当年生活在塔亭医院的老一辈人回忆讲述而成。其中最活跃的口述者，是当年塔亭医院总务长陈为信的儿子陈兆奋。

To ensure the best clinical experiences, Takding Hospital had strict rules and regulations for its staff of medical profession, all based on the medical ethics which stayed unchanged in the historical documents and still holds true today. In four sentences, the conduct codes read: "Emergency aid should be given to the critical patients before they are charged; No arguments or fights should be given back to any patients; No distinction between on and off duties in severe cases; No talk of patients' incurable diseases unless in a group consultation." What was required of the staff members in Takding Hospital was indicative of the familiar principle in medical field—"to heal the wounded and rescue the dying under the guidance of humanitarianism".

The funds Takding Hospital could depend on was never comparable to the abundance most private hospitals enjoy today, and the 1921 annual report provides a glimpse of its tight financial situation: Some detailed calculations with the mention of "expenses have increased considerably" while "subscriptions have fallen off". Nonetheless, it kept practicing medication free of charge the way most missionary hospitals did, especially on its early stage when local people still cast doubt upon Western medicine. There was, therefore, no charge for outpatients, and for inpatients only a five-jiao silver coin for any length of hospitalization exclusive of fees for nursing and board. Later in the 1930s the hospital started to charge both outpatients and inpatients with a package fee inpatients needed to pay on a weekly basis that included expenses in bed, medicine, meals and three routine blood tests, excluding injection and special blood test, but gratuitous diagnosis still kept open on the afternoons of Monday and Wednesday, and for people in poverty, free medical services were still applicable. Other contributions Takding Hospital had made, to the local residents' advantage, included free vaccination against, say, chickenpox, and its efforts in disseminating knowledge about public health while playing a part in the prevention and control of epidemics such as bubonic plague, cholera, small pox, etc. Through its charitable gesture, the hospital brought to the local community relief, care and knowledge, making itself a potent catalyst to accelerate the modernization of Fuzhou.

In recent years, the legacy of the hospital has been further explored and the moving stories that took place during the War of Resistance Against Japanese Aggression are luckily recollected through the reminiscence of some elders who once lived there and one of them, Chen Zhaofen, whose father was Chen Weixin, Director of General Affairs of Takding Hospital, is the most vigorous story teller.

在如今 90 高龄的陈老先生眼里，抗日战火中的塔亭医院是一座无惧蛮敌、救济百姓的"战地医院"。1938 年抗日战争全面爆发后，福建省会福州处于日本侵略军的海空威胁中，频频遭遇敌机轰炸。为防空袭，烟台山各国驻福州领事馆以及洋行宅第纷纷在房顶刷上各国国旗标志，城里民众纷纷逃往仓山避难。塔亭医院不仅房顶上刷上英国国旗标识，大门口也插着英国国旗，日军不敢贸然进入，因此成为当地人的避难所，经常有人跑进塔亭医院躲避空袭。1939 年，中洲岛梅花道和港头遭袭；1941 年，龙潭角被炸。在这两次重大事件中，塔亭医院旋即成为"战地医院"，4 位医生黄约翰、陈颂磐、陈宗磐和陈为信迅速展开伤员急救。他们连续奋战 36 小时，挽救了许多生命。据说在连续不眠不休的状态下，为了补充体力，他们只能在手术台上快速咽下护士递来的鸡蛋。为了更好地实施救助，帮助难民，塔亭医院的医生们主动与福建国际红十字会联系，自发组成了一支红十字会急救队。他们戴着国际红十字会臂章，组织人员运送粮食、药品等紧急救济物资，还亲自开车，冒着枪林弹雨往返于城内各医院、学校和难民所，提供各种援助，其中城里的协和医院和柴井医院受到重点支援。

塔亭医院后期三位主要中外医生，从左到右是陈颂磐、陈宗磐、黄约翰
Three important doctors at the late stage of Takding Hospital standing from left to right: Chen Songpan, Chen Zongpan, John Webster

Mr. Chen Zhaofen now in his early nineties refers to Takding Hospital in the wartime as a "field hospital" that, according to him, braved all the risks in order to save people's lives. In 1938 when the War of Resistance against Japanese Aggression escalated into its comprehensive stage, Fuzhou, the capital city of Fujian, became a target of attack by Japanese forces at sea and from the air. To avoid air strikes, all foreign consulates, hongs and residences in Yantai Mountain had their roofs painted with their national flags, making Cangshan a sanctuary city dwellers fled to. Takding Hospital was no exception. With painted British national flags seen from above and some real ones put up at the entrance to keep Japanese aggressors out, it made itself a shelter from air strikes for locals. Among all the incidents, widely reported were two events of bombardments that caused many casualties, respectively in 1939 at Meihuadao of Zhongzhou Island and Guangtou and in 1941 at Longtanjiao, when four doctors of Takding Hospital——John Webster, Chen Songpan, Chen Zongpan and Chen Weixin——worked for thirty-six hours without any rest in order to save as many lives as they could, and to save time they simply swallowed the boiled eggs passed from the nurses for energy without leaving the operating table. On other occasions, they made contacts with Fujian International Red Cross and formed a Red Cross rescuing team for the sake of a better rescue for the refugees. Wearing a Red Cross armband, they were busy organizing delivery of relief supplies of food and drugs, or driving cars in person through shots and shells to and fro among hospitals, schools and refuges inside the city offering aids of different kinds, with priority assistance to Foochow Christian Union Hospital and Cha-Chang Christ's Hospital.

1944 年，福州二次沦陷期间，城里医院被占或迁往他处，塔亭医院成了全市唯一承担医疗任务的医院。日军的宪兵队驻地就在离医院几步之遥的汇丰银行，医院如处虎口，经常遭到日本宪兵无端挑衅。好几次，恰逢危急关头，院长陈颂磐和总务长陈为信总能急中生智，演绎出一幕幕临危不惧、化险为夷的精彩交涉。陈为信曾巧妙设置暗号，用"大十"表示"日本"，在医院内通风报信，成功保护了年轻女护士和抗日义士。医院不仅积极收治抗日伤员，还巧妙地把义士伪装成伤员，将他们安置在早已撒上白石灰的"疫区"或"太平间"。准备好的鼠疫患者死亡的照片吓退了不少日本宪兵。很多时候，会讲日语的陈为信在大门处和日军周旋，受保护的人员则从窑花井后门撤离。1934 年，中共仓山地下党组织受到破坏时，叶飞同志遭到追捕，也是从塔亭医院进入，在医院的保护下，从窑花井后门逃出。救护生命、保护正义，塔亭医院在烽火岁月书写了感人至深的福州版"辛德勒"传奇。抗日战争结束后，塔亭医院收到了福建省政府主席刘建绪赠送的牌匾，牌匾悬挂在病房走廊上方。"见义勇为"四个大字正是塔亭医院在危急时刻挺身而出的真实写照。

三位曾在塔亭医院生活或工作的受访者应邀在福建电视台节目讲述塔亭医院抗日战争故事
Three interviewees that once lived or worked in Takding Hospital telling stories that happened in Taking Hospital in a television program produced by Fujian Television Station

In 1944 when Fuzhou was under Japanese invaders' control a second time, hospitals in the city were either occupied or forced to relocate elsewhere outside the city, leaving Takding Hospital the only institution in Fuzhou that shouldered the medical responsibility. Despite the threat posed by the Japanese Military Police who were stationed at HSBC, a few steps away from the hospital, doctors headed by Chen Songpan, Director, and Chen Weixin, Director of General Affairs, were brave and resourceful enough to confront and deal with the police who often came and demanded threateningly for a search of anti-aggression fighters. Chen Weixin, who could speak some Japanese, for example, would keep the Japanese in negotiation for some time at the gate while the ingenious code word he devised—"dashi", literally "big" and "ten" in Chinese characters that can be put together to form another Chinese character "ben" meaning Japanese—was passed on to warn of the arrival of the Japanese police so that the young nurses and patriotic fighters could be timely relocated to safety, sometimes to the outside through Yaohuajing, a narrow lane close to the small exit at the back door. The similar escape was also successfully planned and carried out for Ye Fei who went into and out of the hospital through Yaohuajing in 1934 when Cangshan branch of the underground organization of the Communist Party was destroyed and he was tracked. Sometimes the police forced an entry into the hospital but ended up in a panic flight when they saw the terrifying photos of death from the bubonic plague, and the Isolation Section or the Mortuary that had been heavily covered with lime, all well prepared in advance without their knowledge as a disguise and thus it became a real sanctuary for the patriots who had been dressed up as the wounded. Such legendary stories make today's people believe that Takding Hospital was a Schindler in Fuzhou, a compliment of no less weight than the inscription that read "Bravery for Righteousness" on the plaque the hospital received after the war from Liu Jianxu, then Chairman of Fujian Provincial Government, for its heroic moments of rising to the occasion that forged for itself an image of a guardian of life and justice.

塔亭护士学校

1918 年，福州女子大学礼堂里，一群女士正在开会热议：女护士是否可以护理男病人？同样的热烈场景四年前在上海也有过一次，当时讨论的是，是否有更好的称呼取代"看护"一词。与会者是全国护士代表，不过，除了一个华人，其余的都是外国护士。在西方，护士作为正式职业在 19 世纪中叶刚刚起步，到 19 世纪末 20 世纪初，传教护士是西方国家对女性开放的少数几种工作之一。这些女传教士千里迢迢来到中国，或办学助教，或护理病人，培训助手，她们冲破闺阁之限的行为，唤醒了中国女性对自身价值的重新认识。这两次会议讨论的结果是肯定的：华人护士钟茂芳提出的"护士"一词，很好地体现了看护从业人员的专业技术性，获得全票通过，载入史册；华人女护士在外国女护士陪同之下行将打破"男女授受不亲"的禁锢。辛亥革命以来渐开的社会风气不断推进，护士正成为女性走出家庭的职业选择。越来越多女性加入护士行列，她们很快就要取代男护士，成为护理队伍中的主要角色。

在仓山，马高爱医院早在 1888 年就开设了小规模的护士培训班。当时福州第一个外国女西医特拉斯克于 19 世纪 70 年代来到仓山，开办岭后妇孺医院（即后来的马高爱医院）。她慧眼识才，推举仓山女孩许金訇西渡学医，造就了中国第一个女博士，也开启了福州地区女性职业之道。不过，信宝珠 1907 年来到马高爱医院时，还是感叹"这里没有医学校，没有护士，没有护士教程，没有护士组织，也没有护士实习的病房"（Lin，2020：78）。人们告诉她，中国不需要也没打算要护士。信宝珠没有打退堂鼓，她很快就着手改变这种状况。当年，她创办了中国的第一所注册护校——佛罗伦斯·南丁格尔护士和助产士培训学校（福建省卫生职业技术学院前身）。两年后，信宝珠发起成立了中华中部看护联合会，后几经易名，成为今天的中华护理学会。西方护士体系从此从零散培训走向正规。民国时期，全国各地开办护校，蔚为大观。到 1920 年为止，150 名中国护士获得中华护士会颁发的文凭，同年注册在案的中外护士总计达 183 人。到 1924 年，中华护士会成员中，中国护士已占比三分之二以上。当时，等待分配职位的注册护校毕业生名单总是长长的一张。

Takding Nursing School

In 1918, a group of ladies were having a meeting in a women's college in Fuzhou and the topic under heated discussion was whether female nurses should be allowed to attend to male patients. A similar hot debate occurred in Shanghai four years before when participants were looking for a better translation for "nurse" to replace the old "kanhu", a term only suggesting the duty of looking after the sick. Discussing nursing matters were nurse representatives from the whole country, all of whom except one were foreigners, who came from afar to China as missionary nurses to help run schools, take care of the sick or train assistants when missionary nursing as one of the few jobs was open to the Western women at the end of the 19th century and the early 20th century shortly after the recognition of nursing as a profession in the West in the mid-19th century. The conclusions both meetings arrived at were affirmative: In one meeting a better term "hushi" put forward by Elsie Mawfung Chung, the only Chinese nurse in the meeting, was adopted unanimously and recorded historically as a proper title that identifies nurses as well-trained technical personnel; in the other, it was decided that Chinese female nurses should be allowed, in the company of a foreign female nurse, to look after male patients, which would break the old social etiquette of a forbidden physical contact between men and women. Greatly awakened by the Western ladies' choice of working outside their homes and also propelled by the improved social convention that had played out since the Revolution of 1911, women in Fuzhou began to choose nursing as their career that they believed could best redefine their value, and as more women joined in, they would soon take on a dominating role in nursing in place of male nurses.

Nursing training in Cangshan has a long history. Back in 1888 a small nursing training class was opened in Magaw Memorial Hospital, a hospital for women and children at Liang Au, Cangshan, run by Dr. Sigourney Trask, the first female foreign doctor in Fuzhou who came in the 1870s and later recommended Hü King-eng to go to America to study medicine before Hü returned as the first Chinese woman with a Doctorate and as a good example to inspire women to work outside their family. The idea of establishing a nursing school, however, came a bit late. Cora Simpson lamented upon her arrival at Magaw Memorial Hospital in 1907, "There was no medical school, no nurses, no textbooks, no nurses' association, and no ward for trained nurses." And there, she was told there was no need of nurses but this grew her desire to change the situation. And there again she soon had the first registered Chinese nursing school established—Florence Nightingale Training School for Nurses and Midwives, the predecessor of Fujian Health College, and two years later she initiated what is now known as Chinese Nursing Association (CNA). Since then Western nursing training in China involved a systematic and formal education, and a nationwide opening of the nursing schools prevailed in the period of the Republic of China. By 1924, 150 Chinese nurses were granted certificates from CNA and there was a total of 183 registered Chinese and foreign nurses; by 1924 Chinese nurses accounted for more than two thirds of CNA members. In those years, the list of nursing graduates waiting for deployment of posts was always a long one.

正是在这种氛围下，塔亭医院也将建立护士学校摆上了议事日程。1920 年医院开始筹备工作，由后来成为总务长的陈为信负责。1921 年 2 月，医院的附属护士学校成立。至 1925 年止，福建省至少 17 家教会医院都办了护校，其中在中华护士会注册的有 11 家，塔亭医院属于私立医院中较早注册的。初期，塔亭护校兼培训医士和护士。近代医学发展促使医院成为集治疗和护理为一体的机构，医护不分家，塔亭医院护士学校就曾在男护士中开办医士班。事实上，塔亭医院历史上一些护校毕业生通过后期学习实践晋升为医生，这并非特例。

护校初期招生不定期，每届招生仅一两名。如，1924 年全院只有 4 名护士，1 名外籍，3 名中国护士。早期仅招收基督徒，由各教区推荐，男女兼收，学生经外国医生面谈认可即可入学。当时，男生多于女生。这是因为 20 世纪初前 20 年，男护士一直是我国医院的主要护理力量，到了 30 年代，护理工作被视为女性的专门职业，男护士才显得不合时尚，必须另谋出路了（刘燕萍，2005）。1936 年塔亭医院开始允许女护士护理男病人，这节奏多少还是比 1918 年的会议决议慢了几拍。塔亭医院一直由圣公会女差会派驻院师姑，师姑就是传教女护士，她们从事医务护理和日常管理。自 1924 年起，巴师姑和留师姑先后担任护校第一任、第二任校长，负责护理业务和护士学校学生管理工作。

塔亭护士学校男护士参加的医师培训班里的学员
Members of a training class for male nurses to be promoted as physicians in Takding Nursing School

On the heels of pioneering efforts in nursing education, Takding Hospital put on the agenda the establishment of its own nursing school and after preparation in 1920 under the charge of Chen Weixin, Takding Nursing School was founded in February, 1921. By 1925, there had been at least seventeen missionary hospitals in Fujian that had their own nursing schools set up, eleven registered in CNA, and Takding Nursing School was among the early private hospitals to register. In its early program, Takding Nursing School offered training to both junior physicians and nurses, reflecting a system of combining treatment and nursing into one and an inseparable relation between doctors and nurses in early modern medical institutions, as the result of development of medical science. Training classes for physicians were once open to male nurses in Takding Hospital; some nursing graduates were indeed promoted to be physicians through proper training and practice and that was never a rare case.

In its early days, the school had irregular enrollments, each time with only one or two students admitted, as evidenced by the data in 1924 where there were only four nurses in all, one foreigner and the other three Chinese. Early students, male or female, had to be Christians recommended by their parishes and interviewed by foreign doctors. Men students were preferred as men nurses had been the dominating force in the nursing profession in the first two decades of the 20th century and it was not until 1930s when women were thought to be cut out for nursing that male nurses were believed out of fashion. Women nurses in Takding Hospital were not allowed to attend to male patients until 1936, which somewhat fell behind the decision of the 1918 meeting. As resident nurses assigned by CEZMS, missionary nurses, better known as home sisters or "shigu" in Chinese, not only took charge of daily nursing routines in the hospital, but also ran the school as the principal, say, Sister Barr and Sister Barron respectively serving as the first and the second principal responsible for the nursing business and the student management.

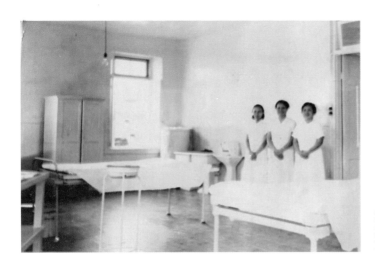

塔亭医院的护士（来源：陈美爱）
Nurses in Takding Hospital (Source: Chen Meiai)

20 世纪 30 年代，护士学校改为公开招生，条件比原来严格，到 40 年代，开始招收非教徒学生，学生生源多了，要求更为严格。此时的学生大多完成了小学初中教育，教会学校毕业的女生摆脱了裹足之缚，更加向往职业之道。如果说 20 年代的护校学生多是靠着家庭宗教渊源举荐入学，以缓解家庭经济状况，那么到了三四十年代，上护校更多表现为女性自食其力的主张。护校学习免费，住宿由医院负责，不过学生入学需交一定保证金，毕业后可退。据记载，几乎没人申请退保证金，看来保证金已不重要，毕业生正跃跃欲试，前途就在眼前。护校的学制 3 年 4 个月，前 4 个月为试读期，合格后转正为正式生。学生半工半读，上午在病房工作，下午晚上读书。从学校后期一份材料看，学生每周听课时间和实习时间分别是第一学年 16 小时和 36 小时，第二学年 10 小时和 42 小时。很显然，护理专业强调操作，重在实践。学生们在学期间称为护生，护生穿蓝袖、白色背心连衣裙，不戴护士帽，根据学习年段分配不同的护理任务，她们承担了医院大部分的简单基础护理工作。

教师则由医院医生兼任。1924 年陈颂磐来院工作，他曾经负责教授解剖学、药物学、内科等。1937 年，陈兆勤来院任护校校长兼课任教师，课程逐步走向正规，当时设护理学、护士心理学、解剖学、内科、外科、国文（后改称语文），后来国际护士课程进一步加入，学生们学习科目还包括生理学、营养学、药学、保健学、病菌理论、家政学、英语、拉丁语等。外语在当时很重要，学生要学会用英文写交班记录，要看懂拉丁文药名。塔亭护士学校的毕业生可自愿留院工作，其中女生可以再进修一年的产科课程后任助产士。早期护士大多受到师姑们以院为家的熏陶，毕业即留院，如包罗以、张美恩等。1924 年到 1952 年医院接办前，塔亭医院的护理人员主要都源于塔亭护校毕业的学生。至 1941 年止，护校共有毕业生 142 名。1949 年，教职工 21 人，在校生 77 人。1952 年医院接办后，护校改名为福州第四护校，同年底护校撤销，并入福州第二护校。

福州塔亭高级护士学校欢迎新教师新同学留念（1950 年 10 月 2 日）（来源：陈美爱）
A group photo taken on the occasion of welcoming new teachers and students to the nursing school (October 2, 1950) (Source: Chen Meiai)

Open to the public in the 1930s and to non-Christians in the 1940s, the school now had more students who, with education background in primary and junior high schools, fared rather well in the stricter recruitment, all eager to enter the nursing field. Unlike students in the previous decade who came mainly for religious and financial considerations for their families, students now, females in particular who had broken the bondage of foot-binding, expressed more of the readiness to earn their own living. There were no tuition fees, and the accommodation was arranged by the hospital; the guarantee deposit payable could be returned upon graduation, but the promising future nursing career would soon bring to them, as they believed, was such that no graduates seemed to bother to claim the reimbursement. During their stay in school, the first four months was a trial period to see if they were qualified enough to be accepted formally as regular students for the following three years' training that was to be carried out on a work-study basis, that is, ward duties in the morning and classroom studies in the afternoon and in the evening. Documents show that students' class hours and internship length per week in the first semester was sixteen hours and thirty-six hours respectively, and in the second, ten hours and forty-two hours, with priority obviously lopsided to the practice. Wearing white shirtdresses with blue sleeves but no nurse's cap on the head, these students, often addressed as nursing students (NS), took on the bulk of basic nursing duties, each with specific tasks based on the grades they were in.

Hospital doctors were assigned to do the teaching jobs. Chen Songpan, for example, was once teaching courses such as anatomy, pharmacology and medicine after his arrival at the hospital in 1924. In 1937 when Chen Zhaoqin came to teach and manage the school as the principal, a formal curriculum gradually came into being which involved nursing, nursing psychology, anatomy, medicine, surgery, Chinese, etc., and later with more international courses added, what students had to learn also included physiology, nutrition, pharmacy, health science, germ theory, home economics, English and Latin, etc. Foreign languages were important subjects because students were required to write nursing report in English and to understand Latin names of medicines. Students were greatly encouraged to work in Takding Hospital after graduation, and Bao Luoyi and Zhang Meien were such representatives who might have been influenced by the sentimental loyalty the resident nurses had to the hospital. For female graduates, they could also choose to stay another year to learn obstetrics before they were employed as midwives. From 1924 to 1952 graduates from Takding Nursing School were the essential source of the nursing personnel in Takding Hospital. By 1941, there were altogether 142 graduates, and in 1949 seventy-seven students and twenty-one staff members. Later in 1952 when the hospital was taken over, the school name was changed to Fuzhou Fourth Nursing School, and again in the same year, the school was merged into Fuzhou Second Nursing School.

护校学生所受训练十分严格，虽然还只是护生，但对于护士一职的严苛规矩，她们都了然于心。比如，护士工作时不准穿硬底鞋；一轮夜班为期一个月，每班 13 小时；护士发错药或饮食，要受到脱帽处分，直到认为改正了，才可重新戴上护士帽。护理工作必须规范，比如，护士要做晨间护理、测体温、病床清洁、打针、发药，重病员从脸清洁、洗涤到分饮食等生活护理，事无巨细，必须面面俱到。而在特护室的护理工作，除了基础护理，如每天给病人洗口腔、翻身、擦背等，每 15 分钟要为病人测一次血压、脉搏、呼吸，还要注意病人的病情变化。特护期间，如果发现病人受压部分皮肤发红或长褥疮，护理人员要受到警告、记过、开除等处分。严苛的规章制度并没有让这群怀揣新时期职业梦想的少女退缩。自食其力，呵护生命，塔亭护校的年轻人奏出了时代最强音。

20 世纪 20 年代成立的塔亭护士学校一直到 1943 年才立案，这或许与二三十年代非基督教运动引发的收回教育权有关。1947 年，学校正式取名为福州私立塔亭高级护士职业学校。其校舍历经几次搬迁。1927 年，医院在靠近窑花井的西向建了一座三层楼房，40 年代学校立案后，汇丰银行旧址曾作为教学楼。据说公园西路 2 号的白鸽楼也曾当过护士学校楼。1946 年，医院新建一座四层砖木结构新楼，是学校的新校舍。地点变迁，不变的是护士的"十心"口号："要有爱心、虚心、耐心、认真的心、同情的心……"（王小虎、游庆辉，2005）

历史车轮滚滚向前，塔亭医院已不再是当初那个以西侨民为中心的社区医院。通过开办护校，医院内涵得以拓展，医院拥有了现代意义的教育功能。这样一来，医院事实上扩大了地方民众受教育的机会，为女性解放提供了实现空间，也为社会输送了人才。为此，它收获了一方民众，融入当地，并扎根于此，在时代大潮中与当地同呼吸，共命运。

福州私立塔亭高级护士职业学校曾经的校址：汇丰银行福州分行旧址（1952）
Fuzhou Takding Advanced Private Nursing Vocational School in the former site of Fuzhou Branch, HSBC (1952)

Strict as the nursing training was, students all had a good understanding and familiarity of the iron-cast rules such as no hard-soled shoes at work or a 13-hour-long night shift for one month. Not yet a nurse's cap on the head, they knew it well that if nurses dispensed wrong medicine or diet the cap would be taken off as a punishment and not be back on until the mistake was corrected. Standardized routines were also well kept in mind such as morning care of taking temperature, tidying beds, giving IV or shots and dispensing medicine, or an all-round service to the severely sick from face washing, clothes changing and washing to arranging diet. Equally well remembered was the duty in wards for special nursing care that entailed a close and constant watch apart from taking blood pressure and checking pulse and breath at an interval of 15 minutes, let alone a basic daily service such as mouth cleaning, turning over, back washing, and, by the way, failure to do the last two, for example, would result in patients suffering from bedsores, and in turn, a warning, a demerit record, or even a dismissal to the nurses concerned. For all the stringent rules and regulations, no young ladies showed any sign of withdrawal from the profession they believed that would carry them far enough to the land where their dream of being able to stand on their own feet while taking care of others would come true and reverberate throughout.

Probably due to the non-Christian campaign in the 1920s and the 1930s that spurred the movement of reclaiming educational rights, Takding Nursing School, although established in the 1920s, was not registered until 1943, and it was in 1947 that the school was officially named Fuzhou Takding Private Advanced Vocational Nursing School. The school premises in history changed several times leaving the trace of its growth. For example, a three-story house was built in 1927 close to Yaohuajing in the west, and in the 1940s after the school's formal registration, the school moved to the hospital's nextdoor, the old site of HSBC, for more space. Another building used outside the hospital was Pigeon Building located at No. 2 West Park Road. In 1946, a new four-story school building inside the hospital was completed. Despite the change of school building, what remained unchanged was the motto nurses always committed to memory and to practice—to serve with "a heart full of love, a mind that is open, an ear always listening, a hand ready to help, the look full of compassion. . . "

Moving forward with the rolling wheel of history, Takding Hospital was no longer the community medical center originally for the interest of Western residents. With a nursing school, the hospital now was able to perform the function of education in the modern sense, producing education opportunities for locals, space of independence for women, and talents for society. In return there came the recognition from and deeper integration into the local people with whom the hospital was to share a common destiny in the coming new tide of the times.

● 时代新篇——福州市第二医院：大医精诚，薪火相传

中华人民共和国成立后，塔亭医院翻开了崭新的历史篇章。20 世纪 50 年代，在政府大力帮助下，医院重获新生，原来教会色彩浓重的私立医院转型为公立"福州市第二医院"，历史上那个属于西侨的"本地医馆"从此改天换地，成为名副其实的人民医院。70 年来，许多科室和业务从无到有，医院实现了跨越式大发展。50 年代中医科、针灸科、60 年代麻醉科、70 年代草药科的成立和建设，使得这个西医肇始的百年医院呈现一派中西医学并重互补相辅相成的文化景观。如今，医院规模层次不断扩大，科室齐全，人才济济，是仓山区起引导作用的市级医院。这里有国家级重点专科骨伤科和重症医学科，是国家中医药管理局确定的三级甲等中西医结合医院。2013 年，医院增加了一个身份——厦门大学附属福州第二医院，医院交流合作范围扩大，科研平台得以提升。新时期，医院走特色专科品牌和全面综合发展道路，每一次前进都铿锵有力，悬壶济世，初心不忘。

"龙头"骨科

"看骨科找二院"，这是福州老百姓的口头禅。在福州医疗界，骨科品牌是二院的一张烫金名片。中华人民共和国成立初期，福州各个综合医院尚无骨科，当时市二医院在外科收治骨科病人，设备简陋。为解决骨科患者就医难的问题，医院组织骨科治疗小组，开展手术。1958 年，医院正式在外科中成立骨科。60 年代，二院已具备骨科专业医师队伍和护理队伍。1977 年，骨科独立分科。同年骨科编写的《骨科检查法》作为内部资料在全国发行，是国内较早的一本骨科工具书。1979 年医院被省卫生厅列为培训正规骨科医师的重点基地，成为全国第一批骨科住院医师规培培训基地。80 年代，骨科继续壮大，开始设行政主任。1984 年，成立省内首家骨科研究所。在接下来的发展中，骨科一路高歌猛进，床位不断增加，目前有骨科床位 650 个，占全院病床数三分之一多，全院 30 多个病区近一半属于骨科。骨科越分越细，医院因此成为省内分科最细、亚专业最全的骨科专科医院，也是全省规模最大、接诊和治疗的创伤病人最多的骨科中心。作为国家中医药管理局骨伤科学重点学科，骨科诊疗水平居全国先进水平，是全省骨科诊疗教学研究中心。

福州市第二医院 155 周年院庆时"龙头"骨科全体医护人员合影
A group photo of Orthopedics Department taken on the occasion of 155th anniversary of Fuzhou Second Hospital

• A New Chapter with Continued High-Quality Medical Services

The hospital entered a brand new stage after the founding of the People's Republic of China. With great support from the government in the 1950s, the private hospital that used to belong to the Foreign Community turned into a public medical institution. With some new departments such as Departments of TCM and Acupuncture in the 1950s, of Anesthesiology in the 1960s, and of Chinese Herbs in the 1970s, the hospital underwent a gradual evolution into a medical culture that was to welcome the combination of Chinese and Western medicine. Now the new hospital remains a leading municipal hospital in Cangshan District, and with the orthopedics & traumatology and ICU as the two state-level key specialties, it enjoys a good reputation as a Grade-A hospital of Chinese and Western medicine authorized by The National Administration of Traditional Chinese Medicine (NATCM). In 2013, a new identity, Fuzhou Second Hospital Affiliated to Xiamen University, has broadened the hospital's cooperation and improved its research level. Now in the present new era, the hospital is working on a strategy of strengthening signature specialties and promoting its overall development, while carrying on its original commitment to the protection of people's life in each stage of its growth.

Orthopedics as a Flagship

"Bone problems? The Second Hospital is surely the best place to go." That familiar talk among folks is no exaggeration because in medical fields in Fuzhou, orthopedics in this hospital is a recognizable signature brand. But back in the early 1950s, there was no bone department in all general hospitals in Fuzhou. To meet the needs of orthopedic patients, the Second Hospital organized a team for bone treatment which later in 1958 became the orthopedics section under the surgical department. Staffed with its own specialized doctors and nurses in the 1960s, orthopedics was able to rise independently in 1977, and its book, *Orthopedic Examination Techniques*, was issued as the internal reference in the whole country and hailed as one of the first reference books of its kind in China. In 1979, the hospital was authorized by Fujian Provincial Department of Health as the key formal training base for orthopedic surgeons and the first national standardized training base for resident orthopedic doctors. Its growth in the 1980s necessitated the position of executive director and the establishment of the first provincial orthopedics research center in 1984. Since then remarkable strides forward have been made with the increasing beds which now reach 650 accounting for more than one third of the total bed counts. Its persistent specialization and division has won it nearly half of the hospital's over thirty wards. With the most comprehensive sub-specialties and specific clinics, it treats the largest number of orthopedic patients in the province, making the hospital the biggest provincial orthopedic specialty hospital. As a key specialty under NATCM, its diagnosis and treatment appraised to the advanced national level, it deserves to be the provincial teaching and research center of orthopedics.

在二院，骨科及骨伤复原是"龙头"，这里有20世纪80年代省内最先开展的关节镜下手术，有2010年省内首例人工全髋关节成功翻修，有2015年在全国率先运用的3D打印技术，成功矫正罕见小腿畸形，技惊业界，还有治愈率达到国际同期水平的计算机辅助导航技术下人工髋膝关节置换手术及置换后相关手术。被戏称为"一科独大"的骨科所获赞誉无数，却不曾妄自尊大，科技迭代让他们更注重学习交流。2021年，骨科通过柔性引进优质医疗资源、科研团队和高端人才，不断提升骨科整体医疗服务、技术水平和科研转化能力，其中教授名医"师带徒"工作室落户福州市第二医院，更是带来了一系列新技术，可谓骨科又一点睛之笔。

特色中西医结合

清末民初，西医东来，中国社会卷入传统医学和外来西医的博弈之中，中西医关系一度含蓄微妙。民国初期，政府大力提倡西医，"废止旧医"引发中西医大辩论，形成传统中医与现代医学双峰对峙的局面。在福州仓山，自古以来就流行草药治病的传统。晚清民国时期，个体中医诊所遍布全区，草药科、骨科和眼科最具特色，中医群众基础良好。中华人民共和国成立以来，政府多次倡导中西医结合，20世纪80年代在卫生部提出"中医、西医、中西医三支力量都要发展，长期并存"的方针下，仓山区普遍采用在西医科学辨病的基础上应用中、西药结合治疗疾病的方法，疗效较为理想。作为仓山区最主要的医疗机构，福州市第二医院在80年代以前就设有分科较细的中医科以及草药科，日均门诊量大。因此，1984年，省政府授予的"福建省福州中西医结合医院"落户福州市第二医院。1989年，六千平方米的新门诊大楼奠基石上"发挥中西医结合特色，创文明医院"揭示了医院进入新的发展时期。1996年，医院被国家中医药管理局确定为三级甲等中西医结合医院。历经二十载建设，2008年5月，医院顺利通过国家中医药管理局专家组评审。

福建省福州市中西医结合医院授牌仪式（1984）
Plaque unveiling ceremony of Fujian Fuzhou Hospital of Integrated Traditional Chinese and Western Medicine, held in 1984

Through efforts of all staff, Orthopedics & Orthopedic Recovery has become the head department that managed many firsts in the province: the application of arthroscope in the 1980s, the revision of total hip replacement in 2010, and the use of 3D printing to correct the rare leg deformity that stunned the medical community in 2015, and computer-aid artificial hip and knee joint replacement with a cure rate up to the international level in 2017. Winner of many prizes and merits as it is, the department never creates a case of "winner take all", although it is sometimes dubbed "the department that is overwhelmingly dominant". Instead, they take themselves as a flagship department that never rests on their laurels but keeps its fingers on the pulse of technology trends. A case in point is a project of soft introduction in 2021 of high-quality medical resources, researching team and top-level talents with an aim to promote medical service, technology level and conversion of research in the department. A studio of apprenticeship led by the well-known doctors in the project was another highlight that was sure to bring in the-state-of-the-art technologies.

Characteristic Integration of TCM and Western Medicine

Traditional Chinese medicine (TCM) and Western medicine had been in a subtle relation since the arrival of Western medicine in the late Qing Dynasty. Early in the Republic of China, a nationwide debate triggered by the government's proposal of promoting Western medicine while "abolishing TCM" resulted in a temporary reconciliation, and later a standoff between the two. In Cangshan, local people had a tradition of using herbs to deal with diseases, and clinics of Chinese medicine run by individuals were everywhere, all known for the use of herbs, especially in the treatment of bones and eyes. Since the founding of the People's Republic of China, Chinese government has encouraged many times the integration of TCM and Western medicine. In the 1980s, guided by the new policy of "coexistence and equal growth of traditional Chinese medicine, Western medicine and integrated Chinese and Western medicine" put forward by the Ministry of Health, hospitals in Cangshan found the satisfactory curative effect lied in the blend of Chinese and Western therapy after a Western diagnosis. Among those hospitals, Fuzhou Second Hospital, the leading medical institution in Cangshan, had specialized departments of TCM and herbs set up long before the 1980s that drew a large number of outpatients every day, and was therefore chosen by the provincial government in 1984 as the site of Fujian Fuzhou Hospital of Integrated Traditional Chinese and Western Medicine. In 1989, the hospital entered a new developmental stage when a new outpatient building covering six thousand square meters was erected with words on its cornerstone that read "For a Better Hospital with Characteristic Integration of Chinese and Western Medicine". In 1996 it was certified by NATCM as Grade-A, and successfully passed the evaluation organized by NATCM in May 2008.

骄人的成绩背后是医院"继承不离古，发扬不离宗"的理念。在这一理念引导下，市二医院找到了独特的发展路径，成为全省唯一一家三级甲等中西医结合医院，拥有国家级重点中西医结合专科两个（骨伤科、重症医学科），以及一批省级市级重点中西医结合专科，此外全院科室还普遍开展中西医结合诊疗工作。如今，医院拥有30多家省市级医疗学术科研机构，其中西医和谐共舞的交响曲更加恢宏大气。

文化兴院

文化是无形的，但也有形可见。"以病人为中心"在二院就是看得见的医疗关爱。"不需要开刀就不要开刀"的原则最大程度保护了患者的健康和经济利益。在"镇痛—无痛示范病区"，手术病人主动参与疼痛评估和处理，术后疼痛大为改善。救治无主病人，名医为保证医患沟通顺畅专门学说福州话等等。看得见的还有医院日益增加的基础设施和设备，缓解了患者就医难的问题。急救大楼自2009年投入使用以来，每天都上演着医者妙手悬壶，与死神赛跑，为生命永不言弃的感人场景。医者托起生命之重的承诺背后，是以精湛的医疗技术为基础的强烈责任心，这是市二医护人员的共识。正是这种"从病人利益出发"的态度，促成了和谐友好的文化生态，丰富了医院的服务文化，塑造着医院的文化气质。

市二院还积极履行社会责任，以医院文化引领社会文明。医院定期或不定期举行各类义诊，宣传科普健康知识；支援区内多项卫生工作，帮扶弱势群体，为街道特困人员施行酌情免费政策，解决其就医难的问题。医院免费救治见义勇为的英雄，极大地弘扬了社会正气。无论是汶川地震还是疫情肆虐，医院总有一批批"召之即来，来之能战"的医护队员。在新的历史时期下，医院在更大范围发挥其技术文化引领作用。除了派医生帮扶乡镇卫生院，市二医院通过托管或合作，帮助一些地区医院发展，其中有鹤龄医院（现为福州市第三医院）、马尾经济技术开发区医院、福清市第三医院等。

What lay behind the remarkable achievements was the belief that "there is no sustainable development without respect to legacy", and it was from the recognition of the value of TCM that the hospital blazed a trail of its own: the only provincial Grade-A Integrated Chinese and Western Medicine Hospital. There is a general application of the integration approach in all departments including the two key national specialties, that is, Orthopedics & Traumatology and ICU, and some specialties on provincial and municipal level. Now with more than thirty medical research societies, the congruity of the two medical sciences will no doubt play out in a broader sense.

Nurture of Culture

However intangible culture may sound, it is perceptible and visible in the patient-oriented medical care Fuzhou Second Hospital is committed to. There is, for example, the guideline of "No surgery is needed unless it is essential" for the benefit of patients' health and their economic interest, and the establishment of "Analgesia Ward" where patients are encouraged to evaluate and decide for themselves to what level they want their pain to be eased. Good examples also include free hospitalization to unidentified patients, and renowned doctors' learning Fuzhou dialect for the sake of smooth communication with patients, etc. Also discernible are the increased infrastructure and equipment in relation to the medical service accessibility. Here in the emergency building since it was put into use in 2009 there have been wars fought by doctors against time to snatch life from the jaws of death each day. At the back of the services the hospital vows to deliver is the strong sense of responsibility bolstered by the exquisite medical technologies, as is the shared belief among the medical personnel who put the interest of patients above everything else and help cultivate the service culture in the hospital.

The social responsibility the hospital has been taking on for years to guide social civilization and progress is another thing that carries its cultural reputation far and wide. Regularly or irregularly, the hospital organizes medical services for the community such as free diagnosis, popularization of health knowledge, sufficient support to the disadvantaged including free medical service to the most needy. Free and best treatments to those who risked their life to protect others have greatly promoted social justice. To save lives in disasters such as Wenchuan Earthquake and the recent pandemic, the hospital has sent its professional teams that are always ready to respond, to act and to accomplish. Cultural influence through technology is not played down either. For a stronger leadership the hospital believes it should assume in the technological culture, it has launched programs of assistance through regular deployment of doctors to medical clinics in small towns, and through trusteeship or collaboration with hospitals such as Fuzhou Heling Hospital (now Fuzhou Third Hospital), Mawei Hospital in Mawei Economic & Technological Development Zone, and Fuqing Third Hospital.

与让患者满意、社会认同一样，职工幸福也是医院文化建设的内容。历史上塔亭医院职工少，是一个小家，如今三千多名员工，组成了团结友爱的大家庭。医院早期有多处职工宿舍，无论是塔亭门诊楼，还是汇丰银行旧址、白鸽楼、蓬芦区，都留下了二院人深情回望的角落。如今职工们在温馨的"职工之家"，在各种丰富的问题活动和慰问活动中，每一次相聚都是幸福的回忆。近年来，医院大力挖掘"塔亭"文化精髓。职工们的归属感、自豪感和使命感不断深化。无论是150周年院庆期间，医院的《塔亭医讯》和《塔亭苑》，还是近年的塔亭骨科国际论坛，以及如今公众号上丰富多彩的报道，二院人向外界传递着尊重历史、继往开来、与时俱进的精神风貌。医院院徽中，主题图案中的"骨"字巧妙地融合在医院历史古建筑塔亭楼中，历史交汇，中西合璧，以骨科为龙头的市二医院和历史起点塔亭医院融为一体，前世和今生托起的百年健康呵护在温暖向上的宫墙红中显得底气十足，令人信赖。

医院 2016 年庆祝 150 周年院庆设计的医院院徽（左）和院歌（右）
The hospital emblem (left) and song (right)to mark its 150th anniversary in 2016

医院原来的院报
The old newsletter of the hospital

A third cultural highlight the hospital has been working on with no less effort is the well-being for its staff, who keep the tradition of taking the hospital as their home that is now growing into a big and harmonious family of more than three thousand members out of a small one in Takding era. In earlier times, the hospital managed to find proper houses for its staff as their dormitories such as the old outpatient building, former site of HSBC, Pigeon Building and Pengluqu, most of which still exist for its previous residents to recall the passing days they spent together. Now staff members meet each other in "Home of Staff", where celebration activities or entertaining get-together bring them happy moments to recollect each time. The hospital's cultural projection of "Takding Culture" in recent years has successfully enhanced its staff's sense of belonging, pride and mission. "Takding" was once used to name the hospital journals and newspapers to mark the hospital's 150th anniversary, and it is now in the name of its annual international orthopaedics forum and some cultural projects. Cultural channels as such, together with colorful updates from today's Wechat official account, help to pass to the outside world the positive atmosphere among the staff that shows not only their respect to the past, but also their pledge to carry forward the predecessor's undertakings and their persistence in keeping up with the times. In its new emblem, the motif pattern in Chinese character "gu", suggesting Orthopedics Department, is well incorporated into the shape of the ancient Takding inpatient building, the historical starting point of the hospital. The design joins the East and the West, past and present to reproduce a reliable cultural power that is destined to sustain the medical care that has been on for more than a century and now still radiates robust warmth against its bottom vermilion.

院刊《塔亭苑》（来源：肖志勇）
Takding Yuan, the new form of the hospital's newsletter(Source: Xiao Zhiyong)

● 建筑中的记忆

建筑是历史的眼睛，透过建筑，遇见历史，这是今天人们的情怀。人生七十古来稀，今天的市二医院就完好地保留着两栋距今 70 余载仍在使用的楼房：当年的护士学校校舍和门诊大楼。

这两栋楼建造年代相近，属于民国时期的砖木建筑，但功能不同，风格迥异。护士学校楼建于 1946 年，20 世纪 90 年代改造成了制剂楼，楼内有生产各种中药制剂的设备，医院许多特效自制方剂就在这里生产。在 90 年代的改造中，楼内的木质结构已由水泥加固，原本护校时期的青砖外墙也贴上了红色瓷砖，倒是可以让人顺理成章地想象这里曾经飘过的欢声笑语。一楼原先是大礼堂，护士学校的集会和表演都在这里进行。当年家住护士楼对面的陈宜英老人清楚地记着，孩童时候，有一次学生们表演戏剧，她被临时"借"到舞台上，当了回那群花季少女的"儿子"。机缘巧合，若干年后，她也穿起了温馨记忆中那身洁白无瑕的护士连衣裙装。黄发忆垂髫，历历在目，依旧那般美好有趣。二楼是当年学生们上课的教室，三楼四楼是学生和医护人员的宿舍，地下室是洗衣间和洗澡房。当年医院靠着业务收入建起的这座学校大楼规模不大，却恰到好处，如今楼内经过再次改造，已经成为医院的信息中心。从学校到制剂楼再到信息中心，大楼的每一次角色转换都紧跟时代步伐。如果不是大楼奠基石上"民国三十五年五月二十日奠基"的提醒，人们恐怕很难想到这是目前医院楼群中年代最为久远的一座了。

∶ 建于 1946 年的塔亭护士学校楼
∶ Building of Takding Nursing School erected in 1946

• Memory Restored in Architectures

When ancient architectures are valued, modern people can borrow an eye to look into the past and have their curiosity met. Like a man in the old times who would be thought to have lived a long life with great wisdom when reaching his 70s, two buildings that have been standing for seven decades in Fuzhou Second Hospital—the Nursing School and the outpatient building—are worth a visit.

Except for the same brick-and-wood structure, the typical architectural style of the Republic of China, the two buildings, although erected in only two years apart, share not much resemblance mainly because of their different uses. One of them initially built as a nursing school and completed in 1946 was converted in the 1990s into a place of pharmaceutical preparation with various kinds of equipment to manufacture traditional Chinese medicine, some of which were produced according to the self-developed formula with desirable effect. The refurbishment in the 1990s also included the wooden structure inside stabilized with cement and the outside blue brick wall installed with red ceramic tiles. Coincidentally, this red wall now becomes an easy association of a nursing school that must have been bustling with chattering and laughing. Some of these lively scenes still remain fresh in the memory of Chen Yiying, an 80-year-old lady who lived opposite the nursing school when young. In her pleasant recollection, there was an auditorium for gatherings and performances on the first floor and there she was once "borrowed" onto the stage to play "son" of the young students. By fate or by chance, years later she put on the same pure white dress that had been in her mind since that indelible experience. Constructed with the hospital income alone, the building was not big but functional enough with classrooms on the second floor, dorms on the third and the fourth for students and the staff, and laundry and baths on the underground floor. To meet the demand for the new development, the building, after another round of renovation, is now used as Information Center. So well adapted to each transition from an educational center all the way now to a technology and information hub, this building is rarely looked upon as an old building, let alone the oldest existing architecture in the hospital, without the reminder of its cornerstone that records the date of its erection: May 12, 1946.

当年塔亭护士学校大楼的奠基石，上面写有当时的院长陈颂磐亲笔题词"乃役于人"及时间"民国三十年五月十二日"
Cornerstone of Takding Nursing School building that reads "To serve" by Chen Songpan, the acting director, on May 12, 1946

顺着当年护士楼所在的小坡底往上走，很快就可以看到当年的门诊楼。这座建于1948年的大屋为长方形建筑，高约11米，占地面积约407平方米。整座楼坐东朝西，一进八开间，第二、三层中间有宽敞的走廊，走廊两侧有分布对称的房间，房间外配有相通的外廊，外廊原无遮拦，为开放式双外廊，西侧可观上藤路，东侧可见院内情况。后来外廊全部装上福州地区较为少见的木制玻璃廊窗，呈现双外廊封闭式。闭窗保暖隔热，开窗通风采光，密闭的廊窗与整座建筑浑然一体，大楼结构上的整齐划一得以呈现。这座砖木结构楼散发出浓郁的民国风，也呈现出20世纪30年代西方建筑古典主义之外的"国际式"，主要表现为几无装饰，无所偏重，力求平面上便利而已（朱永春，2001），是一种现代主义简约风格。当年大楼的设计师是福建协和建筑部的林缉西。

　　屋顶采取中国传统歇山式，符合当地多雨潮湿的气候特点，也与当地建筑融为一体。细看一些19、20世纪在中国的西方学校建筑，会发现许多类似的中式大屋顶。据说当年西方建筑师为实现传教士们朦胧而美好的中式校舍梦，展开了"各显神通的富有东方情调的尝试"，结果设计师们无一例外都选择了中式大屋顶（董黎，2001）。看似"混搭"的背后，折射出的却是建筑界里十分热闹有趣的"折衷主义"。各种建筑元素打散开来，玩转于设计师手中，洋为中用，古为今用，常常令人眼前一亮。外墙使用本地青砖，与中国古时传统建筑一致，既低调也实惠。

　　医院在20世纪50年代完成公有制转变后，基础设施不断完善，门诊大楼随着新楼的建造几度搬迁，这座楼遂改为他用。这里曾被当作医院职工的居家宿舍，锅碗瓢盆，人间烟火，十分热闹。近年来该建筑已纳入政府保护修复项目，"修旧如旧"，让人耳目一新，如今大楼已作为医院体检中心交付使用。

左图：修复一新的旧门诊大楼（2021）（来源：池志海）
Left：The newly renovated outpatient building in 2021 (Source: Chi Zhihai)
右图：旧门诊大楼东面外廊呈开放式（20世纪80年代）（来源：陈美熙）
Right：The old outpatient building with open balconies in the east in the 1980s (Source: Chen Meixi)

A path uphill from the nursing building leads to the outpatient building erected in 1948. About eleven meters high, this rectangular structure, facing west with an area of 407 square meters, has three stories. Inside the building is a stretch of eight rooms on each side of the hall. Upstairs through a staircase in the middle to the second and the third floor are even more spacious passages, both sides of which are rooms opposite in parallel, all sharing long balconies that were previously open either to Shangteng Road in the west or to the inside part of the hospital in the east. Now covered with glass windows set in wooden frames that create an impressive unity of the entire building, a rare architectural style in Fuzhou, this closed balcony on both sides can keep colds out or have light and fresh air in with open windows. This brick-wood house reflects another popular architectural style—internationalism—that prevailed in the Republic of China, apart from classicism, in the 1930s, which "gave neither room for decorations nor priority to any part, but a convenience to the image of architectural plan", a pure style of simplicity under the influence of modernism. The architect in charge was T. Seth Lin who worked in Union Architectural Service.

The building has the traditional Chinese saddle roof that best suits the local wet weather and matches the native architecture. Indeed, the similar roofs are often seen in Western school buildings in China in the 19th and 20th centuries when Western architects were said to have agreed unanimously on this choice after they tried in vain to find the best in various attempts full of oriental sentiments to satisfy the misty dream the missionaries held about the Chinese-style school buildings. Behind this apparent Mix & Match lies eclecticism in which all elements are at the architects' disposal often for an amazing effect. The use of local blue bricks fit in with the code of traditional ancient Chinese buildings and gave the building a low profile and an economical use of funds.

With infrastructure improvement since the hospital's transformation into public ownership in the 1950s, the building for outpatient services had changed several times from one new building to another, but the old was never abandoned. It was once used as staff's living quarters, full of boisterous atmosphere with sounds of pots and pans, walk and talk. Put on the list of governmental projects of protection and renovation a few years ago, the building has now been restored to the past as it was, and with a pleasantly fresh look, it is now welcoming people to experience its new role as the physical examination center.

旧门诊大楼现有的木窗封闭式外廊（2022）
The present balconies with glass windows set in close wooden frames in the old outpatient building（2022）

旧貌换新颜的门诊大楼留给现代人一个真实的历史空间。徜徉旧楼之际，不免让人心生好奇：更早的门诊楼，还有最早塔亭楼是否有迹可循？150 载花开花落，沧海桑田，寻觅塔亭楼并非易事。幸运的是，在一些老照片、文献资料和几位当年生活在医院生活区有着共同记忆的口述者的帮助下，我们找回了 20 世纪四五十年代的塔亭空间，勾勒出了塔亭医院大楼的模样和改制前后的医院布局，历史回望因此多了几分真实。

　　下图中占地面积最大的建筑楼群是塔亭医院诊疗区，包括了相互连通的四栋楼，建造时间有所不同。其中靠着西大门与上腾路平行的这栋就是前面提到的 1948 年建造的门诊楼（图示⑤），此时它是建筑群中最新的一栋。与这座新门诊楼垂直的这座（④）就是更早的门诊楼，该楼建于 1915 年，为纪念 1912 年去世的首任院长连尼而建（李文巍，2014：59）。新门诊楼建起后，这座旧门诊楼的二楼主要做化验室。接下来诊疗区的楼群就是呈"八"字型的塔亭楼，即病房大楼。当年，建造病房大楼是西人开设医院而非诊所或药房的重要标志，这栋楼的主体部分（①②）就是 1886 年医院迁来时建造的最早的塔亭大楼，右翼部分（③）是 1894—1895 年间增建的女病房楼。整座大楼呈现典型的殖民地单外廊式建筑风格。19 世纪下半叶，中西建筑文化交流频繁，西式建筑以迅雷不及掩耳之势迅速传遍整个中国建筑界。这种建筑形式以带有外廊为主要特征，通常有一至二层楼，是英国殖民者将欧洲建筑传入印度、东南亚一带，为适应当地炎热气候而形成的一种建筑形式。外廊通风空气好，利于病人恢复。

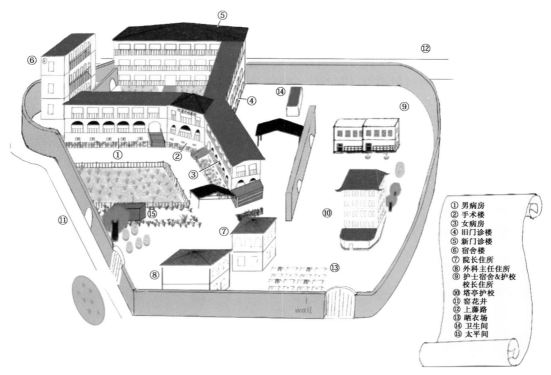

：塔亭医院 20 世纪四五十年代布局复原图（绘制：刘可欣）
：A restored layout of Takding Hospital in the 1940s‐1950s (Drawn by Liu Kexin)

The ancient building with a new look gives a physical historical site for visitors to wander around and to wonder as well where its predecessor was and what it looked like. Vicissitudes of one and a half centuries make things beyond recognition and this exploration of the oldest Takding building, a fanciful idea. Yet fortunately, with old pictures, literature and the help of people who were brought up in Takding Hospital with common memory of the 1940s and 1950s, a sketch of the Takding space became possible and a look back at Takding building, real and rich.

A cluster of four buildings (①～④) connected to each other, some built in different years, was the medical section that covered the largest area of the hospital. Standing parallel to Shangteng Road and next to the west gate was the aforementioned outpatient building (⑤) constructed in 1948 when it should be looked at as the newest of all. Vertical to that was the even earlier outpatient building (④) set up in 1915 in memory of Thomas Rennie, the first superintendent of the hospital who died in 1912. Its second floor was once used as a laboratory. The A-shaped structure was the inpatient building, the then important mark of a hospital rather than a dispensary or a clinic in the early days of Western medicine in China. As the earliest construction built in 1886 (①②) when Takding Hospital relocated here, this building, which later in 1894 and 1895 had a right wing added as women's wards (③), represented more of a typical colonial style with a veranda on one side only as the result of a rapid spread of Western style in the architectural exchange in the second half of the 19th century. One-or-two-storey buildings with a veranda was a choice by the British colonists to adapt to the local hot weather conditions when they first arrived in India and Southeast Asian countries with European architecture, and such well-ventilated veranda was no doubt good for the recovery of patients.

塔亭病房大楼女病房部分（来源：陈美爱）
Part of the wing of women's wards in the inpatient building (Source: Chen Meiai)

呈"八"字型的塔亭病房大楼共两层，外加地面一个地基层。单面外廊位于八字形的"内院"一面，"内院"部位立面高处写有"闽省塔亭医院"字样，立面造型简洁，半圆形券窗。"八"字型两侧分别是男女病房区，对称分布，每层各有门廊 6 间，呈新古典主义风格。楼前空地宽敞，种有各种花草树木。中间是手术楼区，体现病区分离的"亭式病区"原则，符合 19 世纪下半叶流行于英国的医院风格。该大楼的"八"字外形与 1912 年重建的马高爱医院有几分相似，反映了通商口岸时期烟台山地区西式医院建筑的样式。

病房大楼各功能区设置合理，之间有廊道和楼道相通。手术室在手术楼区二层，20世纪 30 年代扩建，一层为女病房，有 2 间；手术区右侧也是女病房区，这里的一楼还有三大间女病房，分别是 Mather、Ladar、Rood Ward，每间 5 个床位（《烟台山史话》，2014：89），还有一间产房，一间医生办公室，尽头是杂物间。二楼主要是师姑住房，师姑们居所的位置考虑与建造由加拿大女传教士玛格丽特负责。男病房区一楼主要是男外科病房，有两大间，分别有 10 个床位，二楼也有一间 10 个床位的病房，是男内科病房。同样在二楼的还有 3 间单人病房，属于急症或特需病患的特殊病房，这里还有一间医生办公室。大楼内廊道相通，但不同功能区之间有门做分隔，楼内还有多处楼梯通往楼外，这里的楼梯是当年人们最喜爱的照相打卡点。女病房侧边还盖有雨遮，避热防雨，便于通行。男病房边上有一座三层楼房，这是 1927 年医院在窑花井（⑪）西向所建的护士学校楼，后来改做医生宿舍，一层是病人的营养室。

以塔亭楼为中心的塔亭医疗楼群在整个院区的西向，院区北侧离女病房较近的则是集合了护士宿舍、校长居所和仓库的楼群（⑨）以及最新的塔亭护士学校（⑩），东侧还有两座住宅，曾经是医生住房和院长住所。医院的诊疗区和生活区之间有不高的墙，墙上有出入门。

从男病房区可见塔亭医院时期的院长住所
Director's residence seen from the wing of
men's wards

This A-shaped Takding building had two floors excluding a ground layer with the veranda in the east facing the inner part of the hospital where the Chinese name of the hospital was clearly seen high on the facade wall—Min Provincial Takding Hospital. A glance of it from the old photos can tell an obvious influence of a neo-classical architectural style: a simple elevation, semicircular arched windows, a symmetrical plan of wards for men and women separate in the two wings of the A-shape with six arched sections in the veranda, and a spacious area full of flowers and trees just before the building. Connecting the two wings was an area for operation, reflecting a clear division and separation of different sections under the principle of "pavilion style" that prevailed among the British hospitals in the second half of the 19th century. The exterior A-shape that resembled Magwa Memorial Hospital reconstructed in 1912 is demonstrative of what a western-style hospital in the treaty port period might look like.

Inside the building was another proper plan of different functioning sections accessible through passages, verandas and staircases. The only operating theatre on the second floor was extended in the 1930s and the two rooms on the first floor were therefore used as women's wards. The right wing next to the operating section was women's wards, three of which on the first floor were Mather, Ladar, and Rood Ward, each with five beds. Also on the first floor was a delivery room, a doctor's office and a utility room at the end while its second floor was the living area for home sisters. It was Margaret Brown, a Canadian female missionary, who built housing for nurses in Takding Hospital to make sure that nurses lived closer to the hospital. On the left wing were men's wards with two ten-bed wards on the first floor for surgical patients, and one ten-bed ward on the second floor for medical patients. Also on the second floor were three private wards for patients in critical situation or with special request, and a doctor's office as well. All passages and verandas were passable with doors as partition of different functioning areas and stairs leading to the outside. Against women's wards was a long awning that made a convenient walkway to keep out rain or heat for people. To the left side of men's wards was a three-storey building built in 1927 to the west of Yaohuajing Lane (⑪) as the nursing school which later was converted to doctors' dormitory with the first floor as patients' dining area.

The medical block that centered around the Takding building was located in the southwestern part while in the northern part near the women's wards was a building (⑨) that combined the nurse dormitory, the house of the school principal and the storage into one, and the new nursing school (⑩). In the east were two houses once used by the hospital directors (⑦) and surgeons (⑧). A stretch of short wall marked the division of the medical block and the living quarters but with doors for people to go in and out.

改制前医院医护人员不多，院长、护校校长和外科医生都住院里。他们和教会派来的师姑一样，以院为家，守护病人和医院，对医院有着特殊的感情。据陈兆奋老人说，抗日战争时期，地方上的流氓经常乘机哄抢放火，对医院的财产造成威胁。医院就组建防卫队，晚上分配医务人员和工友值班巡逻，通宵护院。院长陈颂磐也经常戴着皮手套，身揣童子军刀在医院各处巡逻。说起对医院的感情，外科医生陈宗磐的女儿陈美熙老人一直记得自己的父亲在新门诊大楼建设期间忙里忙外的身影。说到父亲在设计图纸上写写画画，在施工工地查看进展，带上亲自做的冰棍请工人们一起吃的情景，老人家说，儿时的父亲是她最崇拜的人。

陈宜英老人从小在院区出生长大。说起塔亭医院，如今八十出头的她，眼里闪烁的满是鲜花和童趣。她是首位帮助我们描绘出塔亭医院20世纪四五十年代图景的老人。在她的图绘中，让人最为意外的竟然不是我们苦苦寻找的建筑楼群，而是医院随处可见的花圃用地。老人对院区及大楼的各个分布区域记得十分清楚，也画得很细致，但她笔下大大小小不下十处的"花园"却是我们最意外的收获。当我们请她儿时院区另一伙伴陈美熙老人凭借回忆也为我们绘一幅塔亭地图时，想不到，这次塔亭医院的花圃更加抢眼。老人为花圃涂上了靓丽的色彩，似乎默默地提醒我们，这是一座花园式医院。19世纪至20世纪的欧洲医院擅长利用花园营造家的氛围，而"亭式"布局的建筑原则也提倡病区之间设计花园（King，1966：364）。当年塔亭楼前的大片空地是大小不一的花圃用地，忙碌的护士偷闲片刻，站在病房的外廊上，满眼鲜花，沁人心脾。站在短短的台阶楼梯上，看着春日的争奇斗艳，此时拍下的照片一定留有余香。就连医院的太平间（⑮）也巧妙地掩藏在由大片花园和鱼缸围绕着的小树丛中。从上腾路医院大门入口进来，左右两个露天花园扑面而来；护士学校通往女病房的路上，一派生机盎然，有绿树、鱼缸和鲜花陪伴，脚步顿时轻盈起来。20世纪八九十年代，因医院新时期建设需要，大部分楼群陆续拆除，百年风云变幻中完成了历史使命的旧塔亭病房大楼，一转身也凝固成了历史，藏身于静谧的历史影像群中。

楼区间的花园
Gardens between buildings in the hospital

站在女病房区外廊上的护士（来源：陈美爱）
Nurses standing on the veranda of the women's wards (Source: Chen Meiai)

Residents in the hospitals before its transformation were a few important members out of a small size of staff such as the director, the school principal and the surgeons, who, like resident home sisters from the church missions, held special attachment to the hospital and took it as their own home. According to Chen Zhaofeng, there was once a defense squad formed to keep away local rogues who often went looting and pillaging, posing great threat to the hospital's property. Each evening, designated personnel including doctors and workers were on patrol the whole night. Chen Songpan, director of the hospital, was said to be often seen on this duty wearing feather gloves and carrying a Boy Scout knife around the hospital. When it comes to the love of the hospital, Chen Meixi, daughter of Surgeon Chen Zongpan, said with undisguised admiration that still vivid in her mind was the busy silhouette of her father in and out of the outpatient building that was then under construction, making notes and sketches on the design drawing, checking progress on site and sharing with workers popsicles he himself made. That image of a father, Chen said, made him the one she admired the most.

When asked about the hospital, Chen Yiying, another lady who grew up in the hospital, beamed with pleasure, her eyes twinkling with childhood joy. She was the first to help to draw the hospital plan of the 1940s and 1950s when she was born and brought up there. Although in her 80s, she has strong memory that gave immediate yet meticulous sketches of the hospital layout. The pleasant surprise that we had from her pictures was not the buildings but no less than ten patches of "gardens". When her childhood playmate, Chen Meixi, who also lived in the hospital, was invited to draw a picture of hers, the lady gave a better-designed painted one with flowers and grass and trees in colors as if to remind people of this necessary existence of flowers in a hospital. Indeed, European hospitals in the 19 – 20th centuries excelled in showing the garden and the attention to home-like atmosphere, and the pavilion principle also suggested the arrangement of gardens between ward blocks. Right before the Takding building were gardens of different sizes that often drew busy nurses to the veranda to "smell the flowers". A photo taken to capture the moment of people standing on the stairs with a gaze at the delightful display all flowers sprang to in spring must smell sweet. Even the mortuary (⑮) was somewhat "hidden" in a garden and shrubs surrounded by some fish tanks. Through the entrance at the Shangteng Road into the hospital one was sure to be welcomed by the gardens on both sides. A walk from the nursing school to the women's wards was certainly full of brisk steps with green trees, fish tanks and flowers on the way to enjoy. Also brisk was the development in the 1980s and 1990s when most old buildings were demolished for further development in the new age. Takding inpatient building that had been in service for more than a century now turned away from sight and buried itself into the richer stock of historical landscape.

说到建筑，用地是绕不开的话题。通商口岸早期来福州的西方人大都有一段租地、买地的故事。塔亭医院自中洲岛火灾搬迁至塔亭路以来，也一直在考虑扩大地盘的问题。随着医院的发展，其实际占地范围也不断扩大。医院百年来与当地民众比邻而居，成功购得用地却没留下纠纷记录，足见医院与当地的关系融洽。在1921年的年度报告中，就有医院向捐资各界提出购买民居作为医院用地的迫切愿望："如果资金足够，建议买下和医院紧挨着的两排民居。这两排民房连着医院现有的两栋楼房，严重影响医院卫生状况，酷暑天这个问题尤为严重，因长期得不到解决，已成为医院的卫生隐患。此外，这种情况还带来火灾风险。如能买下，不仅能解决上述问题，还可使现有医院地盘扩大至院外大路。"塔亭时期，医院的发展受到包括资金和人员等诸多方面限制，其发展规模和速度也十分有限。

公立制后的市二医院就幸运多了，多年来在政府支持协调和自身努力下，周围一些民居用地经过友好协商，陆续划归医院。20世纪70年代医院盖了内科大楼，80年代有了新外科大楼。随着基础设施建设的持续更新，医院也不断突破为民众服务的高度和广度。2009年投入使用的21层福州市急救中心大楼已然成为仓山地区地标式急救航母，2023年4月落成的端庄大气的康复大楼已交付使用，再一次展示了医院集医疗、科研、教学、预防、康复为一体的深刻内涵。2022年，仓山区政府启动68亩土地征收，即将在城南建一所重磅三甲医院，这个投资达36亿元的项目就是福州市第二医院南台分院。届时，一个半世纪的市二医院将首次走出塔亭地块，到更靠近福州南大门的地方再辟一方杏林。2023年，市二医院响应政府医改举措，牵头整合福州神经精神病院和市妇幼保健院，成立福州市第二总医院，医院在"大科室""一院三区"的新视角下，开拓创新，为健康保驾护航，更为塔亭今生再续华章。

航拍下的医院主要用地和建设中的康复大楼项目
（2021）
Dronestagram: Main premises of the hospital and
the rehabilitation building under construction in 2021

刚投入使用的康复大楼
The new rehabilitation building just put into use

Premises are also a subject that should be touched upon when it comes to architecture. Stories are many about how Westerners in the treaty port era rented or purchased local lands for their business and similarly there had long been deliberations on the land expansion since Takding Hospital's relocation to Takding Road after it was burned down in a fire at Zhongzhou Island. The hospital's actual enlarged area went along with the hospital development and a close relationship with locals from whom the hospital managed to procure the land without any records of dispute. At the beginning of the *1921 Medical Report* was a plea to contributors for their subscriptions of a land purchase: "If sufficient funds are forthcoming it is proposed that the hospital should purchase two Chinese houses which will enable it to extend its boundaries to the public road. The two houses are part of a row of four, of which two are already in the possession of the hospital. This row of houses constitutes a fire menace to the Institution and is a great source of annoyance during the hot weather owing to the unsanitary conditions."

Unlike Takding Hospital whose development was subject to the provision of funds and personnel from others, Fuzhou Second Hospital since its transformation into a public institution has enjoyed much more advantageous conditions and successfully included more of its neighboring sites into its blueprint with the supportive coordination from the local government and the great efforts it has made. New buildings for medical services in the 1970s and for surgery in the 1980s, and the 21-story landmark-like emergency center in 2009, are examples of breakthroughs on the part of infrastructural construction that the hospital has made to the height and breadth of its service to the people. Its new depth is now being displayed in a recently completed grand building for rehabilitation that has just been put into use, as a center that has medical services, scientific research, teaching, public health and rehabilitation all well incorporated into a medical institution. In 2022, a piece of land covering about 45,333 square meters, or 68 *mu* in Chinese measurement, in the south of the city, was expropriated by Cangshan District Government for the future construction of a second Grade-A hospital in Cangshan District, and this hospital project with an estimated investment of 3.6 billion CNY will be Nantai Branch of Fuzhou Second Hospital. Never before has the hospital in its past one and a half centuries ever gone beyond its original site to seek new premises. Now driven by the call of the medical reform and the confidence it has built, Fuzhou Second Hospital this year has just upgraded to Fuzhou Second General Hospital by integrating medical resources with the other two facilities—Fuzhou Psychiatric Hospital and Fuzhou Maternal and Child Health Hospital. Experimenting with the innovative concept of taking each of its three member hospitals as a distinctive medical department, the hospital is now poised to take the lead again in the new voyage of life protection to its people and to continue a fresh chapter that is destined to be richer in the thick book of Takding Hospital about its past, present and future.

● 塔亭故事汇

1866—1951 年近百年间，塔亭医院在"晚清衰、民国乱"的社会剧烈动荡之中创立、发展和变化。在明暗晦变、变幻莫测的时代大背景下，一群有着良好职业操守的医护人员秉承医者仁心，呵护地区卫生健康。他们的故事汇集起来，形成塔亭前世的重要文脉，成为后人宝贵的精神财富。

情驻榕城的外国医护

晚清民国时期，仓山是外国人活动的主要区域，塔亭医院周边有教堂、银行和学校，出入的外国人很多。这些人中，有负责诊疗病患的塔亭医院医生，还有负责护理的师姑。19 世纪下半叶至 20 世纪中叶，这些文献记载总数 10 人左右的外方医护人员成为塔亭医院抹不去的历史叙事，他们的生活和中国近代的社会命运紧密相连。与那些服务于教堂、教会学校以"疗灵"皈依为己任的传教士有所不同，治病救人、护理病患是他们的主要职责，但随着时间流逝，他们都逐渐淡出人们的记忆，一些人的真实姓名也有待确认。所幸，通过文献耙梳、访谈口述，他们的过往总算有迹可循，在若隐若现中，成为丰富后人想象空间和精神世界的历史人物。

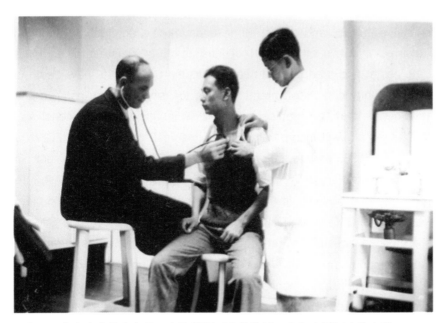

：中西医生为病人检查身体（左为外国医生黄约翰，右为中国医生陈宗磐）
：Foreign and Chinese doctors seeing a patient（Left: foreign doctor John
：Webster；Righ：Chinese doctor Chen Zongpan）

第一章 CHAPTER ONE 从塔亭医院到福州市第二医院 From Takding Hospital to Fuzhou Second Hospital

• Stories of Medical Staff

During the period from 1866 to 1951, the late Qing Dynasty was in decay, the Republic of China was in disarray, and the society was undergoing tremendous transformation. Amidst this turmoil of nearly one century, Takding Hospital was established, evolved and transformed. With the establishment of the hospital, a group of medical professionals emerged. They conducted themselves with professional ethics and compassion, dedicated to the health and well-being of the local people. Their stories have formed the cultural and historical skeleton of Takding Hospital and served as a valuable spiritual treasure for future generations.

Foreign Medical Professionals in Fuzhou

During the late Qing Dynasty and the Republic of China, foreign residents in Fuzhou were most often seen in the churches, banks and schools, not far from Takding Hospital, in Cangshan District, a foreign-settlement-like area. Among them were doctors and nurses from Takding Hospital who provided medical diagnosis and treatment or took charge of nursing and management. From the second half of the 19th century to the mid-20th century, these foreign medical professionals, totaling about ten in documents, became the important narrators of the history of Takding Hospital, and their lives were closely linked to the fate of the early modern Chinese society. Unlike the missionaries who served in churches and missionary schools to "heal souls" and convert people, these medical workers devoted most of their time and energy to the mission of treating diseases and taking care of patients, yet with the passage of time most of them were buried into oblivion and some remained unidentified. Fortunately, marks of their lives and work can still be tracked in various documents and interviews, making them historical figures that enrich the imagination and spiritual world of succeeding generations.

外国医生
A foreign doctor

师姑在医院的居所
A home sister in her residence
in the hospital

19世纪八九十年代，一位三四十岁模样的英国人骑着一匹灰色斑点母马往返于南台街道上，据说这是当年南台地区一道引人注目的风景。骑着马匹的这位正是塔亭医院第一任院长连尼（或译"任尼"）（1850—1912）。

这位行事一向低调的苏格兰医生并不知道自己成了那一道风景的主角，在榕31年，他关注的是福州地区的医疗卫生情况。1872年连尼在苏格兰阿伯丁大学获得"最高荣誉"医学博士学位，毕业后他先到台湾海关工作了7年。1880年4月，连尼被派往福州并委以重任，这一年他30岁，身兼数职——闽海关医员、英国驻福州领事馆馆医和主要医务代表、传教医生、塔亭医院首任院长。作为闽海关医员，他曾为闽海关撰写多份年度《福州地区健康报告》，报告笔墨详尽，覆盖面广，是后人了解当时福州情况不可多得的材料。不过，当年血气方刚的青年才俊在经年累月的繁忙中，似乎没有时间精力对自己的医务实践来一番学术论证，并诉诸笔端寄回英国。"他不喜欢写作，故而没能在医学研究上作出贡献"，这是《英国医学报刊》（1912：983）1912年发表的连尼悼词中所提及的唯一憾事。如果时光倒流，连尼会重新规划他的学术生涯吗？

1880—1911年，连尼见证了福州地区西医从无到有，从被抵触、怀疑到尝试、认可的历史瞬间。三十载岁月，领事馆的人早已换了一波又一波，他却长情留守福州，期间仅有三次短暂回国休假。与那些热衷于受邀演讲的回国休假传教士不同，连尼频频走访伦敦和其他地区的医学中心，以了解最新医学动态。在晚清中国社会的背景下，担任英国驻通商口岸领事馆主要医务官，这个担子非常人可挑。有的时候，连尼不免陷入孤军奋战，身边却没有同行、助手或护士。仪器设备严重不足，很多时候，他需要一人独当一面。白内障、剖腹术、接生等手术，他都驾轻就熟，其诊治惠及西侨团体和本地人。

连尼后人萨利·帕克斯深情拥抱鼓岭一处别墅（2012年9月）（来源：鼓岭管委会）
Rennie's descendant, Sallie Parks in Kuliang in September 2012
(Source: Kuliang Administration Committee)

In the 1880s and 1890s in Cangshan, there was an attractive sight: A Briton in his 30s or 40s riding a gray spotty mare to and from the streets of Nantai. The man on the horse was none other than Thomas Rennie (1850 – 1912), the first director of Takding Hospital.

The humble Scottish doctor might have been unaware of the attention he was getting for he had paid all his attention to local health care throughout his 31-year stay in Fuzhou. A Doctorate in Medicine with "highest honors" in 1872 from the University of Aberdeen, Scotland, Dr. Rennie first worked in Customs in Taiwan for seven years before he was sent to Fuzhou and entrusted with heavy responsibilities in April 1880. At the age of 30 in that year, he was wearing several hats: a medical officer of the Fukien Customs, a principal medical representative of the British Consulate in Fuzhou, a missionary doctor, and the first director of Takding Hospital. In the earnest manner as a medical officer, he wrote for the Fukien Customs annual reports—*Dr. T. Rennie's Report on the Health of Foochow*—in details, making them invaluable sources for future generations to learn about Fuzhou in the 1880s and 1890s. For all his vigor and youthful talent, Rennie seemed to have little time and energy in many years of busy work to produce academic papers on his medical practices and send them back to England for publication. "Dr. Rennie made no serious contribution to medical literature. He dislikes writing." was somewhat the regret expressed in his obituary on a 1912 *British Medical Journal*. Would Rennie have re-planned his academic career if he could turn back the clock?

From 1880 to 1911, Dr. Rennie witnessed the Western medicine in Fuzhou grow from scratch, from being resisted and doubted to being tried and recognized by the locals. His thirty years in Fuzhou saw consular staff members come and leave, yet his attachment to the city let him stay except for three holidays back to the UK. In those brief visits back home, quite unlike most missionaries on furlough who were preoccupied with giving lectures, he kept himself busy making frequent visits to medical centers in London or elsewhere in the country, for he did not want to lose this opportunity to learn about the latest medical developments. Serving as the chief medical officer of the British Consulate at the treaty port in the late-Qing Chinese society was never a job one could easily take. There were times when Rennie had to fight alone. Caught in serious medical situations where no trained nurses at command nor colleagues or adequate appliances around, he would manage to handle on his undivided responsibility. His rich experience in medical services enabled him to tackle a cataract, a midwifery case or a laparotomy, etc., all to the benefit of the European Community and the local patients alike.

连尼到福州当年，就被委任为当时还在中洲岛的福州本地医院及药房（后称塔亭医院）的负责人。但他身兼多职，活动范围广，经常出现在各个医务场所。他擅长打交道，无论西侨团体还是中国人，都与他交往甚密，关系良好。他合理调配当时较为有限的医疗资源和人员，有效地促进了当时正在发展中的多家西式医院间的联系，客观上拓展了当地西医院的发展空间。1884年，中法马江海战，1885年，福州城霍乱横行。这两年间，病人数量增加，当时业务规模较大的保福山医院一时人满为患。此时连尼二话没说，和亚当一起接过重任。1899—1901年福州鼠疫大流行，前后三年，死亡人数不计其数，但他没有嫌弃离开。1900年，他的小儿子在福州出生。巧的是，同年年底，他的搭档亚当也在福州当了爸爸，其妻子在闽江一艘疍民船上临盆，孩子取名为乔治·闽。这个有纪念意义的名字多少见证了那个时代一批执着于救死扶伤的西医对福州的感情。

近年来，福州鼓岭成为当年在榕西人之后辈探寻先辈足迹的历史旅游胜地，殊不知，连尼正是这个当年外国人避暑胜地的第一建造人。19世纪60年代中期，已有外国人夏日上鼓山租寺庙避暑，而鼓岭为西人所知则缘于一次意外发现。1885年一个酷暑难当的日子，有西医接到连江急诊通知，为抄近路，他翻越鼓山，途径鼓岭时，这里凉爽宜人，让他印象深刻。后来这事传开了，外国人开始在鼓岭租房避暑。这位医生，一说是美国医生伍丁，一说是英国医生连尼。1886年，连尼成了第一个在鼓岭上盖度假别墅的外国人。不过连尼很快就让人把别墅拆了，因为当地人发现房屋选址过于显眼，破坏了当地风水。第二年事态缓和下来，连尼这才又选了处不起眼的地方盖起了别墅，再没遭阻拦，却引得一批批外国人争相效仿，最终在鼓岭地区形成了一处外国人居住区。高峰时期这里至少有330座别墅、一家医院和其他设施，外国人与当地居民相处融洽。1903年，美国领事格雷曾邀请了80多位鼓岭当地人参加了他在鼓岭举办的69岁生日派对，场面十分热闹。

鼓岭上的外国人别墅区（1900—1910）（来源：池志海）
Foreigners' residences in Guliang during 1900–1910（Source: Chi Zhihai）

鼓岭上的外国人别墅区（1925）（来源：池志海）
Foreigners' residences in Guliang in 1925（Source: Chi Zhihai）

The year Rennie arrived in Fuzhou, he was appointed head of Foochow Native Hospital and Dispensary still located on Zhongzhou Island (later known as Takding Hospital), but as a multi-tasker, he also made regular presence at other medical institutions. With excellent social ability, he was a great favorite and had good relations with both the Westerners and the Chinese. His rational allocation of limited medical resources and personnel proved instrumental for better connection between several developing Western-style hospitals, facilitate their progress. After the 1884 Sino-French Majiang Sea Battle and the 1885 Cholera outbreak, the number of patients soared to an extent that even a larger hospital such as Ponasang Hospital was overloaded with people. Without a second thought, Rennie took over the burden with Adam. During the 1899 - 1901 Plague that claimed countless lives, he stayed and chose Fuzhou as his youngest son's birth place in 1900. Coincidentally, at the end of the same year, his partner Adam's first child was also born in Fuzhou. Adam's wife, Isabella Elizabeth B. Robertson, gave birth on a boat in the the Minjiang River, and the child was named George Min B. Adam. This memorable name somewhat testifies the deep attachment to Fuzhou this group of Western doctors had formed in their dedication to life saving.

In recent years, Kuliang has become a historical tourist attraction for descendants of Westerners to trace the footprints of their ancestors in Fuzhou. Unbeknownst to many, the construction of this spot as a summer resort for foreigners back then was started by Rennie. Back in the mid-1860s, some foreigners rented temples in Gushan Mountain in the hot summer days to seek refuge from the heat in the city, but Kuliang was not known until the discovery of some doctor, Rev. S. F. Woodin or Rennie, on a scorching hot day in 1885, who was impressed with the pleasant coolness when going over Kuliang as a shortcut for an emergency call in Lianjiang. Since then, foreign residents began to use local houses in Kuliang in summer. In 1886, Rennie became the first foreigner to build a house in Kuliang, but he soon had it torn down because the locals complained that the house was in such a conspicuous site that it destroyed the local *feng shui*. A year later when things smoothed down, Rennie picked a less noticeable place for his villa and was not stopped this time. His fellows soon rushed to follow suit, and eventually, a foreign community was formed. In its heyday, there were at least 330 villas, a sanitarium and other facilities. The Westerners lived in peace with local communities. It is said that at American Consul Gracey's 69th birthday party in Kuliang in 1903, he invited his Kuliang neighbors, over 80 people.

左上角为连尼的别墅，是鼓岭上第一栋外国人建的度假别墅（来源：布里斯托大学）

Dr. Rennie's house on the top left, the first villa for holiday built in Kuliang by foreigners (Source: University of Bristol)

塔亭医院的外国医务人员与当地人相处融洽，诀窍之一便是能说福州话。连尼在台湾七年学会了闽南话，在福州又学会了福州话。国外文献中可以找到不少夹杂着福州话的表达，十分有趣，比如"Dong Ciu Island""Dr. Ding"分别表示"中洲岛"和"陈医生"。

会说福州话的还有塔亭医院的师姑们，由于师姑们住在院区（事实上她们住在女病房楼上）需要和本地人打交道，因此她们多数能讲一口流利的福州话。小时候在医院生活区长大的陈宜英老人至今记得师姑们呼唤她和伙伴到师姑住的二楼家里"食冰箸"（福州话"吃冰棍儿"）。当年除了施师姑讲普通话外，其他4位师姑都会福州话。据说早期传教士若是语言能力太差，教会十有八九是不会派遣其来华的，因此当年多数传教士一到福州，就得先张罗着学习当地方言。

"入乡随俗"，当年塔亭医院的外国医生护士大多有中文名，这些名字有的留在了医院的档案里，有的则深深地刻在了当年认识他们的人的脑海中。每每提及，这些白发苍苍的老人常常流露出与老邻居不期而遇的亲切。其中师姑的名字最有意思，塔亭医院曾经有巴师姑（"巴"音在福州方言中有"白"的意思，因此一些材料此处误写为"白师姑)、留师姑、俞师姑、宝师姑、施师姑。其中三位有全名记载，即俞和平、宝快乐和施多霖，其他几位大致以其英文姓的谐音加上"师姑"而成。在中国，佛教出家女信徒称"尼姑"，道教则有"道姑"，"师姑"一词少了"尼"和"道"的宗教色彩，多了"师"和"姑"传递的中国文化中特有的礼仪人际关系，表达了尊敬之意。"姑"字更是很好地回应了姐妹称呼，是个世俗味儿更浓的词。在塔亭医院，人们也称师姑为 home sister。在一些老照片中，师姑和当地人合影，宛若一家人。

：师姑和当地人一起，如同一家人
：Home sisters with natives as if they were family members

At Takding Hospital, the key to befriending locals was Fuzhou dialect. Rennie learned to speak Hokkien during his seven years in Taiwan, and while in Fuzhou he also picked up the local dialect. In documents written by these foreigners, unique expressions with a distinctive flavor of the local dialect are not rare. For example, "Dong Ciu Island" and "Dr. Ding" are Zhongzhou Island and Doctor Chen respectively.

Not just doctors, missionary nurses also picked up the local dialect. Since they lived in the hospital, to be more exact, on the upper floor of the female ward, they should have more daily contacts with the locals and their language. Chen Yiying, who grew up in the hospital's living quarters, still remembers being invited by the resident nurses whom they called "shigu" to go to the second floor of their house to "Siǎh Bǐng Dêu" ("eat popsicles" in Fuzhou dialect). Back then, except Miss Shi (probably Miss Skegg) who spoke only Standard Chinese, all the other four sisters could speak Fuzhou dialect. It is said that the early missionaries were unlikely to be sent to China by the Church if their language skills were too weak, so most missionaries resolved to learn the local dialect as soon as they arrived.

"Do as the locals do." Most of the foreign doctors and nurses at Takding Hospital had Chinese names, some of which are found in the hospital's archives, while others stick in the minds of those who were just kids or teenagers back then. Now gray and old, these people look radiant and young when names of their old acquaintances are mentioned. Much mentioned and most interesting are the names of home sisters. For example, Miss Barr is often mistakenly taken as "Sister White" and written in Chinese characters as "白师姑" because the English sound of "Barr" is the same as "white" in Fuzhou dialect. Among the often-mentioned five sisters—Miss Barr, Miss Barron, Miss Walters, Miss Chamber and Miss Skegg—three of them have their full Chinese names recorded, namely Yu Heping (literally peace), Bao Kuaile (literally happiness), and Shi Duolin (literally much rain), but all were referred to as someone with a general name "shigu" and a Chinese surname coming from the approximate transliterations of their English surname. Why are female missionaries here called "shigu"? In China, Buddhist nuns are called "nigu" and Taoist nuns are called "daogu". Devoid of religious context, "shigu" conveys the meaning of respect and courtesy in Chinese culture. "Gu" corresponds to sisters in Christianity, yet retains an earthly connotation of girls or women in Chinese. At Takding Hospital, "shigu" was also called home sisters. They looked like family members to the locals in some old photos.

师姑受英国圣公会女差会派遣,监督并参与塔亭医院管理。这群单身女传教士既亲切也严格。巴师姑曾经在一次外出路上遇到一位刚刚丧夫的妇女要上吊殉情,她和同行师姑伊达赶忙上前劝说开导,并将这位妇女带回自己的住所,对其关爱有加。俞师姑对护士要求严格,要求护士至少半小时查房一次,这样才能确保护士时时监测病人,有情况随时汇报医生。她有一个检查绝招:用眼睛瞄下护士服的臀部裙摆部分,如果这里皱了,说明护士病房巡查不到位,坐着的时间太长。师姑们对于医院的卫生管理也十分有效,卫生间总是整洁有序,毫无异味。福州的夏天暑热难挨,塔亭医院自1917年起规定,医院每年8月份暂时关闭,给员工休假,师姑们则利用这段时间对医院展开卫生休整。师姑们在塔亭医院的工作涉及护理和管理的方方面面,如留师姑还管理医院财务和职工生活。史料提及的师姑不多,但她们对塔亭医院长情不仅言,让人印象深刻。比如,俞和平驻院时间最长,太平洋战争时她离开回国,抗日战争胜利后又回来,直到1952年才和施多霖师姑最后回国。塔亭医院一定是她们回国后常常想起的地方吧。

1944年中国人接手院长以前,塔亭医院的主管院长并不多。除了前面提到的多年担任院长的连尼,之后还有慕惠德、戴满、高伦、黄约翰。作为最后一任外籍院长,黄约翰亲历抗日战争硝烟,他和塔亭医院的中国医生们一起冒着生命危险实施人道救助。他们戴着国际红十字会臂章,筑起一道牢固的生命防线,为后人称道。

三位师姑从左至右:俞和平、留师姑、宝快乐
Three home sisters from left to right: Irene Walters, E. A. Barron, Ida Chamber

Most home sisters were single female missionaries dispatched by CEZMS to supervise and manage Takding Hospital and they were both amiable and strict in discipline. Miss Barr, for example, once encountered a woman who had just become a widow and wanted to hang herself. Together with Miss Ida Chamber, she talked the lady out of the suttee, and took her back to her hospital residence where she showed much kindness and care for her. Miss Walters was strict with nurses who were required to make rounds at least once every half an hour to ensure a close watch over patients at all times and timely reports of patients' changing conditions to the doctors at any time. Judging from the wrinkles on the nurse's uniform, she could immediately tell whether the nurse had fulfilled her duty or had been sitting too long. Efficient in the hygiene management, they always kept the bathrooms clean and odorless. Since 1917, Takding Hospital would temporarily close every August to avoid summer heat. While other staff members were on vacations, home sisters stayed and cleaned the hospital thoroughly. Their job responsibilities were many and varied. For instance, Miss Barron was in charge of the hospital's finances and staff matters. Although not much had been found about their life in the available materials, their attachment to the hospital was impressively infinite. Irene Walters, the longest-serving home sister in the hospital, went back to her country during the Pacific War, and returned after the victory of the War of Resistance Against Japanese Aggression. It was not until 1952 that she and Miss Skegg left China for the last time. Takding Hospital must have always remained in their memories.

Before Chinese doctors took over the position of hospital director in 1944, foreign doctors in charge at Takding Hospital could be counted on the fingers of one hand. Successors of the aforementioned Thomas Rennie, who served in the post for many years, were J. Moorhead, Dai Man, Eric Callum, and John Leslie Atherton Webster, some of these names being Chinese transliterations or incomplete English names for want of proper literature. John, locally known as John Huang, is worth a mention because, as the last foreign director, he worked actively with Chinese doctors at Takding Hospital especially during the War of Resistance Against Japanese Aggression to combat life-threatening hazard, risking their lives to provide humanitarian aid to those in need. Wearing Red Cross armbands, together they were strong protectors of life. Their feat has been greatly honored by all the succeeding generations.

勇挑大梁的中国医生

　　塔亭医院从一家西方教会参与的私立医院，逐步演化成中国人自己的公立医院，这个过程既是西医在中国发展的缩影，也是中国医护人员前仆后继、扶伤救众的医护凯歌。值得一提的是，塔亭医院时期的中国医生虽然总数不过十人，但多数毕业于"高进严出"的著名西式医学校，确保了医生素质和医院的诊疗水平。比如上海圣约翰大学医学院就是一所淘汰率很高的学校。据记载，自 1896 年成立到 1952 年，该校平均每年毕业生 8.3 名，而头 45 年的毕业生更少，每年仅 5.2 人（何小莲，2006：237），而塔亭医院就有三位医生是从这个学校毕业的。当年医生少，病人多，医生们每天工作强度大。据当年护士回忆（王小虎、游庆辉，2005），抗日战争期间，医院仅有三名医生，有时碰到大手术，三个医生一起上。他们忙得连打杯水的时间都没有，有时只好一边啃着馒头一边给病人看病，每天工作十几个小时，但却从无怨言，笑容总是挂在脸上。塔亭时期的医生在改制后继续在福州市工人医院和福州市第二医院发挥着重要作用，他们在没有护士学校的情况下成功地举办了助理护士班，医护力量不断增强。

塔亭医院部分医务人员合影（1953 年前后）
A group photo of some medical personnel around 1953

Chinese Doctors Who Took the Lead

The gradual evolution of Takding Hospital from a church-related private foreign hospital to a public local hospital owned by the Chinese people is not only an epitome of the development of Western medicine in China, but also a triumph for a succession of Chinese health care personnel who dedicated themselves to healing wounds and saving lives and thus strengthened national consciousness. What's worth mentioning is that although there were less than 10 Chinese doctors in Takding Hospital, most of them graduated from famous Western-style medical schools with strict admission and graduation criteria to ensure competence of doctors and high quality of medical care. For instance, three doctors graduated from St. John's University in Shanghai, a school noted for its high elimination rate with an average 8.3 graduates per year from its establishment in 1896 to 1952, and only 5.2 per year in its first 45 years. Back then, a rather low ratio of doctor to patient caused a heavy workload to doctors and nurses. As recalled by a nurse, during the War of Resistance Against Japanese Aggression, there were only three doctors who had to perform together in times of major surgeries. Doctors had so many patients that they didn't even have time for a glass of water when busy, or sometimes, they would simply have a steamed bun to chew while continuing seeing the patients without a lunch break. More than ten hours a day at work was not unusual, but never did they complain; they smiled. They continued their important roles after the hospital transformation and helped to organize training classes for assistant nurses to ensure the growth of medical personnel and service.

助理护士班结业照（1953）（来源：陈美爱）
A group photo taken in 1953 on the occasion of the completion of assistant nurses training (Source: Chen Meiai)

塔亭医院首位中国医生林叨安（1871—1922）是中国早期西医的代表。林叨安的父亲是福宁（今霞浦）渔民，早年他带着妻儿来到福州，在大英教会安立甘会开办的教堂担任厨师，曾在乌石山一带外国人寓所帮忙做事，是福州地区较早信仰基督教的家庭。林叨安在当地教会学校读书期间，聪明勤奋，很快就被传教医生雷腾看中，招为自己的助手。早期传教士在中国医务传教，通常在当地物色合适人选，作为自己的传教员兼医务助手，这是西式医学院出现前，中国早期西医的主要成长模式。林叨安于是和另一位中国学生一道，跟随雷腾医生学习英语、科学和药学。五年间，林叨安帮助雷腾在莆田兴化开办并管理圣路加圣教医院，这是当时教会所办最大的医院。后来，林叨安回到福州，担任连尼的首席中国助手，成了塔亭医院第一位华人医生（Doyle，2017）。据他的后人林良民说，自己曾经见过一张羊皮纸的圣公会医师资格证，上面写着祖父的名字。而在家族相册中，一张 1918 年塔亭医院的英文传单上，印着"HOUSE SURGEON·LING TO ANG"，即外科住院医生——林叨安（郑芳，2020：84—85）。当年林叨安还在仓山开办屈臣氏大药房。到 20 世纪 20 年代初，福州地区至少有 30 家西药房，这些药房是西医推广的有益补充。

1893 年，林叨安与詹爱美成婚，婚后两人继续从事福州地区安立甘会事务，他们任塔亭路上明道堂的董事会成员，负责捐钱维护和管理明道堂。他们同时也参加了 1905 年成立的基督教青年会。两人重视十个孩子的教育。其中长子林步基和三子林步瀛学业突出，后成为民国时期有名的人物。1921 年 5 月 4 日这一天，林家在三一学校户外操场为这兄弟俩同时举行了一场极为轰动的五百人参加的盛大婚礼。今天，在居安里七号的"林步瀛故居"遗址还住着林医生的后代。如果主人在家，或许可以在家族老照片中找到林医生。2011 年，林叨安的曾孙女 Jennifer Lin 曾从美国费城来福州寻根，饶有兴致地记录下了林家五代人百多年的变迁和信仰。

1922 年，林叨安患肺炎逝世（当年福建省内该病的死亡率仅次于肺结核）。至此，"他在塔亭医院服务了整整二十年，他的离世是塔亭医院的重大损失，"医院在悼词中这样写道。

：林叨安
：Lin Dao'an

The first Chinese doctor in Takding Hospital was Lin Dao'an (1871 – 1922), or Foochow Romanized Ling To Ang, an early representative of local doctors of Western medicine in China. Lin Dao'an was raised in a Christian family in Fuzhou. His father, a fisherman from Funing (now Xiapu), brought his wife and children to Fuzhou in his early years, where he first worked as a cook in an Anglican Church and later ran errands for foreigners in Wushan Mountain. During his studies in the local missionary school, Lin Dao'an's intelligence and diligence caught the attention of the missionary doctor Birdwood van Someren Taylor who was then looking for suitable locals as his assistants like most missionary doctors did before the emergence of Western-style medical schools during the initial development of Western medicine in China. Lin Dao'an and another Chinese student therefore studied English, science, and medicine from Dr. Taylor. After working with Dr. Taylor for five years, during which Lin helped to open and run the biggest missionary hospital, St. Luke's Hospital in Xinghua, Putian, he returned to Fuzhou and became the principal Chinese assistant of Dr. Thomas Rennie and the first Chinese doctor in Takding Hospital. Lin Liangmin recalled seeing his grandfather's name on a medical license in parchment issued by Anglican Church and "HOUSE SURGEON · LING TO ANG" printed on a 1918 English flyer of Takding Hospital tucked in a family album. Lin also ran Watson's Pharmacy in Cangshan. By the early 1920s, there were at least 30 Western pharmacies in Fuzhou, and they greatly promoted Western medicine.

After his marriage in 1893, Lin continued to work with his wife Zhan Aimei as board members of Mingdao Church (the Anglican Church) on Tating Road, responsible for tithing and donations to support the church's management and maintenance. They had also active roles in YMCA in Fuzhou, founded in 1905 on Guanyinjing Street. They attached great importance to the education of their ten children. Their first son, Lin Buji, or Romanized Ling Pu-chi, and Lin Buying, their third son, were brilliant students and later turned out to be the well-established figures in the Republic of China. It is said that the Lin family held a sensational wedding ceremony for the two brothers at the same time in the outdoor sports field of Trinity College on May 4, 1921, with five hundred attendees. Today at No. 7 Ju'anli Lane, also labeled as the site of the official residence of Lin Buying, chief of Fukien Postal Bureau, still live Dr. Lin's descendants. If the present owner is at home, visitors may have the luck to meet Dr. Lin in their old family album. In 2011, Lin Dao'an's great-granddaughter, Jennifer Lin, came to Fuzhou from Philadelphia to seek her ancestral roots. She recorded with great interest the changes and beliefs of the five generations of the Lin family for well over a century.

In 1922, Dr. Lin died of pneumonia, whose mortality rate was second only to tuberculosis at that time in Fujian Province. In eulogy of Dr. Ling, the hospital stated, "He faithfully served the hospital for twenty years and his death has been a great loss to this Institution."

1923 年，塔亭医院迎来了第一位医学校毕业的西医王灼祖（1892—1983）。王灼祖，福建仙游人，12 岁到福州求学，先后就读于福建高等学堂、北京协和大学医科、山东齐鲁大学医科。1923 年由山东齐鲁大学附属医院到塔亭医院任医师，一年后离职。1925年，他赴美学习参观，1926 年回国时，福州城已摆脱军阀统治，城内一派民族自强独立的气氛。王灼祖在烟台山对湖路家中开办灼祖医院，开始个体行医。30 年代初，王灼祖与王兆培等人组织福州市医师公会。1942 年，福州时疫流行，福州医师公会集资筹办"时疫医院"，王灼祖任院长。当时塔亭医院与其紧密合作，为时疫医院提供各方面支持，时疫医院则分担塔亭医院繁重的防治传染病任务（陈兆奋，2015）。由于初创资金困难，王灼祖自愿义务工作，他不计个人安危，经常深入病人家中抢救。1943 年，时疫医院改名合组时疫医院，利用日本博爱医院旧址，方便台江市民就医，名重当时。中华人民共和国成立后，王灼祖先后出任福州市卫生局副局长、福州市红十字会副会长、福建省卫生厅副厅长兼任福建省中医药学术研究委员会副主任和福建省红十字会副会长。

1944 年，塔亭医院有了第一位华人院长陈颂磐（1899—1955）。陈颂磐为医院服务了整整 32 年，巧的是，这与塔亭医院第一任外籍院长连尼在榕 31 年相似，为医院历经百年风雨仍得以延续立下了汗马功劳。陈颂磐，籍贯古田，毕业于上海圣约翰大学，医学博士，1923 年曾在上海同仁医院任医师，1924 年入职塔亭医院。他的出现改变了多年来塔亭医院由一名外籍医生主导的局面。由于塔亭医院外籍院长一职多为兼职职位，院长并不驻院，因此医院规模较为有限。陈颂磐作风扎实，勤勤恳恳，深得外籍院长信任。30 年代起，医院工作慢慢开始转由陈颂磐负责。以实干之风闻名的陈颂磐爱院如家，对医院做了许多建设性改革，如科室分工和建设；他还精简机构，设立总务长和总护士长两职位，由中国人担任，开启中国西医主导外国私立医院的时期。在他的影响下，三四十年代越来越多的中国医生护士加入塔亭医院，为后来塔亭医院转型成为中国人自己的医院打下了坚实的基础。

陈颂磐院长（来源：陈美爱）
Chen Songpan, director of the hospital (Source: Chen Meiai)

In 1923, Takding Hospital had its first practitioner with formal education in Western medicine, Wang Zhuozu (1892 - 1983). Born in Xianyou, Fujian, Wang received secondary education in Fujian Advanced Academy at 12 in Fuzhou and later his tertiary education in Peking Union Medical College and Cheeloo College of Medicine. In 1923, he transferred from Affiliated Hospital of Cheeloo College to Takding Hospital, where he served as a physician but resigned in the second year for his further study in the US in 1925. When returning in 1926 he found a different city that had been freed from the reign of the Beiyang Warlords. Inspired by the spirit of national independence, Wang opened Zhuozu Hospital at home on Duihu Street near Yantai Mountain, and began private medical practice. In the early 1930s, Wang started Fuzhou Medical Doctors Association with other doctors such as Wang Zhaopei. In response to the epidemic that struck Fuzhou in 1942 the Association raised money to build Fuzhou Cholera Hospital, Wang serving as the hospital director. Working closely with Takding Hospital, the Cholera Hospital received support in all aspects from Takding Hospital and at the same time shared with it the burdensome responsibilities in the fight against epidemics. Due to financial difficulties, Wang volunteered for all duties irrespective of personal safety, say, visits to patients' homes for emergency treatment whenever necessary. In 1943, Fuzhou Cholera Hospital was renamed Fuzhou Joint Hospital of Cholera and later relocated to the former site of a Japanese hospital named Pok Oi Hospital in today's Taijiang District where it was highly reputed for the medical services it rendered to the locals. After the founding of the People's Republic of China in 1949, Wang took on leadership responsibility in the following municipal or provincial departments such as Fuzhou Municipal Health Bureau, Fuzhou Red Cross Society, Fujian Provincial Department of Health, Fujian Provincial Academic Research Committee of Traditional Chinese Medicine and Fujian Red Cross Society.

In 1944, Chen Songpan (1899 - 1955), a native of Gutian, Fuzhou, became the first Chinese director of Takding Hospital, and his 32-year service, a coincidentally similar length of Rennie's service in Fuzhou, witnessed his special contributions in the continuity of a hospital that just survived through the past decades. Chen joined Takding Hospital in 1924 after his graduation from Saint John's University with Doctorate in Medicine and a short stay in Shanghai Tongren Hospital in 1923 as a physician. His presence and persistence changed the longstanding one-foreign-doctor-in-charge situation in Takding Hospital whose development was also restricted for want of a full-time resident director. Chen's earnestness and conscientiousness in work quickly earned the foreign director's trust. Since the 1930s, Chen began to take charge. Known as a down-to-earth person who viewed the hospital as his home, Chen devoted himself to many constructive reforms, including the division, construction and streamlining of departments. He created two new positions—Secretary of General Affairs and Chief Nursing Officer—for Chinese to take, ushering in a new period when Chinese doctors of Western medicine began to play a major role in a foreign private hospital. Under his influence, more Chinese doctors and nurses joined Takding Hospital during the 1930s and 1940s, making for its transition to the hospital owned by the Chinese people.

1944 年，塔亭医院最后一任外国人院长黄约翰回国，陈颂磐接任代院长，1947 年正式出任院长。抗日战争期间，塔亭医院在陈颂磐的带领下，不仅担负鼠疫、霍乱等流行时疫的防治工作，更是挑起了福州唯一一所承担全市民众医疗任务医院的重担。据当年的护士林敏庄回忆（王小虎、游庆辉，2005），陈颂磐院长每天提早一个小时到医院上班，门诊之前他先用 1 个半小时处理当时流行的肺鼠疫，全身消毒后去看儿科门诊，又继续巡病房、看门诊，看诊到下午一两点是常事。据他的孩子回忆，家里的大门装着一个方便护士报告的电铃，夜里常有铃声响起，夜间急诊，父亲总是随叫随到。

抗日战争结束后，陈颂磐马上投入医院基础设施建设中，于 1946 年和 1948 年主持修建两座大楼。1949 年，塔亭医院发展成为中华圣公会福建教区各大教会医院中住院病人和门诊量最大的医院。医院许多重要时刻，无论是 1947—1950 年间医院的管理和产权的变更，还是 1951—1952 年中华人民共和国对医院的接收改造，他都扮演了举足轻重的作用。三十载风雨，他为医院发展殚精竭虑，尽管常年受高血压和头痛折磨，但仍靠服药和浓茶坚持工作，在患者面前态度和蔼，谈笑风生。1955 年 1 月，陈颂磐在办公室过劳离世。如今市二医院信息中心楼（原护士学校）奠基石上还有他亲笔题写的"乃役于人"的字样。

和院长陈颂磐一起工作最长时间的是陈为信（1898—1983）。陈为信 20 世纪 20 年代末期进入塔亭医院，多年来，主要从事院务管理协调等诸多重要工作。1928 年，福州基督教协和医院成立时，陈为信曾帮助为其培训护士。1931 年，陈为信进修后，承担手术麻醉任务。他也曾任护校教师，并负责建设住院病人的营养室（《烟台山史话》，2014：90）。20 世纪 40 年代，陈为信任总务长，负责行政事务、对外医务、药物采购等。抗日战争时期，他和陈颂磐、陈宗磐一起，组织医院职工，想方设法掩护、转移受伤抗日志士。会日语的他经常想办法与日本兵周旋。他们不顾安危，实施人道主义救助的行为为塔亭医院赢得了荣誉，成为塔亭医院光辉历史的一部分。他的儿子陈兆奋退休后，非常注重仓山地区历史文化遗产的保护，做了大量资料整理工作，为后人翻看塔亭医院历史提供了许多有价值的线索和材料。

：陈颂磐（1954）（来源：陈天如）
：Chen Songpan（1954）（Source: Chen Tianru)

：陈为信
：Chen Weixin

In 1944, Chen Songpan replaced John Webster, the last foreign director who had returned to his own country, first as the deputy and then in 1947 the officially designated director. During the War of Resistence Against Japanese Aggression, the Hospital, under Chen's leadership, was shouldered with a mantle of responsibility as the only medical institution that could render medical services in Fuzhou, apart from its arduous efforts to prevent and control epidemics like plague and cholera, etc. According to Lin Minzhuang, a former nurse, Chen had a tight daily schedule. Coming to work one hour early, he would first spend one and a half hours for cases in the rampant pneumonic plague and then disinfect himself and go to see pediatric outpatients before he made ward rounds and returned to see outpatients often until one or two o'clock, nearly without a break in a day. In his children's memory, their father had one doorbell installed to the door of their house for the night emergency call and their father never missed the call.

Immediately after the war, Chen lost no time in working on the infrastructure and had two buildings completed respectively in 1946 and 1948. In 1949, the hospital had the largest number of inpatient and outpatient visits among the missionary hospitals in Fukien Church. At every crucial juncture of the hospital evolution, including the change of management and ownership from 1947 to 1950, and the takeover and transformation from 1951 to 1952, Chen played a decisive role. For three decades, the strenuous efforts he made for the hospital development had never been in the least reduced, nor even when he suffered from high blood pressure and headache, which he would take medicine and strong tea to overcome in order to create a positive and cheerful atmosphere before his patients. In January 1955, Chen passed away in his office from overwork. Today, his personal inscription "To Serve" still lies in the cornerstone of the Information Center building.

Working with Chen Songpan the longest time in the hospital was Chen Weixin who had been engaged in various important managerial duties since his first arrival at Takding Hospital in the late 1920s. Chen helped to train nurses for Foochow Christian Union Hospitals in 1928. When back from his further study in 1931, he concurrently served as an anesthetist. Once a teacher in the nursing school, he was appointed in the 1940s Secretary of General Affairs to take charge of managerial tasks and liaison with medical affairs outside and drug purchase. During the War of Resistence Against Japanese Aggression, he worked with Chen Songpan and Chen Zongpan and organized staff in the hospital to try all means to cover and transfer the wounded soldiers. He leveraged his advantage of speaking Japanese to deal with Japanese soldiers. Their efforts to provide humanitarian aid irrespective of personal safety won glory for Takding Hospital, becoming a part of the illustrious history of the hospital. His son Chen Zhaofen has owed it to himself to protect the historical and cultural heritage of Cangshan since his retirement, and the extensive materials he has sorted out provide valuable clues and documents for succeeding generations to review the history of Takding Hospital.

另一位陈医生被当地人亲切地称为"细陈"（福州方言中的"小陈"）或"二陈"，他就是"大陈"陈颂磐的弟弟陈宗磐（1908—1969），号称"塔亭一刀"，闻名当年福州医务界。1934年从上海圣约翰大学毕业后，他来到塔亭医院担任外科医师，极大地充实了医院外科力量。陈医生技术过硬，问诊后凭借西医基本功望、触、扣、听，即能做出准确诊断。业务扎实的他经常有奇思妙法解决困难。抗日战争期间，医院医疗物资紧缺，他通过观察，反复试验，发现医院老樟树上毛虫的肠子通过处理消毒可以取代手术急需的羊肠线。1956年，他作为代表到北京参加全国科技人员大会。他主持外科工作要求严格，培养学生也是一丝不苟。他培养的许多医生日后成绩斐然，成为所在县市的"一把刀"。尽管医术高明，他依旧不断学习，家里书橱中全是英文版的医学参考书。孩子们印象中的父亲经常研读至深夜。"类似手术做过无数，但对不同病人体质症状都得有不同的手术方案，做好充分准备才能应万变"，如今也是医生的女儿陈美爱至今仍记得父亲当年的话。

　　1949年，陈宗磐获得到英国伦敦学习的机会，1951年，他决定提前回国，以实际行动支持中华人民共和国。回国前，他上街演讲，募捐钱款购得手术台等一批医疗器械。他知道新政权将面临很多困难，作为外科医生，这是他朴素的帮助。途中经过新加坡和中国香港时，他谢绝了旧日老同学让他留在局势稳定、待遇优厚的地区从医的邀请，毅然决然地回到纵有万水千山也阻不断牵挂的家国。背弃祖国是他难以容忍的，在他的灵魂深处，热爱祖国、热爱家乡是做人起码的品格。1955年"一二零"大轰炸，台江一片火海，伤员被悉数抬入市二医院。正在柴井医院开会的陈宗磐冒着生命危险往回赶，途经中亭街桥头时险些中弹。到了医院，他二话没说，和抗日战争时期抢救伤员一样，又一次投入不眠不休的伤员救治中。"医生娘"，小时候陈美熙跟着妈妈上街总能听到陌生人这样呼唤自己的妈妈。这个称呼几十年来一直留在她的心中，每当想念父亲，她总会想起这一声饱含深情的呼唤。

：陈宗磐（来源：陈美爱）
：Chen Zongpan（Source: Chen
：Meiai)

Another Dr. Chen, affectionately known to the locals as "Se Ting", meaning "Small Chen", or "Second Chen", was Chen Zongpan (1908 – 1969), the younger brother of Chen Songpan who was "Big Chen". Fresh from Saint John's University, Chen Zongpan joined the Hospital in 1934 and his excellence in surgery soon won him the nickname "No. 1 Scalpel of Takding Hospital" meaning the best surgeon. His command of Western checking methods such as inspection, palpation, percussion and auscultation was good enough to enable him to make accurate diagnoses. His remarkable expertise sometimes went so far as to the blue-sky thinking that would solve tricky problems. When short of catgut sutures during the war, for example, he thought on his feet and proved that the intestines of the fat worms on camphor trees in the hospital, after proper process and sterilization, was a good alternative. In 1956, as a representative, Chen attended the National Science and Technology Conference held in Beijing. As a specialist, Chen had students who, after his strict instruction, later became the leading surgeons in their own county or city. Expert as he was, he impressed his children as a learner who had a bookshelf full of English books of medicine and would read late into midnight. "No matter how many similar surgeries a surgeon has performed, a specific operation plan to each patient should always be on hand in advance for any contingencies," are the words clearly remembered by his oldest daughter, Chen Meiai, a retired doctor.

In 1949, Chen was granted a chance to study in London, but in 1951 he decided to make an early return to work for the People's Republic of China. Before his journey, conscious of the possible difficulties the new establishment might face, he purchased a batch of medical equipment including an operating table with the money he raised by giving speeches in the street, hoping to pitch in as a surgeon. During his stopovers in Singapore and Hong Kong, China on his voyage back home, he declined the invitation from his former classmates who asked him to stay and work where the political situation was stable and the remuneration was attractive. But he missed his family and his country so much that nothing could stop him from coming back. For him, abandoning his motherland at this critical moment was nothing but a betrayal he would never condone, as deep in his heart love of one's homeland was the essence of humanity. It was this strong belief in humanity that guided him to save lives whenever possible. On 20 January 1955, he was having a medical meeting in Cha-Chang Hospital when an air raid struck Taijiang, all set ablaze and many wounded people carried to Takding Hospital. He knew he should lose no time flinging himself into the same hectic rescue he once joined during the War of Resistance Against Japanese Aggression. When the meeting was stopped, he risked his life to hurry back to the hospital and he didn't mention to anyone the narrow death he escaped on his way back that day until several days later to his family members. His youngest daughter, Chen Meixi, still remembers a special name local people would use to address her mother, "Dr. Nuong" meaning Wife of Doctor, a title full of people's respect to her father and his wife as well, and a title she has cherished for years as part of pleasant memories of her dear father.

生活中的陈医生富有情趣，温馨美好。有护士家在外地，结婚出嫁时不方便，他家就成了护士的娘家；无依无靠的老园丁退休了，他请他吃太平面，给他盘缠回家乡。忙里偷闲，他会在雨天收集青蛙卵放到小水缸里，让孩子们观察青蛙的孵化过程；工作再忙，他也不忘给孩子们购买课外书；每年一次带着孩子们上桃花山，亲近大自然。有时他叫上院里大点的孩子一起在家里为医院制作所需的药膏；而为了孩子们的安全，他敢于与当时"高人一等"的师姑们理论，要求她们拴好、管好自己的狗。他了解中国古代器乐合奏之美，也能在合唱《波兰圆舞曲》时，即兴在"啦啦啦"后面加上"哈哈哈"，营造欢乐祥和的气氛。这位热爱生活的青年才俊还在摄影中表达他对艺术的追求，他与附近的天真照相馆老板结缘，为后人留下许多珍贵影像。1957年他被错划为"右派"，"文革"时期被打成"黑帮"，但他没有抱怨，依然埋头苦干，一如他埋头在自己心爱的胶卷暗房中冲洗照片。如今这些照片让不断远去的历史，无意间留给后人回望的瞬间。

20世纪三四十年代陆续加入塔亭医院的医生护士们都有值得一说的轶事，此处仅提一二。陈兆勤毕业于汉口普爱医院护士学校护士师资培训班，是塔亭护士学校的校长，曾经进修学习麻醉，继陈为信后兼负责麻醉工作。他对学生要求十分严格，但爱好文艺的他经常组织文艺汇演，让学生在一张一弛中收获学习的快乐。有时碰到节日，他会请护生把脚踏风琴抬到每间病房，由他亲自为病人弹奏乐曲，为学生示范良好的医患氛围。他富有幽默感，每次被迫卷入"运动"中时，他告诉别人，自己是"老运动员"。他的妻子张美恩是塔亭护士学校的早期学员，后来成为总护士长。

陈兆勤，塔亭护校校长（来源：陈宜英）
Chen Zhaoqin, principal of Taking Nursing School（Source: Chen Yiying）

In daily life, Chen Zongpan was interesting, full of love and care to his fellow workers and his children. Once a nurse needed a place as her parents' home for her wedding ceremony, and he and his family members were happy to oblige doing what a bride parents' side should do. Another time in order to comfort an old gardener who had no relatives around when retired, he treated him to a typical local meal of thin and long noodles to wish him all the best and gave him some money for his travelling expenses. Busy as he was, he would remember to do what a father could for his kids: collecting frog eggs and putting them in a small water tank for them to observe the incubation, buying books for them to read and taking them to Taohua Mountain for their annual spring outing and a closer touch to nature. Sometimes he made ointment for the hospital at home and would welcome older kids to pitch in; for the safety of all kids, he would reason with home sisters and asked them to have their dog chained. Talented and intelligent, he talked the beauty of traditional Chinese instrumental ensemble, and he also performed the essence of Western waltz: once in a chorus of *Poland Waltz*, his ad-lib adding a Chinese sound of "Ha Ha Ha" to the original line of "La La La" left a memorable festive atmosphere. His love of life and art saw him enthusiastic about photography and acquainted well with the owner of a nearby well-known photo studio—Innocence Photoshop. Although wrongly labeled as a rightist in 1957 and mistakenly treated as a member of sinister gang during the Cultural Revolution, he complained nothing; instead, he kept his nose to the grindstone the way he developed films in his beloved darkroom. Thanks to the photos this handsome young doctor had taken, the history that is all the time drifting into obscurity without conscious or unconscious capture of special moments, is now partly visible.

Also worth mentioning are the stories of doctors and nurses who successively joined Takding Hospital in the 1930s and 1940s. Chen Zhaoqin, principal of Takding Nursing School, was a graduate of Nursing School at Hodge Memorial Hospital in Hankou in its nursing teachers training program. His further study in anesthesia made him an anesthetist in succession to Chen Weixin. Strict as he was, he understood so well the use of art in education that he, himself an art lover, frequently organized performances so that his students could relax and have fun in between studies. On festivals, he would play the reed organ for the patients in their wards to showcase healthy doctor-patient relationship to the students who would help carry the instrument from one ward to another. He had a great sense of humor and would make fun of himself by calling himself a "senior campaigner" for all the political campaigns he was subjected to. His wife, Zhang Meien, was among the first nurses in the early years and later became the head nurse.

同样有着幽默天性，被称为"开心果"的是陈尚娟。她 1948 年毕业于成都华西协和大学医学院即入职塔亭医院，工作至退休。她擅长儿科，深受人们喜爱，是继全科"大陈"、外科"二陈"后的"三陈"。西医出身的她，喜欢向老中医请教，经常为病人开出实惠单方，效果奇佳，十分受病人欢迎。她选择不婚。同样选择不婚的是为人称道的妇科专家、共产党员薛德英，她毕业于上海女子医学院。她们代表了学院派第二代西医医护女性。当时，教会医院有成文或不成文的规矩：护士不能结婚，如要结婚，必须先辞职。如果女大夫选择了内科、外科、妇产科这样的大科，就必须做好不婚的准备。无论被动还是主动，她们都代表了那个时期的新女性。她们选择职业而非婚姻，家庭已经不再是约束她们的场所了，她们开始在更广泛的意义上关注家庭、儿童与女性自身问题，成为时代进步的标志。

：塔亭"三位陈医生"（来源：陈美熙）
：Three Dr. Chens in Takding Hospital（Source: Chen Meixi）

　　20 世纪 50 年代初，塔亭岁月画上了句号，但中国医护人员在艰苦卓绝的岁月中为国家独立、民族自强所进行的不懈努力却从未泯灭。这股催人奋进的新时代塔亭精神在二院新的发展时期不断发扬光大，其内涵也不断拓展。1956 年，市二医院迎来了中华人民共和国成立后政府任命的第一任院长，具有划时代的意义。骨外科专家何祖焕（1912—1964）接下了这份沉甸甸的担子，演绎了新时期共产党员的模范典型，为后人敬仰。

Another doctor who would bring joy and laughter to people around was Chen Shangjuan, a graduate of School of Medicine of West China Union University in Chengdu. As a pediatrician, her popularity can be well understood from the nickname she enjoyed, "Third Chen", a special recognition to a trio of highly-respected doctors: the previously mentioned "Big Chen" as a general practitioner and "Second Chen", a surgeon. Though well trained in Western medicine, she learned from senior Chinese medicine doctors for inexpensive but effective prescription to her patients. She chose to stay single her whole life. So did Xue Deying, a well-reputed gynecologist and a CPC member who graduated from Women's Christian Medical College in Shanghai. They were the second generation of women educated in Western medicine. At that time, there was an unspoken rule in Christian hospitals that nurses were allowed to get married only after they quit their jobs. Likewise, a woman doctor who chose to work in major departments of internal medicine, surgery, gynecology and obstetrics must understand that she was not expected to get married. Whether they were forced or opted to pursue careers instead of marriage, as typical women of the new era delivered from the bondage of family life, they directed their focus on problems of family, children and women in a broader sense, which can be seen as a sign of social progress.

In the early 1950s, stories under the name of Takding Hospital came to an end. However, the unremitting efforts the Chinese medical staff made for national independence and national self-reliance in hard times continued to shine. The new era saw enrichment and expansion of Takding spirit. 1956 witnessed the epoch-making event when Fuzhou Second Hospital had its first director appointed by the government of the People's Republic of China. He Zuhuan (1912 - 1964), an expert in orthopedics, took over this mammoth task and set up a typical example for his followers to learn, of a Communist Party member dedicating all his life to the construction of a better society in the new age under the leadership of Chinese Communist Party.

院长何祖焕，骨外科专家
He Zuhuan, director of the hospital and an orthopedic expert

何祖焕，曾用名何光耀，原籍福建晋江，出生于福州。1932年福州三一中学毕业后，留校任教。1933年考入福州协和大学化学系，两年后考入上海圣约翰大学医学院，1941年毕业获医学博士学位。1941年6月进入上海仁济医院任外科住院医师。1945年3月，追求进步的他接受新四军驻沪组织的聘请，到新四军七师卫生部任医师兼抗日战争创伤队队长。同年8月，与新婚妻子回杭探亲，此时新四军北上抗日，遂与新四军失去联系。回上海先后在沪东医院、中美医院任主治医师。1947年，任杭州广济医院外科主任。1948年，母亲生病，回到榕城。1949年8月，应聘到福州塔亭医院，此后常年担任医院的外科主任，1956年加入中国共产党，同时被任命为院长。

何祖焕初到塔亭医院时，全院仅有9名医师，其中3名为外科医师，医疗设备较差。何祖焕不畏困难，先后进行大量手术治疗，从普通外科手术发展到泌尿外科、颅脑外科、胸外科等。由于他诊断准确，医术高明，尤其是术前准备充分，手术过程中认真细致，因而疗效良好，深受患者称道。据说，何医生在手术中，有时护士递线的速度赶不上他手术线打结的速度。"妈妈告诉我，这是父亲从前在小小扁扁的火柴盒里刻苦练习打结练就的功夫"，女儿何以敉解释说，"为了增加手指灵敏度，他还跟着犹太人学小提琴。他做手术创面清楚，上石膏效果特别好。"

何祖焕发现，骨病患者多，但当时福州各综合医院并无骨科，于是他克服困难，开始筹建骨科。1956年，何祖焕到天津人民医院骨科进修，回来后大大加速了骨科建设步伐，1958年，二院率先在外科中成立了骨科，很快又有了骨科专业医师队伍和护理队伍，为后来市二的"龙头"骨科打下了坚实的基础。何祖焕在繁忙医务实践和医院事务中，也积极从事学术研究和人才培养。除了在《中华医学杂志》发表论文，作为福建医学院教授，他长期讲授《骨科学》，为省、市培养大批骨科人才。他注重培养新人，鼓励年轻人敢于自我挑战。当时医院有一对医生夫妻，双双被鼓励学习骨科。妻子对于女性从事骨科心存顾虑，何祖焕积极引导，最终妻子的骨科技能超过自己的丈夫，一时成为美谈。

何祖焕去天津进修前集体照（1956）（来源：陈美爱）
A group photo taken before He Zuhuan went to Tianjin for further study
(1956)(Source: Chen Meiai)

He Zuhuan, formerly known as He Guangyao, was born in Fuzhou, though he had his family origin in Jinjiang, Fujian. He was kept to teach after his secondary education in Trinity College Foochow in 1932. A year later, he attended the Department of Chemistry of Fukien Christian University and was admitted, two years later, to St. John's University School of Medicine in Shanghai. In June 1941, he became a surgical resident in Shanghai Renji Hospital immediately after graduating with a Doctorate in Medicine. In March 1945, in pursuit of progress, he accepted the appointment of the New Fourth Army in Shanghai, and served as a physician in the Department of Health of the Seventh Division of the New Fourth Army, and was also the leader of the trauma team in the War of Resistance Against Japanese Aggression. In August, he and his newly-wed wife went back to visit their family in Hangzhou and consequently lost contact with the New Fourth Army that headed north to fight against the Japanese army. When back in Shanghai, he worked as an attending physician first in Hudong Hospital and later in Sino-American Hospital. In 1947, he served as director of surgery of Hospital of Universal Benevolence in Hangzhou. In 1948, he returned to Fuzhou to care for his mother who had fallen ill. In August 1949, he began his work at Takding Hospital serving as the director of surgery for many years. In 1956, he joined the Communist Party of China and was appointed director of Fuzhou Second Hospital.

When he first arrived at Takding Hospital, there were only nine doctors, three of whom were surgeons. There was also a lack of up-to-date medical equipment. Undaunted, He Zuhuan performed a wide range of surgeries including general surgery, urological surgery, brain surgery, thoracic surgery, etc. He was well-known for his accurate diagnosis, excellent medical skills, and particularly his meticulousness before and during the operation. It is said that Dr. He could tie surgical knots so fast that sometimes nurses could hardly keep up with him. "My mother told me that my father used to practice tying knots in tiny, flat match boxes," He Yimi, his daughter, explained, "He even learned to play violin from a Jewish friend to increase the dexterity of his fingers. He kept surgical wounds clean and applied casts effectively."

When He Zuhuan discovered there were no orthopedic departments in general hospitals in Fuzhou to meet the demand of patients with bone disorders, he decided to make a change. In 1956, he went to the Orthopedic Department at Tianjin People's Hospital for further study. In 1958, Fuzhou Second Hospital took the lead in establishing the Department of Orthopedics with a professional team of orthopedic surgeons and nurses assembled afterwards, which laid a solid foundation for the department's later noticeable growth. Although busy with medical practices and administration, Dr. He also engaged himself in academic research and talent cultivation. Besides a contributor to *Chinese Medical Journal*, he taught Orthopedics as a professor of Fujian Medical University, cultivating orthopedic talents for the city and the province. He encouraged young doctors to challenge themselves. Once under his guidance, a doctor couple decided to learn orthopedics and the wife dismissed her misgivings about being a woman orthopedic doctor and later proved a better surgeon than her husband in actual performance.

何祖焕任劳任怨，追求进步，除了钻研专业，还坚持阅读马列著作，学习辩证唯物主义和历史唯物主义。何祖焕工作中几乎无休，每天晚上工作到凌晨1点，24小时待命。女儿何以籹说，周六晚陪孩子看场电影是爸爸唯一难得的放松，也是当时年幼的她心中所存不多的与爸爸共度的美好时光。据何以籹回忆，父亲当年连周日也不休息，总是一头扎在办公室，或是和年轻医生谈心，或是读书、查资料。童年时的以籹偶尔周日跟着爸爸来到办公室，印象最深的就是摆在爸爸办公室的那具人体骨骼模型，还有爸爸抽屉里写满密密麻麻文字的本子和画得整整齐齐的表格，文字中有不少有关关节研究的内容。二院后来出的一部全国通用的内部资料《骨科检查法》，就是在何祖焕多年手稿的基础上编订的。

1963年，积劳成疾的何祖焕患病住院。住院期间，仍有一些病人慕名而来，到病房求他诊治。每次看诊，他的额头总是布满豆大的汗珠，身体严重透支的他，为病人服务的热情却丝毫不减。1964年9月，何祖焕患肝癌医治无效逝世，临终前他交代，为了科学，希望捐献自己的遗体，不要对家属搞特殊化。他的妻子也一直遵守丈夫遗愿，在多年手术室护士的工作压力之下，她患有植物神经紊乱性高血压症，但直到退休前几年，她一直没有要求调换岗位。她以实际行动纪念自己的爱人，诠释并延续着塔亭医护们的大爱无私的崇高精神。

在新旧制度过渡时期成长起来的杰出塔亭人物还有不少，如马来西亚出生的黄腓力（1919—1987）就是其中一个。1937年，怀揣一颗赤子之心，他回国求学。1948年，他从上海同济大学医学院毕业后，到塔亭医院担任内科主治医师。他医术高明，医德高尚，诊疗过程中为病人着想，病人少花钱且疗程短，见效快、治愈率高。1964年，他服从分配，被调往20公里之外的马尾马江医院加强乡镇医疗力量。在那里，他深受群众爱戴。

斗转星移，半个世纪后的2013年8月28日，马江医院已发展成开发区医院，它需要新一轮的扶持，此时市二医院正与它签订托管合作协议，双方正式"联姻"。从一个人的帮扶到整个医院的参与，塔亭故事续写着精彩纷呈的市二新篇：前世今生，初心如磐，笃行致远。十年后的2023年6月19日，市二医院迎来了新时期的又一次成长蜕变，为了更好地服务人民，医院整合福州神经精神病防治院和福州市妇幼保健院，成为福州市第二总医院，其精彩故事也将留待后人采撷。

Diligent at work and progressive at heart, He Zuhuan was an avid reader: He read not only medical updates but works of Marx and Lenin as well. With so much to do, He Zuhuan worked almost non-stop. One o'clock after midnight was his usual bedtime and he was on call 24 hours a day. Recalling the few happy moments she spent with her father, He Yimi, said the only ewe lamb of pleasure her father had was going to a movie with her on Saturday nights. According to He Yimi, her father would stay in the office even on Sundays, talking with young doctors, reading books, or consulting references. Occasionally she was allowed to follow him to the office where she was impressed with the skeleton model, the fully-written notebooks, well-drawn diagrams and papers with words about joints. Part of those was Dr. He's manuscript he kept working on for many years, on which Fuzhou Second Hospital later compiled *Orthopedic Examination Techniques* for the exclusive use by the health care workers nationwide.

In 1963, He Zuhuan was hospitalized from years of overwork, but his reputation still drew patients to his ward for treatment. Whenever such patients came, he would forget his own status as a critically ill patient and examined his patients as earnestly as he did before despite the heavy exhaustion and the clearly seen drops of sweat oozing from his forehead. He Zuhuan died of liver cancer in September 1964. In his last words, He expressed his will to donate his body to science and insisted that the hospital grant no favors to his family. To fulfil his last wish, his wife, who worked in the same hospital many years as a surgical nurse and suffered from working stress and hypertension caused by autonomic dysfunction, did not ask for a change of position until a few years before her retirement. In this way, she commemorated her husband and continued to hold high the banner of selflessness of Takding spirit.

Takding Hospital witnessed the rise of many professionals in its transition. One of them was the Malaysia-born Huang Feili (1919 - 1987). In 1937, as a patriotic young man, he returned to China for further study and after graduating from Shanghai Tongji University School of Medicine in 1948, he worked in Takding Hospital as an attending physician. With great skills and ethics, he brought quicker recovery at lower cost and a high cure rate, and enjoyed great popularity among the patients. In 1964, he was dispatched to serve in Majiang Hospital in Mawei, 20 kilometers away, to improve local medical conditions and was honored and respected by people there.

Half a century went by in a twinkling. On August 28, 2013, Majiang Hospital evolved into Hospital of Mawei Economic and Technological Development Zone. In need of a new round of support, it signed a trusteeship cooperation agreement with Fuzhou Second Hospital, ensuring a mutually beneficial relationship for both sides. From the help of one person to the involvement of the entire hospital, Fuzhou Second Hospital opened a new chapter for Takding's stories: Stay true to the original aspirations while forging ahead. Another new chapter began ten years later on June 19, 2023 when the hospital was officially announced to be Fuzhou Second General Hospital taking Fuzhou Psychiatric Hospital and Fuzhou Maternity and Child Health Hospital as its members in the context of medical resources integration for the benefit of the people, and that will surely produce more inspiring stories to tell.

回望百年，一怀缱绻，流年碎影，散落心头。一个半世纪的历史，风尘翕张。塔亭与二院，前世今生，时光作渡，眉目成书。这样的心照不宣，应是源于对生命的理解、尊重与呵护。

时光匆匆，不觉中，百多日的历史探寻也行将告一段落。这段时空之旅，以塔亭路为起点，史料为车，时光厮磨中，穿越晚清民国，及至当下。途中幸遇塔亭老者，拓路踏歌，一路相伴，数风流人物，看房前屋后，尽现云卷云舒。遇见历史，忝列其中，与有荣焉。

历史是现在与过去的对话，这种对话可以在"宏大叙事"中展开，近几十年来，对话发生了"记忆的转向"，回忆成为历史叙事的重要部分。历史和记忆一样，既关乎过去，更关乎现在。人们对于当下处境的关切，往往自觉不自觉地影响着他们对于过往记忆的选择和诠释，记忆也因此不再是消极的事实存储，而是积极的意义再造。本章的塔亭往事正是在史料的基础上，汇入了一批生动真实的回忆。当回忆者以不同角度讲述历史时，我们看到的是一个更为丰满的历史空间。限于能力和篇幅，此次塔亭叙事仍留有较大空间等待开拓，而眼前的福州市第二医院正在书写的岁月不褪青春，正是现世人们不忘历史、继往开来的历史新篇。

● 特别鸣谢

本章写作过程中，得到以下单位和个人的大力支持，特此鸣谢。

福州市第二医院办公室主任唐卫红、总务主任余力、工会主席戴恩泽、档案室金瑾、宣传科朱玉、五官科主任肖志勇、总务办徐小龙等为本章提供了十分宝贵的历史档案资料、图片和宣传材料，及相关人事信息。原院长吴和木先生接受访谈，热情提供资料，并对内容做了部分批阅。

A wistful look at the thinly-veiled fragmented episodes that one's eyes can capture and his minds would read. Such is the typical scene in a historical travel back into one and a half centuries where clouds of dust are certain to blow out of the past events. Out of the dust is a delightful finding that Takding Hospital and Fuzhou Second Hospital, the latter being the former's afterlife, are in such a bond that a glance one casts is sure to meet with the other's immediate acceptance as if they have long been familiar to each other, so much so that they have developed minds that think alike, that is, life should be treated with recognition, respect and care.

Unwittingly, this journey of more than one hundred days now has to come to a conclusion. This is a ride on a carpet of historical documents, starting from Tating Road all the way through the late Qing Dynasty and the Republic of China to the present time. The adventure became an interesting and lucky one when some old witnesses of Takding period joined us and gave vivid accounts of what people were like and how houses were planned. Their narration for the sake of recollection and their help without any private request made us feel humble and honored.

History is a dialogue between the present and the past and can be related in the "grand narrative", or as recent decades see, in the small narrative with "a turn of memory". Like memory, history is concerned with the present as well as the past because the concern one has for the current situation will affect, in one way or another, the choice and the interpretation of the past stories. Memory, therefore, is a positive reconstruction rather than an inactive stock of facts. The past of Takding times in this chapter depends on historical documents and also real stories that are told from different perspectives and thus add richness to its historical space, yet due to the writer's limited ability and writing space, this narrative of Takding Hospital still has a lot left to be desired. Nonetheless, we are happy to see that a greater new historical chapter is now being written in Fuzhou Second Hospital about how to stay true to the original commitment, the way people today vow to carry forward the undertakings of the predecessor and forge ahead into the future.

• Acknowledgments

I should like to acknowledge the tremendous support the following institutions and individuals have provided to help bring this chapter into completion.

My first debt of gratitude is owed to Fuzhou Second Hospital, the first institution I went for information and have since then been given assistance in the whole process. All valuable materials that included archival documents, old and new photos, hospital journals, updates for publicity, etc., are the understanding and the kindness from the following people: Tang Weihong, Director of General Office, Yu Li, Director of General Affairs, Dai Enze, President of Trade Union, Jin Jin in charge of Archive Office, Zhu Yu of Publicity Office, Xiao Zhiyong, Director of ENT Department, and Xu Xiaolong, etc. My gratitude also goes to Wu Hemu, the former director of the hospital who gave important details in the interviews, and offered materials and advice for the revision of the draft.

接受访谈的还有陈兆奋、陈美爱、陈宜英、陈美熙、何以籹等人，他们中大部分人虽是古稀耄耋之年，但十分健谈，对曾经生活过的塔亭医院印象深刻，感情深厚，他们为书中的建筑和人物部分提供了重要、生动的讲述和图片文字材料。其中陈美爱医生提供了大量老照片，陈宜英和陈美熙为20世纪四五十年代塔亭医院建筑布局的复原图做了大量工作，该图由福建师范大学外国语学院2020版学生刘可欣多次修改绘制而成。此外，在各方面帮助协调人物线索和提供资料内容的还有陈星、陈建中、戴显群、徐心希、唐希、陈天如、池志海，以及鼓岭管委会的工作人员。

本章在文本资料查阅过程中，得到上海医药博物馆（集团）总馆长上官万平先生的慷慨相助，他提供了十分宝贵的塔亭医院1921年的原版英文年度报告，目前存放于上海月湖中西医博物馆。此外，福建师范大学社会历史学院郭荣刚老师也为我们的资料查阅提供了便利，其中已故史学大家陈增辉先生30多年前编写制作的《来华外人汉名录》卡片柜为我们提供了不可多得的百年前外国人在中国的"身份证明"。

本章的英文翻译得到福建师范大学协和学院的周秦超老师、福建师范大学2017级毕业生梁书尧和2018级毕业生何宇喆的大力协助。他们一起负责本章节"人物故事汇"部分的翻译和校对。

My special and deepest gratitude should also go to the following interviewees: Chen Zhaofen, Chen Meiai, Chen Yiying, Chen Meixi and He Yimi, most of whom are at their great age but enthusiastic and supportive about the narrative of history. It is hard to put into words the gratitude I owe them for their vivid accounts, without which stories in this chapter would have been impossible. Particular thanks to Chen Meiai for her provision of the precious old photos, to Chen Yiying and Chen Meixi for their great patience in checking the details about the layout of Takding Hospital in the 1940s and 1950s, and to Liu Kexin, a student of Class 2020 of College of Foreign Languages of Fujian Normal University, for her tireless revisions on the drawing of the restored plan. I also thank those from whom I have been privileged to make more contacts and get materials. Among these faces and voices are Chen Xing, Chen Jianzhong, Dai Xianqun, Xu Xinxi, Tang xi, Chen Tianru, Chi Zhihai and people in Kuliang Administration Committee.

I am profoundly grateful to Shangguan Wanping, General Curator of Shanghai Pharmaceutical Museum (Group), for the most gracious help he offered in providing photos of the original English version of *1921 Medical Report* of the Hospital, a rare authentic document that is on display in Moonlake Chinese and Western Medicine Museum in Shanghai. Similar thanks go to Guo Ronggang, a teacher of College of Sociology and History of Fujian Normal University, for his generous assistance and his introduction of a card cabinet, in which foreign residents in China decades ago have their "identity" cards with corresponding foreign and Chinese names. These cards were made more than thirty years ago by Chen Zenghui, the late expert in history, to whom much should be owed as well.

And finally, a particularly warm thank-you is due to the following teacher and students for their crucial efforts in providing translations and later revision in the most efficient manner for the final part of *Stories of Medical Staff*: Zhou Qinchao, a teacher of Concord University College of Fujian Normal University, Liang Shuyao, and He Yuzhe, graduates in 2021 and in 2022 respectively of College of Foreign Languages of Fujian Normal University.

CHAPTER TWO

从马高爱医院到福建①
医科大学附属协和医院

From Magaw Memorial Hospital to Fujian
Medical University Union Hospital

第二章 福

● 地理风貌

福建协和医院位于福建省福州市新权路 29 号，坐落于福州市中心风景宜人的于山之麓，地理环境优越，为八闽现代医学的发祥地。福州协和医院所依偎的于山有着悠久的历史传统和丰富的文化内涵，对协和医院有天然的孕育之蕴。于山又称九仙山、九日山，位于福州城区中心鼓楼区东南。传说中，战国时古民族"于越氏"的一支在此居住，于山因此得名。汉代时，临川的何氏九兄弟在此炼丹修仙，因此于山又名九仙山。闽越王无诸曾经于九月九日在这里宴会，于山因此又名九日山。于山曾改名红岩山，1977 年复名于山。于山与乌山、屏山并称"三山"，作为国家 4A 级旅游景区，备受游客青睐，主要景点包括戚公祠、白塔、状元峰、兰花圃、狮子岩等，是福州的一张旅游名片。于山风景区风景秀丽，遍布摩崖石刻、古榕"根抱石"等景观，留有戚继光等众多名人史迹。

：福州于山白塔
：White Tower, Yushan Mountain, Fuzhou

院内有代表协和医院悠久发展历史的旧楼——红楼。这座楼始建于 20 世纪 20 年代，20 世纪 30 年代开始使用。20 世纪 20 年代美国基督教美部会与美以美会决定合并两教会办的圣教医院和马高爱医院，共同筹建一所规模更大的新医院，取名为"福州基督教协和医院"，寓意为同心协力，和衷共济，共同办好社会福利事业。英文名以捐款人姓名命名为 Willis & Pierce Memorial Hospital。自 1928 年 10 月 1 日起，福州基督教协和医院作为一个联合机构开始运转，一部分在城里，一部分在仓山，院长为美国人邱永康医生。

1937 年建成新病房大楼，一色的红砖砌成，楼中央部分为五层楼，西翼四层，东翼三层。西翼地下一层临街为门诊，设候诊室、诊疗室、药房、挂号、收费处。一层至三层为病房，设病床 120 张，最多可收治 150 个病人，分为特等、一等、二等、三等 4 类病房，按照当时最现代医院的设计，配备手术室、隔离室、接生室、私人病房、X 光室、教学手术看台，并设有小儿、妇产专科，五楼专供治疗肺结核病人。

Scan for more
扫码了解更多

• Location and Landscapes

At the foot of Yushan Mountain in the center of Fuzhou with beautiful scenery, Fujian Medical University Union Hospital is located at No. 29, Xinquan Road, Fuzhou City, Fujian Province. The hospital is superior in geographical environment and is the birthplace of modern medicine in Fujian Province. Yushan Mountain, in which Fujian Medical University Union Hospital is nestled, has a long historical tradition and rich cultural connotation and is a natural breeding land for the hospital. Yushan Mountain, also known as Jiuxian Mountain or Jiuri Mountain, is located in the southeast of Gulou District, the center of Fuzhou City. According to the legend, during the Warring States period, a branch of the ancient nationality "Yu Yue" lived here, and Yushan Mountain was named after part of the name "Yu". In the Han Dynasty, the nine brothers of the He family in Linchuan made alchemy and tried to cultivate themselves to immortals here, so Yushan Mountain is also known as Jiuxian Mountain. King Wuzhu of Fujian and Yue once held a banquet here on September 9, so Yushan is also known as Jiuri Mountain. It was once renamed Hongyan Mountain and was renamed Yushan again in 1977. Yushan Mountain, Wushan Mountain and Pingshan Mountain are known as "Three Mountains", which is a national 4A-level tourist attraction favored by tourists. The main attractions include Qigong Temple, White Tower, Zhuangyuan Peak, Orchid Garden, Lion Rock, etc. "Three Mountains" is a card for the tourism of Fuzhou. Yushan Mountain Scenic Area has beautiful scenery including Cliff Stone Carvings, Ancient Banyan Trees with "Roots Embracing Stones", etc., and keeps historical sites of Qi Jiguang and many other famous figures.

In the hospital, an old building, Red Building, shows the long history of Fujian Medical University Union Hospital. It was built in the 1920s and opened in the 1930s. In the 1920s, the American Board of Commissioners for Foreign Missions and the Methodist Episcopal Church decided to merge the Foochow Missionary Hospital and the Magaw Memorial Hospital run by the two churches to build a larger new hospital, named "Foochow Christian Union Hospital", which means "work together and help each other to do a good job in the social welfare". The English name was also called Willis & Pierce Memorial Hospital after the donor's name. On October 1, 1928, the newly merged hospital with Dr. Thomas H. Coole, an American, as the director, started operating as a joint institution, partly in the city and partly in Cangshan.

In 1937, a new ward building of red bricks was built. Its central part had five floors, the west wing four and the east wing three. The basement of the west wing, with street access, was the outpatient department, in which there were a waiting room, a consultation room, a pharmacy, a registration office, and a toll office. Wards were on the first to the third floors with 120 beds, which could accommodate up to 150 patients. Those wards had 4 types: special, first, second, and third. Thanks to the most advanced design at that time, the ward building was equipped with an operating room, a quarantine room, a delivery room, private wards, the X-ray room and the platform for teaching operations, and had department of pediatrics, and department of obstetrics and gynecology. The fifth floor was specially used for the treatment of tuberculosis.

卫生间装有抽水马桶，病房的纱窗、门把手等部件是铜质的，不锈钢餐具、托盘、蚊帐、毛毯都是美国货。整个院舍有电灯及冷热水装置设备，水源是离医院半英里外125尺深的井水，并经检验证明没有大肠杆菌。电力能够保证进口的先进镭射设备、X光机、显微镜、化验仪器等医疗设备的用电，并设置了护士用电系统，所有夜间灯光都装在墙内的地线板上。为保证不影响病人的睡眠，走廊和病房隔墙装了防音板，消除噪音。医院办公室连接各个护士站有院内电话系统，调配厨房与各楼层服务间有专门的送餐升降梯，食品用装有热水箱的小车保温分送。医院还配有专用汽车。协和医院是当时福建规模最大、设备最好的医院。

红砖楼又叫红楼，当时成为福州的标志性建筑，是福州人的骄傲。同时这栋大楼也是一栋命运多舛的大楼。在抗日战争期间，红楼遭到了极大的破坏，其中有生活用品——"一半可移动的家具；所有的地毯、床单和毛巾"；有医学药品和仪器——"三分之二的药物，所有实验室的试剂和染色剂，一半的手术仪器"，还有病例、图书等文字资料。（耶鲁档案 r8b138f7 pp27）

协和医院的新院徽在2009年7月启用，以代表协和医院悠久历史的独特建筑红楼为主体背景，彰显了古朴、典雅和庄严的特质。院徽上的红十字寓意为助人于危难之中，弘扬"人道、博爱、奉献"的精神，一方面象征着护佑人民的生命和健康，促进整个人类的和平发展，另一方面体现了协和医院作为教会医院的特殊历史背景。协和医院致力打造安宁、祥和与充满活力的医院，崇尚"绿色人文"，营造良好就医环境并积极实现"以病人为中心"的服务宗旨。橄榄枝蕴含着生命、健康与希望，是医院愿景的象征。

协和医院新院徽（来源：福建医科大学附属协和医院）
The new emblem of Fujian Medical University Union Hospital （Source：Fujian Medical University Union Hospital)

The lavatories were equipped with a flush toilet, and the screen windows and door handles of the ward were made of copper. The stainless-steel tableware, trays, mosquito nets, and blankets were from America. The entire facility was equipped with electric lights and installations for hot water and cold water. The water source, free of bacterium coli, was a 125-foot-deep well located half a mile from the hospital. The power ensured the working of advanced laser equipment, X-ray machines, microscopes, laboratory instruments and other medical equipment that were imported, and an electric system for nurses was also set up. All night lights were installed on the ground plate in the wall. In order not to affect the patient's sleep, soundproof panels were installed in the corridor and partition walls of the ward to eliminate noise. The hospital office was connected to each nurse station by an in-hospital telephone system. The kitchen and service rooms on each floor had elevators for food delivery. Food was distributed by trolleys with hot water tanks. The hospital also had a car. It was the largest and best-equipped hospital in Fujian.

As a landmark in Fuzhou at that moment, this red-brick building, also called Red Building, became the pride of Fuzhou people. Red Building also experienced twists and turns. During the War of Resistance Against Japanese Aggression, it was greatly damaged: the daily necessities, "half movable furniture, all carpets, sheets and towels"; medical drugs and instruments, "two-thirds of drugs, all laboratory reagents and dyes, and half of the surgical instruments", as well as written materials such as case reports and books.

The new emblem of Fujian Medical University Union Hospital was put into use in July 2009. With the unique Red Building representing the long history of the hospital as the main background, it highlights the characteristics of simplicity, elegance and solemnity. The red cross on the emblem means helping others in danger and disaster, and advances and enriches the spirit of "humanity, fraternity, and dedication". It symbolizes the peaceful development of human beings through the protection of people's lives and health. Meanwhile, it reflects the special historical background of Fujian Medical University Union Hospital as a church hospital; the hospital creates a tranquil, peaceful and vibrant medical institution, advocates the "green humanity", produces a good medical environment and actively realizes the "patient-centered" service tenet. The olive branch in the new emblem contains life, health and hope, and is a symbol of the vision of this hospital.

• 历史沿革

　　西方医学与福州结缘要从 19 世纪中叶讲起。1850 年，英国圣公会差会首次向福建福州派遣了两名传教士，即温敦和札成。（耶鲁档案：*Fukien—Then and Now*，p2）传教士来到福州后，出入于百姓之中，学习福州方言，并以己所能帮助福州百姓。其中，温敦的医术成了他与当地百姓互动交流的重要桥梁。"温敦开了一家诊所，各阶层的人都前来问诊。"（Ibid：6）这些医生是第一代在福州行医的西方传教士，他们的医学活动为后来马高爱医院和圣教医院以及二者合二为一的协和医院的诞生和发展开创了历史。

　　百年协和，源远流长。19 世纪 70 年代是西方教会在福州开展医学工作的一个转折点。医学博士西格尼·特拉斯克小姐于 1874 年随美以美会使团抵达福州。她的行医仅限于妇女和儿童，美以美会于 1877 年为特拉斯克小姐开了一家医院，即马高爱医院。1870 年 1 月 22 日，奥斯古德受美部会派遣，作为一名医学传教士与妻子海伦·W. 奥斯古德来到福州。抵达后，他开始兼职行医，不久，他建立了临时医院，在那里投入了大量精力。1878 年，在福州太平街，一所新的 50 张床位的医院在外国商人、中国商人和福州官员的资助下建成，福州圣教医院正式开设，旧的建筑变成了鸦片戒烟所。1877 年建成的马高爱医院和 1878 年正式开办的圣教医院于 1928 年合并成立协和医院，即今天的福建医科大学附属协和医院前身。

马高爱医院的医生、护士和患者（来源：福建医科大学附属协和医院）
Doctors, nurses and patients in Magaw Memorial Hospital
(Source: Fujian Medical University Union Hospital)

• Past and Present

The story of the relationship between Fuzhou and Western medicine started from the middle of the 19th century. In 1850, the Church Missionary Society sent two missionaries, William Welton and R. D. Jackson, to Fuzhou, Fujian, for the first time. After the missionaries came to Fuzhou, they lived among the local people in Fuzhou, learned the Fuzhou dialect, and helped the locals with what they could do. William Welten's medical skills became an important bridge for him to interact with the locals. "W. Welten opened a clinic, and people of all classes arrived for treatment. " These doctors were the first generation of Western missionaries who practiced medicine in Fuzhou. They had a historic influence on the birth and development of Magaw Memoriary Hospital and Foochow Missionary Hospital, as well as the late Foochow Christian Union Hospital, which was a combination of the former two hospitals.

Fujian Medical University Union Hospital has a long history. The 1870s was a turning point in the history of the work by Western churches in Fuzhou. Miss Sigourney Trask, MD, arrived in Fuzhou in 1874 with the mission of the Methodist Episcopal Church. Her medical practice was limited to women and children, and the Methodist Episcopal Church opened a hospital for Miss Trask in 1877, which was called Magaw Memorial Hospital. On January 22, 1870, Osgood was dispatched by the American Board to come to Fuzhou as a medical missionary with his wife, Helen W. Osgood. Upon arrival, he began practicing medicine part-time, and soon he established a makeshift hospital, where he devoted a great deal of energy. In 1878, on Taiping Street, Fuzhou, a new 50-bed hospital was built with the help of foreign businessmen, Chinese businessmen and Fuzhou officials. That meant Foochow Missionary Hospital was officially opened, and the old building was turned into an opium smoking cessation center. Magaw Memorial Hospital built in 1877 and Foochow Missionary Hospital officially opened in 1878 merged to form Foochow Christian Union Hospital in 1928, which evolved into Fujian Medical University Union Hospital at the present time.

福建协和之前身马高爱医院——中国最早的妇孺医院

　　医学博士西格尼·特拉斯克小姐 1874 年随美以美会使团抵达福州。1875 年，使团寻求拨款 5 000 美元购买一处场地，为这位医生修建一所医院以及住所。这一要求很容易得到了批准，其中 4 000 美元由纽约分行提供，500 美元由费城分行提供，500 美元由巴尔的摩分行提供。1876 年 8 月，购买第一批土地，建筑工程开始。这栋楼高 98 英尺，宽 57 英尺。这是一座坚固的两层住宅，在各方面都适合其预定用途。它包括下层客厅、图书馆和供住院医生使用的餐厅；药房、手术室、特殊病房、检查室、病人候诊室；有地方给本地助手。楼上有三间卧室，与医生的住所相连，还有两间大病房、浴室、护士室等。在这栋建筑落成之际，有大量知名人士在场，包括欧洲人和当地人。美国领事德拉诺先生主持会议。范泰先生在几名福建省专员的陪同下出席了会议。在开幕式的整个过程中，这些官员留了下来，并表现出对建筑细节的极大兴趣以及对其慈善目的的兴趣。在如此有利的条件的支持下，女子外国传教士协会开始了在福州的医疗工作。药房每天都为临时病人开放。（Wheeler，2018：168）

1910 年重建的马高爱新医院（来源：福建医科大学附属协和医院）
Magaw Memorial Hospital rebuilt in 1910（Source：Fujian Medical University Union Hospital）

　　1877 年 4 月 18 日，医院建成开业，为纪念捐款人而命名为马高爱纪念医院。因特拉斯克医生的行医对象限于妇女和儿童，当地人习惯称其为"岭后妇孺医院"。（Carlson，1974：88）这是一座简易的两层砖楼，仅用屏风把女医生的住所与病人分开。西格尼·特拉斯克医生为第一任院长，有 6 位外国医生和 1 位护士。医院收治的第 1 位病人是一个 28 岁的已婚妇女，因膝关节摔伤未及时治疗，造成骨胶着弯曲僵硬，5 年不能行走。手术矫正后，她三个月就能走着回闽清老家。根据 1891 年的文献，当年马高爱医院的病人总数达 6 215 人，处方量 6 975 张，出诊 1 088 次。1910 年前后，老楼房遭台风袭击倒塌，在原址上盖起了三层的新洋楼。

　　马高爱医院通过创办护士学校推动了当时中国的医疗事业发展。"教会医院是基督教在华医疗事业的重要组成部分，也是基督教开展公共卫生事业的主要力量。"（牛桂晓，2019）

Magaw Memorial Hospital, the Earliest Hospital for Women and Children in China

Miss Sigourney Trask, MD, arrived in Fuzhou in 1874 with the Mission of The Methodist Episcopal Church. In 1875, the mission sought a grant of $5,000 to purchase a site to build a hospital and residence for the doctor. This request was easily approved, with $4,000 provided by the New York branch, $500 by the Philadelphia branch, and $500 by the Baltimore branch. In August 1876, the first piece of land was purchased and the construction work began. The building was 98 feet tall and 57 feet wide. This was a solid two-storey building, fit for its intended purpose in every respect. It included the lower living room, library and dining room for residents as well as pharmacy, operating room, special ward, examination room, and patient waiting room; there also were rooms for local assistants. There were three bedrooms upstairs, connected to the doctor's residence, as well as two large wards, bathrooms, nurse's rooms, etc. The building was inaugurated in the presence of many prominent personalities, including Europeans and locals. Mr. Delano, the American consul, presided over the meeting. Mr. Fan Tai and several Fujian provincial commissioners attended the meeting. In the opening ceremony, the officials showed great interest not only in architectural details but also in its charitable purpose. Therefore, with such favorable support, the medical work of the Women's Foreign Missionary Association started in Fuzhou. The pharmacy was open daily for temporary patients.

On April 18, 1877, the hospital was completed and opened, and was named Magaw Memorial Hospital in honor of those donors. The medical work by doctor Trask was only given to women and children, so the locals used to call it "Liang Au Woman's Hospital". It was a simple two-storey brick building with only screens separating the female doctor's residence from the patients. Besides the first director, Dr. Sigourney Trask, there were 6 foreign doctors and 1 nurse. The first patient admitted was a 28-year-old married woman who was unable to walk for 5 years for a knee injury not treated in time. Three months after surgical correction, she was able to walk back to her hometown in Minqing, a district in Fuzhou. According to the record about the hospital in 1891, the total number of patients, prescriptions and visits was respectively, 6,215, 6,975 and 1,088. Around 1910, hit by a typhoon, the old building collapsed, and a new Western-style building of 3 storeys was built on the original site.

Magaw Memorial Hospital promoted the development of medical care in China at that time by establishing a nursing school. "Church hospitals are an important part of Christian medical care in China, and they are also the main force for Christianity to carry out public health work."

马高爱医院是中国最早的护士和护士培训学校的诞生地之一，其护士培训主要由美国护士信宝珠来主导运作。内布拉斯加卫理公会医学院是信宝珠女士的母校，波士顿西蒙斯学院是她获得护士资格证书的学校。1908 年，她作为奉美国基督教卫理公会差遣来华的第一批资格完备的护士之一来到福州，任职于马高爱医院。（施德芬，1946：116－117）信宝珠来华后深入调查，发现中国当时人口众多，但医院极少且条件极差，医院大量缺少护士，甚至有的医院没有护士，因而医院大都不能正常开展护理工作。"护士"一词在当时的中文中还未出现。信宝珠觉得很有必要成立一个机构来培养中国护士。1910 年夏，马高爱医院的病房因福州遭遇台风倒塌。1912 年，在信宝珠的监理下，砖木结构的三层医院大楼在原址上得以重建。在这座哥特式风格的大楼里，设有多个医疗科室，如内科、外科、妇产科、小儿科等，还设有附属用房，病床 84 张，配有医生 7 人、护士 20 人，医院条件得以大大改善，成为当时全国最好的教会医院之一。同年，信宝珠正式创办了福州马高爱医院附设看护学校，并亲自担任校长。在师资力量上，由在外国取得专业学位的医生、护士担任学校教师；在学习内容上，设置三年的国际护士课程和一年的产科课程，还设置了包括解剖学、生理学、按摩、保健学、营养学、家政学、英语等在内的主要课程，做到了学习内容充实。学校注重培养医德素质，南丁格尔人道主义精神主导了学校风气。但因条件所限，学校每年培养的护士只有几名至十几名。（洪常青等，2012：75－78）

福建协和之前身——圣教医院

多芬·威廉·奥斯古德博士于 1845 年 11 月 5 日出生于美国新罕布什尔州的纳尔逊。1866 年，他在鲍多因医学院学习医学，1869 年在纽约大学获得医学博士学位。在家乡有过短暂实践后，奥斯古德作为一名医学传教士和妻子海伦·W. 奥斯古德来到中国，于 1870 年 1 月 22 日抵达福州。他从兼职行医开始了在福州的生活，1878 年，他主导建立了圣教医院。由此可知，福州圣教医院可能正式建立于 1878 年，这与 1860 年的说法有异。（Carlson，1974：87－89）

Magaw Memorial Hospital was one of the birthplaces of the earliest nurses and nurse-training schools in China. Its nurse training was mainly operated by Miss C. E. Simpson, an American nurse. Nebraska Methodist Medical College was her alma mater, and Simmons College Boston was where she received her nursing certificate. As one of the first fully qualified nurses sent to China by the Methodist Church, she came to Fuzhou and worked in Magaw Memorial Hospital. Through the in-depth investigation she made after coming to China, she found China had a large population at that time, but the hospitals were very few and the conditions were extremely poor. There were a large number of hospitals lacking nurses, and there were also hospitals without nurses. Most of the hospitals were unable to carry out normal nursing work due to the lack of nurses. The word "nurse" did not appear in Chinese at that moment. Simpson felt the need to set up an institution to train Chinese nurses. In the summer of 1910, Fuzhou was hit by a typhoon, and the ward of Magaw Memorial Hospital collapsed. In 1912, under the supervision of Simpson, the three-storey hospital of the brick-wood structure was rebuilt on the original site. In this Gothic-style building, there were several medical departments, such as internal medicine department, surgery department, department of obstetrics and gynecology, department of pediatrics, etc., and attached rooms, 84 beds, 7 doctors, 20 nurses. The hospital conditions were greatly improved, and it became one of the best church hospitals in the country at that time. In the same year, Simpson officially founded the Nursing School Affiliated to Fuzhou Magaw Memorial Hospital and served as the principal in person. The doctors and nurses who had obtained professional degrees in foreign countries served as school teachers. There were three-year international nursing courses, one-year obstetrics courses, and anatomy courses, physiology, massage, health science, nutrition, home economics and English, etc., as well as other major courses. The learning content was enriched. The school paid attention to cultivating the medical ethics, so Florence Nightingale's humanitarian spirit permeated the school. However, due to limited conditions, the school trained only no more than a dozen nurses every year.

Before Foochow Christian Union Hospital—Foochow Missionary Hospital

Dr. Dauphin William Osgood was born on November 5, 1845 in Nelson, New Hampshire, USA. He majored in medical science at Bowdoin's School of Medicine in 1866 and later received his M. D. in New York University in 1869. After a brief medical practice in his hometown, Osgood came to China as a medical missionary with his wife Helen W. Osgood. After his arriving in Fuzhou on January 22, 1870, he began his life there as a part-time doctor. In 1878, he established Foochow Missionary Hospital. So it can be inferred that Foochow Missionary Hospital was officially established in 1878, which is different from the statement of its being established in 1860.

奥斯古德在福州工作了十多年。在他生命后期的医疗实践中，他对鸦片成瘾者的治疗产生了浓厚的兴趣，并设计了一个治疗方案，让大多数鸦片成瘾者戒掉烟瘾。每个月大约有 60 人申请鸦片成瘾的治疗。到 1880 年，他已经为大约 1 500 名吸食鸦片的病患提供医疗服务。1880 年夏天，奥斯古德的健康状况恶化。在他十年的劳动生涯中，诊治过 78 697 名患者，为病人做过 4 015 次手术。（耶鲁档案 r8b139f1 p11）1880 年 8 月 17 日，奥斯古德在闽江河口附近的尖峰岛上的一家疗养院中暑去世。在他去世的前一天，完成了一本解剖学标准著作的五卷中文译本，中文名为《全体阐微》。

奥斯古德博士去世后被安葬在福州的美国传教公墓，靠近公墓大门右侧的围墙。墓头有一个白色大理石十字架，坟墓周围有一条黑色铁链，铁链嵌在一个低矮的花岗岩基座上。他的墓碑上的铭文是：

> 我的荣耀在基督的十字架上
> 我是多芬·威廉·奥斯古德
> 1870 年 1 月 22 日抵达福州
> 1880 年 8 月 17 日与世长辞
> 福州外国人协会立碑以示敬意。

协和医院命名之后

1928 年 10 月，1877 年创建的福州马高爱医院与 1878 年创建的福州圣教医院合并为福州基督教协和医院，同时，分别附设于两个医院的护士学校合并为福州基督教协和医院护士职业学校，并扩大了学校规模。从 1928 年 10 月 1 日起，福州基督教协和医院作为一个联合机构开始运转，一部分在城里，一部分在马高爱医院。1931 年，卫理公会美国传教士亨利·维·勒希任院长，聘请福建建设所的美国建筑师范哲明为新医院的建筑师，开始着手筹建新医院。1936 年，医院的附属学校成立董事会，同年 9 月向国民政府福建省教育厅办理立案，定名为福州基督教协和医院高级护士职业学校，益慧修任校长。1937 年新病房大楼落成，共五层楼。1938 年 4 月 23 日至 6 月 18 日，医院的病床、病人和设备迁往协和新院址，科室合并，并新增设了供应室等科室。

Osgood had worked in Fuzhou for more than ten years. During his medical practice later in life, he developed a keen interest in the treatment of opiate addicts, devising a treatment regimen that would allow most opiate addicts to quit smoking. About 60 people applied for treatment for opium addiction each month, and by 1880 he had provided medical treatment to approximately 1,500 opium addicts. Osgood's health deteriorated in the summer of 1880. In his ten-year medical career, he has treated 78,697 patients and performed 4,015 operations on patients. On August 17, 1880, Osgood died of heatstroke in a sanatorium on Sharp Peak Island (Jianfeng Island) near the mouth of the Minjiang River. The day before his death, he completed a five-volume Chinese translation of a work on anatomy standards, titled "Comprehensive Interpretation on the Body".

Dr. Osgood was buried at the American Mission Cemetery in Fuzhou, close to the wall at the right of the cemetery gate. The head of the tomb had a white marble cross, and surrounded the tomb was a black iron chain on a low granite pedestal. The English inscription on his tombstone was:

> In the cross of Christ I glory
> Dauphin William Osgood
> Arrived at Foochow January 22, 1870
> Died at Sharp Peak August 17, 1880
> Erected by the foreign community of Foochow as a token of respects.

After the Naming of Foochow Christian Union Hospital

Since October 1, 1928, the Foochow Christian Union Hospital had been operated as a joint institution. In 1931, serving as the director, Henry V. Lacy, an American missionary of the Methodist Church, hired the American architect Paul P. Wiant of the Fujian Construction Institute as the architect, and began to prepare for the construction of the new hospital. In 1936, the school affiliated to Foochow Christian Union Hospital established a board of directors. In September of the same year, it filed a case with the then Fujian Provincial Department of Education and named it Foochow Christian Union Hospital Senior Nursing Vocational School, with Yi Huixiu serving as the principal. In 1937, the new ward building was completed. From April 23 to June 18, 1938, the beds, patients and equipment of the hospital were moved to the new site, the departments were merged, and the supply room and other departments were newly established.

1943 年，医院的附属学校改名为私立福州基督教协和医院高级护士职业学校。1944 年抗日战争期间，医院曾一度被日军占领，院内一切器械、物品损失殆尽。协和医院的业务暂停，部分医务人员及器械迁至永泰，在县城设置门诊，并在县私立桐仁学校内收治少量病人。1945 年 5 月福州解放，6 月协和医院迁回福州，收集一切散乱家具，于是年 7 月正式开门诊，9 月底开始收治病人。1948 年山东解放前夕，美国教会办的齐鲁医学院教授带着部分学生迁至福州，并把协和医院作为教学基地。协和成为齐鲁医学院附属医院，一批著名的教授参加协和医院的临床工作，医院增设了一些新的科室，开始有专科医师，医疗、教学水平得到显著提高。

1942 年的《福建省中等学校概况调查表》记载，福州马高爱医院护士学校当年的在校生 64 人，年龄在 15～22 岁之间，其中包括护士预科 20 人，护士一年级 18 人，二年级 8 人，三年级 18 人。学校管理严格、教学规范并组织实施大量的临床实践，让毕业生成为非常优秀的护士。至 1950 年，共有 300 余人从学校毕业。（洪常青等，2012：75－78）

中华人民共和国成立之后

1951 年 5 月 27 日，福建省政府正式批准接管协和医院，与院方代表院长李温仁签字，福州基督教协和医院正式更名为福州中国协和医院。医院的工作人员除一名专职牧师外，全部按原职原薪接收。外国人全部回国，原董事会聘请的院长李温仁继续留任。同时，协和护校改称为福州第三护校。

1951 年底医院成立团支部。1952 年成立了中共党支部。1959 年成立了党、团总支。1952 年 11 月建立了工会，属福州市医务工会。解放后，人民政府重视发挥协和医院的技术优势，在财力物力上给予尽可能的支持，医院在人民政府的领导下有了长足进步。

：红楼建筑设计图（来源：福建医科大学附属协和医院）
：The design of Red Building（Source：Fujian Medical University Union Hospital）

In 1943, the school affiliated to Foochow Christian Union Hospital changed its name to the Private Foochow Christian Union Hospital Senior Nursing Vocational School. During the Chinese People's War of Resistance against Japanese Aggression in 1944, the hospital was once occupied by the Japanese army, and all the equipment and items in the hospital were lost. The business of the hospital was suspended, and some medical staff and equipment were moved to Yongtai, where an outpatient clinic was set up in the county of Yongtai, and a small number of patients were treated in the county's Private Tongren School. Fuzhou was liberated in May 1945, and the hospital moved back to Fuzhou in June, so the outpatient clinic was officially opened in July of the same year, and patients began to be treated at the end of September. On the eve of the liberation of Shandong Province in 1948, the professors of Cheeloo College of Medicine, run by the American church, moved to Fuzhou with some students, and used Foochow Christian Union Hospital as a teaching base. The hospital became the Affiliated Hospital of Cheeloo College of Medicine. A group of famous professors participated in the clinical work of the hospital, which added some new departments and began to have specialist doctors, and the level of medical treatment and teaching was significantly improved.

In 1942, the "Fujian Provincial Secondary School Survey Table" recorded that there were 64 students in the Nursing School of Fuzhou Magaw Memorial Hospital, aged 15 – 22, including 20 preparatory nurses and 18 first-year nurses. There were 8 students in the second grade and 18 students in the third grade. The school had strict management and standardized teaching, and organized and implemented a large number of clinical practices, so that graduates become very good nurses. By 1950, more than 300 people had graduated from the school.

After the Founding of the People's Republic of China

On May 27, 1951, Fujian Provincial Government officially approved the takeover of Foochow Christian Union Hospital, and signed with Li Wenren, the representative of the hospital. From then on, Foochow Christian Union Hospital officially changed its name to Fuzhou Union Hospital of China. Except for a pastor, all the hospital staff received salary as before. All foreigners left China, and Li Wenren, the director hired by the former board of directors, continued to serve in the hospital. At the same time, Union Nursing School was renamed Fuzhou No.3 Nursing School.

A branch of Communist Youth League of China (CYLC) was established at the end of 1951. In 1952, a branch of the Communist Party of China (CPC) was set up. In 1959, the general branch of CPC and CYLC was established. In November 1952, a labor union was established, which belongs to the Medical Labor Union of Fuzhou City. Since the founding of the People's Republic of China, the people's government attached great importance to the technical advantages of Fuzhou Union Hospital of China, and gave as much support as possible in terms of financial and material resources. Great progress has been made under the leadership of the people's government.

20 世纪 50 年代中期，医院外科开始向专业分科发展，成立了省内最早的胸外科和麻醉科，率先建立了泌尿专业及病房、小儿外科和整形外科。1955 年 6 月，首先在省内成功开展了肺叶切除、食管癌切除、贲门癌切除等手术。1957 成功开展了全国首例结肠代食道根治食管癌手术、省内第一例心脏外科手术——缩窄性心包炎手术。1958 年首例二尖瓣狭窄闭式分离术获得成功。在省内首先成功施行了胰十二指肠切除术及脾肾静脉分流、肝切除治疗肝癌手术、经脾肝穿胆道造影术。1959 年协和医院成为福建医学院附属医院。

1960 年 5 月，李温仁院长与国内知名专家吴英恺、黄家驷三人代表中国赴莫斯科参加全苏外科会议，介绍了"结肠代食道"的经验并手术示范，为国家争得了荣誉。1964 年，医院自行设计建造了世界第三台、亚洲第一台高压氧治疗舱，并在舱内成功施行了低温麻醉心内直视手术以及体外循环下心内直视手术，治疗危重病人，达到世界领先水平。此外普外科肝胆手术、胰头癌根治术以及脾肾静脉吻合术均在全省居领先地位。内科血液病治疗在华东地区享有良好声誉。协和医院外科成为福建省外科的名牌和医疗、教学、科研的中心，在全国外科学科中享有一席之地。

∴ 福建医科大学附属协和医院大楼一瞥
∴ Fujian Medical University Union Hospital

1969 年 11 月，协和医院人员、设备等内迁清流、明溪、宁化三个山区县。1970 年 1 月，福建中医学院附属人民医院及中医研究所迁入原协和医院院址，与协和医院留下的少数外科、内科、儿科人员合并组成以中医为主的中西医结合医院，更名为福建省人民医院，床位 200 张，职工 180 人，日门诊量 300 至 400 人次，由福建省卫生厅领导。

In the mid-1950s, surgery in the hospital began to develop into sub-disciplines. The earliest thoracic surgery and anesthesiology departments were established, and urology departments and wards, pediatric surgery and plastic surgery were the first to be established. In June 1955, the hospital carried out the first lung lobectomy, esophageal cancer resection, and spout cancer resection, in Fujian. In 1957, the hospital successfully carried out the first colonic esophagus radical operation for esophageal cancer in China and the province's first cardiac surgery—constrictive pericarditis operation. In 1958, the first closed mitral valve stenosis was successfully separated. In the province, the hospital did the first successful implementation of pancreaticoduodenectomy and spleen-renal venous shunt, liver resection for the treatment of liver cancer, cholangiography of biliary tract through the spleen and liver. In 1959, Fuzhou Union Hospital of China became the Fujian Medical College Union Hospital.

In May 1960, Director Li Wenren, together with well-known domestic experts Wu Yingkai and Huang Jiasi, attended the Soviet Surgery Conference in Moscow, introduced the experience of "replacing the esophagus with colon" and demonstrated the operation, winning honors for the country. In 1964, the hospital designed and built the world's third and Asia's first hyperbaric oxygen therapy cabin, and successfully performed hypothermic anesthesia and intracardiac . Vision surgery and open-heart surgery under cardiopulmonary bypass in the cabin. Till that moment, the treatment of critically ill patients had reached the world's leading level. In addition, general surgery hepatobiliary surgery, radical resection of pancreatic head cancer and splenorenal venous anastomosis were all in the leading position in the province. Blood disease treatment was very professional and enjoyed a good reputation in East China. The Department of Surgery of Fujian Medical College Union Hospital had become a famous brand of surgery in Fujian Province and a center of medical treatment, teaching and scientific research, and enjoyed a place in the national surgical discipline.

In November 1969, the personnel and equipment of Fuzhou Union Hospital of China moved to three mountainous counties, Qingliu, Mingxi, and Ninghua. In January 1970, the People's Hospital Affiliated to Fujian College of Traditional Chinese Medicine and the Institute of Traditional Chinese Medicine moved to the site of the former Fuzhou Union Hospital of China, and merged with a few personnel of surgical medicine, internal medicine and pediatric left by Fuzhou Union Hospital of China to form an integrated hospital of traditional Chinese medicine and Western medicine, which was mainly based on traditional Chinese medicine, and the new hospital was named Fujian Provincial People's Hospital, with 200 beds, 180 employees, and a daily outpatient volume of 300 to 400 people, led by the Fujian Provincial Department of Health.

1981 年医院开始招收研究生，内科血液病专业被授权为硕士研究生培养点，成为我省医疗卫生系统最早开始招收、培养研究生的机构。1984 年 7 月 1 日，经福建省政府批准正式恢复福建医学院附属协和医院的名称，原人民医院所属编制人员全部划归中医学院。1985 年 2 月，人民医院迁至吉祥山。部分原协和医院职工陆续调回。

1986 年，医院占地总面积 22 065 平方米，建筑面积 17 798 平方米，编制床位 550 张，实际开放床位 625 张，人员 850 人，其中医师 285 人，护士 265 人，高级职称 40 人。临床实行二级分科，有 32 个科室，10 个医技科室，11 个行政科室，附设省级研究所 3 个，医科大学研究机构 5 个；有日本岛津放射诊断设备、B 超诊断仪、血液透析机、德国西门子心脏急救装置、八导脑电图机等万元以上大型设备 72 件。图书馆藏书 22 591 册。日均门诊 1 340 人次，日均出院人数 21 人，住院死亡率 2.1%。全年业务收入 697.07 万元，平均住院每日每人 11.11 元，门诊每日每人次 4.76 元。率先在省内成功开展了骨髓移植治疗白血病。

1995 年 8 月，成功开展了福建省第一例心脏移植手术。随着福建医学院于 1996 年 4 月更名为福建医科大学，福建医学院附属协和医院更名为福建医科大学附属协和医院。

目前，医院处于振兴发展的大好时期，在医疗、教学、科研等各方面都位居全省医疗系统前列。作为福建医学院的主要教学基地之一，协和医院在完成福建医科大学高年级学生的临床教学和毕业生实习任务的同时，承担了大量本省进修医师的培训和再教育，并向地市医院派出专家会诊、指导以及输送技术骨干，为福建省医疗卫生事业的发展作出了重要贡献，被誉为"福建省医学人才的摇篮"。

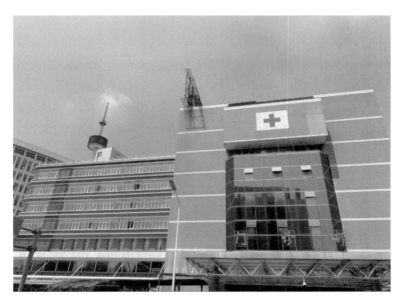

：福建医科大学附属协和医院大楼一瞥
：Fujian Medical University Union Hospital

In 1981, the hospital began to offer postgraduate programs in internal medicine hematology. The hospital then became the first institution in the province's medical and health system with such programs. On July 1, 1984, with the approval of Fujian Provincial Government, the name of Fujian Medical College Union Hospital was officially restored, and all the staff members of the former Fujian Provincial People's Hospital were assigned to Fujian College of Traditional Chinese Medicine. In February 1985, Fujian Provincial People's Hospital moved to Jixiang Mountain. Some former employees of Fuzhou Union Hospital of China had been transferred back one after another.

In 1986, the hospital covered a total area of 22,065 square meters, with a construction area of 17,798 square meters, 550 beds (625 actually available), and a staff of 850, including 285 physicians, 265 nurses, and 40 with senior titles. There were 32 departments, 10 medical technology departments, 11 administrative departments, 3 provincial research institutes and 5 medical university research institutes. There were 72 large-scale equipment, each of which valued more than 10,000 yuan, such as Japan's Shimadzu radiological diagnostic equipment, B-ultrasound diagnostic equipment, hemodialysis machine, German Siemens cardiac emergency equipment, and eight-lead EEG machine. The library contained 22,591 volumes. There were 1,340 outpatient visits per day, 21 discharged per day, and 2.1% of in-hospital mortality. The annual business income was 6,970,700 yuan, the average payment for one inpatient per day was 11.11 yuan per person, and one outpatient 4.76 yuan. The hospital was the first to successfully carry out bone marrow transplantation in the province to treat leukemia.

In August 1995, the first heart transplant operation in Fujian Province was successfully carried out in Fujian Medical College Union Hospital. With the renaming of Fujian Medical College to Fujian Medical University in April 1996, Fujian Medical College Union Hospital was renamed Fujian Medical University Union Hospital.

At present, the hospital is in a good period of revitalization and development, and ranks in the forefront of the province's medical system in terms of medical treatment, teaching and scientific research. As one of the main teaching bases of Fujian Medical University, Fujian Medical University Union Hospital has undertaken the training and re-education of a large number of advanced physicians in the province while completing the clinical teaching of senior medical students and internships for graduates, and dispatched experts to prefectural hospitals for consultation. It has made important contributions to the development of medical and health care in Fujian Province, and is thus known as "the cradle of medical talents in Fujian Province".

如今，历经百余年风雨的洗礼，走过了漫长而曲折的道路，凝聚着几代人创业艰辛的老院已旧貌换新颜，焕发出勃勃生机。新一代医院领导人以科学发展观的思路、国际化的眼光谋划医院发展的新篇章，认准了科技兴院才是协和腾飞的唯一道路，以舍得投入、肯花气力的大手笔加强学科建设和人才培养，实行现代化科学管理，以老协和严谨、求精的传统狠抓内涵建设，努力打造一流的医疗质量、一流的服务，光大协和的老字号品牌，使医院发展步入了快车道。

近十年，医院逐渐形成大型现代化综合医学中心，规模不断扩大，床位、人员及工作量增长迅速，在医疗、教学和科研上都取得了长足的发展。医院目前有2 300余张床位开放，每年有大约150万人次门诊病人，约4万余人次住院病人，开展近5万台各类手术。医院技术力量雄厚，2 000多名员工中，4人为国家突出贡献专家，9人为省部级优秀专家，32位专家享受政府特殊津贴，68人入选国家及省厅级"百千万人才工程"。拥有400余位正副教授、主任医师，60%以上医师具有博士、硕士学位。

4个学科入选全省首批10个重点学科，分别为血液内科、内分泌科、普通外科、心外科；福建省内10个医疗特色专业中有3个在协和：烧伤外科、心血管内科冠心病专业、小儿内科医学心理学专业。血液病学专业成为福建省"211工程"唯一的西医临床重点学科。福建省超声医学、院内感染、烧伤治疗质量控制中心挂靠协和医院。

近年来，医院涌现大量新技术、新项目，在同种异体心脏移植手术上居于全国领先地位，儿童心脏移植更是填补了国内空白；心脏移植后包括肝移植、双肺移植等在内的多项技术已达到国内先进水平。

协和医院是福建医科大学的临床医学院，现设有教研室39个，临床医学博士后流动站1个，博士学位授权点18个以及硕士学位授权点32个。

：协和医院的红楼和现代建筑与白塔交相呼应
：Red Building（left），Modern Building（right）and White
：Tower（middle）in Fujian Medical University Union Hospital

Today, after more than 100 years of trials and hardships, and going through a long and tortuous road, the original hospital, which has embodied the painstaking hard work of several generations of medical workers, has taken on a new look and is full of vigor. The new generation of administrative personnel plans a new chapter in the development of the hospital with a scientific outlook on development and an international perspective, and insists that the only way for Fujian Medical University Union Hospital to thrive is to rely on science and technology. Therefore, it has been strengthening the construction of disciplines and the cultivation of talents, and implementing modern scientific management by willing to invest both money and efforts. Besides, it has been enhancing internal construction by inheriting the Union tradition of rigorous refinement. It has been striving to build first-class medical quality, first-class service, and carrying forward the time-honored brand of the hospital so as to position the hospital in the fast lane of development.

In the past decade, the hospital has gradually developed into a large-scale modern comprehensive medical center. The scale of the hospital has been expanding. The hospital beds, personnel and workload have increased rapidly, and great progress has been made in medical treatment, teaching and scientific research. Currently the hospital offers more than 2,300 beds, and reports approximately 1.5 million outpatient visits, over 40,000 inpatient visits, and nearly 50,000 operations of various types on yearly average. The hospital boasts strong technical strength. Among the more than 2,000 employees, 4 are experts with outstanding national-level contributions, 9 are outstanding experts at provincial and ministerial levels, 32 experts enjoy special government allowances, and 68 are selected into "Ten Million Talents Project" at national and provincial levels. There are more than 400 full-time associate professors and chief physicians, and over 60% of the physicians have a doctoral or master's degree.

Four disciplines were selected as the first batch of the 10 key disciplines in Fujian Province, namely, the hospital's departments of hematology, endocrinology, general surgery, and cardiac surgery; three of the 10 medical specialties in Fujian are in this hospital: the specialty of burn surgery, coronary disease specialty of cardiovascular medicine, medical psychology specialty of pediatric internal medicine. The specialty of hematology has become the only key clinical discipline of Western medicine in the "Project 211" in Fujian. Fujian Quality Control Centers of Ultrasound Medicine, Nosocomial Infection, and Burn Treatment are affiliated to the hospital.

In recent years, a large number of new technologies and new projects have emerged in the hospital, taking the leading position in our country in allogeneic heart transplantation. Children's heart transplantation has taken the lead in our country. In addition to heart transplantation, many technologies, including liver transplantation, double lung transplantation, etc., have reached the advanced level in China.

Fujian Medical University Union Hospital is the clinical medical school of Fujian Medical University. At present, it has 39 teaching and research offices, 1 post-doctoral mobile station for clinical medicine, 18 doctoral degree programs and 32 master's degree programs.

福建医科大学临床医学、医学影像学、医学检验学、药学、护理学等专业的临床教学任务由协和医院承担，每年招收培养博士及硕士学位研究生 120 余名。2006 年开始承担 7 年制学生研究生阶段培养任务，现有在读研究生 377 人，以现代化大型综合医院为依托的研究生教育为推动福建省高等医学院校高学历教育不断发展发挥积极的促进作用。

今天的福建医科大学附属协和医院（来源：福建医科大学附属协和医院）
Fujian Medical University Union Hospital at the present time（Source：Fujian Medical University Union Hospital）

医院拥有高水准的科研平台。11 个省级研究所及 10 个校级研究机构挂靠协和医院，涵盖了福建省血液病、内分泌、肝胆外科、胸心外科等学科。协和医院承担了大量国家自然科学基金及其他省部级科研课题，在国内外著名学术刊物发表的论文数量及获得国家、省部级科研成果奖均在全省卫生系统中居于前列。

● 协和人物与事迹

许金訇——最早的留洋女医学博士

许金訇（1865—1929）出生于福州，是福建省第一位留学生。她是首批归国人员中的中国女医生，也是中国第一位参与国际事务的女性代表。她的人生故事始于她的父亲许扬美——美以美会的一名牧师，在那里他一直工作到 1893 年去世。许金訇的父亲认为女性缠足这种普遍而古老的习俗是错误的。因此，他做出了一个在该地区前所未有的勇敢决定：他的女儿应该有天然的脚，并且应该脱掉绷带。后来，许金訇成为自然足的热心倡导者，并经常讲述她作为福建自然足运动先驱的经历。

当许金訇长大到可以上学的年龄时，她去了英国人设立的英格女子学校，这是一所由卫理公会圣公会管理的寄宿学校。离开寄宿学校后，她去了建于 1877 年的马高爱医院，这是中国最早也是当时最大的妇幼医院。她对医疗工作的适应能力和对病人的同情给马高爱医院院长特拉斯克博士留下了深刻印象，院长希望许金訇能得到更全面的医学教育。因此，她给外国女传教士协会执行委员会写了一封信，赞扬了许金訇的能力和性格，并敦促为她安排赴美学习。如果有必要的话，她可以在美国待十年，以便回国后作出更大的贡献。

The clinical teaching tasks of clinical medicine, medical imaging science, clinical laboratory science, pharmacy and nursing of Fujian Medical University are undertaken by the hospital, and more than 120 doctoral and master graduate students are recruited and trained every year. In 2006, it began to undertake the task of cultivating 7-year program students at the postgraduate level. There are currently 377 postgraduates in the training scale. The postgraduate education based on the modern large-scale comprehensive hospital has played an important role in promoting the continuous development of higher education in Fujian Province.

The hospital has a high-level scientific research platform, 11 provincial-level research institutes and 10 school-level research institutions affiliated to the hospital, covering hematology, endocrinology, hepatobiliary surgery, cardiothoracic surgery and other disciplines in Fujian Province. The hospital has undertaken a large number of scientific research projects of the National Natural Science Foundation of China and other projects at provincial and ministerial levels. Its papers published in domestic and overseas renowned academic journals and the awards of scientific research at state, provincial and ministerial levels rank the top in Fujian Province.

● **Figures and Deeds of Foochow Christian Union Hospital**

Hü King-eng—the Earliest Female Overseas Student with a Doctor of Medicine Degree

Hü King-eng (1865 – 1929) was born in Fuzhou and was the first student who studied overseas in Fujian Province. She was a Chinese female doctor in the first batch of overseas returnees and the first female representative of China to participate in international affairs. Her life story began with her father, Hü Yangmei. Her father was a minister of the Methodist Episcopal Church, where he worked until his death in 1893. It was customary for girls to have their feet bound from an early age at that time. However, Hü King-eng's father believed that this common and ancient custom was wrong. So, he made a brave decision never seen before in the region: His daughter should have natural feet, and the bandage should be taken off. Later, Hü King-eng became an ardent advocate of natural foot and often recounted her experience as a pioneer of the natural foot movement in Fujian.

When she was old enough, Hü went to Uk Ing Girls' School, a boarding school run by the Methodist Episcopal Church. After leaving the boarding school, she went to Magaw Memorial Hospital, founded in 1877, the earliest and largest women's and children's hospital in China. Her adaptability to medical work and compassion for patients impressed Dr. Trask, then the head of the hospital, who hoped she could get a more comprehensive education than she had received in Fuzhou. Therefore, she wrote a letter to the Executive Committee of the Women's Foreign Missionary Society, praising Hü's abilities and character and urging that arrangements be made for her to study in the United States. She could stay in the US for a decade if necessary, so that she could make a greater contribution when she returned.

对于这个只有 18 岁的年轻女孩来说，决定离开家乡和祖国，去一个对她来说完全陌生的国家学习是不容易的。她的父母告诉她，她在国外会感到孤独，她必须经历远洋航行的危险，以及十年后她就 28 岁了，远远超过了适婚年龄。但是，许金訇怀着坚定的信念和决心毅然去美国攻读学位。

1884 年春天，许金訇踏上了美国之旅。抵达纽约后，她立即去费城看望基恩夫人，在那里她遇到了塞茨一家。塞茨一家来自福州，她从小就认识他们。许金訇在费城参加了卫理公会圣公会的一次会议，并和他们一起度过了夏天。塞茨夫妇帮助许金訇学习英语。秋季学期开始时，许金訇成功进入俄亥俄卫斯理大学。有人想知道，在美国生活这么多年是否会改变她对祖国的眷恋，事实上是她并没有改变。

几年后，在向一些第一次去美国的女孩告别时，她说："我们得到的越多，我们欠中国妇女和女孩的就越多。因此，无论我们走到哪里，都必须考虑如何造福人民，而不是变得傲慢。"1892 年秋，许金訇进入费城女子医学院，于 1894 年 5 月 8 日毕业。第二年，她很幸运地被费城普通诊所选为外科医生助理，这使她参加了所有诊治和讲座。

许金訇（来源：福建医科大学附属协和医院）
Hü King-eng（Source：Fujian Medical University Union Hospital）

1895 年，她回到福州，立即开始在马高爱医院工作。第二年，莱昂医生请假返回美国，让她全权负责医院的工作。一位传教士描述了她对许金訇的印象："她在医院和家里都很忙，但她总是很快乐，乐于助人。"大约在这个时候，许金訇有幸被李鸿章任命为 1898 年在伦敦举行的世界妇女大会的两名中国代表之一。她不仅是一位成功的医生，也是一位很好的医学教师，深受当地人和外国人的喜爱。

It was not easy for this young girl, who was only eighteen years old, to decide to leave her home and her country and go to study in a foreign country that was completely new to her. Her parents told her at length about the loneliness she would experience in a foreign country, the perils of the long ocean voyage which she must undertake, and the situation she would face when she returned ten years later, at 28, well past her marriageable age. However, Hü decided to go to the United States to study for a degree with firm belief and determination.

In the spring of 1884, Hü started the journey to the United States. After arriving in New York, she immediately went to see Mrs. Keene in Philadelphia, where she met the Seitzes, who had come from Fuzhou, where she had known them since she was a child. Hü King-eng attended a meeting of the Methodist Episcopal Church in Philadelphia, and spent the summer with them. Mr. and Mrs. Seitz helped Hü learn English. When the fall semester began, Hü King-eng successfully entered Ohio Wesleyan University. Some wondered if living in the United States for so many years would have changed her love for her motherland. Actually, she didn't make that change happen.

A few years later, saying goodbye to some girls who went to the United States for the first time, she said, "Some people don't want girls to study in the United States because they think that when girls are educated, they will get proud. I don't think we really have anything to be proud of. We Chinese girls have such a good chance to study abroad not because God love us more than anyone else, but because God love all of us Chinese. That is why He sent us first to learn about all the good things that we can do to help our people. The more we receive, the more we owe to the women and girls of China. So, wherever we go, we have to think about how we can benefit our people and not become arrogant." In the fall of 1892, Hü entered the Women's Medical College of Philadelphia. She graduated on May 8, 1894. She was fortunate enough to be selected as a surgeon's assistant at the Philadelphia General Clinic, which gave her the privilege of attending all the clinic treatments and lectures.

In 1895, after returning to Fuzhou, she immediately began working at Magaw Memorial Hospital. The next year, Dr. Leon took a leave for the United States, and Hü was entrusted with full responsibility for the hospital's work. One missionary described her impression of Hü, "Although very busy at the hospital and at home, she was always happy and helpful." Around this time, Hü had an honor of being appointed by Li Hung Chang as one of two Chinese delegates to the World Congress on Women held in London in 1898. As a successful doctor and good teacher in medicine, she was popular among locals and foreigners.

1899 年许金訇接管了伍尔斯顿纪念医院。这是一家距离福州三英里的妇幼医院。在伍尔斯顿纪念医院，她有四项主要工作：在药房工作、与医院病人合作、探访那些病得太重而不能来的病人，以及监督医学生的培训。在她领导伍尔斯顿纪念医院的 9 年里，她几乎不间断地工作，很少休假。许金訇从未结婚，并将一生奉献给了医学事业。1926 年，她前往东南亚，3 年后在新加坡去世。她曾经谦恭地说："我只是告诉病人'请抬起头来伸出手'。"

信宝珠—中国护士会之母

被誉为"中国护士会之母"的信宝珠，1880 年出生于美国医生家庭，受父亲影响，信宝珠从小学习医学知识，后来在波士顿西蒙斯学院取得护士资格证书。1907 年，美以美会妇女部派遣信宝珠来到中国福州，担任马高爱医院的护士长。信宝珠创办了第一所在中国注册的护校——佛罗伦斯·南丁格尔护士和助产士培训学校，1907 年开始教学，1909 年颁发首份毕业文凭。

信宝珠（来源：福建医科大学附属协和医院）
C. E. Simpson（Source：Fujian Medical University Union Hospital）

在马高爱医院，信宝珠女士务实肯干，倡导英美护理的先进理念，以英美规范的护理工作标准为参照制定了培养方案，推进了医院的各项工作。她一边从事临床护理和护理管理工作，一边开展护理培训，同时兼管麻风病人，表现出了吃苦耐劳、甘于奉献的医学精神。

鉴于当时中国已有从事学术活动和出版医学刊物的"中国博医会"，信宝珠认为中国有必要成立一个护士组织，统一全国护理教育的标准，为中国培养护士，从而提高护理服务水平。后来，她给英国长老会派遣来华的高士兰医生写信商讨此事。高士兰时任"中国博医会"出版委员会编辑兼秘书，有一定的影响力。信宝珠、高士兰等几位外籍护士、医生在江西牯岭创建了全国性护理组织"中国中部看护联合会"，后更名为"中国看护组织联合会"，它是中华护理学会的前身。

In 1899, Hü King-eng took over the Woolston Memorial Hospital, a women's and children's hospital, three miles from Fuzhou. Here, she had four main jobs: working at the pharmacy, working with patients, visiting those too ill to come, and supervising the training of medical students. The hospital records tell many stories of what happened in the hospital. During the nine years of her leading the hospital, she had few holidays. Hü never married and devoted her whole life to the cause of medicine. In 1926, she left for Southeast Asia and died 3 years later in Singapore. She used to humbly say, "I just tell patients to 'Please hold up your head and stretch out your hand'."

Cora E. Simpson—Mother of the Chinese Nurses Association

Cora E. Simpson, known as "Mother of the Chinese Nurses Association", was born in an American doctor's family in 1880. Influenced by her father, Cora E. Simpson learned medical knowledge from an early age and later obtained a certificate in nursing at Simmons College in Boston. In 1907, the Women's Department of the Methodist Episcopal Church dispatched Simpson to Fuzhou, China, to serve as the head nurse of Magaw Memorial Hospital. Simpson founded the first nursing school ever registered in China, Florence Nightingale Training School for Nurses and Midwives, which started offering training courses in 1907 and awarded its first diploma in 1909.

In Magaw Memorial Hospital, Ms. Simpson was pragmatic and hardworking. She advocated the advanced concept of British and American nursing, formulated a training plan based on the nursing standards of the United Kingdom and the United States, and promoted various work of the hospital. While engaged in clinical nursing and nursing management, she carried out nursing training and meanwhile took care of leprosy patients, exemplifying the medical spirit of hard work and dedication.

In view of the fact that China already had the "Chinese Medical Association", which was engaged in academic activities and published medical journals, Simpson believed that it was necessary for China to establish a nurse organization to unify the standards for national nursing education and train nurses for China, so as to improve the level of nursing services. Later, she wrote a letter to discuss the matter with Dr. Gao Shilan (P. B. Couslan) who was sent to China by the British Presbyterian Church. Gao Shilan, the editor and secretary of the publishing committee of the Chinese Medical Association at that time, has some influence in the field. Thus, several foreign nurses and doctors, including Cora E. Simpson and Gao Shilan, established a national nursing organization, Nursing Federation of Central China in Guling, Jiangxi Province, which was later renamed Chinese Nursing Federation, the predecessor of the Chinese Nursing Association.

得益于信宝珠女士的多年努力，1914 年 6 月，中国看护组织联合会第一届全国代表大会在上海召开，翻开了我国护理学新的一页。这次大会期间，钟茂芳作为第一位出国接受培训的护士提出了一个想法——将英文"nurse"由原中文翻译"看护"改译为"护士"，"护"意为照顾或滋养，"士"乃学者，"护士"即是深谙如何滋养和照顾别人的人。中国从此才有了"护士"一词。这一提法是她经过查阅《康熙字典》、请教许多中国学者之后才形成的，具有一定的权威性，所以得到了与会者的一致赞同。此次大会决定将"中国看护组织联合会"更名为"中华护士会"，"看护学校"也相应改名为"护士学校"。信宝珠女士在这次大会上被选举为中华护士会兼职总干事，对她而言越发任重道远。那时候她住在上海的一小间出租屋中，每月租金 30 元，过着俭朴的生活。对她而言最艰辛的是出访考察，但却意义非凡。通过出访考察她可以指导各地的护士学校，让它们在中华护士会注册。两年时间里她风尘仆仆，足迹遍布全中国。

信宝珠女士富有远见、思维活跃并且高效务实，要求注册学校将照片和校史交存备查，注册后每两年检查一次，同时关注护士毕业生谋职，主动为护士介绍工作。当时国内护理教科书匮乏，信宝珠女士想尽办法筹措出版了大量护理、医药书籍作为教学之用。她向中华护士会提议将 5 月 12 日南丁格尔诞辰定为"医院纪念日"，得到了中华护士会的同意，这是现在我国庆祝"5·12"国际护士节的最早雏形。（陈美者，2016：79 – 81）

佛罗伦斯·南丁格尔护士和助产士培训
学校旧址附近的一处历史建筑
A historical building near the old site of
Florence Nightingale Training School for
Nurses and Midwives

1937 年抗日战争全面爆发，信宝珠女士奔走于硝烟炮声之中，坚持工作，冒着生命危险，辗转各地处理学会会务。1944 年 12 月，时局动荡，美国政府安排 64 岁的信宝珠女士离开了她服务奉献了近 40 年的中国。我们可以想象，当轮船远去时，信宝珠定是眼含热泪，毕竟她一生最美丽的时光、最饱满的热情、最卓越的智慧都留在了中国。历史也会将她铭记。

1946 年，第十五届中华护士会全国会员代表大会授予信宝珠女士"中华护士学会荣誉总干事"称号。后来，信宝珠被誉为"中华护士会之母"，因为她为中华护士会作出了突出贡献并对中国护理事业的发展产生了重要影响。

Thanks to Ms. Simpson's years of hard work, the first National Congress of Chinese Nursing Federation was held in Shanghai in June 1914, ushering in a new chapter of nursing in our country. During this conference, Zhong Maofang (Elsie Mawfung Chung), the first nurse to have been abroad to receive nursing training, put forward the proposal to translate the English word "nurse" into "hushi" in Chinese rather than the original translation "kanhu" (nursing). "Hu" (nurse) means to take care of or to nourish, and "shi" refers to a scholar. Therefore, a "hushi" is someone who knows well how to nourish and take care of others. Since then China has the word "hushi". This proposal was conceived after Zhong Maofang looked the words up in *Kangxi Dictionary* and consulted many Chinese scholars, so it was authoritative to some extent. Therefore, it was unanimously approved by the participants of the conference. The conference decided to change the name of Chinese Nursing Federation to Chinese Nurses Association, and accordingly Nursing School to Nurses' School. Ms. Simpson was elected as the part-time director general of the Chinese Nurses Association at this conference, which, in her eyes, meant she was supposed to shoulder more responsibilities. At that time, she lived in a small rental house in Shanghai, with a monthly rent of 30 yuan, and led a simple life. The most difficult thing for her was the fact-finding trips, but they were so significant. Through the trips, she could guide nursing schools in various places, helping them to register with the Chinese Nurses Association. In two years, she had traveled all over China.

Ms. Simpson was farsighted with an active mind, efficient and pragmatic. She required registered schools to submit photos and school history for future reference. After registration, they would be inspected every two years. At the same time, she paid attention to nurse graduates' job-seeking, and took the initiative to introduce jobs to nurses. At that time, there was a shortage of nursing textbooks in China. So Ms. Simpson tried her best to publish a large number of nursing and medical books for the sake of teaching. She proposed to the Chinese Nurses Association that May 12th, Nightingale's birthday, should be designated as the "Hospital Memorial Day", and her proposal was approved.

Despite the outbreak of the War of Resistence against Japanese Agression in 1937, Ms. Simpson persisted in her work, risking her life and travelling to various places to handle the affairs of the Chinese Nurses Association. In December 1944, when the situation was turbulent, the US government arranged for 64-year-old Ms. Simpson to leave China, where she had served for nearly 40 years. We can imagine that Simpson must have tears in her eyes when the ship sailed away. After all, she devoted the most beautiful time in her life, her fullest enthusiasm, and her most brilliant wisdom to China. People in China will always remember her.

In 1946, the 15th National Congress of the Chinese Nurses Association conferred the title of "Honorary General Director of Chinese Nurses Association" to Ms. Simpson. Cora E. Simpson is known as "Mother of the Chinese Nurses Association" for her outstanding contributions to the Chinese Nurses Association and has had an important impact on the development of China's nursing cause.

蒲天寿与他的后裔

蒲天寿是协和医院最后一位外籍院长，任职于 1945 年至 1950 年。他在福建兴化出生，父母是最早来华的传教士。蒲院长对第二故乡福州有深厚的感情，对当时福建缺医少药的民众非常同情，他恳切地呼吁朋友们向协和医院健康基金会捐款，用于购置病人所需医疗器物。

蒲天寿（来源：福建医科大学附属协和医院）
Harold N. Brewster（Source：Fujian Medical University Union Hospital）

蒲天寿是著名的外科大夫，能手术治疗当时的绝症"结核病""溃疡病"。他在哈佛公共卫生学院取得公共卫生硕士学位后，回到福州依托协和医院创建了妇幼诊所、巡回医疗队、麻风病院等公共卫生服务机构，为当地民众的健康做了大量的工作。

蒲天寿院长的儿女们都在福建出生，他们自 1950 年离开中国后，多次回到福建。1984 年，蒲天寿院长的女儿与家族中多人一起回到福建莆田，庆祝祖父母来华 100 周年。21 世纪以来，他们也多次回榕，寻找记忆中的童年。2010 年，蒲天寿院长的女儿与其家人回到福建，走访了在古田的旧居，并来到协和医院参观。2017 年，蒲天寿院长的女儿再次来榕，参访协和医院红楼，了解医院近年来的变迁发展，与院领导亲切交谈。

● 协和精神

协和精神之严谨求精

协和医院在一代代薪火相传中形成了独特的文化理念和传统精神。特别是 20 世纪初，福州基督教协和医院引进美国的标准化医院管理模式，形成了治院严格、医风严谨的作风。

当时，医院逐步建立起了严格的人才培养和管理制度。医师等级分明：主任-主治医师-总住院医师-住院医师-实习医师。实习生实行淘汰制，经过各科轮转一年，筛选后仅个别成绩突出者留在协和。

Harold N. Brewster and His Descendants

Harold N. Brewster was the last foreign director of the Foochow Christian Union Hospital, holding his post from 1945 to 1950. He was born in Xinghua, Fujian. His parents were among the first missionaries who came to China. Director Brewster had a deep affection for Fuzhou, his second hometown, and was very sympathetic with the people in Fujian who lacked doctors and medicines at that time. He earnestly appealed to his friends to donate to the Health Foundation of Foochow Christian Union Hospital so as to purchase medical equipment needed by patients.

Harold N. Brewster was a famous surgeon who could surgically treat diseases such as tuberculosis and ulcer diseases which seemed to be incurable at that time. After obtaining a master's degree in public health from Harvard School of Public Health, he returned to Fuzhou and, with support from Foochow Christian Union Hospital, established some public health service institutions such as Women's and Children's Clinic, Mobile Medical Teams, and Leprosy Hospital. He did a lot for the health of the local people.

Harold N. Brewster's sons and daughters were all born in Fujian. After they left China in 1950, they returned to Fujian many times. In 1984, Brewster's daughter and many members of his family came back to Putian, Fujian, to celebrate the 100th anniversary of her grandparents' visit to China. In the 21st century, they also returned to Fuzhou many times in search of their childhood memories. In 2010, they returned to Fujian, and revisited the old residence in Gutian and Fujian Medical University Union Hospital. In 2017, the daughter of Director Brewster came to Fuzhou again to visit the Red Building, learned about the changes and development of the hospital in recent years, and had a cordial conversation with the hospital leaders.

• The Spirit of Fujian Medical University Union Hospital

Rigorous Refinement of the Spirit of Fujian Medical University Union Hospital

Fujian Medical University Union Hospital has gradually formed its own unique cultural idea and traditional spirit from generation to generation. Especially in the early 20th century, Foochow Christian Union Hospital introduced the standardized hospital management system of the United States into the hospital, and formed its own style of strict hospital management and rigorous medical style.

At that time, the hospital gradually created a strict personnel training and management system. Physician classification was distinct: chief physician—attending physician—chief resident physician—resident physician—intern. The elimination system was implemented. The interns would rotate through the departments in the hospital for one year. After screening, only those with outstanding performance would stay.

担任院长、主任、护士长的美国专家对医务人员要求极高。住院医师实行 24 小时负责制，随叫随到，不能离开医院，没有较长的节假日，每周放假半天，可以外出购物、看电影。晚饭后要到病房查房，有时要工作到晚 11~12 点。晚上门诊医生既要看急诊，又要给病人打吊瓶。第二天，主任查房，拿着病历。值班医师要背诵昨晚病人的病情，查完房，所有事情都处理完才能下班。

医生和护士们在手术（来源：福建医科大学附属协和医院）
Doctors and nurses worked together to do the operation（Source：Fujian Medical University Union Hospital）

当时的检查设备很简单，诊断主要靠听诊器和医生的临床经验，因此非常注重临床观察。衡量一个医师的水平就看他对病人入院时检查得出的初步印象与出院的诊断结果符合率的高低。内科三大常规、静脉输液由临床医生自己操作。外科手术也由医生自己做麻醉，大多施行腰麻，麻醉完成后再洗手上台开刀，术中内科医生负责观察血压等情况。全麻则由内科医生执行。

福建省著名心血管专家胡锡衷教授生前深为感慨，正是协和医院整整 20 年严格的医学训练，为他打下了扎实的内科基础，影响了他的一生。他回忆道：协和医院管理制度严格，学术风气浓厚，每天查房分早查房、午查房、晚查房，由主任带着。病房有英文打字机，病历书写、病史报告、交班、病例讨论等都用英文进行；体检从头到脚，病史要问三代，病历书写要清楚，查房时下级医师要背病历，包括心电图等检查结果。X 光报告出来，医生拿着片子分析病情，提高下级医生的诊断水平，培养扎实的专业基础。

American experts who served as the director of the hospital, chief physicians, and head nurses were extremely demanding with the medical personnel in the hospital. Resident physicians, who must stay within call, and could not leave the hospital, worked according to a 24-hour responsibility system. They did not have long holidays. They only took half a day off every week, during which they could go shopping or go to see the movies. After dinner, they had to do their rounds in the wards, and sometimes worked until 11 - 12 o'clock at night. In the evening, the outpatient doctor not only had to see the patients at the emergency department, but also needed to give the patients intravenous injections. The next day, when the chief physician did his rounds in the wards, with the medical records in hand, the doctor on duty must recite the patient's condition the night before. After checking the wards, he could not be off work unless he handled all the matters.

At that time, medical equipment was so simple that the diagnosis mainly depended on the stethoscope and the experience of the doctor, so clinical observation was valued. A physician's competence was measured by the extent to which the initial impression that he derived from the check results when the patient was hospitalized matched the diagnosis results when the patient was discharged from the hospital. The three major routines of internal medicine and intravenous injections were operated by clinician. Anesthesia, most of which was spinal anesthesia, was also done by the surgeons. After the anesthesia was completed, they washed their hands and began doing surgery. During the operation, the physicians were responsible for monitoring the blood pressure and other conditions. The general anesthesia was performed by a physician.

Professor Hu Xizhong, a famous cardiovascular expert in Fujian Province, thought that it was the 20 years of strict medical training in Fujian Medical University Union Hospital that laid a solid foundation for his knowledge and practice in internal medicine and had a profound influence on his whole life. In his memory, the hospital had a strict management system and a strong academic atmosphere. Led by the chief physician, daily rounds were further divided into the morning round, the afternoon round, and the evening round. There was an English typewriter in the wards. Writing of medical records, reports of medical history, shift handover, case discussion, etc. were all conducted in English. The physical examination was carried out from head to toe, and the history of illness was traced back to the patient's three previous generations. Medical records must be written clearly, and the junior doctors must keep the medical records, including the check results of electrocardiogram, in mind when doing their rounds in the wards. As soon as the X-ray report came out, the doctors analyzed the patient's conditions with the help of the X-ray film, aiming to improve the diagnosis level of junior doctors, and help them build a solid professional foundation.

：马高爱医院的配药室（来源：福建医科大学附属协和医院）
：Dispensary in Magaw Memorial Hospital（Source：Fujian
：Medical University Union Hospital）

每周三全院医师大查房，各科室提出疑难病例供大家讨论会诊。讨论非常热烈，既保证了医疗质量，对实习生又是很好的带教，是实习生最喜欢的一课。协和的疑难病例讨论会很有名。所有死亡病人都要进行尸检，临床诊断不符合的，由病理科提供病例，先把病理报告遮盖起来，各科都参加讨论分析。先由住院医师发言，然后是主治医生、主任讲，最后再由病理科主任公布结果，相互对照。这对提高业务水平很有帮助，大家很感兴趣。医院还发给医生每人一把图书馆的钥匙，自己可以随时去查资料。

当时，医院对护士的管理也同样借鉴了美国医院的管理模式，总护士长下设病区护士长。医护人员早上七点半上班，八点之后开始日常工作，口头汇报、书写病历、护理记录及处方等都使用英语。护士长负责调配工种，抄写病历、药方、护理记录，还兼给实习医生上护理课。老护士负责带领护校的学生为病人打针、发药、洗澡、换衣。有专门的夜班护士长负责夜间巡视全院各病区，处理特殊病情。医院还规定，护士如犯错会受罚，而在医院实习的护校的学生则会被罚延期毕业，留校察看。

当时的总护士长雅各布斯女士是美国加利福尼亚人，身材瘦高，说话很慢，举止端庄，40多岁仍单身。她在中国居住多年，会说福州话。她工作极认真、严格，整天在全院病房、门诊巡查；检查护士工作是否合格；拜访病人，征求意见。她甚至经常半夜三更查房，如发现护理有不规范之处，看到护士在闲谈、看小说、织毛衣，便会严厉批评处罚，毫不留情。由于她认真负责和严谨求精的态度，没有人敢犯规。她还要求护士必须穿软底鞋，走路要用脚尖。医生护士的白大褂都必须熨烫平整，进病房楼要先在大厅对着镜子整装。就连实习医生量血压后血压计没折好，杰克女士都要叫来重新做。她对自己同样很严格。按照合同规定，美国医护人员在中国工作每三年可以回国休假一年，但她因工作需要放弃了与家人团聚的机会，一直坚守岗位。

：等待求医的病人（来源：福建医科大学附属协和医院）
：Patients waiting for the good physician（Source：Fujian Medical
：University Union Hospital）

Every Wednesday, the doctors of the hospital had a grand round. Each department presented difficult cases for everyone to discuss and consult. The discussion was very lively, which not only ensured the quality of medical care, but also provided a good teaching to the interns. The discussion on difficult cases in Fujian Medical University Union Hospital was very well-known. All dead patients must undergo autopsy. If there were disagreements concerning the clinical diagnosis, the pathology department would provide the case. With the pathology report veiled, all departments would participate in the discussion and analysis. The resident physicians presented their analysis first, followed by the attending and chief physicians, and finally the director of the pathology department announced the results and compared their analysis with the results. The process was very conducive to the improvement of their professional level, so everyone was very interested. The hospital also gave every doctor a key to the library so that they could search for the information they needed any time.

At that time, the hospital's management system of nurses was also borrowed from America. The medical staff went to work at 7:30 in the morning, and started their daily work at 8:00. The oral reports, writing of medical records, nursing records and prescriptions were all in English. The head nurse was responsible for allocating work, transcribing medical records, prescriptions, and nursing records, as well as giving nursing classes to trainees. The senior nurse was responsible for guiding the students of the nursing school to give injections, dispense medicines, bathe patients and change clothes for patients. The head nurse on night shift was responsible for patrolling all wards at night and dealing with patients' conditions. The hospital also stipulated that if nurses made mistakes, they would be punished, while the students of nursing schools who were doing their internship in the hospital had to postpone their graduation and stay on school probation as their punishment.

Miss Jacobs, the head nurse at that time, who was tall and thin, and spoke slowly, was from California, USA, and had a dignified manner. Still single in her forties, she had lived in China for many years and could speak Fuzhou dialect. She, extremely conscientious and strict, patrolled the wards and outpatient clinic of the hospital every day. She examined whether the nurses were qualified and visited patients to seek opinions from them. There were even frequent ward rounds in the middle of the night. If she found irregularities in nursing care, or saw nurses chatting, reading novels, or knitting sweaters, she would severely criticize and punish them. Seeing her conscientiousness, sense of responsibility and rigorous attitude, no one dared to foul. She also required nurses to wear soft-soled shoes and to walk on their toes. The white coats of doctors and nurses must be ironed flat, and they must be dressed up in front of the mirror in the hall before entering the ward building. Even when the sphygmomanometer was not folded properly after the interns took the blood pressure, Miss Jacobs would call them in to do it again. She was also very strict with herself. According to the contract, American medical staff who worked in China for three years could return to America for one year's vacation. However, she gave up the opportunity to reunite with her family due to work needs and had been sticking to her post.

协和精神之勤奋奉献

老协和的许多外国医生富有爱心，有的甘愿放弃优越的生活，到贫困偏远的地区治病救人，奉献自己的青春甚至生命。20世纪40年代任院长兼内科主任的戴毓昭是一位50岁左右的美国白人女性，中等身材，待人和善，说得一口流利的福州方言，能直接和病人深入交谈。抢救危重病人时，戴主任一般都要在场，总是交代下级医生："电话就在我的枕头边，任何时候有事都可以找我。"她说到做到，不论三更半夜，一旦病房或门诊有危重病例，电话一打她很快就到，马上投入抢救工作中。

1943年4月，日军发动细菌战，在江西铅山一带用飞机投放带菌的老鼠，造成鼠疫大流行。鼠疫蔓延到福州，每日发现数例，传染性极强，死亡率很高。协和医院腾出一个病区专门收治鼠疫病人，规定发热病人必须由护士先检查全身有无淋巴结肿大，然后由专职医师诊治。大家都害怕传染，戴院长不顾危险亲自检查病人，穿着白色特制的防护服，连鞋子也套入长裤里。她每看一个病人，就要到光亮处从上到下检查一遍全身有无跳蚤，再看下一个病人。

1946年夏秋，福州霍乱大流行，协和医院的小病房住满了霍乱病人。一天，戴医生正给刚入院的霍乱病人体检时，病人突然控制不住，喷射性地吐得戴医生脸上和身上都是污物。戴医生沉着镇静，没有半句怨言，稍加清理，坚持处理好病人再去清洗。

戴毓昭在中国行医30多年，直到1949年才依依不舍地离开协和医院回到美国，把一生中最美好的年华献给了中国人民，救治了许许多多病人。她终身未婚，仅领养了一个中国小姑娘。

The Spirit of Diligence and Dedication of Fujian Medical University Union Hospital

Many foreign doctors in Foochow Christian Union Hospital were caring, and some were willing to give up their comfortable life and dedicate their youth, even their lives to curing diseases and saving people in poor and remote areas. Dr. Laura G. Dyer (Dai Yuzhao), director of Foochow Christian Union Hospital and director of internal medicine in the 1940s, who was a white woman in her fifties with a medium build, treated people kindly. She spoke fluent Fuzhou dialect, and could directly communicate with patients at length. When rescuing critically ill patients, Director Dai was usually present and she always told the junior doctors, "The phone is right next to my pillow, and you can call me anytime if you need anything." She acted on her words. Even at midnight, once there was a critical case in the ward or outpatient clinic, she would arrive as soon as a call was made, and would immediately throw herself into the rescue work.

In April 1943, the Japanese army launched a bacteriological war, and used planes to drop bacteria-carrying mice in the Qianshan area of Jiangxi Province, causing a plague pandemic. The plague spread to Fuzhou, and several cases were detected every day. It was extremely contagious and had a high mortality rate. Foochow Christian Union Hospital set aside a ward for the treatment of the plague patients, and stipulated that patients with a fever must be checked by nurses to see if there were swollen lymph nodes, and then they would be diagnosed and treated by physicians. Everyone was afraid of the infection, but Director Dai checked the patients by herself in spite of the risk. She wore a special white protective suit and her shoes were tucked into her trousers. Each time after diagnosing a patient, she went to the bright place to check the whole body from top to bottom to see whether there were fleas or not, and then went for the next patient.

In the summer and autumn of 1946, the cholera epidemic broke out in Fuzhou. The small wards of the Foochow Christian Union Hospital were full of cholera patients. One day, Dr. Dai was examining a cholera patient who had just been admitted to the hospital. The patient suddenly couldn't control it and vomited so much that Dr. Dai's face and body were dirty. However, Dr. Dai was calm and composed. She did not complain, and insisted on attending the patient before cleaning herself.

Dai Yuzhao practiced medicine in China for more than 30 years. It was not until 1949 that she reluctantly left Foochow Christian Union Hospital for the United States. She devoted her best time to the Chinese people, and cured numerous patients. She never got married and adopted a Chinese girl.

• 协和医院大事记

- 1877 年，福州圣教医院成立，由美国基督教美部会创办，为八闽现代医学的发祥地
- 1884 年，中国最早的留洋女医学博士——许金訇赴美留学
- 1907 年，佛罗伦斯·南丁格尔护士和助产士培训学校成立，为中国第一所护士学校
- 1957 年，中国第一例结肠代食道根治食管癌手术
- 1964 年，亚洲第一台高压氧治疗舱
- 1978 年，中国第一部血液病学专著——《临床血液病学》
- 1980 年，最早发现和报告我国铁粒幼细胞性贫血，并对该病的病因、发病机理、诊断和治疗进行系统研究，获卫生部医药卫生成果一等奖
- 1981 年，创建福建省首个医学（内科血液病学）硕士点
- 1987 年，国际首创"三尖杉酯碱治疗真性红细胞增多症"，研究成果获"国家级科技进步三等奖"
- 1997 年，最早发现我国福建省沿海地区人类 T 细胞白血病小流行区，获"国家科技进步三等奖"
- 1988 年，最早开展血小板释放功能同步测定法，对白血病患者的血小板功能、环核苷酸和凝血八因子的变化及其临床意义进行研究，获得"福建省科技进步一等奖"
- 1990 年，创建福建省首个医学（内科血液病学）博士点
- 1991 年，在国内率先进行了细菌内毒素对 Corti 氏器及神经成分损伤的研究，成果获"卫生部科学技术进步三等奖"
- 2001 年，与中国医学科学院血研所合作，率先对巨核细胞和血小板的病理生理学特征及其生长调节进行研究，成果获得"国家自然科学二等奖"
- 2003 年，中国第一例全腹腔镜下大肠癌切除术
- 2003 年，亚洲第一例换心人再换肝的高难度手术
- 2006 年，首创超声介入无水酒精量化治疗肝癌，研究成果获"福建省科学技术一等奖"

• Major Events of Fujian Medical University Union Hospital

- In 1877, the founding of Foochow Missionary Hospital by the American Board of Commissioners for Foreign Missions, the cradle of modern medicine in Fujian

- In 1884, Hü King-eng, the first female doctor of medicine in China to study abroad went to the US

- In 1907, the founding of Florence Nightingale Training School for Nursing and Midwives, the first nursing school in China

- In 1957, the first case of colonic replacement of esophagus for esophageal cancer radical operation in China

- In 1964, the first hyperbaric oxygen therapy cabin in Asia

- In 1978, China's first monograph on hematology——*Clinical Hematology*

- In 1980, the first discovery and report of sideroblastic anemia in China, and systematic research on the etiology, pathogenesis, diagnosis and treatment of the disease, winning the First Prize for Medical and Health Achievements of the Ministry of Health

- In 1981, the first master's program of medicine (internal hematology) in Fujian

- In 1987, the world's first "harringtonine in the treatment of polycythemia vera", with the research results winning the "Third Prize of National Science and Technology Progress"

- In 1997, the first to discover the small endemic area of human T-cell leukemia in the coastal areas of Fujian in China, winning the "Third Prize of National Science and Technology Progress"

- In 1988, the first to carry out the simultaneous determination of platelet release function, and to study the changes of platelet function, cyclic nucleotides and eight coagulation factors in leukemia patients and the corresponding clinical significance, winning the "First Prize of Fujian Provincial Science and Technology Progress Award"

- In 1990, the first doctoral program of medicine (internal hematology) in Fujian Province.

- In 1991, taking the lead in the research of bacterial endotoxin damage to the organ of Corti and nerve components, with the results winning the "Third Prize of Science and Technology Progress of the Ministry of Health"

- In 2001, in cooperation with the Institute of Hematology, Chinese Academy of Medical Sciences, taking the lead in researching the pathophysiological characteristics and growth regulation of megakaryocytes and platelets, winning the "Second Prize of National Natural Science"

- In 2003, the first case of total laparoscopic colorectal cancer resection in China

- In 2003, the first difficult operation of liver transplant for a heart-transplant patient in Asia

- In 2006, pioneering the quantitative treatment of liver cancer by ultrasound intervention with anhydrous alcohol, with the research results winning the "First Prize of Science and Technology of Fujian Province"

- **特别鸣谢**

本章写作过程中，得到以下单位和个人的大力支持，在此特致以真诚的感谢。

感谢福建医科大学附属协和医院授权使用部分图片，这些图片是对文字所阐述历史的一个很好的回应。

感谢福建师范大学外国语学院陈榕烽老师以及就职于福建医科大学附属协和医院的陈榕烽老师的爱人郑培焱先生，感谢他们在协调与福建医科大学附属协和医院沟通方面给予的大量帮助。感谢福建医科大学附属协和医院宣传统战部副部长苏萍女士，她为本章顺利开展影像拍摄工作提供了大力支持。

● Acknowledgements

I would like to express my sincere gratitude to the following institutions and individuals for their irreplaceable support during the writing of this chapter.

My first gratitude goes to Fujian Medical University Union Hospital who authorized the use of some pictures provided by the hospital in the chapter. These pictures play the role of good response to the history described in the text.

My gratitude also goes to Chen Rongfeng, a teacher from College of Foreign Languages of Fujian Normal University, and her husband, Zheng Peizheng, who works in Fujian Medical University Union Hospital, for their great help in coordinating communication with the hospital. I would also like to give special thanks to Ms. Su Ping, Deputy Director of the Publicity and United Front Work Department, Fujian Medical University Union Hospital, who has provided strong support for the production of the video about this chapter.

CHAPTER
THREE

从毓英女校到福州第十六中学①

From Uk Ing to Fuzhou

No. 16 Junior High School

第三章

福

---

① 本章图片除标注来源的以外，均由福州第十六中学提供。

"闽江之滨，烟山南麓，林木葳蕤，华宇丹阁；麦园菁菁，师尹赫赫，钟灵毓秀，英才辈出"。这是 2017 年 158 华诞之际，福州第十六中学所得献辞的发端之句，起首便是扬今日芳华，忆往昔岁月的气势与格局。

　　坐落在福州市仓山区麦园路 35 号的福州第十六中学，一眼看去和其他福州中学并没什么大不同——三栋棕红色外立面的现代大楼占据了中轴位置，墙面上金色的大字在阳光下熠熠生辉，"教学楼""图书馆""行政楼"让我们瞬间明白它的身份；标准的塑胶环形跑道上，每到大课间就有学生浩浩荡荡地跑操。跑道中心是足够大的绿茵球场，供学生课余练习排球或篮球——这些都是一所省级初中示范校该有的配置。大概只有细心的来访者才能发现校园内的百年古树，静默犹胜言语，启发人们去探究隐藏在校内"毓英馆"中的校史。馆中的《毓英辞》有云："忆昔初创，咸丰九年，毓英女子，东亚首校；开化民智，尤重女学，筚路蓝缕，功莫大焉。西人办学，亦为我而造多士，计迁四度，实立志并不移。"

：福州第十六中学
：Fuzhou No. 16 Junior
：High School

：校史馆：毓英馆
：School history museum:
：Uk Ing Museum

"Onshore the River of Min/At the southern foot of Yantai Mountain/ Stand with grandeur several teaching mansions/Right on the Road of Maiyuan./As the leading public junior high school in the District of Cangshan/With brilliant teachers and students/Generations of talents are bred, as abundant/As the luxuriant trees and flowers on campus, vibrant/When nourished and nurtured by a unique civilization."Preluding the dedication to Fuzhou No. 16 Junior High School on the occasion of its 158th anniversary in 2017, the above lines celebrate its present accomplishments while recalling the past momentum. Fuzhou No. 16 Junior High School, located at No. 35 Maiyuan Road in Cangshan District, Fuzhou City, appears like other ordinary middle schools at a glance. Its status as a model provincial middle school is self-evident with a closer look at all its facilities on campus. Any visitor will find at random the three modern buildings occupying the pivotal position with their brownish-red facades inscribed with prominent gilded Chinese characters glittering in the sunlight, representing the names of the buildings respectively as " Teaching Building " " Library " and "Administrative Building", the standard plastic circular runway filled with students running drills every recess, and a game court big enough for students to practice volleyball or basketball for extracurricular activities. What else to be found probably counts on observant visitors when those century-old trees on campus, which are thought-provoking with deep silence rather than loud words, leap to eyes and inspire them to explore the history locked up in the "Uk Ing (a historical name of the school) Museum" of the school. Written on the wall at the gate of the museum is an "Ode to Uk Ing" which reminds visitors that the initiation of the school was in the ninth year of Emperor Xianfeng in the Qing Dynasty when Uk Ing, as the pioneer of girls' boarding school inaugurated by the Westerners in East Asia, first blazed a trail in Fuzhou, China and devoted itself to women's education, a determination that had never changed and had ever since contributed to the cultivation and civilization of many Chinese women scholars through the four stages undergone and accompanied by its relocations.

这样一所老校，跨越一个多世纪时长，始于清末，走过民国，又历经改制，从一所旧时西方教会私立闺阁式女校变成而今男女兼收的政府公办学校，在新中国各个时期踔厉奋发，笃行不怠，跻身福州知名公立校之列，其前世今生，不说是屈指可数，也定含章可贞。这样一所老校，纵使旧貌换新颜，落地扎根，但也历经浮沉，依然裹挟着历史的烟云。

鸦片战争后，清政府于1724年所颁布的"禁教令"（沈艾娣，2013）解除，西方传教士乃有机会来华。19世纪西方开始工业革命，蒸汽机船、电报等新发明用科技手段为来华西人提供了便利。对于美国人而言，1869年后，有了横跨整个美国大陆的太平洋铁路，加上蒸汽轮船，20多天便可抵达中国。他们从开放的五个沿海通商口岸之一进入内地城市，再深入郊区和农村。

早在1825年，美国美以美会就有意愿来华，并成立了专门的委员会进行规划。1835年，美以美会在卫斯理大学正式通过了在中国设立差会（基督教新教差派传教士进行传教活动的组织）的法案。1842年8月，中英《南京条约》签订后，广州、厦门、福州、宁波、上海被迫开放为通商口岸。5个开放的通商口岸当中，福州处于中心位置，北望宁波，南接厦门，与广州和上海几乎等距。美以美会看到福州如此优越的位置所能带来的交通优势和辐射能力，断定其必将成为"繁盛之市场"。

石版画：福州埠，1847年伦敦迪恩出版公司出品（来源：池志海）
Foo Choo Foo (Fuzhou port), one of the five treaty ports opened to British commerce—A lithograph published by Dean and Co., London, 1847 (Source: Chi Zhihai)

A venerable school it truly is! It is definitely the one with many a story to tell about its past and present that may constitute one of the brightest pages in the glorious records of the few schools in Fuzhou with so long a history spanning over a century. With its initiation in the late Qing Dynasty and continuation in the Republic of China, it has finally taken root and come to fruitage in the People's Republic of China after finding its way to restructuring. Evolving from a former private girls' school of a Western mission to the existing public school for co-education of men and women, it has ever since made continual progress through vigorous and determined endeavors and ascended to the list of the best public schools in Fuzhou. It is truly a time-honored school that can be traced back to the mists and clouds of history in the late Qing Dynasty.

After the First Opium War, the ban on Christianity issued by the Qing Government in 1724 was lifted, and the Western missionaries regained their opportunity to set foot in China. Meanwhile, the 19th-century Western Industrial Revolution also enabled the Westerners to have easier access to China with all its means of science and technology, bringing about inventions such as steamships and telecommunications that may provide convenience for their journey. A typical example worth mentioning is that after 1869, it took the American missionaries only more than twenty days by the Pacific Railway across the American continent, coupled with steamships, to travel from home to China, then entered the mainland cities from one of the five treaty ports and, at last, went further to the suburbs and rural areas.

As early as 1825, the American Methodist Episcopal Church (hereinafter referred to as the AMEC) had appointed a special committee to plan for sending a mission (an organization of protestants to spread Christianity) for evangelization in China, the approval of which was finally voted for in 1835 at Wesleyan University in the United States. When *The Treaty of Nanking* following the First Opium War was imposed upon China in August 1842, five ports, known as Guangzhou, Xiamen, Fuzhou, Ningbo, and Shanghai, were to be opened to foreign trade and residence. Facing Ningbo in the north and Xiamen in the south, Fuzhou is in the central position, almost equidistant from Guangzhou and Shanghai. Seeing the superior position of Fuzhou, the AMEC concluded that it might accordingly bring advantages in transportation and prepare Fuzhou as the "point d'appui" for the AMEC's proposed policy of evangelization in China.

1847 年 4 月 15 日，美以美会派遣柯林牧师和怀德夫妇乘"赫伯尔"号邮轮从波士顿港口出发，前往福州设立差会。历经约五个月的航行，他们最先抵达广州，之后在厦门停留了一段时间，随后向北进入闽江流域。罗星塔映入眼帘的那天，他们欣喜不已，因为目的地福州即将到达。第二天傍晚，他们在福州海关附近靠岸登陆（Lacy，1948：38），开始以福州为中心设立差会，之后再向西推进和发展。

　　远渡重洋来到福州的美以美会第一批传教士们和洋商一样，集于南台郊区，租用中洲岛上一座本地居民的木屋落脚。

Kgu Kang Parsonage.

：美以美会传教士租住的第一所当地民房（来源：池志海）
：The first Chinese house rented in Fuzhou by the Methodist missionaries (Source: Chi Zhihai)

　　传教士们入乡随俗，开始采用文化协商和调适的策略：他们学习研究福州方言，达到能和本地人流利对话的程度，因为愿意听演讲的百姓要远多于能看懂并愿意看手册的人；他们不囿于在民房改造的小教堂布道，不管是在街市陌巷，还是酒楼茶肆，传教士们入乡随俗，力图找到民众们感兴趣的话题，甚至适时穿上当地服装，还有牧师剃头编长辫。

Then on April 15, 1847, Rev. J. D. Collins and M. C. Whites, who set out from the Boston Harbour on board the American ship *Herber*, were sent to establish a mission in Fuzhou. A nearly five-month voyage led the missionaries to China and landed at Guangzhou first, and after a stop at Xiamen, they went north along the Minjiang River. They couldn't help rejoicing on the day when they caught sight of the Pagoda Anchorage signifying their upcoming destination. The following evening, the missionaries went ashore near the Foochow Custom House. Taking Fuzhou City as the starting point, the missionaries organized the Foochow (Fuzhou) Mission of the AMEC and decided that the evangelization and expansion of the missionary work from then on should necessarily be westward.

The first missionaries of the AMEC, who traveled a long way to Fuzhou across the ocean, were in no better circumstances than foreign merchants and had to gather in the suburbs of Nantai and fit themselves up by renting a Chinese wooden house for residence.

The missionaries in this foreign culture therefore succumbed to cultural negotiation and adaptation. Aware that the local people were more interested in public discourse than printed books, they studied the native language earnestly in order that they could preach fluently to the local people in the Fuzhou dialect. Without being confined to humble Chinese houses adapted to their purposes, the missionaries wandered through streets and restaurants, where they would learn from the locals and find topics of public interest to hold forth to the natives their sermons. They also accustomed themselves to dressing in Chinese costumes in due course. Some missionaries even shaved the head and braided the cue.

这些尝试逐渐让本地百姓对他们不再那么排斥。之后，他们通过一些重要的日常行为建立起和当地民众的密切联系，例如通过医疗、教育等和生存状态息息相关的方面融入当地生活，以图缓和教会与当地的关系，逐渐得到百姓信任。1857 年 5 月，美部会在福州南台距万寿桥约一公里处建起了第一座砖木结构的基督教堂"救主堂"。同年进入福州的美以美差会则在 1856 年新建了两处基督教堂，一处是位于茶亭的"真神堂"，另一处则是位于闽江南岸的"天安堂"（Maclay，1861：214）。美以美会传教士们由此悟得实业宣教胜于空口论道，于是开始大力出版书籍，发行刊物，兴办各式医院和学校。

茶亭真神堂（来源：池志海）
Ching Sing Dong（Church of the True God）at Iongtau（Tea Pavilion）（Source: Chi Zhihai）

天安堂（来源：池志海）
Tien Ang Dong（Church of Heavenly Peace）（Source: Chi Zhihai）

正是在这个背景之下，福州第一所女子寄宿学校诞生了。作为福州第十六中学的前身，它隶属于美国基督新教卫斯理宗派往福州传教的美以美差会。其筹建款来自当时美国巴尔的摩中国女布道会，它的筹建者是这个女布道会派出的两名美以美会女传教士，她们都受过高等教育。在接下来的讲述中，我们将带您走进一段文化阈限，去回顾这所学校的历史。在这段办学历史中，身为学校主理的美以美会传教士们所信仰的西方教育理念及宗教思想与福州当地民众所奉行的中国文化间经历了排斥与交流、疑拒与接纳的过程，这其中每一个阶段和当时的历史环境一起，都将这所学校推入不同的办学目标和状态。所以，我们在关注它外在发展变化的同时，也将探讨它不同发展阶段所处的文化阈限及成因，因为这是伴随这所学校的历史记忆的。基于这样一种立场，我们诚邀您加入我们的时光之旅，一起探究福州第十六中学——这所历经沧海桑田仍静处一隅的学府，其前世之沉浮变迁，今生之与时俱进。

All those attempts had helped, to some extent, the natives hold a more receptive attitude toward them, but more significant progress came from some other measures of the mission, such as medical treatment, education, and other practices closely related to the improvement of living conditions, by which the missionaries hoped to win the trust of the local people and integrate themselves into the local life. Thereby the missionaries made some achievements. The first brick-and-wood Christian church, "Dudley Memorial Church" was built by the American Board of Commissioners for Foreign Missions about one kilometer away from the Bridge of Ten Thousand Ages in Nantai in May 1857. The Methodist Episcopal Mission (hereinafter referred to as the MEM), which followed the Mission of the American Board to arrive in Fuzhou in 1847, had two new Christian erections in 1856, one of which was "Ching Sing Dong" (Church of the True God) at Iongtau (Tea Pavilion), the other of which was situated at the southern bank of the Minjiang River and named Tien Ang Dong (Church of Heavenly Peace). The missionaries of the MEM, who were convinced that orderly religious practices catering to the needs of the natives were doing better than oral sermons in paving the way to the general introduction of Christianity in Fuzhou, then began to prepare themselves for the establishment of various institutions including publishing and printing, healing and teaching.

It is against this background that Uk Ing, the historical existence of Fuzhou No. 16 Junior High School, has come into being. As the first girls' boarding school in Fuzhou supervised by the MEM of the Protestant Wesleyan denomination and sponsored by the Ladies China Missionary Society of Baltimore in the United States, it is inaugurated by two American Christian women, who are both graduates of higher education. In retrospection, the story of this school will unfold at its different historical stages in a cultural liminality heterogeneous with both Western and Chinese cultures, under the joint forces of which different religious ideologies and educational concepts in their constant interactions with all other external historical factors have led to isolations and exchanges, suspicions and acceptances and evolved the school into its various manifestations and orientations. Therefore, besides introducing its external status quo in different historical stages, the internal factors embedded in the specific cultural liminality will be treated as a constituent part of the school's history. The present chapter is intended for readers interested in exploring Uk Ing's historical transformation to see how it has been keeping pace with the times after all historical vicissitudes and has come into existence as the present Fuzhou No. 16 Junior High School in its peaceful being.

Scan for more
扫码了解更多

● 历史沿革

回顾福州第十六中学至今 160 多年的办学历史，前世今生之分水岭应在 20 世纪 50 年代。1952 年，它与寻珍女校合并，同时将福州私立邮电学校的女生一并归入，由"福州私立毓英女子初级中学"更名为"福州第二女子中学"。从此，它不再是一所教会拥有的私立初级中学，而是新中国福州的一所公立中学。1956 年，"福州第二女子中学"再次更名为"福州第十六中学"，男女学生兼收，结束了其近百年来的女校历史，至此脱胎换骨。

在此，我们将按阶段梳理出福州第十六中学的缘起、发展和变化，形成较为清晰的历史发展脉络。我们将把它置于美以美会在中国布道的四个发展阶段和新中国成立改制之后的几个时期所形成的时间横轴之上，而文化阈限作为纵轴贯穿其中。我们作为在其中自由移动的视点，兼顾学校外在发展变化及内在驱动因素，由此形成一个三维的、有事件、有内涵、有述评的发展沿革。

改制前：美以美会所属的教会私立学校

十六中的前身是美国美以美会在福州、也是东亚的第一所私立女子学校，其校名在发展过程中历经多次更改。为了叙述方便，以下提及时，凡 1952 年前，一律称（毓英）女校；1952 年至 1956 年间，称为福州第二女子中学；1956 年后至今的福州第十六中学在本章则简称为十六中。毓英女校自 1859 年（清咸丰九年）问世伊始，直至 1952 年合并更名后收归公办，这 93 年始终是美以美会所属的教会私立学校。

: 20 世纪 20 年代福州美以美会成员合影（来源：池志海）
: A group photo of Fuzhou Methodists in the 1920s（Source: Chi Zhihai）

• Evolution of Fuzhou No. 16 Junior High School

An overview of the over 160-year history of the school from Uk Ing to Fuzhou No. 16 Junior High School finds the 1950s a vital era to tell its past from the present. In 1952, the former Uk Ing Girls' School restructured itself to become Fuzhou No. 2 Girls' Middle School by merging with Sing Ding Girls' School and the girls' department of Fuzhou Private Post and Telecommunications School. This watershed event marked its transformation from a private mission school to a public school of the new China while remaining a girls' school. It was in 1956 that the ultimate transformation came when it went further to enroll both male and female students and was renamed Fuzhou No. 16 Middle School, thus ending its century-old history of female education.

The following elaborates on the causes and effects of its evolution under different circumstances along a historical development continuum. Readers will be given a comprehensive review of the school's origin and transformation, with its developments along the horizontal time-base as the first dimension suggesting the four stages of the MEM's evangelization in Fuzhou and the restructuring periods of the school in new China, the historical events along the vertical cultural liminality as the second dimension all the way providing for underlying factors, and the analyses and comments in this part will serve as the third dimension establishing bidirectional ties from the interplay of the first and second dimensions, thus forming a three-dimensional and all-around presentation of its evolution.

Before Restructuring: Uk Ing as a Private Mission School of the MEM

Uk Ing, one of the historical names of Fuzhou No. 16 Junior High school, was the most well-known among many others after its establishment by the MEM as the first girls' school in Fuzhou and East Asia. For this reason and for the sake of convenience, it will be referred to in the following of this chapter as Uk Ing or the Girls' School when it is mentioned before its restructuring in 1952. It is called Fuzhou No. 2 Girls' Middle School between 1952 – 1956, while after 1956 till now, it is just referred to as No. 16 Middle School for short. It should also be noted that throughout the 93 years of its history as Uk Ing, from its existence in 1859 (the ninth year of Emperor Xianfeng in the Qing Dynasty) to its restructuring in 1952, it is in nature a missionary school under the supervision of the MEM.

改制前的毓英女校自 1859 年创立，作为美以美会所属的教会学校，其办学之起步、发展之起落皆处在由西方基督教文化和东方儒、释、道及地方民俗文化交汇所逐步形成的文化阈限之中。在其改制为新中国公立学校以前，先后由美以美会之巴尔的摩中国女布道会及海外女布道会拨款解决大部分的办学经费，以及指派传教士负责学校的日常管理和教学。

女校之破冰初创

前文已说明毓英女校创立之前，美以美中国差会传教士们第一个十年（1847—1857）间在福州破冰播种之背景，此处不再赘述。几乎与此同时，在美国本土成立发展的巴尔的摩中国布道会成为毓英女校创办的关键。

1858 年，巴尔的摩中国布道会收到母会转来的一封求助信。已在福州传教 4 年的万为牧师在信中向母会求助 5 000 美金用于女校办学。巴尔的摩中国布道会不仅接受了这个请求，积极筹措经费，而且将布道会的名称改为"巴尔的摩中国女布道会"，明确了布道会"女性工作为女性"的宗旨和方向，自此正式拉开了美以美会在福州创建东亚第一所女子寄宿学校的帷幕。

1858 年 10 月 4 日，美以美会派娲标礼和娲西利两姐妹及宝姑娘前往福州负责女校的筹办事宜。她们于 1859 年 3 月 19 日抵达目的地福州。对三位女传教士而言，适应福州当地的风土习俗、学习福州当地方言实为不易，但安定校舍和寻找学生需要更大的努力。三人团队中的宝姑娘到福州不久就和万为牧师结婚，主要协助万为的传教事务，开办女校的任务几乎全由娲氏姐妹负责。

: 娲氏姐妹之一
: One of the Woolston sisters

1859 年 11 月 28 日，娲氏姐妹主理的女子寄宿学校正式成立，《福州美以美年会史》记载其"以前男校为校舍"（林显芳，1936：21）。因美国美以美母会在开设女校的钱款和人员方面均未安置妥当，为不浪费资源，1856 年 11 月便先安排牧师基顺办起一间男寄宿学校，该校于 1857 年 12 月 30 日停办（Lacy，1948：142）。自娲氏姐妹抵达福州到女校开设时隔不过数月，自然来不及购置地块新筑校舍，只能以前男校所在地先行过渡。

Therefore, the management of Uk Ing by the MEM in a foreign city of Fuzhou after its debut in 1859 was involved in the process of development symbiotic with the formation of a cultural liminality involving the American Methodism and Chinese Confucianism, Buddhism, Taoism, and the indigenous customs and habits. In the meantime, the Ladies China Missionary Society of Baltimore and Woman's Foreign Missionary Society (hereinafter referred to as the WFMS) were successively responsible for appropriating most of its school funding and appointing missionaries as administrators and teachers in Uk Ing.

Uk Ing in Its Infancy

The first ten years (1847 – 1857) for the missionaries of the MEM to toil and sow the seeds of Christianity in Fuzhou has been foregrounded in the introductory part as a trigger for the inception of Uk Ing and will not herein be repeated. What should not be neglected now is a catalyst almost of the same period and importance for the birth of Uk Ing—the organization of the China Missionary Society of Baltimore in the United States.

In 1858, from the Parent Board, the society received a letter by Rev. E. Wentworth, then missionary to China, who appealed for $5,000 to build and sustain a female school in Fuzhou. Not only had the China Missionary Society of Baltimore taken and completed the task by actively raising funds to meet the note for the five thousand dollars pledged to the school, but it also renamed itself to be Ladies China Missionary Society of Baltimore to make specific its goal as "woman's work for woman". Henceforth, the first girls' boarding school in Fuzhou and also in East Asia officially got underway.

On October 4, 1858, Beulah Woolston and Sallie. H. Woolston, along with Miss Potter, sailed for Fuzhou to arrange for the school's founding, and reached Fuzhou, their final destination, on March 19, 1859. It had been an endeavor for them to acquire a knowledge of the local dialect and adapt to Fuzhou's local culture and customs, let alone settle the school buildings and secure students. When Miss Potter afterward became the wife of Rev. E. Wentworth and mainly assisted Wentworth in his missionary affairs, it was on the part of the Woolston sisters to see to the school's founding.

On November 28, 1859, the first girls' boarding school supervised by the Woolston sisters in Fuzhou was opened in the building that the former boys' school had occupied, as was specified in *Historical Records of the Foochow Methodist Annual Conference*. Anxious to make the most efficient use of the facilities on hand, the MEM had previously resolved to authorize Rev. Gibson to open a boys' boarding school, believing there would be ample time to get a new compound for the girls' school after the reception of money and teachers from the American Parent Board. However, the Girls' School opened no more than a few months after the Woolston sisters arrived in Fuzhou. It was too short a time for the Woolston sisters to find a new site for the school; therefore, the only choice available for the Woolstons was the building occupied by the former boys' school.

由于美以美会的贝弗利·沃主教 1858 年在巴尔的摩去世，巴尔的摩中国女布道会便以建女校纪念主教的名义来筹得毓英女校建校所需的 5 000 美金。故而女校最初的名字为"沃女子学校"（Maclay，1861；Lacy，1948：144）。

女校新立，诸事皆备，唯缺学生。彼时富贵人家的女儿，但凡有读书识字的，也是自设家塾，请先生私授。更何况商埠初开，洋商洋教士等由此源源而入，如乱石穿潭，给福州百姓的经济与生活都带来了一定冲击，处于文化休克状态的当地百姓对洋教士带来的新鲜事物毫无了解，且静观其所为。鉴于招生之难，女校初期非但不收学费，还为学生提供食宿、书籍及一应所需，以此吸引学生入校。饶是这般，进展还是极为缓慢。据娲标礼 1860 年的办学报告记载（Maclay，1861：255），学校成立时只收到一名中国学生。据毓英前校长李淑仁回忆，这第一名女学生是她的伯母黄晖钦。8 天后才又有 6 名女孩入学，但没过多久就辍学回家了。到了第 8 个月，共收了 10 名女生，年龄在 7 岁至 13 岁。为了留住生源，差会和其中九个订了契约，有 3 名学生订了 5 年，4 名订了 6 年，其余两名则订了 7 年。到了 1860 年 10 月，办学已足足 10 个月时，"共收得了十五名小女生，但只八名留在校中，余不久都退学了"（林显芳，1936：21）。到了 1861 年，女校又收了两名学生，一名大概在待嫁之龄，她的未婚夫"懂道理"；另一名已 68 岁，头发皓白，入校前也听讲过"十诫"（林显芳，1936：21）。

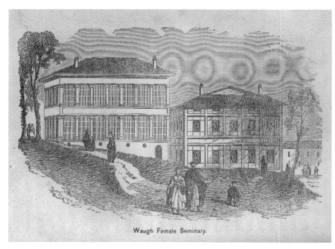

沃女子学校（来源：池志海）
Waugh Female Seminary（Source: Chi Zhihai）

女校招收的第一名学生，刊于毓英女校 50 周年校庆手册
The first student enrolled in the Girls' School, a photograph in the 50th anniversary report of Uk Ing

The Girls' School was then called "Waugh Female Seminary" owing to the fact that five thousand dollars were raised by the Ladies China Missionary Society of Baltimore in the name of opening the Girls' School as a memorial to Bishop Beverly Waugh, who had passed away in Baltimore in 1858.

The difficulty for this newly-established Girls' School was nothing but the insufficiency of pupils. Girls from the local wealthy official-gentry families, as long as they could gain permission to literacy, were more ready for private schooling at home from private teachers. As for the common people in Fuzhou, with the influx via the newly-opened trade ports of foreign merchants and missionaries, like stirring fish in the water, causing disturbance to the indigenous life and economy, they found themselves perplexed by those new things introduced by the missionaries and chose to adopt a wait-and-see attitude, thus leaving the school in want of pupils. In view of the low enrollment, the Girls' School promised to provide their pupils food, clothing and shelter, not to mention free books and tuition, which, however, had contributed little to soliciting students. According to the annual report from Beulah Woolston in 1860, the Girls' School opened with only one Chinese student, whose name was Huang Huiqin, aunt of Li Shuren, one of the former principals of the Girls' School , as was recollected by Li Shuren herself. Eight days passed before another six girls joined in, but they were all taken home in a short time. It was not until the eighth month that the Girls' School had enrolled ten little girls, all between seven to thirteen years of age, and nine of them were committed to the mission under a written agreement, three for five, four for six, and two for seven years. By October 1860, when the Girls' School had been running for ten months, "Fifteen Chinese girls have been received in school, only eight of whom now stay, with a quick drop-out of the other seven". The Girls' School received two more students in 1861, one of whom was probably at the age of marriage, and her fiancé understood the Christian doctrines. The other, who was then 68 years old and white-haired, had attended the sermons of the Ten Commandments before she entered the school.

1862 年，女校搬到了由巴尔的摩中国女布道会捐助的新校舍，故又改名为"巴尔的摩女子中学"，新校舍位于仓前山太古坪（今仓山小学内）。又因其为当时美以美会在福州唯一的女子寄宿学校，也常被称为"福州女子寄宿学校"，在福州的美以美差会亦称其为"内女学"。美以美会在福州所创办之"外学"一般设在乡村，学生人数较少，教员男女皆可；"内学"则多设在府县，教员、学生人数较多，学生在校内住宿，课程班级更有秩序。因此可知，"内女学"的含义也就等同于女子寄宿学校（林显芳，1936：21 - 22）。1865 年，主教爱德华·汤姆生访问参观了毓英女校，他留下的描述为我们提供了女校办学初期的一个粗略剪影：家具简单粗糙但整洁，学生们衣着朴素却干净，用长条凳当座椅，床上铺有席子，放着竹编的枕头。学校已有 23 名女学生入学，娴氏姐妹由此信心倍增（Lacy，1948：144）。

士教和利麥

　：麦利和牧师（来源：池志海）
　：Rev. R. S. Maclay（Source: Chi Zhihai）

　　1859 年成立的毓英女校在《福州美以美年会史》中被描述为"闽省女子学校之开山祖"（林显芳，1936：37）。不过，也有他人撰文，认为麦利和夫人所开学堂是美以美会在福州所办的第一所女学校。麦利和在其所著的《生活在中国人中间》一书中对这所学校有比较详细的描述。1850 年秋，麦利和夫妇在自家住宅后院耗资 55 美金盖起一座中式房屋，由麦利和夫人负责管理，专门招收一些女学生。学生们不在这里住宿，只在日间一定时段学习经文，传教士们称之为"日学"。以传教士妻子身份协助传教的麦利和夫人应该只能把部分的时间精力投入其中，因而 1857 年美以美会年度报告中将其描述为"谦逊的投入"（Maclay，1861：245）。

In 1862, the Girls' School moved to a new place called Taiguping, where the present Fuzhou Cangshan Primary School is located. Since the Ladies China Missionary Society of Baltimore donated the new school building, the Girls' School was officially renamed "Baltimore Female Academy". It was, more often than not, referred to as "Foochow Girls' Boarding School" in that it was the only girls' boarding school in Fuzhou at that time. For missionaries in Fuzhou, it was the typical "Nei-NÜ-Xue". According to the MEM's different programs for schooling, compared with the so-called Wai-Xue, or rural education, which was usually opened in small villages and enrolled with a comparatively smaller number of students in the care of both male and female teachers, Nei-Xue, or urban education, was normally instituted in prefectures and intended to provide accommodations and more extensive courses for a comparatively greater number of students. Hence in this sense, Nei-NÜ-Xue, meaning urban female education, was simply a different way to define a girls' boarding school. We can derive a sketch of the interior of the Girls' School in mind from Bishop Edward Thompson's brief description during his visit to the school in 1865: the furniture was plain, rough, and cheap, but clean; the children were plainly but neatly dressed. There were benches for chairs, mattresses for beds, and bamboo frames for pillows. Misses Woolston were much encouraged by accessions recently received. There were now twenty-three girls under instruction.

Uk Ing, founded in 1859, was ranked as "the pioneering girls' school in Fukien Province" by Lin Xianfang in his Historical Records of the Foochow Methodist Annual Conference. However, others argued in their articles that the school managed by Mrs. Maclay should be the first school for girls run by the Methodists in Fuzhou. For an answer, let's first turn to the details of Mrs. Maclay's school recounted by Mr. Maclay in his Life Among the Chinese People. During the autumn of 1850, a small building in Chinese style costing fifty-five dollars was erected on the rear portion of the lot occupied by Mr. and Mrs. Maclay, and a school for Chinese girls was commenced under the care of Mrs. Maclay. The students lived at home, but they spent some time during the day reading the scriptures in the school, which might well account for its being called "day school" by the missionaries. As a missionary's wife, Mrs. Maclay could just devote a portion of her time to the day school, which was described as "unassuming labors" in the annual report of the MEM in 1857.

1851—1858 年，女日学的办学过程也是断断续续。1858 年因为女校开始筹办，麦利和夫人的女日学便停办了。相较而言，我们感觉麦利和夫人所办的更像是女校筹办之前一种过渡的启蒙学塾。其实，等级更高的女子寄宿学校一直是美以美会希望达成的目标，因为日间学校难以做到对学生规范的管理和系统的学科输入，很难达成美以美会通过培养本土女信徒来扩大教会影响的初衷，而寄宿女校的学生则全程在校，避免了朝闻"道"而夕改之的尴尬。

女校之步入正轨

1866 年（同治 5 年），美以美福州差会在福州首次召开布道年会，这标志着福州布道会即将由差会时代步入年会时代。1877 年 12 月 20 日，福州美以美年会正式成立。在省内，美以美会迅速将传教区域往福州各郊县及闽北扩张，省外则往西、往北，分别在江西和北京开辟了教区。

传教事务的稳步推进，一方面减少了地方百姓对传教士各种活动的排斥，同时也让美以美会可以腾出更多余力来关注办学，为毓英女校的稳定和发展创造了条件。耶鲁大学的相关资料中记载了一则关于毓英女校的趣事。薛承恩牧师去福州 50 里外的一个村子布道，当地村民竟毫不犹豫地将房子租给他。这破天荒的待遇让薛牧师很吃惊，因为两年前由美国领事馆出面都租不成功的房屋，现在居然一问就租到手中。问及缘由，才知几年前邻村一名女孩被送进了毓英女校读书，回村后村民们见她不仅安然无恙、吃穿无忧，还学到了东西，因而对毓英女校的偏见有所改观，觉得这所学校并非如初闻之传言，故而由此及彼，对教士传教自然也不如之前那样抗拒。

From 1851 to 1858, the day school was continued with occasional interruptions and was finally suspended in 1858 with a view to the organization of a boarding school for Chinese girls. From the above, it seems that Mrs. Maclay's day school was, in fact, a transition from an attempt at family schooling to a formal operation of full-scale female education. However, a higher-level boarding school such as Uk Ing had always been the pursuit of the MEM. Students in a day school without a strict observation of tenets and a systematic input of disciplines could hardly meet the goal of the MEM to expand the mission with cultivated native Christian women. The students in a boarding school, nevertheless, with their presence at school day and night, could avoid the embarrassment of acquiring the Christian doctrines in the morning and reverting to their own idolatry at night.

Uk Ing in Its Growth

The first annual conference held in Fuzhou by the MEM made 1866 (the fifth year of Tongzhi's reign) a significant year, leading the Foochow Mission to an epoch of the Foochow Conference of the Methodist Episcopal Church. Then on December 20, 1877, the Foochow Methodist Annual Conference was founded. With the establishment of the Methodist Episcopal Conference (hereinafter referred to as the MEC) structure, the influence of MEC was radiated to the surrounding towns and hamlets of Fuzhou and farther to the northern part of Fujian, while in the meantime it also pushed its entry westward and northward into other parts of China and later opened the Kiangsi and Peking Conferences.

The progressive advances in evangelization saved the missionaries from handling native opposition to Christian practices, thus the missionaries could spare more of their time and energy for running schools, which undoubtedly created favorable conditions for the steady growth of Uk Ing in all aspects. An anecdote about Uk Ing showing the school on its proper track of development is kept in the record of Yale University. When Rev. Nathan Sites was preaching in a village fifty miles from Fuzhou, he was surprised at the willingness of a man to rent him a place for a chapel without fear. Two years before that, the American Consulate had tried in vain to secure for him what was now granted on merely a private request. When inquiring the man, he was told that a girl in the neighboring village had been received into Uk Ing and was seen well fed, clothed, and instructed after her return home safe and sound. The spreading news, being different from the previous rumors, had somewhat dispelled the villagers' prejudice and fear toward the education of Uk Ing and therefore toward the preaching of the missionaries.

1873 年，毓英女校迁往仓前山土地庙街（现麦园路），买下琉球在福州开设的太茂茶行作为校舍，因此更名为"太茂女斋"，即现在福州第十六中学所在之仓前山麦园路35 号。同年，毓英女校学生人数已增长至 28 人，其中含 7 名基督教徒的女儿，2 名来自非基督徒家庭，余下 19 人均为弃婴。女校弃婴基本来自娟氏姐妹开设的保生堂，附属于毓英女校。被弃女婴进入保生堂后，先由雇来的奶娘照顾，稍大些则指派老师对其进行教导。等到入学年龄，便直接进入毓英女校就读，直到肄业。保生堂于 1913 年发展、改置为毓英幼稚园。保生堂的开设算是一举多得：一则对当时的社会陋习起到了一定的劝诫作用；二则可以保证女校生源无忧，稳定办学；三则客观上为福州幼儿学前教育积累了一定经验，发挥了先导实践的作用。

: 太茂女斋校内雨盖操场
: The rain-cover playground in Tai Maiu Girls'
: School

: 太茂女斋校内 26 教室走廊
: Corridor of 26-classroom building in Tai Maiu
: Girls' School

: 太茂女斋内景（来源：UMC
: Digital Galleries）
: The interior of Tai Maiu Girls'
: School（Source: UMC Digital
: Galleries）

1879 年，毓英女校应该算有了值得一提的进展。我们在一篇题为"二十年之后"的毓英办学报告中，看到了当年毓英女校小学低年级师生的一张合照。照片下方的文字很详细地介绍了照片上站在正中的两名女老师和分列在她们身前和左右的 8 名学生，包括她们的名字、特点和身份等。从文字介绍得知，照片中的两名女教师——保恩和秀金——本身就是毓英女校最早的学生，肄业后留任女校教师，分别负责上下午课程，这算是间接向我们透露了女校当时的办学状况。

In the year of 1873, the Girls' School was renamed Tai Maiu Girls' School after it moved to Tu-Di-Miao Street (today's Maiyuan Road), Cangqian Mountain (today's Yantai Mountain), and was situated on the premises bought from Tai Maiu & Co., a tea trading company of the Ryukyu Kingdom in Fuzhou, the exact location of which matches No. 35, Maiyuan Road, Yantai Mountain where Fuzhou No. 16 Junior High School now stands. As of that year, the number of students received into the school had increased to twenty-eight, among which seven were from native Christian families, two from non-Christian families, and nineteen others were foundlings, mainly from the Foundling Asylum affiliated to the Girls' School run by the Woolston sisters. The abandoned baby girls in the Asylum were first under the care of a nurse employed and then guided by a designated teacher when they grew older. After they reached school age, they were readily admitted to Uk Ing and stayed until graduation. The Foundling Asylum, after years of development, had become a kindergarten of Uk Ing in 1913. The operation of the Foundling Asylum at that time might have served its multiple purposes in the following aspects: to have given an exhortation for the removal of backward social customs, to have ensured a stable enrollment for the Girls' School, and to have furnished a prototype of and accumulated experience in preschool education in Fuzhou.

The small progress of Uk Ing's schooling in 1879 deserves our mention. It is captured in a report entitled "After Two Decades" and a picture of teachers and students from a primary class in Uk Ing. In the picture, two teachers, Po-ong and Swoi-king, are standing in the center, with eight students positioned either before or on each side. Beneath the picture are detailed accounts of their names, characters, and identities, revealing that the two teachers were the earliest students of Uk Ing and were kept as teachers in the school after finishing their courses, one teaching in the morning, the other in the afternoon. The picture, therefore, is a piece of substantial evidence for the steady growth of the Girls' School in its undertaking.

1888 年，女校有 6 名学生完成了小学、初中和高中的全部课程，从学校毕业，拿到了女校颁发的第一批毕业证书，证书上印有一盏明灯、一本翻开的书和一朵莲花，象征着女校对学生的训诲和期待，即"真理明，学问好，德行全"。这 6 名毕业的学生之后全都在天安堂受洗入教。

总之，在这一阶段，毓英女校虽然从办学规模和学生数量上看，尚不算繁荣，但其逐渐扭转了门庭冷落的局面，保生堂的女童到了入学年龄便直接转到女校就读。从 1870—1880 年间女校有较为稳定的生源，基本保持在 30 人左右。此外，办学经费亦呈递增之势，如 1872—1873 年是 658.32 美金，1879—1880 年得海外女布道会拨款 877 美金，平均每位学生约 30 美金（Ford，1936：57），同时也有了符合办学期望的毕业生产出，算是步入了正轨。

女校之规模扩大

19 世纪末 20 世纪初，美以美会在福州乃至中国的发展越来越好，进入了传教事务的发达时代，一直持续至 1919 年五四运动前。这期间，教会的高层人士开始出任一些当地社会职务，拥有一定的社会影响力；中方牧师人数日益增长，能力出众，在美以美年会拥有和西方牧师同等的话语权。文化调适之后，东方和西方文化开始逐步进入交流阈限。美以美年会财库充盈，更加注重人才培植，在办学上不仅注意区域布局之完密，更注重学制之完善。

1892 年 11 月 28 日（光绪十八年十月十六）建校 33 周年之日，女校的师生以及受邀的牧师齐聚一堂，聆听谢锡恩牧师关于在女校开设大学的设想，心潮澎湃，备受鼓舞。这个梦想从 1896 年开始不再遥远，因为女校不用再费心寻找学员，相反还有了挑选学员的余地。

In 1888, the Girls' School granted diplomas for the first time to six girls after they had done the work at the primary, grammar, and high school levels. Admonitions and expectations for the graduates were tacitly symbolized by a bright lamp, an unfolded book, and a lotus flower painted on the diploma, meaning the pursuit of truth, learning, and virtue respectively. Afterward, the six graduates were all baptized at Tien Ang Dong and received into the church.

To sum up, the Girls' School had yet to enter into a period of prosperity given its limited scope of education and number of students. Nevertheless, attendance steadily increased, largely because the children of the affiliated Foundling Asylum were transferred to the school as they reached school age. During the decade from 1870 to 1880, the attendance remained fairly constant, averaging about thirty. On the other hand, school funding is on escalation. For example, expenses from 1872 to 1873 were 658.32 dollars in total, while the average appropriation by the WFMS from 1879 to 1880 was 877 dollars per year, or an average expense per pupil of nearly thirty dollars. Last but not least, the number of graduates meeting the expectations is also strong evidence for the normal operation of the school.

Uk Ing in Its Heyday

From the turn of the 19th century through the beginning of the 20th century till around 1919 before the May Fourth Movement, the MEC had been gaining momentum in Fuzhou, or rather China and thus had ushered in its heyday of missionary enterprise. It's notable that under this phase, some senior figures of the MEC began to hold local positions and exerted a certain influence of Christianity on local people. Meanwhile, it's remarkable that, with their increasing numbers and outstanding competence, the ordained Chinese elders began to hold equal status with Western missionaries in the church. It seemed that the East and the West were stepping into a cultural liminality of exchanges. The MEC, rich in its financial resources, invested more of its assets and efforts into cultivating talents. Not only had it emphasized a full array of schools in every missionary region, but it also paid attention to the perfection of its educational systems.

Rev. Sia Sek Ong was invited to talk about the future of the Girls' School in celebration of its 33rd anniversary held at the school on the 28th day of November 1892—the eighteenth year of Guangxu, the tenth month, sixteenth day. The women and girls were so inspired and encouraged when assembled with the presence of some of the missionaries and native elders to listen to Sia Sek Ong's dream of changing the Girls' School into the Girls' College. The dream had become a prophecy since 1896 when the Girls' School no longer bothered to recruit students, but there was a pool of applicants to choose from.

之后，随着生源增多，设施更加完善，教育程度逐步提高，1898 年开始以"毓英"冠名，那时已经有了小学、中学、大学三个层级。年会史记载的原话为"一八九八年始改为毓英女学。时分为大学、中学、小学三部。及华南女校产生，大学中学并归于彼。本校专办初级中学、高小、初小、幼稚园四种。女学生额数约三百余人"（林显芳，1936：37）。可见 1898 年对于女校而言是一个极特别的年份，相较之前，学生人数极大幅度增长，由几十至几百，学制也逐级达到完善。

毓英女校主体建筑视角之一
A view of the main buildings in Uk Ing

毓英女校主体建筑视角二（来源：福建师范大学图书馆）
Another perspective of the main buildings in Uk Ing（Source: Fujian Normal University Library）

据十六中现任教务副主任李萍老师介绍，"毓英"谐音"育婴"，即既不忘从保生堂起步的办学历史，又寓意其培育钟灵毓秀之英才的宗旨。此说法是否确凿暂且不论，凭着从西文校名到直白朴实的"太茂"，再到引人联想的"毓英"这一发展变化，我们似乎也可以窥见东方文化对西方文化的影响。美以美会内部对此的评论大致可概括为：东方和西方开始直面的交流，它们权衡着彼此的距离和实力，互相靠近，互相影响。

With its increase in enrollment and improvement in facilities and schooling, the dream finally came true in 1898 when it began to be named Uk Ing and boasted its three educational levels, the primary, the middle, and the higher, which was recounted in *Historical Records of the Foochow Methodist Conference* as "It is in the year 1898 that the Girls' School was renamed Uk Ing, whose education incorporated the primary, middle and higher departments. Both the middle and higher departments were designated to Hwa Nan Women's College after its establishment, while the Girls' School was devoted to its recruitment of junior high, higher primary, and lower primary as well as kindergarten students, totaling about three hundred girls". The year 1898, therefore, meant much to the Girls' School. It witnessed the most notable achievements compared with those of the preceding years, including the surge of its enrollment from dozens to hundreds and the gradual perfection of its educational system.

According to Li Ping, the current deputy dean of the academic registry office of Fuzhou No. 16 Junior High School, Uk Ing meaning "cultivating talents" is homophonic to "nurturing babies" in Chinese, therefore the naming of the Girls' School as "Uk Ing" might have indicated "cultivating talents" as well as "nurturing babies", which would not only remind people of the early days when it had started from the Foundling Asylum but also suggest to people its ultimate goal of educating elegant and graceful women scholars. It still needs time and further evidence to confirm whether her statement is true, but a juxtaposition of those early English names to the ready-made Ryukyuan pronunciation of "Tai Maiu" and finally to the connotative Chinese naming of "Uk Ing" would readily demonstrate an impact of the oriental culture on the occidental culture, as was put by missionaries of the MEC: The East and the West have come in direct contact. They are measuring lengths and weighing forces. The Occident and the Orient are meeting and interfusing.

1904 年女校的年度办学报告为我们提供了这种双向交流中的诸多细节，女校办学之日新月异可见一斑。从民间层面看，越来越多的殷实之家开始将自家女儿送进毓英读书，所有学生都可以自行支付所需的学杂、被褥、服装等费用，绝大多数学生能付得起住宿费。对于经济有困难的学生，学校用手工劳动等办法让其实现"自养"。这种做法颇切合实际，故而学校乐于招生，父母愿意送读，办学开始良性循环起来。1909 年时，女校已有 60 个自费生，能收入学费 100 美金，从母会处收到 250 美金，又有海外女布道协会拨款 2 200 美金，对比 19 世纪末增长了三倍之多，基本能达到收支平衡；女校生源整体素质和风貌也有极大提高，不缠足已成为基本入学条件。19 世纪末，女校学生有三分之一是童养媳，到 1909 年，只有两名，即每 80 个女生才有一名童养媳。自 1888 年颁发毕业证书起，毕业生已达 117 人，很大一部分成为医生和老师。值得一提的是，已有 9 位学生先后赴美、日留学，亦有 5 位毕业生在政府的公立学校任职。回首办学初期，谁又能想象原先被要求缠脚的中国女学生现在竟能走出国门，而被冷落的教会女校培养出来的学员也能进入政府学校任职？从官方层面看，1909 年 50 周年校庆之际，学校的小教堂插满了中式旗帜，福建省议会有 19 名官员应邀出席庆典，议长在庆典上简短发言表示祝贺，另一名议员则发言表示宪法将允许女性拥有投票权利，欢迎女校学生承当起为国家效劳的重任。这一发言说明官方对女校及女校学生开始认可。

女校第三代学生
Third-generation students of Uk Ing

1907 年的女校学生
Students of Uk Ing in 1907

Some details of the bilateral contact between the local people and Uk Ing were collected in the annual report of the Girls' School in 1904. After an increasing number of well-off families became willing to send their daughters to Uk Ing for education, a large number of the students could pay for their board, and all could supply their own books and bedding as well as clothes. Those who had difficulty paying for their education were encouraged to do some manual work for their self-support. The fact that students could help to pay for their education had caused many parents to send their daughters to the Girls' School, thus producing a virtuous circle for both sides. A few years later in 1909, there were already sixty self-supporting students enrolled. The Girls' School had accumulated an income three times as much as that of the end of the last century—with $100 from tuition, $250 from the Parent Board, added with an appropriation of $2,200 from the WFMS, the total income of the Girls' School was $2,550, which basically covered its expenses. The students enrolled had an improvement in their deportment and attainment, because unbinding of feet was made a condition for entrance, and infant-betrothal was rarely found among girl students. At the turn of the 19th century, one out of three of the students were subject to infant-betrothal or commonly spoken of as "little daughter-in-law", while in 1909, there were only two little daughters-in-law in school or one in eighty. Since the granting of diplomas in 1888, one hundred and seventeen girls had graduated, most of whom were engaged in different branches of work including physicians and teachers. Of the especially promising graduates to be mentioned, nine had gone abroad for further studies, and five others were employed as teachers in government-sponsored public schools. Had it been back to fifty years before when the Girls' School was inaugurated, who could have envisioned that those Chinese girls having been required to bind their feet in earlier days should go abroad with their feet unbound, and graduates from the Girls' School having been doubted and neglected should one day be employed as teachers in the government-sponsored schools? With the local government, a closer relationship was also established for the Girls' School. In 1909, the fiftieth anniversary of the Girls' School was held in the school chapel where Chinese flags figured conspicuously in the decorations, and 19 officials of the Provincial Assembly were invited to visit the school. The President of the Assembly addressed the faculty and students briefly, saying it was a pleasure for them all to visit the school on this occasion, while another speaker from the Assembly said among other things that the constitution would grant the girl students equal rights with men of voting on all matters, and at the same time rendered them the responsibility of serving the country. This announcement might be reckoned as official recognition of the school and the girls by the government.

民国（1912）之后，女校的发展逐渐达到建校以来的鼎盛时期，主要体现在以下六个方面。①学生人数大幅增长，1888 年颁发毕业证开始至 1913 年已有 150 名毕业生。民国后女子学风日盛，寻常在校生便有 250 人左右。②校园扩建，校园较 19 世纪末已扩大三倍，加盖了音乐楼和小学教学楼。③学制完善，将原先的育婴堂加以改置，在原来八年学制的基础上增设幼儿园。在课程设置上，参照美国本土学校安排，添加了许多之前没有的科目，学生所受教育更加全面。④卫生健康管理进步，尽一切可能增强学生体质，鼓励学生进行体育运动和培养良好的饮食习惯。女校在每学期初均举办一次茶话会，茶中加入驱蛔虫的药，保持学生肠胃健康，因此那时女校从无霍乱病例。⑤生源非常稳定，拥有众多生源的女校不再免费招生，另外还设条件对报名者加以选拔。⑥学生素质日渐提高，从最早时的怯不敢言到踊跃发言，积极参与学校和社会事务。

⫶ 民国前后女校毕业生（来源：池志海）
⫶ Graduates of Uk Ing around the establishment of the Republic of China（Source: Chi Zhihai）

女校之立案搬迁

20 世纪 20 年代后，国际国内形势风云变幻。一战后世界经济疲软，美以美会美国布道部因捐输骤减，分配给各海外布道会经费呈今非昔比之态，美以美福州年会原定各项发展因开支不足而渐显萧条气象。1922—1927 年，国内发起非基督教运动，这场由"中国知识界人士对西方宗教文化的相对理性的批判"（杨天宏，2005：2），作为新文化运动民主与科学思潮在不同时代和领域的延伸，一浪高过一浪，终于掀起各地的"收回教育权运动"。

In general, the founding of the Republic of China in 1912 witnessed the Girls' School in its prime time of development, which could be seen from the following six aspects. First, there was a massive increase in the number of students. Despite that there was only one student admitted at its establishment, it had sent out 150 graduates in total from 1888 to 1913, all with granted diplomas of the Girls' School. With the boom of female education after the founding of the Republic of China, the number of students had ever since continued to grow with a regular attendance of about 250 in school. Second, there was an expansion of the school quarters. After two more buildings were added, one for music, and the other for the primary department, it had by then three times outgrown its original accommodation at the turn of the 19th century. Third, there was perfection in educational systems. To the original eight-year course of study was added a kindergarten, which had been developed from the Foundling Asylum, hence a broader scope of education was covered. Meanwhile, there had been decided changes in the curriculum. Various new courses opened in the native American schools were introduced to the Girls' School to provide the students with a more liberal education. Fourth, there was an improvement in hygiene and health care. Everything possible was done to build up the students' constitution. Students were encouraged to take physical exercises and cultivate good eating habits. To ensure the students' intestinal health, a "tea party" consisting of a dose of santonin would be held at the beginning of each semester, which greatly contributed to protecting the students from the epidemic of cholera. Fifth, there was consistency in its recruitment. With its far-reaching opportunities in recruiting students, rather than promising free enrollment, it had begun to select from the applicants with preset conditions. Sixth, there was an overall upgrade in the abilities of the students. Contrary to the earliest days when they were too timid to speak a word, the students were audacious to express their opinions and enthusiastic to participate in various school and civic activities.

Uk Ing in Its Turbulence & Recession

The 1920s ushered in a rapidly changing world with a sagging economy after the First World War. The American Parent Board, therefore, suffered a drastic decrease in donations and had to cut its planned budget for its foreign missions. For lack of funds, the MEC in Fuzhou had to reduce all its normal expenses, for which its missionary enterprise was undergoing a slump. Then emerged the Anti-Christian Movement, "a comparatively rational critique of the Western religious culture launched by the Chinese intellectuals" from 1922 to 1927 in China. This movement, echoing in uplift the call for democracy and science of the New Culture Movement in different times and tides, had finally reached its climax of a nationwide Regaining Education Rights Movement.

1927 年春，收回教育权运动委员会与福州各教会学校师生取得联系，敦促他们向国民政府立案。1927 年下半年，毓英女校完成向国民政府立案，首要之重大举措即女校管理由"校长制"改为"委员制"。立案之前，按美以美会教育制度，女校管理历来为"分任制"，校长总理校政，且均由美以美会女传教士担任，只有负责教务的监学和教员会聘任福州当地人（林显芳，1936：22）。立案后的毓英女校奉福建省政务委员会批转的教育部指示，由郑惠碧、陈佩德与吴芝兰三人组成委员会共同管理校政。1928 年 6 月，吴芝兰赴美国密歇根大学深造，三人委员会解散，校董会（由美以美教会重要成员组成）任命郑惠碧出任校长，历时 3 年。

：郑惠碧
：Dang Hie Pek

　　立案后的第二个整改涉及教学与考核层面。
　　（1）学制：立案后，女校学制与民国时期公立学校一致，小学分设初小 4 年、高小 2 年；中学分初、高两级，各 3 年。
　　（2）课程设置：1931 年在福州美以美女教士第 47 届年会上，时任毓英女校校长的兰醒球（Carleton，1931：51）在其年度报告中说明，立案后女校不再正式开设宗教课程，而是使用国民政府统一颁布的教材，但依然坚持和注重一些特色课程。英语和音乐尤受重视。比如英语每周不少于 7 课时，提倡课内英语发言和校内英语会话；注重音乐素养训练，除了学习乐理、练习合唱外，学生们还学习各种乐器，如小提琴、管风琴、曼陀铃等（Wilson，1926：24）。劳作和家政也是女校极具特色的课程，女校为此专门盖起一座"家政楼"作为家政实训的场地（Carleton，1931：52）。

In the spring of 1927, teachers and students of each Christian school in Fuzhou were contacted and urged by the Committee of Regaining Education Rights Movement to register with the government. In the second half of 1927, after Uk Ing was approved for its registration with the government, the first significant rectification was to replace "the principal system" with "the commissioner system" in its administration. Before its registration, the Girls' School followed the so-called "split appointment system", which was stipulated in the educational by-laws of the MEC that the Girls' School should be in the full charge of a woman missionary who was appointed the principal, while the local people could only be employed as superintendents or teachers. After its registration, in compliance with the instruction of the Ministry of Education, which was proclaimed via Fujian Provincial Committee of Government Affairs, the administration of the Girls' School was transferred to a commission of three members, including Miss Dang Hie Pek, Miss Ding Buoi Daik and Miss Ngu Cie Lang. In June 1928, the commission was dismissed when Miss Ngu was going to Michigan University for her graduate study, and Miss Dang was later appointed principal for a three-year term by the Board of Directors consisting of senior members of the MEM.

Then followed the rectification of teaching and evaluation schemes.

The first thing was the educational system, which was modified to be consistent with that of the government-sponsored schools of the Republic of China, with a scheme of four years for lower primary, two years for higher primary, and three years respectively for junior high and senior high schooling.

The second thing was the readjustment of the curriculum. For this issue, Mary Sing-Gieu Carleton, then principal of the Girls' School, claimed that religion would not be taught during regular school hours in her forty-seventh annual report to the Foochow Woman's Conference of the MEC in 1931. Although courses in the Girls' School were opened with unified teaching materials in conformity with those enacted by the Nationalist Government, some featured ones still topped the list of its curriculum design. Special emphasis was put on English and Music. For example, there were no less than seven school hours every week for English, and English speaking in class and English conversation on campus were also encouraged. It is also reckoned important for students to have an ear for music. In addition to learning music theory and practicing singing in chorus, students were required to take lessons on the violin, organ, and mandolin. Other characteristic courses in the Girls' School were labor work and home economics, for which the Domestic Science Building was erected as the venue for practicing homemaking.

（3）教、学评估：各学科均组织教学研究会，接受福建省教育厅教学研究会和教会的"福建省教育会"的指导，下设各学科，如社会、国文、理化、数学等研究组，每月定期开会一次，研究教学方法。女校每月举行成绩展览会一次，作业无论优劣，全部陈列，由各级学生互相参观；每学期举行一次学科竞赛、运动会和时事测验。

（4）毕业考试：女校学生要经历"双考"。她们首先要参加美以美教育部的考试，测试科目包括公民、卫生、音乐、体育、绘画、生物、家政等，之后还得参加政府方面的会考，科目包括国文、算术、物理、化学、地理、历史、英语等。通过双考的学生有两张毕业证书，一张由国民政府教育部颁发，一张由福州美以美会教育部颁发。

立案后国民政府教育部颁发给女校学生许道锋的毕业证书（来源：许道锋遗物，池志海扫描自福建华南女子职业学院）
Diploma granted by Ministry of Education of The Nationalist Government to Xu Daofeng of Uk Ing Girls' School after its registration with the Nationalist Government （Scanned by Chi Zhihai. A bequest of Xu Daofeng to Fujian Hua Nan Women's College.）

立案前福州美以美会教育部颁发给女校学生郑惠碧的毕业证书（来源：许道锋遗物，池志海扫描自福建华南女子职业学院）
Diploma granted by Foochow Board of Education of The Methodist Episcopal Church to Dang Hie Pek of Uk Ing Girls' School before its registration with the Nationalist Government （Scanned by Chi Zhihai. A bequest of Xu Daofeng to Fujian Hua Nan Women's College.）

立案之事方歇，卢沟之变乍起。1937—1945 年间，中国大地烽烟四起，山河动荡，福州亦遭日军两度侵袭。女校为师生安全，数度搬迁，两次更名。

The third thing is the evaluation of teaching and learning. Under the guidance of the Teaching Research Association of Fujian Provincial Education Department and the MEC's Christian Educational Association of Fujian Province, seminars were organized for teachers to meet once a month to discuss teaching methods of various disciplines such as Society, Chinese, Physics & Chemistry, Mathematics and so on. For students, a monthly exhibition of academic achievements would be held with their assignments, whatever their merits, being displayed and assessed among themselves. Besides, academic competitions, sports meetings, and current affairs tests were held every semester.

The fourth thing is the graduation examination. The students of the Girls' School would have a double dose of final examinations for their graduation. They first took the examinations issued by the Board of Education of The Methodist Episcopal Church, involving Civil Citizens, Hygiene, Music, Physical Exercises, Drawing, Biology and Home Economics, and then the examinations issued by the Nationalist Government, including subjects such as Chinese, Arithmetic, Physics, Chemistry, Geography, History and English. Having passed all those examinations, the students were awarded two diplomas, one granted by the Ministry of Education of the Nationalist Government, and the other by the Foochow Board of Education of The Methodist Episcopal Church.

No sooner had the problem of registration settled in peace than the Lugou Bridge Incident occurred all of a sudden. For nearly a decade from 1937 to 1945, while China had suffered from turbulences in flames of war rising everywhere, Fuzhou was twice invaded by the Japanese troops. For the safety of teachers and students, the Girls' School had been relocated on several occasions and twice renamed.

1938 年，时任校长兰醒球带领师生迁往闽清十四都。1940 年，为解决经费与师资短缺，女校迁到闽清六都毓真女校，与闽清毓真、福州进德两所女子学校合办，校长为刘宫鹦。1941 年 4 月，福州第一次沦陷之际，为避战火，举迁闽清五都。同年 8 月，各校生源大幅减少，毓英女校学生仅剩 20 名。为了继续办学，美以美会遂将福清、古田、长乐、连江等地美以美会所属的 16 所中学合并后迁往顺昌元坑，更名为"卫理联中"，新立校长杨昌栋。1943 年，卫理联中解散，8 月毓英女校迁回闽清县城，由郑珍珠担任校长，以天儒中学名义招生办学。1943 年底，改由周苏藤任校长，次年女校迁回福州原址后未足一月，福州再次沦陷，无奈再迁闽清六都，直至 1945 年 8 月日本无条件投降，才回到福州原址。1946 年，周苏藤校长出国进修，由李淑仁接任校长直至 1952 年改制。

　　抗日战争期间，毓英女校学生爱国精神高涨，组织各种抗日战争宣传队、抗敌后援队，进行时事讲演、歌剧表演，激励民心，鼓舞士气。爱国精神之外，女校学生的自立自强也值得一提。在动荡搬迁中，女校学生依然积极乐观，时常进行野外生活训练，在校园内种玉蜀黍、甘蔗、香蕉等，在家政教室实习烹饪、裁缝，自给自足。

：刘宫鹦
：Liu Gongying

：郑珍珠
：Zheng Zhenzhu

：杨昌栋
：Yang Changdong

：周苏藤
：Zhou Suteng

：毓英学生抗敌班（来
：源：池志海）
：The Anti-enemy Class
：of Uk Ing（Source：Chi
：Zhihai）

In 1938, Mary Sing-Gieu Carleton, then principal of the Girls' School, led the faculty and students to move to the Fourteenth *Du* (an administrative sub-division of Mintsing county in the Qing Dynasty) of Mintsing County. Two years later in 1940 when the Girls' School was relocated to the Sixth *Du* of Mintsing County, to address the problem of finance and faculty, it was operated in coordination with the other two girls' schools, Uk Cing of Mintsing and Ceng Daik of Fuzhou, with Liu Gognying as principal. In April 1941, when Fuzhou was occupied by the Japanese for the first time, to escape the flames of war, Uk Ing, Uk Cing and Ceng Daik were all moved to the fifth *Du* of Mintsing County. Then in August of the same year, the number of students in each Methodist school decreased significantly, and there were then only twenty students left in Uk Ing Girls' School. To keep its educational enterprise running, the MEM merged sixteen of its schools in Futsing, Gutien, Diongloh, Lien Chiang and other places into one and moved it to Yuankeng, Shun Chang. It was renamed Methodist United Middle School and Yang Changdong was appointed as its principal. In August of 1943, with the dissolution of Methodist United Middle School, the Girls' School moved back to Mintsing County and operated by recruiting students in the name of Tien Ju Middle School, with Zheng Zhenzhu as its principal. In late 1943, Zhou Suteng replaced Zheng Zhenzhu to be principal before the Girls' School returned to its campus in Fuzhou one year later. Nonetheless, in less than one month, Fuzhou fell again and the Girls' School was forced to move once again to the Sixth *Du* of Mintsing. It had stayed there since then and was finally able to move back to its original location in Fuzhou City until the Japanese unconditional surrender in 1945. In 1946, as Zhou Suteng went abroad for further study, Li Shuren succeeded her to be principal until the restructuring of the Girls' School in 1952.

During the War of Resistance Against Japanese Aggression, patriotic feelings surged among the girl students of Uk Ing and drove them to organize various anti-enemy propaganda teams and support teams, by which they gave current affairs lectures and opera performances to inspire the people and to boost morale. Another thing worth mentioning other than patriotism is their self-reliance. Despite the upheavals of relocating back and forth, they stayed optimistic and positive in a difficult time: Field life training was conducted, maize, sugar canes, bananas and so on were planted on campus, and cooking and dress-making were practiced in their home economics classrooms, all being guarantees for their self-sufficiency.

1946 年至改制前后的女校相关记载着实难觅。几经周折，我们访得叶益昭女士，她自 1946 年幼稚园入学直至初中毕业，均在女校就读，是这段历史的亲历者。年逾 80 的叶女士看起来不过 60 出头，步伐矫健，行止得当。拜访当日，还冒雨走出小区引领我停车，让我感动不已。交谈中，叶女士思路清晰，记忆甚佳，侃侃道来。据她回忆，当时女校含幼稚园、小学和初中教育，幼稚园以外按九年学制设置课程，小学六年，初中三年，每年级都只有一个班。每周一早上师生在礼堂做礼拜，初中生每天早上有升旗仪式。当时女校幼稚园和小学校长为黄乃裳之长女黄端琼，1948 年下半年开始由李淑仁兼任小学和中学校长。

：毓英幼稚园师生合影（来源：叶益昭）
：Teachers and children of Uk Ing Kindergarten（Source：Ye Yizhao）

　　以下两张奖状由叶女士提供，前后相差不到一年，但校长签名已从黄端琼变成了李淑仁。

：两张叶益昭女士就读于毓英女校时的奖状（来源：叶益昭）
：Two certificates of merit awarded to Ye Yizhao by Uk Ing Girls' School（Source：Ye Yizhao）

Though chances were rare for us to acquire complete records on Uk Ing during the phase from 1946 to the restructuring around 1952, we managed to interview Ye Yingzhao, who studied in Uk Ing from kindergarten in 1946 to graduation from junior high in 1958, to get some fragmented information. Ms. Ye, who is over eighty years old, looks like in her early sixties with her vigorous steps and proper conduct. On the day of my visit to her, she was so considerate to wait for me in the rain outside the residential quarters and lead me to the parking lot. With her clear mind and good memory, she was quite responsive and eloquent during the interview. As was recollected by her, the Girls' School provided a nine-year program at that time, which included six years for primary and three years for junior grades, and each grade had only one class. Teachers and students were assembled for worship every Monday morning in the school chapel, and there were flag-raising ceremonies specially for junior high students. Wong Tuan Keng, the eldest daughter of Wong Nai Siong, had once been the principal of both the kindergarten and the primary school at that time. However, in the second half of 1948, Li Shuren was at once the principal of the primary school and the junior high school.

As can be seen from the two certificates of merit on the previous page provided by Ms. Ye, although their awarding dates were less than a year apart, the principal's signature had changed from Wong Tuan Keng to Li Shuren.

1949 年后，新中国开始逐步接管各教会私立学校。女校在 1950 年已着手改制事宜。当时女校学生虽同在一个校园，实则已分立为两所学校。小学部分称福州市麦园小学，派以徐言欢为首的三人工作组先行驻校管理。初中部则更名为福州第二女子中学，校长依然是李淑仁。麦园小学办学不到一年，到 1952 年下半年，小学被拆散分至仓山其余几所小学，如麦顶小学、三一小学等。原校址作为福州第二女子中学校园，只剩初中部。

　　后页插图可体现当时较为完整的毓英女校建筑布局。手绘图耗时一个多月完成，是叶益昭女士根据她 1946—1958 年在毓英女校近 12 年学习生活中依然深刻的记忆、对母校的深厚感情绘制而成。电脑绘图则根据叶女士的手绘图及其补充描述和修改要求，融入一定艺术表现进行绘制。鉴于年代久远以及记忆与资料的留白，无法做到毫无误差。现存照片几乎只涉及女校局部或特定建筑，这两张电脑绘图一可提供女校内部全景，以飨读者；二则以其清晰的线描勾画弥补了现存黑白老照片细微处模糊不清之缺憾。

Scan for more
扫码了解更多

After liberation in 1949, the People's Republic of China began its plan for taking over all missionary schools. Restructuring of the Girls' School had been actually underway since 1950, during which time it was divided into two schools, a primary school and a junior high school. The primary school was called Fuzhou Maiyuan Primary School, with a three-person working group headed by Xu Yanhuan being sent to take charge of it. The junior high school was renamed Fuzhou No. 2 Girls' Middle School, whose principal remained to be Li Shuren. However, the existence of Fuzhou Maiyuan Primary School lasted less than a year. In the second half of 1952, the students of Maiyuan Primary School were split up and dispatched to several other primary schools in Cangshan District, such as Maiding Primary School and Trinity Primary School. Left on the original campus were those junior high students who constituted Fuzhou No. 2 Girls' Middle School.

The following drawings attempt to give an interior panorama of Uk Ing. The hand-sketched illustrations are from her former student Ye Yizhao, who had studied for nearly twelve years from 1946—1958 in Uk Ing. Based on the cherished memory of her life and study on the campus, Ms. Ye, with her deep affection for her alma mater, spent more than one month to finish the sketch, which was artistically revised by our digital version with more details and some corrections according to further information in her later communications with us. Try as we might, due to so long a lapse of time in its history, a precision recovery plan is impossible to be guaranteed for unavoidable failures of memory or lack of necessary information. However, with its panoramic perspective, faithful color rendition, and clear delineation of the buildings and landscape, it is truly a blessing for readers who are not content with a partial or tintless view of the school provided by those ancient black and white photos blurred in time.

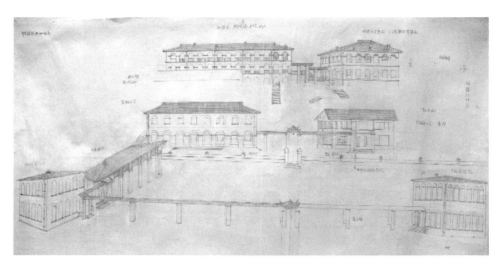

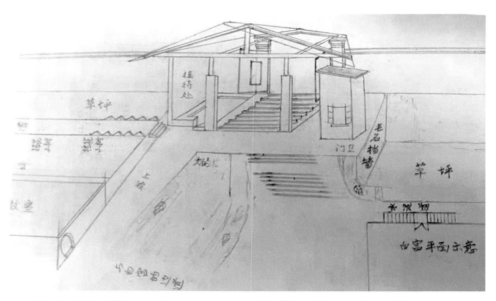

毓英女校学生叶益昭女士手绘 1946—1958 年间毓英校内建筑（作者：叶益昭）
Hand-sketched buildings and school gate of Uk Ing during 1946 – 1958 by Ye Yizhao, a
former student of Uk Ing（Dessinateur: Ye Yizhao）

根据叶益昭女士手绘图制作的电脑彩绘图：1946—1958 年间毓英女校内部全景（作者：涂志钢、郑芝琳）
The colored digital picture of the interior panorama of Uk Ing during 1946 - 1958, realized according to the sketches of Ye Yizhao（Dessinateurs: Tu Zhigan & Zheng Zhilin）

根据叶益昭女士手绘图制作的电脑彩绘图：1946—1958 年间毓英女校校门（作者：涂志钢、郑芝琳）
The colored digital picture of the school gate of Uk Ing during 1946 - 1958, realized according to the sketches of Ye Yizhao（Dessinateurs: Tu Zhigan & Zheng Zhilin）

改制后：新中国的公立学校

1952 年 7 月，按福州市人民政府指示，毓英女校、福州私立寻珍女子中学与福州私立邮电学校女生部合为福州第二女子中学（以下简称"福二女中"），由教会私立初级中学改制为政府公办完全中学。这一举措革故鼎新，可谓是千头万绪待收拾，而今迈步从头越。

: 福二女中少先队员合影（来源：叶益昭）
: The young pioneers of Fuzhou No. 2 Girls' Middle School
: (Source: Ye Yizhao)

蜕变与摸索的年代

遵照中央"谨慎地有步骤地改造私立学校"这一指示，福二女中先暂维持毓英女校原状。待师生人心日渐稳定，觉悟逐步提高，公立福二女中的第一"越"便从跨越招生的阶层限制开始，扩大招生对象，向工农女子开门。福二女中的第二"越"则跨越了性别隔阂。1956 年下半年，福二女中开始男女学生兼收，从此结束了其近百年的女校历史，福二女中亦正式更名为福州第十六中学（以下简称"十六中"）。可以说，改制后的这两项举措让我们看到了真正的教育普及和平等。从理性过渡到顺利改制，再到德育、智育与体育建设初现雏形，十六中在 20 世纪 50 年代末完成了蜕变，进入了新中国教育计划管理体制。

: 福二女中初三乙组毕业班师生合影（来源：叶益昭）
: Teachers and junior high graduates from Class B, Grade 3, Fuzhou No. 2 Girls' Middle School
: (Source: Ye Yizhao)

After Restructuring: A Government-Sponsored School in the People's Republic of China

In July of 1952, following the instructions of the Fuzhou Municipal People's Government, the former Uk Ing Girls' School merged with Sing Ding Girls' School and the girls' department of Fuzhou Private Post and Telecommunications School to become Fuzhou No. 2 Girls' Middle School, indicating its transformation from a private missionary school to a government-sponsored school. The transformation by discarding the old system and introducing the new one was a thorough reform, which, however, should be started from the very beginning with small steps other than bold strides, since it involved a myriad of things to be addressed.

The Era of Transformation and Exploration

Following the instructions of the Central Committee of the Communist Party of China to "reform private schools prudently and step by step", Fuzhou No. 2 Girls' Middle School temporarily maintained the original state of Uk Ing Girls' School. It was until the teachers and students were in a steady state of mind with their gradually awakening political consciousness that the first "stride" of transcending the enrollment limit to specific industries and classes was taken, that is, to expand its enrollment by admitting daughters of workers and peasants into the school. Then followed the second "stride" of transcending the enrollment limit to different genders. In the second half of 1956, Fuzhou No. 2 Girls' Middle School became a co-educational school, thus putting an end to its nearly century-old history as a girls' school. Thereafter, Fuzhou No. 2 Girls' Middle School was officially renamed Fuzhou No. 16 Middle School. The above two "strides" were significant measures to realize popularization and equality of education. From the rational transition to the smooth implementation of restructuring, No. 16 Middle School, with its achievements in the transformation, was under the new management system of China's education program at the turn of the 1950s.

1963 年秋，在福州市教育局的规划下，十六中高中停止招生，集中精力于初中办学。1966 年"文化大革命"开始，学校已建立的教学秩序被干扰，常规教学中断，师生们进入茫然摸索时期。1969 年 9 月，十六中的学生们回到课堂，学校又恢复为初高中兼设的完全中学。1976 年"文化大革命"结束后，翌年即恢复高考，这一举措掀起了学习热潮，教师的积极性也得以重新释放。十一届三中全会召开后，十六中遵循拨乱反正和改革开放的精神，采取一系列措施，让学校各项工作重回正轨。

改革与特色的年代

20 世纪八九十年代，十六中举头奋进，初中教育、旅游职业教育和校办企业三管齐下，皆取得喜人成绩。从其历年中考成绩来看，十六中的初中教育教学成果在市属非重点中学中遥遥领先。校办企业一直朝高水平、高质量方向发展，不仅为学校办学发展提供了强有力的经济支撑，还为国防事业作出了一定贡献。校办企业和旅游职业教育可谓是十六中紧密结合社会发展需求，以教育服务于社会经济发展和职业需求的两大特色，尤以其旅游职业教育为傲。

1986 年 4 月，十六中经福州市教育局批准开办了"福州旅游职业学校"。基于学校领导前期的调研取经、教材编写、师资组建等方面的周密筹备，特色办学大获成功，首届毕业生供不应求。1988 年，已发展为福建省培养旅游服务人才的重要基地。1992 年，被国家教委认定为省级重点职业高级中学。2000 年，被教育部认定为国家级重点职业中专学校。2001 年，成为首批"五年专"试点学校。2002 年因发展需要，福州旅游职业中专学校与福州第十六中学分设，各自独立办学，十六中再次改为初级中学。

福州旅游职业学校 91 届旅游英语毕业生与老师合影
Teachers and Tourism English graduates of 1991 from Fuzhou Tourism Vocational School

In the autumn of 1963, conforming to the policy of the Fuzhou Education Bureau, No. 16 Middle School stopped its enrollment for senior high students and concentrated on junior middle school education. However, with the start of the Cultural Revolution in 1966, the established teaching order was disrupted, and the teachers and students were both at a loss as to how to deal with the interruption of regular schooling. The good news was that in September 1969, the students of No. 16 Middle School resumed classes, and the school was restored to a full high school. The following year after the end of the Cultural Revolution in 1976, the National College Entrance Examination was resumed, which set off a learning boom for students and aroused teachers' enthusiasm. After the Third Plenary Session of the Eleventh Central Committee of the Communist Party of China was held, No. 16 Middle School, following the spirit of bringing order out of chaos and the policy of reform and opening up, took a series of measures to get the school right on its track.

The Characteristic Era of Reform

In the 1980s and 1990s, No. 16 Middle School adopted a three-pronged strategy. It made great efforts to move headway into junior high education, tourism vocational education, and school-run enterprises, all achieving gratifying results. Its achievements in Junior high education went far ahead of other municipal non-key middle schools. As for the school-run enterprises, they had been developing towards a high-level direction with products of high quality, which not only provided sustained financial support for the school's development but also made specific contributions to national defense. Though the school-run enterprises and tourism vocational education were both distinctive in adapting to the social needs of career development and the economic worth of educational service, No. 16 Middle School especially boasted of its achievements in tourism vocational education.

In April 1986, No. 16 Middle School was approved by the Fuzhou Education Bureau to open the "Fuzhou Tourism Vocational School". Thanks to the preparatory work of survey and investigation organized in the early stages by school leaders, coupled with its careful design for textbook compilation and teaching team building, No. 16 Middle School achieved great success in its spectacular vocational education, the first graduates being in short supply to meet the urgent demand of the society. In 1988, the vocational school became an important base for tourism service training in Fujian Province. It was recognized in 1992 by the State Education Commission as a provincial key vocational high school. In 2000, it was recognized by the Ministry of Education as a national key vocational secondary school, and in 2001, it became one of the first batches of pilot schools of "five-year junior college". The finishing touch of the story was in 2002 when Fuzhou Tourism Vocational School was separated from No. 16 Middle School and became an independent school in its own right to meet the needs of its further development. No. 16 Middle School, therefore, has once again become a junior high school.

蓄势与进发的新世纪

历经近半个多世纪的摸索、磨砺与实践，结合社会发展与教育政策之需求，进入21世纪后，十六中开始崭露头角，潜心专注于初中教育，秉持"用完整的现代教育为每一个学生终身发展奠基"的办学理念，承前启后，让德育"扎根"，将其融入社会、历史、生活的大事小情，提倡眼观耳闻，用心领会；谨守"笃实、求知、力行、致远"之校训，吐故纳新，让智育"生花"。学校以学生为主体，以教师为引领，师生素养并重，开创智慧课堂；以提高核心素养为标杆，铸造身体，陶冶精神。排球作为学校的优秀体育项目，不仅让学生们勇于拼搏，团结协作，还积极为国家输送优秀人才，如我国知名沙滩排球运动员薛晨。毓英合唱团作为十六中的艺术名片，屡获赞誉，让学生以歌咏志，借曲抒怀，用旋律来表达对一切美好事物的感悟。

: 沙排世界冠军薛晨回母校指导
: Xue Chen, Champion of the World Beach Volleyball
Competition, coached in Fuzhou No. 16 Middle
: School during her visit to her alma mater.

: 毓英合唱团
: Uk Ing Choir

在21世纪，十六中厚积薄发，已成为仓山区最好的公立初中，先后获得福建省文明校园、福建省首批义务教育教改示范性建设学校、全国青少年校园排球体育传统特色学校等荣誉称号。十六中有了更稳健的脚步，更长远的目光，更博大的胸襟，在自身发展的同时，还打开了国际交流的大门，先后与英国兰开夏郡的圣贝德斯和达拉姆两所中学建立了友好往来关系。此举既能培养学生的国际视野，增强全球意识，又能开辟让世界了解中国优秀、深厚文化的一个窗口。博观约取，积跬步以致千里；厚积薄发，集众力得育英才，这应该就是21世纪福州第十六中学执着的方向。

The New Century with Momentum and Spurt

After nearly half a century of explorations, endurance, and endeavors, combined with its adaptation to the needs of social development and educational policy, No. 16 Middle School has carved out a name with its concentration on junior high school education when entering the 21st century. Adhering to the concept of "laying a foundation for every student's lifelong development with comprehensive modern education", the school requires teachers and students to inherit fine traditions and let them take root in their hearts. Moral cultivation is achieved by using their minds to observe what they see and hear so that they may follow examples of virtuous people in history and then by learning from them, set criteria by personally taking part in the significant events in society or small affairs in study and life. Following the school motto of "honesty, knowledge, practice and progress", No. 16 Middle School eliminates all outdated teaching methods and introduces new ones to stimulate sparks of intelligence. The teachers' attainment and the students' expertise are infused to create an innovative classroom. Its benchmark of consolidating the students' core literacy also attaches great importance to building up body health and cultivating temperament. Volleyball, as an excellent sports event of No. 16 Middle School, has not only played a role in training the students to be brave, united, and cooperative but also delivered topnotch athletes to the national team, one of whom is Xue Chen, a well-known beach volleyball player in China. Uk Ing Choir, a traditional artistic asset of No. 16 Middle School, gathers the students to sing for their aspirations and express their deep feelings toward the surrounding beauty with touching melodies.

For its achievements in the past twenty years, No. 16 Middle School has now become the best public junior high school in Cangshan District, winning honorary titles one after another, such as Fujian Civilized Campus, the First Demonstration School for the Construction of Compulsory Education Reform in Fujian Province and National Traditional Characteristic School for Youths' Campus Volleyball Sports. Furthermore, with its achievements in various aspects, No. 16 Middle School now develops steadily in the new era. Adopting a foreseeing and open-minded attitude, it has opened its door to international exchanges and established friendly relations with two foreign secondary schools, St. Bede's Catholic High School and Durham High School, in Lancashire, the UK, which can not only broaden the students' global vision and enhance their global awareness, but also open up a window for the world to understand China's excellent and profound culture. In the new era, Fuzhou No. 16 Middle School has set out a grand vision by taking every small step towards learning from the outside world. It also makes every prudent decision to nurture talents for society by gathering abundant wisdom.

● 女校课程设置之"变"与"辩"

娲氏姐妹开办毓英女校之时，尚在美以美会福州传教初期。当时作为传教辅助的女校教育以向当地民众传教，达到"教化"为其终极追求。从其创办到步入正轨，再到发展，整个过程如何摆脱文化休克，进行文化调适，达到某种程度的文化交流，各届主理校政者在东西方两种不同文化和思想的碰撞中，必然会介入自己的观点和方式，努力在其间形成一种暂时的稳定与平衡。在苦寻散落各处、支离破碎、细节几乎遗失殆尽的毓英女校办学历史时，我们幸运地梳理出了美以美会内部一场关于女校课程设置的辩论。导向辩论的深层原因是美以美会女性传教士与男性传教士之间、不同女性传教士之间，以及西教士和中教士所代表的不同思想、文化的碰撞。这场辩论不管对于深入了解女校历史本身，还是了解福州美以美会传教内部"教化"与"开化"思想分歧所带来的变化，都极有意义。

升入华南女子学院的女校学生在上数学课（来源：池志海）
Students upgraded from Uk Ing were having a math class in Hwa Nan Women's College (Source: Chi Zhihai)

娲氏姐妹时期的课程设置

娲标礼于 1828 年 8 月生于美国新泽西州伯灵顿县的一户基督教家庭，娲西利既是她的妹妹，也是她传教生涯的终身助手。姐妹一起就读于维明顿市的卫斯理安女子学院，之后一起接受美以美会的派遣，于 1859 年在中国福州创办了毓英女校。女校初办时期，正是鲁弗斯·安德森提出的基督教"三自"理论盛行时期。该理论认为海外传教士的职责就是"教化"，讲经布道，培养本地信徒，最终让他们实现"自养，自为，自宣"。"开化"是"教化"后的自然伴生物，而不是传教士必须做的事情。娲氏姐妹在女校办学宗旨上应该是秉持宗教教育这一原则的，具体执行到女校的教育方向则是培养女信徒，以便一方面拓宽基督教传播的渠道，另一方面为美以美会的乡村日间学校培养师资。

• The Curriculum of Uk Ing: "Transformation" and "Confrontation"

Uk Ing was founded by the Woolston sisters in the early years of the MEC's evangelization in Fuzhou when its educational work was just started and subject to the ultimate goal of evangelizing the natives and implanting Christianity. The Girls' School, involved in different cultures of the East and the West in its various phases from its initiation through gaining its foothold to its growth, was up to different principals, who would inevitably manipulate quite different strategies representing their deviating philosophies during their tenures, to get out of different cultural quandaries and stay in compromise. While we were struggling in piecing together the fragments of Uk Ing's history scattered everywhere and almost lost in detail, a typical case in point concerning the curricular debate arising in the MEC was sorted out, which was deemed rewarding and significant not only for us to dig into the history of the Girls' School, but also to understand changes within the MEC aroused by the dispute of evangelization and civilization. The underlying factors of the debate were very complicated and entwined, embracing the conflicts and deviations between male and female missionaries of the MEC, between different female missionaries, and between missionaries and the Chinese pastors due to their diverse ideologies and cultures.

The Woolstons' Curriculum Design in Uk Ing

Beulah Woolston was born in August 1828 and raised in a Christian family in Burlington County, New Jersey. She went with Sallie H. Woolston, her younger sister and life associate in missionary work, to the Wesleyan Female College at Wilmington and later responded to the call from the AMEC to set up Uk Ing in Fuzhou, China in 1859. The reigning mission theory among American protestants at that time was the "three-self" theory pioneered by Rufus Anderson. The cardinal tenet of the three-self theory was that the purpose of the mission was evangelization by preaching and raising a native ministry that was self-supporting, self-governing, and self-propagating, while civilization, deemed as a natural outcome of evangelization, was not a must for missionaries. The Woolston sisters must have been upholding this principle of Christian education in their supervision of the Girls' School, which, to be specific in its daily practice, was to train female disciples to enhance the possibility of Christian dissemination on the one hand and to train teachers for the Methodist day schools opened in the villages on the other.

女校创立之初，生源基本来自穷苦人家孩子或是孤儿。她们年纪不大，很多学生入学时没有名字，只有像"小妹""大妹"这类绰号。娲氏姐妹先按中国习惯，帮她们取一些寓意较美的名字，如彩云、爱月、紫菊等，首先唤起学生对她们情感上的认同；之后，教她们简单地识字，学会主祷文和十诫，而后慢慢进入读和写的学习；另外还要培养她们讲卫生、勤劳节俭及忠诚的习惯。

林显芳牧师（1936：46-47）记录了女校早期常用的一些教材，比如仿照中国《三字经》编写的基督教《三字经》："自太初，有上帝；造民物，创天地；无不知，无不在……"；还有以福州方言诵读的榕腔《三字经》："元早早，毛天地。凡人物，昧切备。当彼时，务上帝。第一先，第一快……"；当然，专为培养贤妻良母而编写的《女学三字经》更是少不了："为女子，异男儿。要端庄，要整齐。治头髻，理裳衣。立无跛，坐无敧。勿大笑，勿高声。勿任性，勿生嗔。勿般唆，勿插事。节饮食，省言语……"。此外，还有诸如《小学四字经》，主要是教诲孩子要懂得父母之爱。女校日常教学还有《依经问答》《真道启蒙》《圣学问答》《信德统论》《初学阶梯》《圣经》等等。每到圣日，行拜日斋，所用教材为《比利亚问答》《依经问答》或《圣经》。这些过关之后，算术、天文、地理、历史等课程再逐步加入。不过，女校最为重视的还是学生品德、举止和卫生习惯的训练（Robert，1996）。女校学生都必须学习家务，参加劳动，比如学会做绣花等针线活，或者是花圃园艺劳动。娲西利曾撰文记载女校为学生提供花圃供其栽植，学生们不挑拣地之好坏，耐心者播种，性急者植株，但皆勤于除草浇水，种出美丽花朵，读起来颇为生动。

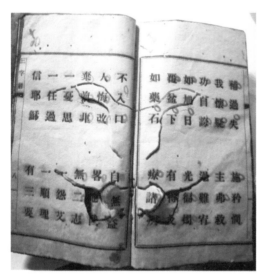 

福州天安堂珍藏的基督教《三字经》（来源：天安堂）
The Christian *Three Character Classic* reserved in the Church of Heavenly Peace in Fuzhou（Source: the Church of Heavenly Peace）

In the nascent Girls' School, most of the school girls were orphans or from the poorest families. They were usually little girls with no names other than "little sister" or "elder sister". To show their affinity with the girls, the Woolstons would first give them what is, from the Chinese point of view, a good name like "Caiyun" (many colored clouds), "Aiyue" (love the moon) or "Ziju" (purple chrysanthemums), and next was to teach them the Lord's prayer and the ten commandments. Finally, they were prepared to do simple reading and writing. School girls were also required to cultivate the habits of hygiene, thrift, and loyalty.

Some textbooks of the Girls' School used in its early days were recorded by Rev. Lin Xianfang. Above all were a few imitative works of the Chinese *Three Character Classic* extolling God's divinity. For example, the Christian *Three Character Classic* wrote, "Since nothing begins, God's been there. Everybody and thing, made by Him; Earth and Heaven, created by Him. He knows everything, and is everywhere..."; similar contents were also embraced in the *Three Character Classic* in Fuzhou dialect like this, "In its earliest, Earth and Heaven, did not exist; Nothing and nobody, in concrete forms. Then and there, God should be. The first one, in fastest being..."; The most indispensable one was *Nü Xue San Zi Jing* (Girls' Three Character Classic), written primarily for cultivating good mothers and virtuous wives, advocating "Born as women, different from men. Be a lady, who is tidy. Buns well-combed, clothes well-groomed. Stand up straight, sit yourself upright. No loud laughter, no noisy speaker. Be not stubborn, be not indignant. No gossip teller, no troublemaker. Plan your diet, eat in quiet...". In addition, there were books to teach children to understand parental love, with *Xiao Xue Si Zi Jing* (The Primary Four Character Classic) being one of them. For their daily lessons, the students were taught with textbooks such as *Yi Jing Wen Da* (The Shorter Catechism), *Zhen Dao Qi Meng* (True Enlightenment of God), *Sheng Xue Wen Da* (Colloquial Catechism), *Xin De Tong Lun* (On Unification of Faith), *Chu Xue Jie Ti* (The Premier of Christianity) or the *Bible*. Students who had gone through these pieces of training were then given courses including arithmetic, astronomy, geography, and history. Moral training, deportment, and hygiene were greatly emphasized. All the girls in the Girls' School were required to do some housework, such as needlework like embroidery, or do some labor work like gardening. One of the writings by Sallie H. Woolston vividly described that a garden on campus had been prepared for the girls, and the grounds were divided among them. Rather than picking and choosing their flower beds, they were all diligent in weeding and watering after sowing, eager for beautiful flowers to come out. However, some could not wait for the seeds to come up and grow, so they picked flowers already in bloom and planted them.

课程设置之"变"

1869年3月，娟氏姐妹因十年办学，体劳神乏，回国休假。将近三年时间，校务皆交予薛承恩夫妇管理。彼时娟氏姐妹应该万万没有想到，她们休假期间，薛承恩夫妇对学校课程进行了重大调整，由此掀起轩然大波，引起美以美会内部的一次重大争执，最终导致美以美会在华办学方针的重大调整。

外籍教师在校园内合影留念
Group photograph of American female teachers in the Girls' School

薛承恩夫人（来源：池志海）
Mrs. Nathan Sites（Source:
Chi Zhihai）

大概是要展示自己的管理成效，薛承恩夫人邀请了1869年福州新按立的七名中方牧师（以下简称"中牧"）到毓英女校观看学生的学期结业考试。中牧们诧异于女校学生出色的表现，同时也发现中国女子教育大有可为，或可培育出既有见识、又有中国传统美德之女性，作为改良社会不良习俗之表率，因此开始关注女校教育。鉴于女校所学科目均为西式学科，中牧们认为女校应增设中国经学，教授中国典籍。薛承恩夫妇因此从香港订购了相关书籍，并为女校聘请了一个中文教师，专门为学生讲授中国经学。1871年底，娟氏姐妹从美国返回福州，发现在自己不知情的情况下，女校已增设了中国经学课程。在为薛承恩牧师所写的传记《东方史诗》一书中，薛承恩夫人（Sites，1912：112）记载，此事最终以薛承恩牧师极力劝说娟氏姐妹采用"让日益壮大起来的本土牧师保持对女校的兴趣"之方式办学而收场，但我们还是能从这种隐晦而间接的表述中依稀感受到娟氏姐妹的不悦。

Transformation of Curriculum Design in Uk Ing

In March of 1869, the Woolstons, after ten years of persevering toil in the Girls' School, returned to the United States for a furlough that lasted almost three years. Rev. and Mrs. Nathan Sites presided over the school during their absence. It was pretty unexpected for the Woolstons that Rev. and Mrs. Nathan Sites would make significant changes in the curriculum, causing a considerable disturbance within the MEC and leading to a substantial dispute that finally triggered the Methodist adjustment of its education policy in China.

Probably to demonstrate her achievements in school running, in 1869 Mrs. Sites invited the seven newly-ordained native pastors to the closing exercises of the Girls' School. Impressed by the intellectual abilities of the girl students, the Chinese pastors found great potential in female education. They became optimistic and concerned about the Girls' School, hoping it could cultivate enlightened women who would play a leading role in abolishing injurious social customs while maintaining traditional feminine morality. Considering that what was given in the Girls' School were mostly Western subjects, the Chinese pastors asked that the Chinese classics be added to the curriculum and taught to the girl students. The Sites hence procured a set of books from Hongkong, and a Chinese scholar was employed to teach Chinese classical literature in the Girls' School. When the Woolstons returned in late 1871, they were appalled to see that the girls had begun their study of Chinese classics while they had not been informed of it. Even though this episode, as was mentioned by Mrs. Sites in her husband's biography, *An Epic of the East*, ended up with Rev. Sites' urge upon the Woolston sisters "the importance of making the school a vital interest of the growing native church", we may still sense the disapproval of the Woolstons from the tactfully evasive expressions of Mrs. Sites.

1879 年，娲氏姐妹再次回美国休假，女校依然交由薛承恩夫妇负责。1880 年 12 月，美以美会信徒张鹤龄因在经商过程中感到"英语必将大行于宇内"（吴巍巍，2007），向美以美会福州主要负责人之一武林吉提出捐资 1 万元，成立一所中英双语书院。1881 年，适逢传教士麦利和在日本传教不顺，转赴福州。麦利和凭借他在日本成功创办美以美会英日双语大学的成功案例，指出"以教会英文学校在该国最占优胜。福州自宜仿行。以培人才而储国用"（林显芳，1936；31）。教会的平信徒们（无教会职位的信徒）也发声赞同（Lacy，1948）。在上下几乎一致的呼声中，1881 年中英双语制的英华书院正式成立。受此影响，中牧们和薛承恩夫妇达成一致，在毓英女校增设英语课程。这一举措掀起了福州美以美会内部关于是否应在教会女子学校中开设英语课程的激烈辩论。以娲氏姐妹和李承恩夫妇为代表的大部分美国传教士均持反对态度，认为此举会削弱传教的力量；而中方牧师及少数美国传教士，如麦利和、武林吉、曾大辟、薛承恩夫妇等则力主其施行，认为此举适合当时中国社会之需求。

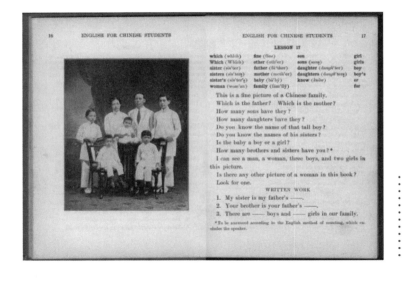

毓英女校英语课程使用材料示例（来源：池志海）
A page from the English textbook for the English course in Uk Ing（Source: Chi Zhihai）

课程设置之由"变"生"辩"

1882 年，娲氏姐妹从美国返回福州，发现薛承恩夫人已在女校增设了英语课程。这一次娲氏姐妹不再像上次增设经学课程时那样勉强接受，而是采取了强硬的手段，撤销了新增设的课程，恢复自己原先的课程设置。娲氏姐妹这一举措引起了中牧们的反对。作为回应，中牧们接管了李承恩夫人负责的女子道学校，根据学生的水平进行分层分班，层级较高者在原有圣经课程外加设英语、经学或医学。1883 年，中牧们向主管毓英女校的美以海外女布道会递交了一份申请，要求改变娲氏姐妹的课程设置，向女校学生提供更为自由开明的教育，比如在女校开设英语课程，并要求布道会派能接受这种开明教育的女教士来主理女校。娲氏姐妹不为所动，依然坚持自己的主张，认为这种教育"不适合女校学生将来所处之境"（McCoy，2004；12），将有害于教会学校的至善追求，对女学生回归自己家园后的生活造成影响。

In 1879, the Woolston sisters went on furlough a second time, and the Sites again took charge of the Girls' School. In December of 1880, an unbaptized Chinese Christian Tiong A-hok, feeling that the English language was bound to be widely used in the world, proposed to Franklin Ohlinger, one of the missionaries-in-chief of the MEC, a subscription of ten thousand dollars for the establishment of an Anglo-Chinese college. It happened that Rev. Maclay's missionary work in Japan was interrupted, and he returned in 1881 to Fuzhou with his successful experience in organizing a Methodist Anglo-Japanese college in Japan. Rev. Maclay pointed out the fact that English Methodist schools were the most successful ones in Japan, so it's appropriate for the MEC in Fuzhou to follow suit to cultivate leaders for China. The laymen (unordained Christians) of the Methodist churches also voiced their approval of this bi-lingual college. Finally, in the unanimous appeal of some leading missionaries and Chinese Christians the Anglo-Chinese College was officially inaugurated in 1881, the impact of whose bilingual mode of education drove both the Sites and Chinese pastors to add English to the curriculum of the Girls' School. This decision had henceforth aroused in the mission field vigorous debates on the need for an English course in a missionary girls' school like Uk Ing. While most American missionaries headed by Sarah and Beulah Woolstons as well as Rev and Mrs. Nathan Plumb opposed it, thinking it would take resources away from the evangelistic task of the mission, the indigenous pastors and some of the Methodist missionaries, such as R. S. Maclay, F. Ohlinger, D. W. Chandler, and Rev. and Mrs. Nathan Sites had spared no effort to provide English courses for the girl students, advocating its conformity to the needs of the Chinese society.

Confrontations Due to the Transformation of the Curriculum Design in Uk Ing

Upon their return to Fuzhou from the United States in 1882, the Woolston sisters found that Mrs. Nathan Sites had opened the English course in the Girls' School. This time, the Woolstons did not settle for the English course as last time they had reluctantly accepted Chinese classics, but took tough measures to cancel the newly introduced English course and restored their original curriculum, which the Chinese pastors heavily disapproved of. They reacted to the Woolstons' reversal by taking over the Woman's Bible Training School run by Mrs. Plumb and dividing the school program into several classes according to the ability of the students so that those competent could study English, Chinese Classics, and medical books. Then in 1883, they prepared a petition for the WFMS, requesting a reformation of the Woolstons' curriculum design and the support for liberal education for Chinese girls. In addition, the Chinese pastors asked that new educational missionaries who favored liberal education be sent to supervise the Girls' School and the course of English be opened to the students. The Woolston sisters opposed those moves and insisted that learning English would "unfit them for life in their future surroundings" and would be prejudicial to the highest good and thus influence the girls when they returned to their homes.

娴氏姐妹所指的女校学生将来所处之境和至善之追求，意即女校初设时的办学宗旨之一：培养女教徒回归家乡担任宗教培训学校的老师，以此加速基督教教义之传播速度与传播范围。一旦在原有的以宗教培训为主的课程中加入英语等课程，将有可能培养出一批有能力介入其他行业领域的精英，从而使其世俗化，削弱其宗教信仰和追求。中牧们的立场则显然不同，他们认为女学生们在神学之外，需要世俗化的教育，以树立自身有能力服务于社会的女性形象，从而让社会改变对女性的定位，进而改变诸如缠足等社会陋习，渐达改良社会之目的。

　　双方各执己见，互不相让，争辩最终白热化。1883年春，在一次领圣餐仪式上，中方牧师貌似无意地略过了娴西利，之后又拒绝娴氏姐妹推举的三名学生入教，僵持之局最终打破。1883年底，娴氏姐妹向美以美海外女布道会递交了辞呈，同时中牧们也向协会提交了一份申请，正式要求协会派出新人选来接替娴氏姐妹。女布道会发文对娴氏姐妹长达25年的海外传教服务表示感谢，同意她们辞职。与此同时，对于女校是否增设英语课程的问题，女布道会用另一种方式间接宣告了它的决定——海外女布道会1883年会代表们经过激烈的讨论，通过了西格尼·特拉斯克医生的一个申请，同意资助毓英女校的一名女学生许金訇赴美学医。

　　这一决定实际上等同于协会对开设英语课程的默许，因为学会英语是赴美留学的先决条件。1884年，海外女布道会派出两名女传教士——凯莉·朱维尔和伊丽莎白·费雪到福州接替娴氏姐妹的位置。毓英女校在美以美会新旧两代女传教士的更替中完成了一次蜕变，从传统保守的循道宗教育开始逐步走向新型的近代开明教育。

By "their future surroundings" and "the highest good" was meant one of the initial goals for the establishment of the Girls' School followed by the Woolston sisters: the education of girls to the point where they could return to their villages and teach others about the gospel so that it could be spread far and wide as soon as possible. They believed that once English was introduced alongside the bible training courses in missionary schools, it might create an elite group capable of joining other fields of work, thus secularizing themselves by weakening their religious beliefs and pursuits. The Chinese pastors, however, held a position entirely different from the Woolstons'. Trying their utmost, the Chinese pastors argued for a liberal education paralleled with missionary education for Chinese girl students to fulfill themselves and contribute to society with their service-oriented femininity, thus wielding an influence on the stereotyped female image prevalent in society at large. In this way, it was possible to do away with irrational social practices such as foot binding and gradually promote social changes.

Hostilities surfaced between those who favored English education for the Chinese girls and those who opposed it, neither giving way to the other. It became a full-blown crisis when in the spring of 1883, the Chinese pastors "accidentally" passed over Sarah Woolston during a communion service and then went further to deny church membership to three students recommended by the Woolston sisters. The deadlock was finally broken at the end of 1883 when the Woolston sisters submitted their resignations to the WFMS, who at the same time received a petition from Chinese pastors asking for new candidates to replace the Woolston sisters. The WFMS documented its thanks to the Woolstons for their 25 years of devoted foreign missionary work and deemed their resignation a great pity. Meanwhile, the WFMS was circuitously coming down on the side of an introduction of English course to the Girls' School—the delegates attending their 1883 annual meeting of the WFMS approved after a vigorous debate the application of Dr. Sigourney Trask and voted to grant Hü King-eng, a young female student of Uk Ing, to go to the United States for collegiate and medical training.

This decision was tantamount to tacit consent to offering English courses, since learning English was a prerequisite for Miss Hü's studying abroad in the United States. In 1884, two female missionaries, Carrie Jewell and Elizabeth Fisher, were sent to Fuzhou to take over the positions of the Woolston sisters. This turnover period witnessed the transition from the old to the new generation of female missionaries of the AMEC and the transformation of the Girls' School from conservative Methodist education to modern liberal education.

由"辩"而"变"，由"辩"见"变"

美以美会内部这一次因课程设置分歧而激发的辩论，其影响和启示是深远且多维的。我们先来看看由"辩"而生之"变"。就辩论所生发的女子教育层面而言，最直接的影响就是以增设英语课程为开端，完善了毓英女校的学科设置，也大大拓宽了女校女子教育的内涵，女校的教育从此走向相对之前更为开明的、实际的近代教育。从之后女校的课程增设情况和校政主理者的教育方针来看，最具意义的变化在于不再将女子设定为传教助手，而是以教育为起始，力求女性地位日益提高，以期逐步与男性平等。

娲标礼之后的毓英主理校政者蒲师母在 1885 年美以美福州年会上，曾就女子教育应该达到一个什么程度公开明确地表明自己的态度，并呼吁"我们必须给予女子等同于男子的教育。男子有初中教育，女子就得有初中教育。男子有高中教育，女子就得有高中教育。男子有大学教育，女子就得有大学教育。如果我们为男子开设医学院，就得为女子也开设。如果我们为男子开设神学院，那么女子也得开设"（McCoy，2004：17）。蒲师母对此教育理念践行甚笃。蒲师母的中文老师是英华男校的学生，有一回他对蒲师母说男生会唱歌，而女生却不会。结果蒲师母立即在毓英女校开设了音乐课程，教女校学生学会识谱，学会唱词，让她们在复活节登台首演，用英语演唱歌曲。笔者写及此处，想到如今十六中的毓英合唱团之名闻遐迩，不禁会心一笑：历史就是历史，纵相隔久远，总有一脉传承。

: 伊丽莎白·费雪，婚后称蒲师母，
: 1884—1889 年间主理毓英校政
: Mrs. Brewster, the former Miss
: Elizabeth Fisher, who presided
: over Uk Ing from 1884 to 1889

The Interactive Effects of "Confrontation" and "Transformation"

The aforementioned confrontation resulting from divergence in the MEC concerning curriculum design deserves a second thought of its ramifications as far-reaching as it was multi-layered. Among the substantive changes following the confrontations, the first and foremost was in the domain of female education, where the conflicts had germinated. With the introduction of English to the course of study, a breakthrough was made in the curriculum design in Uk Ing, whereby initiated in the Girls' School a liberal and practical female education more eclectic than before. As indicated by subjects subsequently added to the curriculum and educational policies adopted by the school supervisors, the most significant change was they no longer trained the girl students solely as missionary helpers but gradually upgraded their social status to equalize with their male compatriots, the first thing being an equitable education for both sexes.

As for the extent to which female education should go, Mrs. E. M. Brewster, the successor who replaced Beulah Woolston to take charge of Uk Ing, had made her attitude clear and openly declared at the 1885 Foochow Conference that "We should give our girls as much education as we give our boys. If we have grammar schools for the boys, we should have grammar schools for the girls. If we have high schools for our boys, we should have high schools for girls. If we have colleges for our boys, we should have colleges for our girls. If we have medical schools for our boys, we should have medical schools for our girls. If we have theological schools for our boys, we should have theological schools for our girls". Mrs. Brewster herself held firm to this educational philosophy. Once, her Chinese language teacher, a student at the Anglo-Chinese College, remarked that Chinese boys could sing, but Chinese girls could not. As a result, Mrs. Brewster soon introduced music to the Girls' School, and the girls were taught to read music and sing in key. Their first performance was to go on stage at Easter and sing in English. Writing here, I am reminded of the famous Uk Ing Choir of today's No. 16 Middle School. I cannot but marvel with a knowing smile at what heritage history should pass down in a continuum from its earliest time!

教育层面另一个明显的"变",则是基督教海外教育不再拘于宗教制约和需求之下的各种衍生课程,而是在实施宗教教育的同时,也开始增设一些传教士们认为符合中国近代社会需求的课程。据最早来福州的三大差会之一美部会记载,教会学校最早于 1888 年开始组织学生开展体育运动,到 1903 年已经开始每两年举办一次田径运动会(Moran,1912:356)。教育领先的美以美会自然不会落后。就毓英女校而言,体育课程的增设即是一个很好的例证。1888 年,白师姑到毓英女校主理校政后,当即增设了体育课程。白师姑为女学生们选择了美国当时流行的体操。

女校课程设置所掀起的辩论风波已让美以美海外女布道会不得不意识到,娲氏姐妹所代表的原教旨主义主导的办学宗旨在中国已行不通,教会教育适当地呼应社会需求才更有助于基督教传播。19 世纪末,以康有为、梁启超为代表的一批有识之士,呼吁通过改革教育制度来引进西方的科学文化,提升女子教育,在社会上引起极大反响,此时亦推波助澜,促使海外女布道会将创办更高层次女子教育提上日程。1904 年,协会派出以柏锡福为首的三人委员会,赴闽考察是否有在福州设立女子大学之必要。经过一系列地理文化调查,决定在福州开设华南女子文理学院。1909 年华南女院招收的五名预科生皆为毓英女校学生。

毓英女校学生在做体操(来源:UMC Digital Galleries)
Calisthenics in the Girls' School(Source: UMC Digital Galleries)

The second dramatic change in the education domain showed that the curriculum of mission-sponsored schools was not just confined to stipulated courses in conformity to the Christian foreign education of the missions, but extended to other courses the missionaries deemed suitable for modern Chinese society. It was evident in the records of the American Board, one of the first three foreign missions arriving in Fuzhou, that athletics were first introduced into China by the missionary schools, with the earliest record at hand being 1888. The practice of holding regular field and track meets twice a year had become firmly established in 1903. The MEC, leading in education in China, would not lag in this respect. A case in point was the introduction of physical training to Girls' School in 1888 when Julia Bonafield was in charge. Miss Bonafield chose for the girls the calisthenics then prevalent in America.

Disputes over the curriculum design of the Girls' School had awakened the WFMS that the fundamentalism-oriented educational principles represented by the Woolston sisters no longer worked in China, and a Methodist education echoing appropriately to the sentiments of the Chinese society at that time would be more conducive to the spreading of Christianity. It so happened that at the turn of the 19th century, some insightful Chinese people led by Kang Youwei and Liang Qichao were appealing for the introduction of Western science and culture through a reformation in the education system, which had struck a responsive chord in society at large for the upgrading of female education. Pushed by the new trends, the WFMS felt it necessary to put the issue of higher female education on the agenda. Therefore in 1904, a three-member committee headed by Bishop Bashford was sent out by the WFMS to investigate the feasibility of establishing a higher institution for female education in Fujian Province. After conducting a series of geographical and cultural surveys, it was decided to open Hwa Nan Women's College of Arts and Sciences in Fuzhou, and in 1909 the college enrolled five pre-higher students, all from Uk Ing Girls' School.

对于我们这些彼时不在场的观众而言，我们还可以看到一些不显山露水，却暗中推波助澜的现象。比如，关于毓英女校课程设置，薛承恩夫人在《东方史诗》一书中提及，在她暂代娲氏姐妹管理毓英女校期间，课程调整皆是薛承恩牧师在中方牧师的要求下拍板决定，女校的事务皆在其掌握之中（Sites, 1912）。对这场风波稍加分析，便可看到几种不同的人物关系。首先，传教士妻子和娲氏姐妹这样的单身女教士是不同的，前者不若后者，可以有自己的传教理念，而是基本执行其牧师伴侣的主张。其次，单身女教士之间亦有传教理念之区别。单身女教士如娲氏姐妹虽主张要改善中国女性之生存状况，但其管理下的毓英女校主要以培养传教助手为主要宗旨。以伊丽莎白·费雪为代表的一批单身女教士则秉持"女性工作为女性"的传教理念，因而其在课程设置和教育方向上都较为开明。更重要的一重人物关系则是中方牧师和西方牧师。回顾前述的整个课程设置之辩，不难发现中方牧师在其中完全不逊于西方牧师的主导作用。翻阅史料可知，1877年福州美以美年会正式成立之际，中方牧师和西方牧师地位完全平等，拥有同等的投票事务决议权，而中方牧师数量超过西方牧师。专注东亚史研究的唐日安教授（Dunch, 2001）认为这是造成这场辩论的重要原因之一。

• 人物撷萃与钩沉

西去复东来：毓英的女留学生们

近百年的毓英女校史，随时随处截取一段时空，抑或选取某个视角，有可言说者何止一二？然限于篇幅，再三估量后，此处仅着重于许金訇、兰醒球二位女士。作为早期的中国女留学生，她们符合本文开篇设定的文化交流视角，尤其是能让我们看到在从清末到民国这段文化交流阈限中动态、螺旋式发展的中西方文化交汇后的反向进程：中国女性进入西方文化地域，复而返回本土文化，或行医济世，或投身教育，以一技之长，尽一己之力。

As readers rather than spectators involved in the historical context, we can easily discern from different sources and perspectives some underlying factors, all contributing to the outburst of confrontation regarding curriculum design in Uk Ing. The records in *An Epic of the East* by Mrs. Nathan Sites revealed that during her administration of Uk Ing for the Woolstons, the adaptation of the curriculum was all implemented by Rev. Nathan Sites at the request of the Chinese pastors, with all school affairs under his control. A brief analysis may help clarify the binary relationships between different people. In the first place were the oppositional roles of missionary wives and single women missionaries like the Woolston sisters. While the latter can insist on their missionary beliefs, the former were followers of their missionary spouses. Then comes the contrasting missionary tenets between single female missionaries. Although the Woolston sisters, as single missionaries, advocated for improving the living conditions of Chinese women, they still preserved in the schooling policy their mission goal of training evangelical assistants in the first place. There were other single missionary women represented by Elizabeth Fisher, however, who adhered to the mission goal of "woman's work for woman", and adopted a more liberal attitude toward the curricula and specific policies in education. Last but not least is the increasingly balanced power distance between the missionaries and Chinese pastors when we look back upon the process of the aforementioned curricular dispute. A dip into history might well serve us that the attainment of the annual conference status of the Fuzhou Methodists meant the equal position held by the missionaries and ordained Chinese pastors. Though each of them had one vote, the Chinese pastors significantly outnumbered the missionary pastors, which was believed to be one of the decisive factors of the curriculum dispute, as was pointed out by Professor Ryan Dunch (2001), a specialist in East Asian history.

• Document Exploration and Interview: Selected Portraits of Female Elites

Reverse Brain Drain from the West: American-Educated Chinese Women from Uk Ing

Over a span of nearly one hundred years, Uk Ing abounded in historical events and figures. Due to the limited space, this article focuses on Ms. Hü King-eng and Ms. Mary Sing-Gieu Carleton, two excellent graduates of Uk Ing. As early female students with study abroad experience, their life and impact echo the intercultural communication perspective of this article, in which the post-liminal rites in the dynamic and spirally developing intersection of Chinese and Western cultures can be especially perceived. These Chinese females were influenced by Western culture, acquired advanced skills, returned to their homeland and dedicated themselves to social work.

仁心圣手，关注女性之许金訇（1865—1929）

　　1884 年春，年方十八的许金訇随同美部会的一对夫妇远赴美国，开启她长达十年的留学生涯。一年多以前，她刚刚结束在毓英女校的学习，到福州岭后妇幼医院担任特拉斯克医生的助手。聪慧沉静的她很快适应了医院的工作流程，成为医生的得力助手。她耐心周到，对病人的关心照顾发自内心。这些特质让特拉斯克赏识不已，做出了一个从未有过的大胆决定：帮助这个中国女孩到美国学医。这确实是个大胆的决定。在此之前，国内仅有浙江的金雅妹被美国麦嘉谛夫妇收养，自幼即学习英语，跟随他们到日本、美国读书（Ye，1994：318）。像许金訇这样，无父母亲属陪伴，只身一人到美国留学的，那当真是第一人。人还未到美国，茫茫大海就给了许金訇第一个考验。惊涛骇浪中，离她不远的一艘轮船翻了，金訇目睹了人生中第一场海难。同行的一位传教士低估了许金訇的求学意志，问她是否害怕，是否想回家。金訇摇头，说从未想过（Burton，1912：26）。所有在异国留学可能遇到的磕绊和考验，出发前金訇便已考虑清楚，做好准备。

　　彼时的金訇尚无丰富的人生与学医经历，也不精通英文。若论起善良聪慧，估计也有不相上下者。那是什么让特拉斯克医生对她格外充满信心呢？或许就是许金訇的那双大脚。那双大脚是父母第一次给予她人生独立选择机会的见证，也是金訇可以留学异国的前提和保证。身为基督徒的父母未让幼时的许金訇缠足。但架不住同伴的嘲笑，金訇同意一位亲戚私下帮她缠了足。当晚，父亲让她自己做一个选择，是缠着足什么也干不了呢，还是不缠足，可以去毓英女校读书，以后当一名老师、医生或是一位健康的母亲？我们不敢断言金訇当时心中所想，只知道她做了一个明智的选择，成为福建省第一个小康家庭出身却不缠足的女孩。在当时，这个选择需要她顶住无数人的议论和指点，但却让特拉斯克医生看见了她独立选择的能力和她的坚强。

许金訇和家人在一起。后排正中站立者为许金訇，右侧坐者为其父亲许扬美。（来源：池志海）
Hü King-Eng, the one standing behind the child, with her family. The man sitting was her father, Hü Yong-mi. (Source: Chi Zhihai)

Hü King-eng: A Professional Doctor Devoted to Women's Health

In the spring of 1884, Hü King-eng, aged 18, following a couple from the American Board of Commissioners for Foreign Missions (the ABCFM), sailed across the Pacific Ocean and set foot in the United States to pursue her overseas study for a decade. Around a year ago, she had just finished her study at Uk Ing Girls' School and assisted Dr. Trask in Liang Au Woman's Hospital in Fuzhou. Brilliant and composed, she quickly adapted to the working environment and became Dr. Trask's right hand. She was genuinely caring for and considerate of her patients. Dr. Trask so appreciated Hü's good qualities that she made an unprecedented decision: She would like to help this Chinese girl receive medical education in the US. This was right a bold decision in that before then in China, only one girl named King Yamei, adopted by the McCartees from the US and acquiring English since little, had followed her foster parents to study in Japan and the US. Hence, Hü King-eng was probably the first to study in the US without relatives to keep her company. On her way to the US, the choppy waters posed the very first challenge. The stormy sea was raging and capsized a ship nearby—it was the very first shipwreck Hü King-eng had ever witnessed in her life. One of her fellow travelers, a missionary, who underestimated her grit and will, asked her if she was frightened and wanted to go home. Hü King-eng shook her head, telling him that she had never had that thought. Before setting off, she had thought through and prepared well for all the potential ordeals that might be happening during her study abroad.

At that time, Hü King-eng was inexperienced both in life and medical education, and neither did she understand English well. In terms of personal qualities and intelligence, there were people on par with her. But what drove Dr. Trask's confidence in her? Perhaps her "big feet". Her big feet were a mark of her very first independent choice in life, and later a premise and support for her overseas study. As Christians, Hü King-eng's parents did not practice foot-binding on their daughter. Her big feet were once scoffed at by her peers. Facing such teasing, one day, she consented to try foot-binding with the help of her relative. That night, her father asked her to make a choice on whether to bind her feet: If she chose foot-binding, she would not be able to do anything later, but if not, she could attend the Girls' School and become a teacher, a doctor or at least a healthy mother when she grew up. It is hard to know exactly what she thought at that moment, but it turned out that she had made a wise choice and became the first middle-class child exempt from foot-binding in Fujian Province. By then, this choice rendered her the center of gossip and even controversy, but her toughness and independence presented in such a situation were perceived by Dr. Trask.

1894 年，许金訇在费城女子医学院完成历时 6 年的攻读，荣获医学博士学位，之后在费城全科医院实习一年，积累、提升其诊疗经验。1895 年，福建省第一位女医学博士回到了她梦想开始的地方——福州岭后妇幼医院，用她出色的医术和一如既往的耐心，帮助患者摆脱疾苦。1896 年，岭后医院莱昂院长回国之际，将医院全权委托给她赞赏与信任的许金訇。1897 年，许金訇主持了一次反对女子缠足大会，会上通过了反缠足七项决议，并提出对坚持不改者施行相应惩罚。这一年，福州岭后医院的许金訇医生声名远播，不仅仅因为她妙手回春、公开呼吁反对女子缠足，更因为她被李鸿章指派为中国妇女代表，参加次年伦敦世界妇女大会。

1899 年，许金訇到城内的娲氏纪念医院担任院长一职，可以说，在这所医院，她付出了毕生之心血。我们从许金訇的医务报告和患者对她的评价可以大概复原她日复一日、年复一年"走马灯"似的工作生活状态：通常天还未亮，就会有焦急的病人打电话来询问各种突发病情。好不容易抽空吃了早饭，方才赶到医院，可能又会因为某个急救电话外出急诊。赶回医院时，来门诊的病人已经苦等良久，许金訇一一耐心问诊，直至下午两三点才吃上午饭。下午又是接二连三的外出急诊，许金訇在福州城里城外地奔波救治，忙到很晚才回家（王尊旺、李颖，2010：157）。这样周而复始的工作强度，连病人见了都忍不住"埋怨"许医生，太不顾惜自己的身体了。可是，当时医院医护人员紧缺，又能有什么办法呢？

许金訇开始在医院开办医护学校。第一批的四个学生在 1905 年毕业了，其中就有她的妹妹许淑訇。医学院为此举办了盛大的毕业典礼，人们对毕业生的表现非常欣赏，不少人表示要把女儿送来这里学医。1906 年，新的医学班准备招生开班。原本教会医院的医学班只有教会学校学生才能报名，但为了让更多的女性同胞得到学医的机会，许金訇突破了这个规定，宣布不需要信教，也不需要文凭，只要通过考试就能被录取。其中有一道考题是"为什么到这里来学医"，被录用者的回答大意是"为了拯救更多没有机会得到医治的姐妹"。

许金訇在娲氏纪念医院开创的医护班正在上课（来源：UMC Digital Galleries）
The nurses attending a training class at Woolston Memorial Hospital（Source: UMC Digital Galleries）

In 1894, Hü King-eng finished her six-year study in Woman's Medical College of Philadelphia and obtained a doctor's degree in medicine. The following year, she served her internship in Philadelphia General Hospital and developed experience in diagnosis and treatment. In 1895, as the first female MD holder (Doctor of Medicine) in Fujian Province, she returned to the very start of her dream—Liang Au Woman's Hospital. There, with her well-commanded medical knowledge and sublime patience, she helped patients get rid of disease suffering. In 1896, when Dr. Lyon, the hospital's chief executive officer, was about to leave, she handed over her administrative work to Hü King-eng, the physician she had always appreciated and trusted. In 1897, Hü King-eng presided over a conference against foot-binding on women. They passed seven resolutions against foot-binding at the conference and proposed related punishment for conservatives. In this year, Hü King-eng's reputation flourished and spread, not just because she rescued patients' lives and made public appeals for foot-binding abolition, but also because she was nominated by Li Hung Chang (the Chinese politician, general, and diplomat of the late Qing Dynasty) as the representative of Chinese women in the International Congress of Women to be held in London the following year.

In 1899, Hü King-eng was appointed to be the chief executive officer of Woolston Memorial Hospital, into which she had put her heart and soul. Based on her medical staff report and the evaluation from patients, her busy working life can be figured out. Usually, before dawn, she would get emergency calls from anxious patients inquiring about all kinds of sudden illnesses. When she finally squeezed out some time for breakfast and had just arrived at the hospital in the morning, she always got house calls. And when she hurried back to the hospital at length, a number of outpatients had been excruciatingly waiting for her. She would then patiently diagnose them. Usually, it was not until two or three o'clock in the afternoon that she could have her lunch. In the afternoon, there would be a succession of home calls for which she had to bustle about the whole city to offer treatment until deep into the night. Her intense but responsible work touched the heartstring of the patients, and they could not help "complaining" that Dr. Hü was too neglectful of her own health. But what else could be done when the hospital was so short of hands?

Hence Hü King-eng started to run a medical school in the hospital. In 1905, the first cohort of students graduated, and her younger sister, Hü Seuk Eng, was one of them. The medical school hosted a ceremonious commencement for them. People appreciated them so much that many decided to send their daughters to receive medical education there. In 1906, the new medical training program started to recruit prospective students. Back then, medical training programs in missionary hospitals could only receive students from missionary schools. But to promote medical education among women, Hü King-eng broke the rule and announced that students were no longer required to be religious or hold a diploma—they could be admitted after passing the examination. In the examination, one of the test items was "why do you apply for medical education?" Most admitted students answered, "I want to save more women who have no access to medical treatment."

到 1920 年，许金訇的医学班共毕业了 47 名医护人员，除了十余人留在娲氏医院，其余去往全国各地医院，治病救人。而许金訇则一如既往，一边救死扶伤，一边向百姓宣传卫生理念，向学生传授医学知识，同时还关注女性地位与健康之提升。从 1899 年至 1927 年，许金訇在福州的娲氏纪念医院，始终秉持希波克拉底誓言之精神，无论男女，无论贵贱，只为病患谋幸福。1927 年，终身未婚的许金訇领着妹妹许淑訇和她们收养的义子远赴新加坡。1929 年，许金訇因脑溢血在新加坡去世。

投身教育，服务女校之兰醒球

2020 年 11 月 25 日，福州第十六中学的毓英馆迎来了一位远道而来的客人——美国知名友好人士、《纽约时报》驻上海分社社长、亚洲区经济与企业高级记者柏凯斯先生。

十六中现任校长郑其瑞赠送柏凯斯先生毓英女校与十六中校徽。
（来源：柏凯斯）
Zheng Qirui, the current principal of Fuzhou No. 16 Middle School, gives the school badges of Uk Ing and No. 16 Middle School to Mr. Bradsher as a present. (Source: Keith Bradsher)

柏凯斯先生千里而来，只因一"绣"而牵。据十六中当时参与接待的李萍老师介绍，挂在家中客厅的一幅"八骏图"刺绣引起了柏凯斯的好奇，这看似有些年代的中国刺绣挂在家中如此重要的位置，引得他忍不住探究背后的故事。母亲告诉他，这是他高祖母杰茜·卡尔顿的姐姐兰玛利亚留下来的东西。据家族史料记载，兰玛利亚曾受美以美海外女布道会派遣，到中国行医。柏凯斯几经周折，终于得知兰玛利亚到中国福州之后的一些情况。苏绣"八骏图"为兰玛利亚养女、毓英女校前校长兰醒球所送。兰玛利亚带回美国后，遗赠给她的侄女，也就是柏凯斯的外婆，最后由柏凯斯的妈妈保留。

By 1920, there were in total 47 medical staff graduating from Hü King-eng's medical program, around ten of whom worked in Woolston Memorial Hospital while the rest served in hospitals around the nation. Hü King-eng, true to form, cured people, promoted health concepts to the public, imparted medical knowledge to students, and concerned herself with improving women's health and enhancing their social status. From 1899 to 1927, Hü King-eng upheld the spirit of the Hippocratic Oath and maintained that she should well serve all patients, male or female, rich or poor. In 1927, the unmarried Hü King-eng set out to Singapore with her younger sister Hü Seuk Eng and their adopted son. In 1929, she passed away there due to a cerebral hemorrhage.

Mary Sing-Gieu Arleton: A Devoted Educator in the Girls' School

On November 25, 2020, the Uk Ing Museum in Fuzhou No. 16 Middle School welcomed a guest from afar—Keith Bradsher, a well-known American friend and the very famous business and economics reporter and Shanghai bureau chief of *The New York Times*.

Mr. Bradsher's interest to visit was triggered by an embroidery. According to Li Ping, the teacher who received him, it was a Chinese embroidery depicting the famous eight horses painting that drew Mr. Bradsher's curiosity. This embroidery was displayed in the living room of his mother's house, so well valued that he could not help exploring its history. His mother told him that it was from his great-great-grandmother, Jessie Carleton's sister, Mary E. Carleton. Based on the family records, Mary E. Carleton was once assigned by the WFMS to practice medicine in China. After much effort, he learned that Mary E. Carleton had been practicing medicine in Fuzhou, and this embroidery was a gift from her adopted daughter Mary Sing-Gieu Carleton, the former principal of Uk Ing Girl's School. After Mary E. Carleton returned to the US, she bequeathed this embroidery to her niece—Mr. Bradsher's grandmother, and finally it was kept by his mother.

2022 年 3 月，我们线上采访了柏凯斯先生，以下内容结合了柏凯斯访谈记录和笔者所查阅的相关资料。

　　1887 年，兰玛利亚受美以美会海外女布道会指派，到福州的医院任职。1888 年 2 月，兰醒球生于福州。当时谁也不知道，她们会有母女之缘。兰醒球两岁时，父母双双去世，成为孤儿，被兰玛利亚收养。1891 年，兰玛利亚通过美国领事馆，办理了正式收养手续，但兰醒球依然保持中国国籍，这也是后来兰醒球能在收回教育权后以中国人的身份担任毓英女校校长的重要前提。

　　兰玛利亚将兰醒球送往美国巴尔的摩女子学院就读。该学院成立于 1885 年，是隶属于巴尔的摩美以美分会的一所女子学校，1913 年后更名为古彻学院。当时巴尔的摩女子学院是一所文科学校，主要是培养、提高学生的整体智识水平，并不着重于某种专业或职业训练。兰醒球在当时表现得极有音乐天分，参加了学校的女子合唱团，成为合唱团首位女高音（赵梅，2019：10）。1912 年，兰醒球从该校毕业，回福州后即穿行于福州各日间学校及读经学校，教授当地妇女读书识字。1915 年，兰醒球任花巷尚友堂女部部长，期间，她积极投入社会服务事务，如举行募捐、反缠足宣传等。1925 年左右，兰醒球在美国哥伦比亚大学攻读社会服务专业的硕士。期间，兰玛利亚回美国募捐，兰醒球作为私人秘书随行，并为此次募捐制作了"中国节日"的手册，内含中国传统节日的文字介绍和插图，现在美国耶鲁大学图书馆、斯坦福大学图书馆、俄勒冈州立大学图书馆及英国西约克郡科克里斯图书馆均有收藏，这应该算非常早期的中国文化传播了。

In March 2022, we interviewed Mr. Bradsher online. The following contains the interview records and resources this article has consulted.

In 1887, Mary E. Carleton was sent to a hospital in Fuzhou by the WFMS. In February 1888, Mary Sing-Gieu Carleton was born in Fuzhou. Neither of them knew that there would be a mother-daughter tie between them. When Mary Sing-Gieu Carleton was only two years old, her parents passed away, leaving her alone in the world. She was then officially adopted by Mary E. Carleton through the consulate of the United States. Although adopted by an American, Mary Sing-Gieu Carleton still retained her Chinese nationality and that was an essential premise for her to be the principal of Uk Ing Girls' School after the Regaining Education Rights Movement in China's modern education.

Mary Sing-Gieu Carleton was later sent by Mary E. Carleton to the Women's College of Baltimore in America. Established in 1885, this college was affiliated with American Methodist Episcopal Mission in Baltimore and later renamed Goucher College. It was a liberal arts school at that time that was not focusing on professional or vocational training but instead aimed to impart general knowledge to its students. Mary Sing-Gieu Carleton was gifted with music. She joined the women's choir in college and was selected to be the first soprano. In 1912, Mary Sing-Gieu Carleton graduated from this college and sailed back to Fuzhou. In Fuzhou, she worked in day schools and bible-training schools and helped local women learn to read. In 1915, Mary Sing-Gieu Carleton was chosen to be the chief of the women and girls' department in the Institutional Church. During her time in office, she actively participated in social work, such as raising funds, opposing foot-binding, etc. Around 1925, Mary Sing-Gieu Carleton pursued her master's degree in social work at Columbia University. During her study period, Mary E. Carleton went back to America for fundraising, and Mary Sing-Gieu Carleton accompanied her as a private secretary. Mary Sing-Gieu Carleton, therefore, made a booklet named "Chinese Festivals", in which Chinese traditional festivals were introduced by words and illustrations. This booklet is now collected in libraries of Yale University, Stanford University, Oregon State University, and Huddersfield Library in Kirklees, the UK. This is an early Chinese culture transmission.

1930 年，兰醒球接受任命，担任毓英女校校长，直至 1940 年离任。十年校长任期，兰醒球以女校之发展、存续为己任，兢兢业业，一日不敢松懈。诚如她在 1931 年妇女年会报告上所说："心怀远大，爱人助人，每日既毕，吾心安乐。"（Carleton，1931：50）其贡献主要体现在以下三个方面。其一，为毓英女校搭建起较为系统完善的课程体系。兰醒球接任校长时，国民政府刚收回学校教育权不久，一些旧的课程需要废除，新的课程则需按要求添设。如何合理地设置课程、课时和考核制度，并合理地保留如英语、音乐、家政等课程，看似简单，实则颇费心神。其二，扩建校园规模，规范学生管理，培养学生社会服务意识。1931 年，女校已经有了三座宿舍楼，按年级高低分开入住。1932 年，家政楼落成，供学生进行家政训练，比如室内布置与陈设、烹调、内务管理等。兰醒球为学校制定了文明、健康、安全的生活守则：不准大声谈笑；不准说话时手舞足蹈；不准涂脂抹粉，一律剪平发；不准私自接待来访者；不准随便吐痰、乱丢杂物。其三，抗日战争期间，兰醒球为女校存续着想，多方筹措，准备船只，护送女校学生撤退到闽清，保存女校教育之火种。而基于女校的家政和社会服务意识训练，女校学生在动荡和硝烟中尚能自力更生，更有毓英学生与华南学生编为女学生军，以赴万里之戎机（林显芳，1936）。

兰醒球（前排右侧）和女校外籍教师
Mary Sing-Gieu Carleton（the right of the front row）and missionary teachers of Uk Ing

In 1930, Mary Sing-Gieu Carleton was nominated as the principal of Uk Ing until 1940. Ten years at the post, she carried the development of Uk Ing upon her shoulder and diligently performed her duties—as she had reported in Women's Annual Conference in Fuzhou, "I love someone more dearly every day, help a wandering child to find his way, ponder over a noble thought and pray and smile when evening comes". Her main contribution resides in the following three aspects. (1) She constructed a relatively comprehensive curriculum system in Uk Ing. When she took over the principal post, the Chinese government had just finished the movement to regain education rights. Some outdated courses needed to be abolished while new courses were required to be added. How to appropriately tailor courses, class hours, and assessments, and in the meanwhile reasonably preserve courses such as English, music and home economics was indeed a huge challenge. (2) She expanded the scale of campus, regulated the management of students, and encouraged students to do social work. In 1931, there were already three dormitory buildings in Uk Ing, where students were accommodated according to their grades. In 1932, the building for home economics was completed, where students received home economics training like interior design, culinary arts, domestic chores arrangement, etc. She also framed school codes of politeness, health, and security for students: no loud laughing; no excessive hand movements while talking; no make-up; uniform haircut; no private visitor reception; no spitting; no clutter littering. (3) She made all efforts to escort students to Minqing county during the War of Resistance Against Japanese Aggression for the survival of Uk Ing and girls' school education. And thanks to the training in home economics and social works in Uk Ing, female students were able to survive the turbulence of war independently and some of them, together with students from Hwa Nan College, formed a female student army and fought on the battlefield.

兰醒球后来在福建协和大学英语系任教，担任过系主任一职。1951 年后赴美国，1966 年去世。访谈结束之际，柏凯斯先生对兰醒球有一番评价，认为她对毓英女校的发展起着重要作用；她作为中国早期的女留学生，无论在当时的中国，还是对于美国来说，都是勇敢开拓的女性。如今，福州第十六中的校史馆中还专门辟出一处空间，极力还原昔日兰醒球校长的办公室陈设，供师生观瞻，不忘兰醒球对女校之孜孜投入。

复原的兰醒球校长办公室（来源：本章作者）
The restored office of Mary Sing-Gieu Carleton, the former principal of
Uk Ing（Photograph by the writer of the present chapter）

从戎再提笔：十六中的功勋老师们

闽地山水，滋育英才。山之厚重，淬炼剑胆；水之灵秀，孕育琴心。在这片土地上，有多少共产党人以其过人胆略和无我精神，历经硝烟战火之洗礼，为新中国的到来努力奋斗，而后，收起锋芒，在和平的祖国，走到每一个平凡又重要的岗位，默默坚守，扎根奉献。福州第十六中学的校园里，就有过他们的身影和足迹。他们的事迹和精神，将不断鼓舞十六中师生昂扬向上、报效祖国之心。

何柏华：战士之心，如柏长青

20 世纪 60 年代在十六中工作学习的师生们，一定都记得他们的何柏华副校长：她面容温和沉静，和蔼大方，从不计个人得失，也从不提自己的过去。认识她的人对她的人品总是钦赞不已；不认识的人也能感受到她身上令人肃然起敬的气场——那是历经数十年解放战争考验，始终坚持的党员战士的胸怀与信念。

Mary Sing-Gieu Carleton later taught at the English Department in Fukien Christian University (now known as the College of Foreign Languages, Fujian Normal University) and was elected dean of the department. In 1951, she moved to America and rested in peace there in 1966. At the end of the interview, Mr. Bradsher highly complimented her, saying that she played a significant part in Uk Ing's development. As an early Chinese overseas student, she was then a brave female pioneer in both China and America. Nowadays, the school history museum of No. 16 Middle School especially displays the restored Mary Sing-Gieu Carleton's office for students and teachers to visit and admire so that her hard work and contribution remain in people's hearts.

From Battlefield to Classroom: Memorable Teachers in Fuzhou No. 16 Middle School

In Chinese culture, the unique features of a local environment always give special characteristics to its inhabitants. Brilliant talents come a long way to Fuzhou's cultural landscape unfolding across the mesmerizing nature of this land. Here, our fearless communist comrades gallantly fought their way out of the war for the establishment of New China. Towering rolling mountains reflect the brave heart of its people and the vast running waters signify their tenderness. With the hard-won peace and tranquillity in this land, they were then unassumingly dedicated their lives to every ordinary but important work to construct the anticipated new life. Fuzhou No. 16 Middle School then witnessed their sweats and toils, deeds and spirits—so far-reaching that every generation in this school will be inspired and encouraged to strive and serve their motherland.

He Bohua: The Heart of a Soldier Lives Long

Teachers and students in No. 16 Middle School during the 1960s would never forget their vice-principal He Bohua—she was always gentle, composed, inclusive, and generous, a woman who embraced the gained and lost, and the come and go. Whoever knows her would admire her moral quality and whoever does not know her can also sense her respectable vibe—it is her everlasting big heart and faith as a communist party soldier through decades of war.

何柏华
He Bohua

何柏华，1911年出生于福州城内文儒坊一户中医人家。药香氤氲，让她可以捧书静读，也让她自小看见了民间疾苦。1924年，何柏华考入福建省立女子师范学校，因思想进步，得到中共地下党组织的关注。据《中国共产党福州地方组织志》记载（石建国，1998：452）。1926年，何柏华加入中国共产主义青年团，为之后成为一名坚定的中共党员做好了思想准备。何柏华深知，要成为一名合格的战士，还必须有过硬的军事理论知识和技能训练。同年，适逢黄埔军校在武汉设立分校，首招女学员，何柏华在共产党人江董琴的推荐下，报名参加考试。1927年1月，何柏华与赵一曼、张瑞华等同批学员一起编入女生队，接受正规、严格的军事理论和技能训练。当时女生队的教官是中共党员恽代英，女生队后来编入国民革命军二十军，军长为贺龙。

1927年8月1日午夜，一声枪鸣，划破南昌城的宁静，中国共产党领导的南昌武装起义打响了！战斗异常激烈，从凌晨2时直到破晓，起义军战士一次一次发起冲锋，突破敌人的火线。枪林弹雨之中，一个敏捷的身影迅速穿行，为战士们传递指挥部的命令；之后，她加入战斗队伍，直至起义胜利。她就是何柏华，南昌起义中唯一的福州女性，于1927年担任国民革命军20军参谋团宣传员，随军开赴南昌，参与起义。经过南昌起义考验的何柏华迅速成长起来，1928年1月，17岁的何柏华正式成为一名共产党员。

南昌起义时期的何柏华（前排右三）
He Bohua（first row，third from the right）during Nanchang Uprising

In 1911, He Bohua was born into a family of Chinese medicine practitioners in Wenru Lane, Fuzhou. The relaxing smell of Chinese medicine provided her with a tranquil reading environment and she also got the chance to witness the bitter life of the coming patients. In 1924, He Bohua was admitted into Fujian Women's Normal School. She was so progressive that she drew the attention of the organization of the then underground Communist Party of China. As written in *Records of Fuzhou Local Organization of Communist Party of China*, in 1926, He Bohua joined the Communist Youth League of China and prepared mentally and faithfully to be a communist party member with solid conviction and will. He Bohua wanted to be a qualified soldier and knew well that she must firmly command military theories and skills. That year, Whampoa Military Academy established a branch in Wuhan and recruited female students. He Bohua, recommended by the communist party member, Jiang Dongqin, took part in the examination. In January 1927, He Bohua, Zhao Yiman, Zhang Ruihua and others were enlisted into the female squad and received formal and rigorous training about military theories and skills. At that time, the commander of the female squad was the Communist Party member Yun Daiying. Later the squad was incorporated into the 20th army group of the National Revolutionary Army under the command of He Long.

At midnight on August 1st, 1927, the thud of a shotgun smashed the silence of Nanchang City and signified the advent of Nanchang Uprising. The battle was extremely fierce. From 2 a. m. to dawn, the uprising soldiers forward the assaults repeatedly and finally broke the enemy's frontline. In the hail of bullets, He Bohua was quite agile in successfully delivering instructions from the military command. Then she joined the battle squads until they won. Since 1927, she was a communicator for the military staff committee and in Nanchang Uprising, she was the only female from Fuzhou. He Bohua grew even faster ever since and in January 1928, aged 17, she officially became a member of the Communist Party.

南昌起义后，部队南下，几番转战后与朱德所率的起义军会师，开拔永定，开展武装斗争。因腿部受伤，何柏华留在了永定，领导一支农民武装队伍，在闽西的崇山峻岭、密林叠嶂中，和敌人斗智斗勇。1929年，何柏华奉命回到福州，负责市委组织工作。18岁的何柏华回到家乡土地时，已积累了一定的斗争经验。一年多的时间里，她领导各种工人和学生运动取得胜利，其中最大的胜利当属收回福州无线电权益运动。1929年，外国公司不甘合同期满后将丧失长期把持的福州无线电，企图通过贿赂国民党政府主管官员，续约15年。何柏华带领工人进行抗争，成功收回了电报权。翌年，何柏华在中共福建省委第二次代表大会上当选为省委候补委员兼省妇女运动委员会书记，数月之后调任上海闸北区妇委书记，同时被派往上海暨南大学读书，以大学生身份配合地下党组织开展工人运动。

革命的道路不可能一帆风顺，在挫折中更能见证革命者的百折不挠。1932年9月，何柏华不幸被捕。尽管遭受严刑拷打，她始终坚守共产党人之气节和信念，严守党的机密，没有一丝屈服。1936年，被上海党组织营救出狱的何柏华回到广东宝安中学任教。她一边积极联系党组织归队，一边自觉履行身为一名革命战士的职责。1937年抗日战争全面爆发后，在广东的东莞、宝安等地，活跃着一位福州女子的身影，她在教很多人唱抗日歌曲。这位才华横溢的女子就是党的革命战士何柏华（陈美者，2015：56），她要以她的革命豪情和爱国思想唤醒国人的斗志。宝安失陷后，何柏华北上寻找党组织，过程十分曲折。她先从宝安前往香港，而后折向泉州，再到浙江，准备由此到安徽寻找新四军。就在此时，组织给她指派了新的任务——加入浙江金华的抗日义勇队。

After Nanchang Uprising, the army marched southward. Undergoing much twist and twine, it finally reunited with the uprising squad led by Zhu De. The reunited army advanced toward Yongding to launch the armed struggle. Wounded in the leg, He Bohua stayed in Yongding thereafter and led a peasant armed force to cleverly fight against the enemy in the forested mountains. In 1929, He Bohua was dispatched back to Fuzhou to take charge of the work in the municipal committee of the Communist Party of China. The then 18-year-old He Bohua had accumulated enough fighting experience when she returned to her hometown. In around one year, she successfully led a number of labor and student movements, and the most successful one was the regaining radio broadcasting rights movement. In 1929, the foreign companies were unwilling to lose control over Fuzhou radio broadcasting after the expiration of the contract and intrigued to bribe the serving officer from the Chinese Nationalist Party for a 15-year extension. He Bohua then organized the workers to wrestle with them, and successfully regain the radio broadcasting rights. In the next year, she was elected the alternate member of the provincial committee and secretary of the provincial committee of the women's movement in the 2nd provincial congress of the Communist Party of China. Several months later, she was transferred to be the secretary of the committee of the women's movement in Zhabei District, Shanghai. In the meanwhile, she was also sent to receive education in Shanghai Jinan University and to assist the campaign launched by the underground Communist Party of China as a university student.

Revolution is bound to be chequered but all the setbacks light up the invincibility of revolutionists. In September 1932, He Bohua was unfortunately arrested. Although she was cruelly inflicted, she abided by her integrity and faith as a Communist Party member, strictly kept the Party's secrets, and did not ever surrender. In 1936, after being rescued by the Communist Party in Shanghai, He Bohua went to teach in Guangdong Bao'an Middle School. She actively contacted the Party organization to rejoin the Party while fulfilling her duties as a revolutionary soldier. After the full-blown outbreak of the War of Resistance Against Japanese Aggression in 1937, she earnestly engaged in the resistance in Dongguan, Bao'an, etc. and taught people to sing anti-Japanese war songs. She was arousing her compatriots' fighting will with her conviction in revolution and her deepest love to the nation in danger. When Bao'an was occupied, He Bohua headed north to rejoin the Party regardless of the dangers and hardships. She first moved from Bao'an to Hong Kong, then to Quanzhou, Zhejiang, and prepared to join the New Fourth Army in Anhui Province. At that moment, she was assigned a task from the Party—to join the anti-Japanese military volunteer squad in Jinhua, Zhejiang Province.

这支抗日义勇队由著名抗日将领李友邦创立。中共地下党组织非常关心和支持这样的正义队伍。何柏华在抗日义勇队堪称"文武双全"，既能执行战斗任务，又能用家传医术救治受伤将士。暨南大学文史系毕业的她，还同时担任抗日义勇队少年团辅导员。她熟练地说着闽南语、粤语、客家话，和队员们亲切交流，赢得了大家的尊敬，"书写了两岸同胞携手抗日战争的历史一页"（卞军凯，2017）。抗日战争胜利后，何柏华随义勇军东渡台湾，先后在几所中学担任教员。

1949 年，何柏华与家人被迫离开台湾，回到大陆。1951 年，何柏华终于又回到了家乡福州，自此一直从事文教工作。1962 年至 1971 年，何柏华在福州第十六中学担任副校长，直至退休。1974 年，63 岁的何柏华走完了她波澜起伏的革命之路。作为南昌起义中唯一的福州女战士，何柏华被《福州党史通讯》誉为"福州妇女界的骄傲"。十六中也没有忘记过她，她的英雄事迹被书写在校史馆中，激励着一代代的十六中人。

2021 十六中师生赴八一南昌起义纪念馆追寻老校长何柏华的足迹
Teachers and students from Fuzhou No. 16 Middle School in memory of He Bohua in Nanchang Uprising Memorial Hall, 2021

杨帼英：福建的阿庆嫂

现代京剧《沙家浜》中春来茶馆老板娘、党的地下联络员"阿庆嫂"在中国可谓家喻户晓，她智斗刁德一，掩护革命同志，"沉着机智有胆量"的形象深入人心，堪称"巾帼英雄"。作为艺术形象的"阿庆嫂"，并非对应现实中某一个具体的人物，而是无数像阿庆嫂这样，在党的革命事业中发挥作用、平凡却不普通的地下联络员。20 世纪 70 年代任职于福州第十六中学的教务处副主任就曾是一位"阿庆嫂"式的人物。她就是杨帼英，是十六中人心目中"福建的阿庆嫂"。

Founded by Li Youbang, the famous general during the War of Resistence Against Japanese Agression, this squad was well supported by the underground Communist Party of China. There, He Bohua was brave and intelligent——she not only carried out military tasks but also treated the wounded soldiers with her family medical practice skills. Graduating from the Department of Literature and History in Jinan University, she also served as the counselor of the young volunteer squad. Fluent in Hokkien, Cantonese, and Hakka, she cordially communicated with squad members and gained respect from them. Bian (2017), a reporter from *Fujian Daily* highly praised her, saying that "she wrote the history of the consolidated cooperation between the Mainland of China and Taiwan compatriots". After the victory of the war, He Bohua sailed to Taiwan with military volunteers and taught in several middle schools.

In 1949, He Bohua and her family were forced to leave Taiwan and return to the Chinese Mainland. In 1951, she eventually moved back to her hometown Fuzhou and continued her education career ever since. Between 1962 and 1971, she was the vice-principal of Fuzhou No. 16 Middle School until she retired. In 1974, He Bohua, aged 63, finally finished her revolutionary path full of ups and downs. As the only female soldier in Nanchang Uprising, He Bohua was regarded "the pride of Fuzhou females" by *Fuzhou Communist Party History Newsletter*. He Bohua will never be forgotten. Her heroic deeds are recorded in the school history museum and encourage every generation of Fuzhou No. 16 Middle School.

Yang Guoying: Fujian's Aunt A Qing

The modern Beijing opera *Shajiabang* depicts the household famous character "Aunt A Qing", the proprietress of Chunlai Teashop and communicator of the underground Communist Party of China. She intelligently fought against Diao Deyi, and covered her revolutionary comrades. Her image of being a composed and witty woman has left a great impression on everyone, making her a national heroine. As an artistic character, Aunt A Qing does not particularly refer to a specific person. Instead, she represents the innumerable plain but great secret communicators that play an important part in the revolution. Yang Guoying, the deputy dean of the Academic Registry Office in Fuzhou No. 16 Middle School during the 1970s was undeniably an "Aunt A Qing" in Fujian Province.

：杨帼英
：Yang Guoying

　　杨帼英 1927 年生于湖南湘潭这一湘中灵秀之地，亦是中国红色文化的摇篮之一。想来这位"辣妹子"自小对家乡的众多能人志士、革命先驱是钦佩景仰的，或许这就是她走上革命道路的内驱力之一。1941 年，杨帼英到省立南平高级中学就读后，认识了一些思想进步的同学，开始参加他们组织的读书活动，传阅《西行漫记》《大众哲学》等进步书籍，打开了认识新世界之门。1945 年抗日战争胜利后，闽江工委大发展，需要新生力量的加入，于是杨帼英在 1946 年到了福州，先后学习了《论持久战》《论解放区战场》等党的先进理论知识，愈发坚定了自己的信仰，怀着热切而向往的心情，提笔写下了自己的入党申请书。

　　1946 年 9 月，杨帼英加入中国共产党，走上了革命道路。曾就读于省立南平高级中学的她，对南平的地理人情较为熟悉，当时主要在南平进行地下革命工作。杨帼英先是担任城工部南平县委宣传委员，将自己从福州带来的《文萃》《新观察》《大公报》《解放区文艺》等进步书刊传播给当地中学的进步学生。1947 年，杨帼英从南平到福州，接受新的任务。回到南平后，杨帼英和母亲一起开起了一家长沙饭店，担任长沙饭店交通站负责人。在这份工作中，她表现得既机智又谨慎，中转、传送了许多重要物资和文件，也迎接、安排了很多同志会面，从未有过差错。长沙饭店成为福州、南平两地信息和人员传送的重要秘密枢纽。

　　中共党史人物传编委会组织编撰的《开国将士》一书中对杨帼英做出如下评价："杨帼英同志在战火纷飞和白色恐怖的岁月里，毅然投身于革命的滚滚洪流中。参加革命后，迅速成长为一名合格的革命战士，为推翻三座大山、建立共和国立下了功劳。"

Yang Guoying was born in the picturesque cradle of the Chinese revolution, Xiangtan, Hunan Province in 1927. She must have admired the revolutionary heroes from her hometown so much that she got inspired to step onto the path of revolution. In 1941, Yang Guoying studied in Provincial Nanping Senior High School and made acquaintance with some student comrades with progressive minds. Then she joined their reading activities and read progressive books such as *Red Star over China*, *Popular Philosophy*, etc., which greatly broadened her horizons. After the victory of the War of Resistance Against Japanese Aggression, Minjiang Working Committee was rapidly developing and expecting youth participants. So, in 1946, Yang Guoying arrived in Fuzhou and studied progressive theoretical works of the Communist Party, such as *On Protracted War*, *On the Battlefield of Liberated Areas* and so on. Through these theoretical readings, Yang Guoying became more firmly convinced of her faith in the Communist Party. Yearning and passionate, she wrote her application to join the Party.

In September 1946, Yang Guoying was accepted to be a member of the Communist Party and embarked on the road to revolution. Once a student in Provincial Nanping Senior High School, Yang Guoying was quite familiar with the geography and local life in Nanping. Therefore, she was mainly engaged in the underground activities there. Yang Guoying was at first the communicator of the Party Committee of the Communist Party of China in Nanping County, and brought to progressive high school students valuable books like *Essays*, *New Observation*, *Ta Kung Pao*, and *Literature in Liberated Areas*. In 1947, Yang Guoying went up to Fuzhou for her new task. Returning to Nanping after accepting the task, Yang Guoying ran a Changsha Restaurant with her mother and she was in charge of the undercover communicating center set in the restaurant. She was so cautious and artful that nothing ever went wrong in the transferring and transmission of important supplies and files, as well as in the reception and arrangement of meetings. Changsha Restaurant became a secret hub for information and members back and forth between Fuzhou and Nanping.

In *National Founders* written and compiled by the Committee of the Communist Party Figures Record, Yang Guoying was highly evaluated—"In the raging flames of the war and the intimidating white terror, Yang Guoying bravely committed herself into the massive flood of revolution, grew rapidly into a qualified revolutionary soldier and contributed greatly to overthrowing feudalism, imperialism, crony capitalism and the founding of the People's Republic of China".

新中国成立后，杨帼英以一如既往的奉献精神，奔赴每一个需要她的工作岗位。20 多年来，她所服务过的部门主要包括宣传部、妇委会、各单位工会、教育部门等。工作中的杨帼英爱憎分明、廉洁奉公，保持和发扬了党的优良传统，时刻同党中央保持高度一致，多次受到上级的肯定和奖励。2019 年，杨帼英荣获中共中央、国务院、中央军委颁发的"庆祝中华人民共和国成立 70 周年"纪念章。

自 1972 年 9 月起，杨帼英在福州第十六中学任教务处副主任。1976 年 12 月，杨帼英在十六中离休，但她在地下工作中不畏艰险、沉稳机警，被誉为"福建阿庆嫂"的革命事迹一直在十六中传颂。离休后的杨帼英时常被邀请回到十六中，为师生们讲述她的故事。2009 年 9 月 16 日的《福建日报》还专门报道了 83 岁的老地下党员杨帼英回到十六中，为十六中学子们讲述当年通过开饭店从事地下工作的经历。2021 年，十六中的师生们还自编自导自演，拍摄讲述"福建阿庆嫂"杨帼英同志地下工作的纪录片，对外弘扬其无畏的革命精神。

钟英希：开出"三枝花"的校长

1979 年，团级退伍转业军人钟英希刚从济南回到福州，就风尘仆仆地赶往福州第十六中学，因为他迫不及待地要看一眼这个他即将工作生活的校园。30 年的军旅生涯，雷厉风行、不辱使命的作风已融入他的血液。1934 年出生于福建连江的钟英希，此时正好 45 岁，正是精力充沛，可以凭借在军队所受教育、所得经验回馈社会的时候。

：钟英希
：Zhong Yingxi

After the founding of the People's Republic of China, Yang Guoying still held on to her spirit of devotion and worked diligently in every position that needed her. For over 20 years, she had served in Publicity Department, Women's Committee, various trade unions, education departments and so forth. She was wholehearted, clean and moral, stood firmly aligned with the Central Committee of the CPC, and therefore received recognition and awards many times. In 2019, Yang Guoying was awarded a commemorative medal in celebration of the 70th anniversary of the founding of the People's Republic of China by the CPC Central Committee, the State Council, and the CPC Central Military Commission.

In September 1972, Yang Guoying was assigned the post of deputy dean of the Academic Registry Office in No. 16 Middle School. In December 1976, she retired from the position. Her honorable deeds of calmly and wittily carrying out undercover tasks during the revolution are still widely told in the school. After retiring, she was often invited back to school and told her story to teachers and students. On September 16, 2009, *Fujian Daily* specially reported her speech about her working experience in Changsha Restaurant in No. 16 Middle School for the underground Communist Party of China. In 2021, students of the school recreated and brought to life the undercover activities of Yang Guoying—the "Aunt A Qing" in Fujian by means of the music video. The video was published to promote her fearless spirit of revolutionism.

Zhong Yingxi: The Realization of Three Blooming Dreams in No. 16 Middle School

In 1979, Zhong Yingxi returned to Fuzhou after retiring from the army regiment in Jinan. He visited Fuzhou No. 16 Middle School immediately as he arrived because he was so desperate to have a look at the campus on which he was going to work. Thirty years of military service had engraved a man of action, mission and responsibility into his soul. Born in Lianjiang, Fujian in 1934, Zhong Yingxi was then a 45-year-old man in his prime day, who was able to give back to the community with all his education and experience gained from his military life.

1949 年 11 月，16 岁的钟英希就参加了中国人民解放军，1953 年 11 月在上海入党。1954 年，钟英希参加国家统一考试，25 门课程，门门都是 5 分。像这样的优等成绩，在当年参加考试的 3 000 多人中，仅有 14 人。因此，重视人才的军校将钟英希作为优秀毕业生留任学校。在高射炮兵学校，钟英希担任军部参谋，协助校长，关注学员的训练情况和思想状况。在军校的培养和个人努力之下，钟英希的军旅生涯，不管作为学员还是干部，表现得都非常出色——自 1950 年 4 月起共立三等功 5 次、四等功 3 次——这让他在 1979 年转业回到福州，即将踏上福州第十六中学这个新岗位时也充满了使命感和责任感。

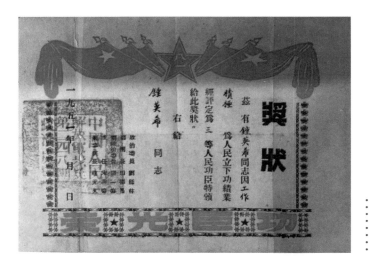

钟英希获三等人民功臣奖状
A certificate of Third-class Merit of People's Hero granted to Zhong Yingxi

1979 年 12 月 26 日，钟英希就任福州第十六中学党委书记、校长。他感到肩上责任重大。学校作为教育基地，是否能够培养国家需要的接班人和有用之才，学校教育是否能够正确贯彻执行党的教育方针，是头等大事。因此，他向学生提出了"四个学会"的校训：学会做人，做个好人，做个有益于人民的人，做个有骨气的中国人，做个善良真诚的人；学会学习，向书本学习，向实践学习，向有本事的人学习；学会办事，父母、老师交代的事要办好，同学互相帮助要办好；学会一技之长，发现和找到自己的兴趣爱好和特长，精通一门技能，可以服务、回报社会。这"四个学会"不乏深刻的内涵，且让人一听就懂，朴实无华，和学生的日常生活、学习紧密结合，易于学生们互相学习和促进。

与此同时，钟英希也非常重视调动教师的积极性，进行师资队伍建设。在这项工作上，钟英希认为要发挥校长的"非权力因素"。首先校长要以身作则，以优秀的品格赢得老师的信赖；校长对老师也要有诚挚的情感，要关心老师的工作状态，尽力解决老师们的实际困难。在任 15 年来，他在师生队伍建设上一丝不苟地践行自己的理念，使学风、教风都不断提高，师生配合日益默契，十六中的初中教育水平也因此一步一个台阶，中考成绩年年在全市名列前茅，成为钟英希在十六中栽培的"第一枝花"。

In November 1949, the 16-year-old Zhong Yingxi participated in the People's Liberation Army of China and joined the Communist Party in Shanghai in November 1953. In 1954, Zhong Yingxi took part in the national examination and obtained full marks in all 25 courses—there were only 14 students out of 3,000 who had achieved such a high score record. Therefore, Zhong Yingxi was invited to teach as an excellent graduate in the college. In Anti-Aircraft Artillery College (nowadays The Airborne Troops Academy of Air Force), Zhong Yingxi was assigned the post of a staff officer in the military force, assisting the principal in guiding students' training and the state of their minds. It is clear that with the cultivation offered in the army and his effort, Zhong Yingxi was exceedingly excellent both as a student and a cadre. He achieved third-class merits five times and fourth-class merits three times, which gave him a sense of obligation and responsibility when he was transferred to civilian work and returned to Fuzhou in 1979 to take the new position in No. 16 Middle School.

On December 26, 1979, Zhong Yingxi was nominated the Party secretary and principal of Fuzhou No. 16 Middle School. In that post, he felt the responsibility on his shoulder. Schools, as the base for education, should prioritize the concern on whether the education policy proposed by the Party can be correctly implemented and whether the whole nation has talents for its development and modernization. Hence, he put forward the "four-learning" school motto: learning to be a man, to be a good citizen, to be good for people, to be a Chinese with integrity and to be moral and honest; learning to learn from books, from practice, and from the talented; learning to handle the work assigned by parents and teachers as well as the help needed by your mates; learning to master a skill, to find your interest and strength, and to serve and give back to the society. There is a profound connotation embedded in the motto. Still, it sounds plain, easy to understand, and closely connected with students' study and life, which could accelerate students' mutual learning and self-developing.

In the meantime, Zhong Yingxi attached importance to teachers' motivation, so he began to build an excellent teaching team. He maintained that the principal needed to influence teachers without imposing authority. First of all, the principal ought to lead by example to gain the trust of teachers; the principal should be sincere to teachers and care for teachers' work and life, and indeed try his best to help them with their problems. During his 15-year term, he meticulously carried out his ideas and improved the school's learning and teaching. Because the teachers and students made a great team, the junior high school education in No. 16 Middle School reached a higher level and ranked in the top percentile in Senior High School Entrance Examination among schools in the whole city. This was his first blooming dream in Fuzhou No. 16 Middle School.

然而钟英希并未就此停下脚步。十六中还有一枝快要枯萎的"花"需要灌溉，那就是1973年开办的校办工厂。当时校办工厂因效益不佳，已是摇摇欲坠。对此，钟英希一方面鼓励老师们进行科研，多做研发；另一方面则团结学校整个领导班子，共同努力，到校外拓展业务，发展合作。到了20世纪80年代初，十六中的校办企业已享誉福州。1989年，仪器仪表成套设备厂受国家国防科工委的委托，为"亚洲一号"通信卫星生产加注设备。卫星发射成功后，十六中收到从西昌发射中心发来的贺电、贺信和锦旗。烟山软件服务部每年开发的软件在90年代更是走在时代前列，扬名国内外。校办企业的成功不仅为社会作出了较为突出的贡献，也为学校提供了充足的后勤保障，同时也提高了教师们的凝聚力和科研创新能力。这就是钟英希在十六中灌溉的"第二枝花"。

1985年，钟英希开始培育十六中的"第三枝花"——创办旅游专业职业高中。这个提议在学校第一届第二次教代会上获得通过后，钟英希立刻组建了"筹备小组"，开展四项准备工作。第一，走入社会调查，进行"人才需求预测"，得出社会第三产业人才有很大需求空间的结论；第二，与福建温泉大厦筹建处接洽，达成了联合办学的协议；第三，外出访问取经，学习其他地区旅游高职办学的经验；第四，组建师资队伍，培训本校老师，并引进外来的专业人才。1986年，"福州旅游职业学校"正式招生办学，自此不断为社会输送专业思想稳定、专业知识较全面、专业技能扎实的旅游、饭店服务人才。《光明日报》曾报道了十六中的这一成功实践，提高了学校的社会知名度。更重要的是，在认真探索、严格办学的过程中，学校也涌现了一大批先进教师和优秀工作者，成为学校可持续发展的宝贵财富。钟英希的这"第三枝花"可谓开得绚烂夺目。

旅游职业学校学生的形体训练课
Body-shaping course for students of Tourism Vocational Technical School

至1994年离休之际，钟英希在福州第十六中学担任书记、校长已整整15年。他始终表现了一个军人的胆略和气质，以开拓、改革、创新的精神，把学校办学水平推上新的台阶，得到广大师生的好评和拥戴。他曾任福州市人大代表、福州市政协委员。1989年被评为全国教育系统劳动模范，被授予"人民教师奖章"。

However, Zhong Yingxi stepped up furthermore. He noticed that the school factory founded in 1973 needed to be brought to life. The factory was almost facing a shutdown because of its poor performance and low benefits. For that, Zhong Yingxi on the one hand encouraged teachers to do more research and creative work and on the other hand consolidated the school's whole leading group to go outside the school to expand the business and seek collaboration. In the early 1980s, the school factory was already well-known in Fuzhou. In 1989, its Instrumentation Manufacturer was authorized by the Commission of Science, Technology and Industry for National Defence of the People's Republic of China to produce filling equipment for the AsiaSat 1 communication satellite. After the successful launching of the satellite, No. 16 Middle School received a congratulatory message, a congratulatory letter, and a silk banner from Xichang Satellite Launch Centre. Every year in the 1990s, the software developed by its Yanshan Software Service Centre was ahead of the time and gained fame at home and abroad. The school factory not only contributed to the society, but also provided the school with sufficient logistical support. At the same time, solidarity among teachers and their creativity were also promoted. This is Zhong Yingxi's second blooming dream in No. 16 Middle School.

In 1985, Zhong Yingxi started establishing a tourism vocational high school. This proposal was passed in the second congress of the first school staff meeting. Then Zhong Yingxi immediately set up a panel in charge of four preparations. Firstly, the panel suggested talent demand forecasting by carrying out social surveys and concluded that the society needs talents for the service industry; secondly, the panel contacted the preparation group of Fujian Wenquan Building and reached an agreement on a joint training program; thirdly, the panel visited other tourism vocational schools and accumulated related experience; fourthly, the panel decided to form a well-trained teaching group in school and bring in professional talents. In 1986, Fuzhou Tourism Vocational Technical School was open to student enrolment. Since then, this school has constantly nurtured professional, moral, and skillful talents in tourism and hospitality for society. *Guangming Daily* once reported this successful practice which increased the school's popularity. More importantly, during the exploration and operation, there sprung up a stream of excellent and progressive educators, which are precious for the school's sustainable development. This is Zhong Yingxi's third glowingly blooming dream.

Until his retirement in 1994, Zhong Yingxi was the Party secretary and principal of No. 16 Middle School for 15 years. As the school history museum lauds, "as a soldier, he demonstrated resourcefulness and courage, and with his spirit of exploration, reform, and innovation, he promoted the education of the school to a new era, which whereby renders him respected and appreciated by teachers and students". Zhong Yingxi was once the deputy of the Fuzhou People's Congress and a member of the Fuzhou People's Political Consultative Conference. In 1989 he was regarded as the Model Worker in national education and awarded the "Teacher of the People" medal.

● 结语

　　历时近百日，回望百多年。行文至此，行将收官，我又想起十六中的"绿色名片"，那棵曾被我错过的百年流苏树。第一次来到烟台山麓时，我步行在幽静的麦园路上，一边寻觅这所百年历史的学校，一边在心里勾画它的样子，尤其是那棵百年古树，名闻遐迩的"飞雪流苏"——传闻每逢花开，叶如华盖，花似浓云。轻风吹过，幽香四溢，飞花如雪，清丽宜人。又听闻这样的百年流苏树在福州仅有三棵，一棵在三坊七巷的衣锦坊，一棵在沈葆桢故居中，另一棵就是在十六中校园内了。如此古树名木，怎不让人心向往之。

：福州第十六中：园林式校园
：Fuzhou No. 16 Junior High School: A garden-like campus

：校园内的毓英亭
：Uk Ing Pavilion on campus

　　迈进十六中校园，沿着大斜坡由南往北而下，一眼望去，发现竟无一条直道，几条小径分往不同方向，幽幽地向校内延伸。石阶边、通道旁摆放的盆栽已是普通点缀，众多的名贵古树看似自拥一处，实则匠心布局，高矮错落，将几座主体大楼环抱，避阳遮阴，赏心悦目。东边修竹繁密，西边夹竹桃树成荫，加上校友捐资新建的"毓英亭"，浑然一个小型植物园，如果说是校园，那也是一个园林式校园。当时只知赞叹，如今从毓英校史中跋涉而回，便知这是当时女校的"闺阁庭院"式布局，只是彼时是作为天然屏障，以防外人窥探，而现在则是天然氧吧植物园，可供观赏，可供标本采集。

• Concluding Remarks

For nearly one hundred days and nights, I have been immersed in the history of No. 16 Middle School, covering more than one hundred years with its past and present. Now it's time to finish my writing. Despite all my rigorous manner and careful wording, it still concerns me that I might have missed something important, just like my experience of searching for the hundred-year-old fringe tree, a well-known green symbol of the school. For the first time last year, when I walked and looked for No. 16 Middle School on the Maiyuan Road, lying and extending quietly along the foot of Yantai Mountain, I was wondering about what this century-old school would be like, while more about the century-old fringe tree famous for its scene of "snowy flying fringes". It is said that every year when it is in full bloom, its spreading crowns are covered with drooping clusters of pure white, wispy and cloudlike flowers. If the breeze blows, the fresh fragrance of the flowers will overflow with their fringy panicles flying like snow in the sky. I also heard that there are only three century-old fringe trees in Fuzhou, with one in the Yijin Lane of the Three Lanes and Seven Alleys, another in Shen Baozhen's former residence, and the third the one in No. 16 Middle School. For such an ancient and famous tree, how can one stop yearning for a look at it?

Stepping into No. 16 Middle School, I walked down the big slope falling from south to north. To my surprise, I could not find at first sight a way straightly leading to somewhere but several divided paths, wandering and winding in different directions on the campus. Rather than those potted plants and flowers placed along the paths or on the stone steps, what enthralled me were those ancient trees standing in profound tranquility on campus, seemingly to keep themselves in repose and peace. Scattered here and there, high and low, the ancient trees were in ingenious layout around the main buildings to provide shade, quite pleasing to the eye. The east side of the campus was lined with elegant bamboos, while on the west side, there were dense oleander trees making a pleasant shade. I found myself in a small botanical garden. If it is a campus, it is a garden-like campus. A unique charm that had added the most important touch to the campus is the delicate newly-constructed "Uk Ing Pavilion", a donation by alumni of Uk Ing. It might be said that the bewitching complex of nature and craft had constituted a "boudoir courtyard" layout of the campus. Knowing nothing before my exploration of its past, I could say nothing but marvel at what I saw then. The "boudoir courtyard" layout of Uk Ing, originally arranged as a natural barrier to avoid outsiders from prying, is now a natural oxygen bar, or a botanical garden either for viewing or for specimen collection.

从毓英馆沿路而行，先是看见百年榕树独木成林，南洋杉掩映相伴。百年香樟树绿荫如盖，树上有多年前老式的打铃钟，还有百年石栗、百年龙眼、番石榴、桂花树、印度橡胶树、白花羊蹄甲……然而，唯独未见我心心念念的流苏树。后来才知，我几次穿行而过、树皮皴裂、虬枝老干、光秃秃不挂一叶的那棵，就是流苏树，那是它花期未到的样子。

四月校园流苏盛开
The fringe tree in full bloom in April on campus

如今，四月将至，流苏花期将至，今年若能如愿看这盛开的流苏，定然会别有一番感受。据说，流苏最早在西方是用以献给加入教会的女性，而后则失去其宗教寓意，代表独立自主的女性。而今的十六中师生，在流苏盛开的季节，在四月的"流苏音乐节"中，唱出最响亮的誓言，赋予了这棵流苏树新的花语：莫负青春，心怀天下！

I walked down the way before the Uk Ing Museum, leading toward the northwest side of the campus. The first to come in sight was a century-old banyan, whopping enough to remind me of a forest. Hidden behind it were a few cook pines, not far away from which stood a camphor tree no less than one hundred years old, with an old-fashioned ringing bell seen high above its trunk. On my way, I also found many other trees, such as the century-old candlenut and logan trees as well as the guava tree, the osmanthus tree, Indian rubber trees, and white bauhinias, all but the fringe tree, the one that had always been lingering in my mind. I was told later that I had missed it many times since it was not in fluorescence then and was easily neglected with its chapped bark, craggy and furrowed trunk, and twisted and curled branches without a single leaf on them.

Now, April is coming, and so is the flowering time of the fringe tree in No. 16 Middle School. Should I fulfill my wish to have a look at it in its full bloom, I would have quite different feelings with my deeper understanding of it. The fringe tree is said to be a dedication in the West to women who joined the church, and the religious meaning is gradually replaced in history by its indication of independent women. In today's No. 16 Middle School, it has derived a new meaning, an oath for teachers and students to sing out loud every year in April at their music festivals, under the fringe tree in its blooming season—to cherish youth and embrace the world!

流苏花瓣
Fringe petals

● 特别鸣谢

本章在写作中得到以下单位和个人的大力支持和帮助，在此特致以诚挚感谢。

福州第十六中学为本文提供宝贵图片和资料。美国卫理公会历史档案总委会允许本章使用经过申请的图片。福州天安堂提供基督教《三字经》图片。

原校长钟英希老师接受笔者电话采访，十六中教务处副主任李萍老师接待笔者参观"毓英馆"及十六中校园。

原毓英女校学生叶益昭女士接受笔者采访，提供女校相关信息和图片。尤其感谢叶女士历时一个多月，根据记忆为本文特别手绘女校全景图。

美国知名友好人士、《纽约时报》驻上海分社社长柏凯斯先生接受线上采访，提供关于兰玛利亚及兰醒球的相关信息。美国卫理公会历史档案总委会的弗兰西斯·莱昂斯先生就图片授权事宜与笔者保持沟通联络，协助完成图片授权工作。

原福建师范大学外国语学院学生、现香港大学硕士生叶张鹏协助完成对柏凯斯先生的采访，下载部分英文文献资料，并完成本章第四部分"人物撷萃与钩沉"的英文翻译工作。

福建农林大学艺术及风景园林学院研究生涂志钢、郑芝琳根据叶益昭女士手绘图完成毓英女校全景电脑彩绘图。

福建师范大学社会历史学院戴显群教授、江振鹏教授，华南女院退休教师董秀苹老师拨冗解答笔者个别疑问。

池志海先生提供文中部分珍贵图片。

• Acknowledgments

I would like to express my gratitude to the following institutions and individuals for their tremendous support, keen intellect and generous sharing of their valuable source materials, personal experiences and collections to help me expand my horizons and refine my ideas in my process of writing this chapter.

Fuzhou No. 16 Junior High School has generously provided many valuable pictures and important data about the past and present of the school. GCAH of The United Methodist Church kindly permitted our use of some of the pictures from its Mission Photograph Album. Fuzhou's Church of Heavenly Peace provided the pictures of the Christian *Three Character Classic*.

The former principal of No. 16 Middle School, Zhong Yingxi accepted our interview on the phone and Ms. Li Ping, the deputy dean of the Academic Registry of No. 16 Middle School, led our visit to both Uk Ing Museum and Fuzhou No. 16 Junior High School.

The former student of Uk Ing Girls' School, Ms. Ye Yizhao accepted our interview, provided the related information and photos about the Girls' School, and drew the panorama of Uk Ing based on her own memory.

Mr. Keith Bradsher, the friendly business and economics reporter and Shanghai bureau chief of *The New York Times*, accepted our online interview and provided related information about Mary E. Carleton and Mary Sing-Gieu Carleton. Mr. Frances Lyons with GCAH of UMC spared his time keeping in touch with the writer and helped a lot by submitting to the general secretary of UMC the writer's application form for the use of pictures from China Albums of GCAH for authorization.

Ye Zhangpeng, an undergraduate student from Fujian Normal University and graduate student from the University of Hong Kong, assisted in the search for some English materials and translated the fourth part of this chapter into English.

Tu Zhigang and Zheng Zhilin, graduate students from the College of Arts College of Landscape Architecture in Fujian Agriculture and Forestry University, realized the colored digital version of the Uk Ing panorama drawn by Ms. Ye Yi Zhao.

Professor Dai Xianqun and Professor Jiang Zhenpeng, both from the College of Social Development in Fujian Normal University, and Ms. Dong Xiuping retired from Hua Nan Women's College helped clear some of our questions.

Chi Zhihai provided some valuable pictures for this chapter.

CHAPTER
FOUR

从三一学校到
福州外国语学校

From Trinity College Foochow to
Fuzhou Foreign Languages School

第四章

福

沿着百米香樟大道，漫步在紫藤花烂漫的校园里，巨榕、塔楼、古钟与葱郁的繁花尽收眼底；顺着闽江之滨，徜徉于象山之麓，"晨辉园""春华园""启明雕塑""硕果雕塑""思万楼"和"俄领馆"古今辉映，无一不述说着这座位于公园路上百年老校的盛世风华。"勤勉、上进、自强、守恒"的校训百十年来激励着无数学子奋进图强。林荫道尽头静默地矗立着一座红砖塔楼，仿如一条时光隧道，带着我们去探访一百多年前那所私立教会学堂，去看那些眼里有光、心里有梦的翩翩少年们。作为福州市唯一的一所公办外国语学校，她和万里之外的爱尔兰都柏林大学圣三一学院之间有着怎样千丝万缕的关系呢？全国足球传统特色校因何结缘于此？圣马可书院、广学书院、榕南两等小学、三一学校、福州九中和福州外国语学校，谁是谁的前世，谁又是谁的今生？

：校门口大道与思万楼（来源：池志海）
：School avenue & Walsh Memorial Tower
：（Source：Chi Zhihai）

　　穿行于仓山的寻常巷陌，随处可见欧式花园洋房，造型各异的医院、学校和教堂，新奇气派的西餐馆与电影院，甚至还有国内少见的跑马场。人们难免疑惑：为什么有着2 200多年悠久历史的福州会在小小南台岛上呈现出完全不一样的欧美风情呢？

　　这恐怕得从100多年前福州被辟为五口通商口岸说起。历经漫漫的百余年时光，福州作为中西文化的交汇点最先接触到当时较为领先的西式思想。中国传统文化的熏陶、淳朴民风的沐浴、当地原有的海洋文化与名人文化的渗透，再加上西方文化的浸润，可谓是古之源融聚今之流，久而久之就形成"有福之州"独特的文化景观，彰显出了不同的气质与风貌。

Strolling along the 100-meter avenue lined with camphor trees, one will marvel at the sight of quaint tower, ancient bells and luxuriant flowers as well as wisteria twining round huge banyan trees. The campus is located at the foot of Xiangshan Mountain where the The Minjiang River runs nearby. Various parts of the school—"Morning Sunlit Park" "Spring Flowers Park" "Statues of Inspiration" "Statues of Achievements" "Walsh Memorial Tower" and "Russian Consulate"—all gleam with glory from the past and the present, unfolding the magnificence of this century-old school, Fuzhou Foreign Languages School. The school motto of "Diligence, Momentum, Self-improvement, Conservation" has inspired countless students to forge ahead over the past century. At the end of the avenue silently stands a red-brick tower, like a time tunnel, leading us to visit the private missionary school more than a hundred years old, to see those young students with glow in their eyes and dreams in their hearts. As the only state-run foreign languages school in Fuzhou, what kind of relationship does it have with Trinity College Dublin of Ireland thousands of miles away? Why is the national football school with traditional characteristics set here? St. Mark's College, Guangxue Academy, Rongnan Primary School, Trinity College Foochow, Fuzhou No. 9 Middle School and Fuzhou Foreign Languages School, who comes before whom and who comes after?

Walking through the winding alleys in Cangshan, you won't miss gardens, schools, hospitals, churches and buildings with novelty and variety, but different in shapes, styles and functions; moreover, a racecourse can even be seen here. You cannot help wondering why the city of Fuzhou, with a long history of more than 2,200 years, is able to present such an Euramerican flavor on the small Nantai Island.

I'm afraid all of these have a lot to do with Fuzhou becoming one of the five trading ports in the 19th century. Fuzhou, the meeting point of Chinese and Western cultures, was the first to get in touch with the comparatively pioneering Western ideology at that time, and more than a century and a half have passed by before we realize it. The combination of traditional Chinese culture, folk culture, local marine culture, celebrity culture, coupled with the infiltration of Western culture, naturally led to the marriage of the past and the present, and over time, the city of blessings with unique cultural characteristics came into being, manifesting diverse glamor and vitality.

Scan for more
扫码了解更多

● 当地教会学校的发展

早期传教士们为了传教创办了教会学校，当时仅是城南一隅的仓山就集中了全市最新式的学堂九所，而其中8所都是教会办的。教会学校出现之前，当地的教育集中在传统的私塾和书院里，一般只有大户人家才有足够好的经济条件供其子女接受较系统的教育。教会学校早期免收学费且提供学生补助，无论贫富贵贱，任何人只要愿意都有机会接受教育。

在近一个多世纪的历史长河里，教会学校在内外因的双重作用下由自发状态逐步向制度化转变，形成了规模庞大、层次多样、涉及面广、从小学到大学的完整教育体系，并与官办学校形成互补，这在某种程度上激发且促进了西学东渐，引发了中西文化的首次碰撞，对多维度且多层面的交流产生了深远的影响。

1842年，美国传教士雅裨理抵达厦门，这意味着新教开始传入福建（葛桂录，2021：102）。几年后，接力赛般入闽传教的有美部会、美以美会和圣公会。《南京条约》允许各国传教士在各个口岸自由传教，但由于千百年来形成的传统观念和信仰根深蒂固，最初十年间不管这些差会的传教士们采用怎样的方式，福州当地居民都对外来宗教毫无兴趣，传教士们进退两难。于是，他们转变了策略，开始建医院，办学校，引进西方生活理念，期望通过各种手段渗透，改变当地居民的观念（施宝霖、秦人，1998）。

美以美会1881年在基督教徒张鹤龄的热心捐助下创办了鹤龄英华中学，而美部会的哈佛大学教育博士弼履仁（即弼来满）则于1890年接任格致书院并将其更名为"榕城格致书院"。这两所学校都率先开展英语教育，并参照欧美中等学府模式进行管理。1850年札成和温敦来榕标志着英国圣公会的到来，但是他们最初把关注点放在了对儿童的教育上。

三一学校教学楼前的大合影（引自《福州老照片》）
Group photo taken in front of the Teaching Building of TCF（Source: *Old Photos of Fuzhou*）

• The Development of Local Missionary Schools

Early missionaries founded missionary schools for preaching. Cangshan, located in the southern corner of the city, was home to nine of the city's most modern schools, eight of which were run by churches. Before the advent of church schools, local education was concentrated in old-style private schools and academies of classical learning, and only rich families could afford a more systematic education for their children. In the early days, the admission was free and missionary schools even offered students' aid, so to speak, education was available to anyone who wanted it, rich or poor, noble or lowly.

Nearly a century had passed before church schools changed step by step, under the dual influence of both external and internal factors, from spontaneous state to institutional transition, and later on formed a large-scale, multi-level, wide-range complete education system covering primary school, middle school and university. This was complementary to government-run schools, which, to some extent, inspired and promoted the eastward transmission of Western sciences, hence triggered the first collision between Chinese and Western cultures. In a word, it had a far-reaching impact on multi-dimensional and multi-faceted communication.

In 1842, American missionary David Abeel arrived at Amoy, which meant that Protestantism had spread to Fujian. A few years later, ABCFM (American Board Of Commissioners For Foreign Missions), MEM (Methodist Episcopal Mission) and CMS (Church Missionary Society) came to Fujian in succession like a relay race. *Treaty of Nanking* allowed the missionaries of various countries to preach freely at each of the five ports. However, due to the deep-rooted traditional ideas and beliefs formed over thousands of years, no matter what methods the missionaries adopted in the first decade, the local residents of Fuzhou showed no interest at all in Western religions, which rendered the missionaries helpless and hopeless. Therefore, they changed their strategy and began to build hospitals and schools, and introduced Western life concepts, all in the hope of permeating all levels of society through various means and changing the notions of local residents.

In 1881, with the generous donation by a Chinese Christian Mr Diong Hokling, the MEM established A-Hok Anglo-Chinese College. In 1890, Lyman Birt Peet, an ABCFM doctor of Education from Harvard University, took over Foochow College and renamed it "Banyan City Institute". Both schools pioneered English education and were run according to the model of European and American secondary schools. The arrival of CMS in 1850 was marked by the coming of R. D. Jackson and William Welton, but their initial focus was on the education of children.

● 三一学校的历史沿革

　　福州外国语学校是由福州九中演变而来的，而九中的前身就是三一学校，三一学校的三个前身（榕南两等小学、广学书院和圣马可书院）其实都隶属于圣公会。三校合一的性质是对这个独特的校名最直观的解读之一；此外，该校与爱尔兰都柏林大学的圣三一学院有十分密切的类似母女的血缘关系；第三是指基督教三位一体的特性。这样的校名简洁凝练，好记易懂。那么，是什么原因，又是什么契机导致这三所学校合为一体呢？

榕南两等小学与广学书院

　　人称"福建英国圣公会之父"的胡约翰在中国待了大半辈子，是圣公会教育事业的主力。1863 年开始他协同他人在乌山陆陆续续创办小学、男校、女校、道学校等各种学校。其中榕南两等小学始建于 1863 年，但后来却毁于 1878 年的乌石山教案。该校的详细情况在历史资料中仅仅一笔带过，并没有多少记载。

　　史荦伯也是圣公会教育事业的奠基人之一：他 1876 年来华后负责教育工作，于教区内陆续创办了上百所小学。1878 年，史荦伯为培养小学师资做准备，在胡约翰夫妇等人创办的男校的基础上成立了具有师范性质的广学书院。但是由于风水、强行租地建房等问题，他们和当地人屡次发生冲突，到了 1883 年，不得不迁至南台施埔重新开校。此后，他们还陆续购买 14 多亩地，并在 1867 年创立的道学校基础上建起了真学堂及真学书院（陈孝杰，2019）。1912 年当三一学校成立时，广学书院已经存在了 34 年，毕业生遍布各行各业。

　　根据史荦伯 1877 年梳理的系统化教育体系，外学（初等小学）的优秀生升入内学（圣教高等小学），而内学优秀生就进入广学书院（相当于中专学校）；年满 20 岁就有机会外派担任小学教员（林殷，2006）；三年后各方面都出色的学生有机会参加选拔，通过者升入真学书院。这算是当时比较系统化的体系。

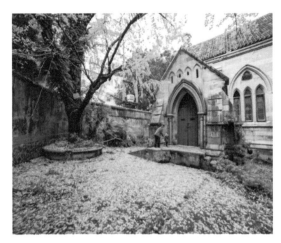

圣约翰堂（来源：池志海）
St. John's Church（Source：Chi Zhihai）

施埔堂（原名真学堂，实际为真学书院的丙座）（来源：池志海）
Shipu Church—A building of Theological College（Source: Chi Zhihai）

● Historical Evolution of Trinity College Foochow

Fuzhou Foreign Languages School (FFLS) has developed from Fuzhou No. 9 Middle School, which was formerly known as Trinity College Foochow (TCF). TCF had three predecessors, namely Rongnan Primary School, Guangxue Academy and St. Mark's College, all of which were affiliated to CMS. The most intuitive interpretation of this unique school name ("Trinity" literally means "three one" in Chinese) actually best presents the nature of the school, that is, the unity of the three schools; in addition, this school has a very close mother-daughter relationship with Trinity College Dublin far away in Ireland; thirdly, the school name also shows the characteristics of the Christianity—three in one—Trinity, more precisely. There is no doubt that this school name is concise and easy to remember and understand. Then, what were the reasons behind it and what was the opportunity that brought these three schools together?

Rongnan Primary School & Guangxue Academy

John Richard Wolfe, known as the "father of Fujian Church Missionary Society", spent most of his lifetime in China and played a leading role in CMS education. Since 1863, he began to establish primary schools, boys' schools, girls' schools and a Taoist school in Wushan Mountain, Fuzhou. Among them was Rongnan Primary School, founded in 1863, but later destroyed during the Wushi Hill Christian Persecution Case in 1878. The details of the school are only briefly mentioned in historical data, and there is not much record to be found.

Robert Warren Stewart was also one of the founders of CMS education. After coming to China in 1876, he took charge of the educational work and successively founded hundreds of primary schools in the diocese. In 1878, in order to prepare for the training of primary school teachers, Robert W Stewart set up Guangxue Academy on the basis of the boys' school founded by John Richard Wolfe and his wife. However, due to geomantic omen, as well as renting land and building houses in a forcible way, they had frequent conflicts with the local people. In 1883 they had to move to Shipu in Nantai Island, and reopen the school. After that, they purchased more than 14 mu of land bit by bit and built Theological School and Theological College on the basis of the Taoist School established in 1867. When TCF came to existence in 1912, Guangxue Academy had already had a history of 34 years, with graduates in all walks of life.

According to the systematic education plan put forward by Robert W. Stewart in 1877, outstanding students from Waixue (lower-level primary school) would be promoted to Neixue (Boarding School, or higher-level primary school), while excellent students from the Boarding School would be admitted to Guangxue Academy (equivalent to technical secondary schools). They also had the opportunity to be assigned as primary school teachers once they were over 20; three years later, students who excelled in all aspects had a chance to participate in a selection test, and those who passed would be promoted to the Theological College. All in all, it was a relatively systematic mechanism at that time.

圣马可书院

1897 年，圣公会传教士万拔文辗转跋涉，抵达了离家万里之遥的中国东南内陆小城福宁府。他先是在福宁府辖区内的霞浦担任作元学校的首任校长，一年后又奉调来到省城福州负责烟台山圣约翰堂等事务。转眼到了 1906 年，贝嘉德担任了圣公会福建教区的首任主教，他认为教育工作是重心，于是便请颇有教育经验的万拔文协助开展学校事务，主持真学书院并担任第四任院长（陈孝杰，2019）。

没多久万拔文就意识到，美以美会和美部会都在开展英语教学，圣公会的真学书院也必须尽快引进英语课程。但是，在圣公会议会上大家一致决定另起炉灶，由他牵头创办一所全新的学校并开设英语课程，定名为圣马可（汉英）书院。1907 年创校伊始只有十个学生，没有合适的校舍就征用自己的私宅教学。师资方面，除了万拔文夫妇两人亲自上阵，近在咫尺的广学书院的老师及一些外商也联手助力（施宝霖、秦人，1998：777）。

第一年，在摸索中还算顺利；第二年，由于学生数增加到了 33 人，书院便开始分为四个班教学，原先的私宅不够大，只能暂时借用仓山施埔（今为盲人福利院）紧挨着广学书院的一所又窄又破的房子（陈孝杰，2019：29）进行教学，不过如今这栋楼早已不见踪影。第三年，虽然报名者多达 150 人，但是由于空间所限，只能录取三分之二。不但教室不够，宿舍也极其紧缺，寻求新的场所已是迫在眉睫的事情了。

三一学校的肇始

圣马可书院创办的第二年即 1908 年，在伦敦举办的世界圣公会代表大会筹集到了一些捐款来资助海外的教育事业。彼时彼刻万拔文为了圣马可书院的持续发展绞尽脑汁，这从天而降的第一笔专款 2 000 英镑正好可以用来扩大书院外加筹建男生新校舍（林殷，2006）。

原俄领馆官邸，现为校友楼（来源：池志海）
Formerly Official Residence of the Russian Consuls, now Alumni Building (Source: Chi Zhihai)

St. Mark's College

In 1897, A CMS missionary named W. S. Pakenham-Walsh from Dublin University Far East Mission finally made it to Funing, a small inland city in southeast China thousands of miles away from his home. At first, he served as the first principal of Zuoyuan School in Xiapu, which was under the jurisdiction of Funing Prefecture. A year later, he was transferred to Fuzhou, the provincial capital, to take charge of St. John's Church in Yantai Mountain. In 1906, Horace MacCartie Eyre Price became the first bishop of the CMS Diocese of Fujian, who firmly believed that education should be the core of his work here. Therefore he asked W. S. Pakenham-Walsh, who was quite experienced in education then, to help handle school affairs and preside over the Theological College and served as its fourth dean.

It did not take long for Mr W. S. Pakenham-Walsh to realize that both MEM and ABCFM were carrying out English teaching with vigor and vitality, therefore it was urgent that Theological College run by CMS should add English to its course arrangement as soon as possible. But in the CMS Council that ensued, it was decided W. S. Pakenham-Walsh take the lead to start a new school with English as the core course, named St. Mark's (Anglo-Chinese) College. When the school was founded in 1907, it had only ten students, and W. S. Pakenham-Walsh had to use his private house for teaching because there was no suitable building. As for teachers, apart from W. S. Pakenham-Walsh and his wife, the faculty of Guangxue Academy nearby and some Western businessmen also joined hands to help them.

The first year went on rather smoothly, but in the second year, since the number of students rose to 33, they had to be divided into four classes. As a result, the original private house was not spacious enough to hold them all, and the school could only temporarily borrow a shabby and incommodious house for teaching, right next to Guangxue Academy in Shipu, Cangshan District, which turned out to be a welfare home for the blind later, but it was a pity that the building has long been nowhere in sight. In the third year, 150 applicants applied, but due to space constraints, only two thirds of them were lucky enough to get admitted. It was obvious that classrooms and dormitories were in great demand, so to find a new place has become impending.

Inchoation of Trinity College Foochow

In 1908, the year after St. Mark's College was founded, the World CMS Congress held in London raised some money to support educational cause overseas. At that time Mr. W. S. Pakenham-Walsh was racking his brain for the sustainable development of St. Mark's College, and the first grant of 2,000 pounds from London came as a godsend, which was used to expand the college and prepare for the construction of a new building for boys.

实际上还有第二笔的 3 000 英镑可以使用，但是按要求只能用在建设医院、教堂或者学校上。为了能够充分利用当年这笔"巨款"，大家经过不断磋商，最终决定把圣公会在福州的榕南两等小学、广学书院同圣马可书院合并在一起，同时请求爱尔兰都柏林三一学院为这个全新的教育机构配备师资。这个决定得到了爱尔兰"母院"的赞同和支持。

师资有爱尔兰方的保证，那么当务之急是尽快找到一个足够大的地方来容纳这三所即将合并起来的学校。恰好当时沙俄在榕的茶叶贸易大幅衰减，俄方决定放弃位于仓山人民公园路的驻榕领事馆。万拔文在福州商界的一位至交偶然得知那块地和那些房子要出售，赶紧为他们获取了优先购买权。他和主教闻讯立刻赶去俄领馆商谈，当天就完成了这个意料之外的交易（万拔文，1935）。

很快，俄国领事馆及周围总共 4 座洋房和园地统一规划为新的校园，兴豫洋行和上海的外国工程师紧接着便开始联手设计施工。到了 1912 年秋，三校合并迁入新址，正式改名为福州三一学校，含小学、中学和汉英三部。俄领馆为中学所用，一座楼作为西方教师和校长的宿舍，另一座作为汉英的校舍，还有一座就给榕南小学使用。从早先筹建位于施埔的圣马可书院到如今三校合一，并入公园路 39 号，并在其新址上成立三一学校，就这么短短 5 年时间，朗朗的读书声便已经此起彼伏。

都柏林三一学院后来捐赠了 1 000 英镑，用以修建史荦伯牧师的纪念堂，大家商量后一致决定在三一学校建个礼拜堂作为他的纪念堂。1913 年，这个承载双重目的的小礼拜堂落成，占地 400 多平方米，模仿上海圣约翰大学礼拜堂的式样，最多可以容纳 400 名学生集会。21 世纪初，该礼拜堂被拆除，校内仅剩"教堂旧址"奠基石碑一块。

根据九中最后一任校长庄才水老先生的回忆，20 世纪 90 年代创建"花园式单位"时，为了实现总体规划，本校美术教师黄鸿恩将"圣马可书院"的石碑和"三一学校"的门柱发掘出来并合理巧妙地安置在了相关景观中，使得它们成了永恒的历史见证者（庄才水，2021）。

Scan for more
扫码了解更多

：福州三一学校教堂（来源：陈华棣）
：TCF Chapel（Source：Chen Huadi）

There was actually a second sum of 3,000 available, but it was required to be spent only on the construction of hospitals, churches or schools. In order to make full use of this "huge sum of money", after continuous negotiations, they finally decided to merge the three CMS schools in Fuzhou—Rongnan Primary School, Guangxue Academy and St. Mark's College, and asked Trinity College Dublin for the faculty backup. This request was endorsed and supported by the "mother-school" in Ireland.

With the faculty guaranteed by TCD, it was imperative to quickly find a space large enough to accommodate the three schools to be merged. Just at that time the Russian tea trade in Fuzhou declined so greatly that the Russians decided to give up the consulate in Fuzhou located in People's Park Road, Cangshan. A close friend of W. S. Pakenham-Walsh's in Fuzhou business circle occasionally got the information that the land and the houses were for sale and achieved the pre-emptive right for them in no time. On hearing this, W. S. Pakenham-Walsh and the bishop immediately came to the Russian consulate for further negotiation and concluded the unexpected transaction on that very day.

Soon, a total of four Western-style houses including the consulate and the surrounding area were integrated into the overall plan for the new campus; Brand & Co., H. S and Western engineers from Shanghai joined their efforts in the design and construction. In the fall of 1912, the three schools were merged and moved to the new site, officially renamed Trinity College Foochow, with the three divisions being respectively primary school, middle school and Anglo-Chinese School. The Russian consulate was used by the middle school, and the Western buildings served as dormitories for the Western teachers and the principal. Anglo-Chinese School requisitioned one building, and the last one became the site of Rongnan Primary School. In retrospect, it was amazing that it took them just five years to witness the whole process, from the establishment of St. Mark's College in Shipu to the founding of TCF on the new site in No. 39 Park Rd, where the cadence of reading permeated far and wide.

Trinity College Dublin donated £1,000 later to build a memorial hall specifically for Robert W. Stewart. After discussion, it was agreed that a chapel be built instead at TCF as a memorial to him. Then in 1913, this dual-purpose chapel came into existence, covering an area of more than 400 square meters. It modeled after the Chapel of St. John's University in Shanghai and could hold up to 400 students at most. It was a pity that at the beginning of the 21st century, the chapel was demolished, and only the foundation stone into which "old Church site" was carved remains.

According to Mr Zhuang Caishui—the last principal of No. 9 Middle School, when the school was busy implementing the overall plan for the establishment of a "garden-style unit" in the 1990s, art teacher Mr Huang Hongen dug out the stele of "St. Mark's College" and the gate post of "Trinity College Foochow" from somewhere and placed them in the relevant landscape properly and skillfully, which makes them eternal witness of history.

三一学校的发展

刚开始时，教会设立的日学和义塾没有固定的学习年限，书院只能参照差会所属国家对应学校的学制来设立自己的学制，至少 6 年，最多 8 年（刘海峰、庄明水，1996：366），重点放在圣经和英文的学习上。1912 年进入民国后，书院陆续改称中学，学制缩短到 4 年或者 7 年。

1912 年合并后的三一学校的三个部分实际上依然保留着各自的特色。榕南两等小学基本保留原有模式。广学书院改称中学，以汉语为主，师范方向的要加读一年，这样培养出来的学子知识储备更加夯实，其优秀毕业生还有机会被保送到山东齐鲁大学，这对当年品学兼优的学生确实是难得的福利。圣马可书院则以英语为主，改称汉英学校，面向社会招生，生源较广泛。据说汉英学校不但英语课时比外校的多，还直接使用英国编的课本；英文课自然毋庸置疑，其他各科亦多采用外教或者外国出版的教材（施宝霖、秦人，1998：771）。此外，汉英学校的五至八年级均使用英语直接教学，教师也基本上来自都柏林大学。所谓严师出高徒，早期的汉英毕业生可以免试升入上海圣约翰大学的三年级（陈孝杰，2019：34），后来根据实际情况只能升入二年级，主要原因是三一学制为 8 年，因此七八年级相当于大学一二年级，这和如今的大学预科班较为类似。

虽然 1927 年立案（即向主管部门备案、注册登记——笔者注）后以上所提及的特殊待遇已经全部取消，学子们升入大学后也必须和其他学生一样读完完整的 4 年课程，但是能一度得到当年齐鲁大学和圣约翰大学的青睐绝非偶然，这和三一学校一向严苛的淘汰制有关。学校坚守优胜劣汰的原则，因此能坚持到毕业的一定是各方面的佼佼者。

Progress of Trinity College Foochow

At the very beginning, the day schools and private schools (charging no tuition) established by churches did not have a fixed period of schooling; and academies could only set their own schooling system according to the corresponding educational system of the countries to which the churches belonged, which usually consisted of six years at the least and at the most eight years, focusing on bible and English learning. After our the establishment of the Republic of China in 1912, "academies" were renamed as "middle schools" and the length of schooling was shortened to four or seven years.

The three parts of TCF have virtually retained their original features even after the merger in 1912—Rongnan Primary School still focused on the elementary education while Guangxue Academy was renamed Trinity High School, specializing in Chinese education; and those who pursued a teaching career were required one more year of schooling so as to enlarge their knowledge reserves; moreover, outstanding graduates were also granted a chance of being admitted into Cheeloo University in Shandong, which was undoubtedly a rare opportunity for students who excelled both in character and learning. St. Mark's College, on the other hand, became Anglo-Chinese School with English as its main language and recruited students extensively from all walks of life. It is said that Anglo-Chinese School not only have more English classes than other schools, but also directly use textbooks compiled by the British. There is no doubt that English classes were taught by Western teachers, moreover, textbooks for other subjects were all published abroad. In addition, students from grade 5 to grade 8 were all taught in English, and the teachers were mainly from TCD. As the old saying goes, capable are pupils trained by strict masters. Earlier Anglo-Chinese School graduates would be exempted from exams and got the direct admission into St. John's University in Shanghai as junior; later on, they could only be enrolled as sophomores based on the actual situation, and the main reason was that TCF's school system covered eight years, so the eighth grade was equivalent to the second year of university, which was quite similar to college-preparatory course.

In 1927 TCF got officially registered by local authorities concerned, and after that all the privileges mentioned above were called off. As a result, students were supposed to complete four years of learning in all when they entered the university. But we could still see clearly that it was not easy, or rather, by no means accidental that students from TCF could get the favor of Cheeloo University and St. John's University at that time, which precisely demonstrated the rigorous elimination system of TCF. The school always adhered to the principle of Survival of the Fittest, so those who could stick to the end must be at the very top in all aspects.

三一学校的锐变与引领

教会学校的创办在某种意义上促进了当时福州文教体育事业的发展，让人们得以窥见西方世界之一斑，取其精华去其糟粕，不断学习前进。可以说三一学子在体育运动、社会服务、生活方式、爱国运动等方面均起到了示范作用。

三一学子的锐变与引领——体育运动

早期的义塾、日学和寄宿学校会利用课外时间组织学生共同打理校内卫生或者从事一些难度不大的手工劳动。进入 20 世纪，教会学校开始日渐重视课外体育运动（施宝霖、秦人，1998），纷纷引进西方体育项目，改变运动风气，形成了独有的体育传统，而三一就是个很优秀的执行者。

三一建校伊始，就实行既规律又严格的生活作息制度。寄宿生每天天蒙蒙亮就得起床洗漱，然后集体列队参加晨练（林殷，2006）。但是，最初学生没有悟到学校的良苦用心，关注点依然是在学习上，所以学校 1919 年后不得不实行强制性的体育训练。学校引进竞技体育必修课，将汉英部的学生与中学部的学生混编为鹰、狮、鲸三队（施宝霖、秦人，1998：773），要求所有学生自由选择足球、排球或者篮球中的一种，然后根据球技高低分为甲、乙、丙组，每天必须参加两节课外运动，直至毕业或离校。

这样的安排其实有着深层的原因。这里我们不得不提及汉英部和中学部（即圣马可书院与广学书院）两部学生多年来的不和：中学部男生主要来自农村，学费低，以中文教育为主；而汉英部男生主要为福州当地人，学费高，意在英语学习，很多来自非基督教家庭，从商、做官者比例高。完全不一样的家庭背景和教育侧重点造成他们之间的摩擦与不和。但是，三一学校对他们进行了强制性的安排和编队，并实施了各种细致用心的计划以确保学生能够获得更强健的体魄，这渐渐缓和了两部之间长期的紧张关系。

福州三一学校（来源：池志海）
Trinity College Foochow（Source: Chi Zhihai）

TCF Students Making Rapid Progress and Taking the Lead

In a sense, the establishment of missionary schools promoted the development of culture, education and sports in Fuzhou at that time, allowing people to catch a glimpse of the Western world, take its essence and discard its dregs, and keep learning and moving forward. It can be said that TCF students have played an exemplary role in sports, social service, lifestyle and patriotic movement.

TCF Students Making Rapid Progress and Taking the Lead—Physical Education

Earlier private schools, day schools and boarding schools would organize students to work together in the maintenance of school hygiene or to do some comparatively easy manual labor as a part of their extracurricular activities. Since the 20th century, missionary schools have begun to pay more and more attention to sports after class. They introduced Western sport programs one after another to the students in the hope of changing the ethos of sports and forming a unique sports tradition. TCF took the lead in this respect.

From the outset, TCF had been implementing a regular and strict system for students'daily life. Boarders were required to get up at dawn every day to wash up before participating in morning exercises together. However, it was not easy at first since students were too young to fully understand the good intentions of the school and their focus was still on study; therefore, since 1919 the school had to put compulsory physical training in practice. After TCF introduced obligatory course of competitive sports, Anglo-Chinese School students and Middle School students were mixed into three teams, namely Eagle, Lion and Whale. All students were given the freedom to choose one of the ball games from football, volleyball, or basketball; and then they would be divided into groups A, B, C according to their specific ball skills. Apart from that, they were supposed to attend two extracurricular class hours every day before they graduated or left school.

In fact, there were some special reasons behind it, and here we had to mention the conflicts between the two divisions—Anglo-Chinese School (St. Mark's College) and Trinity Middle School (Guangxue Academy) for many years. The boys in the Middle School were mainly from rural areas, and the tuition was relatively low; students from the Anglo-Chinese School were mainly local boys, and they were charged a higher tuition and aimed at English learning, among whom many came from non-Christian families, whose parents were mainly businessmen and officials. Completely different family backgrounds and varied educational focuses unavoidably led to friction and disagreements between them, but TCF's quick response, mandatory arrangement, as well as the formation and implementation of a variety of detailed plans ensured that all the students could benefit in the long run, therefore it gradually eased the long-term tension between the two divisions.

慢慢地，学生们逐步改变了观念，懂得要劳逸结合，动静相宜，学业与体育要兼顾。此后，足球、篮球、排球、乒乓球等各种球类运动也得以流行开来。

由于三一学校是英国教会学校，而足球是英国人最普遍的运动，因此足球就成了三一学校最负盛名的项目。1924年秋，都柏林布道会拨款600英镑，再加上上海英国商会的捐助，很快就在学校东面建起一个十亩大小的标准足球场（施宝霖、秦人，1998）。这算福州当时最好的运动场了。有了这样的天时地利，这项运动顺势推广开来并且发展迅速。不但学生们有机会从小学起就接触足球，教师们也有相应的组织架构与培养目标。在多名默默奉献的名师们的悉心指导下，三一足球健儿们时常和外校学生比赛，获得校际冠军是家常便饭，球技与体育精神也逐渐誉满榕城。渐渐地，足球在福州乃至全省流行开来，三一足球队在与美国教会学校的比赛中曾多年保持不败记录，树立了"为体育而体育"的精神和"胜不骄败不馁"的良好心态，并且还勇敢地走出去与外省健儿们较量。原国家足球队主力李国宁就是在这个运动氛围浓厚的校园里逐步成长起来的，他还曾走出国门与球王贝利切磋球技并合影留念（史晓洪，2007）。

三一学子的锐变与引领——社会服务

三一学校严格按照西方的标准来进行整体课程设置和日常教学的实践与管理，无形中也给学生灌输了完全不同的理念。学生们通过甄别、接纳、学习与实践，推动了社会方方面面的进步。

平时课内的学习提升是学生们的头等任务，此外，他们课余还不忘投身社会工作，培养自身的服务意识。自我管理能力和为他人服务的精神不是天生的，需要明确且有效的指导与监督。学校恰恰就是这样的培养人才的地方。学校指导学生成立膳食委员会，按照规定所有成员都必须由学生担任。他们不仅得负责柴米油盐等相关食品的采购、分配和使用，还得承担卫生清理工作，久而久之，这些学生们对营养搭配都十分在行。

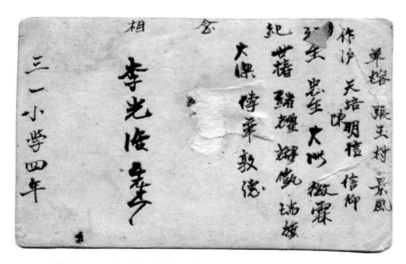

三一学校童子军合影背面名单（来源：池志海）
List of the TCF Scouts Members at the Back of the Group Photo（Source: Chi Zhihai）

With the time passing, students changed their concept, and fully understood that they should keep a balance between study, rest and sports. Since then, soccer, basketball, volleyball, table tennis and other ball games caught on.

TCF originated from TCD, a world-renowned missionary school belonging to UK then. Football was the most popular sport in England, and naturally it won over TCF students and became the most prestigious sport here. In the autumn of 1924, a grant of £600 from the Dublin Mission and a donation from the British Chamber of Commerce in Shanghai soon led to the erection of a ten-acre standardized football pitch in the east of the school, which proved to be the best stadium in Fuzhou at that time. With such favorable conditions, football was promoted and developed rapidly. Not only did students have the opportunity to play football from primary school onwards, but teachers also had an organizational structure and development goals. Under the guidance of some experienced teachers who were always devoted and never asking for rewards, TCF football players often competed against students from other schools, and it was common for them to win the interscholastic championship. Gradually, football became a fashion in Fuzhou and even in the whole province. TCF football team had kept an undefeated record in the competitions with American missionary schools for many years, and established the spirit of "sports for sports" and the good mentality of "winning with pride and losing with grace", and even bravely went out to compete with athletes from other provinces. Li Guoning, the then dominant player of the national football team, grew up on this campus enjoying a prevalent sports atmosphere. He even went abroad to exchange footballing skills with the Brazilian superstar Pelé and took photos with him.

TCF Students Making Rapid Progress and Taking the Lead—Social Service

TCF carried out overall curriculum and daily teaching practice and management in strict accordance with the Western standards, in the meantime imperceptibly instilling completely different ideas into students. In turn, students promoted the progress of the society in all aspects through screening, acceptance, learning and practice.

Study should always be students' top concern. In addition, they did not forget to devote themselves to social work after school so as to cultivate their own service consciousness. Self-management ability and the spirit of serving others were not innate, and both need explicit and effective guidance and supervision; luckily the school was exactly such an ideal place to train people. Under the instruction of the school, students set up a committee of catering services, all members of which must be students according to the regulations. They were not only responsible for the purchase, distribution and the use of daily necessities like firewood, rice, oil and salt as well as other related food, but also in charge of the daily sanitation. Over time, these students became experts at nutrition collocation.

三一学校还是福州第一家成立童子军组织的学校，这是英美很普通的青年学生课余活动组织，通过这种组织可以对学生进行训练，培养他们为社会服务的意识。三一童子军组织有一整套由西方传入的周密体系，学生们会学习各种各样丰富实用的课外知识——从侦察、急救、野炊等户外生存技能到养鸡等日常生活技能都一网打尽。每周至少训练两次，特别是周六下午如果没有别的安排就去郊外实地演练。

学生们在这样的不断实践中茁壮成长，也得到了各方的鼓励与肯定。学校日常的治安维护，会议期间的特别纠察任务、通讯、警戒等都离不开他们忙碌的身影。医护人员紧缺时，他们也往往第一时间挺身而出，协助救护，轮班照顾。（林殷，2006）。

随着三一学子们自身学识的增长与回馈社会意识的提升，他们每晚挤出宝贵的一小时来办"校工识字班"，最初纯粹是为了帮助那二三十个目不识丁的校工学会读书写字。没想到好评如云，影响力不断扩大，越来越多校外的人要求加入，于是学生们牺牲自己的课余时间，排除各种困难，借用校外场所组织夜校（林殷，2006），每晚都会轮流为附近没有接受过任何教育的老百姓义务授课一个半小时。据说受益者前后不下 300 人。这是造福社会的大善事，也体现了三一学子的社会担当。

三一学子的锐变与引领——生活方式

英国素来讲究各种礼仪，隶属于圣公会的三一学校自然而然地按照英国传统制度培养学生，最雷打不动的就是服饰礼仪。与当时非教会学校学子们的长衫马褂截然不同，汉英部和中学部的学生不论寒暑都必须穿统一的黑色校服入校，上衣两袖有白色花纹以示"三一"（林殷，2006：30）。学生们平时有固定校服，运动时也有专门服装。学校还要求老师们上课也要穿戴黑色礼服和方帽，后来由于酷热，炎夏时才能免除这礼仪（施宝霖、秦人，1998：779）。除了外在的服饰，教师们的教学不仅不局限于书本知识，他们还时常在日常生活中创造条件，培养学生们的西方风度和礼节。

三一教学楼前的鸡尾酒会（拍摄者不详，唐希藏品）
Cocktail party in front of the Teaching Building of TCF (Source:
Unknown, Tang Xi's collection)

TCF was also the first school in Fuzhou to establish the Boy Scouts Organization, which was originally a common movement base after school for young students in Britain and America. Through this organization, students could be trained and their awareness of serving the society could be strengthened. TCF Scouts Organization had a complete set of carefully-planned practice from the West, so that the students would acquire a variety of practical extracurricular knowledge—from reconnaissance, first aid, picnic and other outdoor survival skills to daily life skills such as raising chickens. They received this kind of training at least twice a week, and especially on Saturday afternoons, they may go to the countryside if nothing was fixed yet.

Consequently, students had thrived in such continuous practice and had received the encouragement and affirmation from all sides. The daily security of the school, the special picketing mission as well as the communication and vigilance during conferences were all a part of their busy work. Moreover, when medical staff was in great need, they were often the first to step forward bravely .

With the accumulation of their own knowledge and the awareness of contributing back to society, TCF students spared a precious hour every night to run a "literacy class" for school workers. Their original motive was purely to help 20 to 30 illiterate workers to master some basic skills like reading and writing. Against all expectations people thought highly of their selfless efforts, and more and more people outside the school begged to be given the same chance of free classes as school workers. At their request, students made another sacrifice of their own free time, eliminated all sorts of difficulties, and borrowed classrooms from outside for night classes. They took turns to tutor people nearby for one and a half hours every night for free, and it was said that more than 300 completely illiterate local people profited, which was a great deed that benefited the society and also reflected the social responsibility of TCF students.

TCF Students Making Rapid Progress and Taking the Lead—Mode of Life

The British always have a particular regard for etiquettes, and TCF affiliated to CMS naturally followed the British tradition, dress etiquette being the focus. Different from the long gowns and mandarin jackets worn by non-missionary school students at that time, Anglo-Chinese School and Middle School students were required to wear black uniforms at school regardless of the seasons, with white patterns on both sleeves to signify "Trinity". Students had regular uniforms on school days and special clothes for sports as well. Apart from that, teachers were also expected to wear black suits and caps in class, which was later called off on scorching summer days. Appearance was not the whole story, and the actual teaching was really worth mentioning, that is, teaching was no longer limited to textbook knowledge. By contrast, teachers often created various conditions in the daily life to develop students' Western graces and etiquette.

据校友江中美回忆，来淑德（传教士来必翰的太太）教英文写作颇用心。开始时学生比较抵触英国的繁文缛节，她就每周六晚上特地腾出一小时私人时间和大家交流英国的风俗习惯和生活礼节，并且答疑解惑，有时还请学生轮流到家里吃饭，全程也完全按照西方的礼仪进行：从发邀请信到接受邀约，再到餐前、餐中、餐后的各种细节都在潜移默化中呈现并传递给学生。这些理论与实践相结合的举动颇有成效，无形中拓宽了孩子们的视野（江中美，2003）。

随着时光的流逝，学生们的生活方式与理念也开始日渐西化，工作后有时也根据需求去洋服店定制考究的衣服，吃西餐，打网球，参加各种各样的派对。三一学校还曾举办过鸡尾酒会，可以想象当年的盛况。当时的仓山逐渐成了福州最洋派的地方，出现了很多"第一"——第一家西餐厅、第一个照相馆、第一台电梯、第一家私人订制服饰店等等。

西方各种习俗、理念与生活方式拓宽了学生们的视野，也让他们在不断甄别优劣与明辨是非中与时俱进，自觉抵制封建陋习，倡导移风易俗，引领方方面面的国际化进程。1920年，福州最早的一场西式婚礼轰动一时。婚礼在教堂举行，两位新娘都穿着西方白色圣洁的婚纱。巧合的是，两位新郎都曾是三一学校的学生，三一见证了他们成长的重要时刻，于是新人们不约而同地选择在三一学校前留影。更特别的是两位新娘都属虎（林殷，2006），这在当时中国传统观念里颇多忌讳。由此可见，三一学校的影响是潜移默化的，给人们带来了全新观念，开西式婚礼之先河，改变了人们的生活方式，体现了中西共融，在推动社会风俗变迁上起到一定的作用。

：婚礼——三一学校前留影（来源：池志海）
：Wedding ceremony in front of TCF (Source: Chi Zhihai)

In alumnus Jiang Zhongmei's memory, Rev. W. P. W. Williams's wife taught English composition whole-heartedly. At the very beginning, students were quite defensive about the British formalities, so she specially spared an hour every Saturday night to share British customs and etiquette with them, answering their questions, and sometimes even invited students home to dinner in turn. The whole process was carried out in accordance with the Western table manners: from the invitation letters to the acceptance of invitations, as well as all the detailed preparation before, during and after dinners, all of which exerted a subtle influence on students' character and temperament. In short, the combination of these theories and practices was quite effective, imperceptibly broadening children's horizons.

With the passage of time, students' lifestyles and ideas had become increasingly Westernized. After they joined the job market, they sometimes went to Western-style clothes stores to have their clothes custom-made; they enjoyed Western-style food, played tennis and attended various parties; TCF even held a cocktail party then and fancy the grand occasion! Cangshan at that time gradually became the most fashionable place in Fuzhou, leading to a series of "the firsts"—the first Western restaurant, the first photo studio, the first elevator, the first customized clothing shop and so on.

Western customs, ideas and lifestyles broadened students' horizons and enabled them to keep pace with the times, and in this process, they constantly guided students in distinguishing good from bad and right from wrong; moreover, they helped students consciously resist feudal vices, advocated transforming established traditions and practices, and led the process of internationalization in all aspects. In 1920, the first Western-style wedding in Fuzhou was really sensational: The wedding was held in a church, and both brides wore Western wedding gowns, white and sacred; coincidentally, both grooms used to study in TCF, which meant TCF witnessed the important moments of their growth. What was more special was that both brides were born in the year of tiger, which was quite a taboo when looking for a "bride" in Chinese traditional concepts at that time. All these details helped us see that TCF was exercising an invisible, formative influence on students' character, bringing new ideas to them. TCF students took the lead in holding a Western-style wedding, changing people's way of life, reflecting the integration of China and the West, and playing a certain role in promoting the change of social customs.

三一学子的锐变与引领——爱国运动

　　虽然是教会学校，爱国主义的熏陶却无所不在。汉英学校的图书室并不大，20平方米左右，书籍却多达一两千本，是学生们遨游知识海洋感受中西碰撞的广阔天地。福州翻译奇才林纾的作品很受欢迎，《东方杂志》《新青年》等杂志也颇有市场，孙中山的《三民主义》也有人关注。高年级的学生更青睐上海的时事报纸，陈独秀、李大钊、杜威、罗素等人的思想理念时时吸引着他们，潜移默化下他们逐渐成长为爱国、有情怀又有知识的热血青年。在紧张严肃的学习之余，学子们积极参加各种活动，弘扬社会正气，成为当年反帝爱国斗争的重要力量（刘海峰、庄明水，1996）。尤其是在民主学生运动如火如荼开展期间，英华、三一等校的学生便起到引领的作用。

　　1904年为反对美国政府虐待旅美华工，英华、格致和三一大批学生退学抗议（施宝霖、秦人，1998）。1911年年底，福州辛亥革命起义爆发，圣马可书院的十来名学生参加红十字军救护伤兵，在战火中与时间赛跑，与生命较量。1919年五四运动期间，北京学生参加游行请愿被军阀残杀的消息也是在汉英学校的"演讲所"传达给城内学生代表的，随后英华和三一等几所学校联合8千多学生举行声势浩大的游行示威（施宝霖、秦人，1998）。

　　1919年底，日本浪人制造的台江事件引起各界愤慨，英华和三一学生再次罢课（林殷，2006），组队到日领馆前面抗议。在各方施压下，日方不得已确认自己是肇事者，撤换了当时的驻闽总领事。可以说这次外交胜利应该大大归功于学生。

:: 三一学校童子军合影（来源：池志海）
:: Group photo of TCF scouts（Source: Chi Zhihai）

TCF Students Making Rapid Progress and Taking the Lead—Patriotic Movement

Although it was a missionary school, patriotism could be felt everywhere. The Anglo-Chinese School's library was not big, about 20 square meters, but there were as many as 1,000 to 2,000 books, which served as a vast ocean of knowledge for students to swim about and feel the collision between China and the West. Lin Shu's works were well received, who was a translation legend in Fuzhou. Magazines such as *Oriental Magazine* and *New Youth* were also popular among students. Sun Yat-sen's *The Three People's Principles* always attracted the attention of students. Upperclassmen preferred Shanghai newspapers on current affairs, and ideas and philosophies of those revolutionists and thinkers at home and abroad like Chen Duxiu, Li Dazhao, Dewey and Russell always attracted them, hence they grew up into patriotic, passionate and knowledgeable hot-blooded youngsters under the gradual and imperceptible influence. In addition to their systematic learning, students actively participated in various activities to promote social integrity and became an important force in the patriotic struggle against imperialism. Especially when the democratic student movement was in full swing, students from Anglo-Chinese College and TCF played a leading role.

In 1904, a large number of students from Anglo-Chinese College, Foochow College and TCF quitted school to show their protest against the American government's mistreatment of Chinese laborers in the States. At the end of 1911, when the Revolution of 1911 was under way, Fuzhou uprising broke out, and about ten students from St. Mark's College joined the Red Cross to rescue the wounded, racing against time and fighting against life in the flames of war. During the May 4th Movement in 1919, the news that some Beijing students who participated in demonstrations and presented petitions were killed by warlords was also conveyed to the student representatives at the "lecture hall" of Anglo-Chinese School. Soon afterwards, Anglo-Chinese College and TCF held a massive demonstration in collaboration with other schools, and more than 8,000 students joined.

At the end of 1919, Foochow Massacre made by Japanese ronin provoked indignation from all walks of life, Anglo-Chinese College and TCF students again went on strike; they marched towards the Japanese consulate and protested, and finally the Japanese could do nothing but admit that they were the trouble-makers and that they should be blamed for the appalling tragedy under the great pressure from the local society. In no time they replaced the consul general in Fujian, which proved to be a diplomatic victory for China; obviously it should be attributed to students.

这些活动影响都不小，体现了年轻一代敢于为正义发声的明确态度和坚定立场。值得一提的是汉英学生还组成三一学生分会（林殷，2006），努力在方方面面展现学子们该有的担当与风貌：他们提倡劳动观念，重视劳动实践，同情劳动人民。他们支持国货，自觉抵制日货，甚至还组织纠察队利用业余时间到学校周边发放传单，希望唤醒普通民众的爱国热情（刘海峰、庄明水，1996）。

1925年初，随着爱国主义思想的觉醒，国人纷纷以不同形式开展活动，要求收回教育主权。传教士们或采取临时措施应对，或想方设法拖延缓和，但是终究得面对现实（刘海峰、庄明水，1996）。运动持续发酵，到1927年初福州也爆发了声势浩大的运动，数百人在仓山麦园顶举行集会游行（施宝霖、秦人，1998）。福建学联纷纷动员学子们转学到非教会学校，因此大部分教会学校只得做出改革来应对，推举国人担任校长。到了年底，英华、三一、培元等多校要求转学的学生已多达数百人。

三一学生一直积极响应收回教育主权的号召。1929年初夏，由于一些小误会，来必翰和第一任华人校长林步基在没有调查的情况下就简单粗暴地开除了两名学生。这件事就像导火线一样引起中学部师生的罢课请愿和示威游行，顷刻间成了社会热点，当地多家报刊连日以头版头条巨幅报道。虽然学潮最终以师生的胜利结束，但事情闹得不可收拾，影响面极大，教育厅最终勒令停办三一学校中学部。学校一关了事，可学生的教育要如何延续？必须得尽快想个两全其美的方案！于是次年初，校方将中学部和汉英部合为一校，改称私立福州三一中学，以此恢复中学部；三一小学也相应改称私立福州三一中学附属三一小学。

1938年因日军侵华，福州危难之时，真学书院、三一学校等校也筹建难民所，学生们发动各界爱心人士捐衣，捐物，捐军资，使仓山成为一方温馨的港湾。这样感人的例子还有不少，都实实在在地体现了三一学子当年与许多热血青年一样以天下之忧而忧的爱国情怀。

：三一学校校徽（来源：池志海）
：TCF School badge（Source: Chi Zhihai）

To sum up, all these activities had achieved widespread impact and demonstrated the unequivocal attitude and the unwavering stance of the young generation who dared to speak up for justice. It is worth mentioning that Anglo-Chinese School students tried their best to show students' responsibility and features in all aspects as a branch of TCF: They advocated the concept of labor, attached importance to labor practice, and sympathized with the working people. They supported domestic goods, and consciously boycotted Japanese goods; they even went so far to organize pickets to distribute leaflets around the school in their spare time, hoping to awaken the patriotism of ordinary people nearby.

At the beginning of 1925, with the awakening of patriotism, Chinese people began to reclaim the sovereignty of education in different forms. Facing this, missionaries either took temporary measures to cope with it or tried every means to delay or mitigate its development, but they had to face the reality sooner or later. The campaign continued to ferment until early 1927, a huge movement broke out in Fuzhou, with hundreds of people holding rallies and parades in Cangshan. The Fujian Students' Union mobilized students to transfer to non-missionary schools, and in response to it, most missionary schools had to make the expected reform and elect Chinese as principals. At the year end, several hundred students requested the transferral from Anglo-Chinese College, TCF and Boys' Boarding School.

TCF students responded positively to the call for reclaiming educational sovereignty. In the early summer of 1929, due to a few minor misunderstandings, Rev. W. P. W. Williams and the first Chinese principal Mr Lin Buji expelled two students in an oversimplified and crude way without investigation, which touched off all the petitions, strikes and demonstrations from teachers and students that came from Trinity Middle School. They caught the attention of the whole society in no time, and were in the headlines for days on end in quite a few local newspapers and magazines. The protest ended with a victory for teachers and students, but the incident became so violent and influential that the Education Department ordered the closure of Trinity Middle School. How could they go on instructing students in that case? Obviously it was necessary for the school authorities to come up with a solution as soon as possible. Early the following year, the school merged Trinity Middle School with Anglo-Chinese School and renamed it Private Fuzhou Trinity College to revive the middle school division; Trinity Primary School was renamed Trinity Primary School affiliated to Private Fuzhou Trinity College.

In 1938, when Fuzhou was in crisis because of the invasion of the Japanese Army, Theological College, TCF and other places also set up refuge centers. The students mobilized people from all walks of life to donate clothes, daily necessities and military supplies, making Cangshan a warm harbor. These touching examples were no exception, on the contrary, all of them really reflected TCF students' patriotic feelings towards the world around them, just like many hot-blooded young people who showed great compassion for those who were in need.

社会各界对三一学子的认可

家长们想方设法把孩子送过来，认为无论如何孩子的未来必然一片光明。一入学，校方就按学生开门考成绩的高低把全年段分为甲、乙、丙、丁等班，各班又按成绩排座位，因此完全可以理解孩子们入学后为什么不敢有丝毫的懈怠。入读三一之后显然未来可期——读得好可以出国留学，学成之后再回来报效祖国，这也确实是不少杰出三一学子的选择；如果愿意留在家乡也很容易找到合适的工作，毕竟他们几年的刻苦学习已经打下坚实的基础，特别是有外语优势。据不完全统计，三一学子里教会子弟，洋行、海关、邮政等机关子弟，外县和农村非教徒子弟这三大群体各占差不多 20%，剩下差不多40% 都是商界和手工艺界的子弟。将近三分之二的学生毕业后选择在邮政、海关、盐务、电报、洋行等洋务部门工作（刘海峰、庄明水，1996）。听说有些洋行银行待遇十分丰厚，一个人就有可能养活一个家族，因此，可以理解当时大家为何趋之若鹜，挤破头也要让孩子来这福州男校中的"三鼎甲"之一镀金。

受过较系统、较严格英语训练的三一毕业生在职场有一定的竞争力，很受各地各行业的欢迎（施宝霖、秦人，1998）。1915 年，中华邮政局、向东电话公司等机构录用三一学子，使三一学校越发成了香饽饽；有些学生太过抢手，甚至到了还没毕业就接受"预定"而提前走上社会岗位的地步。

三一的优秀学子早期有直升圣约翰大学和齐鲁大学的机会，1916 年福建协和大学创办后，部分学生也可以直升协和大学（施宝霖、秦人，1998）。再后来，三一、英华和格致都成为协和大学完全承认的合格中学（刘海峰、庄明水，1996），所有毕业生均享有升学资格，这也是对三校教学实力的认可。

：福州九中学子（来源：陈华棣）
：Students of Fuzhou No. 9 Middle School（Source: Chen Huadi）

Approval of TCF Students from All Walks of Life

Parents tried their best to send their children to TCF, believing that their children's future would be bright on all accounts. Once admitted, the students would be rated A, B, C, D according to their entrance exam results, hence being assigned to different classes and different rows of seats respectively; therefore it was completely understandable why students dared not have the slightest slack during the school days. In many people's eyes, the future was promising once you stepped into TCF: If you work hard enough, you can go abroad for further study before you come back to serve the motherland upon graduation. This was indeed the choice of many outstanding TCF students. If they were willing to stay in their hometown, it was easy for them to locate a satisfactory job. After all, they had laid a solid foundation through years of hard work, especially their advantage in English got the upper hand. According to incomplete statistics, there were mainly three groups among TCF students, namely, the children of missionaries, the children of employees from foreign companies, customs and post offices, and the children of non-Christian believers in rural areas, each accounting for about 20% of the total respectively; and the rest, about 40%, were children from families in the handicraft industry. However, nearly two-thirds of the graduates later chose to work in such Westernization departments as post offices, customs, salt industry, telegraph companies and Western banks. Some Western banks were said to treat their employees so generously that even an employee was able to support the whole family; so it was easy to understand why people at that time spared no efforts sending their children to one of the "Top 3" boys' schools in Fuzhou.

TCF students had received a systematic and strict English training before graduation, which endowed them with a competitive edge over others in the workplace, therefore they were very popular in various industries. In 1915, Chinese Postal Service and Eastern Extension Telegraph Company recruited some TCF graduates, winning the school a better reputation. Some students were so popular that they couldn't wait to complete their study before they accepted "pre-offers" to enter workforce.

Earlier, TCF students had the opportunity to be admitted to St. John's University and Cheeloo University for further study if they met the required conditions. And after the establishment of Fukien Christian University in 1916, some lucky students were granted the similar chance to study in it. Later on, TCF, Anglo-Chinese College and Foochow College all became qualified secondary schools fully recognized by Fukien Christian University, because of which their graduates were all entitled to the admission for further study, which was also recognition of the teaching quality of the three schools.

三一学校之地标——思万楼的故事

1919年，万拔文辞职回国，临行前全家应邀参加在三一学校举行的一个奠基仪式，由恒约翰主教主持，师生朋友们济济一堂。学校将仿照他的母校都柏林大学圣三一学院的钟楼建一座塔楼。

这座哥特式三层建筑的顶层为白色，下面均由红砖砌就；立面为中世纪罗马风格，底层相对较大，越往上越小，二三层间有退化成装饰性线脚的出挑，而顶部女儿墙的造型颇有城垛口的感觉。塔楼坐南朝北，占地约25平方米，高约18米，正对校门的百米大道，进校门抬头便可以望见，有种穿越时间隧道的一眼百年的感觉。塔楼1925年才竣工，俗称"思万楼"，用来纪念圣马可书院的创始人——三一学校首任校长万拔文。

这座城堡形红砖楼里悬挂了从爱尔兰万里迢迢运来的一个紫铜大钟。大钟是都柏林李逊公园基督教堂赠给校方的，于1914年在都柏林铸造，却被一战耽搁，一直到了1921年才运到福州。百年来，这个钟也命运多舛，但所幸每次都安然度过。据说1944年抗日战争时期，仓山驻扎的大批日军想把钟拆除搬走。学校提前得到风声，几位师生争分夺秒把钟取下藏起，才逃过一劫，抗日战争胜利后才把钟完璧归赵。这一历史性建筑多次逃脱可能的厄运，如今那悠扬的钟声使人静心，催人上进，温馨恒久。

思万楼（来源：池志海）
Walsh Memorial Tower（Source：Chi Zhihai）

Landmark of TCF—Walsh Memorial Tower

In 1919, William Sandford Pakenham-Walsh resigned and planned to return home. Before leaving, his family was invited to attend a foundation-laying ceremony held in TCF, which was presided over by his friend Bishop John Hind. Quite a few teachers, students and friends got together to witness this memorable occasion. The school was to have a tower established, modelling on the bell tower of his alma mater, Trinity College Dublin.

The three-story gothic architecture is white on the top and has a red-brick bottom; the facade is in the medieval Roman style, with a relatively large base that gets smaller as it goes up, then degenerates into decorative moldings between the second and the third storeys, while the parapet at the top has the feel of a crenel. The bell tower stands in the south facing north, covering an area of about 25 square meters and about 18 meters high, just opposite the 100-meter avenue of the school gate, and the first sight of it may give you a feeling of one hundred years flying through the tunnel of time. It was completed in 1925 and is known as the "Walsh Memorial Tower" (Siwan Lou) in memory of W. S. Pakenham-Walsh, the founder of St. Mark's College and the first principal of TCF.

Inside the castle-shaped red-brick building would hang a large copper bell brought all the way from Ireland. The bell was donated to the school by the Christian Church in Harrison Park, Dublin. It was cast in Dublin in 1914, but was delayed by the First World War and was not brought to Fuzhou until 1921. The bell has had its fair share of vicissitudes over the past hundred years, but has survived every one of them. It is said that during the War of Resistence Against Japanese Agression in 1944, a large number of Japanese troops stationed in Cangshan wanted to tear down the bell and move it away. The school got the message in advance, and their fast reaction saved the bell from an unpredictable fate—to be exact, some teachers took down the clock and hid it somewhere with the help of students in a great hurry. Only after the war was finally over did they return the bell to the school, safe and intact. Similarly, this historic building escaped potential impending misfortunes several times, and now the melodious ringing of the bell brings peace and warmth to people, thus urges people to move on forever.

三一学校之芳邻——跑马场的故事

南台岛不大不小，当年的三一学校在规模上也根本算不上大，可是为什么后来就成了全国足球传统特色校呢？说起这个，不得不提起附近一个后人俗称"跑马场"的地方。这片大约350亩的大平地就在学校不远处，五口通商后，使领馆人员、商人和宗教人士云集仓前山，带来了西方文化，也打破了这里世代的平静生活。出于对赛马的狂热，他们将这块地辟为跑马场，而跑马场中的足球场，却不经意间成了附近三一学子的天堂。

据本土知名作家谢冕的回忆，这里不设边墙也不卖票，学生们可以自由进出，是他们课外常去玩耍的地方，就像是三一学校设在校外的一座特大操场。学生们非常荣幸，不但校内有个标准的足球场，校外还有这么一个天赐的大场所。跑马场外围椭圆形，中间长方形，和球场差不多，其实是双重用途。比赛场地很规范，外围跑马，中间的草地绿油油的，长得特别好，尤其吸引周边精力旺盛的孩子们，可以说他们的童年闲暇时光基本都在这里度过。

三一学校算是中国最早开展现代足球运动的学校之一，如今成为国家级足球传统学校也是水到渠成的事。据老校友回忆，但凡三一校队与马尾的外国水手举办足球赛事，跑马场毫无疑问是最佳选择。早期来比赛的以外国人居多，后来就以国人为主。校际间以及不同单位、不同群体、专业或非专业的人，都在这里体会到酣畅淋漓努力拼搏的体育精神。

• 时局变迁

抗日战争爆发后，时局动荡不安，很多单位、机构纷纷迁往内地暂时躲避战乱，三一中学高中部也内迁至古田县。到了1939年初夏，整个中学部内迁至崇安县。虽然奔波不定，但乱世中教工子女的教育也不能落下，所以原本只收男生的三一学校也顺应时势开始招收女生。

陶淑女子学校（来源：池志海）
Do-seuk Girls' School（Source: Chi Zhihai）

Neighborhood of TCF—Racecourse

Nantai island is neither big nor small, and TCF was not at all big, then why did it grow up to be a school famous for its centuried national football education? Speaking of this, we have to mention a place nearby commonly known as "Racecourse". This flat ground is about 350 mu and not far from the school, and after China entered the period of five-port trading, embassy staff, businessmen and religious personages flocked to this tiny island, bringing Western culture and in the meanwhile breaking the peaceful life here that had lasted for generations. Out of the mania for horse racing, they turned the land into a racecourse, and the football field in the racecourse inadvertently became a paradise for TCF students in the vicinity.

According to Mr. Xie Mian, a well-known native writer, there used to be no sidewalls and no ticket booth at all, therefore students enjoyed such great freedom that they came and went freely, which made it their favorite place after school. In a sense, it was more like a large playground off campus, and students were very honored to have not only a standard football field on campus, but also such a fabulous place nearby. The racecourse is oval in the periphery and rectangular in the middle, similar to a football field, and actually served dual purposes. Horses ran freely in this standardized arena, while grass in the middle turned glossy and green, which especially attracted energetic children nearby, who practically spent their leisurely childhood here.

TCF took the lead in China to advocate and develop modern football education, hence it was natural for TCF to become a state-level traditional football school. As alumni recalled, the racecourse was the best place to host a football match between TCF and Western sailors in Mamoi, Fuzhou. In the early days, most of the competitors were from the West, but later on, more Chinese are seen on the pitch. Professional or non-professional, people from different units, groups or schools all experience the uniqueness of sports spirit which best shows the combination of ease and verve, effort and struggle.

• Changes of Current Political Situation

After the outbreak of the War of Resistance Against Japanese Agression, the general situation was characterized by turbulence and intranquility. Many units and institutions moved to the inland areas so as to temporarily escape the war, and Trinity Middle School also moved to Gutian County. And in the early summer of 1939, the entire middle school division moved to Chong 'an County. Despite the unrest and uncertainties, people began to worry about the continuation of their children's education, so TCF, which originally recruited boys only, began to open their door to girls in response to the call of the times.

1941 年，三一还与同为圣公会负责的陶淑女子学校联合办学（林殷，2006），名为"三陶联中"，这也算得上强强联手。当时，三一学校校长陈世钟先生兼任联中校长，三一中学高中部主任薛平西先生被推举为联中副校长兼陶淑女中校长，直至 1944 年两校分开。1945 年抗日战争胜利，三一学校全部回迁，一切日趋正常。

1952 年底，福州市政府接收三一中学为公立学校，定名福州市第九中学，1993 年更名为福州外国语学校。三一小学先更名为象山小学，后与仓山小学合办。1992 年的 85 周年庆典时，时任福州市委书记的习近平和时任福州市长的洪永世也曾发来贺信；1997 年的 90 周年庆典，习近平还亲笔写下"百年树人，桃李芬芳"的贺词，师生们受到了极大的鼓舞。

2003 年，在热心校友林本椿教授的积极牵线下，福州外国语学校恢复了与都柏林大学圣三一学院的合作，学生成绩达标后可直升该校深造。这和早期部分优秀毕业生直升圣约翰大学与齐鲁大学有异曲同工之妙，是历史的传承与时代的见证。

三一创校之初，就非常重视中国古典文化与欧洲文学作品的比较与研究，通过共同认知来互相学习对方文化。万拔文校长非常重视中国典籍，他亲自教授《论语》《大学》《中庸》《孟子》等经典（陈孝杰，2019）。如今福州外国语学校逐步发展成为以"外语见长，文理兼优，全面发展"的学校，培养出具有中国情怀与国际化视野的代代学子。这无疑是该校前瞻性与包容性的完美体现，也是当代中国开放、包容与进步的一个缩影。

九中校门（来源：陈华棣）
Gate of No. 9 Middle School（Source: Chen Huadi）

TCF even joined efforts in 1941 with Do-seuk Girls' School ("Taoshu" in Chinese phonetic transcription), which was also in the charge of CMS, and was renamed "San-Tao Lianzhong", the literal meaning of which was "Trinity-Taoshu Joint Middle School". There was no doubt that this was a win-win cooperation under that condition. Mr. Chen Shizhong, principal of TCF then, was asked to be in charge of Trinity-Taoshu Joint Middle School at the same time; and Mr. Xue Pingxi, director of Trinity senior middle school, served as vice principal of Trinity-Taoshu Joint Middle School and principal of Do-seuk Girls' School until 1944 when the two schools were separated. After the victory of the War of Resistence Against Japanese Agression in 1945, TCF moved back to Fuzhou and everything returned to normal.

At the end of 1952, the Fuzhou Municipal Government took over Trinity College as a public school and named it Fuzhou No. 9 Middle School. In 1993, it was renamed Fuzhou Foreign Languages School with some new focuses and adjustments. Trinity Primary School was first renamed Xiangshan Primary School and later was jointly-run with Cangshan Primary School. In 1992, the then municipal Party secretary Mr. Xi Jinping and Mayor Hong Yongshi sent a letter of congratulation on the 85th anniversary of the founding of school, and then during the 90th anniversary celebration in 1997, Xi Jinping again sent an autographed inscription, "It takes ten years to grow trees but a hundred years to rear people", which greatly encouraged both teachers and students alike.

In 2003, with the help of Professor Lin Benchun, an alumnus and the associate dean of College of Foreign Languages, FJNU, Fuzhou Foreign Languages School resumed its cooperation with Trinity College Dublin, and students who pass the stipulated exams could go to Dublin for further study. This is very similar to the mechanism in early time that some outstanding TCF graduates were granted the admission to St. John's University in Shanghai and Shandong Cheeloo University after graduation due to their excellence in academic field, which best witnessed the inheritance of history and the similarities of the times.

In retrospect, we could see that since the beginning of its establishment, TCF attached great importance to the comparison and study of Chinese classical culture and European literary works, in the hope of learning from each other on the basis of common perception. W. S. Pakenham-Walsh placed such great emphasis on Chinese classics that he taught classics such as *The Analects of Confucius, The Great Learning, The Doctrine of the Mean* and *The Mencius* in person. Nowadays, Fuzhou Foreign Languages School has gradually developed into a school with principles of "being expert in foreign languages, excelling in both Arts and Sciences, and focusing on all-round development". It has cultivated generations of students with Chinese feelings and international vision, which is undoubtedly the perfect embodiment of the foresight and inclusiveness of the school, and also an epitome of the openness, tolerance and progress of contemporary China.

三一学校之所以能够培养出在各行各业有突出贡献的专家学者，很大程度上得益于办学伊始就引进了当时较为先进的国外办学模式，建立起了雄厚的师资队伍，重视英语教学，博采众长，从严治学，努力引导学生开智开眼，打造良好的学风校风。比如因"陈氏定理"而享誉国内外的世界著名解析数论学家陈景润，曾参与阿波罗登月计划的物理大师陈哲人，由司徒雷登先生引荐赴美深造后成为中国第一个发现抗生素药品的王岳博士，中国著名教育家陈景磐，当代国画大师郑乃珖，世界第一个终生在海上船舶工作的中国唯一的远洋船舶女轮机长王亚夫，当代诗歌理论权威、北大博导谢冕，曾任国家青年足球队教练的足坛名将李国宁（史晓洪，2007：67）。可以说优秀校友层出不穷，数不胜数。2021年福外教育集团成立的景润班、谢冕班等，就是对这些校友的最高肯定。现在福州外国语学校的精彩我们静待未来回溯，那么当年校友们眼里的三一学校和九中，又是什么样的存在呢？

● 杰出校友的三一映像

谢冕的三一情缘

　　文学家谢冕是福州本地人，他在校时，陈景润是高一个年级的学长，但当时两个人并不认识。多年后的两人各自成为自己领域里的大师，不得不让人感叹是什么样的环境能培养出这么优秀的人才。令谢冕印象深刻的是那座镶有彩色玻璃的尖顶教堂，遗憾的是多年后回到故乡时它却早已不见影踪，只余记忆里陪伴着他度过中学时光的悠扬歌声。

谢冕先生（来源：陈骋）
Mr. Xie Mian（Source：Chen Cheng）

When asked why TCF was able to cultivate so many experts and scholars who have made outstanding contributions in all walks of life, we should attribute this largely to the introduction of the then advanced education mode from the very outset of the school. After TCF set up a whole team of highly competitive teaching staff, it put great emphasis on English teaching, sought the advantages of various schools, kept an eye on the academic work strictly, guided the students to broaden their horizon and foster their international vision, and tried to create a good atmosphere as well as school ethos. For example, Chen Jingrun, the world-famous expert in analytic number theory who achieved great prestige at home and abroad for his "Chen's theorem"; Chen Zheren, the big shot in the physics field who used to participate in the Apollo moon-landing program; Dr. Wang Yue, who went to the USA for further study with the recommendation of Mr. John Leighton Stuart and later became the first Chinese who discovered antibiotics; Chen Jingpan, a well-known Chinese educator; Zheng Naiguang, the contemporary Chinese painting master; Wang Yafu, the world's first female chief engineer of ocean vessels and the only woman in China who had been working in ships all her life; a doctoral tutor in Peking University, Xie Mian, also a contemporary writer and authority in poetic theories; distinguished football player, Li Guoning, the former coach of the National Youth Football Team as well. It can be said that there is a very long list of those famed alumni and here we named just a few. Jingrun Class and Xiemian Class established by FFLS Education Group in 2021 were undoubtedly the highest recognition of achievements made by these alumni. In a sense, we couldn't wait to look back at the splendor and brilliance of it in the near future, and similarly we couldn't help wondering how both TCF and No. 9 Middle School had impressed the alumni in those days?

• Prominent Alumni's Feelings Towards TCF

Inseparable Tie Between Mr. Xie Mian and TCF

Mr. Xie Mian, a well-known litterateur in China, was a native of Fuzhou. When he became a seventh-grader in TCF, Chen Jingrun was an upperclassman, to be exact, one grade higher, but they did not know each other then. Many years later, both of them turned out to be masters in their respective fields, which makes people wonder what kind of environment was able to cultivate such outstanding talents, as well as who and how. The TCF chapel crowned with a spire and inlaid with beautifully colored glass always haunted him in his dreams, and what a pity that it had long disappeared before he came back to his hometown years later. Only reassuring and melodious singing wafted and accompanied him through the teenage years, as lingered in his memory.

谢冕考入三一学校是在 1945 年秋季，幸运的是他在这里碰到了自己的文学启蒙老师余钟藩先生和林仲铉先生。3 年初中加上高一总共 4 年的三一时光，为他的语文打下了坚实的基础，其余各科的根基自然也是在这里扎深。学校鼓励勤学的孩子，还为品学兼优的学子提供奖学金。这样轻松自由的环境自然对学生的成长大有裨益。高一时，他碰到了同样来三一求学的张炯先生，二人成了同班同学。1949 年 8 月底福州解放后，热血少年谢冕入伍。1955 年，谢冕复员回福州后紧锣密鼓地复习备战当年的高考并于 8 月被北大录取，与张炯的缘分再续，再次成为同门。两人先后成为当代文学研究的著名学者和三一不无关系。解放前，这一批十几岁的青少年对时代的艰辛感受特别深刻，因此特别青睐文学作品，常常阅读五四运动以来的文学作品，希望在书中找到共鸣，找到出路。三一图书室丰富的藏书和自由的学习环境给了他们很大的空间，梦想于此悄然生长。

不可否认的是，在三一学校的短短 4 年时光对谢冕一生影响极大，学校建校伊始就按照西式的理念与培养方式，尊重每个学生的个性，尊重他们的追求，让他们自由发展，尽可能地给予认可与支持。谢冕既不擅长外语，体育也不强，按理说在以外语与体育见长的学校里是得不到重视的，但他对文学的敏锐与天赋很快就得到老师们的赏识，他的作品常常在学校作文比赛中脱颖而出，荣获嘉奖。有此"特权"，他可以尽情沉浸在自己心仪的文学世界里，对学校日渐感情深厚，与大家共度时艰。学校让他学会了爱，学会了感恩，意气风发而忧国忧民。

陈景润的三一故事

福州城门胪雷村里的陈氏祠堂宽敞古朴，近些年来以每年一度的千叟宴远近闻名。回溯历史，这里人杰地灵，世世代代出过不少名人，闻名世界的数学家陈景润就是其中最知名的一个。

It was in the autumn of 1945 that he was admitted to Trinity College, where he was lucky enough to meet literary mentors Mr. Yu Zhongfan and Mr. Lin Zhongxuan, who introduced him to the profound world of literature. During the four school years in TCF, he laid a solid foundation for the Chinese language and that of other subjects as well. The school always inspired diligent children and offered scholarships to those who excelled both in conduct and academic performance. Such a relaxing and free environment was of great benefit to the growth of students. When he was in Grade 9, a Mr. Zhang Jiong became his classmate. After the liberation of Fuzhou in August 1949, Xie Mian joined the army as a hot-blooded young man. And he returned to Fuzhou soon after demobilization in 1955 and went all out to prepare for the college entrance examination that year. Admission to Peking University made it possible for him to resume his friendship with Zhang Jiong, and once again they became classmates. Both of them have become distinguished scholars in contemporary literary studies, which is more or less credited with the education and guidance of TCF. Adolescents like them before liberation had an in-depth understanding of the hard times then and they could do nothing but immerse themselves often in reading literary works published after the May 4th Movement, in the hope of finding resonance in the books and a way out afterwards. The rich collection of books and free environment in the school library witnessed their dreams setting sail silently into the immense world outside.

There is no denying that the four years in TCF has a great impact on the rest of his life. From the very beginning of its establishment, the school followed the ideas and approaches of the Western world, respecting each student's personality and pursuit, as well as offering them much space to develop freely; moreover, it gave them as much recognition and support as required. Xie Mian was poor at both English and sports, which happened to be the strong points of the school then, and this meant that he might not get taken seriously in that case. As a matter of fact, his keen observation and talent for literature soon won the appreciation of his teachers, and his works won popularity and awards in various composition competitions. With this "privilege", he was able to indulge himself in his favorite field and became increasingly attached to the school and shared the weal and woe with others, for the school has taught him to love, to be grateful as well as compassionate.

Chen Jinrun's Destiny with TCF

Chen Ancestral Hall in Lulei village near the city gate of Fuzhou is spacious and primitive, and in recent years was known far and wide for its annual Qiansou Banquet which literally means a banquet specifically held for about 1,000 elderly people in the neighborhood. Looking back, we could see a land of abundance and celebrities from generation to generation, among whom was Mr. Chen Jingrun, the world-renowned mathematician.

陈景润的出身并不显赫，但至少他的大伯、二伯和父亲都在邮局任职，算是邮政之家。邮政当时与海关都是香饽饽，这也解释了 20 世纪三四十年代时局动荡下他为什么有幸接受比较良好的教育，并为一辈子的研究打下坚实的基础。

五岁时，陈景润进入三一小学求学，当时接二连三来榕的各国传教士齐聚仓山建教堂，盖医院、办学校，使得这个小小的南台岛暂时远离战争的喧嚣，他也因此得以心无旁骛地读书。年纪虽小，他的慧心和悟性却很快显山露水，接受力和知识储备量远超同龄的学子，于是两年后就开始跳级。遗憾的是，1944 年冬福州第二次由于日军侵略而沦陷，很多人不得不举家逃往内地山区，陈景润家也不能幸免。他们前往三元县避难，开始了奔波劳顿的生活。在当地学习生活了几年，形势好转后他们便回到榕城。1946 年初，陈景润插班进了三一学校初一，1948 年初，从三一学校初中部毕业后随即到英华书院上高中。

虽然频繁转学，但他一直名列前茅。生活的艰辛造就了他内向敏感但又坚韧的个性以及超人的勤奋。逃难的老师们带来渊博的知识，也常常向学生灌输科学救国的理念。他对文史不是很感兴趣，唯独对数学情有独钟，他深信数学是万学之源，救国不可以没有科学，尤其是数学。启蒙老师陆宗授引他进入神奇的数学世界，常人眼里枯燥无味的代数方程式是他颠沛流离生活里唯一的乐趣。代数老师林宜荣、几何老师陈鹏远对他的影响和教诲调动了他全部的数学细胞（林殷，2006），日渐显露出这方面的才能。值得一提的是，当年清华大学的航空系主任沈元老师关于数论难题的两节课无意中在年仅 16 岁的他的心里种下了摘取数论皇冠上明珠的梦想。这实现梦想的过程之艰辛坎坷无须赘述，但我们不能否认三一中学是他向数学高峰攀登的起点，应该说这一切得益于当时教师们自始至终严谨的作风与严格的要求。

Chen Jingrun did not come from the upper class, but at least his uncles and his father all worked in the postal system, when both postal service and customs were among the most popular. And that explains why he was fortunate enough to receive a relatively good education after becoming a primary school student in TCF at the age of five, laying a solid foundation for a lifetime of research even during the turbulent years in the 1930s and 1940s.

At that time, a succession of missionaries from different countries gathered in Cangshan District to build churches, hospitals and schools, which temporarily kept the small island away from the hustle and bustle of the war, so that he could concentrate fully on his studies. Although he was young, his wisdom and comprehension soon became apparent, and his capability of absorbing and storing knowledge far exceeded that of his peers, which enabled him to skip grades two years later. Unfortunately, in the winter of 1944, many people had to flee to the mountainous areas in northern Fujian Province with their families because of the War of Resistence Against Japanese Agression. Chen 's family was no exception; they took refuge in Sanyuan County and experienced the twists and turns of life. Several years later, when the situation took a turn for the better, they returned to Fuzhou. In early 1946, Chen transferred to Trinity College and became a student of Grade 7 and moved up to Anglo-Chinese College two years later.

He soon got ahead of the others even after frequent changes of schools. The hardships of life endowed him with introverted sensitivity but tough personality and exceptional diligence. The teachers who fled to the mountainous areas had brought along profound knowledge and often instilled in students the idea of saving the country with the help of science, which greatly broadened his horizon. He showed little interest in literature and history, but had a fondness for mathematics, fully convinced that mathematics is the root of all learning and that we cannot save the country without science, especially mathematics. The teacher who led him into the magical world of mathematics was Mr. Lu Zongshou, and it was also Mr. Lu who made boring algebra equation the only fun in difficult and unsettled times as far as Chen was concerned. Besides Mr. Lu, both his algebra teacher Mr. Lin Yirong and geometry teacher Mr. Chen Pengyuan had had great influence on him and had dug out and mobilized all his mathematical potentials. It is also worth mentioning that, Professor Shen Yuan, head of the Department of Aeronautics at the then National Tsing Hua University, unconsciously planted in Chen's mind the dream of doing profound research into the world-renowned Number Theory after only two class hours' brief introduction to this specific field when Chen was only 16, which totally changed his life hereafter. It is unnecessary to go into details as to the bumpy process of realizing his dream, but we cannot deny that Trinity College was the starting point for him to approach the Peak of Mathematics. And it should be said that all this was due to the rigorous teaching style and strict requirements of the teachers at that time.

三一学校对英语的重视程度甚至超过本国母语，陈景润和其余学生一样狠下功夫背单词，理解课文，培养语感。如果没有这些长期打下的坚实牢固的英语基础，他日后就不可能自如高效地阅读外文数学杂志原文，吸收世界数论精华了。这实实在在的童子功以及严谨的治学态度为他借鉴外国数学成就赢得了宝贵时间，使他一直处于世界数学科学前沿阵地，直到向那最难攻破的数学堡垒之一——哥德巴赫猜想——进军。

林本椿教授的九中情结

曾在九中初中就读的福建师大外国语学院原副院长林本椿教授说起母校时眼里满是温暖的笑意。如果没有 20 世纪 60 年代初短短三年的九中情缘，师大图书馆中那两本薄薄的毫不起眼的传教士回忆录也不会吸引他的眼球（庄才水，2017）；如果没有他极高的敏锐性与学者习惯性追根溯源的探究精神，他也不可能联系上万里迢迢之外的爱尔兰都柏林大学；如果没有这样的机缘巧合应邀前往爱尔兰"母校"进行长达十天的访问并为天各一方的两所三一学校牵线搭桥，就不会有这百年后 21 世纪的两校再续前缘。那座有着 430 年悠久历史的欧洲著名高等学府牵挂着位于中国东南部的"女儿校"，时任校长海格蒂先生欣然接受林教授之约回访福州外国语学校（以下简称为"福外"），这在 21 世纪初是一件激动人心的大事。2003 年，爱尔兰一行人在林教授等人的陪伴下参观校内的爱尔兰文化中心，并与英语实验班学生倾心交流，为这段特别的缘分画上了美好的一笔。

90 年代初，在九中申办福州外国语学校的过程中，林教授作为热心的"少壮派"校友，协助陈中新老校长等人联络海内外校友，自始至终不遗余力。1994 年起福建师大外国语学院与福外联办的"五年专"以及商务英语培训，还有后来陆续引进美澳等国外教这类"外事"，都离不开林教授的大力支持与帮助。

：林本椿教授（来源：陈琳）
：Prof. Lin Benchun（Source：Chen Lin）

Moreover, Trinity College attached more importance to English than to our own mother tongue, therefore, like other students, Chen put lots of work into reciting words, appreciating texts and cultivating a good sense of language. Without this solid English foundation, he would not be able to read the original texts of Western mathematical magazines freely and efficiently later on, and wouldn't be able to absorb the essence of Number Theory either. This consistent and rigorous academic attitude won him precious time to learn from Western mathematical achievements and remain in the forefront of the world mathematical science, until in the end he marched towards the most difficult part of the mathematical fortress—Goldbach Conjecture.

The Predestined Link Between Prof. Lin Benchun and No. 9 Middle School

Before he retired, Professor Lin Benchun was vice dean of College of Foreign Languages, Fujian Normal University, and he used to study in No. 9 Middle School when young. At the mention of his alma mater, he always wears a warm smile. Had it not been for the three years' study there in the early 1960s, the two plain and inconspicuous missionary memoirs in the school library of FJNU would not have attracted his attention. Had it not been for his great sensitivity and the spirit of academic inquiry as a revered scholar, he would not have been able to get in contact in the shortest possible time with Trinity College Dublin, Ireland, which is thousands of miles away. Had he not been invited to the "mother school" in Ireland for a ten-day visit and acted as a bridge between the two Trinity schools soon afterwards, there would have been no connection at all in the 21st century. Being a renowned institution of higher learning in Europe, TCD enjoys a history of 430 years and shows great concern for its "daughter institution" in the remote area in Southeast China. Mr. John Hegarty, the then provost of TCD gladly accepted Prof Lin's invitation and paid a visit to Fuzhou Foreign Languages School (hereinafter referred to as "FFLS"), which was a stirring event in the early 21st century. In 2003, accompanied by Professor Lin and leaders of the school, the distinguished guests from Ireland visited the Center of Irish Studies in FFLS and had a face-to-face talk with the students of the English Experimental Class, which added a touch of warmth and harmony to this special relationship between the two institutions.

In the early 1990s, when No. 9 Middle School was to be renamed Fuzhou Foreign Languages School, Proffesor Lin, as an enthusiastic "young" alumnus, spared no efforts all the way through in assisting Mr. Chen Zhongxin, the former principal, and some others in contacting alumni at home and abroad. Since 1994, College of Foreign Languages in Fujian Normal University has joined efforts with FFLS in establishing the "5-year junior-college program" and starting the Business English training, and later on introduced in succession Western teachers from abroad to help with the language teaching, all of which are inseparable from Professor Lin's consistent instruction and timely guidance.

此外，为了增加福外的外语特色，提高福外的外语教学软实力，他紧锣密鼓地联系、组织、安排福建师大外国语学院的外籍教师、本院教授以及有经验的资深老师们有计划地到福外指导外语教学，提高教学质量。美国语言学教授琳达还深入课堂听课，尽力帮助任课教师提高语言能力，掌握讲课艺术。

在林教授的印象里，当年大部分老师都是老三一出身，治学严谨，言传身教。比如毕业于燕京大学新闻系的郑锡安教授分别在三一学校和师大外院任教过，也曾是英华英语学校的首任校长，可谓是桃李满天下；曾任北大数学学院院长的79届校友王长平教授现在是福建师大校长，他的梦想也正是在这里腾飞。这些老师得益于当年三一学校那一套严格严谨到近乎严苛的教学方法，也将此治学精神自然而然地传给了后面一代代的学子，为培养人才树立了一个独特的标杆。据说在英文课上，如果老师反复强调过的语言点，学生复习不到位、掌握不扎实犯了不该犯的语法错误的话，即使是非常微小的错误，老师也会在其作业或者卷子上盖个三角形的印戳，二话不说让其从头再做。这样几次下来，大家都纷纷吸取教训，再也不敢犯低级错误了。

这种对完美细节的貌似吹毛求疵的把控为学生们未来治学、工作与生活打下了良好基础。很多三一学子后来有机会前往福建协和大学、圣约翰大学、齐鲁大学、燕京大学等名牌学府深造，应该说在很大程度上归功于他们青少年时期在三一学校时所受到的独一无二的训练。

身为中国译协理事兼福建省译协副会长的林教授，是翻译理论与实践领域的著名学者，对中外文化交流与中英互译颇有造诣。九中的庄才水老校长1963年刚刚分配到福州高级中学教书时，林教授是他的第一届学生，多年后他提起自己这个学生的文学底蕴与翻译功底时依然赞不绝口。

In addition, in order to reinforce the school's language features and improve its soft power in many facets, he went all out to contact and invite experienced teachers at home and abroad to assist the teaching in FFLS in a planned and systematic way. Linda, a linguistics professor from the United States, has done a superb job in attending lectures in person to help improve teachers' language skills and master the art of lecturing.

In Professor Lin's memory, most of the teachers in those days graduated from TCF and were noted for their meticulous scholarship, and they always taught by precept and example. For example, Professor Zheng Xi'an, a journalism major of Yenching University, used to teach successively at TCF and the College of Foreign Languages, FJNU, and was also the first principal of Private Anglo-Chinese College; Professor Wang Changping, a former dean of the School of Mathematics at Peking University, is now the president of Fujian Normal University, and his dream took root right here at TCF. These teachers benefited a lot from the strict, rigorous or even stern teaching methods of TCF at that time, and they, in turn, passed on this spirit to the following generations of students, setting a unique benchmark for cultivating students. It is said that in some English class, some students did not work hard enough and therefore did not have a good command of the language points teachers repeatedly emphasized, and they tended to make grammatical mistakes sooner or later. In that case, even if they were only minor mistakes, the teacher would stamp a triangle on their exercisebooks and ask them to do it all over again. No bargain! It happened several times and everyone had learned tough lessons, so they dared not make this kind of careless mistakes any more.

This seemingly fastidious focus on details prepared students for a lifetime pursuit in both work and life. Thanks to the unique training they received in their teenage years at TCF, many students later went on to study at prestigious universities such as Fukien Christian University, St. John's University, Cheeloo University or Yenching University.

As a member of the China Translators Association and vice president of the Fujian Translators Association, Professor Lin is a master in the field of translation theory and practice, with profound knowledge of Sino-foreign cultural exchanges and bilingual translation. Professor Lin is one of the first students of Mr. Zhuang Caishui, when Zhuang was first assigned to teach at Fuzhou Senior High School in 1963 after graduation from university. Mr. Zhuang is the last principal of No. 9 Middle School many years later, and he always speaks highly of Prof. Lin's profound literary foundation and translation skills.

庄校长依然记得那是在 20 世纪 90 年代，他们一起陪同悉尼大学李科林教授到鼓山参观，他还没琢磨透那些摩崖石刻里对联等文字的含义，林教授已经在一旁用流畅的英语解释得头头是道，让外国人对我们博大精深的中国文化与文字魅力有了生动而直观的印象。这些日积月累的功底多少得益于中学时代的双语文化浸染，尤其是那一口纯正的英语语音让人怀疑他是否曾旅居国外多年？对于笔者的疑惑，林教授依然是那副"弥勒佛"般处事不惊又淡然内敛的笑容——其实他是"土生土长"的九中人。可以这么说，当年严师们传递给代代学子严谨治学的三一精神与"激励后世历代"的爱尔兰母校校训在温厚儒雅的林教授身上得到了完美的呈现。

陈华棣会长的三一足球人生

福外校友会会长陈华棣先生是林本椿教授的初中同学，人称"中国足球收藏第一人"的他在采访中曾多次提起，他的一切都是足球给的；如果没有九中的培养，没有三一的情缘，就不会有如今的多彩经历。与足球结缘始于童年，他家附近就是跑马场，跑马场的另一头就是三一学校。长方形的足球场外面是椭圆形的跑马场，还有长满绿草皮的空地，外面还有内河，再外面还有很多活动的空间，这无疑是物质匮乏年代孩子们的天堂。那里常常有各式各样的比赛，孩子们都在周边玩，频频感受视觉盛宴后，不禁萌生了在球场肆意奔腾的念头。

遗憾的是跑马场是大人的天下，很少有机会轮到小朋友们；孩子们大部分时间都只能在稻田瞎折腾，或者趁大人忙着春播秋收无暇顾及时，偷偷跑进去撒野一番。最早应该是五六岁的时候，从小天性活泼好动的陈华棣初次在跑马场接触到足球，从此一发不可收拾。

He can still clearly recall the day when they accompanied Mr. Colin Pears, a professor from the University of Sydney, to the Gushan Mountain, where lots of inscriptions on precipices scattered here and there. For most people it is not in the least an easy job to figure out the subtle meanings of those couplets and ancient poetry, and before he could even make it to discern what Chinese characters were engraved on stones, Professor Lin had already been explaining in fluent English the charm, extensiveness and profoundity of the Chinese culture and characters, leaving an intuitive impression on the Western expert. There is no denying that his knowledgeability comes from the daily accumulation, and that he benefited a lot from the bilingual culture in his middle school. It is also fun to mention that his pure English pronunciation always makes people wonder whether he has been abroad for many years. In response to my doubts, Professor Lin wears the same smile as that of the Maitreya Buddha. In fact, he was absolutely indigenous—born and raised nearby—and spent his most ignorant years in No. 9 Middle School. It can be said that the Trinity spirit of rigorous scholarship and the Irish alma mater motto of "inspiring future generations" passed on by severe teachers in those days are perfectly shown on Professor Lin, a learned and refined gentleman.

Mr. Chen Huadi's Football Romance with TCF and No. 9 Middle School

Mr. Chen Huadi, president of FFLS Alumni Association, used to be the classmate of Professor Lin Benchun in junior middle school. He is known as "the first football collector in China" and has mentioned many times in the interview that he owes everything to football. Without the cultivation of No. 9 Middle School and the convenience brought by TCF, he would not have had the colorful experience now. He took a fancy to football since his childhood, since there was a racecourse near his home, and TCF was just opposite it. Outside the rectangular football field is the oval racecourse as well as the open space covered with green turf, and there was an inland river beyond. This spacious plain in the vicinity had undoubtedly become a paradise for children in the age of material scarcity. A variety of matches were held there, and children playing nearby witnessed the visual feast again and again, because of which they could not help conceiving of the fun and fulfilment of running freely in the football pitch.

What a pity that the racecourse belonged to adults most of the time, and there were few opportunities for children to set free their dreams. Children spent most of their time fooling around in the rice fields, or sneaking into the racecourse when the adults were fully-occupied with spring sowing or autumn harvest. The first time Chen Huadi got in touch with football, he was only five or six years old, and he fell in love with it and took actions in no time.

于是他空余时间发动小伙伴们抓抓螃蟹，捡捡树上掉下的橄榄。卖出去的几分钱几毛钱日积月累，买了足球印了背心后，一个民间足球队——海鸥队就这么成立了。这应该是当年福州最低龄的足球队吧！颇有天赋的他，小学毕业就被保送到爱才惜才并被誉为"福州现代足球发源地"的福州九中，在那里他确定了成为专业足球运动员的梦想，也在恩师何馨朝老师的悉心教导下茁壮成长。

何老师是老三一出身，黄埔军校毕业，当时是他们的班主任兼体育老师。作为足球界的元老与伯乐，他慧眼识珠、因材施教，培养了无数的足球人才，其中就有李国宁等国家级足球健将。建国七十周年时，国家还因为他的独特经历与卓越贡献为他颁发了荣誉勋章，这是一份殊荣，是对他一辈子提携无数体育人才的嘉许。小小年龄的陈华棣正是因为得到何老师的全心教导才进步神速，足球人生才得以全面开启。在九中的几年时间里，他作为校队一员参加过福州市以及福建省各种赛事，南征北战，甚至到国外进行交流，收获满满。令他至今难忘的是，在 20 世纪 60 年代物质条件并不宽裕的情况下，何老师总是想方设法记录他们成长的瞬间，为他们留下了许多珍贵的老照片。思万楼下孩子们满眼的憧憬与光芒，一号楼、二号楼旁小运动员们的意气风发，都定格成了永远的财富。

福州九中一号楼二号楼（来源：陈华棣）
Building No. 1 and Building No. 2 of No. 9 Middle School（Source: Chen Huadi）

后来作为高中生的陈华棣顺利进入省队，遗憾的是一年后他的足球生涯不得不戛然而止。回到老家的他仍旧把足球梦深藏于心，同时不断寻求好机会，很快就办起了东升印刷厂。改革开放后这个民办工厂如火如荼，为许多人提供了就业机会。转眼到了 1978 年，这是陈华棣人生中又一个重要的转折点。离开省队整整 12 年没有碰过足球的他，因为伯乐何老师的召唤又回到绿茵场，作为福州队的一员参加了第七届省运会，与九中的一生缘也再次续上。

He encouraged his buddies to catch crabs and collect olives which fell off the tree in their spare time and sold them all, by which they accumulated money, a few cents per time. With this small sum increasing over a period of time, they bought a football and had their uniform (vests, to be exact) printed, thus a civilian football team—Seagull—came into existence. This must be the youngest football team in Fuzhou! After graduating from primary school, he was recommended to Fuzhou No. 9 Middle School, known as "the birthplace of modern football in Fuzhou", where he got a clear vision of becoming a professional football player and developed well under the devoted guidance of his respected teacher, Mr. He Xinchao.

Mr. He used to be a student in TCF and finally graduated from the Huangpu (Whampoa) Military Academy. He was Chen's class adviser and physical education teacher. As the founding member and a talent scout of the football circle, he has trained and fostered numerous football talents, including Li Guoning and other national football players. In the 70th anniversary of the founding of the People's Republic of China, our government awarded him the Medal of Honor for his unique experience and outstanding contributions. This is undoubtedly a special honor, and a tribute to him for guiding and cultivating countless sports talents in his life. Chen Huadi was lucky in that he got Mr. He's whole-hearted instruction at a young age and made rapid progress, bringing his great potentials into full play. During his years in No. 9 Middle School, he participated in various matches in Fuzhou and even in Fujian as a member of the school team. He even went abroad to exchange experiences and gained a lot. What makes him unforgettable is that in the 1960s, when few people were materially well-off, Mr. He always tried to record the moments of their growing up, leaving many precious old photos for them. The vision and light in the eyes of the children in front of Walsh Memorial Tower, and the vigor and the high spirits of the young athletes standing next to Building No. 1 and Building No. 2 have all become frozen moments just as eternal and memorable heritage.

Later, as a high school student, Chen Huadi was admitted into the provincial team without a hitch, but his football career had to come to an abrupt end unfortunately one year later for some reason. He went back to his hometown and buried his football dream deep in his heart, while constantly seeking good opportunities for a better life. Very soon he set up Dongsheng Printing Plant and with the deepening of reform and opening-up, this private factory was in full bloom, providing employment opportunities for many local people. Time went by quickly. In 1978 Mr. Chen came across another important turning point in his life. Since he left the provincial team 12 years ago, he had never touched football any more. And now because of Mr. He's summon, he came back to the familiar football pitch and participated in the 7th Provincial Games as a member of Fuzhou team without hesitation, thus his lifelong attachment to No. 9 Middle School was continued.

老师的长期认可与不断提携，再加上省队一些好友的支持，让他的足球梦再次点燃，但是这一次他不再满足于自己踢球。20世纪80年代，他组织志同道合的球友成立校友队，紧接着创立了东升足球俱乐部，再后来创办了足球学校来招收有天赋的中小学生。这些举措其实都是效仿当年恩师，重在发现人才、挖掘人才，为他们提供各种可能的机会与平台，让他们为自己的梦想拼搏。这种对可塑之才的敏锐、重视和用心得益于三一的传承，只要一发现好苗子就会尽力创造条件去培养。这就是所谓的传帮带吧。

在三一和九中众校友的联手助力下，当年的庄校长带领校领导班子为申办福外而不懈努力。在此期间，陈华棣先生总是积极主动，有求必应。九中第一任老校长陈中新曾以"母校近况"为内容起草过一封给海内外校友的中英文信，该信经由薛平西和陈鹏远两位老领导共同讨论修改签名后，由陈会长的东升印刷厂承印600份（庄才水，2017：43），并第一时间向国内外校友寄发。这是何等重要的一封信，它见证了重要的历史时刻，意义非凡。

曾经的足球健将和企业家，在古稀之年急流勇退，创办起了私人博物馆，并以福建省收藏家协会会长的身份续写精彩人生。他的五个分馆各个都独一无二——体育的历史与文化、足球的周边、印刷设备的衍变、知青岁月的记忆以及红色珍藏品，件件都让人赞叹，引人遐思。馆内和足球有关的藏品最为丰富，有名人签名的足球、不同国家各年代的足球宣传画、比赛门票、秩序册、徽章、邮票等大约2万多件，让人叹为观止。或许它们不完全是大众眼中的稀世之宝，但对于陈会长来说，每一件都是无价的宝贝。它们无声地讲述着与足球有关的故事，见证着跌宕起伏的体育史，感受着纵横百年的体育精神，让我们不知不觉回想起百年前在南台小岛的球场上奔跑的那些少年。

何馨朝老师和学生们于思万楼前（来源：陈华棣）
Mr. He Xinchao and his students in front of Walsh Memorial Tower(Source: Chen Huadi)

Mr. He's long-term recognition and continuous guidance, coupled with the support of some friends in the provincial team, ignited his football dream again, but this time he was no longer satisfied with his personal participation only. In the 1980s, he formed an alumni team with like-minded players, followed by the establishment of Dongsheng Football Club, and later established a football school to recruit primary and secondary school students who are talented in football. In fact, he modeled after his mentor and role model Mr. He in taking these measures, focusing on the discovery of talented students, cultivating them and providing them with all the possible opportunities and platforms, so that the kids can fight for their dreams, just as what Mr. He did to them many years ago. Thanks to the instruction of TCF, which had a sharp eye for students with great potentials and which valued them and cared for them, he has followed the example and has done his utmost to nurture the children with football dreams. I guess that's what they call mentoring and inheritance.

With the help of the alumni of TCF and No. 9 Middle School, the then Principal Mr. Zhuang led the leading body of the school to make unremitting efforts for the transferral to FFLS in the late 1980s. During this period, Mr. Chen Huadi always took the initiative and granted whatever was requested. The first principal of No. 9 Middle School Mr. Chen Zhongxin had drafted a letter to the alumni at home and abroad with "Recent Developments of Alma Mater" as the main content in both Chinese and English, and then two of the former school leaders, Mr. Xue Pingxi and Mr. Chen Pengyuan, had an in-depth discussion before making some proper modification and signing the letter. Later on, Mr. Chen Huadi instructed his Dongsheng Printing Plant to undertake the printing mission of 600 copies, and immediately sent them to alumni both here and abroad. What an important letter it is, for it witnessed a very uncommon moment in the history of the school.

Once a football player and entrepreneur, he retired in his prime when he was about seventy. In no time he set up a private museum, and continued his wonderful life as the president of Fujian Collectors Association. The museum has five branches and each of them is unique—Sports' History & Culture, Football Peripherals, Evolution of Printing Equipment, Memory of School Graduates as well as Revolutionary Collection. People can't help gasping in admiration at the sight of the various exhibits that set them thinking. The museum has the most abundant collection related to football, altogether more than 20,000 pieces, including footballs signed by celebrities, football posters of various countries, tickets for matches, programs of matches, badges, stamps and so on. They may not be exactly what the public thinks of as rare treasures, but in Chen's eyes, each piece is priceless, which silently tells stories concerning football, witnesses the ups and downs of sports history, feels the spirit of sports throughout a hundred years, and reminds us unconsciously of those boys running on the pitch a century ago in the small Nantai Island.

庄才水校长"教书育人"的双重情怀

听闻庄才水校长参与并见证了福州九中转变为福州外国语学校的发展历程，我满怀期待。这样一位传奇又低调的老人，会是什么样的呢？眼前戴着鸭舌帽的庄老清瘦矍铄，反应敏捷，逻辑清晰，完全看不出已经 83 岁高龄。说起一生热爱的教育事业，他眼里满怀激情与信念。爱国、爱校、爱学生是学校办学的永恒主题，也是他半辈子教育生涯中一直努力践行的。在教学育人和行政管理方面，他一向有着自己独特的理念与方法。

从大学毕业分配到福州高级中学从教开始，他就致力于学科的钻研，很快便在福州市化学教育界有了一定的影响力。他擅长用生动直观的手段来激发学生学习兴趣，还时常根据教学需要精心制作教具。2003 年，教育部编写新教材课本时，已经退休的他作为省里化学学科三位代表之一应邀再次出山。不管是常规教学还是编写教材，他都遵循同样的理念：要贴近生活，贴近实际，不搞贴标签；老师们不可能事事讲深讲透，但要把概念讲清楚，让学生准确理解，学会应用。

庄老的教育理念和别人也不太一样，体现了与时俱进。他曾提出一个观点，要给学生一杯水，教师必须有一桶水。后来他自己批判了这个论点：教师是一桶水，学生应该是一条河；老师不一定得比学生强，相反，学生一定要比老师强；而且一杯水是注入，不是启发；河流奔涌着，更有生命力，意味着学生可以大大超过老师。这样一代胜过一代，我们这个社会才能发展、才能前进。此外，他不赞同"教学是指老师教学生学"，他认为老师的任务重在教会学生怎么去学，而不仅仅是为学生传授知识；也就是说老师不是给学生野猪肉，而是给学生一把猎枪教他怎么去打猎。老师与学生在教学活动中要共同成长，同理，家长和孩子在家庭关系中也应该是共同成长。

Principal Zhuang Caishui's Dual Expectation of "Imparting Knowledge and Educating People"

I am looking forward to meeting Principal Zhuang Caishui, who has participated in and witnessed the transferral of Fuzhou No. 9 Middle School to Fuzhou Foreign Languages School. What does such a legendary old man look like? Wearing a cricket-cap, Mr. Zhuang looks hale, hearty and agile, and his quick wit and good logic deny him showing his 83 years of age. Speaking of his lifelong love of education, his eyes are full of passion and faith. Patriotism, love of the school, love of the students have become the school's eternal theme, and he has been trying to practice these in his education career over a half century. We can credibly say that he always has his own unique ideas and methods in both education and administration.

After graduation from university, he was assigned to teach in Fuzhou Senior High School, and he devoted himself to this holy cause since then. Soon, because of his undivided attention in teaching and research, he has had a certain influence over the chemical education circle of Fuzhou; he is skilled at using vivid and visual means to stimulate students' interest, and often makes teaching aids according to the real needs. In 2003, when the Ministry of Education was preparing for the compiling of new teaching materials, he was invited as one of the three representatives of the provincial chemical circle, even though he had already retired then. Whether it is routine teaching or compiling textbooks, he always follows the same philosophy of being close to life and reality. He objects to labeling, and he is well aware that it is impossible for teachers to explain everything profoundly and thoroughly, but that we should at least make them explicit, so that students could have a better understanding and learn to put them into use step by step.

Mr. Zhuang's educational concept is quite different from that of others, in some way reflecting "advancing with the times". He once put forward the idea that if we want to give students a glass of water, we need to equip ourselves with a bucket of water. But very soon, he refuted this argument. He further argued if teachers are a bucket of water, then students should be a river. Teachers don't have to be better than students, on the contrary, student are expected to do better and achieve more. The glass of water is more an infusion, not an inspiration; while the river is surging and gushing, vigorous and alive. Likewise, students can vastly surpass their teachers, which means each generation will prevail over the former one, and only then can our society develop and advance in the right way. In addition, he does not agree with the idea that "teaching means teachers teach while students learn"; he thinks that a teacher's task is to teach students how to learn, not just to impart knowledge to students. Let's put it another way, instead of giving students wild boar meat, teachers should hand over shotguns and teach them how to hunt whatever they want. Teachers and students should make progress together in teaching activities, similarly parents and children should also grow up together in family relations.

庄校长还认为学生不应是标准件而应是百花园，不能用同一个标准来约束他们，要根据不同学生的特点与特长因材施教。在他整个教学生涯中，吸引学生靠的是自信，是内容，是多年对学生群体的潜心研究，是掌握学生跳动的思想脉搏。

作为教育工作者，他认为做人做事要怀有敬畏之心，要持续更新和丰富知识体系，并且不断弥补短板。他几十年如一日的深度学习思考与知识的迭代更新就是给师生们树立的最好的榜样。如今年逾80的庄老在求知若渴的同时还保持着批判性思维。每年高考结束，他都把全国各地的化学卷做一遍，一旦发现有疑虑、有生疏的地方，立马查经据典，追根溯源。

2016年，他应邀参加首都师范大学的学术研讨会，其他教授专家都是从文科的角度来阐明哲学课题，唯独他是从自然科学角度展开论述，独特的见解得到与会专家的重视和一致认可。谈及各门学科的关系时，他提出：物理、化学、生物等是自然科学，提高科学素养以求"真"；语文、政治、历史等属于人文科学，提高人文素养以求"善"；音乐、美术等属于艺术门类，提高艺术素养以求"美"。"真善美"和"德智体"完美呼应，这也正是他多年教学的思考与观点的提炼。

1988年是一个重要的转折点——他从福州高级中学教务主任的位置上直接被调到福州九中当校长兼书记。万事开头难，摆在他面前的困难是多方面的，好在来自各级领导、各方师友以及众校友的大力支持，让他克服重重困难，顺利渡过各种难关。庄老知道信心比金子还珍贵，因此要逐步扬正气，让处于低谷期的老师们能够看到希望，树立信心，这是学校走出困境的关键。而学校要找出路，首先得要先有思路，大家集思广益得出的新思路就是创建外国语学校。

He also holds that students should not be like standard parts but should be like hundreds of flowers blossoming in the garden; in other words, they should not be restricted by the same standard, by contrast, they should be cultivated according to what they are good for. We should put emphasis on characteristics and expertise of different students. Throughout his teaching career, what attracts students most is his confidence, the knowledge, years of research into the student body as well as keeping pace with their minds.

As a senior educator, he believes that whatever we do, we should hold in awe and veneration; moreover, we should constantly update and enrich our stock of knowledge, and continuously strengthen our weak links. He has set the best example for teachers and students alike with his decades of in-depth learning, profound thinking as well as iteration and renewal of knowledge. Now even in his 80s, Mr. Zhuang still keeps a critical mind while staying intellectually curious. Every year right after the national college entrance examination, he will do all the chemistry paper in person that he could collect from all over the country, and once he has any doubts or finds something unfamiliar to him about the paper, he will immediately consult reference books and trace them to the source.

In 2016, he was invited to participate in the academic seminar in Capital Normal University. While other professors and experts elaborated philosophical issues from the perspective of liberal arts, he was the only one who expounded from the perspective of natural science. His unique views were valued and unanimously accepted by the experts present. Talking about the relationship between various disciplines, he holds that subjects like physics, chemistry and biology belong to natural sciences, hence we need to boost our scientific literacy so as to keep the "true"; subjects like Chinese, politics and history belong to the humanities, so we need to uplift our humanistic quality in order to keep the "good"; subjects like music and art belong to classes of arts, so we need to improve artistic accomplishment in order to keep the "beautiful". "Truth, Goodness and Beauty" perfectly echoes "moral, intellectual and physical education", which is exactly what he has reflected and refined after years of teaching.

The year 1988 was a memorable turning point, since he was transferred directly from the position of academic director in Fuzhou Senior High School to Fuzhou No. 9 Middle School as the principal. As the old saying goes, all things are difficult before they are easy. He faced many difficulties to start with, but thanks to the substantial support from leaders at all levels, teachers, friends and alumni, he was able to overcome them all one after another and successfully pulled through all kinds of crises. Mr. Zhuang was well aware that confidence was more precious than gold, so the school should gradually encourage upright force and let the teachers who had been at low ebbs see the hope and build up confidence, which was the key for the whole school to get out of dilemma. In order to find a way out, the school should come up with new ideas, and here it is—to re-establish a foreign language school.

为什么呢？当时福州九中还是个薄弱校，转变极其不易。所幸上级政策发生了变化——20 世纪 70 年代末的集中力量办重点校到 80 年代末的扶持一般校——给学校带来了契机，可谓是天时地利人和。

"生源、师资和管理"是办好一所学校最重要的三个要素。在改变生源素质方面，1991 年，市教委允许提前跨区跨片招收英（日）语特色班，这是很重要的举措，也是创办福外的"前哨站"。庄老刚刚来时，每年初中留级将近一百人，合格率只有 36.7%。庄老意识到留级救不了九中，必须减少留级的人数，直至完全消除这种现象。12 年后他退休时优秀率已超过 80%，及格率更是飙升到 99%，这是显而易见的进步。把情况摸清楚继而对症下药，生源问题就迎刃而解。紧接着提升教师素质成了十分紧迫的任务，为此他带领团队参加集体备课，深入课堂听课。除了给学生上课，他也两次为老师们作"如何上好一堂课"的演讲。管理的关键是律己，公正无私才能致远。1991 年被评为省优秀校长并获得千元奖金后，他毫不迟疑地悉数捐给了学校。

师生同心协力，经过几年的筹备和努力，福州九中于 1993 年 6 月 25 日更名为福州外国语学校。在薄弱校的起点上创办外国语学校，这在全国极其罕见，长路漫漫。他对老师们说，如果把福外比喻成一台戏，他更像是搭建舞台的木工和泥水匠，演员得由师生们联手来担当，而且要经过几代人的艰苦努力，一步步推进，才把学校办好。

：庄才水校长与笔者（来源：陈琳）
：Principal Zhuang Caishui and the author（Source：Chen
：Lin）

Why so? At that time, No. 9 Middle School was still a weak school, in other words, schools which were not built and operated in a desirable way; worse still, it was extremely difficult to make changes. Fortunately, the policy of higher authorities has changed, to be exact, at the end of the 1970s, the focus was on the concentration of various efforts to run key schools while at the end of the 1980s it shifted to support ordinary schools. This momentous reform brought rare opportunity to No. 9 Middle School, which can be said to be at the right place and at the right time.

"Students, teachers and management" are the three key elements to run a school well. In terms of changing the quality of students, in 1991, the Municipal Commission of Education allowed the school to recruit students of English (Japanese) major in advance, which was a very important move and an "outpost" for the establishment of Fuzhou Foreign Languages School. When Mr. Zhuang just took office here in 1988, nearly 100 ninth-graders failed to go up to the next grade for poor performance every year, and only 36.7% of them passed all the required courses and moved up as planned. As an experienced teacher, Mr. Zhuang realized that repeating a year could not save No. 9 Middle School and that they could eliminate the phenomenon completely if they were able to reduce the number of detained students by all means. By the time he retired 12 years later, the school had achieved an over 80% excellence rate and a 99% pass rate, which was an obvious improvement. It is clear that once we figure out where the root-cause lies and then take appropriate measures, most problems will be solved, just as the efforts which were made to improve the quality of students. With the solution of the first problem, it became an urgent task to improve the quality of teachers, so he led the faculty to participate in collective lesson preparation and in-depth class attendance, in the hope of enhancing their all-round capabilities. In addition to giving lectures to students, he successively gave two lectures specifically to teachers on How to Give a Good Lesson. There is no doubt that the key to management is to be self-disciplined and impartial, and he has always been a great example. In 1991, he was awarded the prize of ¥1,000 for his excellent work as a principal but he donated all to the school without hesitation.

After years of detailed preparation and great efforts, Fuzhou No. 9 Middle School was renamed Fuzhou Foreign Languages School on June 25, 1993. It was extremely rare in China to establish a foreign languages school on the basis of a weak school, and obviously there was still a long way to go. He said to the teachers that if FFLS was compared to a play, he was more like a carpenter and a mason who built the stage, while the roles of actors should be played by teachers and students together; apart from that, only by the hard work of several generations can they move on step by step, and finally make the school better, stronger and more popular.

在创办福外的过程中，有原来九中老领导的支持，有老三一校友真心实意的帮助，有九中少壮派校友不遗余力的支持，这些感人的细节让他自始至终深受鼓舞。薛平西、陈中新、陈鹏远是原三一已退休多年的老校长，他们主动上门跟庄校长共商复兴母校大计，第一时间联名写信给国内外校友并广为寄发，号召广大校友出力献策，并强调：现在母校由庄校长主持，是校友支持母校的最佳时期。84 岁的陈鹏远老校长主动帮助学校写校志，写回忆录到三更半夜，还不让家人打扰；旅居美国、已经 103 岁高龄的原三一老校长童志柔几次为学校捐款；以著名月老刘含怀为代表的不少老校友也奔前跑后，用各自的方式表达对母校复兴的支持。

每个人一生中至少四分之一的美好时光是在校园里度过的。如果我们有幸遇见了点亮我们人生之旅、指引我们砥砺前行的导师，那是莫大的幸运。庄校长深以为然，他也一直如此践行。近半个世纪以来，爱国、爱校、爱学生的情怀早已内化成为他的信念。他殷切期望在福州外国语学校的校园里、在我们民族的土地上，能涌现出代代优秀学子，让我国的教育事业迎来更加美好的明天！

● 结语

绘着宗教故事的彩色窗棂早已不在，耳边依稀传来平和的圣洁音乐，思万楼的钟声催人奋进，足球场的汗水是曾经飞扬的青春。那座曾经风光一时的东欧风格双层砖木结构静静矗立着，原先的白墙黑瓦历经风吹日晒雨打本已斑驳，但在热心校友捐资修复下却再一次焕发新颜。安着木框玻璃、嵌着铁栅的拱形窗户依然在，重新粉刷过的灰蓝色外墙在阳光下时常衍射出奇幻的光影，仿佛在诉说它昔日的辉煌，在遥想未来的灿烂。

必翰楼（来源：池志海）
Rev. W. P. W. Williams Memorial Hall（Source: Chi Zhihai）

In the process of founding FFLS, Mr. Zhuang was deeply moved and greatly inspired by the steadfast backup from the former leaders of No. 9 Middle School, the sincere help from the TCF alumni, and the alumni of No. 9 Middle School who spared no efforts in various assistance. Mr. Xue Pingxi, Mr. Chen Zhongxin and Mr. Chen Pengyuan all retired from Trinity College many years ago as principals, and when they heard about the reforms that were carried out by the then principal Mr. Zhuang, they couldn't help taking the initiative to meet Mr. Zhuang and hold joint discussions about reviving their alma mater. In no time they wrote a letter in joint names and sent it to alumni at home and abroad, calling upon them to offer advice and make contributions, for the common goal of revitalization of the prestigious school. They didn't forget to convey the idea that with the guidance and supervision of Principal Zhuang, it was the best time for alumni to serve their alma mater worthily. Looking back, we won't miss some touching details really worth mentioning: The 84-year-old former principal Chen Pengyuan offered to write annals and memoirs for the school, and he was so immersed in it that he worked far into the night and didn't allow his family to disturb him throughout; Mr. Tong Zhirou, the 103-year-old former principal of TCF who has moved to the United States, has donated willingly for the school several times. Many other alumni, represented by the well-known match-maker Mr. Liu Hanhuai, also made every endeavor to show their support for the school's revival in their own ways.

Everyone spends at least a quarter of their life on campus, so if we meet mentors who light up our journey and guide us on our way, that is surely our utmost luck. Principal Zhuang firmly believed in that, and he has been practicing so. For nearly half a century, his love for his country, his school and his students has been internalized into his faith, and has naturally become an indispensible part of his life. He sincerely hopes that on the campus of Fuzhou Foreign Languages School and on the land of our nation, generations of outstanding students will emerge in large numbers to usher in a better future for China's educational cause.

• Concluding Remarks

The colored window lattice painted with religious stories has long gone, and the serene and holy music can be faintly heard. The bell of Walsh Memorial Tower is inspiring, while the sweat on the football field witnesses the youth that released their vigor and enthusiasm in the air. The eastern-European-style double-decker structure with brick and timber used to be so fashionable but stands still now, and its original white walls and black tiles were weather-beaten. Luckily it was restored to its original condition due to donations from enthusiastic alumni. Arched windows with wooden frames and glass and iron bars are still there, and the gray-blue façade, which was newly painted, often diffracts fantastic shadows in the sunlight, as if telling of its past glory and imagining its future splendor.

● 特别鸣谢

笔者于 2022 年 2 月中到 3 月底的采写过程中，有幸得到福州外国语学校林建校长的热心指导，先后采访了福建师大外国语学院原副院长林本椿教授、福州外国语学校校友会会长陈华棣先生以及福州九中最后一任校长暨福外第一任校长庄才水先生。他们跌宕起伏的人生经历和深情感人的母校情结给我留下了难忘的印象，也为本章节的撰写提供了丰富有趣的宝贵资料。此外，也特别感谢池志海先生、唐希先生、陈华棣先生等人不吝赐图，他们是百年烟台山的热心记录者，更是两千两百年闽都文化的虔诚守望者。

：从南台岛俯瞰中洲岛（来源：池志海）
：Overlooking Zhongzhou Islet from Nantai Island（Source: Chi Zhihai）

• Acknowledgements

From February to the end of March 2022, I had been occupied with the interviews and all kinds of preparations for the writing. In the process, I had the great honor to get the instruction and guidance from Mr. Lin Jian, the principal of Fuzhou Foreign Languages School. Moreover, I had the opportunities to successively meet Professor Lin Benchun, the former associate dean of College of Foreign Languages, FJNU; Mr. Chen Huadi, the present president of FFLS alumni association; as well as Mr. Zhuang Caishui, the last principal of Fuzhou No. 9 Middle School and the first principal of FFLS, from whom I have learnt a lot and benefited as much. Undoubtedly their life is full of ups and downs, but they still have a strong attachment to their alma mater, which has left an unforgettable impression on me, and also provided varied and valuable information for the writing of this chapter. Apart from them, I would like to give my special thanks to Mr. Chi Zhihai, Mr. Tang Xi and Mr. Chen Huadi and others for their generosity in offering those very precious pictures and memorable details. They have been zealously recording the charm of the centuried Yantai Mountain, and have naturally matured into devout watchers of time-honored local culture noted for a history of more than two thousand and two hundred years.

CHAPTER
FIVE

从英华到附中（一）

The Anglo-Chinese College（1）

第五章

福

有人会因为一个人或一栋建筑而爱上一座城，而我们完全有理由因为烟台山（仓山）而爱上整个福州城。因为得天独厚的地理条件，烟台山在 1842 年福州被辟为通商口岸之后成为外国商人、领事、传教士和归侨的聚居地，从而给榕城福州增添了独具特色的历史文化。鹤龄英华书院就是这独特历史文化的一部分，是教会在福州创办的诸多中学中的佼佼者。英华校歌的歌词"雄踞闽江滨""闽山苍苍，闽水泱泱，济济萃群英""婀嬛福地"，道出了英华乃山水环绕之美境和群英荟萃之福地。让我们踏着历史足迹，去领略英华不平凡的历史过往。

● 上篇：历史过往不平凡

鹤龄英华书院原位于福州市仓山区鹤龄路，是 1881—1952 年间基督教卫理公会（美以美会）所办的一所私立教会中学。该校是在美以美会牧师麦铿利的倡导下于 1881 年 2 月建立的，定名为英华书院。1883 年，基督教徒、商人张鹤龄捐款银元 1 万，购置仓前山池后路有利洋行的一座洋楼及周围场地作为校址。为纪念他，中文校名改为"鹤龄英华书院"，福州话俗称"英华斋"（平话字 Ĭng-huà-că），书院曾一度改名为福州大学，1890 年决定仍用"英华书院"这一校名。书院于 1916—1920 年转型为六年制中学（前 2 年为预科，后 4 年为正科），1924 年定校名为"鹤龄英华中学校"。1927 年，鹤龄英华书院向中华民国教育部办理立案，改名为"私立英华中学"。也有的史料将 1881—1918 年间的称为英华书院，将 1918—1952 年间的称为英华中学。

Scan for more
扫码了解更多

Just as one may fall in love with a city simply for the sake of a person or a building, so do we have every reason to fall in love with Fuzhou for the sake of Yantai Mountain. Owing to its unique geographical conditions, Yantai Mountain was the very area accommodating foreign merchants, consuls, missionaries as well as returned overseas Chinese since Fuzhou became one of the first five treaty ports in 1842, and has ever since added much difference to the history and culture of Fuzhou. And part of this uniqueness and difference is attributed to Anglo-Chinese College（ACC）, the top among the missionary schools established in Fuzhou at that time. As its school song suggests, ACC was located on the Yantai Mountain close by the famous Minjiang River, a place where hill and water join and a blessed land where countless talents come out. Let's follow the footsteps of history and revisit the brilliant past of ACC.

• ACC History: A Brilliant Past that Lingers

Situated on Heling Road（named in honor of Tiong A-hok）in Yantai Mountain, Anglo-Chinese College was a private missionary school founded in February, 1881, by the Methodist Episcopal Mission（MEM）on the earnest suggestion of its priest Rev. R. S. Maclay, D. D. In 1883, Tiong A-hok, a Christian as well as a merchant, donated 10,000 silver dollars to help purchase as its school campus the fine property belonging to the Chartered Mercantile Bank together with its adjoining area, and in his honor, the school was once named A-hok Anglo-Chinese College, commonly known as Ĭng-huà-că in Fuzhou Dialect. For a time it was renamed Foochow University until 1890 when it went back to its original name, Anglo-Chinese College. During 1916 – 1920, the school was transformed to a six-year high school, with the first two years for the preparatory department and the next four for the college department proper. In 1924, it was designated as Anglo-Chinese High School, and in 1927 the school was officially registered as the Private Anglo-Chinese High School by the Ministry of Education of the Republic of China. Some other historical data divided the school into two, Anglo-Chinese College （1881 – 1918）, and Anglo-Chinese High School（1918 – 1952）.

办学规模

书院创办初期，虽然有教会的支持和赞助，但也是设施简陋，师资匮乏，后面才得以逐步发展。第一，我们可以从学校招生人数的变化来了解一下其办学规模的发展。1881年开班时仅4人入学，1883年学生人数增加到30人，1884年为60人，在1907年春季学期结束时，学生达257人，1921年增至540人。1927年秋季因学校改组停课半年，一批学生转学他校。1928年陈芝美就任校长时，全校学生188人，翌年增至342人。此后办学规模有较大发展，1937年，在校生人数增至650多人。1938年内迁洋口时，学生人数大约为550人，1939年为741人，1947年上升至最高峰1128人，为当时福州规模最大的中学之一。福州解放前后回落至800人左右。

第二，从学费来看，英华作为教会创办的一所私立学校，学费自然是不低的。1883年学费为6块银元；1906年3月，由于物价上涨，学校学费翻了一番；1934年，每学期学生膳宿各费总共要138元左右，约折谷子30多担。解放战争爆发后，协和大学每学期的收费是大米320斤，格致中学除学杂费交钱之外，还加收大米150斤，而英华中学的学费和收米比这两所都要高一些。可见，只有家庭条件相对富裕的人才能上得起英华，但对于家庭条件确实困难而又品学兼优的学生，经老师推荐，校长审批，可以减免一半学费，还可以享受奖学金或者清寒助学金，教会也会给贫困生一定的补助，有的贫困生还可以为学校做些杂工挣点收入。

第三，从毕业人数上看，从英华开办第一年坚持读到1890年第一届八年制毕业的，仅有一人。从1881年至1900年的19年中，计有九届毕业生共23人，其中仅毕业一人的有三届。1916年英华书院八年制毕业生9人，1917年16人，1918年31人，最后一届1919年17人。1918年，六年制第一届高中学生毕业，人数为49人；1919年第二届毕业生42人。难能可贵的是，在洋口的8年艰难时期，英华却排除万难，持续发展。据统计，8年间，毕业（包括肄业）生一千多人，并培养出了大批优秀人才。而从毕业生就业去向来看，根据耶鲁大学档案资料（1899），书院的毕业生就业主要是当教师，或在海关、邮局任职，或当牧师，或当译员，有的则升入大学或出国留学，继续深造。比如，英华第一届唯一的毕业生陈孟仁毕业后就是留校任教的。

School Size

At its initial stage, even with the financial support of churches, the school was faced with simple and crude facilities as well as teacher shortage, and was made possible to develop gradually only years later. In the first place, changes in the school attendances may help us to trace its development. In 1881 at the opening of the College, only 4 students were admitted, in 1883, the number increased to 30, in 1884, 60, and the enrollment added up to 257 at the end of its spring term in 1907, and soared to 540 in 1921. In 1927 the school was suspended half a year for reorganization, and as a result, many students were transferred to other schools. In 1928 when Chen Zhimei, whose English name was Dr. James L. Ding, was made president, the total attendance was but 188, and 342 the following year, and tended to have a rapid growth ever since. In 1937, the whole enrollment was approximately 650. In 1938 when the school moved inland to Yangkou (Yankow), the attendance was 550, in 1939, 741, in 1947, 1, 128, making it among the largest of its kind in Fuzhou, and wend downward to 800 or so shortly before and after the liberation of Fuzhou.

Next, we can take a look at changes of its tuition. As a private missionary school, the tuition it charged, of course, was not low. In 1883, it was 6 silver dollars, and in 1906 it was doubled in correspondence with the great increase in the cost of living. In 1934, the all-inclusive fees totaled 138 silver dollars, the equivalent of 60 buckets of unhusked rice. Shortly after the outbreak of China's War of Liberation, the tuition charged by Fukien Christian University (1915 – 1951) was 320 *jin* of rice, and Foochow College charged additional 150 *jin* of rice apart from its tuition and fees. Comparatively, Anglo-Chinese College seemed to charge even more. Therefore, it was obvious that only children from rich and well-off families could afford to attend ACC. Of course, there were some exceptions. Those who were from families with limited means but excellent in both moral character and academic learning were granted half the tuition on the recommendation of a teacher and approval of the president. Besides, they could apply for academic scholarship and special grants for student in poverty, as well as some financial subsidies from churches. They could also choose to do some chores for the school and receive some earnings to make up for their tuition.

Thirdly, in terms of graduates, only one student managed to go through the eight-year study from the opening of the College in 1881 right to 1890, and during the 19 years from 1881 to 1900, its graduates from nine classes totaled 23. Among the nine classes, three had only one graduate from each. In 1916, only 9 graduates finished the eight-year study, in 1917, 17, in 1918, 31, and in 1919, 17. In 1918, 49 students graduated from the first class of the six-year learning, and 42 students from the second class in the following year. Amazingly, during the tough eight years in Yankow, the College was able to develop steadily, despite all difficulties and hardships, bringing out more than one thousand graduates (including undergraduates). In terms of jobs, most graduates served as teachers, clerks in the customs or the post office, clergymen, or interpreters. Some were admitted into universities or went abroad for further study. For example, Mr. Ding Maing Ing, the first graduate, was invited to stay at school as a teacher.

第四，从学校面积和校舍方面看，1881年刚成立时，暂时借用美以美会印书馆楼上和天安堂的几间房子为教室，1884年仅有一幢楼。后来随着办学规模的扩大，校舍也逐步扩建，至1916年书院占地面积约35亩以上，建有洋楼7座，其中教室两座，为施教室和鹤龄楼，礼堂1座，为力礼堂，宿舍3座，为沈宿室、卢宿室和薛宿室，还有藏书楼、实验室、操场等设施。1937年，校址面积初中部35亩，高中部14亩。1937年后，英华又扩充部分场地校舍，全校面积50多亩，楼房十多座，其中高中部的代表建筑有保志楼、克廉楼和校友楼，初中部的代表建筑有鹤龄楼、施教室、美志楼、力礼堂和钟楼。英华刚迁到洋口时，起先是借用福州会馆、汀州会馆等作为校舍。据校友回忆，福州会馆大厅作集体卧室，戏台两侧楼下作教室，两侧楼上作医务室，东侧和南侧楼上分隔起来作部分教师的住房，馆前空地是活动场所。汀州会馆是食堂，迴龙阁是图书馆和实验室。

　　在洋口前后8年中，英华又先后建了林吉楼（为纪念英华第一任校长武林吉而命名）、高智楼（为纪念英华第四任校长高智而命名）、平和楼（为纪念英华第五任校长夏平和而命名）、文渊图书馆（为纪念卫理公会会督陈文渊而命名）、哲明医院（为纪念英华书院董事会董事、卫理公会建筑师范哲明而命名）、心公科学楼（为纪念当时福建省教育厅厅长郑贞文而命名）等，还修缮了借用的福州会馆、汀州会馆、复龙祠、三元殿、八角楼、敦善社、蜚江小学等作为校舍。

　　从以上各方面数据可以看出，英华在20世纪20年代前处于发展的初期，而从20年代至新中国成立前处于发展的鼎盛时期，在学生人数和校舍等方面均达到一定的规模，这在当时的历史条件下还是罕见的。

In terms of the College plant, in 1881 when the College was founded, the rooms borrowed from the Press of the MEM in Fuzhou and from Church of Heavenly Peace functioned as its temporary classrooms. Later on, large additions had been made to it. In place of the one building in 1884, it covered in 1916 an area of 35 *mu*, with seven buildings in total, two for classrooms, namely, Symth Hall and A-hok Hall, one for chapel, namely, Nind-Lacy Memorial Chapel, three for dormitories, namely, Simester Hall, Lu Hall, and Sites Hall, and one for school library. Besides, there were such facilities as laboratories and playgrounds. In 1937 the Junior Division covered an area of 35 *mu*, and the Senior Division, 15 *mu*. Since 1937, the College plant was further expanded, with a total area of 50 *mu* and more than 10 buildings. Among them, Boise Hall, Cleveland Hall and Alumni Science Hall are the representative buildings of the Senior Division, and A-Hok Hall, Symth Hall, Nind-Lacy Memorial Chapel and Alamni Clock Tower are the representative buildings of the Junior Division. At the time ACC moved to Yankow, Foochow Guild Hall and Tingchow Guild Hall were vacated for its use. As one alumnus put it, the hall room of Fuzhou Guild Hall served as the collective living room for students, the downstairs on both sides of the stage as the classrooms, the upstairs as the infirmary, the upstairs in the east and the south of the Hall was cut out for teachers' residence and the space in front of the Hall was used for activities. Tingchow Guild Hall served as the dining hall of the College, and Jionglong Garret as the school library and laboratory.

Of course, ACC also contributed some new buildings to Yankow during the eight years, including Linji Building (named in honor of its first president D. Rev. Franklin Orlinger), Gaozhi Building (named in honor of its fourth president Dr. John Gowdy), Pinghe Building (named in honor of its fifth president M. A. F. C. Harighorse), Wenyuan Library (namend in honor of Mr. Chen Wenyuan, superintendent of the Methodist Church), Zheming Hospital (named in honor of Mr. Paul Prince Wiant, a member of the Board of Trustees of ACC as well as an architect working for the Methodist Church), Xingong Science Building (named in honor of Mr. Zheng Zhenwen, Minister of Education of Fujian Province). It also helped to maintain and restore such buildings it borrowed for temporary use as Foochow Guild Hall, Tingchow Guild Hall, Fulong Ancestral Hall, Sanyuan Temple, Octagon, Dunshan Society, and Feijiang Primary School.

From all the aspects mentioned above, it can be seen that ACC was in its early stage of development before the 1920s, but had ever since developed rapidly and achieved its prime till 1949 when the People Republic of China was founded, with an impressive size of both enrollment and school plant, which was quite rare under the historical conditions of the time.

诚然，英华并非对广大平民百姓的孩子开放，对招收的学生资格有比较高的要求，一是学费比较高，这就决定了贫穷家庭的孩子几乎上不起英华；二是对学生的知识基础也有一定的要求——"通晓汉文，或论义，或诗碎，亦预习五经一二部及四书注……"。据英华老校友、马来西亚归侨李挺章回忆："英华中学的门槛很高，不仅学费昂贵，还要求学生有很好的成绩，几乎可以说是千军万马过独木桥了；而我在马来西亚才学到四年级，马上报考英华中学显然是不明智的。为了实现父亲的愿望，我小学毕业之后，又到补习学校学了一年，专攻英语和数学。1938 年，在英华中学的入学考试上，我一举成功，圆了父亲的英华梦。英华中学是当时口碑甚佳的好学校，我能成为其中的一员，心中自是充满了喜悦。"可见，英华在当时有比较高的社会声誉，这主要归功于它较为完善的课程设置和优良的教学传统。

课程设置演变

鹤龄英华的课程设置，最早是参照美国中学的模式。"在中国的传统教育中缺失中学层次，没有模式可供参考。而福建的传教士主要来自英、美差会，他们创办的中学模式均直接源于英、美中学，是西方近代教育的中国版。"（陈明霞，2012：77）除英文教学外，教会学校还开设中文、数学、地理学、历史、逻辑学、宗教，以及其他辅助课程（林金水，1997：427）。除了语言教学外，英华在引领科学知识方面，也可以说是福建省的先驱者。1889 年英华就有自己的科学实验室，配备欧美仪器，包括天文望远镜。1897 年，英华书院曾公开向社会表演电话，让福州人第一次见到了电话，后来校友刘一清还成立了一家小规模电话公司，开创了福建省公共电话的先河。同时，施美志主理还公开向社会讲述并演示电学以及其他科学，向社会群众传授科学知识。

概括起来，英华的课程设置经历了由预科到"八年四"学制到"六年一贯制"的演变。

预科

1881 年英华书院创办时只开设预科，为两年，课程分国文和英文两类。第一学年，英文课主要有练读、文法（语法）启蒙、心算启蒙、翻译浅文、读华文圣经等；国文课主要读《论语》、《小学》、论说文范等。第二学年，英文课主要有练读、文法启蒙、谈论、翻译浅文等；国文课主要读《上孟》《左传》《战国策》等。

Undoubtedly, ACC was not open to all children from common families, for it set high standards for its enrollment. In the first place, the tuition, as mentioned above, was high, which left out a majority of children from poor families. In the second place, its enrolled students were supposed to be proficient in Chinese, meaning, and poems or had learned one or two of the Four Books and the Five Classics. As Mr. Li Tingzhang, an alumnus as well as a returned overseas Chinese from Malaysia, put it, "Chances of getting admitted to ACC were slim, and only those from well-off families and with good scholarship stood a chance. Before I came back to China, I was in the fourth grade in Malaysia, so it would be unwise of me to apply directly for ACC. I had to go on and finish the primary school first, and went to a cram school for another year to improve my English and Math before I dared venture ACC admission tests, and luckily, I did make it." It is obvious that ACC was highly acknowledged by the society at that time, owing to its perfect curriculum and fine teaching tradition.

Curriculum Evolution

The curriculum of ACC was originally in reference to that of the American high schools, for high school education was seriously lacking in the traditional Chinese education, and thus no reference was available to ACC. Moreover, most of the missionaries in Fujian were of British or American missions, and quite naturally the high schools they founded in Fujian were similar to those in Britain or America, or rather the Chinese version of modern Western-style education. Apart from the subject of English missionary schools also opened such courses as Chinese, math, geography, history, logic, and religion, along with some auxiliary courses. A pioneer in language teaching, ACC also took the lead in imparting scientific knowledge in Fujian. As early as 1889, it boasted its own science lab with equipment from Europe and America, including the telescope. In 1897, ACC demonstrated the telephone to the public, and that's the first time the local people saw with their own eyes such an invention. It came as no surprise that later on Mr. Liu Yiqing, an alumnus of ACC, set up a small telephone company, thus pioneering public telephone service in Fujian. Meanwhile, Dr. George B. Smyth, the then president of ACC, lectured and demonstrated to the public the mechanism of electricity and other sciences, keeping them informed of scientific knowledge.

On the whole, the curriculum of ACC underwent a shift from the original preparatory department to the eight-year-and-four-month system and eventually to the six-year system.

Preparatory Department

At the opening of ACC in 1881, it offered only two years of preparatory courses, including Chinese courses and English ones. The first year English courses covered reading, basic grammar, arithmetic, translation, and Chinese Bible while the Chinese courses comprised classics such as *the Analects of Confucius*, *Xiao Xue*, and writing. The second year English courses mainly involved reading, grammar, talks, translation, and for Chinese courses there were *Mencius*, *The Chronicle of Zuo*, and *Strategies of the Warring States*.

"八年四"学制

书院学制为八年制，后两年相当于大学一二年级，毕业后如赴美深造，可升入大学三年级。所谓"八年制"实际上是"八年四"学制，因为学生在完成八年学业后，最后一学期还要进行四个多月的总复习和总考试，成绩合格，才能获得毕业文凭。八年制课程分侯进英文班四年和书院班四年，除英文、《圣经》、汉文为必修外，侯进班学算术、历史、地理、自然、代数；书院班学几何、三角、化学、物理、生理、植物、矿物、天文、历史、伦理学、国际公法等。同时开设体育课，由外籍教师兼任，以队列、拔河、篮球、网球等为主。还购置了天文、理化、生物实验仪器，设有科学实验室。

书院班规定："入本班者，须先得侯进英文四年班文凭方可。"也就是说，前四年是侯进班，后四年是书院班。英华书院还同时开设五年制侯进译文班和五年制道学班。入学年龄、程度与侯进英文班同，区别在课程和培养目标上。译文班每日学西学、儒学课各半天，学英文一小时。修完五年课程，"考得优分者……给一文凭卒业"，卒业后学生直接到社会就业，不再升入书院班继续学习。

道学班的培养目标是"教人考究圣经要道与教会来历规矩及传道之法、牧师之工"，学生修完五年课程后，考核合格，发给文凭。学生"无论在学几年，出院后必须任年会之传道五年方可"，否则以"违约"论处。1906年，道学班从英华书院独立出去，成为美以美会道学院，后与基督教会的其他单位合并成立福建协和道学院，1945年改称福建神学院。

英华书院还在1910年开设了五年制土木工程科，学生修完书院班头两年课程后方可进入此科。此外，又在1905年、1912年、1919年分别开设过商科、研究班和一年制医学先修班。商科入学资格与土木工程同；研究班、医学先修班皆为书院班毕业生继续深造而设，后均或停或转。

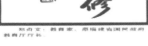

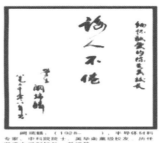

知名校友为母校题词（来源：廖基远）

Inscriptions of renowned ACC alumni (Source: Liao Jiyuan)

The Eight-Year-and-Four-Month System

The full regular course required eight years, with the last two equaling the first and second year of university study, and that's why students would be admitted into the third year of a university if they went to America for further study. What was meant by eight years was, indeed, eight years plus four months, as students had to go through an additional four-month general review and examination even though they had finished the eight years of study, and only when they passed the general exam could they be granted the diploma and graduate in the real sense. The eight years were divided into two, with the first four years covering the work of the preparatory department, and the last four covering the work of the collegiate department. The preparatory courses included English, the *Bible*, Chinese, which were compulsive courses, as well as arithmetic, history, geography, nature, and geometry. Collegiate department opened such courses as algebra, triangle, chemistry, physics, physiology, botany, mineralogy, astronomy, history, ethics, and international law.

The collegiate department made it clear that, "To get admitted, the candidate first had to finish the four years of study in the preparatory department and earned a diploma." In other words, work in the preparatory department was a must before one was allowed to move on to the collegiate department. ACC ran simultaneously a five-year preparatory interpreting class and a five-year theological class. Students of the preparatory interpreting class had to spend half a day every day on Western learning and Confucianism, and one hour every day on English. At the end of the five-year study, an exam would be required and those who passed the exam with good grades would be granted a diploma and graduated. After graduation, they went on to work directly instead of getting promoted to the collegiate department.

The theological class aimed to "teach the essence of the *Bible*, the origin of the church, the way of preaching, and the work of a pastor". In the same way, students in this class should have an exam after finishing the five-year study and they would be granted a diploma only if they successfully passed the exam. As was regulated, the graduates from this class must work as a clergyman at the annual conference of the MEM for five years, not matter how many years they stayed in the class, otherwise it would be regarded as a default. In 1906, the theological class was separated from ACC and became an independent theological seminary of the MEM, which was later merged with other Christian units as Fukien Union Theological Seminary, renamed again in 1945 as Fukien Theological Seminary.

In 1910, ACC also set up a civil engineering course, and to be admitted, students would have to finish the first two years of study in the collegiate department. In addition, business course, graduate course, and preparatory medical course were also offered in 1905, 1912 and 1919 respectively. The same admission qualifications went to business course and civil engineering course, and graduate course and preparatory medical course were designed for further study for graduates from the collegiate department, which were later closed down or transformed.

六年一贯制

1915 年，福建基督教各差会联合创办了福建协和大学，成立后，英华书院七八年级就并入这个大学，所以 1916 年，英华书院改为中学六年制。1918 年 2 月六年制第一届学生毕业，我国著名经济学家、教育家陈岱孙就是这一届毕业的。据陈岱孙回忆，书院还有一个"专读生"制度，就是学校对一些上过几年私塾的要考入英华的学生开的方便之门。申请"专读生"的学生，须参加中文特别考试，包括三场中文作文考试，写三篇不同性质的文章——经义、史论、时事对策。考试合格被录取后，"专读生"可以免修各年级全部中文课程，专读外文课程，这样缩短了上学的年限。所以，陈岱孙 1915—1916 年始业时，考入英华学校三年级后通过"专读生"制度得以在 1917—1918 学年上学期结束时毕业，缩短了原本需要四年的学习时间。他在考入英华之前的九年，上的是旧式的私塾，读经、史、诗、文，所以转入英华后便有了申请"专读生"的资格。

英华学校自 1920 年起才完全转型为六年制中学。1927—1928 年，仓山人民发起了收回教育权运动，教会中学做出改革，课程与公立中学的基本相仿，宗教课成为选修课，由中国人担任校长，董事会成员中中国人占三分之二以上，学校受政府制约并贯彻政府的教育方针与政策。1928 年 1 月，陈芝美任英华首任华人校长后，对英华行政管理和课程设置等做了一系列改革，如 1928 年至 1929 年春，课程增加党义课，将宗教课改为选修课。自 1929 年春至 1932 年秋，课程采取分科制度。预科分工具、知识、技术三科；初中分国文、英文、数学、自然科学、社会科学、艺术、体育等科；高中则分文、理、数、商四科。高中二年级上学期开始时，学生应选定一科为主修科。学科分公共必修科、分科必修科和选修科，学生必须修满 166 学分才能毕业。文、教、商三科学生，三年中必须修完生物、化学、物理中的两门学科；理科学生必须修完以上三门学科方准毕业。各科课程均十分完备，程度和普通初级大学相比，实有过之而无不及。

The Six-Year System

Since the founding of Fukien Christian University in 1915 by Fukien Christian missions, incorporated into it were ACC students of the seventh and the eighth grades, and as a result, ACC became a six-year high school, and had its first graduates in February, 1918, one of whom was Mr. Chen Daisun, a famous economist and educator. Mr. Chen Daisun mentioned that, ACC endowed some "special students" with certain privilege. That is, it offered some preferential policies to those who had attended some years of old-style private school. They had to pass a specially designed exam including three separate writings of different genres, one about the understanding of the classics, one about comments on history, and one about comments on and strategies of current events. And these "special students" could be exempted from all the Chinese courses and specialize in the English courses, which shortened their years of study at ACC. That's why Mr. Chen Daisun was able to graduate at the end of the spring term in 1917 – 1918, three years after he was admitted into ACC in the autumn term in 1915 – 1916 as a "special student", which would otherwise have taken him four years. The reason why Mr. Chen was qualified for a "special student" was that he had spent nine years learning the classics, history, poetry, and writing in an old-style private school before he applied for ACC.

It was not until 1920 that ACC became thoroughly a six-year high school. In response to the campaign launched by the local people to restore education rights to the Chinese in 1927 – 1928, the missionary schools in Fuzhou, including ACC, made corresponding reforms, changing the curriculum to match that of the public schools, and religious course became optional instead of obligatory. Above all, the president of ACC must be Chinese, and two-thirds of the members of ACC Board of Trustees should be Chinese as well. The College should be subject to the government and carry out its relative policies and guidelines. Dr. James Ding, President of ACC, went about making a series of reforms in ACC administration and curriculum. Between 1928 and early 1929, the religious class was made an elective course, and in its place was a new course, Party doctrine education. Between 1929 and the autumn of 1932, ACC adopted a division system for its curriculum. The curriculum of the preparatory department is divided into tool, knowledge and technology. Courses of the junior classes consisted of Chinese, English, math, natural science, social science, art and physical education, while those of the senior classes are broadly divided into liberal arts, science, mathematics, and business. And senior two students were supposed to choose one of the four as their major. All courses fell into three groups: public courses, compulsory courses, and elective courses, and a total of 166 academic credits should be obtained for graduation. Students specializing in liberal arts, education, and business should take two of the following three courses, biology, chemistry, and physics, and students specializing in science must take all the three courses and get the required academic credits. As we can see, the courses provided were adequate, and in terms of difficulty, the equivalent of, if not more challenging than, the first and second year courses of university.

自 1932 年秋至 1937 年秋，课程皆以教育厅颁发的课程标准为依据，尤其重视基本学科。国文、数学、史地等科均聘请专家担任教师。此外，对劳作、美术、园艺等科做了整顿，使学生能够学好工艺技能。军事教育课有军事教学、军事训练、童子军操练等。体育被列为正课，而且每日下午三时后，学生都要参加课外活动，有球类、拳术、爬山、田径等。寄宿生每日早晨还要参加健康操。1940 年，由于教育厅下令不准开设中学预科，英华中学增办了六年制英华小学，由陈芝美兼校长。

教学传统

英华学校在当时的福州城乃至整个福建省都有着较高的声誉，又因为培养出了很多具有国内和国际影响力的人才，加上学校常年聘请外教和名师，所以在海内外颇具声誉。这样一所不一般的学校，自然有着其独特的教学传统。英华教师治学严谨，教学灵活多样，注重因材施教、注重学生的全面发展；学生勤奋好学，师生关系融洽，校园风气民主又和谐。英文教学是它的传统，名师教学是它的传统，注重德育和爱的教育是它的传统，追求民主和自由是它的传统，丰富多彩的课余活动是它的传统。

英文教学

在福建，有的学校虽然比英华创办得早，但最先读英文的学校还是英华书院。英华书院自创办以来就一直秉持学习英文对沟通世界各国的思想与文化起着重要作用这一理念，因而突出英文教育是英华书院的传统特色。当时张鹤龄捐资建校的一个条件就是要求用英文教学。《福州鹤龄英华书院章程》明文规定："若英文月考不及格者，次月另开特别夜班。"还规定："头五年中，半天学英文，半天学中文，但在后四年中，所有的学科都用英文。毕业生能够写和说地道的英文。"

Between the autumn of 1932 and the autumn of 1937, all courses met with the curriculum standards issued by the Provincial Department of Education, and special importance was attached to such basic subjects as Chinese, math, history and geography, all of which were instructed by experts and professionals invited to teach at ACC. Moreover, courses such as labor, fine art, and gardening were rearranged to enable students to master relative crafts and skills. When it came to military education, three courses are involved, military theory, military training and Boy Scouts training. Physical education was made a regular class, and students were all out to have sports like balls of all sorts, boxing, mountain climbing, and track and field; the school boarders were expected to do physical exercises every morning to keep fit. In 1940, as the Provincial Department of Education expressly prohibited the opening of preparatory department in all schools, ACC replaced it with a new primary school, with ACC President Dr. James Ding as its part-time principal.

Teaching Traditions

As a school that engaged through the year experts and famous teachers as well as foreign teachers, ACC was able to cultivate countless influential talents and thus enjoyed great reputation both at home and abroad. A unique school as such definitely had its own select teaching style and precious teaching traditions. ACC teachers were noted for their meticulous scholarship and flexible teaching methods, who tried every means to suit their instruction to different levels of students and attached great importance to students' all-round development. ACC students were as diligent and eager for learning, and they got along well with their teachers, and hence a democratic and harmonious atmosphere came into being on campus. Instruction in English was its tradition; instruction from famous teachers was its tradition; moral education and love education was its tradition; the pursuit of democracy and freedom was its tradition, and colorful extracurricular activities were its tradition as well.

Instruction in English

Despite the fact that long before the advent of ACC some other schools of its kind had been in existence, ACC was surely the first to conduct teaching in English, as it had always been upholding the notion that English learning played a vital role in bridging thoughts and cultures among countries. And it was worth mentioning that Mr. Tiong A-hok donated to help build the College on the sole condition that all courses should be instructed in English, a proof of his wisdom and foresight. The Constitution and Bylaws of Anglo-Chinese College expressly stipulated that, "Those who failed in English in the monthly test are required to attend the special night class in the following month to brush up their English," and "for the first five years, half a day every day is spared for English, and the other half for Chinese, but for the last four years, all courses will be instructed in English. The graduates are expected to speak and write in idiomatic English."

这种英文教学模式成绩显著。1896 年，英华书院毕业生谢天章就曾在天安堂用英语演讲，开创了学生用英语演讲的先例；1893 年的毕业生何天增和 1897 年的毕业生许世光还担任福州苍霞精舍的英文教员，这样福州才有了第二所学习英语的学校。陈芝美接任英华后，仍然注重英文教学，英文课时比其他中学要多。初中开设四门英文课，每周 10 课时，其中练读 4 课时，文法 3 课时，会话 2 课时，作文 1 课时。高中也是开设四门英文课，每周也是 10 课时，其中文学 3 课时，修辞学 2 课时，作文 2 课时，阅读与会话 3 课时。

从教材选用和教学方法来看，英华学校的英文教材多是英文原版教材，包括一些英文故事、经典演讲和小说，如林肯在葛底斯堡的演讲、莫泊桑的《项链》，等等，还有"活的英语"，即学校将从美国新闻处得到的新闻电讯贴在教室走廊上，学生从中学到了一些军事术语和其他英文知识。学校还订有一些英语杂志，如《英语周报》《中国评论》，以扩大学生英语知识面，提升其语言能力。英文老师对学生的语音、文法、作文、诵读等都严格要求，学生还得定时去美籍教师家进行英语会话。此外，还时不时有英语话剧表演、英文诗歌欣赏等活动。美籍教师沈维德在周末常邀请学生到她家做客，通过许多游戏让学生练习英语口语，寓教于乐。

经过这样的培养，学生高中毕业时已经具备了英语听说读写的能力，并能翻译一般的短文和小说。就英华学生的英语水平，这里举两个例子。其一，英华 1928 届校友、著名的民族学家、人类学家、历史学家、社会学家和民族教育家，中央民族大学终身教授林耀华，1944 年就著有英文专著 *The Golden Wing-A Chinese Chronicle*，现收藏于哈佛燕京学社。该书讲述了福建两个普通家庭黄、张两家的兴衰和截然不同的命运，而黄家的兴盛靠的就是教育，特别是在英华中学接受的教育。其二，笔者于 2021 年 1 月 28 日采访了 97 岁高龄的英华惊涛级学生陈世明老先生，他英文书写极具规范和美感，英文发音清晰、准确，他还送给笔者一本他和几位同学当年用英文写的记录英华生活的小册子，英文表达流畅，文体自然。英华学生英文水平由此可见一斑。

英华校友陈世明手迹和编著的英文小册子（来源：陈世明）
ACC alumnus Chen Shiming's English handwriting and the English pamphlet he complied (Source: Chen Shiming)

As could be expected, such kind of English instruction did pay off. In 1896, Mr. Sia Tieng Ciong, graduate from Class 1896, delivered a speech in English at Church of Heavenly Peace, unprecedented before. Mr. Ho Tieng Ceng and Mr. Hu Sie Guong, graduates from Class 1893 and Class 1897 respectively, worked as English teachers in Cangxia Elementary Technological School, the predecessor of today's Fujian University of Technology, and thus there came the second school in Foochow that taught in English. After Dr. James Ding took over ACC and became its president, he carried on its tradition of highlighting English, and the class hours for English were far more than those of other schools. The junior students had four English courses to cover, with a total of ten class hours every week, of which 4 for reading, 3 for grammar, 2 for conversation, and 1 for writing. The senior students also had four English courses to cover, with a total of ten class hours every week, of which 3 for literature, 2 for rhetoric, 2 for writing, and 3 for reading and conversation.

The English teaching and learning materials fell into several kinds. First, for classroom instruction, ACC chose for its students the original English textbooks, such as English classic novels like *the Necklace* and influential speeches like Lincoln's speech at Gettysburg. Besides , on the corridor of the classroom were news posts of different kinds, news that the school managed to retrieve from the press office in America, a sort of "living English" that acquaint students with military terms as well as other English knowledge. Moreover, to help students broaden their horizons and sharpen their language skills, ACC had in its possession a collection of magazines in English, such as *English Weekly* and *China Critic*. As for the English teachers, they tended to be very strict with students in pronunciation, grammar, writing and reciting, and students were supposed to go to their English teacher's house to have conversations in English, and engage in English activities such as drama performances and poetry readings. For example, Miss Eidth W. Simester, the English teacher from America, used to invite students to her residence and arranged games and activities for the purposes of both education and amusement.

Under such diverse modes of training, students were well-equipped with the basic English skills of listening, speaking, reading and writing, and were able to translate some short stories and novels into English. Here, two examples may suffice to exemplify the English proficiency of ACC graduates. One is Mr. Lin Yueh-hwa, a graduate of Class 1928 of ACC, a noted ethnologist, anthropologist, historian, sociologist and a national educationist, and a tenured professor of Minzu University of China, who had his treatise in English published in 1944, *The Golden Wing—A Chinese Chronicle,* which depicts the different destinies of two ordinary Chinese families, the Huang's and the Chang's, and what made the Huang family prosper was the fact that its children received good education, in particular, education at ACC. One more example is Mr. Chen Shiming, a graduate of the Tide Class(1943), who can speak fluent English and write beautiful English even though he is now 97. In the interview, he also gave me a pamphlet in English that he and his classmates compiled, *ACC Traditions Shine On*, a precious little book in fluent and smooth English that depicts their life and study at ACC.

师资配备上，英文教学主要是美籍教师，外教的阵容也很强大，如沈师姑、顾师姑、华师姑、毕理先生、毕理夫人、德辟孙等。也有一些中国老师教英文，如教初中的庄家锋老师、王穆和老师和教高中的杨镜清老师。还有一位王干酥老师，在有外国传教士来讲道的时候，常被叫去当翻译。除英文外，学校也教法文和德文（陈毓贤，2013：63）。

名师教学

在英华，陈芝美校长时常跟学生提起："英国有一所著名的第一流的伊顿中学，它的毕业生很多都进了第一流的牛津大学和剑桥大学。"看来陈芝美校长正是以伊顿中学作为英华中学的办学标准。他提出要把英华办成第一流的学校，培养出第一流的人才。为此，他认为，"光有第一流的设备还不够，重要的还必须有第一流的师资"。这就是他的"三个第一"的教学思想。为此，他高薪聘请海内外高水平、德才兼备的优秀教师来英华任教。1928 年 1 月 24 日，他就任英华校长第五天，就聘请日本早稻田大学政治学学士王复初为国文系主任，美国西北大学文科硕士河爱榄女士为英文系主任，美国爱荷华大学数学硕士陈拯为数学系主任，美国西北大学理科硕士河威廉为科学系主任，美国密歇根大学政治学硕士梁孝忱为史地系主任。他还聘请留美博士刘强，硕士林升华、李可敏、蔡公椿、王钰杰等担任主科教员。同时，为纠正外籍校长执政时期轻视国文的做法，他还聘请国学大师陈遵统、林行陀、魏建祥、王孝泉、何叔静等教授国文，也请来著名作家萧乾讲授新文学。1936 年，著名作家郁达夫来闽工作，陈芝美校长邀请他到英华参观并做题为"文艺大众化与乡土文化"的讲演。1935 年，聘请浙江大学数理系讲师周恒益来榕讲授数学，对学生数学程度的提高有很大裨益。在英华执教的大多是大学毕业生，或者是留学生，或者是外籍教师，或者是国内外知名学者。据统计，1931年 40 个教师中，美籍教师占 6 人，留学的占 8 人。这种高水准的师资队伍，即使今日来看，也是相当了不起的，这也是英华人才辈出的一个重要原因。

ACC had quite many devoted English teachers, mainly from America. The teaching faculty included Miss Edith W. Simester, Miss Gu, Miss Worley, Mr. John A. Pilley, Mrs. Murvel C. Pilley, Mr. Sydney Arthur Davidson Jr. Apart from them, some Chinese teachers were also engaged in English teaching, such as Mr. Zhuang Jiafeng in the Junior Division and Mr. Wang Muhe and Mr. Yang Jingqing in the Senior Division. There was also a teacher named Wang Gansu, who was asked to do the interpretation for foreign missionaries who came to preach at ACC. It should be noted that besides English, French and German were also taught at ACC.

Instruction from Eminent Teachers

At ACC, President James Ding used to mention Eton College in Britain, a first-rate British independent boarding school for boys aged 13 to 18, most of whose graduates were admitted to Oxford University and Cambridge University. It could be seen that he looked upon Eton as a model for ACC and devoted himself to its perfection. Accordingly, he put forward the notion of "three firsts" in the management of ACC, namely, to make ACC a first-rate school that cultivated first-class talents, to equip it with first-rate facilities, and to endow it with first-class faculties. To achieve these goals, he spared no efforts to engage high-level teachers with both integrity and ability at home and abroad to teach at ACC. On 24, January, 1928, five days after he was made President, he set out to appoint Mr. Wang Fuchu, bachelor of political science in Waseda University as Dean of Chinese Literature Department, Ms. He Ailan, master of arts in NorthWestern University as Dean of English Department, Mr. Chen Zheng, master of mathematics in University of Iowa as Dean of Department of Mathematics, Mr. William He, master of science in NorthWestern University in America as Dean of Department of Science, and Mr. Liang Xiaochen, master of political science in Michigan University as Dean of Department of History and Geography. He also invited Dr. Liu Qiang from America, Mr. Lin Shenghua, Mr. Li Kemin, Mr. Cai Gongchun and Mr. Wang Yujie, all of whom had a master's degree, to be in charge of the main courses. Meanwhile, to correct the long-term tendency of inadequate attention to the Chinese literature during the reign of the six foreign principals, President James Ding also invited great scholars of Chinese national culture such as Mr. Chen Zuntong, Mr. Lin Xingtuo, Mr. Wei Jianxiang, Mr. Wang Xiaoquan, and Mr. He Shujing to teach Chinese classics. Mr. Xiao Qian, a prominent writer, was also invited to give students lectures on new literature. In 1936, Mr. Yu Dafu, a well-known writer, came to work in Fuzhou and was invited to visit ACC and give a speech on popular literature and the local culture. In 1935, Mr. Zhou Hengyi, a lecturer from Department of Mathematics in Zhejiang University came to teach math at ACC for a time, a blessing indeed to the students. On the whole, ACC faculty members were mainly college graduates, or graduates with a degree earned abroad, foreign teachers, or scholars widely known at home and abroad. According to statistics, of the 40 teachers of ACC in 1931, 6 were Americans, 8 were graduates who came back to China from abroad. Such high-level teaching faculty, even by today's standard, are remarkable, which made ACC the very place where talents of all kinds came out.

严谨与民主相得益彰的传统校风

治学严谨是英华的优良传统，这种严谨体现在对学生的严格要求上。英华对学生的学习生活、考试考察和奖惩都有严格的制度，达不到要求者，轻则记过，重则留级或退学。如学校规定，考试成绩两门主科不及格者留级，一科不及格者为"积欠"，一科补考不及格或者两科"积欠"者均要留级。对于犯错误的学生，学校从不姑息，但也不粗暴训斥，总是动之以情、晓之以理，让学生懂得自尊、自爱、自重、自强。此外，为了激励学生，学校规定每个班级都要取一个富有寓意的班名，如"七七级"班名意在"不忘国耻，抗日救亡"；1943届（英华第57届）为惊涛级，原先为"夏云级"，后来随着他们颠沛流离到洋口，改名为"惊涛"，取"惊涛骇浪"之意，抒发他们在逆境中奋发图强之决心；又如1948届（英华第64届）"嘤求"级，级名出自《诗经》"嘤其鸣矣，求其友声"，意在鼓励同学们友爱互助。这种"严"同时也体现在学校对教师质量的严格把关。除了聘请德才兼备的名师之外，学校规定到英华任教的大学毕业生，要从初一初二教起，合格的才能升入高年级，不合格的给予及时解聘。这样，师资得以不断更新和补充，确保了高质量教学。

这种"严"还体现在对师生品德的严格要求上。"育人先育德"是陈芝美校长的一贯主张。他认为成绩差可以弥补，但道德品质有问题就很难弥补。因此他在重视教学的同时，更是强调教师要"育人"，勉励师生努力做到无愧于己、无愧于人、严于律己、宽以待人。

A Rigorous But Democratic School Spirit

Rigorous scholarship had always been a tradition at ACC, which was for one thing, embodied in its strict requirements for students. ACC set rigid rules for students' life and study, for tests and examinations, and for rewards and punishments. Those who failed to meet the requirements would, in mild cases, be given a demerit, but in acute cases, repeat the term or even be dropped. The school rule had it that students who failed in two or more subjects could not pass into the next grade. Those who failed in one subject would be regarded as in arrears, and those who failed in the makeup exam or had two major subjects in arrears had to repeat the term. On the other hand, ACC would never be indulgent towards students' mistakes, but would never dress them down in a crude way. Instead, it always moved them with love and educate them with reason and got it across to them the sense of self-esteem, self-respect, self-discipline and self-improvement. In addition , to motivate students, ACC encouraged each class to choose a name for itself that carried particular significance. For example, Class 1940 was named "Seven-Seven Class" to remind themselves not to forget national humiliation and to rise up and resist the Japanese invasion. Class 1943 was originally named "Summer Clouds", but as they drifted from Fuzhou to Yankow through all kinds of hardships, like a boat sailing against roaring waves and fierce tides, they decided to rename it "Tide Class" to express their determination to rise up against every adversity. Class 1948 was named "Yingqiu Class", indicating their eagerness to find like-minded friends. *ying* meaning "bird chirps", *qiu* meaning "seeking", both derived from a poetic sentence in *the Book of Songs* "The birds are chirping to seek the echoes of their friends". This rigorousness was also reflected in the rigid control over the quality of ACC teachers. Besides engaging famous teachers with both ability and moral integrity, ACC made it a rule that the new teachers fresh out of colleges should start with the junior one or junior two courses, and could be promoted to senior classes only after they had proved themselves qualified in the junior classes, and those who turned out to be unqualified would definitely be dismissed. In this way, the teaching faculty were replenished and revitalized, thus ensuring the high quality of teaching.

This rigorousness was, above all, highlighted in the great importance attached to moral characters on the part of both teachers and students. President James Ding firmly believed that moral education was more important and thus should come first in the process of nurturing well-rounded school graduates. It was his faith that one could make up for his poor performance in studies, but could never make up for his poor moral character. Therefore, he paid attention not only to good teaching, but ever more to cultivating good people. He encouraged each and every teacher as well as student to try to be worthy of himself and of others, be strict with himself but lenient with others.

在这样的氛围下，教师上课既严谨，又活泼。许世晖老师上物理课时，为了让学生更好地了解电的性能，让学生手拉手围成一个圆圈，然后突然在圆圈中间接上低压直流电源，结果霎那间大家全身为之一振，手都松开了。许由恩老师上生物实验课时，采用的是大学生物系的教材，要求学生背记动植物解剖后的全部组织、细胞、遗传、基因等英语名称和拼写，要求学生了解生物进化、生殖、生存竞争等道理，并让学生用牙签从自己的口腔中刮下颊细胞，然后放在显微镜下观察，并画出细胞结构图。林行陀老师讲解国文，博古通今、引经据典，虽已年迈，但诲人不倦，批改作文认真及时。陈衡庭老师讲代数时常夹杂着英语，而且他还开设了当时中学中绝无仅有的本是大学的课，即逻辑学。陈衡庭老师的逻辑学不但讲了形式逻辑、符号逻辑，还讲了辩证法，而且从亚里士多德一直讲到马克思，涵盖了整部逻辑哲学史。

沈维德和毕理夫人讲授英文，方法多样，有时是学生问、老师答，有时是老师问、学生答，有时是写作文，有时是英文辩论会，还每年至少一次邀请学生到家里做游戏，规定用英文交谈。结果到了高中三年级，学生不仅可以阅读《读者文摘》《生活》等英文杂志和小说，并且能用英语写作文、会话，还能排演莎士比亚话剧。

许多老师不仅课上得好，还有业余爱好和专长，如陈景汉老师不仅文章写得好，还擅长演讲；何铭朝老师会演话剧；徐志德老师擅长演奏小提琴、吉他等乐器；陈苣洲老师是太极高手，写得一手柳体好字，还教学生作旧体诗的一种形式——"折枝诗"。老师们的高尚品德和多才多艺对学生的学习和生活乃至整个人生有着潜移默化的影响。老师们在给学生灌输科学知识的同时，也跟他们讨论人生，谈论理想和抱负，给学生灌输爱国思想，培养他们的正义感、集体感、奉献意识和吃苦精神。

Under such an atmosphere, ACC teachers had formed their unique and lively teaching styles. In his physics class, Mr. Xu Shihui had his students stand hand-in-hand in a circle, and without warning, he had the circle connected to AC with low voltage, forcing them to drop their hands. Mr. Xu Youen, in his biology class, chose the equivalent of college-level teaching materials, and students were required to commit to memory all the English terms related to animal anatomy, such as tissues, cells, inheritance, and genetics, and they should acquaint themselves with such concepts as evolution, reproduction and the Survival of the Fittest. To make his class vivid and direct, he had his students swab the inside of their mouths with toothpicks and observe under a microscope their own cell structures. And Mr. Lin Xingtuo, an eminent scholar, was extremely erudite and well-informed, and could quote the classics to meet every need in class. Even in his old age, he corrected students' compositions as passionately and always handed them out in time. Mr. Chen Hengting was liable to dot his lecture on geometry with one or two English terms, and he opened a unique college course, logic, one and the only one in all the high schools at that time, which covered the whole history of logical philosophy, including formal logic, symbolic logic and dialectics, running from Aristotle through to Marx.

The foreign teachers Miss Simester and Mrs. Pilley also adopted a variety of teaching methods to help students learn English, such as questions-and-answers between and across the teacher and students, writings, English debates. They also invited students home at least once every year to have games and conversations with them in English. And their hard work did pay off. The Senior Three students could read the English issues of *Reader's Digest*, *Life*, as well as English novels, and they could speak and write in English without difficulty, and they even could perform dramatic plays by Shakespeare.

It is also worth mentioning that ACC teachers were not only skilled in teaching, but also equipped with hobbies and specialties. For example, Mr. Chen Jinghan was an expert in writing and public speaking. Mr. He Mingchao was good at drama performing. Mr. Xu Zhide could play such musical instruments as the violin and the guitar. Mr. Chen Qizhou was a master of Tai Chi and Chinese calligraphy, and he even got students to know about an old-style poetry named "Zhezhi Poetry". The versatility and noble moral character of ACC teachers exerted a subtle influence on students in their study, in their daily lives, and even in their world outlook. Besides imparting knowledge, ACC teachers also took great trouble to talk with students about life, ideals and aspirations and to inspire their sense of patriotism, justice, teamwork, dedication and diligence.

丰富多彩的学术文化活动

英华除了重视课堂教学，还很注重开展各种学术文化活动，以扩大学生的视野，激发他们的活跃思维，以及探索知识、追求真理的欲望。即便在学校内迁洋口的艰难时期，虽然生活艰苦、学习紧张，但全校师生仍然齐心协力，克服各种困难，开展了丰富多彩的学术文化活动。在初中阶段，就有语文、数学等学习组，到高中阶段则有文学研究会、英语研究会、音乐研究会、美术研究会、体育研究会等机构，聘请教师当顾问，开展各种学术活动，出文学、英语专刊，举办音乐会、美术展、球赛等。学生会办有《日日新闻》墙报，报道校内各种动态，后来发展为对开铅印周报《英华消息》。青年会办有《日日格言》。此外，各班级成立学术会（级会），办墙报是级会主要活动之一，一般每学期出三四次，内容涉及学习心得交流、文艺创作、专题笔谈、生活小品、批评建议等。惊涛级墙报不定期创办文学评论专刊，还跟其他班级合作出过一期英汉双语的《平达》（Pinta 是哥伦布发现新大陆所乘的船号），表达他们因为鼠疫期间洋口学校停课，学生被迫回榕，之后回来复课的经历和感受。此外，1941 年，惊涛级同学在美籍英语教师穆蔼仁的指导下，出了英语月刊 *Tide* 创刊号，这是英华在洋口的唯一英文墙报。

学校还经常举办各种辩论会，如曾组织过"印度是否应该独立?"的辩题，可见当时学校一直在引导学生关心世界政治大事，培养他们的博大胸怀。惊涛级学生还组织了一次题为"中学男女生合校好还是分校好?"的辩论题，结果主张男女合校的一方胜出，这是对教会办学长期坚持男女分校传统的否定。有趣的是，后来英华还真招收女生了。荟蔚级学生薛谋洪在学校演讲比赛和辩论会上舌战群儒，屡屡夺冠，后来成为外交家和国际关系专家。还有美籍教师组织的各种英语辩论赛和英文话剧表演，如表演莎士比亚名剧《罗密欧与朱丽叶》。此外，学校规定每周一上午第一节为"总理纪念周"，以纪念孙中山先生，学校还常常邀请学者、名流或本校教师做演讲。

Rich and Colorful Academic and Cultural Activities

In addition to classroom teaching, ACC also held all kinds of academic and cultural activities to broaden students' horizons, activate their thinking and arouse the desire to explore knowledge and pursue truths. And such activities were undisturbed and went on as usual even at the time of adversity when the school moved inland to Yankow. The junior students formed among themselves study groups of such subjects as Chinese and Math, while the senior students had seminars of all kinds, Literature Seminar, English Seminar, Music Seminar, Art Seminar, and P. E. Seminar, which had the teachers as consultants and carried out a variety of academic and cultural activities such as releasing special issues on literature and English, holding concerts, art exhibitions and ball games. The Student Union edited a wall newspaper entitled "Daily News" to report various events on campus, which was later on developed into a folio printing "ACC Weekly News". The YMCA had their "Daily Motto". Every class had its Class Union, mainly responsible for the work of the wall newspaper, three or four issues every term, with information ranging from exchanges of learning experiences, literary creations, thematic comments in writing, life sketches, and criticisms and suggestions. Tide Class had a periodical on literary review published at irregular intervals, and they also cooperated with other classes to publish an issue of bilingual Chinese-English "Pinta" to voice their bitter feelings and unusual experiences at the time when the school was closed for a time because of the plague and they had to go back to Fuzhou and then take the return trip to Yankow when the school resumed. Moreover, under the direction of their American teacher, Mr. Donald MacInnis, Tide Class issued an English literary newspaper called "Tide" in 1941, the only English journal of the war-time ACC in Yankow.

ACC had students participated in debates on a wide range of topics. For example, debates on topics closely related to the great international events of the time, like "Should India be made independent?", were held with the intention to encourage students to be more concerned about the global affairs and have a broader mind. In view of the fact that boys and girls should go to separate schools, Tide Class had a debate on "Should boys and girls receive separate education in different schools or should they be mixed together?", and it turned out that the winner went to the side for the opinion that both sexes should be admitted into the same school, a sign of students' disapproval of the separate education of boys and girls, an enduring tradition of missionary schools. Interestingly, years later ACC did do away with the tradition and started to admit girl students. Mr. Xue Hongmou from Huiwei Class was greatly eloquent and stood out in most speeches and debates and therefore it came as no surprise that he turned out to be a great diplomat and an expert in international relations. Besides, the American teachers also organized English debates as well as English drama performances. Also, ACC spared a special week, the "Memorial Week", in memory of President Sun Yat-sen, during which time famous scholars, eminent people and some ACC teachers were invited to give a variety of speeches.

特别值得一提的是，地下党办了一个秘密的"小小读书会"，便于同学传阅进步书籍，大多是苏联和中国解放区的小说、诗歌、戏剧，还有一些科普读物，如邹韬奋的《萍踪寄语》《萍踪忆语》以及他主编的《全民抗日战争》，斯诺的《西行漫记》，马克思和恩格斯的《共产党宣言》，列宁的《国家与革命》。

学校同时也很重视培养学生的音乐、体育和美术素养。英华学生对音乐有特殊的爱好，个个都喜欢唱歌，他们经常唱的歌曲有《夜半歌声》《黄河大合唱》《流亡三部曲》《中华颂》等。学校还常常举办小型音乐会，让学生欣赏留声机放出的世界名曲，如贝多芬交响曲、肖邦小夜曲等。还有一个风靡一时的"英华铜乐团"，举行过三次大型的演奏会，为顺昌全县仅有。著名闽剧作家林亨仁 1939 年寒假在洋口英华就读期间，为开展抗日爱国宣传编写了歌颂史可法英勇不屈、坚持民族气节的闽剧《梅花岭》，组织同学演出。这是他创作的第一个闽剧剧本，演出轰动了整个顺昌县城。

此外，英华还一向重视体育运动。一方面做到体育运动的普及化，一方面做到体育运动的技能化。英华学校篮球队尤为出名，经常赴将乐、沙县、南平等地与兄弟学校或其他团体进行友谊赛。1917年，英华学生就在校内与来访的美国水兵举行篮球比赛。在 1928 年的福州市公私立学校运动会中，英华夺得球类冠军。在 1930 年的闽侯县第一届运动会中，夺得排球和篮球双冠军。1935 年获得青年杯户内篮球冠军。1937 年获得闽师杯篮球冠军。此外，英华还设有游泳场，让学生有组织地前往游泳，并有较好的安全防护措施。

英华这些丰富多彩的活动确保了学生身心的全面发展和综合素养的提高，为他们的成才提供了保障。笔者采访的英华校友陈世明老先生和李青藻老先生分别为 97 岁和 92 岁高龄，却身姿矫健、思维清晰、谈吐自如。据了解，英华校友中长寿者数量颇多。

In particular, the secret underground Party organization established a "Miniature Reading Group" and circulated progressive revolutionary novels, poems, dramas, and periodicals from the Soviet Union and China's liberated areas, such as *Ping Zong Ji Yu* and *People's War of Resistance* by Zou Taofen, and *Red Star Over China* by Snow, *The Communist Manifesto* by Marx and Engels, and *State and Revolution* by Lenin.

ACC also attached great importance to enhancing students' appreciation of and achievement in music, sports and fine art. Students were enthusiastic about music and songs, and songs popular among them included "Midnight Singing" "The Yellow River Cantata" "The Trilogy of the Exiles", and "Ode to the Chinese". In addition, there were small concerts from time to time, at which students could indulge themselves in the world classical music from the gramophone, like Beethoven's symphony and Chopin's serenade. ACC also boasted a copper band, which had three concerts, the only band at that time in Yankow. In 1939 when he was a student of the war-time ACC in Yankow, Mr. Lin Hengren, the playwright of Min Opera, had, for the sake of arousing people's patriotism during the War of Resistence Against Japanese Agression, created a drama entitled "Meihua Ling" to sing high praise for Mr. Shi Kefa, a brave and unyielding national hero who adhered to national integrity. It was his first work, which was put on stage later and caused quite a sensation in Yankow, or even the whole Shunchang County.

As with music and art, sports also gained the same weight at ACC. Efforts were made to make it popular with all students and a technical skill for some. Of all sorts of sports, basketball was the most popular, and ACC Basketball Team went around to Jiangle, Shaxian, Nanping to have friendly matches with fraternal schools or teams. And the achievements of ACC Basketball Team were quite fruitful. In 1917, ACC students had a basketball game on campus with the visiting American sailors. In 1928, ACC won the basketball championship in the intercollegiate sports competition in Fuzhou. In 1930, ACC won the championships of both basketball and volleyball in the first sports meeting of Minhou County, in 1935, the championship of the Youth Cup Indoor Basketball Match, and in 1937, the championship of the Minshi Cup Basketball Match. In addition, ACC also had a swimming pool on campus with good security facilities, and students were allowed to go swimming in an organized fashion.

Such rich and colorful extracurricular activities ensured ACC students' physical and mental development, thus paving the way for their future success. It is really amazing, during my interview, to see ACC alumni Mr. Chen Shiming, aged 98, and Mr. Li Qingzao, aged 94, were still sound in health, agile in gait, clear in thinking, and poised in chatting. Actually, quite a number of ACC alumni tend to live long.

"家庭式"的爱的教育

　　陈芝美校长是个有大爱的人，他用一生来阐释爱，正如他常说的"Love never fails"（爱永远不会失败）。他的名言是：爱教育如同生命，爱学校如家庭，爱同事如手足，爱学生如自家孩子，这就是他的"四爱"办学思想。抗日战争全面爆发后，许多学生与家庭失去联系，连伙食都无着落。陈芝美校长在学校动员会上安抚大家："只要我在，你们就有书念；只要我有饭吃，你们也有饭吃。"因为好多学生还小，而且是第一次离开父母，都很想家，学校给低年级的学生配了一位保姆，照顾他们，陪他们聊天，以解他们的思乡之苦，并且每晚在宿舍内巡视，为学生盖被子，或催促起来小便。大家都亲切地称呼她"依奶"（福州话"母亲"），这充分体现了学校的"家庭氛围"。1943年福州沦陷，很多学生断了家庭的经济支持，面临困苦和饥饿，于是，陈校长这位"大家长"身先士卒、无私奉献，除了想办法节省学校各种开支外，更是把自己的薪金从200元降为130元，在学校最困难的时候，还曾主动停薪。英华校友陈景润成名后，到处有人请他作报告、演讲，照例给他的酬金，他都坚决退回了。他说："我已有了工资。"这是受英华学校"爱的教育"所影响的。在陈芝美的领导下，全校展开勤俭节约、自力更生的活动，如种菜、养家禽、拾柴火，还到附近的泰宁一带买价格相对便宜的大米和大豆、建立学生储蓄所等。学生们还自己印刷书籍、粉刷墙壁、写标语等，齐心协力度过难关。教师们自愿无偿轮流看护学生宿舍，校长和老师的太太们还自愿帮孩子们缝补衣服，节假日还邀请学生去家里小聚。师生关系极其融洽，一起做礼拜，一起倾心交谈、郊游、野炊，一起参与娱乐和运动。学生之间也团结友爱，互相帮助，亲如兄弟姐妹。在学习上，他们建立互助组，帮扶学习后进生，学期末还组织由优秀生辅导的复习工作。生活上，家庭条件好的会捐钱物给家庭贫困的孩子，生病的学生会被送往校医院（哲明医院）并有同学们主动轮流护理，老师们也会来医院慰问，甚至还会每天给送一瓶鲜牛奶（当时是奢侈品）。

陈芝美校长与全体英华中学教职员合影

1941年陈校长与英华中学第一届教育参观团合影

1938年，陈校长与全家及亲属合照。

: 英华教师及家属（来源：廖基远）
: ACC teachers and their family dependents（Source: Liao
: Jiyuan）

Family-Style Love Education

President James Ding was a great man with universal love. As he used to mention time and again, "Love never fails", and indeed his whole life was devoted to giving and expounding love. His notion of "four loves" for education had far-reaching impact on ACC, namely, to love education as you love your life, to love the school as you love your family, to love your colleagues as you love your brothers, and to love your students as you love your own children. With the outbreak of the War of Resistence Against Japanese Agression, many students lost contact with their families and could hardly pay for their daily meals. At this critical moment, President James Ding firmly declared at the school's mobilization meeting, "As long as I am here, your will have food and schooling." After ACC moved to Yankow because of the war, students in the Junior Division, still in their early teens, suffered from homesickness. As a result, a "house mother" was employed to take care of them, to have talks with them to take their minds off homesickness, and to watch over them at night lest they kick off their covers or wet the bed. And as a result, most students were very close to her and addressed her affectionately as their "Mama". All this mirrored the family warmth of ACC. After Fuzhou fell into the hands of the Japanese invaders in 1943, the majority of students were cut off from their family's financial support, and were faced with bitterness and hunger. To cope with all these difficulties, President James Ding, the head of the ACC family, tried every means to minimize the expenditure necessary for the working of the school, cut his own salary down to an average teacher's level, and even took the initiative to suspend his own salary. Inspired by the example of the president, Mr. Chen Jingrun, the world famous mathematician, an ACC alumnus, denied and returned all the money given to him as pay every time he was invited to give a speech. Under the president's leadership, many effective measures for frugality and self-reliance were taken, such as growing their own vegetables, raising their own poultry, gathering firewood on their own, going to the adjoining area Taining to purchase rice and soybean at a lower price, and setting up a student savings bank. Students were actively involved in other chores for the school, things like printing, whitewashing walls, and writing slogans, all working together to pull through. ACC teachers took turns watching the dormitories without extra pay, and wives of the president and teachers pitched in to mend clothes for the students, and even invite them home for a treat. Therefore, ACC teachers and students were on good terms, and they enjoyed various activities together, such as church fellowship, heart-to-heart talks, outings, picnics, recreations and sports. Students also loved and helped one another as if they were brothers and sisters. In their studies, a Mutual Help Group was organized to help students who had difficulty in their studies, and, when term exams drew near, to help them with the review work with top students as tutors. In their daily lives, rich students would contribute money to the poor ones, and any seriously-ill student would be sent to the school hospital at once for proper treatment. Faculty members would, time and again, pay visits to the sick, and would even give away their precious daily share of milk, a luxury at that time.

因此，尽管生活条件不好，物资紧缺，师生们却以极大的热情进行有条不紊地学习和生活，在洋口度过了艰难而又充实、令他们终生难忘的几年。学生毕业时，学校为毕业生举办"毕业钱宴"，老师和学生们坐在标着"尔、乃、世、之、光"的五张圆桌旁，桌上放着陈芝美校长赠送的卡片"爱永远不会失败"和节目单，畅所欲言、相互赠言，依依惜别。即便毕业了，英华师生也常常找机会相聚。如林观得校长去北京的时候，曾约在北京的校友聚会，看到其中有个学生衣裳单薄时，还给他买衣服；而那时已回到清华航空系当主任的沈元老师也抽空跟他们聚会，陪他们逛圆明园，还给他们看他在英国学习和工作的照片。英华一届又一届的毕业生犹如展翅高飞的鸟儿，虽离了巢，却永远不忘自己是"英华大家庭"的一员。

英华之光

英华办学成绩卓著，远近闻名，培养出了一大批优秀的人才，他们都是英华的骄傲，是英华之光，也是民族之光。那些为英华无私奉献、辛勤育人的老师们，更是英华之光，是学生们的指路明灯，其中尤为值得一提的是那些热爱中国、为英华教育和中外友好往来作出贡献的外籍教师，他们也是文明的使者，是英华之光。

英华英烈

英华不仅是知识的摇篮，也是革命的摇篮。1902 年，英华校友陈能光、林馥村等许多人秘密参加福建最早的革命社团"益闻社"（后改称"桥南公益社"，骨干分子均加入同盟会）。1906 年，英华学生发起了福州学生运动史上最早的一次爱国运动。1909 年，英华教员黄乃裳创办《左海公道报》，积极宣扬革命。1920 年，为抵制日货，校友筹益部在本校鹤龄楼创立"中华国货陈列室"，由校友吴养贤向各工厂商店征集标本，此为福州有国货陈列室之始。校友吴养贤、周宗颐改良雨伞、牙刷等国货，推动了福建国货促进会的成立。他们筹募捐款，在南公园兴建福建国货促进会大楼，在南门兜和南公园门口树立"请用国货"石碑各一面。后来，福州南公园"国货陈列馆"的创立和"国货路"的命名均源于此。

：请用国货石碑（来源：福建博物院）
：A stele that reads "Please use domestic products"
：(Source: Fujian Museum)

In spite of the poor living conditions and material shortages, ACC teachers and students carried on with great enthusiasm and optimism, and lived through those arduous but fruitful and unforgettable years. To mark the special moment of students' graduation, ACC would hold a graduation banquet. On this special occasion, both teachers and graduates would be seated at five round tables respectively marked with each of the five Chinese characters of the school motto, *er* (you), *nai* (are), *shi* (world), *zhi* (of), and *guang* (light), in the middle of which were placed the playbill as well as the card that read "Love never fails" as a gift from President James Ding. They chatted joyfully and bid farewell with best wishes, all reluctant to leave. Even after they graduated from ACC, the alumni would seize every opportunity to have a reunion with their teachers, and vise versa. For example, Mr. Lin Guande, the second Chinese President of ACC, would gather together the alumni working in Beijing and when he saw one of them dressed thinly, he offered to buy some clothes for him. And Mr. Shen Yuan, the former ACC teacher who had ever since come back to Tsinghua University and served as Dean of Department of Aeronautics, would spare time for them, showing them around the Summer Palace and sharing the pictures he took during his stay in Britain for further study and work. ACC graduates of one class after another, like full-fledged birds on the winds, have left the nest for the pursuit of their ideals, but in their hearts is cherished forever the love for their alma mater.

Lights of ACC

As a first-rate school, ACC raised quality graduates of one class after another, who contributed a great deal to their motherland and earned honors for their alma mater. They are the light of ACC. And ACC teachers, who made selfless sacrifices for the school and were devoted heart and soul to their teaching career are also the light of ACC. Among them, the foreign teachers, who held a sincere love for China and dedicated themselves to the education of ACC students and the good relations between China and other countries, were the ambassadors of civilization. They are definitely the light of ACC as well.

如果说英华培养出了十几位院士在全国中学里是罕见的，那么，在政治上英华的成绩同样也是罕见的。不论是在民族解放战争、抗日战争，还是建立新中国的人民解放战争，英华师生都是时代的先锋。他们不畏艰险，不怕牺牲，谱写了一曲又一曲可歌可泣的英雄篇章。1930年春，英华学生叶光明加入了中国共产党，是学生中最早的党员。第二年，王助、郑维新也加入了中国共产党。1939年，许世华在洋口秘密创建了中共英华特别支部，这是英华第一个党支部。到1945年，成立了两个党支部，一个是闽江工委调委领导下的支部，书记为郑锡基，一个是闽江工委学委领导下的支部，书记为陈学仕。随着革命形势的发展，英华党组织不断发展壮大，党员人数逐渐增多。到1949年，英华已有四个党支部，其中嘤求一个班级就有30多个党员。在党组织的外围，还涌现了"古田同乡会""工友夜校""灯塔社""民间社"等群众组织和十多个马列主义学习组。

方尔灏 (1904~1927.5)　郑维新 (1911~1932.11)　吴大麟 (1911~1940.2)　王　助 (1913.2~1941.9)

邱文凯 (1923~1941.8)　曹维新 (1923~1942.6)　黄回良 (1929~1948)　杨申生 (1919~1948)

何友礼 (1925~1948.4)　孙道华 (1922.5~1948.4)　傅孙焕 (1924~1948)　陈文相 (1925~1948)

部分英华英烈校友（来源：廖基远）
Part of ACC martyr alumni（Source: Liao Jiyuan）

ACC Martyrs

ACC was not only the cradle of knowledge, but also the cradle of revolution. The list of ACC participation in revolutionary activities is endless. As early as 1902, Mr. Chen Nengguang and Mr. Lin Fuchun, both alumni of ACC, joined the earliest revolutionary organization of Fujian, *Yiwen* Club, later on renamed *Qiaonan* Club, the key members of which became members of the subsequent Fujian Branch of the United League of China. In 1906, ACC students launched a patriotic movement, the first of its kind in Fuzhou. In 1909, Mr. Wong Nai Siong established a periodical named *Cau Hai Kung Dao Pao* to propagate the revolutionary cause. In 1920, to boycott Japanese goods, the Alumni Fundraising Department of ACC set aside an exhibition room in A-hok Hall to display China-made commodities, collected by ACC alumnus Mr. Wu Yangxian from different factories and stores in Fuzhou, the first exhibition room of domestic products in Fuzhou. Besides, Mr. Wu Yangxian, together with another alumnus Mr. Zhou Zongyu also dedicated themselves to the improvement of such domestic products as the umbrella and the toothbrush and thus helped the establishment of the Promotion Association of Domestic Products of Fujian, and they raised funds to build an office building for the association in Nan Gongyuan and put up a stele that read "Please use domestic products." in Nanmen Dou and Nan Gongyuan respectively. In honor of their great work, later in Nan Gongyuan was established the Exhibition Hall of Domestic Products and a road nearby was renamed Guo Huo Road, Guo Huo meaning domestic products.

If it can be seen as extremely rare for a single school like ACC to produce more than ten academicians of CAS and CAE, it is equally amazing for ACC to have achieved that much politically. Whether in the National Liberation War, in the War of Resistance against Japanese Agression, or in the People's Liberation War, ACC teachers and students were pioneers, who, afraid neither of adversities nor of self-sacrifices, kept shouldering one heroic mission after another. First, a large number of students chose to join the Communist Party, with Mr. Ye Guangming being the first , followed in the next year by Mr. Wang Zhu and Mr. Zheng Weixin. In 1939, ACC alumnus Mr. Xu Shihua established an underground Party branch in ACC, the first in ACC. Up to 1945, there were two Party branches, one under the leadership of the Commission of Inquiry of Minjiang Working Committee, with Mr. Zheng Xiji as its secretary, the other under the leadership of Student Work Commission of Minjiang Working Committee, with Mr. Chen Xueshi as its secretary. ACC Party organizations developed further as the revolution carried on, and ACC Party members increased rapidly. In 1949, there were four Party branches in ACC, with a total of over 30 Party members in the single Qiuying Class. Apart from the Party organizations of different ranks, some mass organizations and Marxist-Leninist Study Groups were developed at the same time, such as Gutian Town Fellowship Association, Night School for Coworkers, Lighthouse Society, and Nongovernmental Society, to name just a few.

许多党员在严酷的对敌斗争中经受住了考验，成为地下党的优秀骨干。有十多人被选送到省委机关工作，或者被派往闽北、闽中、闽赣边工作。王助、杨申生、孙道华、曾焕乾等同志被委以重任，分别担任新四军驻榕办事处主任，中共福建省委常委、宣传部长，福州市委书记，城工部所属地下军副司令等要职。

据统计，一共有 40 名英华校友为民族解放事业献出了宝贵的生命，成为革命烈士，其中包括黄乃模、方尔灏、郑维新、王助、何友礼、杨申生、真树华、魏品团、孙道华、郑锡基、曾焕乾、李继藩、林城良、柯海燕、陈学仕、陈东岚等。

我们不禁要问，一所教会学校，为何能培养出如此之多的爱国志士？这首先得益于陈芝美校长的开明和包容的民主办学思想。他坚持以民主精神办学，在不危害学校的基础上，支持学生参加进步活动。他常说，"只要番薯灶不被推倒，你们可以选择应走的道路。"他为进步教师陈衡庭在课堂上讲授社会发展史和辩证法提供方便，即使在国民党顺昌县党部提出警告的情况下，仍然坚持让衡庭老师在校继续授课。陈芝美校长还想方设法不让国民党派来的军训教官对进步学生进行监视和控制。其次是英华进步教师，如陈衡庭、陈景汉等，对学生革命思想的启蒙。在解放战争时期，陈景汉老师经常给学生们介绍国内外的形势，还积极组织学生参加读书会，指导他们学习进步书籍和文件，如《大众哲学》《政治经济学大纲》《论联合政府》《新民主主义论》《中国革命和中国共产党》等，还开办了工友夜校，帮助工友学习文化知识，以及组织学生参加福州的学生运动。

Many Party members of ACC withstood tests of all kinds in the bitter fight against the enemies and turned out to be the backbone of the underground Chinese Communist Party. More than ten people were sent to work in agencies of Provincial Party Committee, or on revolutionary mission to such areas as Minbei(the north of Fujian), Minzhong(the middle of Fujian), and Mingan Bian(the border area between Fujian and Jiangxi). Among them, Wang Zhu, Yang Shensheng, Sun Daohua and Zeng Huanqian were respectively entrusted with such important posts as Office Director of the New Fourth Army in Fuzhou, Member of the Provincial Standing Committee, Head of the Publicity Department, Municipal Party Secretary of Fuzhou, and Deputy Commander of the Underground Army attached to the City Work Department.

In total, there were 40 ACC alumni who sacrificed their lives for the national liberation cause and became revolutionary martyrs, including Huang Naishang, Fang Eryi, Zheng Weixin, Wang Zhu, He Youli, Yang Shensheng, Zhen Shuhua, Wei Pintuan, Sun Daohua, Zheng Xiji, Zeng Huanqian, Li Jifan, Lin Chengliang, Ke Haiyan, Chen Xueshi, Chen Donglan, and so on.

At this, one can't help wondering how come such a missionary school as ACC could bring out so many patriots. The reasons are as follows. For one thing, it was owing to President James Ding, who held democracy and freedom in high regard. He insisted on running ACC on the spirit of democracy, and tacitly supported students in their progressive activities, as long as they didn't threat the operations of ACC. As he put it, "As long as ACC is not threatened, you can follow your own belief." He provided convenience to Mr. Chen Hengting, a progressive ACC teacher, for his lectures on history of social development and dialectics, and chose to have Mr. Chen continue his teaching in ACC even in the face of the warnings from the Shunchang Branch of the Kuomintang (KMT). President James Ding also made efforts to get ACC students away from the monitor and control of the military training officer sent by the KMT. For another, it was owing to the enlightenment of students' revolutionary thoughts given by such progressive teachers of ACC as Mr. Chen Hengting and Mr. Chen Jinghan, who, during the period of China's War of Liberation, kept students updated about the situations at home and abroad, and encouraged them to take part in the Reading Group, guiding them to read such progressive books and documents as *Popular Philosophy*, *An Overview of Political Economy*, *On the United Government*, *On New Democracy*, and *The Chinese Revolution and the Chinese Communist Party*. They also contributed to the establishment of a night school for coworkers to help them with their study, and organized students to participate in student movements in Fuzhou.

关于英华革命传统这个问题，作者在采访李青藻老先生时，他的见解可谓客观和严谨。他说："英华中学作为载体，培养和输送了一批革命志士，体现了光荣的革命传统。这当然与英华中学作为培养人才的摇篮有密不可分的关系，但同时又不能简单地把这件事与中学当局画等号。英华中学中共地下党员多的根本原因是社会教育的效果。应该肯定，这是中共地下组织扎根基层、艰苦努力，对进步青年长期教育和指导的结果。当然，与当时的大背景也有关系，国民党反动派和帝国主义势力相勾结，搞得腐败透顶、民不聊生，从反面激励进步青年走上革命道路。"

外籍教师

英华的成就，也应归功于英华的外籍教师。他们大多热爱中国，热爱中国文化，精通中国话和福州方言。他们潜心教学，开导学生，在各个方面帮助学生，还为学生出国留学等提供便利条件。他们当中，有夫妻都在英华工作的（毕理夫妇），为英华人才培养作出了贡献。范哲明在陈芝美担任校长前到中华人民共和国成立，一直担任着英华中学的董事，对英华的发展作出了贡献，其夫人也曾任过英华英语教师。所以，洋口英华校医院取名为哲明医院，并且福州英华高中部有"哲明门"。抗日战争期间，范哲明曾经几次去洋口，对英华怀有深厚的情感，更是重视人才培养，曾资助中国人林缉西留学美国，还资助英华学生陈世明读英华中学和协和大学。1948年，陈世明被捕入狱的时候，范哲明和毕理先生相继到狱中看望，还送给他英语读物，供他在狱中阅读。

As for the school's fine tradition of patriotism, Mr. Li Qingzao, in the interview, made his insightful comments as follows, "ACC nurtured a large number of revolutionaries for the country, which embodied its fine revolutionary tradition. This is, of course, closely related to ACC as the cradle of talent cultivation. Nevertheless, we can never attribute it all to the school itself. The fact that ACC boasted so many underground Party members was the result of social education, or, to be specific, the meant-to-be achievement of the underground Chinese Communist Party that took root among the masses and made every effort to guide progressive ACC students. Of course, the general background of the time also came into play, in which Kuomintang reactionaries colluded with the imperial power, resulting in social corruption and dire poverty. These negative social elements prompted students to rise up and take the revolutionary cause."

Foreign Teachers

The remarkable accomplishments of ACC should, in part, be attributed to the dedication of the foreign teachers, who loved China and the Chinese culture and were versed in the Chinese language and the Fuzhou dialect. They put all their heart on teaching and directing students, helping them in every possible way and providing convenience to students' pursuit of further study abroad. Among them were couples Like Mr. and Mrs. Pilley, who both worked for ACC. Mr. Paul P. Wiant, whose Chinese name was Fan Zheming, had been a director of the Board of Trustees of ACC for many years, from the time before Dr. James Ding was made president up to the time right before the founding of the P. R. C., and contributed a lot to ACC, and his wife also worked for a time for ACC as an English teacher. To commemorate his dedication, the school hospital was named after him, and the Senior Department had a gate named after him as well. During the War of Resistence Against Japanese Agression, Mr. Wiant went several times to Yankow, where the war-time school was located, which showed his affection for ACC. He did all he could to help ACC students. He contributed money to the ACC student Lin Jixi in support of his going abroad for further study. He also provided money for Chen Shiming so that he was able to finish his education at ACC and moved on to Fukien Christian University. In 1948 when Chen Shiming was arrested by the KMT, Mr. Wiant and Mr. Pilley went to see him in prison, and to pull him through, they gave some English books for him to read.

抗战期间，美籍教师沈维德和毕理夫妇满怀对英华的高度爱心，不畏艰险，毅然回绝了美国大使馆要他们撤退回国的通知，自愿与英华同患难、共命运，随校迁到洋口继续任教。沈维德4岁的时候，父亲在福州病故，她跟随母亲回国。1930年，她大学毕业后，来福州英华她父亲工作过的地方任教，长达16年，可谓把自己的青春献给了英华，为英华培养了许多优秀人才。她同情中国革命，支持进步学生活动，曾把自己的住处作为进步学生订阅《新华日报》的投递地址和进步书籍的藏放处，并让她的家成为一些学生阅读进步书籍的场所。此外，她还帮助英华学生润色旨在呼吁美国人民制止美国政府支持蒋介石实行内战的《告美国人民书》的英译，定稿后由她带回美国发表。1946年，曾任英华特支书记的马绍永从崇安集中营释放回福州，被特务跟踪，曾在她家隐蔽一个月。1980年，时隔34年后，沈维德携其夫保罗先生来福建师大附中参观访问，受到学校和昔日同事和学生的热忱欢迎和接待。1984年，嘤求级校友林奔访美时，与沈师姑偶遇，相谈甚欢，他还将这次戏剧性场面写进他的访美通讯里，刊登于《福建日报》。

　　德辟孙二十八九岁来英华任教，教授修辞学、英文写作等，期间跟陈衡庭老师结下了深厚情谊。他热爱学生，更热爱中国，常穿中国长衫，还组织学生上课间操，让学生们身心都得到放松。他还资助学生完成学业，临终前还将仅有的300多元余款汇给协和大学会计室保管，以资助两位学生（周伟骅和叶明勋）完成学业。

During the War of Resistence Against Japanese Agression, Ms. Simester and Mr. and Mrs. Pilley, chose to stay in China even though they were requested by the American embassy to embark on the return journey to America, and moved inland with the school. They shared discomforts and hardships, trials and tribulations with ACC teachers and students. Ms. Edith W. Simester had to go back to America with her mother after her father passed away in Fuzhou, but in 1930 when she graduated from an American college, she decided to go back to China and had been working in ACC ever since for 16 years, dedicating her youthful years to ACC to help nurture numerous great talents. She identified herself with the Chinese in their revolutionary cause and supported students' progressive activities. She made her residence the delivery place of students' subscription for *Xinhua Daily*, the hiding place for students' progressive books and also the place where students gathered together to read the books. She even helped students improve the English version of "To the Americans" drafted by ACC students with the intention to appeal to the American government to stop supporting Chiang Kai-shek and Kuomintang in launching the civil war in China, and when it was finalized, she took it back to America to have it published. In 1946, Ms. Simester offered to take in for a month ACC alumnus Mr. Ma Shaoyong, who used to be Secretary of ACC Special Party Branch and was being shadowed by Kuomintang spies on his return trip to Fuzhou soon after his release from Chongan Concentration Camp. In 1980, 34 years after she left Fuzhou, Ms. Simester, together with her husband Paul, paid a visit to the Affiliated High School of Fujian Normal University, with ACC as one of its predecessors, and was warmly welcomed and received by her former colleagues and students. It so happened that later in 1984, Lin Ben, an ACC alumnus of Qiuying Class, had a chance meeting with Ms. Simester on his visit in America and they had pleasant chats for a good while and this unexpected and dramatic encounter was noted down in detail in his article about his visit to America and was published in *Fujian Daily*.

Mr. Sydney Arthur Davidson Jr. came to teach at ACC in his late twenties, and forged a deep friendship with Mr. Chen Hengting, a progressive teacher at ACC. Mr. Davidson had a devoted love for China and that was why he used to dress himself in a Chinese long gown. He had a sincere love for his students, organizing them to do exercise during the break to make sure they were properly relaxed and refreshed for the following study. He gave what money he had to support students to go through college, and as he was dying, he had all the money he had on him, 300 yuan in total, delivered to the Accounting Room of Fukien Christian University to help support two of its students Zhou Weihua and Ye Mingxun to finish their college education.

许多外教后来虽然回国了，却心系福州，情在英华。1989 年 10 月，毕理夫人及其孙女到福州英华英语学校参观访问。据去机场接她的成渊级学生李恩至回忆，因为一生清廉简朴又乐善好施，她们几乎没有什么积蓄，所以她们的往返路费还是由在美国的校友筹集的。她们回国时，还把节省下来的 500 元路费赠送给英华学校。毕理夫人的父亲是柯志仁，美国传教士，1900 年来华，先后在延平（南平）和福清传教，曾任培元书院（福清三中前身）校长。2012 年，毕理夫妇的两个女儿再次来到福州，走访了英华（附中）和福清三中。2017 年 9 月 22 日，师大附中迎来了 19 位美国友人，他们大多是在英华工作过的美籍教师的后代，有穆蔼仁家族、蒲天寿家族、柯志仁家族等。他们在师大附中校史馆内看着父辈的照片，感受先辈曾经在英华的工作环境。蒲美珠在馆内一张名为"私立福州鹤龄英华中学全体教职员摄影纪念"大合照中找到了自己的父母。"这是我的母亲，"蒲美珠指着老照片的人物，激动地说着。

2004 年，已至耄耋之年的穆蔼仁再次来闽。曾是美国飞虎队成员的穆蔼仁（唐迈克）被陈芝美校长在美募捐和演讲所感动，来英华任教，与英华师生结下了深厚情谊。课余时间他还成立了一个有关时局讨论的社团，极大地激发了学生们的抗日热情。他还帮惊涛级学生陈世明等审校英文墙报 *Tide*，回国后还把他珍藏多年的墙报寄回给陈世明。他和妻子后来在协和大学任教，还在鼓岭买了房子。他常说："我的根在中国。"穆蔼仁 2004 年还去武夷学院任教，当时《福建日报》以"一位 84 岁美国志愿者的福建情缘"为题报道了穆蔼仁。2005 年穆蔼仁在美国家中病逝。遵照他生前的遗愿，2015 年，他的家人将其一半骨灰带回福州，撒入闽江（陈世明，2014：72）。

Many foreign teachers still kept ACC and Fuzhou in mind even though they had long gone back to their motherlands. In October, 1989, Mrs. Pilley and her grand-daughter came to visit Fuzhou Anglo-Chinese College, reestablished in 1988 in memory of Anglo-Chinese College established in 1881, and as Li Enzhi, an ACC alumnus from Chengyuan Class who went to the airport to pick them up, recalled it, they didn't even have enough money for their trip, which was all funded by ACC alumni in America, as the Pilley family were all clean and honest and were given to doing charitable work. And true to their moral character, before they left for America, they offered the remaining 500 yuan to Fuzhou Anglo-Chinese College. Mrs. Pilley's father was Harry Russell Caldwell, who came to China in 1900 and did missionary work in Yanping (Nanping) and Fuqing in Fukien Province. He used to be President of Boys' Boarding School in Fuzhou, the predecessor of Fuqing No. 3 Middle School. In 2012, the two daughters of Mr. and Mrs. Pilley arrived in Fuzhou, and they visited the Affiliated High School of Fujian Normal University, and Fujian Fuqing No. 3 Middle School. On September, 22, 2017, the Affiliated High School of Fujian Normal University had a special group of 19 American visitors, most of whom are the descendants of the former foreign teachers at ACC, including the MacInnis Family, the Brewster Family, the Billing Family and the Caldwell Family. They were shown around the School History Museum, in which were displayed old pictures of their parents or grandparents as well as ACC students and teachers. Ms. Brewster stopped at a group photo, and, pointing to one lady in it, said excitedly, "This is my mother!"

In 2004, Mr. Donald E. MacInnis, a former teacher of ACC in his eighties, came back to Fuzhou for a visit. While he was a member of the American Flying Tigers, also called American Volunteer Group, he was greatly touched by ACC President Dr. James Ding, who came to America to deliver speeches to raise funds for his school. As a result, Mr. MacInnis chose to quit his job and came to Fuzhou and became an English teacher at ACC. There, he befriended many teachers and students, and together they organized a society dedicated to the discussions of and comments on the international affairs, which greatly aroused the patriotism and enthusiasm to fight against the Japanese. Mr. MacInnis also offered to improve the wall newspaper in English created by Chen Shiming and his classmates from Tide Class, and later when he came back to Fuzhou, he gave back to Chen Shiming the precious copy of the wall newspaper he had kept over the years. Later, Mr. MacInnis and his wife moved on to teach at Fukien Christian University and bought their own house at Kuliang, a place in Foochow where most foreigners resided. As he put it, " I have my root in China. " In 2004, when he came back to Fuzhou at the age of 84, he offered to teach at Wuyi University for a year, and was featured into *Fujian Daily* with the headline "The Affection a 84-Year-Old American Volunteer Had for Fujian". In 2005, Mr. MacInnis passed away. In accordance with his will, in 2015, his family took half of his ashes back to Fuzhou and had them scattered into the Minjiang River.

英华知名校友

英华具有优良的办学传统，培养了数以千计的著名政治家、专家、学者，如前国民政府主席林森，著名历史学家、燕京大学和哈佛大学教授洪煨莲，经济学泰斗陈岱孙，国际法学家王铁崖等。特别是新中国成立后，有17位英华校友先后当选中国科学院和中国工程院院士。一个中学培养出如此之多的院士，这在全国范围内也是首屈一指的。以下以院士侯德榜、政治家林森、史学家洪业为例，让读者领略英华各级各类名家的风采及其在英华的成长历程。

侯德榜（1890—1974）

福州市人，化学家，化工专家，中国科学院院士。1903年起就读于鹤龄英华书院，1907年进入上海闽皖铁路学校。1911年进入清华留美预备学堂，以10门功课1000分的特优成绩创下了清华园的一个奇迹。1913年公费留美，获麻省理工学院化学硕士学位，哥伦比亚大学化学硕士、博士学位。1921年接受爱国企业家范旭东的诚聘，回国出任天津永利制碱公司总工程师等职，历尽艰苦，振兴民族工业。1926年终于打破外国苏尔维集团历时70年之久的技术垄断，制成中国自己的"红三角"牌纯碱，获美国万国博览会和瑞士国际商品展览会金奖，享誉全球。1933年，侯德榜把索尔维制碱法的全部技术和实践经验写成专著《纯碱制造》在美国以英文出版，把制碱的奥秘分享给全世界，为世界制碱工艺增添了绚丽的篇章。美国化学家威尔逊教授称这本书是"中国化学家对世界文明所作的重大贡献"，轰动了国际化学界。

Scan for more
扫码了解更多

Prominent ACC Alumni

With excellent teaching traditions, ACC nurtured hundreds of prominent statesmen, professionals and scholars, such as Mr. Lin Sen, the former President of National Government of the Republic of China, Mr. Hong William, Professor of both Yenching University and Harvard University, Mr. Chen Daisun, the prince of economists, and Mr. Wang Tieya, an international jurist. In particular, after the founding of the People's Republic of China, a total of 17 ACC alumni were made academicians of Chinese Academy of Sciences and Chinese Academy of Engineering, which was second to none among all high schools in China. The following are a brief introduction of Mr. Hou Debang, Mr. Lin Sen and Mr. Hong William (Hong Ye), who may serve as typical examples of ACC elites in all fields.

Hou Debang (1890 – 1974)

Hou Debang was a native of Fuzhou and a distinguished chemist and expert in chemical industry. He was enrolled in ACC in 1903, and in 1907 moved to Minwan Tielu School in Shanghai. In 1911, he was admitted into the Preparatory School of Study in America in Tsinghua University, and got full marks in all the ten courses, a miracle in the history of Tsinghua. In 1913 he went to study in America at state expense, and earned a master's degree of Chemistry in MIT, and a master's degree and a doctorate degree of Chemistry in Columbia University. In 1921, he accepted the invitation of Mr. Fan Xudong, a patriotic entrepreneur and was appointed as Chief Engineer of Tianjin Yongli Soda Co., Ltd., and devoted himself to revitalize national industry. The year 1926 witnessed a breakthrough in his career, when he broke the 70-year technical monopoly of Solvay Group of Belgium by manufacturing China's own soda under the brand name Hong Sanjiao (Red Triangle), an invention that won the Gold Medal of American World Exposition and of Swiss International Commodities Fair, and thus he became world-renowned. In 1933, Mr. Hou had his book *Manufacture of Soda* published in New York, in which he shared the secret of soda manufacturing by offering technology and experimental practice of Solvay Alkali Process, and opened up a new chapter in the world soda production. The book was highly honored by the American chemist Prof. Wilson as a remarkable contribution of a Chinese chemist to the world civilization, and caused quite a sensation in the international chemical circle.

1937 年 1 月 31 日，一座绵延 5 千米、规模宏大、工艺先进、在亚洲首屈一指的化工联合企业在南京长江北岸建成。至此，基础化工的两翼酸和碱，在中华大地崛起，奠定了我国化学工业奋飞的基础。抗日战争期间，侯德榜坚决顶住敌人的威逼利诱，凛然宣布"宁肯给工厂开追悼会，也决不同日本人'合作'"，在日军轰炸声中，将南京和天津塘沽酸碱两大厂的设备与人员迁往四川。为解决永利入川后原盐成本增加导致索尔维法高耗低产的问题，他赴德国洽谈购买察安法专利。洽谈失败后，侯德榜决心自主研究制碱新法。他用 3 年时间，试验 500 余次，提炼成品 2 000 余份，终于成功研究出制碱新工艺，其优越性远超索尔维法和察安法，食盐利用率从 70% 提高到 96%。1941 年 3 月，新的制碱法被命名为"侯氏制碱法"。它是 20 世纪一项伟大的科技创新，不仅开创了世界制碱工业的新纪元，更为抗日战争时期的军工业及大后方的工业发展作出了巨大贡献。抗日战争胜利后，侯德榜为了民族和永利的利益，亲赴日本，无所畏惧地和日军司令谈判，历尽艰辛，全胜而归，被日本掠夺走的设备终于回归祖国。由于在科技上的卓越成就，侯德榜获中国工程师协会首枚荣誉金牌、哥伦比亚大学一级奖章、英国皇家学会化工学会名誉会员（当时全球共 12 名，亚洲仅中国、日本各 1 名）等殊荣。1949 年 7 月，侯德榜正在印度指导化工建设，接到党中央的召唤，旋即回京，受到毛主席、周总理的专门约见。新中国成立后，他历任国务院重工业部技术顾问、化工部副部长，当选为中国科学院首批学部委员（院士）、中国科协副主席、中国化学会会长、化工学会理事长，为社会主义建设事业作出重大贡献。他还把新中国成立后出版的《制碱工业》上下两卷的全部稿费缴了党费，把珍藏图书和个人储蓄捐赠给国家和公益事业。

On January 31, 1937, a large-scale first-rate chemical complex with advanced technology was established in the northern bank of the Yangtze River in Nanjing, thus achieving the domestic manufacture of acid and soda, the two wings of basic chemistry, and laying a solid foundation for the takeoff of China's chemical industry. During the War of Resistance Against Japanese Agression, with a heart of patriotism, Hou firmly withstood the coercion of the enemies and sternly declared that he would rather hold a funeral for his factory than cooperate with the Japanese. And amid the enemy's air raids, he systematically arranged for transferring to Sichuan the equipment and staff of the acid factory and soda factory in Nanjing and Tanggu of Tianjin. After the move to Sichuan, the factories were faced with the rising cost of salt, which resulted in the high consumption and low yield of Solvay Alkali Process. To solve the problem, Hou embarked on the journey to Germany to negotiate for the buying of the patent of Zahn Process, but was frustrated. As a result, Hou was determined to invent his own process of soda manufacturing. He spent three whole years doing 500 times of experiments and refining 2,000 pieces of products and eventually worked out the new technology of soda manufacturing, with its advantages far surpassing those of Solvay Alkali Process and Zahn Process and the utilization of salt increasing from 70% to 96%. In March 1941, his new technology of manufacturing soda was acknowledged and named Hou Process, a great scientific and technological innovation of the twentieth century, which not only ushered in a new era of soda manufacturing, but also made tremendous contributions to the military industry and the industrial development of the Rear Area (the area under KMT rule during the War of Resistance Against Japanese Agression). After the victory of the war, to take back the equipment plundered by the Japanese army, Hou fearlessly went to Japan to reason with the Japanese commander on behalf of the Chinese people and Yongli Co., Ltd. He tided over innumerable difficulties and trials and in the end came back a victor. In reward for his splendid achievement in chemistry, he was granted a lot of national and international honors and awards, such as the first honorary gold medal ever given by Chinese Engineers Association, the first-class medal given by Columbia University, honorary membership of Chemical Society of British Royal Society (only 12 in total globally, with one from Japan and China each). In 1949 while Hou was in India directing chemical construction, he was called back by the central authorities and was warmly received by both Chairman Mao and Premier Zhou, and was henceforth entrusted with vital positions. He was successively appointed as Technical Advisor for Ministry of Heavy Industry of the State Council, Deputy Minister of Chemical Industry, among the first batch of academicians of the Chinese Academy of Sciences, Vice Chairman of China Association for Science and Technology, President of the Chinese Chemical Society, and Chairman of the Chemical Society, and had ever since made a significant contribution to the cause of socialist construction. In his late years, Hou gave away all his author's remuneration of his two books, the first and second volume of his *Soda Manufacturing Industry*, to the Party in the form of Party membership dues, and his life-time collections and savings to the country for public welfare undertakings.

1974 年 8 月 26 日，侯德榜逝于北京，终年 85 岁，被誉为"科技泰斗，士子楷模"。为缅怀其丰功伟绩和高风亮节，侯德榜故乡福州市台江区宁化街道的一条公路被命名为"德榜路"，并设有"侯德榜故居"，供后人参观和瞻仰。

侯德榜在英华期间就表现出了极大的爱国心和科技救国的抱负。侯家世代务农，祖父是个读书人，希望他长大能金榜题名、求取功名，故为他取名"德榜"。幼年随祖父受启蒙教育，平时还要参加田间劳动，过着半耕半读的生活。侯德榜自幼勤奋好学，学习之余要干农活，然后又抓紧时间学习，放牛时带着书看，甚至连帮妈妈烧火时也口中念念有词。有一次，祖父远远看到他伏在水车上车水。祖父一边走一边高声喊他，可他却没有应答。走近一听，祖父发现他正一边车水，一边拿着从姑妈家借来的《古文观止》诵读里面王柳的诗句，"挂车攻读"的故事由此而来。

1903 年，13 岁的侯德榜在姑妈的资助下，进入英华书院就读。那一年，放学归来的侯德榜看到蓬头垢面、衣衫褴褛的几百名中国劳工被手持皮鞭的洋人驱赶着登上了洋人庞大的远洋船。这些苦力上身裸露，每人胸上都烙有号码，他们在暴雨中拖着沉重的脚步，艰难地向轮船移动。他愤慨不已，去跟他最敬佩的、刚从国外回来的黄先生讨论这事。黄先生告诉他这是因为清政府腐败无能，国弱遭欺，并激励他说唯有刻苦学习科学技术，振兴民族，国家才有希望。从此，侯德榜意识到只有科技才能救国，只有发展中国人自己的民族工业，才能摆脱列强的压迫和剥削，自立自强。

侯德榜晚年学习不辍（摄于侯德榜故居）
Hou Debang in his late years（Source: Former residence of Hou Debang）

On August 26, 1974, at the age of 85, Mr. Hou Debang passed away in Beijing. He was highly regarded as the prince of scientists and the role model of scholars. To commemorate his great contribution and noble character, a road in his hometown in Fuzhou was named after him and his former residence was restored and rebuilt where people can go and revere his greatness.

Since his early years, Hou had demonstrated great patriotism and the ambition to revitalize the nation through science and technology. For generations, the Hou family was a farming one, except that his grandfather was an intellectual. and as his name Debang suggested, his grandfather expected him to stand out in the imperial examinations and win an official rank. As a result, the young Hou Debang could be said to live a half-farming and half-reading life, going to the farm most of the day and sparing some time for studying under the guidance of his grandfather. To manage both tasks successfully, Hou tended to be studying while he was doing such work as herding the cow or cooking. Story had it that once his grandfather saw him on a waterwheel wheeling water, but he didn't seem to hear his grandfather calling for him, and as his grandfather went near, he realized the young Hou was reciting the poem by Wang Liu in the book *The Finest of Ancient Prose* borrowed from his aunt.

In 1903, the 13-year-old Hou Debang was able to be enrolled at ACC with the financial support of his aunt. On his way home from school, he saw with his own eyes the Chinese laborers in rags whipped to get on board the huge steamer. They were bare on their upper body, each with a number branded on the chest, and moved with great difficulty in the rain toward the steamer. At this, Hou was filled with indignation, and went to consult his most revered teacher, Mr. Huang, who had just come back from overseas. Mr. Huang told him that the corruption and incompetence of the Qing Government resulted in a weak nation falling prey to the brutal foreign countries, and encouraged him to study hard and arm himself with knowledge of science and technology; only in this way was it possible to revive the country and rejuvenate the nation. Hou was awakened to the truth that the only way to save the country was the mastery of science and technology and the only way to break away from the oppression and exploitation of the foreign powers was the rise of the Chinese national industries.

1906 年，侯德榜就读的英华书院发生了福州学生运动史上最早的一次爱国运动，起因是 1904 年清政府与美国续订华工禁约，排斥和迫害旅美华工。这激起了中国各界的反美爱国运动。同年 6 月，英华书院学生推出庄考文等代表，要求时任主理高智和福州美领事葛尔锡转电致美国抗议书，遭高智训斥，并以停膳、开除相威胁。高智的高压手段激起学生们更大义愤，侯德榜、林鼎章等主张退学以示抗议，广大学生纷纷响应。

林森（1868—1943）

福建闽侯县人，原国民政府主席。1881 年进入刚创办的英华书院就读，1884 赴台，在台北电报局工作，1888 年重返英华续完学业后再赴台任职。1895 年，台湾被割让给日本，林森参加抗日军，失败后回到福州。期间，曾在英华母校任教并广泛联络海内外革命志士，遭清政府通缉后于 1898 年再度赴台，与孙中山取得联系，加入兴中会，并创立兴中会台湾支会，进行抗日反清活动。1899 年，因遭日本侦缉而返回家乡。1902 年，林森到上海海关供职，组织旅沪福建学生会，任会长。1905 年，加入同盟会，先后组建同盟会福建支会、江西九江分会等。武昌起义后，策动新军及海军主力舰队起义，在稳定辛亥革命大局中功勋卓著。

In 1906, there occurred at ACC a large-scale patriotic student movement, the first and the earliest in Fuzhou. The trigger was that in 1904 the Qing Government renewed the treaty with America to exclude and persecute the Chinese laborers in America, and hence the patriotic anti-American movement coming up in all parts of the country. ACC students also acted in response. Represented by Zhuang Kaowen, they appealed to Mr. Gowdy the then President of ACC and Mr. Samuel L. Gracey the then American consul in Foochow to extend to the American government ACC students' "Letter of Protest to America". To their bitterness and disappointment, President Gowdy refused all their appeals and instead, threatened them with stopping their meals and discharging them from the school. His high-pressure means aroused greater indignation among ACC students, and Hou Debang and Lin Dingzhang proposed to quit school in protest, and was echoed by many ACC students.

Lin Sen (1868 – 1943)

Lin Sen, born in Minhou County in Fuzhou, was the former President of the National Government of the Republic of China. In 1881, he was admitted into ACC established that same year, and in 1884 he went to work as a clerk in the Taipei Telegraph Office in Taiwan. In 1888 he came back to ACC to finish his study before he went back again to Taiwan. In 1895, Taiwan was ceded to Japan, and in protest, Lin Sen joined the Anti-Japanese Army, which was frustrated, so he came back again to Fuzhou. During his stay in Fuzhou, he worked for a time as an ACC teacher while at the same time he busied himself making contact with revolutionaries at home and abroad and was consequently put on the wanted list of the Qing Government. As a result, Lin Sen had to go back to Taiwan once again and there he met Mr. Sun Yat-sen and joined the Renaissance China Association. Later, he established Taiwan Branch of the Renaissance China Association, and carried on the anti-Japanese and anti-Qing activities. In 1899 he was hunted down by the Japanese army and had to go back to his hometown Minhou County. In 1902, Lin Sen took a job in the Customs House of Shanghai, and he established Union of Students with Fujian Nationality in Shanghai. In 1905, he joined the United League of China (1905 – 1912, the predecessor of the Kuomintang), and helped to establish its Fujian Branch and Jiujiang Branch in Jiangxi. After the outbreak of Wuchang Uprising, he engineered the uprising of both the New Army and the main navy fleet and performed noble exploits in stabilizing the overall situation of the Revolution of 1911 (the Chinese bourgeois democratic revolution led by Sun Yat-sen which overthrew the Qing Dynasty).

中华民国成立后，林森历任临时参议院议长、大元帅府外交部长、国民党中央执行委员、国民政府常委、立法院院长、代理国民政府主席、国民政府主席。林森曾先后主持修建黄花岗七十二烈士墓和南京中山陵。西安事变时，他极力主张和平解决，并以国民政府主席的名义于 1937 年初先后两次下令赦免张学良并恢复其原职，但蒋介石拒不执行。抗日战争期间，林森立场坚定，始终恪守反对日本侵略的原则立场，为坚定国人抗日斗志、阻挡恐日投降逆流做出了杰出贡献。林森对光复台湾十分关心，1943 年因车祸受重伤，弥留之际仍嘱收复台湾。1943 年 8 月 1 日林森病故于重庆，享年 76 岁。林森一生为官清廉，淡泊名利，重视教育，严于自律。在官场从不结党营私，对亲友之事、政事方面的请托，都一律拒绝。

林森能从一介平民走向国民政府主席的高位，与他在鹤龄英华书院读书期间所接受的"西化"教育有紧密的联系。事实上，当时很多人就是因为英华书院这个学习平台而脱胎换骨，彻底改变命运的。林森在 1881 年进入英华书院读书之前，已经在美国教会办的培元学校接受过 6 年西学教育的熏陶，英华更高层次的西学教育让他在青春期就形成了正确的世界观、人生观和价值观，所以他离开英华后就报考台湾西学堂，而不是选择参加科举考试。

The victory of the revolution led to the founding of the new government, the Republic of China under the leadership of Sun Yat-sen, and Lin Sen was appointed successively to such important positions as President of the Provisional Senate, Foreign Minister of Generalissimo Sun Yat-sen's Mansion, Central Executive Member of the Kuomintang, Member of the Standing Committee of the National Government of the Republic of China, Head of the Legislative Chamber, Acting President of the National Government of the Republic of China, and eventually, President of the National Government of the Republic of China. He also took charge of the construction of Tomb for 72 revolutionary martyrs of Huang Hua Gang and Sun Yat-sen Mausoleum. In the Xi'an Incident, which occurred in Xi'an on December 12, 1936, General Zhang Xueliang and Yang Hucheng took Chiang Kai-shek hostage and demanded that he cease the civil war. The incident was settled peacefully, but as a result General Zhang Xueliang was imprisoned. Lin Sen strongly advocated a peaceful solution to the incident, and he, in the name of President, ordered twice the pardon of General Zhang Xueliang and the resumption of his posts, which was rejected by Chiang Kai-shek. During the War of Resistance Against Japanese Agression, Lin Sen invariably kept the firm stand to fight against the Japanese invasion, which was of vital significance in strengthening the nation's resolve to fight against Japan and preventing the surrender and submission due to the horror of Japan. Lin Sen also cherished in his heart a great aspiration for the recovery of Taiwan from the rule of Japan, and in 1943 when he was severely injured in a car accident, he even made this his deathbed wish. Lin Sen passed away in 1943 in Chongqing at the age of 76. In his whole life, he had always been an honest and incorruptible official, took his personal fame and fortune lightly, attached great importance to education and practiced stern self-discipline. He never banded together with other officials for personal purposes, nor did he ever take advantage of his post to benefit his family and relatives in any way.

That Lin Sen was able to promote from a civilian to a high-ranking government official was closely related to the Western-style education he had received at ACC. As a matter of fact, he was by no means the only one who was transformed and completely changed his fate thanks to his education in ACC. Before he was admitted into ACC in 1881, he had been in Boys' Boarding School, also a missionary school in Fuzhou during that period, and received six years of Western-style education, and his enrollment in ACC, a school with higher level of Western education made it possible for him to form right values, worldview, and outlook on life in his teens. And that was why he chose to apply for Taiwan Western Learning School after he left ACC, instead of attending the traditional Imperial Examination.

众所周知，英华课程注重英文教学和科学教育，包含自然科学和社会科学，而学生们在学习西方知识的同时，也受西方民主、自由、平等、博爱思想的熏陶，思想积极，加上当时能及时了解国际上的一些政治偏见和争端，很容易激发他们的反抗精神和革命思想。林森对当时英华学校要求学生上圣经课以及每天早上要做晨祷等很是不满，曾向书院主理提出将圣经课改为学生自由选择的课，不列为主修课，其他基督教活动也应让学生自主选择，结果均遭到校方拒绝。后林森因"触犯天条"肄业离开英华（王亮，2020）。从中，他懂得了国家强大和民族独立才是硬道理，从而走上了救国之路。

洪业（1893—1980）

福建闽侯县人，号煨莲，取其英文名 William 的同音字，博士、教授、历史学家，与钱穆、顾颉刚、陈寅恪齐名。1910 年进入英华书院，1915 年毕业后赴美留学，获哥伦比亚等大学文学学士、硕士、博士及神学博士学位。1923 年起应聘燕京大学历史系，培养了大批史学家，如研究汉史的瞿同祖、研究辽史的冯家升、研究方志的朱士嘉，还有考古的郑德坤、研究佛教的陈观胜等（陈毓贤，2013：8）。1924 年，受燕京大学之命与哈佛大学协商，为创立哈佛燕京学社和争取查尔斯·马丁·霍尔的亚洲文化教育事业基金作出了重要贡献。1925 年，赴哈佛大学讲学，1930 年回国，任燕京大学国学研究所所长兼导师。1933 年和 1940 年先后获美国俄亥俄卫斯理安大学名誉文学博士和名誉神学博士。1937 年，获巴黎茹理安（儒莲）奖金。1945 年，燕京大学复校，仍任历史系教授。

As was known, ACC was noted for its English teaching and emphasis on science education, including natural science and social science, and while ACC students were receiving the Western-style education, they were at the same time nurtured with the Western spirit of democracy, freedom, equality and universal love, which made them positive in thinking. Besides, they were able to be informed of the latest political discrimination and disputes over the world. Therefore, it was natural for ACC students to derive the spirit of rebellion and revolution. And Lin Sen was a typical example. He strongly objected to ACC students having to attend the Bible class and do morning prayers every day, and proposed to the president that the Bible class, together with other religious activities, be made elective instead of compulsory, which was, as could be imagined, rejected. Later, he had to quit in the midst of his study due to the so-called violation of the school rules, and he realized that a powerful country with its independent nation was the utmost principle and henceforth embarked on the cause of revolution for a new and independent country.

Hong William (1893 – 1980)

Hong Ye, also named Hong Wei Lian, a homonym of his English name William, born in Minhou County of Fujian, was a PhD, a professor, a great historian who enjoyed equal fame with Qian Mu, Gu Jiegang and Chen Yinke. He was enrolled in ACC in 1910, and went on to American for further study in 1915, where he earned successively a degree of BA, of MA, of D. L (Doctor of Letters), and of D. D (Doctor of Divinity). From 1923 on he had been working for Department of History in Yenching University, where he trained and brought up many historians. Among them were Qu Tongzu, dedicated to the study of Han Dynasty, Feng Jiasheng, dedicated to the study of Liao Dynasty, Zhu Shijia, dedicated to the study of local records, Zheng Dekun, dedicated to archaeology, and Chen Guansheng, dedicated to the study of Buddhism. In 1924, he received instructions from Yenching University to seek cooperation with Harvard University, and contributed to the establishment of Harvard-Yenching Institute with the fund bequeathed by Charles Martin Hall dedicated to promote higher education in Asia. In 1925, he was invited to Harvard University as a lecturer and in 1930 came back to Yenching University where he was made Director and Supervisor of the Institute of Chinese Studies. In 1933 and 1940, he was granted respectively the honorary degree of Doctor of Letters and of Doctor of Divinity by Ohio Wesleyan University, and in 1937 he was awarded the Prix Stanislas Julien, a prize that recognizes outstanding Western-language scholarship in the field of Asian humanities. In 1945 with the end of the War of Resistance Against Japanese Agression, Yenching University resumed its usual operation, and Hong Ye remained a professor of the Department of History.

洪先生一生著书立说，成果丰硕，编撰出版经史子集各种引得64种81册，著有中文著述40多种，英文著述21种（陈毓贤，2013），其中有关刘知几《史通》的专题研究（英文）和《蒙古秘史源流考》（英文）成为世界各国大学讲授蒙古史的必读参考教材。他著有中英文专著几十部，其中英文专著《中国最伟大的诗人杜甫》1952年由哈佛大学出版社出版，被士林推为权威之作。洪先生一生爱国，1941年太平洋战争爆发后曾遭日军逮捕入狱近半年。他坚持民族气节，拒绝为日伪工作，即便后来定居美国，仍心系中国。1979年，他嘱其后人将他毕生珍藏的中外珍本三万册图书赠予北京图书馆和中央民族学院，并将其中文论著《洪业论学集》50余万字交北京中华书局出版。1980年12月23日，洪业病逝于美国，终年87岁。

洪业幼年大半在福州度过，祖父在南台（仓山）开有"永吉茶行"。1910年，在其父的朋友、商务印书馆总编辑高梦旦的建议下，进入英华书院学习，直到1915年毕业，与陈芝美、王穆和是同班同学。当时英华书院的校长是高智。在英华书院，穿着一身旧蓝布衫的洪业与身穿丝绸的大部分同学形成鲜明反差，在同学中特别显眼，加上他喜欢引经据典，被同学笑称为"孟子"，意思是当孔子是不够格了，当孟子还是可以的。因为入学英文口试成绩很差，他被安排在一班。但他天资聪明，勤奋好学，学业突飞猛进，每几个月就升一班，毕业时全校成绩最高，被奖励了一本商务印书馆出版的颜惠庆的《英华大辞典》。

Hong Ye was devoted to writing scholarly books and was remarkably prolific, having compiled and published a total of 81 tomes of 64 kinds of index to classical works, historical works, philosophical works and belles-lettres, the four traditional divisions of a Chinese library. Besides, he authored scores of books in English and in Chinese, one of which was his English work entitled *Du Fu: China's Greatest Poet*, published in 1952 by Harvard University Press, and well received as an authority by the literati. In his whole life, Hong loved China sincerely. In 1941 when the Pacific War broke out, he was arrested and imprisoned half a year by the Japanese army; there he adhered firmly to national integrity and refused to work for the Japanese. And even though he had settled down in America, he still held his mother country dear in his heart. In 1979, he had his offspring give away all the 30,000 volumes of books he had collected in his life to Beijing Library and Minzu University of China, and entrust Zhonghua Book Company with the publication of his book *Collection of Hong Ye's Theories*. Hong Ye passed away on December 23, 1980 in America at the age of 87.

Hong Ye spent most of his childhood in Fuzhou, for his grandfather ran a tea shop there. In 1910, on the advice of a friend of his father's, Mr. Gao Mengdan, Chief Editor of Commercial Press in Beijing, Hong Ye enrolled in ACC with John Gowdy as president, in the same class with Dr. James Ding and Wang Muhe, until he graduated in 1915. At ACC, Hong Ye, always dressed in a worn-out blue shirt, was in sharp contrast with, and stood out conspicuously among, other students wearing silk. Since he was inclined to quote the classics, he earned the nickname Mencius from his classmates, who joked that he was well qualified to be the second Mencius, if not the second Confucius. As Hong Ye did poorly in the oral English test at the entrance examination of ACC, he was assigned to Class One. But as he was greatly talented and diligent, he was promoted to a better class every few months, and on graduation, he ranked the first in academic achievements and was thus rewarded with an *English-Chinese Dictionary*, compiled by Yan Huiqing from Commercial Press.

关于英华办学的思考

鹤龄英华书院是教会在福州创办的诸多学校中较出名的一所学校，其校训"尔乃世之光"也带有一定的宗教色彩，取自圣经《马太福音》第五章第 14 节。据《战事期中之基督教教育》记载，福建教会中学生人数 1936—1937 年间是 5 343 人，1939—1940 年间增至 9 344 人。但学校数基本保持原来水平：抗日战争前 42 所，1938—1939 年间 39 所（陈明霞，2012：74）。

那么，教会为何要在福州创办这么多学校呢？自然就是为教会服务的。对此，英华书院理事高智直言不讳："教会学校与一般学校不同，它是宗教和教育的结合体，是为宗教而教育。"（刘海峰、庄明水，1996：291）从教会的立场看，其办学目的大致可以分为以下几种：一、性格塑造：培养真诚的人、有同情心和爱心的人、积极努力的人；二、获取知识，锻炼身体；三、基础知识的传授和培训；四、专业知识的传授；五、培养神职人员；六、培养好公民。传教士狄考文在 1877 年关于"基督教会与教育"的发言中提到了教会办学的几个目的：一、培养当地牧师；二、为教会学校提供教员；三、培养精通西方科学、艺术的中国人才；四、提升社会阶层；五、使本地教会自力更生（林金水，1997：418）。基于以上目的，教会办学有一套完整的体系，涵盖初等教育、中学教育和高等教育（大学），甚至包含学前教育，如在福建创立的协和幼稚师范学校（协幼）。当然，从政治的角度来看，当时教会在中国办学并不仅仅出于宗教目的，更重要的是通过教会办学，扩大西方在第三世界国家的影响，在思想上进行垄断和控制。

应该说，教会在中国的办学客观上扩大了国人的视野，提高了国人的文化素质，对中国近代教育有一定的促进作用。鹤龄英华中学是教会学校的典型代表。

Reflections of the ACC Mode of Education

Anglo-Chinese College stood out among the scores of schools founded by Western missionaries, whose religious characteristics are well reflected in its school motto, "You are the light of the world", adapted from Matthew 5:14. It was recorded that the number of students from missionary schools in Fujian was 5,343 during 1936 – 1937, and 9,344 during 1939 – 1940, while the number of missionary schools tended to hold, with a total of 42 before the outbreak of the War of Resistance Against Japanese Agression, and 39 during 1938 – 1939.

Then, here comes the question. Why is it that there were so many missionary schools in Fuzhou? The answer, of course, is self-evident: to serve the purposes of Christianity. For that matter, John Gowdy, President of ACC, was frank by saying that missionary schools differed from other types of school in that the former were a combination of religion and education and were intended to educate for religious purposes. In the perspective of Christian churches, the purposes of running missionary schools, as mentioned in many religious works, are, more or less, the same: character building, namely, to train sincere, sympathetic, loving and diligent people; knowledge acquisition and physical buildup; the impart and training of basic knowledge; the impart and training of professional knowledge; the training of clergymen; the training of good citizens. Missionary C. W. Mateer, in his speech on Christianity and education, pointed out a few purposes of missionary schools: to train the local clergymen, to train teachers for missionary schools, to cultivate the Chinese talents versed in Western science and art, to help students promote to higher social class, and to make the local Christian churches self-reliant. For these purposes, the Christian education was highly sophisticated, covering different stages, ranging from primary education (elementary schools), secondary education (high schools) and high education (colleges and universities), even preschool education like Union Kindergarten Training School founded in Fuzhou. Of course, from a political perspective, the missionary schools are a means to exerting the influences of Western countries on China, so as to ultimately monopoly and control the Chinese people ideologically.

There is no denying that all these missionary schools founded in Fuzhou or in other parts of China were helpful in that they broadened the nation's horizons, improved the cultural quality of the people, and promoted the national education.

当然，我们也应该看到英华的局限性，如过于重视基督教育、过于依赖西方国家导致奴化教育，以至于遭到很多学生（如林森）的强烈抗议，甚至有传闻说陈芝美校长聘请教师时把是否为基督教徒当作一个考量标准。但是，英华学生并没有一味地皈依基督教。有数据显示，福州英华中学1934年初中毕业生38人中，信仰基督教的只有4人，占10.5%，信仰佛教的1人，占2.6%，其余为无信仰者，占86.9%（陈明霞，2012：92）。学生们并没有一味地崇洋媚外，反倒是更坚定了爱国信念（Dunk，1996：204），其中不少人成为优秀的共产党员。所以，我们要客观评价英华，既要充分肯定它的积极作用和贡献，也要看到它的局限性。

对于英华的成就，我们也应该客观评价。对此，李青藻老先生提出要用"历史唯物主义看'英华'"。他指出："英华中学的办学时间很久，规模逐渐扩大，经验逐步积累。其办学成果最突出的是在后期。抗日战争胜利后，英华中学迁回福州，呈现出一派欣欣向荣的景象。当时在福州地区，乃至在全省，英华中学都是鹤立鸡群、一枝独秀。这是与当时的大背景有关系的。当时的国民党反动又腐败，以至于物价飞涨、民不聊生，造成教育事业空前凋零。那时的公办学校没有像样的校舍，教师待遇低，致使教学质量下降。而英华因为有教会的经费支持，设施齐全、设备一流，能聘请一流的教师，所以能培养出一流的学生。英华中学与公办学校相比，客观上衬托和成就了英华的辉煌。"（李青藻，2016：76）

● 下篇：一脉相承续情缘

中华人民共和国成立后，由教会创办的私立英华中学被政府接收并改制，后迁到桃花山，之后发展演变成为福建师范大学附属中学，而在英华原校址的基础上又建立了福州高级中学。在英华老校友的努力下，福州英华英语学校和英华职业学院得以创立。而英华在抗日战争期间迁往顺昌县洋口镇的8年间，与洋口中学结下了情缘。由此，这五所学校与曾经的鹤龄英华书院结下了情缘，它们在传承英华优良传统的基础上，不断创新和发展，书写新时代的新篇章。

：福州英华职业学院
：Anglo-Chinese College

ACC as a typical example of the missionary schools had, of course, its own limitations, such as too much importance attached to religious education, excessive dependence on and copy of Western modes of education, which was as much as enslavement, and hence the protests from ACC students like Lin Sen. It was said that President James Ding, in hiring ACC teachers, would take it into consideration whether the applicant was a Christian. Nevertheless, ACC students were not blind to Christian tenets, nor were they converted to Christianity massively. One solid evidence was that statistics showed that of the 34 ACC junior students in 1934, only 4 believed in Christianity, accounting for 10.5%, and only one believed in Buddhism, accounting for 2.6%, the rest being atheists. ACC students, far from being submissive all the time and blindly worshiping foreign things, loved their country all the more, and quite a few of them became highly qualified members of CPC. Therefore, an objective view is needed in judging ACC, one that takes into consideration both its positiveness and limitations.

As regards ACC accomplishments, we need to take a proper attitude. For this matter, as an ACC alumnus, Mr. Li Qingzao said that a perspective of historical materialism is needed. In his remarks, ACC had a long history, and in the process it was able to develop step by step and accumulate precious experience. That's why ACC was at its best in its later period. In particular, with the victory of the War of Resistance Against Japanese Agression, ACC moved back to Fuzhou and took on a new look, coming out as the top of nearly all schools of its kind. Its achievement should be put under the general background of the then China. The Kuomintang, the government in power at that time, was reactionary and decayed, and hence the inflation. As a result, people had no way of making a living, and school education was likewise suffering from unprecedented decline. The public schools at that time were left with no decent school buildings, and teachers received extremely humble pay, which in turn gave rise to the sharp decline in the teaching quality. In contrast, ACC, with regular funds from Christian missions, could well afford first-class facilities as well as first-rate teachers, and thus was able to bring out quality students. From the above, it is obvious that the glory of ACC was in a comparative sense, in comparison with the backward public schools.

• ACC Lineage: Schools that Carry On

After the founding of the P.R.C., ACC was taken over and reformed by the local government, and later on moved to Tao Hua Shan. Afterwards, ACC was developed into the Affiliated High School of Fujian Normal University, while in its original location was founded Fuzhou Senior High School. And, to commemorate ACC and its contribution, its alumni tried all means to establish ACC lineage, Fuzhou Anglo-Chinese College, a school of secondary education, and Anglo-Chinese College, named after the former ACC, a vocational school. Besides, it is known that, during the War of Resistance Against Japanese Agression, ACC moved to Yankow in Shunchang County, and was thus closely related to Yankow Middle School there. As can be seen, these five schools are magically attached to ACC in one way or another.

福建师范大学附属中学

1951年，英华中学与华南女中、陶淑女中三个学校由政府接办，成为"福州第二中学"，迁到麦园路桃花山原寻珍中学旧址。1973年起，正式更名为福建师范大学附属中学。

鹤龄英华书院作为福建师大附中的前身之一，经常被人和后者作比较。在新中国成立前长达几十年的时间里，英华和格致是公认的福州最好的中学，而现在，提起福州中学教育，人们脱口而出的便是"一三附"，即一中、三中和附中，近年来，附中更是赶超了三中。可见，师大附中依然是中学教育的佼佼者。关于这个问题，李青藻老先生也作了客观的评价："英华接办以后，师大附中这所学校继往开来办得很好，是可以给老校友们一个满意的答案的。据我了解，附中先后被评为特级教师的人数居全省之首。新中国成立以后，教学质量好的中等学校越来越多，反映出整体教育水平的提高，但附中始终处于这类学校排头兵的位置。附中重视德育教育和坚持全面发展，在高考成绩和各项课外活动中都走在各校前列。尤其在国际奥林匹克学科竞赛中，获奖数超过全省的二分之一，成绩突出。"

: 福建师范大学附属中学
: The Affiliated High School of Fujian
: Normal University

The Affiliated High School of Fujian Normal University

In 1951, ACC, Hwa Nan High School, and Do-seuk Girls' School were taken over by the government and merged into a new public school, Fuzhou No.2 Middle School. The new school was situated on the original location of Sing Ding Girls School on Tao Hua Shan of Maiyuan Road, and ever since 1973 it has been known as the Affiliated High School of Fujian Normal University.

As ACC is known to be one of the predecessors of the Affiliated High School of Fujian Normal University, there is a tendency to compare the achievements of the two, even though they belong in different times. For decades before the founding of the P. R. C., ACC and Foochow College were generally acknowledged as the best schools around Fuzhou. But now, when it comes to the best schools in Fuzhou, three come out, namely, Fuzhou No. 1 High School, Fuzhou No. 3 High School, and the Affiliated High School of Fujian Normal University. Therefore, it is obvious that just as ACC used to be a top school, so the Affiliated High School of Fujian Normal University remains a leader in secondary education of Fuzhou. Mr. Li Qingzao, as an ACC alumnus, also offered his objective comments on the achievements of the Affiliated High School of Fujian Normal University, "Since the take-over of ACC by the government, in its place has been the new Affiliated High School of Fujian Normal University, which carries forward the ACC cause and forges ahead into the future, with achievements up to the expectations of ACC alumni. As far as I know, the school boasts the largest number of teachers granted with the title 'Master Teacher' in Fujian. As we can see, after the founding of the P. R. C., there have emerged more and more schools with high teaching quality, a reflection of the improvement of the general education level, and over time the Affiliated High School has always been the pacesetter. It also carries on the fine tradition of ACC by attaching great importance to moral education and students' comprehensive abilities and excels both in the entrance examination for colleges and universities and in extracurricular activities. In particular, it's worth mentioning that its students of one class after another have received the greatest number of medals in the International Academic Olympiad, accounting for half of the total of its kind won by all high schools in Fujian. "

福州高级中学

英华中学迁走后，在原址处设立了福建省工农速成中学，是福建师范学院的附设，后于1956年正式定名为"福州高级中学"。虽然英华中学迁走了，可是它的建筑，如美志楼、力礼堂和校友钟楼，却是迁不走的。正是这些因教育得以传承的建筑及其背后的故事紧密联系着如今的福州高级中学（下文简称"福高"）与曾经的鹤龄英华书院，使两校结下了前世与今生的不解之缘。笔者采访福州高级中学校办公室周晓文副主任时，他提及"文革"期间福高的师生们为了保护英华留下的美志楼和力礼堂，作了很多努力，如用土灰覆盖建筑上面的英文字符等，后期更是与省文物保护管理单位一起保护和修缮这些古建筑。这些建筑也成了激励福高师生的一面旗帜，鼓舞他们不断努力、"志当存高远"、创造辉煌，正如曾任福高历史老师的方宝璋所说，"建筑是凝固的历史，是内在精神文化的形象化，是校友思念母校的载体"。（转引自福高校史馆文稿）

美志楼现为福高学术艺术中心。力礼堂曾作为福高的体操馆使用，在2018年修旧还旧之后，又从体操馆恢复成了礼堂风貌，作为学生的文艺活动中心，在功能和风貌上更接近当年设计者的初衷。而为纪念被拆除的鹤龄楼，在原址上福高又重建了一栋四层楼的"鹤龄图书馆"，设计者从原有的建筑中提取元素建设新的外观，形成新的建筑外立面，设计典雅、美观大方，曾获福建省土木建筑学会组织的"第十三届优秀建筑创作奖"，与美志楼和力礼堂呈三足鼎立的态势，是校园重要的三个建筑景观节点。

福高的校标更是完美结合了现代与历史两个元素，寓意深远。校标主体为FG，取福高的拼音首字母。字母F的形状，是力礼堂哥特式建筑的符号式提炼，也是"志当存高远"校训的凝练；字母G是美志楼罗马式拱门的写意，代表着福高莘莘学子迈向人生艺术的"高雅之门"。校标右上方的数字1881是福高校园的前身鹤龄英华书院的办学年份，彰显着福高校园积淀深厚的悠久历史，象征着锐意进取、勇攀高峰的昂扬气势。

Fuzhou Senior High School

As ACC moved elsewhere, in its place was founded Fuzhou Accelerated Middle School for Workers and Peasants, attached to Fujian Teachers' College, and renamed as Fuzhou Senior High School in 1956. As a result, the buildings left behind by ACC, in particular, Symth Hall, Lacy Ninde Memorial Chapel and Alumni Clock Tower, have been in the care of Fuzhou Senior High School, since it would be out of the question for ACC to take these buildings in its move. And it's exactly these buildings that link the two schools in an amazing way. In the interview with Mr. Zhou Xiaowen, Office Manger of Fuzhou Senior High School, he mentioned the great efforts made by both teachers and students of this school during the Cultural Revolution to protect these buildings in that they put ashes over the English words carved at the top front of each building so that they would not be demolished. Besides, the school has been working together with the provincial cultural relics protection unit to maintain and restore these old buildings. These magical buildings, in turn, serve as a banner to inspire teachers and students to carry on. As Mr. Fang Baozhang, who used to be a history teacher in Fuzhou Senior High School, put it, "Architecture mirrors history, embodies the spiritual culture and bonds the alumni and the alma mater."

Symth Hall now functions as the academic and artistic hall, with such function rooms inside as Academic Meeting Room, Interview Room, Calligraphy Room, Geography Virtual Lab, Electronic Piano Room, Fencing Hall, Music Classroom, Art Classroom, and Activity Room. It is a well-cherished place where students are able to remember the history, activate their thinking, pursue knowledge and wisdom, and perfect their moral character. Another building, Lacy Ninde Memorial Chapel, was, for a time, used as gymnastics hall, but in 2018, it was restored to its original exterior and redefined in function and was changed back to be an auditorium, serving as the students' cultural activity center, which ran closer, in terms of appearance and function, to the initial intention of its design. In honor of the A-hok Hall that had long been demolished, the school library building was named as A-hok Library. Based on the exterior of the original A-hok Hall and extracting its key elements, the new building of four stories takes on a new look, elegant and artistic in design, and was thus granted "The 13th Outstanding Architecture Design Award" sponsored by Fujian Civil Engineering & Architectural Society. The three buildings, Symth Hall, Lacy Ninde Memorial Chapel, and A-hok Library, stand on three directions of the playground, embodying the notion of triangular balance.

The school logo represents a perfect combination of the present and the past and is pregnant with meaning. The two phonetic alphabets F and G, the abbreviations of the name of the school, comprise the main body of the logo. F is in the symbolic shape of the Gothic-style Lacy Ninde Memorial Chapel, and implies the school motto "To Aim High". G is in the shape of the Romanesque arch of Symth Hall, indicating the elegant door through which to go toward the art of life. On top stands the number 1881, the year ACC was founded, indicating the long history of the school plant, and inspiring students to aim high and to forge ahead in high spirits.

新英华

英华优良的办学传统和光荣的革命传统堪称教育界的精神遗产。虽然英华中学于1951年由政府接办合并成今日的师大附中，但广大英华校友都有着怀念母校的赤诚之心，都希望英华能复办起来。在广大海内外校友多年的不懈努力下，陈霖校友承诺为新校捐资。从1987年10月至1988年3月，福州校友会协同北京校友会努力向福建省教委、福州市教委申请办校，在北京的沈元会长、高放副会长、陈秋凡秘书长也努力向国家教委反映，并在此期间由沈元主持召开多次理事会，分析研究情况，找出解决办法，最终于1988年3月，英华英语学校获批，成为福州市最早的私立普通完整中学，并建成了两座大楼——陈霖楼和芝美楼。英华以崭新的面貌呈现在人们眼前，英华校友们多年来的夙愿终于实现了。校友郑锡安为首任校长，沿用英华中学的校训、校歌和校徽，继承英华优良的办学传统和芝美校长的教育思想，全面贯彻教育方针，突出德育和英语教学，保持英华固有的特色。

1994年，福州英华外国语学院获批，列为福建省民办高校首批"国家学历文凭考试"试点单位；2001年，成为首批普通高等职业学院，更名为"福州英华职业学院"，并纳入了国家统一招生计划。英华的复办，是英华校友不懈努力的结果，彰显了英华的不凡的影响力，体现了时至今日社会对英华优良传统的认可，更体现了我国教育在传统基础上的进步和发展。

：福州英华职业学院
：Anglo-Chinese College

The New ACC

ACC, with its fine traditions, especially its glorious revolutionary tradition, can be said to be a wonder in academic circles. Even though ACC was taken over by the government in 1951 and merged with other schools into today's Affiliated High School of Fujian Normal University, its alumni, with a sincere love for and a deep loyalty to their alma mater, all hoped that they could establish a new ACC, one that carried on the fine traditions of the former ACC. For this dream, a great majority of ACC alumni at home and abroad had worked persistently. In particular, Mr. Chen Lin promised to offer funds for the founding of the new ACC. With everything well underway, ACC Alumni Association in Fuzhou, together with ACC Alumni Association in Beijing, applied consistently from October of 1987 to March of 1988 to both Fujian Provincial Education Commission and Fuzhou Municipal Education Commission for the resumption of ACC. Meanwhile, Mr. Shen Yuan, President of ACC Alumni Association in Beijing, together with Mr. Gao Fang, Vice-president, and Mr. Chen Qiufan, Secretary of the association, presented a relative report to the State Education Commission. In response to the problems and inadequacies as exposed in the application work, they held several councils presided over by Shen Yuan, trying to find out solutions and make up for the deficiencies. Eventually, their hard work paid off and their dream came true. Fuzhou Anglo-Chinese College (ACC) was officially approved in March of 1988, the first private regular secondary school with both junior and senior stages in Fuzhou. The new ACC, with two typical buildings, Chen Lin Building (in honor of Mr. Chen Lin, the donator) and Zhimei Building (in honor of Chen Zhimei, also named Dr. James Ding, president of the former ACC), takes on a new look while retaining the school motto, school song and school badge of the former ACC. Headed by Zheng Xi'an, and fully implementing the education policies, the new ACC carries forward the fine traditions of the former ACC under President James Ding by attaching the same importance to moral education and English teaching.

Afterwards, in 1994, a second school named after ACC was founded, Fuzhou Anglo-Chinese College of Foreign Languages, listed as the first batch of "National Diploma Examination" pilot units of the provincial colleges and universities run by the local people. In 2001, it became the first batch of general higher vocational colleges, and was renamed as Anglo-Chinese College, included in the National Unified Enrollment Program. The resumption of ACC should be attributed to the persistent efforts of ACC alumni, to the lasting social recognition of ACC and its fine traditions, and to the progress and development of the national education on a traditional basis.

洋口英华学校

1937年，日军发动了侵华战争，作为教会学校的英华被日军许诺在校舍上方挂上一些标志性的物件，就可以不受炸弹的滋扰。学校起先确实保持了一段时间的宁静，但没过多久，日寇变本加厉，在福州上空疯狂轰炸，整个福州城惨不忍睹。为避免无谓的损失，学校不得已做出内迁的决定。在几经考察内迁地之后，最终确定了商业较发达、水路交通较便利的顺昌县洋口镇。1937底，开始分批迁往洋口，直到1945年8月开始分批迁回福州。在洋口的8年间，英华传统继续发扬光大，培养了许多人才。毕业、肄业学生达千余人，占英华1881—1951年70年学生总数2 500人的40%。其间，涌现了大批的人才，有革命志士仁人，如中共闽江工委委员杨申生、傅孙焕，福州市委书记孙道华，中共省委闽浙赣地下军副司令曾焕乾等；有数以百计的专家、教授、学者，以及企业家，如南京紫金山天文台台长陈彪，著名中科院学部委员高由禧、曾融生、林亲基，国务院学术委员会第二届学科评议组成员高放，中国驻肯尼亚全权大使、北大教授薛谋洪，中国电影家协会副主席、国际影评委员石方禹，国家领导人保健医生罗慰慈、林友华主任医师，美国商务部经济学家陈乃润，美国化学专家李联欢和著名教授江祖贻，土木工程专家美国肯塔基大学教授黄仰贤，曾受邓小平等领导人接见的美国普渡大学教授林本铭，泰国棉花大王丁政曾，菲律宾女企业家邱以芝，企业界知名人士陈炎生、黄萃源等。

英华中学内迁洋口的8年期间，除招收福州地区的学生以外，还广为招收顺昌洋口的本地学生入学。数年间，共有60余名本地学生从英华中学毕业，其中也不乏许多优秀人才，如官希吉（小儿科专家、教授）、洪斯同（外科创伤急救专家、主任医师）、黄仰贤（教授）。

Yankow ACC

In 1937, Japan launched the war of aggression against China. As a missionary school, ACC was promised to be exempted from air raids on the condition that some identifiable objects were put up above the school plant. For a time, ACC did manage to keep things going, but soon afterwards, the Japanese invaders intensified its air raids over Fuzhou, and the whole city was in turmoil. In such a situation, to avoid deadweight loss, the school made the hard decision to move to the interior of the province. After investigations of several places in consideration, Yankow, a town of Shunchang County, with its convenient water transportation and relatively prosperous business, became its first choice. In the late 1937, ACC moved to Yankow in different batches, and stayed there for 8 years until it moved back to Fuzhou in 1945. During the 8 years, ACC traditions carried on, and graduated more than one thousand students, including those who chose to quit in the midst, accounting for 40% of its total graduates from 1881 to 1951. And countless talents of all kinds in all fields were brought out. Among them were Yang Shensheng and Fu Sunhuan, members of CPC Minjiang Working Committee, Sun Daohua, Secretary of the Fuzhou Municipal Party Committee, and Zeng Huanqian, Deputy Commander of the Fujian-Zhejiang-Jiangxi Underground Army of the CPC Provincial Committee. There were also hundreds of prominent experts, professors, scholars, and entrepreneurs, such as Chen Biao, Director of Nanjing Purple Mountain Observatory; Gao Youxi, Zeng Rongsheng, and Lin Qinji, members of the Chinese Academy of Sciences; Gao Fang, member of the second subject evaluation group of the Academic Committee of the State Council; Xue Mouhong, Chinese ambassador to Kenya and professor at Peking University; Shi Fangyu, Vice Chairman of China Film Association and International Film Critics Committee; Luo Weici and Lin You Hua, doctors entrusted with the healthcare of the national leaders; Chen Nairun, an economist at the US Department of Commerce; Li Lianhuan, an expert of chemistry in America; Jiang Zuyi, an eminent professor; Huang Yangxian, an expert in civil engineering and professor at the University of Kentucky; Lin Benming, a professor at Purdue University who was received by Deng Xiaoping and other national leaders; Ding Zhengzeng, a cotton king in Thailand; Qiu Yizhi, a female entrepreneur in the Philippines; Chen Yansheng and Huang Cuiyuan, well-known figures in the business circle.

The war-time ACC in Yankow, enrolled students from Fuzhou as well as the local students in Yankow, and succeeded in graduating more than 60 local students during the eight years, many of whom turned out to be social elites, such as Guan Xiji, a pediatric specialist as well as a professor, Hong Sitong, a chief physician and first-aid expert in surgical trauma, Huan Yangxian, a professor in America.

此外，考虑到当时随英华内迁洋口的教职工的女儿们升中学有困难，陈校长于1939年打破英华历史上只招收男生的常规，接纳了当义务校医的丘英三大夫的女儿丘以芬加入高二（七七级）学习，成为英华有史以来第一位女生，她后来成为一名针灸大夫。此外，还有图画老师白瑞进的三个女儿，以及语文石老师的女儿石美芬和石春航等。学校也招收本地女生入学，如官希吉于1940年插入初二蓓蕾级（高中改为荟蔚级）。

　　总的来说，学校招收的女生人数不多，有的班级没有女生，有的班级只有两三位女生。据统计，英华在洋口的8年中，共招收女生38人。这些女生受到学校特别的优待。陈芝美校长强调她们是"英华的宝贝"，号召英华这个大家庭的成员们都要爱护女生，在妇女节的时候为她们举行庆祝活动，还让女生们扮演话剧中的女主角，让她们真正融入学校，和男生们亲如兄弟姐妹。后来，英华搬回福州后，继续招收女生，为女子教育作出了贡献。总之，英华在洋口的8年间，对洋口的政治、经济、文化、教育等方面都产生了很大的影响，为顺昌历史写下了光辉的篇章。

　　英华很多师生多年后，仍念念不忘洋口，时不时回洋口（英华）中学参观，其中最大规模的一次是1990年6月荟蔚级毕业45周年之际校友参观访问洋口，受到顺昌县政府和洋口镇政府的热情接待。校友们参观了当年英华母校初中部旧址和高中部旧址，找到了高中部学生宿舍福州会馆旧址右侧的沈葆桢的三个金字题名。座谈会上，校友们向顺昌县政府赠送了两幅字画，菲律宾的程光还捐资3 500美元，赞助顺昌县教育基金，而顺昌县政府还赠送给每位校友一套（12只）出口日本的木碗和檀香扇作为校友们此次顺昌寻根的纪念品。校友们说："这是一种类似母爱的细腻感情，我们太感动了。"

福建师大附中与顺昌洋口英华学校结为友好学校（来源：廖基远）
A group photo on the occasion where the Affiliated High School of Fujian Normal University and Yankow ACC signed up as sister schools(Source: Liao Jiyuan)

In addition, considering that the daughters of the teaching faculty of ACC in Yankow had no school to attend for their secondary education, President James Ding broke the ACC routine of recruiting boys only by admitting Qiu Yifen, the daughter of the school volunteer doctor Qiu Yingsan into Senior Two (Class Seven Seven), the first female student in the history of ACC, who was made into an acupuncture doctor. Afterwards, the three daughters of Bai Ruijin, a drawing teacher, as well as the two daughters of Mr. Shi, an instructor in Chinese, were admitted into ACC, followed by some local female students, like Guan Xiji, enrolled into Junior Two (Class Beilei), which was later renamed Class Hui Wei of the Senior Division.

On the whole, the number of female students was not large, with a total of 38 through the 8 years. These female students received preferential treatment from the school. President James Ding called them the treasures of the school and asked that they be taken good care of by all members of ACC. On Women's Day, special activities were held in their honor and they played heroines in the drama performance. In this way, the female students fit into ACC naturally and were on good terms with the male students, as good as brothers and sisters. And this practice of recruiting girl students went on after ACC moved back to Fuzhou, thus contributing to female education in general. To sum up, during the eight years in Yankow, ACC had great impacts on Yankow politically, economically, culturally, and academically, making a glorious chapter for the history of Shunchang.

Many ACC alumni could never ever forget their time at Yankow, and they would go back there for a visit whenever possible. One of the major visits by probably the largest number of alumni was the visit by Class Hui Wei on the occasion of their 45th anniversary of graduation in June of 1990. They were warmly received by the county government of Shunchang and town government of Yankow. They visited the site of their former Junior Division and Senior Division as well as what used to be their dormitory building, the Fuzhou Guild Hall on which was inscribed the three Chinese characters of the name of Shen Baozhen in his own handwriting, who was a national hero as well as a great statesman, a military strategist, and a diplomat. In the informal discussion, the alumni presented two paintings as a gift and one of the alumni, Cheng Guang, from the Philippines, offered $3,500 as education fund for Shunchang County. In return, the county gave each alumnus a set of 12 wooden bowls as well as a sandalwood fan as souvenirs of their visit, sort of a maternal love in the eyes of the alumni, which moved them deeply.

作为英华学校"后世"的福建师范大学附属中学和福州英华英语学校，也没有忘记洋口。1993 年 6 月 6 日，由顺昌县政府牵头，在英华内迁洋口 55 周年、洋口中学建校 35 周年的庆典上，福州英华英语学校与洋口中学签约结为姐妹校。两校同宗同源，一脉相承，通力合作，共谋发展。"尔乃世之光"的校训，又镌刻在顺昌洋口当年英华旧址石碑上。1996 年 2 月 28 日，顺昌县政府发文同意洋口中学再定名为洋口英华中学。2015 年 5 月，福建师范大学附属中学又与顺昌洋口英华学校结为友好学校。

● 特别鸣谢

笔者在写作过程中，有幸先后采访了福州高级中学行政办公室主任周晓文、师大附中英语组退休教师郭圣光、英华老校友李青藻和陈世明、顺昌县洋口英华中学校长廖基远，他们为本章节提供了许多宝贵的资料，在此致以诚挚的感谢！也特别感谢福州英华职业学院董事长江澜博士为本章提供了《尔乃世之光：福州鹤龄英华中学校史》等内部资料，以及进校拍摄等相关支持。

As ACC lineage, Fuzhou Anglo-Chinese College and the Affiliated High School of Fujian Normal University also showed great concern for Yankow Middle School and made efforts to do something for it. On June 6, 1993, on the occasion of the 55th anniversary of ACC move to Yankow as well as the 35th anniversary of the establishment of Yankow Middle School, with the efforts of the County Government of Shun Chang, Fuzhou Anglo-Chinese College and Yankow Middle School signed up as sister schools, committed to cooperating with each other and developing together, and the ACC school motto "You are the light of the world." was once again engraved on the stone tablet of the former site of ACC in Yankow. On February 28, 1996, The County Government officially approved that Yankow Middle School be renamed as Yankow ACC. In May, 2015, the Affiliated High School of Fujian Normal University and Yankow ACC signed up as sister schools.

• Acknowledgments

Sincere and heart-felt thanks are to be extended to Mr. Zhou Xiaowen, Office Manager of Fuzhou Senior High School, Mr. Guo Shengguang, a retired teacher at the Affiliated High School of Fujian Normal University, Mr. Chen Shiming and Mr. Li Qingzao, alumni of ACC, Mr. Liao Jiyuan, Principal of Yankow ACC, and Dr. Jiang Lan, Vice President of Anglo-Chinese College, all of whom the author was lucky enough to interview during the writing process, for their selfless help and the precious materials and clues they provided. In particular, the author was greatly touched by Mr. Chen Shiming and Mr. Li Qingzao, who are well in their 90s, and despite the storms they've weathered, are still sound in health and active in thinking. It is a rare treasure to be able to get to know about their unusual life experiences, their devotion to the country, and their broad-mindedness.

福建历史文化外译丛书

总主编 葛桂录

岳峰 章琳 主编

Fuzhou's Cangshan District: Past and Present at the Crosspoint of China-Western Cultures

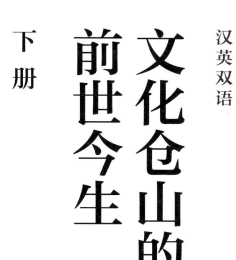

下册

汉英双语

文化仓山的前世今生

上海交通大学出版社
SHANGHAI JIAO TONG UNIVERSITY PRESS

目　录

CONTENTS

CHAPTER
SIX

从英华到附中（二）①

From Anglo-Chinese College to
the Affiliated High School（2）

第六章 福

---

① 本章所用照片，除特殊标注外，均由福建师范大学附属中学提供。

这是一所走过了百年岁月的老校，有着优良的办学传统，秉承"以天下为己任"的校训，弘扬"文明、勤奋、求实、创新"的校风，不断追寻着教育之真谛，如今依然青春焕发。习近平总书记在福建工作时曾夸奖她"历史悠久，具有优良的革命传统和学习传统……英才辈出，硕果累累，久负盛名"。她就是位于福州市仓山区对湖路的福建师范大学附属中学，人们亲切地简称她为"附中"。

附中前身为福州鹤龄英华中学（创办于 1881 年）、华南女子文理学院附属高级中学（创办于 1908 年）、陶淑女子中学（创办于 1903 年）三所私立教会学校。三所学校课程设置和课外活动都与当时多数本土学校不同，遥领时代之先。教师多为大学毕业生，其中相当一部分还是归国留学生，教资因此也颇为优良，这在客观上为培养我国人才、促进现代科学文化知识的传播作出了贡献。侯德榜、陈景润、沈元、高由禧、王仁、陈彪、曾融生、阙端麟、卢耀如、黎念之、萨支唐、王世中、王铁崖、刘广京等院士均出自英华学院。这也是部分国人参与建校的原因，如辛亥革命先驱、英华校友黄乃裳在 1891 年为《鹤龄英华书院章程》所作的序言中提道："鹤龄英华书院何为而设也？为我国培育有用之才而设也……知英华书院之大有关我国富强，与夫各与国交涉事务，故乐为之叙。"

Scan for more
扫码了解更多

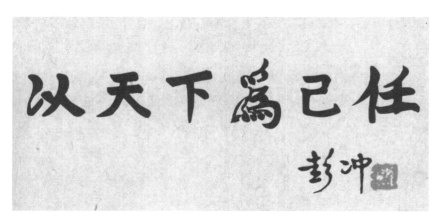

附中校训：以天下为己任
The affiliated High School of Fujian Normal University adopts as its
motto "OUR WORLD, OUR DUTY"

The Affiliated High School of Fujian Normal University, situated in Duihu Road of Cangshan District in Fuzhou, is a hundred-year-old school vigorously probing the essence of education. Carrying on its fine tradition, it devotes to the ideal of a humanistic education by adopting as its motto "Our World, Our Duty" and promoting as its guiding values "Civility, Diligence, Practicality, and Creativity". President Xi Jinping sang high praise of it when he worked in Fujian, remarking that "it has a long history and a fine revolutionary tradition and learning tradition...a great alma mater for a large number of talents, a school with great achievements and a long-standing reputation". As such, it is admired by people in Fuzhou and called as "Fuzhong (The Affiliated High School)" in short in Chinese.

The Affiliated High School of Fujian Normal University has as its predecessors three church-owned schools: Anglo-Chinese College (founded in 1881), Hwa Nan High School (founded in 1908) and Do-seuk Girls' School (founded in 1903). The three church-owned schools designed distinct and pioneering curriculum and extracurricular activities, and, with sufficient fund, equipped themselves with well-educated teachers, quite a lot of them ever studying abroad. Therefore, they won great fame for the outstanding teaching quality. It should be admitted that the education offered by them did somehow contribute to the cultivation of Chinese talents, the dissemination of modern scientific knowledge and eventually the development of modern China. Lots of talents valued for their later contribution to the country established their solid basis of knowledge in these schools. Alumni honored greatly nowadays by the Affiliated High School including Hou Debang, Chen Jingrun, Shen Yuan, Gao Youxi, Wang Ren, Chen Biao, Zeng Rongsheng, Que Duanlin, Lu Yaoru, Li Nianzhi, Sa Zhitang, Wang Shizhong, Wang Tieya, Liu Guangjing all owed their education to Anglo-Chinese College. Such cultivation of talents is the force that motivated some Chinese people at that time to participate in the establishment of these schools. Wong Nai Siong, an alumnus of Anglo-Chinese College and pioneer of the Revolution of 1911, mentioned in the preface to *the Constitution of Anglo-Chinese College* in 1891: "What could Anglo-Chinese College serve? It can help cultivate useful talents in our country... I am willing and happy to write the preface for it because I hold that Anglo-Chinese College can help promote the prosperity and competitiveness of our country and smooth the negotiating affairs with countries around the world."

中华人民共和国成立后，1951年7月9日，福建省文教厅把私立鹤龄英华中学与华南女子文理学院附属高级中学合并接办，派中教科科长李执为组长，带领工作组进校宣传党的政策，贯彻群众路线。7月18日定校名为福建省福州市第二中学，任命中共党员郑书祥为校长，共产党员叶振汉为副校长。这是中华人民共和国成立后福建省首次接办教会中学，因此非常轰动。《福建日报》发表了报道和评论，为福建福州市第二中学回归人民的怀抱而欢欣鼓舞。8月1日，省文教厅又按照华东军委会教育部要求，接办私立陶淑女子中学，与福建省福州第二中学合并，同样由李执带领工作组完成接办工作。到此，三校合并成为公立学校。

新中国成立初期，各级教育都处在调整之中，校名也随之几经变化。1952年8月，因为学校归福州大学（现福建师范大学）领导，福建省福州第二中学更名为福州大学附属中学。1953年9月，由于福州大学更名为福建师范学院，福州大学附属中学也随之更名为福建师范学院附属中学。1970年9月3日，因为福建师范学院停办，附中更名为福州第二十七中学，归市革委会政治处宣教组领导。1972年夏，福建师院复办，更名为福建师范大学。1973年11月27日，经福建省革委会决定，福州第二十七中学划归福建师范大学直接领导，更名为福建师范大学附属中学，该校名沿用至今。

1980年底到1981年初，附中整理校史，筹备校庆。经过慎重考虑，决定以英华中学（书院）的创办年，即1881年，作为校史的起始年，定1981年为福建师大附中建校100周年，定10月3日为校庆日。此后逢五逢十周年，学校都举行庆典。1991年第110周年校庆，庆祝活动改在10月2日举行，之后就一直沿用这个时间。

The three church-owned schools were taken over by the government of the People's Republic of China in 1951 and merged into one new public school. On July 9, 1951, Fujian Provincial Department of Culture and Education announced to merge the Anglo-Chinese College with Hwa Nan High School. A working team, with Li Zhi, the chief of the Chinese education section, as leader, was assigned the task of publicizing the party's policies and helping the new public school to come into being. On July 18, 1951, the new school, named as Fuzhou No. 2 Middle School in Fujian Province, were officially on the stage, with Zheng Shuxiang, as the headmaster and Ye Zhenhan, as the vice principal. Both of them were Communist Party members. This was the first attempt of the province to transform the church-owned middle schools since the founding of the People's Republic of China. *Fujian Daily*, rejoicing at the birth of Fuzhou No. 2 Middle School in Fujian as a school of Chinese people, devoted a report to the sensational event. On August 1, according to the requirements of the Ministry of Education of the East China Military Commission, the Provincial Department of Culture and Education took over Do-seuk Girls' School and merged it into Fuzhou No. 2 Middle School. Li Zhi again took charge of the task. This is how the three schools were merged.

The name of the Affiliated High School of Fujian Normal University underwent several changes, influenced by the exploration for appropriate education systems in the People's Republic of China. As we mentioned above, it was first named as Fuzhou No. 2 Middle School. In August 1952, as Fuzhou No. 2 Middle School was put under the leadership of Fuzhou University (now Fujian Normal University), it was renamed as the Affiliated Middle School of Fuzhou University. In September 1953, as Fuzhou University was renamed as Fujian Teachers College, the Affiliated Middle School of Fuzhou University was accordingly renamed as the Affiliated Middle School of Fujian Teachers College. On September 3, 1970, due to the closure of Fujian Teachers College, the Affiliated Middle School was renamed as Fuzhou No. 27 Middle School, in the charge of the Publicity and Education Group of the Political Department of the Municipal Revolutionary Committee. In the summer of 1972, Fujian Teachers College was reopened and renamed as Fujian Normal University. On November 27, 1973, the Fujian Provincial Revolutionary Committee decided to put Fuzhou No. 27 Middle School in the charge of Fujian Normal University. The school thus got its name as the Affiliated Middle School of Fujian Normal University, which has been used until now.

At the turn of 1981, the Affiliated High School began to compile the history of the school to celebrate its anniversary. After careful consideration, it was decided that the year 1881, the founding year of the Anglo-Chinese College, should be taken as the first year of the school. They decided to celebrate the 100th anniversary in 1981, and settled on October 3 as the date for school anniversary. Since then, the school holds anniversary celebrations every 5 years. In 1991, the 110th anniversary celebration was held on October 2 instead of October 3, and this date continues until now.

百年校庆之后，因为省内外有些原教会学校考虑恢复原来的校名，附中的一些老校友也提出类似提议，想要把名字改为英华中学或者福建师大附属英华中学。附中考虑到本校是由三校合并，华南女中和陶淑女中当时也颇有名气，使用英华之名不能反映附中的完整历史。同时，1984 年，教育部发布"（84）教中字 009 号"文件，文件本着尊重历史的态度，允许在现校名后面注明原学校名称，以纪念历史。因此，现在附中的校史（2021）上显示的是"福建师范大学附属中学校史（含原英华中学、华南女中、陶淑女中）"。

● 校址

1951 年三校合并后，按照省文教厅的通知，陶淑女中校舍拨给福州大学使用，英华书院初中部校舍拨给工农速成中学使用，而附中则使用原英华高中部（地址在今海军基地院内，原校舍已拆除）和华南女中的校舍。1954 年，因为福建师院对各系各单位的校舍进行大调整，师院院方认为桃花山地区最适合扩建为附中的校园，于是把位于对湖路桃花山的原寻珍女中校区和"洋墓亭"及前德国驻福州领事馆的两栋附属建筑物划给附中作为校舍；同时将原福建神学院校舍（地址在现福州十六中学对面）给附中作为二部校舍（师生住所生活区和初中部教学区）；之后，又将陶园里一座宿舍拨给附中。1958 年，师院又将二部移到原省总工会所在位置，与一部相邻，另租用蔡氏洋房一座。

After the 100th anniversary celebration, influence by the call for restoring original names of the missionary schools in some provinces, some elder alumni of the Anglo-Chinese College put forward similar proposals to change the school's name to Anglo-Chinese High School or Anglo-Chinese High School affiliated to Fujian Normal University. Considering that the school has three predecessors and that the other two of them, Hwa Nan High School and Do-seuk Girls' School, were not less famous than Anglo-Chinese College, the school decided that the name of Anglo-Chinese High School could not reflect the complete history of the school. In 1984, the Ministry of Education issued "(84) Education of Middle School No. 009" document, which allowed the names of the predecessors to be indicated with parentheses after the current school name to show respect for history. The Affiliated High School were happy with this solution. That is how *The School History of the Affiliated High School of Fujian Normal University (including the former Anglo-Chinese College, Hwa Nan High School and Do-seuk Girls' School)* (2021) got its title.

• Location

Following the merger of the three church-owned schools in 1951, the Provincial Department of Culture and Education allocated the school buildings of Do-seuk Girls' School to Fuzhou University, and the school buildings of the Junior Middle School Department of Anglo-Chinese College went to the Middle School of Workers and Peasants, while the Affiliated High School got the school buildings of the Senior Middle School Department of Anglo-Chinese College (located in today's Naval Base, having been demolished), together with the school buildings of Hwa Nan High School. In 1954, Fujian Normal University reallocated the school buildings among its departments. Considering the Taohuashan area (peach blossom mountain) was more suitable as the campus site for the Affiliated High School, it assigned to the Affiliated High School the school buildings originally belonging to Sing Ding Girls' School, as well as the Foochow Mission Cemetery and the two buildings of the former German Consulate in Fuzhou. At the same time, the former school buildings of Fujian Theological Seminary (located opposite the current Fuzhou No. 16 Middle School) were also allocated to the Affiliated High School, serving as dormitories for teachers and students, as well as the teaching buildings for its junior students. It was called as the second campus. A dormitory in the Taoyuanli Community was also allocated to the Affiliated High School. In 1958, Fujian Normal University decided to relocate the second campus on the site where the former Provincial Federation of Trade Unions stayed, as it was closer to the main campus of the Affiliated High School. The Affiliated High School also rented a Western-style house of Cai clan.

● 学制变化

三校合并后，根据全市统筹安排，实行初、高中"三·三"学制。当时分春秋两季招生。那时候国家建设需要人才，因此 1952 年让本来还差半年的春季班三年级同学也与前一届的秋季班一起毕业。郭孔辉院士就是当年秋季班的毕业生。春秋两级共 4 个班，100 多人一起参加高考（中国工程院科学道德建设委员会，2010：2）。1953 年起取消春季招生，实行单一的秋季始业。

1960 年，受时任省教育厅厅长王于畊的鼓励，附中设定"赶超福州一中""达到全国一流"的教学目标，实行初、高中"三·二"教改实验，在实际授课中，减免历史、地理和生产基础知识科，同时高中第一学年授课周比省规定增加 3 周，第二学年增加 2 周。1962 年，不再对入学新生继续该实验，恢复初、高中"三·三"学制。

1966 年"文革"开始，全校停课。1969 年复课，根据当时省革委会政治部的决定，学制改为"二·二"学制（初中两年，高中两年）和春季招生，原有传统的编班方式被取消，改为部队的连排番号编制，"连"表示年段，"排"表示班级（黄松生，2010），课程也随之改变，物理和化学改为工业基础知识课，生物改为农业基础知识课，地理、体育等课程被取消。这一番变化对附中教学影响很大，但附中在困难之中坚持"以教学为主"，顶住了极左思潮的干扰，坚持文化课的教学，同时还顶住了"不学 ABC，照样干革命"的乱局，坚持开设英语课。

• Changes of Schooling

The "three · three" schooling system was implemented in the new public school at the very beginning, that is, three years for junior schooling and three years for senior schooling. Students had two chances to get enrolled, one in spring, the other in autumn. In 1952, as the new country was in urgent need of talents, the grade-three students of the spring batch, who still had six months to go, were asked to enroll for the college education together with the autumn batch of 1951. Academician Guo Konghui was one of the graduates of the autumn batch that year. All together, there were four classes, more than 100 people, participating in the college entrance examination. After that, spring enrollment was cancelled, and students were enrolled only in autumn.

In 1960, Wang Yuchen, director of the Provincial Department of Education at that time, encouraged the Affiliated High School to catch up with and, if possible, overtake Fuzhou No. 1 Middle School to make itself the national first-class school. To achieve the goal, the Affiliated High School began to implement the "three · two" teaching reform experiment among its junior and senior students, that is, three years of junior schooling and two years of senior schooling. To meet the challenge, the Affiliated High School cut off the subjects of history, geography and basic knowledge of production. What's more, senior students were to study for 3 more weeks and 2 more weeks than required during the first academic year and the second academic year separately. Such practice caused high pressure. In 1962, the experiment was stopped with the freshmen and the "three · three" schooling system of junior and senior high schools was restored.

The schooling was interrupted by the Cultural Revolution in 1966 and remained so until 1969. In 1969, as required by the Political Department of the Provincial Revolutionary Committee, "two · two" schooling system was adopted (two-year junior schooling and two-year senior schooling) and students were enrolled in spring. The traditional numbering of classes was replaced with the units adopted in the armies, such as "company" and "platoon". "Company" was used to refer to the grade, while "platoon" was used to designate class. The curriculum changed accordingly. Physics and chemistry were renamed as "basic industrial knowledge" and biology as "basic agricultural knowledge". Geography and physical education were cancelled. Such change had quite a negative impact on the teaching of the Affiliated High School. But the Affiliated High School survived the chaos by insisting on "focusing on teaching" in the midst of difficulties, and continuing providing regular courses, including English course. Considering the interference of the Ultra-Left Trend of Thought and the popular claim that "ABC is not needed for revolution", such insistence deserved all the honor.

1973 年起恢复秋季招生，到了 1978 年又恢复了生物、化学、物理等课程，不过地理课直到 1987 年才正式恢复。据校史所记，1980 年，附中高中过渡到三年制，然而，福建省《仓山区志》（1994：368）记载：1981 年，福建师范大学附属中学率先开始转向"三·三"学制。就该学制变动，笔者询问了冯玮老校长，他说：

> 我当时担任 1980 届段长，这届学生是最幸运的。他们初中是两年制，高中也是两年制，所以他们中学只读四年就毕业了，毕业当年就参加高考，1980 届刚好是我们师大附中最辉煌的，文科理科高考平均分都是全省第一名，还出了一个全省的理科状元。1980 年考完后，福建省执行中央教育部的决定，初高中均改为三年制，这样一来，1981 年就没有毕业生。当时省教育厅就做一个决定，1980 年高考没有考上的，继续留在学校，作为高二生再读一年高三，这样 1981 年的学生就初中两年，高中三年。

1984 年，随着首届三年制初中和三年制高中学生的毕业，附中完成从"二·二"制向"三·三"制的转变。1998 年，市教委要求福州市一级、二级达标学校实行初高中分离，不设初中部，扩大高中规模。附中于是停止初中招生。2000 年最后一届初中生毕业后，附中只剩下了高中部，不再是完整的中学。

2022 年 8 月 27 日，附中复办初中。福州市推进"公参民"学校建设工作，民办名校福州时代中学转为福建师范大学附属初中部，归福建师大管理。

• 学生人数

英华中学开班时仅有 4 名学生，1921 年增至 540 人，到 1937 年又增长到 608 人。华南女中刚开始只有 13 名学生，1937 年有高中生 108 人；而陶淑女中开班时仅有 3 人，到 1937 年中学部学生有 140 人。

In 1973, autumn enrollment was resumed, and in 1978, courses like biology, chemistry and physics were resumed. However, geography was not officially resumed until 1987. According to the school history of the Affiliated High School of Fujian Normal University, the Affiliated High School adopted the "three·three" schooling system again in 1980. However, according to the records of *Cangshan District Chronicle* of *Fujian Province*, the turn to the "three·three" schooling system began in 1981. The former headmaster of the Affiliated High School, Feng Wei, explained the incongruence between the two dates:

> I was in charge of the teaching for the 1980 batch then. This year's graduates were the luckiest. They spent two years in junior study and another two years in senior study. Only four years in total and then they graduated. They took part in the college entrance examination in the year of graduation. The graduates of the 1980 batch happened to be rather brilliant. Both liberal arts and science classes harvested the best average score of the college entrance examination in the province, and one of the graduates in science class even ranked the top in the province. After the examination in 1980, to follow the instruction of the Central Ministry of Education, Fujian Province decided to adopt the "three·three" schooling system, which means there would be no graduates in 1981. The Provincial Department of Education thus made a decision, allowing those who failed the college entrance examination in 1980 to continue the study in school as sophomores for another year. So, the graduates in 1981 were those who spent two years in junior study and three years in senior study.

In 1984, with the graduation of the students who were the first to spend three years in junior study and three years in senior study, the Affiliated High School completed the transformation from "two·two" schooling system to "three·three" schooling system. In 1998, the Municipal Education Commission required schools of the first and second level in Fuzhou to stop enrolling junior students so as to train more senior students. The Affiliated High School thus stopped junior high school enrollment as required. After 2000 when all the junior students graduated, the Affiliated High School turned into a senior-only high school.

On August 27, 2022, the Affiliated High School resumed its junior high school. In response to the demand of promoting the participation of the public schools into the compulsory education offered by private schools, Fuzhou Shidai Middle School, a famous private school, has been transformed into the junior high school, affiliated to Fujian Normal University.

• The Number of Students

Anglo-Chinese College had only four students to begin with. The number soon increased to 540 in 1921 and 608 in 1937. Hwa Nan High School had only 13 students at the beginning, but soon attracted 108 high school students in 1837; Do-seuk Girls' School had only 3 students at the beginning, but by 1937, there were 140 students in its Middle School Department.

到 1948 年，鹤龄英华中学共有 15 个班级，学生总人数为 1 088 人，华南女子文理学院附属高级中学有 6 个班级，学生总人数为 183 人，陶淑女子中学有 9 个班级，学生总人数为 326 人，办学经费来源为教会募捐及学费，彼此招生没有地域限制，各县生源都有，甚至还有部分生源来自外省。

1951 年，三校奉令合并时，英华有学生 814 人，华南有学生 101 人，陶淑有学生 187 人，三校学生总数为 1 102 人，第二年学生数就增长为 1 722 人。此后到"文革"前，平均每年学生数在 1 700～1 900 人之间，大大超过了历史上三校学生数之和。20 世纪 70 年代，由于实行地区划片，就近入学，学生数剧增，1975 年全校学生数甚至达到 3 370 人。1980 年起实行初中本区择优录取，高中全市择优录取，学生数标准定额为 1 854 人，每年级 6 个班，共 36 个班，初中每班 55 人，高中每班 48 人。

到 1989 年，福建师大附属中学有 38 个班级，学生数 1 769 人，教职工数 199 人。学校占地面积 93 亩，校舍面积 30 412 平方米，为仓山区中学之首。

1998 年，师大附中初中部停止招生。2000 年起只有高中年级，每个年级 10 个班。2001 年增加至每个年级 12 个班，三个年级共 36 个班，每个班级 48 人，学生数标准定额为 1 854 人。目前，师大附中有高一 16 个班，高二、高三各 17 个班，共 50 个班。2022 年 8 月接收福州时代中学为初中部，共有初中部学生约 2 640 人。

从学生人数可见中国教育的逐渐发展。

By 1948, Anglo-Chinese College had 1,088 students, divided into 15 classes; Hwa Nan High School had 183 students, divided into 6 classes; and Do-seuk Girls' School had 326 students, divided into 9 classes. These schools were funded by church donations and tuition fees. As there were no geographical restrictions for the enrollment of the students, their students came from all over the province, some of them even from other provinces.

In 1951, when the three schools were merged, there were 814 students from Anglo-Chinese College, 101 students from Hwa Nan High School and 187 students from Do-seuk Girls' School, 1,102 students in total. One year after the merger, the number of students soon increased to 1,722. Since then, they enrolled 1,700~1,900 students per year, far more than what the three predecessors could achieve together. The enrollment remained stable until it was interrupted by the Cultural Revolution. In the 1970s, due to the requirement of *Nearby Enrollment Policy* that public schools should enroll students from designated areas which were close to the school, the number of students enrolled increased sharply, rocketing to 3,370 in 1975. Since 1980, preferential admission for talented junior students in the designated areas and talented senior students in the city has been implemented. The quota of enrollment was 1,854 for the Affiliated High School, with 6 classes per grade, thus 36 classes in total, 55 people per class in the junior section and 48 people per class in the senior section.

By 1989, the school had had a total of over 1,769 students divided into 38 classes, 199 faculty members and occupied an area of 93 *mu*, with its buildings covering a total floor space of 30,412 square meters, which made the school stand out among the schools in Cangshan District of Fuzhou.

In 1998, the enrollment for the junior section was stopped. Since 2000, the school has only provided education for the senior section. It had 10 classes per grade in 2000. In 2001, it was allowed to have 12 classes per grade, thus 36 classes in total. Each class could accommodate 48 students according to the requirement, and thus they had 1,854 students in total. At present, there are 16 classes in senior grade one, and 17 classes in senior grade two and in senior grade three separately. In total, the senior department now have 50 classes. In August 2022, the Affiliated High School had another 2,640 junior students as Fuzhou Shidai Middle School was transformed into the junior high school of the Fuzhou Normal University and thus became the senior department of the Affiliated High School.

As we can find from the increase of the number of students, Chinese education has been advancing continuously.

● 学校校舍建设

原有楼舍：寻珍楼、灰砖楼

三校刚合并时，可做教室之用的仅有原属于寻珍女中的红砖楼（寻珍楼）和灰砖楼。红砖楼具体建造时间不明，应早于1926年寻珍女中建校那一年，有说法是1904年建成的。寻珍女中把该楼作为校舍。

寻珍楼为砖木结构，欧洲券廊式风格，呈凹字形状，连地下室共三层，木制楼梯，本无名，因外墙为红砖铺砌，因此被师生们昵称为"红砖楼"（林涛，2021）。附中接管后，把"红砖楼"设为行政办公楼，也有部分作为教室使用，到20世纪80年代又将其命名为"寻珍楼"，以纪念该楼之渊源。根据校友回忆，20世纪60年代，红砖楼旁边有个布告栏，上面总是张贴着一期又一期的《苏联画报》（叶令炀，2021）。

寻珍楼东立面，1904年建，1996拆
The east facade of Sing Ding Building, which was possibly built in 1904 and demolished in 1996

寻珍楼
Sing Ding Building

《寻珍楼记》石碑
The stone tablet telling the story of Sing Ding Building

后红砖楼因年久失修而破损严重，1996年8月，上级同意申请，允许由政府拨款拆掉该楼。1998年，在原址建成了一幢六层教学楼与一幢四层图书馆楼，两楼用走廊连接为一体，共7 460平方米，花费681万元。为慰藉校友对老校舍的怀念之情以及铭记历史，学校将此两楼统一命名为"寻珍楼"。在原址新建的综合楼墙上镶嵌有《寻珍楼记》石碑一方。

- ## School Buildings

Inherited School Buildings: Sing Ding Building and Grey Brick Building

The year the three schools were merged into Fuzhou No. 2 Middle School, the buildings available that can serve as the classrooms are no more than the red brick building ("Sing Ding Building") and grey brick building, both inherited from Sing Ding Girls' School. The public belief holds that the red brick building was constructed in 1904 but such saying has not yet been confirmed due to the lack of historical record. But it is obvious that the red brick building had existed before 1926 when Sing Ding Girls' School was established. It was used as a school building in Sing Ding Girls' School.

The three-story brick and timber structure with an underground basement and wooden stairs was in a concave shape and in the style of European arcade. It was not officially named. But the faculty and students of Sing Ding Girls' School called it "red brick building" as its outer wall was paved with red bricks. After the Affiliated High School, called as the Fuzhou No. 2 Middle School at the time, took over the campus, the main part of the "red brick building" was used for administrative purpose, and the rest of it as classrooms. In the 1980s, it was named "Sing Ding Building" officially to commemorate the origin of the building. One alumnus recalled that, in the 1960s, there was a bulletin board next to the "red brick building" (Sing Ding Building), on which one can find issues of *Soviet Pictorial*.

In time, the "red brick building" fell into disrepair. In August 1996, the application for permission to dismantle the building was approved and funded by the local government. In 1998, on the site of the dismantled "red brick building", a six-story teaching building and a four-story library building were built, covering a total area of 7,460 square meters, and costing 6.81 million yuan. The two buildings were connected by a corridor. In response to alumni's nostalgia for the "red brick building" and to remember the history, the school named both buildings "Sing Ding Building". On the wall of the newly-built buildings, one can find an inset stone tablet telling the story of Sing Ding Building.

三校合并接管寻珍校舍时，已有的校舍除了红砖楼外，还有一栋双层的灰砖教学楼（灰砖楼），后曾专用为生物实验室。寻珍楼房间多为小面积的房间，可用作上课教室的房间太少，因此上课多在灰砖楼。后为补充教室，又增盖了五四楼等校舍，灰砖楼就专门辟为生物实验室之用。

中间露出屋顶的是原寻珍楼，左边就是双层灰砖教学楼，右边是合并后搭建的双层木结构教室楼，时为初一楼
The building in the middle is the original Sing Ding Building. Its roof could be seen among the trees. On the left is the two-story grey brick teaching building, and on the right is the two-story wooden structure classroom building built after the merger, which served the teaching of Senior-One students at that time.

鸡爪槭树盛开时，原生物楼，即灰砖楼一景
The Acer palmatum was in full bloom. The building behind it was the biological laboratory building, that is, the grey brick building.

原德国领事馆之谜

除了这两栋楼外，位于"洋墓亭"南侧属于前德国驻福州领事馆的两栋楼房也拨给了附中做校舍之用，附中后来把它改为了图书馆、音乐教室等。1996 年，两栋楼房拆除，改建为五层的时代教学楼。

需要注意的是，这里的两栋楼属于前德国驻福州领事馆，而非前德国驻福州领事馆所在地。根据《福州老建筑百科》，前德国驻福州领事馆

位于仓山禅臣花园（现程埔路 172 号）内，建于清末，为禅臣洋行的办公楼，因创办者禅臣任领事而兼做德国领事馆使用。1917 年因一战爆发被当时的北洋政府没收。1939 年划拨给新创办的福建省自然科学研究所使用；1951 开始由师大生物系使用。1983 年左右建筑被拆毁，仅余附属禅臣花园。

Besides the red brick building (Sing Ding Building), the other building inherited from Sing Ding Girls' School was a two-story grey brick teaching building (grey brick building). As most of the rooms in Sing Ding Building are not big enough to serve as classrooms, the "grey brick building" shouldered the responsibility. Later, with more school buildings built to meet the teaching need, the grey brick building finished its task and was used mainly as biological laboratory.

The Mystery of the Former German Consulate

In addition to these two buildings inherited from Sing Ding Girls' School, two buildings of the former German Consulate in Fuzhou, located in the south of the "Foochow Mission Cemetery", were also allocated to the affiliated High School, who used them as the library and then music classrooms. In 1996, the two buildings were demolished to make way for a five-story teaching building, whose name is "Times Teaching Building".

It should be noted that the two buildings here originally belonged to the former German Consulate in Fuzhou, but they were not the office of the former German Consulate in Fuzhou. According to the *Encyclopedia of Fuzhou Old Buildings*, the former German Consulate in Fuzhou

was located in Siemssen Garden in Cangshan District (now No. 172 Chengpu Road). It was built in the late Qing Dynasty and served as the office building of Siemssen & Krohn. As its founder G. Siemssen was appointed as the consul, the building was used as the German Consulate. In 1917, it was confiscated by the Beiyang government due to the outbreak of World War I. In 1939, it was allocated to the newly established Fujian Institute of Natural Sciences. It then came into the possession of the Biology Department of Fujian Normal University in 1951. In 1983, the building was demolished, leaving behind only the attached Siemssen Garden.

这是前德国驻福州领事馆，1983 年拆毁，为一座三层半砖木结构的殖民地外廊式建筑。建筑带有一座四层塔楼，立德国国旗；主体建筑和塔楼顶部均做雉堞式女儿墙。

清末或民国时期发行的印有德国驻福州领事馆照片的明信片（来源：池志海）
Postcards printed with photos of the German Consulate in Fuzhou, issued in the late Qing Dynasty or by the Republic of China(Source: Chi Zhihai)

林正德校友（2021）说时代教学楼所在位置上最早应该是前德国驻福州领事馆，后来成了福建省研究院动物研究所，再后来才是附中原图书馆：

从附中校史节外生枝，引出个不是本文的话题，如果附中校史没说错的话，前德国驻福州领事馆是在桃花山校园内，以前李元松老师就跟我提起这事，我想来想去，从建筑风格上看，最大可能就是以前附中图书馆乃前德国驻福州领事馆，附几张照片供考证。不过，近日附中退休老教师陈金武告诉我说，附中原图书馆以前是福建省动物研究所，其对马路是福建省植物研究所，他以前上学时经常路过此地，曾到动物研究所参观过，从石阶上去，看见房间玻璃橱窗里摆满了老虎、豹子等各种动物标本。这是 20 世纪 40 年代末的事，那么时间再往前推移，追溯到第一次世界大战之前，这幢建筑物是谁建造的？据网上搜索说："1864 年德国首任领事居茹在程埔路旧洋墓陵附近（现福州程埔路 172 号）建领事馆。中国对德宣战后，该馆舍和谦信洋行住宅作为敌产，拨给福建省研究院作为院所。"在洋墓亭附近唯一的洋楼就是这幢建筑，它后来是福建省研究院动物研究所，这推理是说得通的，但尚待进一步考证。

就林正德校友这个说法是否确切，我们咨询了冯玮老校长。他说：

What is described above was the former German Consulate in Fuzhou, which was demolished in 1983. It was a three and a half-story colonial corridor architecture with brick and timber structure. The building had a four-story tower attached to it, on the top of which was the German flag. The top of both the main building and the tower were decorated with battlement parapets.

Alumnus Lin Zhengde（2021）said that the location of the Times Teaching Building should have been the site of the former German Consulate in Fuzhou, which served later as the Institute of Zoology of Fujian Academy of Sciences, and then the library of the Affiliated High School:

Let's stray from our topic into a story related to the history of the Affiliated High School. According to the history of the Affiliated High School, the former German Consulate in Fuzhou was located in Taohuashan（Peach Blossom Mountain）campus. Mr. Li Yuansong had even mentioned it to me. And I turned it over in my mind many times. Judged from the architectural style, it is most likely that the former library of the Affiliated High School used to be German Consulate in Fuzhou. At the bottom you can find several photos attached for reference. However, recently, Chen Jinwu, a retired teacher of the Affiliated High School, told me that the old library used to be the Fujian Institute of Zoology. On the opposite side of the road was the Fujian Institute of Botany. He used to pass by the Fujian Institute of Zoology when he was at school and had visited it. Going up the stone steps, he saw in the room glass-windowed closets full of animal specimens such as specimens of tigers and leopards. What he described was the situation in the late 1940s. But then, who built this building before the first World War? According to an online article, "In 1864, H. Krüger, the first consul of Germany, built a consulate near the Foochow Mission Cemetery on Chengpu Road（now No. 172 Chengpu Road, Fuzhou）. After China declared war on Germany, the consulate and the dormitory of China Export Import& Bank Co., Ltd. were confiscated and then allocated to Fujian Research Institute. " The only foreign building near Foochow Mission Cemetery was this building. It was later used as the Fujian Institute of Zoology. This connection makes sense, but more evidences are needed to confirm it.

The statement of Lin Zhengde is somehow confusing. To work out the confusion, we consulted Feng Wei, the former headmaster of the Affiliated High School. He said:

原德国领事馆有两个地方，其主体部分在现在时代中学的校区，新中国成立前是福建的植物研究所，那里面高大的树很多，再之前为德国的领事馆。而附中时代教学楼那里原有两栋楼，也是德国领事馆的一部分。所以德国领事馆是两部分，主体在生科院，过了条路到我们这边的，估计是作为住宅楼，一栋是两层楼，还有一栋是一层的。到了老三校合并，成为师院附中，定校区在桃花山，原来寻珍楼的两栋，一栋是寻珍楼，一栋是双层的灰砖结构的，给我们了。还不够，又把这边洋墓亭划归起来，跟洋墓亭紧靠的原来属于德国领事馆的这两栋楼，也给了我们，都变成附中的校园。而对面福建省植物研究所占地就归师院生物系所有。

原德国领事馆的两座附属楼房之一，"文革"前是图书馆

One of the two buildings of the former German Consulate used as the school library before the Cultural Revolution

原德国领事馆两座附属楼房之二，单层的砖房，"文革"前是音乐教室

The other building of the two buildings of the former German Consulate, a single-story brick building, used as music classrooms before the Cultural Revolution

仿建的德园（来源：池志海）

The duplicate of Morals Garden（Source: Chi Zhihai）

福州老建筑百科又说聚和路 15 号德园有一座红砖双层洋楼，原是领事官邸。德园于 2007 年 11 月在程埔头拆迁中被拆除。福建省建筑科学研究院进行了测绘，并在 2010 年在聚和路另外择址（靠近时代中学后门）仿建一座。这个说法是否正确，有待考证。

The former German Consulate had two locations. The main part was located on the campus of Fuzhou Shidai Middle School. Before the founding of the P. R. C., it belonged to Fujian Institute of Botany. Many tall trees grew there. Before it became Fujian Institute of Botany, it was the German Consulate. While the two dismantled buildings, which were located where the Times Teaching Building of the Affiliated High School stayed, were the other part of the German Consulate. So the main part was located where the Fujian Institute of Botany stayed, while the other part, the residential part, I think, included the two buildings here, across the road, opposite to the Fujian Institute of Botany. One was a two-story building and the other was a one-story building. When the three schools merged into Fuzhou No. 2 Middle School attached to the Teachers College, the campus was set in Taohuashan area (Peach Blossom Mountain). They inherited two buildings, one was Sing Ding Building, the other was a two-story grey brick building. But these two buildings could not accommodate the students we had. So, the area around Foochow Mission Cemetery was allocated to us too. The two buildings close to Foochow Mission Cemetery, which originally belonged to the German Consulate, became ours, and the Fujian Institute of Botany on the opposite side was allocated to the Biology Department of Normal University.

According to *Encyclopedia of Fuzhou Old Architecture,* a two-story red brick Western-styled building called Morals Garden on the No. 15 Juhe Road was the office building of the German Consulate. Morals Garden was demolished together with the demolition of Chengputou community in November, 2007. Fujian Academy of Architectural Sciences duplicated the building on Juhe Road (near the back door of Fuzhou Shidai Middle School) in 2010. But based on the information above, more evidences are needed to check whether Morals Garden is part of the Consulate.

20世纪五六十年代桃花山校区新盖楼舍：五四楼、双层木结构教学楼、旧科学实验楼与梯形教室

三校刚合并为附中时，四周荒芜杂乱，校舍零星。为满足教学要求，1954年迁入桃花山时，学校花费7万元左右建造了一幢面积1448平方米的三层教学楼（五四教学楼）供高中一年级学习，后作为初中楼，2000年为了盖双层框架体育场馆而拆除。

建完五四楼之后又陆续在五四楼西侧建了两间木结构教室，在今日校前区附近建了两间临时竹棚教室，在校门口附近建了一座竹棚雨盖灯光球场，在寻珍教学办公楼西南侧建了一间梯形教室。在今日校前区西侧土坡附近建了一座466平方米的双层木结构教学楼，作为初一的教学楼，花费1.84万元，1986年拆除。1958年又建了科学楼，花费5.81万元，为三层砖木结构，位于桃花山西北侧，面积1301平方米，内设9间实验室。1963年建高中教学楼，半框架结构，水泥地板，花费11.5万元，1966平方米。

五四楼，1954年建，2000年拆
May Fourth Teaching Building, built in 1954 and demolished in 2000

双层木构教室，建于20世纪50年代，1986年拆
A double-layer wooden teaching building, built in the 1950s, and demolished in 1986

旧科学实验楼，1958年建，1983年拆
The old Science Experiment Building, built in 1958, and demolished in 1983

New Buildings Built in Taohuashan Campus in the 1950s and 1960s: May Fourth Teaching Building, Two-Story Teaching Building of Wooden Structure, Science Building and Lecture Theatre

The new school was obviously in great need of school buildings. Thus, the year it moved to Taohuashan area in 1954, the school spent about 70,000 yuan in building a three-story teaching building (May Fourth Teaching Building) for Senior-One students, with an area of 1,448 square meters. Later, it was used as a teaching building for the junior students. It was demolished in 2000 and replaced by a double-layer frame stadium.

Following the May Fourth Teaching Building, two wooden classrooms, two temporary bamboo classrooms, a bamboo lighted court with rain cap and a lecture theatre were built, which are located separately to the west of the May Fourth Teaching Building, in the front area of today's campus, near the school gate, and in the southwest of Sing Ding Building. A double-layer wooden teaching building, which covered 466 square meters, was built near a slope on the west side of the front area of today's campus, costing 18,400 yuan. It was used as the teaching building for junior one. It was demolished in 1986. In 1958, the Science Building, a three-story brick and timber structure equipped with 9 laboratories, was built in the north west of Taohuashan, covering an area of 1,301 square meters and costing 58,100 yuan. In 1963, the Senior Teaching Building was built, with a semi-frame structure and cement floor, costing 115,000 yuan and covering 1,966 square meters.

原高中楼 1964 年建，2010 年拆除
The old Senior Teaching Building, built in 1964, and demolished in 2010

寻珍教学办公楼西南侧的梯形教室最为校友所怀念。梯形教室为砖木结构独栋建筑，面积约 100 平方米。形状像个火柴盒，内侧是白色薄板灰墙，地面由方形棕红色地砖铺就，美观大方（叶令炀，2021）。

1957 届校友王锦燧（中国照明学会原理事长、研究员）（2021）撰文回忆该梯形教室说：

教室内配有学士椅，大约有 110 个座位。教室明亮通透，南北墙面均有窗户，东面是一扇大门，西面墙上有一块大黑板。东面门口外斜坡下面当时是一块菜园，可通向大操场（位于现在游泳池北面几个篮球场所在地，当时地面是裸露的泥沙地）。西面的斜坡通往"五四教学楼"。平时学校上大班课都在这大阶梯教室里进行。记得全校教职工大会也在这里召开。阶梯教室盖好后，校领导决定晚上把它作为高年级学生的晚自习教室。晚自习休息的时间，我们都到山上眺望远处夜景，呼吸新鲜空气。上世纪五十年代，台湾国民党飞机经常到福州城区骚扰，这座简易教室离防空壕很近，一有防空警报，我们就迅速跑到防空壕躲避。令人兴奋的是在 1956 年夏季的一个夜晚，当我们在这座教室晚自习时，福州市区四周山上的解放军突然把探照灯全部打开，将整个夜空照射得分外明亮夺目。这时我们都跑出教室欢呼，这件事给我留下深刻的印象。自从那时起，敌机再也不敢飞进福州城市上空，我们也开始在这座教室度过清静的晚自习时光。

"文革"中的建设：古山里分校

"文革"期间，附中的发展有所停滞，但也并非毫无故事。

What alumni recall frequently is the lecture theatre in the southwest of Sing Ding Building, a single-story brick and timer structure, covering an area of more than 100 square meters. It was a beautiful building in the shape of a matchbox, with its inside wall covered by white thin gray sheet, and the ground paved with square brownish red floor tiles.

Wang Jinsui, an alumnus graduating in 1957 (once served as director and researcher of the China Lighting Society), wrote an article recalling the lecture theatre:

> The classroom was equipped with about 110 seats. There were windows on the north and south walls, allowing in ample sunlight. There was a gate in the east and a large blackboard on the west wall. A vegetable garden spread under the slope outside the gate, leading to the playground (now it has been turned into the basketball courts, in the north of the swimming pool. But at our age, it was bare, muddy ground). The slope in the west led to the May Fourth Teaching Building. We tended to have lesson together in this large lecture theatre. The staff meetings were also held here. And it served as a self-study classroom for senior students in the evenings, as expected by the school leaders. During the self-study break in the evening, we would climb to the top of the mountain to enjoy the night scene in the distance and breathe fresh air. In the 1950s, Kuomintang planes from Taiwan often harassed Fuzhou City. As this lecture theatre was very close to the air defense trench, whenever there was an air defense warning, we rushed to the air defense trench to take shelter. One night in the summer of 1956, when we were studying in this classroom, the People's Liberation Army stationed on the mountains around Fuzhou suddenly turned on all the search lights. They illuminated the whole night sky. We ran out of the classroom and cheered excitedly. You can picture the scene. Very impressive. Since then, enemy planes have never dared to fly over Fuzhou. We welcomed quiet evenings for self-study in this classroom.

Construction in the Cultural Revolution: Gushanli Campus

The Cultural Revolution somehow froze the development of the Affiliated High School, but not totally.

附中在"文革"期间有一个特殊的分校。1970 年 5 月，根据市革委会宣教组要求，各中学要在北峰办农场，后来改称"分校"。附中最初在北峰的桂湖建农场，后迁址古山里建设分校。古山里分校地处山坡上，距福州的校本部 96 华里，没有长途车可以直达。福州去分校的长途汽车只到 193 号公路的竹坪路口，从这里沿着蜿蜒盘旋的 194 号公路要步行 4 公里路才能达到分校。师生们自带干粮，按连队（1971 年后改成年段）集合徒步往返，单程费时 10 余小时。附中当时叫第二十七中学，花了大约 10 万元在这里建设校舍，约可容纳 6 个班 300 多名师生轮流劳动和上课。初二以上每个班级轮流上分校，一般每个学期一个月（李青藻，2021）。

校舍位于公路的左上方，几排一层的宿舍楼和一栋两层的办公楼依山坡而建。一条小石径位于房屋的左侧，通向一个小拦水坝，沿着拦水坝的流水沟向下，越过马路再下一条小路，便是分校的教室区了。农田散落在附近的山上。分校有个大食堂，是师生们用挖来的花岗石砌成的，可容纳约三四百位学生吃饭。

前往北峰古山里分校拉练途中
Walking to the Gushanli Branch School in the Beifeng Mountain area

开荒
Reclaiming wasteland

初创时期的古山里分校，几年间，在图中的位置和附近地区，先后建起了办公住宿大楼、学生住宿房、三间大教室、一座大食堂
The office building, the student accommodation building, three large classrooms and a large canteen in the early days of Gushanli Branch School

The Affiliated High School had a special campus during the Cultural Revolution. In May 1970, the Publicity and Education Group of the Municipal Revolutionary Committee required that all middle schools "farm" lands in a mountain area called Beifeng. The movement was later renamed as "building branch school". The Affiliated High School set its farm firstly in Guihu village, in about the middle part of Beifeng mountain area, and then soon moved to Gushanli village and settled down there. Gushanli Branch School was located on the hillside, 48 kilometers away from Fuzhou. There was no direct bus from Fuzhou to Gushanli village. The coach from Fuzhou ran no further than the Zhuping intersection along the Highway 193. To get to the branch school, one still needed to walk along the winding Highway 194 for 4 kilometers. The teachers and students would bring solid food and walked for more than 10 hours to the branch school in military formation of company (After 1971, the military formation was canceled and the division of school grade was restored). The Affiliated High School, called as No. 27 Middle School at that time, spent about 100,000 yuan in building school buildings there, which can accommodate about 300 students, divided into 6 classes. Teachers and students from Junior Grade Two to Senior Grade Three worked and studied there in turn, usually for one month per semester.

The school buildings were at the upper left of the road, consisting of several rows of one-story dormitory buildings and a two-story office building along the mountain slope. On the left side of the buildings was a small stone path leading to a small dam. Down the ditch behind the dam, across the road and then along a path, one could find the classrooms, with the farm lands nearby on the mountain. The campus was also equipped with a large canteen, built of granite excavated by teachers and students. It could accommodate about three to four hundred students.

学生们在这里除了要上课，还要劳动，打草、养猪、上山砍柴、下地种田，生活颇为清苦艰辛，但也是一种特殊的磨练。青春在这里依然是飞扬的，师生们不怕苦不怕累，时有欢声笑语。水坝拦起的水库边是少年们戏水时的欢声笑语，空余时间的会演上是青春的歌声，远处的篮球赛场上是同学们的豪情万丈。青春，并不因艰苦的生活条件而褪色。

1978年9月，随着"文革"结束，古山里分校这个"文革"时期的特殊产物也随之停办了。

岁月已逝，当年的纷扰与喧嚣都已销声匿迹，但在那里度过的青葱岁月，那里的苦、那里的乐趣、那里的生活，依然为当年的学子怀念着。2010年，75届12班的潘志刚、林津、陈永荣、吴钦师、李秀玲、吴绵先6名同学多方活动，想要保护和建设师大附中原北峰古山里分校，并于2010年9月28日与日溪乡政府、点洋村村委会、古山里林场承包者签订了《关于租用师大附中原北峰分校土地使用经营权合同》，将分校原校部、教室及操场、养猪场等山坡地租用35年零9个月，想要把原古山里分校建设成参观游览的好景点、传统教育的好场所、休闲疗养的好家园。但可惜，由于种种原因，还未做成。

2018—2019年，福州晋安区组织"重拾芳华遇见美好"系列活动，邀请当年的学子重返北峰山区，去寻找当年各分校的旧址（何佳媛，2019）。一时间，怀旧之情风卷而至。回想当年北峰山区"晴天一身灰，雨天一腿泥"的艰苦生活，而如今，在政府和人民的共同努力下，晋安区已经打造出北峰山区的全新面貌，这里有了风光无限的全景公路。飞驰在这条现代之路上，遥想着当年的学子之歌在山间回荡，过往今昔，不由让人既感慨当年的峥嵘岁月，也惊叹如今乡村的振兴。

数学组教师在分校测量
Mathematics teachers conducted
survey at the branch school

Besides taking classes as they did on the campus in Fuzhou, on Gushanli Campus, students also did physical labor, mowing grass, raising pigs, cutting firewood and raising crops in the fields. Life is quite hard there, but it also turned out to be a special kind of education. Youthful joy was still ringing in the air regardless of the hardship. Those teenagers found happiness in playing with the water in the reservoir by the dam, singing songs in the spare time and playing basketball on the ground.

In September 1978, with the end of the Cultural Revolution, Gushanli Branch School, a special product of the Cultural Revolution, came to the closure.

In 2010, Pan Zhigang, Lin Jin, Chen Yongrong, Wu Qinshi, Li Xiuling and Wu Mianxian, six alumni from Class 12 of 1975 batch, committed themselves to protecting and rebuilding the former Gushanli Branch School, out of the nostalgia of the hard and yet joyful youth. On September 28, 2010, they signed the contract with the Rixi Township Government, Dianyang Village Committee and the contractor of Gushanli forest farm, renting the land use and management right of the land where Beifeng Branch School was located. The contract allowed them to use the land where the office building, classrooms and playground and the pig farms of the branch school were ever located for 35 years and 9 months. They intended to rebuild the former Gushanli Branch School into a scenic spot for sightseeing, an education base and a place for leisure. The big plan still has a long way to go, however.

From 2018 to 2019, Jin'an District of Fuzhou organized a series of activities under the theme of "regain youth and meet beauty". Students ever studying in the branch schools were invited to return to Beifeng mountain area to find the former sites of the branch schools. The old memories flooded in and people were surprised to find that Beifeng mountain area were no longer the poor and undeveloped place in their memories, which "covered them with dust on sunny days and spattered them with mud on rainy days." Instead, with the joint efforts of the government and the villagers, Beifeng mountain area takes on a new look. The muddy winding road has been replaced by a panoramic highway with charming scenery. People participating in the activities organized by Jin'an District couldn't help marveling at the revitalization of today's countryside while reflecting on their old days.

"文革"给附中带来了一定的冲击，但即便如此，这所青春校园也并未完全停止发展的步伐。除了上述古山里分校的建设外，校本部也多了供学子挥洒青春汗水的场地。

1972年，因为全国排球分区赛和全省篮球比赛的部分赛事在附中举行，于是便在校门口内路旁的空地上突击建成了一座简易灯光球场，场内共有1 000多个看台座位。1974年，又投入2.4万元，通过师生无私的劳动，在校园西侧利用山体斜坡建成了一座可容纳5 000名观众的露天灯光球场，于是校前区的简易灯光球场便被拆除了。1974—1978年间，该球场举行了多场全国及全省的篮球赛、排球赛，球场对外售票，票价为0.2元，当时还出现了一票难求的盛况。

20世纪七八十年代改革开放新发展：胜利楼、校大门、科学楼

随着"文革"结束，百废待兴，同时改革开放带来了蓬勃生机。在政府的关心支持下，附中着手校园建设，拆除破旧建筑，建起新建筑，着力改善师生的工作学习条件，解决生源爆满、教室紧缺的问题。

: 胜利楼
: Victory Building

1979年，学校将竹棚雨盖灯光球场拆除，又将学校大门沿围墙向东移动了20米，建起了一栋5层混砖结构的楼舍，共22间教室，取名为"胜利楼"。胜利楼原为初中教学楼，1996年起改为办公楼。2004年行政办公楼落成后，拆除了胜利楼。

同年，不但建了胜利楼，也改建了学校大门，扩展了校前区，附中校园焕发出了新的面貌。

: "文革"前老校门
: The old school gate before the Cultural
: Revolution

: 旧校门，1979年建，2006年拆
: The old school gate, built in 1979, demolished in
: 2006

The Cultural Revolution did impact the Affiliated High School, but even so, it couldn't halt its development completely. In addition to the construction of Gushanli Branch School as mentioned above, there were other constructions.

In 1972, some of the national volleyball Division Series and the provincial basketball matches were to be held in the Affiliated High School. To meet the demand, a plain lighted court with more than 1,000 bleachers was built on the ground beside the road behind the gate of the school. In 1974, an unroofed lighted court that can accommodate 5,000 spectators was built on the mountain slope on the west of the campus, costing 24,000 yuan as well as the unpaid labor of both teachers and students. The plain lighted court in the front area of the school was demolished after the new court was built. From 1974 to 1978, a number of national and provincial basketball and volleyball matches were held in the court. Tickets for the matches were very cheap, costing only 0.2 yuan. They sold out quickly as people were so enthusiastic about the matches.

Development Brought by the Reform and Opening-up in the 1970s and 1980s: Victory Building, New School Gate and New Science Building

With the end of the Cultural Revolution and the implementation of the reform and opening-up policy, the whole country was full of vitality. Supported by the government, the Affiliated High School set out to replace old buildings with new ones, aiming to improve the working and learning conditions of teachers and students and to accommodate more students.

In 1979, the bamboo rain-capped lighted court was demolished, and the school gate was moved 20 meters eastward along the wall. On the ground vacated, a 5-story brick building with 22 classrooms was built. It was named "Victory Building". Victory Building was originally used as the teaching building for senior students, but then serves as office building since 1996. In 2004, as a new office building was built, the Victory Building was demolished.

Not only the Victory Building was built, but also the school gate was rebuilt in 1979. With the construction of the new school gate, the campus took on a new look.

1983 年拆除并重建了科学楼，1986 年新科学楼完工，从 3 层砖木结构变为 6 层框架结构，总面积 5 325 平方米，造价 156 万元。1993 年，又在科学楼顶层建成天文圆顶，科学楼内含物理、化学、生物实验室、电教、计算机中心、多媒体大教室及可容纳 300 人的小礼堂等。

20 世纪 90 年代的大气发展：教学大楼、图书馆、时代教学楼

时光荏苒，不知不觉到了 20 世纪末，中国的经济正在腾飞，附中也越来越有底气了，又新又气派的现代建筑也如雨后春笋般涌现，这为附中的进一步发展打开了新的局面。

1996 年，附中梯形教室和灰砖楼与原寻珍楼同时拆除，取而代之的是崭新大气的教学大楼与图书馆。新图书馆馆舍面积 3 000 多平方米，藏书约 14 多万册，订有 400 余种期刊及 100 多种报刊，备有 2 000 多种音响资料及 600 多种数字视听材料，有图书借阅室、期刊借阅厅、电子阅览厅、音响视听室、学生茶座、读者论坛室、师生校友著作室、教师电子备课室、书画摄影展览室、校史展览室等。2007 年，被评为福建省中学示范图书馆。

：图书馆
：The library

：新寻珍楼
：The new Sing Ding Building

：时代教学楼
：Times Teaching Building

同年，时代教学楼也在原图书馆和原音乐教室（即前文所说的前德国领事馆所属楼房所在之处）旧址上拔地而起，5 层框架结构，面积 1 750 平方米，含 15 间教室、4 间办公室，造价 148 万元。

In 1983, Science Building, the three-story brick wood structure, was demolished. In its place was the new Science Building, completed in 1986. It is a six-story frame structure, covering an area of 5,325 square meters and costing 1.56 million yuan. In 1993, an astronomical dome was placed on the top of the Science Building. The Science Building contains physics, chemistry and biology laboratories, audio-visual education center, computer center, multimedia classrooms and an auditorium that can accommodate 300 people.

Development in the 1990s: Teaching Building, Library and Times Teaching Building

With the rapid development of the 20th century, new buildings sprang up in the Affiliated High School.

In 1996, the lecture theatre, the grey brick building and the original Sing Ding Building were demolished at the same time and replaced by a brand-new and grand teaching building and a modern library. The new library covers an area of more than 3,000 square meters. It has a collection of more than 140,000 books, more than 400 periodicals, more than 100 newspapers and periodicals, more than 2,000 kinds of audio-visual materials and more than 600 kinds of digital audio-visual materials. It consists of a book reading room, a periodical reading hall, an electronic reading hall, an audio-visual room, cafeterias for students, a room for readers' forum, an exhibition room of teachers, students' and alumni's writings, an electronic room for teachers to prepare lessons, an exhibition room for calligraphy, painting and photography, a school history exhibition room, etc. The library is so brilliant that in 2007, it was rated as the model library of middle schools in Fujian Province.

In 1996, the Times Teaching Building was also built on the ground where the old library and the old music classroom were (that is, where the buildings belonging to the former German Consulate were, as was mentioned above). It is a five-story building with a frame structure including 15 classrooms and 4 offices, covering an area of 1,750 square meters and costing 1.48 million yuan.

21 世纪的美丽现代建设：双层体育场馆、新大门

2000 年，附中拆除了灯光球场的西、南看台和部分北看台，五四楼及周围的木教室、木工场、厕所等建筑也被拆除，建成了一座双层体育场馆。该体育场馆总面积 15 500 平方米，于 2002 年竣工，上层为全塑胶 300 米环形跑道和足球场，下层为篮球场、60 米室内塑胶跑道及乒乓、体操、羽毛球等运动场所，在二层还有一座人行天桥，连接一部教学区与二部生活区。除体育场馆外，2000 年也建造了一座附有用房与看台的游泳池，共 8 泳道，面积为 21×50 平方米，造价 150 万元。因为 1968 届初高中校友为其建造捐资近 50 万，因此该游泳池被命名为"六八游泳池"。2008 年，1968 届初高中校友又捐资 57 万多元，用于建造 4 个塑胶篮球场，并将新建的塑胶篮球场与游泳池合称为"六八运动场"。校友会会长、朱旭老校长为六八运动场撰写碑文，著名书法家朱以撒为运动场碑石题字，著名书法家、校友吴酒光题写了"开启碑"碑名。

灯光球场，1974 年建，2000 年拆
Lighted court，built in 1974 and demolished in 2000

双层体育场馆
Double-decker stadium

2003 年，附中建造综合教学实验楼、行政办公楼以及大型报告厅，2004 年竣工，其中教学实验楼为 7 层框架结构，与 1998 年在原寻珍楼地址上建起的教学大楼连在一起；行政办公楼为 6 层框架结构，大型报告厅有 800 多个座位，底层为停车场。竣工后，拆除了用作行政办公的胜利楼。

报告厅外观
The exterior of the lecture hall

报告厅内部
The interior of the lecture hall

Modern Construction in the 21st Century: Double-Decker Stadium and the New Gate

In 2000, stands in the west and the south and some of the stands in the north of the lighted court were demolished, together with the May Fourth Teaching Building, the wooden classrooms, the carpentry work shop, and the toilets near the May Fourth Teaching Building. In their place is a double-decker stadium with a total area of 15,500 square meters, which was completed in 2002. The upper decker of the stadium includes a full plastic circular track, 300-meter long, and a football field, while the lower decker consists of a basketball court, 60-meter-long indoor plastic track and sports venues for table tennis, gymnastics and badminton. There is also a platform bridge on the upper layer, connecting the teaching area with the living areas.

In addition to the stadium, a swimming pool with rooms and stands was also built in 2000. It has 8 lanes, covering an area of 21×50 square meters and costing 1.5 million yuan. The alumni of the 1968 batch donated nearly 500,000 for it, and thus the swimming pool was named "68 Swimming Pool". In 2008, The alumni of the 1968 batch donated another 570,000 yuan to build four plastic basketball courts, and so the newly-built plastic basketball court and swimming pool were collectively referred to as the "68 Playground". The former president Zhu Xu of the Affiliated High School, also the president of the Alumni Association, composed the inscription for the "68 Playground", and the famous calligrapher Zhu Yisa inscribed it on the tablet. The famous calligrapher and alumni Wu Naiguang inscribed the name of the "Opening Monument".

In 2003, the construction of a comprehensive teaching and experiments building, an administrative office building and a large lecture hall was under way, which was completed in 2004. The teaching and experiments building is a 7-story architecture with a frame structure, connected with the teaching building that replaced Sing Ding Building in 1998; The administrative office building is a six-story architecture with a frame structure, equipped with a large lecture hall that has more than 800 seats and a parking lot on the ground floor. After the construction was completed, the Victory Building was no longer needed for administrative office work and was thus demolished.

2006 年，由 1980 届与 1986 届校友共同捐资，又建了一个新大门。

随着时代的进步，国家对中学教学楼有了抗震的要求，要求中学把没有达到抗震指标的楼舍拆掉重盖。2010 年，拆除高中楼，盖了新楼，并于 2012 年落成。2012 年，也对原"科学楼"进行了重建。学校为了对新盖的楼舍进行命名，就把新修建的科学楼命名为"润德楼"，以纪念陈景润和侯德榜这两个优秀校友，并把新盖的高中楼命名为"英华楼"，以纪念英华中学这个历史最久、影响最大的前身学校。

新校门，2006 年建
The new school gate built in 2006

润德楼，即科学楼，2012 年改建完成
Runde Building, i.e. Science Building, rebuilt in 2012

英华楼，原高中楼，2012 年重建
Anglo-Chinese Building, i.e. Senior Teaching Building, rebuilt in 2012

● 主要景观

110 周年校庆建立的侯德榜塑像（作者：胡汉平）
The statue of Hou Debang set on the 110th anniversary of the school, designed by Hu Hanping

侯德榜塑像，建于 1991 年，汉白玉雕像，塑像高 1.4 米，基座 1.7 米，位于科学楼前的草坪上，基座上镌刻着聂荣臻元帅的题字。

求索碑，建于 1993 年，由著名科学家、教育家、全国政协副主席钱伟长题名，碑体上镌刻着附中在国际中学生学科竞赛中获奖的学生和他们指导老师的名字。

2001 年，建陈景润塑像、烈士纪念碑、立志亭、思源亭。2001 年 10 月 2 日，在 120 周年校庆上，举行了英烈校友纪念碑和陈景润铜像揭幕典礼。全国人大常委会原副委员长、中国科协主席、中国科学院院长周光召为陈景润铜像题写碑名，并题词："科教兴国，人才为本"。后英烈校友纪念碑被正式命名为"英雄墙"。

求索碑
The Quest Monument

In 2006, with money donated by alumni from the 1980 batch and 1986 batch, a new gate was built.

With the development of our country, it is required that the buildings in the middle schools should have strong seismic resistance. Those which fail to meet the requirement are strongly advised to be demolished and rebuilt. Consequently, in 2010, the Teaching Building for senior students was demolished and a new building was built, which was completed in 2012. The Science Building was also rebuilt in 2012. The school named the newly built Science Building "Runde Building" to commemorate two outstanding alumni Chen Jingrun and Hou Debang, and named the newly built Teaching Building for Senior Students "Anglo-Chinese Building" to commemorate Anglo-Chinese Middle School, the oldest and most influential predecessor.

Scan for more
扫码了解更多

● Landscape

Hou Debang statue, built in 1991, is a white marble statue, 1.4-meter high and with a 1.7-meter-high base. It is located on the lawn in front of the Science Building. The inscription of Marshal Nie Rongzhen is engraved on the base.

The Quest Monument, built in 1993, was inscribed by Qian Weichang, a famous scientist, educator and Vice Chairman of the National Committee of the Chinese People's Political Consultative Conference. The monument is engraved with the names of the students who won prizes in the international competitions and their instructors.

In 2001, the statue of Chen Jingrun, the monument to martyr alumni, Ambition Pavilion and Source-worship Pavilion were built. On October 2, 2001, on the 120th anniversary of the University, the unveiling ceremony of the monument to martyr alumni and the bronze statue of Chen Jingrun was held. Zhou Guangzhao, former Vice Chairman of the Standing Committee of the National People's Congress, Chairman of the China Association for Science and Technology and President of the Chinese Academy of Sciences, inscribed the bronze statue of Chen Jingrun, which reads: "Developing the country through science and education; reinvigorating China through human resource development." The monument to martyr alumni was officially named "Heroes Wall".

英雄墙
The Heroes Wall

思源亭
Source-worship Pavilion

立志亭
Ambition Pavilion

立志亭，由 1975 届校友在校庆时捐建，亭名由 1957 届校友、福建省政协原主席陈明义命名并亲笔题写。楹联"躬行止至善，力学致新知"由附中语文老师张可珍撰文，由 1964 届校友、著名书法家蒋平畴书写。思源亭，由学校出资建成，由院士校友郭孔辉、张钺题写。楹联"入吾校长知报国，登斯亭不忘尊师"由 1955 届校友高芝臻撰文，由 1964 届校友、著名书法家蒋平畴书写。2006 年，1966 届校友补认捐"思源亭"。

2005 年，由 1985 届校友捐建，在校大门附近建造假山瀑布，命名为"润"，寓意"润物细无声"。同年，建环校路。

：瀑布：润
：Waterfall: Run

2012 年，1962 届校友毕业 50 周年时献给母校一块感恩石，题名"桃山成蹊"。1962 届校友金青撰文介绍说感恩石的外形像一颗籽粒饱满的花生。花生的正式名称叫"落花生"，寓意学生布满天下，落地生根，开花结果。花生又有"长生果"之雅称，代表学生对母校的良好祝愿，希望她永远生机勃发！"桃山成蹊"即应和附中的代称桃花山之名，也是表达对附中蓬勃发展、桃李满天下的骄傲之情。感恩石上刻有一双脚印，寓意学子和慕名取经的人"接踵而来"，同时也暗指附中的成就是一步一个脚印走出来的。感恩石原位于附中现存唯一的历史建筑即旧传达室门口。2012 年 10 月 2 日，朱旭老校长、林瑜校长和李绚书记亲手为感恩石揭幕。现在这块感恩石被移至校园最南面的土坡上，与英雄墙共同组成了校园中一个重要的场所。

：感恩石
：Gratitude Stone

The Ambition Pavilion was built with the money donated by the 1975 batch during the school celebration. Its named was inscribed by Chen Mingyi, alumnus from the 1957 batch and former chairman of the Fujian Provincial CPPCC. The couplet "practice until you achieve the perfection, work hard until you gain the knowledge" was composed by Zhang Kezhen, a Chinese teacher of the Affiliated High School, and inscribed by Jiang Pingchou, an alumnus from 1964 batch and famous calligrapher. Source-worship Pavilion was inscribed by academician Guo Konghui and Zhang Bo, both alumni of the school. The couplet reading "when you enter our school, you should learn to serve the country; when you approach the pavilion, you should be reminded to respect the teachers" was composed by Gao Zhizhen, an alumnus from 1955 batch and inscribed by Jiang Pingchou, an alumnus from 1964 batch and famous calligrapher. In 2006, the 1966 batch donated and claimed "Source-worship Pavilion".

In 2005, with the money donated by the 1985 batch, a rockery waterfall was built near the school gate, named "run" in Chinese, which means "moisten things silently". In the same year, a road that circles the school was built.

In 2012, on the 50th anniversary, alumni of the 1962 batch presented a Gratitude Stone to their alma mater, entitled "footprint along the peach blossom mountain". According to Alumnus Jin Qing, the gratitude stone is in the shape of a peanut because peanut's full Chinese name is "luohuashen (flowers fall and fruits grow)", which indicates that students will take root and blossom and then bear great fruits in the school. Peanut also has the nickname of "longevity fruit", which represents the students' good wishes to their alma mater that she will always be full of vitality. The title of "the peach blossom mountain" also echoes the name of Taohuashan (peach blossom mountain), where the Affiliated High School is located. "Peach", together with "plum" in Chinese culture symbolizes the students. It thus expresses the pride of the students for the vigorous development of the Affiliated High School, with a huge number of outstanding and talented students graduating from the school and pursued their dreams and ambitions all over the world. There is a pair of footprints engraved on the Gratitude Stone, which means that one after another student are attracted into the school. At the same time, it also implies that the achievements of the Affiliated High School are won by step-by-step effort. The gratitude stone was once located in front of the janitor's room. On October 2, 2012, the former principal Zhu Xu, principal Lin Yu and Party secretary Li Xuan unveiled the Gratitude Stone. Now this Gratitude Stone has been relocated on the southernmost slope of the campus, together with the Heroes Wall.

2015 年 8 月 15 日，1985 届校友在母校举行主题为"梦回青春"的高中毕业 30 周年庆典，并为母校捐修了校友接待室，该室由母校唯一的老建筑"门房小木屋"改建而成。2021 年，附中 140 周年校庆时，又在这个旧门房的边上修建了一小栋具有现代化风格的建筑，共同作为陈景润纪念馆，门房也就成了纪念馆的入口。这是国内首家陈景润纪念馆，收藏了丰富的图文资料，由 1993 届校友欧生设计，外观朴素低调，象征陈景润的为人。

陈景润纪念馆，左边新建筑建于 2021 年，与右边旧门房相通，旧门房为纪念馆入口
Memorial Hall of Chen Jingrun, the building on the left was built in 2021, connected with the old janitor's room on the right, which now serves as the entrance of the Memorial Hall

● 著名校友

这个美丽的学校孕育了许多出色的校友，培育了许多国家栋梁。到目前为止，附中有 17 位院士，他们分别是我国近代化学工业的奠基人之一侯德榜，空气动力学家沈元，气象学家高由禧，固体力学与地球动力学家王仁，天文学家、天体物理学家陈彪，固体地球物理学家曾融生，数学家陈景润，半导体材料专家阙端麟，汽车工程专家郭孔辉，计算机专家张钹，喀斯特学家及水文工程与环境地质学家卢耀如，美国化学工程学家黎念之，美国微电子学家萨支唐，农业科学家王世中，法学家王铁崖，美国研究中国近代史学家刘广京，加拿大工程院院士邓力。其中郭孔辉、张钹、邓力为三校合并之后培养的人才。

On August 15, 2015, alumni of the 1985 senior batch held a celebration of the 30th anniversary of graduation in their alma mater with the theme of "return to youth in the dream". They donated money to rebuild the janitor's room into a reception room for the alumni. The janitor's room is the only surviving old architecture. On the 140th anniversary of the Affiliated High School in 2021, a small modern building designed by Ou Sheng, an alumnus of 1993 batch, the Memorial Hall of Chen Jingrun, was built next to the old janitor's room, which serves as the entrance to the memorial hall. This is the first "Memorial Hall of Chen Jingrun" in China, whose external appearance is a mirror of Chen Jingrun's personality—simple and pure. One can find a rich collection of graphic materials.

• Famous Alumni

The school has graduated tens of thousands of outstanding students, many of whom have made great contributions to the country. Its distinguished alumni include 17 academicians. They are: world-famous chemist Hou Debang, aerodynamicist Shen Yuan, meteorologist Gao Youxi, leading scientist in solid mechanics and geodynamics Wang Ren, astronomer and astrophysicist Chen Biao, solid geophysicist Zeng Rongsheng, mathematician Chen Jingrun, expert in semiconductor materials Que Duanlin, expert in automobile engineering Guo Konghui, computer scientist Zhang Bo, karst scientist and hydrogeologist and environmental geologist Lu Yaoru, American chemical engineer Li Nianzhi, American microelectronics scientist Sa Chitang, agricultural scientist Wang Shizhong, jurist Wang Tieya, Liu Guangjing, an American historian studying modern China, and Deng Li, an academician of the Canadian Academy of Engineering. Among them, Guo Konghui, Zhang Bo and Deng Li graduated from Fuzhou No. 2 Middle School after the merger of the three predecessors of the Affiliated High School.

陈景润

　　从附中建筑的命名以及景观塑像等不难看出，侯德榜与陈景润对附中意义非凡。侯德榜院士发明的"侯氏制碱法"对中国的工业发展作出了巨大贡献，侯德榜及"侯氏制碱法"的介绍早已编入新中国的中学化学科教材中，是学生非常熟悉的著名科学家。陈景润是全中国家喻户晓的数学家，是青年学者学习的榜样，是激励他们向科学进军的力量。因此，附中在众多院士中突出展现侯德榜和陈景润，作为激励青年学子的力量。侯德榜的故事我们前面已介绍，现在我们来细说陈景润与附中的故事。虽然陈景润在附中的前身英华中学求学，但他与三校合并后的附中仍有很强的互动。

　　陈景润院士与沈元院士的故事几乎家喻户晓。1948 年，陈景润到英华中学读书时，时任班主任兼数学、物理、英语教师的正是沈元。沈元本来在清华大学任航空系教授、系主任，那一年夏天，回福州奔父丧，要回校时因为正赶上解放战争，三大战役即将爆发，北方战乱频仍，南北交通受阻，无法成行。沈元的母校英华中学得知后，请他回母校执教，沈元因此暂时在英华中学任教，所带的班级恰好就是陈景润所在的班级。沈元知识渊博，教学有趣，常常跳出教材，天马行空，信手拈来，风格颇为生动幽默，因此深受同学欢迎。有一次在上课的时候他提到了著名的哥德巴赫猜想，提到这个猜想还未有人能证明。沈元说："数学是自然科学的皇后，数论是数学的皇冠，哥德巴赫猜想就是皇冠上的明珠。"（叶青、叶蓓，2019）这堂课对陈景润触动极大，在他心中种下了摘取明珠的梦想。经过 20 年的艰苦努力，他终于成功地证明了"1 + 2"，并完成了它的改进和简化（黄启权，2009）。

　　陈景润读书时并不是特别突出的学生。据陈景润的中学老师陈荫慈老先生（2020）回忆，陈景润那时候沉默寡言，并不活跃，只是一个平常而又普通的学生，成绩不是特别拔尖，也没显示出特别的天赋。后因偶然得知和他有点"表兄弟"关系，陈荫慈老先生才开始关注这个学生，逐渐发现陈景润只是不喜争抢，不善表达，其实早已心知答案。

Chen Jingrun

The Affiliated High School of Fujian Normal University admired Hou Debang and Chen Jingrun so much that it has many of its buildings and statues named in honor of them. It is natural as Academician Hou Debang made great contributions to Chinese industrial development with his invention, Hou's process for soda production. High school students are familiar with the scientist as his achievement has been introduced in their chemistry textbooks since the founding of the People's Republic of China. While Chen Jingrun, a well-known mathematician in China, has set an inspiring example for young scholars to commit themselves to the research. As Hou's story has been covered before, now let us talk about Chen Jingrun, who maintained a close relationship with the Affiliated High School, even though he graduated from its predecessor Anglo-Chinese College before the merger.

The story between Academician Chen Jingrun and Academician Sheng Yuan is widely known. Chen entered Anglo-Chinese College in 1948, when Sheng happened to be his class teacher as well as his math, physics and English teacher. Professor Sheng was once the head of the Department of Aeronautical Engineering of Tsinghua University, but he could not make his trip back to Beijing after he returned to Fuzhou for his father's funeral that summer as the transport was blocked by the imminent outbreak of the three major campaigns in the War of Liberation. Sheng was therefore invited by Anglo-Chinese College to teach in the school temporally, where he coincidentally became Chen Jingrun's teacher. Sheng's erudition and humor won him popularity among students as his teaching often went beyond textbooks. In his class, he once mentioned the unsolved problem—Goldbach's conjecture, saying that mathematics is the queen of sciences, number theory is the queen's crown, and Goldbach's conjecture is the pearl on the crown. What the teacher said sowed the seed of dream to catch the pearl in the heart of Chen. Eventually, after twenty years of strenuous efforts, he succeeded in proving "1 + 2" and having it improved and simplified.

Chen was in no way a standout when he was at school. As his high school teacher Mr. Chen Yinci recalled, Chen Jingrun, silent in class and mediocre in academic performance, showed no sign of a talented student at that time. Later when Mr. Chen Yinci learned by chance that the student was a distant cousin of his, he started to pay attention and found that Chen Jingrun had always known the answers to teachers' questions, but he was just not of fan of competition and not good at expressing himself.

陈景润喜欢学习，平日读书相当用功，一副近乎痴迷的状态，因此被同学们戏称为"bookworm"（书虫）。他经常去英华中学图书馆借书，比如大学教材《微积分学》《物理学》《哈佛大学讲义》《高等代数引论》《实用力学》等，其中《微积分学》这本书他曾借过两次，可见他非常热爱数学（叶青、叶蓓，2019）。陈景润高二时，陈荫慈的同学及同事陈金华成了陈景润的老师，陈景润时常向陈金华讨教数学问题，并向他借阅书籍。在陈金华老师眼中，陈景润可不是一些报纸杂志上说的"booker"（书呆子）。陈景润去厦大读书时，还特意来向陈金华老师道别。1981 年，附中 100 周年纪念时，陈金华老师专程到北京给陈景润送校庆邀请书。陈景润那时候已经家喻户晓了，但在送陈金华坐公交车的时候，还特意细心叮嘱司机："这是我的老师，请帮忙照顾一下哦。"1989 年陈金华老师逝世时，作为学生的著名数学家陈景润先生特意发来了唁电（施焕军，2007）。

　　在英华的学习显然是陈景润攀登数学高峰的起点。陈景润和老师们的感人故事被附中的一代代学子反复演绎，以别致的形式教育并激励了一代代学子。2002 年，时任福建省省长的习近平同志到附中时，还特别认真地瞻仰了陈景润塑像和英烈碑，并实地考察了双层田径场。2010 年，在省教育厅主办的教师节晚会上，附中以情景诗朗诵《陈景润和他的老师》参演，获得了教育厅的"突出贡献奖"。2013 年，《陈景润和他的老师》又在全国第四届中小学生艺术展演活动中荣获一等奖。2021 年，附中 140 周年校庆时，情景诗朗诵《陈景润和他的老师》再次生动讲述了陈景润和沈元的故事。

情景诗朗诵《陈景润和他的老师》
Poetry recitation performance *Chen Jingrun and His Teachers*

陈景润参加福建师大附中 110 周年校庆
Chen Jingrun participated in the 110th anniversary of the Affiliated High School of Fujian Normal University

　　1981 年，附中建校 100 周年校庆，沈元、陈景润都应邀出席，发表了热情洋溢的讲话。陈景润在讲话中回顾了在母校学习的难忘记忆，说很骄傲看到母校的发展，并认为这归功于共产党，没有共产党就没有新中国，也就没有母校的今天，祝愿母校发扬光荣传统，进一步提高教学质量，办成有特色的、有优良作风的、高质量的、全国第一流的学校。

Chen Jingrun was obsessed with studies and nicknamed "bookworm" by his classmates. He often borrowed college textbooks like *Calculus, Physics, Harvard Lecture Notes, Introduction to Advanced Algebra* and *Practical Mechanics* from the school library. Among them *Calculus* was borrowed twice, showcasing Chen's passion for math. When Chen Jingrun entered Senior Two, he met Mr. Chen Jinhua, Chen Yinci's colleague and old classmate. Chen Jingrun often asked him questions in math and borrowed books from him. In Chen Jinhua's eyes, Chen Jingrun was far more than a "booker" as defined in some newspapers and magazines. When Chen Jingrun was leaving for Xiamen University, he said his farewell to Chen Jinhua in person. To celebrate the centenary of the Affiliated High School in 1981, Mr. Chen Jinhua managed the trip to Beijing to send an invitation letter to Chen Jinrun, who was already a celebrity by the time. But Chen Jingrun stayed a respectful student. When he saw his teacher off, he spoke to the bus driver, "This is my teacher, please help take care of him." When Chen Jinhua passed away in 1989, the mathematician, feeling sad for the loss, sent a message of mourning to his family.

It could be said that years at Anglo-Chinese College is a starting point for Academician Chen to set his trip in math. His story was so popular that when Xi Jinping, then Governor of Fujian Province, visited the Affiliated High School in 2002, he paid special attention to the statue of Chen Jingrun, besides the *Monument to the Martyr*s and the double-decker track-and-field stadium. The touching stories between Chen and his teachers have also been staged time after time, inspiring generations of students in a unique way. In the Teachers' Day Ceremony hosted by the Provincial Department of Education in 2010, the Affiliated High School was given the "Outstanding Contribution Award" for its poetry recitation performance *Chen Jingrun and His Teachers*. The performance also won the first place in the Fourth National Primary and Middle School Art Exhibition and Performance Event. In 2021, the performance was put on stage again in the school's 140th anniversary.

In 1981, Sheng Yuan and Chen Jingrun attended the 100th anniversary celebration of the Affiliated High School, and delivered passionate speeches. Chen recalled his unforgettable days studying here and expressed pride in the school's development. He believed it was the leadership of the Communist Party of China that made everything possible, without which the establishment of New China would be a faraway dream, not to mention the prospect of a school. He further extended his genuine wish that the alma mater would further promote its glory and rank among the nation's finest schools with its unique, distinctive and high-quality teaching.

1991 年，附中建校 110 周年校庆，陈景润阔别 10 年后再次回到家乡，专程参加了 110 周年校庆，时任省委书记陈光毅很关心陈景润的健康状况。10 月 4 日，时任福州市委书记的习近平、市长洪永世、市委副书记金能筹在于山宾馆会见了陈景润、高由禧等。习近平握着陈景润的手高兴地说："我们又见面了，欢迎你们，你们都是福州出去的大人才，对国家作出了很大贡献，为家乡争了光，家乡人民感谢你们。"陈景润感谢家乡的热情款待，他感慨地说："福州变化真大，真漂亮。"（陈国华，1991）

2001 年，附中 120 周年校庆时，举行了陈景润塑像和英烈碑落成揭幕典礼，陈景润夫人由昆携子参加了典礼。2021 年，附中 140 周年校庆时，落成了陈景润纪念馆。

陈景润铜像，2001 年建
The bronze statue of Chen Jingrun, built in
2001

Ten years later in 1991, Chen went back to Fuzhou for the school's 110th anniversary. Chen Guangyi, then Secretary of Fujian Provincial Party Committee, met Chen Jingrun and showed great concern over his health. On October 4th, then Municipal Party Secretary Xi Jinping, Mayor Hong Shuishi and Vice Municipal Party Secretary Jin Nengchou met Chen Jingrun, Gao Youxi and other outstanding alumni of the Affiliated High School in Yushan Hotel. Xi Jinping held Chen's hands and expressed his joy, saying, "I'm glad that we meet again, welcome back. You all are great talents growing in Fuzhou and making contributions to the whole nation. You have won honor for us Fuzhou people and we really appreciate that." Receiving the hospitality, Chen showed his gratitude. "So many changes have taken place in Fuzhou, and it has become even more beautiful," said Chen in delight.

When the Affiliated High School celebrated its 120th birthday in 2001, the inauguration ceremony for the statue of Chen Jingrun and the Monument to the Martyrs was held. Among the attendees were Chen's wife You Kun and their son. In 2021, in the school's 140th anniversary, the Memorial Hall of Chen Jingrun was inaugurated.

郭孔辉

郭孔辉院士，汽车工程专家，中国工程院首批院士，出生在福州仓山盖山镇郭宅村的一个华侨家庭。读初中时，"公民课"老师感慨中国落后挨打，认为中国需要民主与科学，让郭孔辉颇为触动。1949年新中国的诞生为国家带来了勃勃生机，郭孔辉看着到处张贴的"人民当家做主""建设新中国"等标语，再次回想起了"公民课"老师的话：坚定信念，要在这人民当家做主的时代，学科学，做"为祖国工业化作贡献的科学家"。郭孔辉从小成绩优秀，但由于受战争的影响，家里与远在马来西亚经商的父亲断了联系，失去了经济来源。福州又两次沦陷，致使郭孔辉两次失学。虽然他以异常的毅力跳级弥补失去的时间，但也造成了他数学基础的不扎实。到了初中，他的数学甚至需要补考，科学之梦遥遥。之后，因是华侨家庭，经历"土改"后家里经济更困难，差点辍学。开学两个月后，郭孔辉想起，学校在他们毕业时说，如果要继续留校念高中，交一笔留额金（保留学生名额）就行。郭孔辉马上跑到学校会计科，找他们退留额金。英华中学之前并未真正这样做过，但幸运的是，遇到的会计科老师曾经教过郭孔辉植物课，疼惜郭孔辉不能继续上学，出面和校长说情，给郭孔辉免半费续读。这样加上留额金，再加上母亲找人凑了一些钱，郭孔辉得以继续学习（葛帮宁，2020）。更加幸运的是，到英华念高中时，郭孔辉还遇到了优秀的老师。郭孔辉的自述里如此说：

我永远忘不了他们的名字。一位是教几何的老师——邵宗周，一位是教代数的老师——陈金华，他们的循循善诱，使我从害怕数学逐渐开始对数学发生了兴趣。老师们常常在课堂上提问让我回答，没想到我竟也开始受到老师的称赞甚至夸奖。那时，每堂数学课开始，老师总是用10～15分钟时间作一次测验，出一两道题目考大家一下，叫做"平常考"，下一次上课时发回卷子与成绩。这种"平常考"的成绩要与期终考试成绩相平均才是成绩单上的最终成绩。从高中的第二学期开始，我的"平常考"成绩常常都是100分。年轻人，越受夸越来劲，于是我开始热爱数学了。数学的突破又大大激发了我的学习劲头与信心，在高中毕业时，我竟然连续两学期都获小班第一名。（中国工程院科学道德建设委员会，2010：2）

Guo Konghui

Guo Konghui, an automotive engineering expert and one of the first academicians of the Chinese Academy of Engineering, was born in a family with overseas Chinese members in Guozhai Village, Gaishui Town, Cangshan District, Fuzhou. When he was a junior-high student, he was touched by his teacher's instruction that only democracy and science could relieve China of being backward and bullied. The founding of the P. R. C. in 1949 brought great vitality to all Chinese people. When Guo Konghui saw the slogans posted everywhere announcing that "The people are the masters of China" and boosting "to build a New China", the exhortation of his teacher "to hold fast to your belief, study sciences and make contributions to the industrialization of China" rang in his ears. Guo demonstrated his talent since childhood, but he dropped out of school twice, for his family couldn't finance his study because the war, the twice occupation of Fuzhou, cut them off from the father who was doing business in Malaysia. Although Guo skipped grades with extraordinary perseverance to make up for the lost time, he couldn't manage to lay a solid foundation in mathematics. In fact, his performance was so poor that he had to take make-up exams in maths in the junior middle school. His dream of becoming a scientist seemed far away. Subsequently, his family was confronted with more serious economic difficulties due to the land reform and its overseas connections, which almost forced him to leave off his study. Two months after the high school semester started, remembering that he had ever paid a retention fee for continuing the senior education in Anglo-Chinese College, Guo contacted the accounting department of the school, applying for a refund of the fee, which had never before happened in Anglo-Chinese College. It was a big turning point for Guo, as the staff member, who was extremely sympathetic to him and felt greatly sorry for such a talented student to drop off, interceded with the principal for charging him half the tuition. With the help, and the money borrowed from others by his mother, Guo was able to continue his study. More luckily, Guo met excellent teachers in Anglo-Chinese College. Guo said in his autobiography,

> I'll never forget their names. One of them is Shao Zongzhou, my geometry teacher; the other Chen Jinhua, my algebra teacher. It was their methodical and patient guidance that helped remove my fear of math and develop instead a love for it. They often asked me to answer questions in class. Unexpectedly, I began to receive praise from teachers. Every time before the math class began, the teacher usually spent 10 – 15 minutes testing us students with 1 or 2 exercise problems (which was called "routine tests") and we would get the exam papers and grades back at the next class period. The final score at the transcript would be the average of grades of "routine tests" and the final exam. From the second semester of high school, I frequently got full marks for routine tests. For this reason, I was praised increasingly by teachers and developed a passion for math. The breakthrough I made in math learning greatly stimulated my motivation and confidence. Before I graduated from the high school, I ranked first in academic performance in my class for two semesters in a row.

郭孔辉入学时，学校还是附中的前身英华中学，1952 年郭孔辉毕业时，英华已然并入附中，那时候叫"省福二中"，即福州第二中学。郭孔辉院士见证了附中从教会学校走向人民学校的过程，见证了附中一以贯之的优良教育，在新时代中继续前进。物理老师李正修也对郭孔辉产生过重要影响。李正修老师对郭孔辉院士如师如兄，他不仅课堂上有趣，还很关心学生，郭孔辉颇喜欢上他的课。此外，上一届学长陈德宜同学也带给他一定的影响。陈德宜学的是航空，暑假他带回了不少航模器材，领着包括郭孔辉在内的几个学弟搞设计、搞制作，进一步点燃了郭孔辉对航空的兴趣。因此，毕业时郭孔辉便报考了清华大学航空系，之后因为全国院系调整等各种因素，转了四个大学，改学汽车。凭着对科学的热爱和好钻研的精神，他迅速成长，成为中国科学院首批院士，为中国之富强作出了贡献。

张钹

张钹院士是福清人，计算机学家，首批人工智能专家之一，中国科学院院士，俄罗斯自然科学院外籍院士。张钹院士 1953 年毕业于附中，高考时，以数理化三科均满分的优异成绩考入清华大学电机系电机电器专业（王永利，2000）。

和郭孔辉相比，张钹院士的青少年比较顺利。出身书香门第，祖父、父亲都是文人，兄弟姐妹也很会读书。在这种家庭环境下，张钹从小就喜欢念书，不仅喜欢数理化，也喜欢文学，对音乐、绘画也有些兴趣。他的求知欲很强，做任何事情都喜欢争第一，精益求精，从小便立志要当像爱因斯坦那样的科学家。他在小学、初中、高中时的学习都很好，考试总是第一名。

Guo Konghui was admitted into the Anglo-Chinese College as a freshman, but graduated from Fuzhou No. 2 Middle School, which is now, as we all know, the Affiliated High School. He witnessed how the Affiliated High School was transformed from a church-owned school to a school of the people. It was lucky that not only the education of high quality continued during the transform, but also the new era brought vitality in which he was able to grow more vigorously. Li Zhengxiu, his physics teacher, had an important influence on Guo. He treated Guo kindly both as a teacher and a brother. Not only did he give interesting lectures but he cared for his students very much, so that Guo really liked to attend his classes. In addition, Chen Deyi, one of his senior fellow students, also exerted a positive impact on him. As an aviation major, Chen always brought back lots of aircraft models during summer vacations and guided his junior fellows, one of them Guo Konghui, to work out some designs, which further aroused Guo's interest in aviation. Therefore, upon graduation, Guo applied for the major of aviation of Tsinghua University. Afterwards, he was transferred to four different universities due to various factors such as the adjustment of colleges and departments across the country and finally changed his major to vehicle engineering. With strong aspiration and deep love for science and perseverance in studies, he has made great contributions to the prosperity and mightiness of China and become one of the first academicians of the Chinese Academy of Engineering.

Zhang Bo

Zhang Bo, a computer scientist, one of the first artificial-intelligence experts of China, academician of the Chinese Academy of Sciences, and foreign academician of the Russian Academy of Natural Sciences, is from Fuqing County. He graduated from the Affiliated High School of Fujian Normal University in 1953 and was admitted to the Department of Electrical Engineering of Tsinghua University as a major of electrical machines with full marks in three subjects of mathematics, physics and chemistry in the college entrance examination.

Compared with Guo Konghui, Zhang Bo enjoyed relatively smooth adolescent years. He was born in a scholarly family with his father and grandfather engaging in humanities and siblings doing well in studies. Cultivated by this family environment, Zhang has been enthusiastic about study since an early age. He has a strong thirst for knowledge, always strives for perfection in whatever he does and aspired to be a scientist like Einstein from childhood. His academic performance was exceptionally excellent throughout the years of primary and junior and senior high school.

1950 年，张钹从福清小镇考到福州读高中。他当时考了两个学校，一个是福一中，另一个是福州市高级工业职业学校，在两个学校都得了第一名。因为当时大家都比较喜欢职业学校，张钹就去了职业学校，但进去不久就发现职业学校的学习对他来说太浅了。于是在读了一个学期之后，他在一些老师的帮助下，改去英华中学读高中（王永利，2000）。张钹同样经历了附中从英华到福二中的过程，在学校期间，得到了许多老师的帮助，以优异的成绩毕业。高考时数学、物理、化学三门都是满分（郝静、佟静，2005）。

作为理工科专家，张钹院士非常强调不应忽视人文教育而"重理轻文"，认为人文教育对于提高人的素质很重要。张钹院士认为人文教育，包括中国传统文化教育、传统美德教育等都非常重要。他对中小学教育也非常重视，对曾经教过他的母校心怀感恩。他说："人们都说清华大学的学生聪明、优秀，清华因此享誉国内外。是清华的优秀老师培养了优秀的清华学生吗？不完全是。这很大程度上要归功于那些默默无闻的中小学教师！是他们，给名牌大学输送了一批又一批优秀的学生，输送了一个又一个将来可能会成为各行各业拔尖人才的学生！"（王永利，2000）前文所提的"思源亭"的亭名就是由郭孔辉院士和张钹院士书写的。其意义不言而喻。正是不忘母校的培养之情，张钹院士一直与母校保持密切联系。附中 130 周年校庆时，举行了隆重的院士广场揭幕仪式，张钹院士非常风趣地跑去和自己的塑像合影（练仁福，2011）。

除了院士之外，附中还有许多著名的社科经济学界校友和党政军警界校友，如"科技战线铁人"陈篪，著名经济学家陈岱孙，历史学家洪煨莲，女教育家余宝笙，翻译家萧乾，历史学家林耀华，社会主义学家高放，国际政治学家薛谋洪，博士研究生导师严书翰，福建省委书记陈明义，第一机械工业部副部长、新华通讯社香港分社副社长曹维廉，九三学社中央副主席陈抗甫等。各届成为社会发展主力与精英的校友更是数不胜数。

In 1950, Zhang registered for entrance examinations of two types of high school. One of them was Fuzhou No. 1 High School and the other one was Fuzhou Advanced Vocational School of Industries. He finished top in both exams and chose the latter as vocational schools were quite popular at that time. But soon he found that what he learnt in the vocational school was too easy for him so that he transferred to Anglo-Chiense College one semester later with the help of some teachers. Zhang also witnessed the process in which Anglo-Chinese College was merged into Fuzhou No. 2 Middle School. During high-school days, he received assistance from many teachers and graduated with honors. Impressively, he got full marks in three subjects of mathematics, physics and chemistry in the college entrance examination.

As an expert in science and engineering, Zhang especially emphasizes that liberal education shouldn't be ignored and that liberal education plays an important role in improving people's ideological qualities. Besides, he also stresses the significance of education on the traditional Chinese culture and traditional virtues. What's more, he attaches a lot of importance on the primary and secondary education and is very grateful to his alma mater where he gained lots of help and training. He once said, "People usually say that the students of Tsinghua University are smart and excellent so that Tsinghua University is famous both at home and abroad. However, is it all because of the excellent teachers of Tsinghua University that the students become so fantastic? Not exactly. To a large extent, the excellence of university students should be attributed to those unknown primary and secondary school teachers. It is they who cultivate a large number of outstanding students for the prestigious universities, who may become top-notch talents in all walks of life in the future. " It is thought-provoking for us to notice that the name of "Source-Worship Pavilion", which was mentioned in the "landscape" part, was written by Academicians Guo Konghui and Zhang Bo. Bearing firmly in mind the nurture and cultivation of this alma mater, Zhang Bo has kept close connections with the Affiliated High School. During the 130th anniversary of the Affiliated High School, a grand opening ceremony of Academician Square was held and Zhang Bo took a picture with the statue of himself happily.

Among its graduates one also finds many other luminaries, such as Chen Chi, the "iron man in the field of science and technology", famous economist Chen Daisun, historian Hong Xianlian, educator Yu Baosheng, translator Xiao Qian, historian Lin Yaohua, socialist scientist Gao Fang, international political scientist Xue Mouhong, doctoral supervisor Yan Shuhan, and Chen Mingyi, Secretary of Fujian Provincial Party Committee, Cao Weilian, Deputy Minister of the First Ministry of Machinery Industry and Vice President of the Hong Kong Branch of Xinhua News Agency, Chen Kangfu, Vice Chairman of the Central Committee of the Jiusan Society. Right now, large numbers of its alumni are playing crucial roles in different fields for the modernization of China.

● 办学成绩

附中自三校合并以来，取得了一系列成绩。1953 年 7 月，被省教育厅确定为首批 10 所省重点中学之一。附中不负众望，教学成果斐然。

1960 年，福建省教育厅厅长王于畊到附中检查工作时，鼓励附中赶超福州一中，这极大鼓舞了附中师生。1963 年 2 月，附中再次被福建省人民政府确定为 14 所首批办好的省重点中学之一。1965 年，附中实现了赶超福一中的目标，势头强劲。

1978 年，福建省革委会授予附中"福建省教育战线先进单位"荣誉称号。1978 年 4 月，附中被重新确定为 16 所首批办好的省重点中学之一。1979 年 5 月，附中被评为"全国学校体育卫生工作先进集体"；同年，附中还获得省革委会（省政府）颁发的"省社会义建设成绩优异嘉奖令"（李青藻，2021）。

由于附中一贯坚持的良好校风和优良的师资与教学，从 1977 年到 1980 年连续四届，高考上线率和高分率都居全省首位。1994 年被确认为省一级达标学校。2003 年，被省教育厅确认为省级首批示范性普通高中。之后，由于成绩突出，附中先后获得"宋庆龄少年儿童科技发明示范基地""五一先锋岗""全国青少年科技活动先进集体""福州市科普教育基地（素质教育基地）""福建省科技教育先进集体""福州市首届科技教育示范校""福建省青少年科技教育示范学校""科技基础性专项重大项目实验学校""福建省普通高中新课程实验样本校""全国青少年科技创新大赛科技教育创新十佳学校"等众多称号。2020 年被评为"全国文明校园"。2023 年，学校被确定为"新时代中小学校党建工作示范学校建设单位"。

• Achievements

The school prides itself on many achievements since the merger of three predecessors. In July 1953, it was identified as one of the first batch of 10 provincial key middle schools by the Provincial Department of Education. The Affiliated High School did live up to such expectations and achieved remarkable teaching results.

In 1960, when Wang Yuchen, then director of the Provincial Department of Education, was inspecting the school, he trusted the Affiliated High School with the prospect of competing with Fuzhou No. 1 Middle School, the top middle school in Fuzhou. The expectation greatly motivated the teachers and students of the school. In February 1963, the Affiliated High School was once again identified by the Fujian Provincial People's Government as one of the first batch of 14 provincial key middle schools. In 1965, the Affiliated High School was strong enough to compete with and even surpassed Fuzhou No. 1 Middle School.

In 1978, the Fujian Provincial Revolutionary Committee awarded the Affiliated High School the honorary title of "Advanced Unit in Fujian Education Front". In April 1978, the Affiliated High School was listed again as one of the first batch of 16 provincial key middle schools, and in May 1979, rated as the "national advanced unit in school physical health work"; It was also awarded by the provincial government for its "outstanding achievements in provincial socialist construction".

Equipped with qualified teachers and diligent students, the Affiliated High School ranked the top of Fujian Province in the college entrance examination admission rate and high grades rate for four consecutive years from 1977 to 1980. In 1994, it was recognized as a provincial level-one school. In 2003, it was recognized by the Provincial Department of Education as one of the first provincial level exemplary high schools. In the following years, due to its outstanding achievements, the affiliated high school has won the titles of "Song QingLing Demonstration Base of Children's Scientific and Technological Invention" "May Day Pioneer Post" "National Advanced Unit of Youth Scientific and Technological Activities" "Fuzhou Science Popularization Education Base (quality education base)" " Fujian Advanced Collective of Science and Technology Education" "The First Fuzhou Science and Technology Education Demonstration School" " Fujian Youth Science and Technology Education Demonstration School" "Experimental School for Major Projects of Science and Tecnology Foundation" "Experimental Sample High School of Fujian for New Curriculum" "Top Ten Schools of Science and Technology Education Innovation in the National Youth Science and Technology Innovation Competition" and many other titles. In 2020, the school was honored as a "National Model Civilized School". By 2023, it has been designated as a "Model Unit for Party Building in Primary and Secondary Schools in the New Era".

1988 年，附中开始组织学生参加国际奥林匹克学科竞赛。高三学生陈岩松在第 19 届国际物理学奥林匹克竞赛中荣获金牌，这是我国中学生首次在该项赛事中获得金牌。截至目前，附中学生已先后获得国际奥林匹克竞赛 8 枚金牌、5 枚银牌、1 枚铜牌，共 14 面奖牌，这在全省同类学校中是最多的。近年来，学校首创竞赛工作室制度，设立五学科竞赛工作室，组建竞赛教练"梦之队"，带领学生入围省赛、国赛，实现永不停歇的自我超越。

附中，走过漫漫百年，不停脱胎换骨，日益现代化，日益漂亮，也日益辉煌。它是无数校友心中引以为傲的精神家园，也是众多后起之秀梦想启航的起点。百年名校，风华正茂。福建师范大学附属中学将继续在传承与创新中前行，培养更多具备全球视野、家国情怀的时代英才，为国家和社会的发展贡献更多力量。

- **特别鸣谢**

冯玮老校长、吴建平老师、王焕蒲老师为本章提供了许多宝贵的资料，冯玮老校长接受了采访，并对本章进行详细修订，在此一并致以诚挚的感谢！

In 1988, Chen Yansong, a Senior 3 student of the school, won the gold medal in the 19th International Physics Olympiad. This was the first time that Chinese middle school students won the gold medal in this event. Since then, the school has won 14 medals, including 8 gold, 5 silver and 1 bronze, accounting for half of the medals of this kind won by all schools in Fujian. In recent years, the school has pioneered a competition studio system, establishing studios for five key subjects and forming a "Dream Team" of competition coaches, cultivating students to qualify for both provincial and national competitions.

With a history of more than 140 years, the affiliated high school has experienced countless transformations, becoming more modernized, more distinguished and more radiant over time. It serves as a cherished spiritual home for countless alumni and the launch pad for many aspiring young talents. As this prestigious institution celebrates its century-long legacy, it continues to flourish with vitality. Fujian Normal University Affiliated High School remains committed to forging ahead through a balance of tradition and innovation, aiming to cultivate future leaders with global perspectives and deep national pride, contributing to the development of the nation and society.

• Acknowledgements

Here, I wish to express my thanks to the former principal Feng Wei, former assistant principal Wang Huanpu and Mr. Wu Jianping, who have provided many valuable materials for this chapter. Former principal Feng Wei has accepted the interview and revised this chapter in detail. I would like to express my sincere thanks!

CHAPTER
SEVEN

从
私
立
华
南
女
子
文
理
学
院
到
福
建
华
南
女
子
职
业
学
院

From Hwa Nan Women's College of
Arts & Sciences to Fujian Hwa Nan
Women's Voc-Tech College

第七章
福

我于 2003 年开始在福建华南女子职业学院兼课至今，对华南这个百年老校的了解愈发深入。华南是个有故事的学校，有许多我敬佩的人。

● 我最钦佩的人——吴梅玉

话说当年有机会到华南女子职业学院当兼课老师的时候，我毫不犹豫就答应了，我最初是在吴梅玉主任的国际经济与贸易专业担任外聘大学英语老师。吴主任当时是位 70 来岁的退休老太太，她是影响我长期到女院来兼课的重要原因之一。她 1953 年毕业于福建农学院，1979—1985 年在福州二轻局下属的服装公司担任副经理。1985 年私立华南女子文理学院校友复办福建华南女子职业学院时，吴梅玉老师就参与到服装专业的筹备建设中，算得上是华南复办的元老了。2001 年，吴老师又负责筹建国际经济与贸易专业。她结合理论和实践，严格要求学生，注重培养应用型人才，70 多岁仍奋战在教学一线，重视自身知识学习，活到老，学到老。复办后新华南的余宝笙院长曾亲自宣布，吴梅玉老师虽然不是毕业于华南，但她一直为华南服务，就是华南校友（潘丽珍，2008：62）。吴老师之前在服装外贸行业，对于英语非常重视。如何提升女孩子们英语学习成效的话题成为我们交流和沟通的重中之重。她出生于香港，全家人除了她都在香港，可是梅玉老师坚守福州，甘于平淡，退休后一直在华南女院工作，每个月只领取 300 元工资达十多年，真的让人佩服。

I have been teaching and working part-time at Fujian Hwa Nan Women's Voc-Tech College since 2003. Two decades of participation facilitates my understanding towards this women's college in respect to its stories and people. In the process I have met many people whom I have come to admire greatly and I would like to present my experience and thoughts of these people to you. I will begin with Wu Meiyu.

• Wu Meiyu—One of the Ladies I Most Admire

Without the slightest hesitation, I welcomed the opportunity to become a part-time teacher in Fujian Hwa Nan Women's Voc-Tech College when the opportunity presented itself in 2003. I reported to Wu Meiyu—Chair of International Economy and Foreign Trade Department. English communication lessons were assigned to me. Ms. Wu was about seventy years old and she had just retired from her full-time job as manager of a clothing company in Foochow (now spelt as Fuzhou). In 1985, she became one of the first professionals that pioneered the rebirth of the original school now called Fujian Hwa Nan Women's Voc-Tech College. Originally she was the Chair of Clothing Department because of her rich experience in clothing and trade industry. She graduated from Fujian Agriculture College. As I worked with her my respect and admiration grew until I could proudly say she probably influenced me more than any other person at Hwa Nan. I grew to cherish my decision of working there. In 2001 she transferred to the Department of International Economy and Foreign Trade. Because of her vast working experience and theoretical underpinnings, she appreciated the importance of being strict with her students. This was quite different from other teachers at that time, and she valued developing students' skills with applied and practical applications. President Yu Baosheng declared in person that Ms. Wu was truly a Hwa Nan alumna and Hwa-Nanese because she kept serving Hwa Nan though she did not graduate from Hwa Nan. Ms. Wu worked in the clothing and trade industry for many years and fully appreciated the importance of English, so she laid enormously heavy emphasis on the mastery of English by her students. Frequently she would come to me for advice on how to improve their language skills. She was born in Hong Kong and all of her family members lived in Hong Kong except for her. Yet after her retirement, Ms. Wu kept working in Hwa Nan for decades and just got 300 RMB each month. Her enduring commitment to the school and devotion to the education of her students earned her undying admiration.

大家一起追忆往昔，特别是提到一起培养学生英语早读的习惯，提升学生英语水平的趣事；也谈及她自己从前的故事。吴老师读小学才从香港回到福州，主要是躲避打到香港的日本侵略军。由于她长期在福州对外服装贸易公司工作，具有丰富的服装贸易实际经验，又刚退休，所以复办的华南女院就盛情邀请她加入新华南建设。吴老师在华南女院从 1985 年一直工作到 2018 年近 90 岁。复办的华南女院一路走来，一直善于引进像吴梅玉这样有工作经验、有社会阅历的人共同致力于女子教育事业。

- ## 寻找程吕底亚

福州通商开埠于第一次鸦片战争后的 1844 年，是清末五口通商中最晚的，按《南京条约》所述："大皇帝恩准英国人民带同所属家眷，寄居大清沿海之广州、福州、厦门、宁波、上海等五处港口，贸易通商无碍；且大英国君主派设领事、管事等官住该五处城邑，专理商贾事宜，与各该地方官公文往来。"源自产茶区武夷山的闽江穿过福州城，直通马尾入东海，因而福州地理位置极其优越。深入中国内陆的外国人会或明或暗地出入于福州。它正好位居上海到广州漫长的海岸线中间，取道上下轻便自由。

We enjoyed good conversation about Hwa Nan challenges twenty years ago. We recalled how we started to assign early morning reading tasks for girls. She related her own life as an elementary school student in Fuzhou after leaving Hong Kong in order to escape from the Japanese invaders that had occupied Hong Kong. She was invited to join the rebuilding of Hwa Nan right after her retirement owing to her long term service in clothing and trade company. Ms. Wu kept working in Hwa Nan till 2018 at the age of ninety. Fujian Hwa Nan's success relied upon its ability to attract talented professionals like Ms. Wu with resourceful minds and vast working experience to build the new Hwa Nan in the image of old Hwa Nan.

• Search for the Trailblazer: Lydia Trimble

Fuzhou was made one of the five treaty ports to openly trade with the West in the late Qing Dynasty. In 1844, Fuzhou was the last of the five ports to open after the first Opium War. Article II of the *Treaty of Nanking* between Great Britain and Qing Dynasty of China elaborates the details: "His Majesty the Emperor of China agrees that British Subjects, with their families and establishments, shall be allowed to reside, for the purpose of carrying on their Mercantile pursuits, without molestation or restraint at the Cities and Towns of Canton, Amoy, Foochow-fu, Ningpo, and Shanghai, and Her Majesty the Queen of Great Britain, etc., will appoint Superintendents or Consular Officers, to reside at each of the above-named Cities or Towns, to be the medium of communication between the Chinese Authorities and the said Merchants, and to see that the just Duties and other Dues of the Chinese Government, hereafter provided for, are duly discharged by Her Britannic Majesty's Subjects." The Minjiang River winds its way from Wuyi Mountain which is abundant in tea and tea processing all the way through the city of Fuzhou, via Mawei port area to the East Sea of China. With its advantageous geographical location, Fuzhou is halfway between Shanghai and Canton. Throughout the history of China there have been many foreigners who went to China's inland to live or do business via Fuzhou port.

罗伯特·福琼在他 1853 年撰写的书——《两访中国茶乡（上篇）》中，描写了 1845 年他行至福州的所见所闻和感受。那时候中国男性还留着长辫子（福琼、敖雪岗，2015：190），叫外国人"番仔"（同上：193）。福州盛产铜锣、铜器、木材、铁器，银行业比其他城市发达，钱票在交易中使用比较多。比起北方各城镇的人，福州人看起来更活泼些，更接近广州人。在福州，吃牛肉甚至喝牛奶的人不在少数。福州妇女特别喜欢用花朵来装饰她们的发型。福琼到鼓山查看茶园，弄清楚了在英国喝的中国红茶和绿茶实际上产自同一种茶树。它们的颜色味道不同，是因为加工方式迥异，并非如当时大部分英国人想象的，红茶绿茶来自不同的茶树。荔枝、龙眼、李子、橄榄硕果累累，随处可见。仓山地区大量种植着芳香的茉莉花。彼时来榕的外国人不算多，但是外国游客对于福州根雕和青铜器很感兴趣。福州精美高雅的脱胎漆器售价昂贵（卢公明、陈泽平，2009：10）。

19 世纪末 20 世纪初，福州人对于洋枪、洋炮、洋货等十分熟悉。新式学堂、自来水、电报等新东西纷至沓来。最著名的电报学堂当属福建巡抚丁日昌于 1875 年设立的福州电报学堂。福州人叶景吕从 1907 年开始，连续 62 年每年到照相馆拍一张个人肖像照，被今人誉为"肖像帝"，说明当时在福州新技术很普遍。

程吕底亚 1863 年出生于加拿大，其父母皆为虔诚的基督徒，家有子女十人，程吕底亚排行第九。20 岁时，她随兄游学于爱荷华州，毕业于西佛尔师范大学，1889 年 12 月 19 日，受美以美女布道会德梅因支会派遣到中国福建，时年仅 26 岁（岳峰，2018：330）。经过在福州短期的语言学习，她开始了在华 50 余年的宣教办学的生涯，足迹遍布平潭、福清、莆田的广大农村。

In his book *Two Visits to the Tea Countries of China and the British Tea Plantations in the Himalaya* (1853), Robert Fortune described his 1845 trip to Fuzhou and recorded what he saw and felt about the city. During those days Chinese men still had a long braid or queue with head shaven, and the foreigners were named "Fan Zai" (nickname of foreigners). Abounding in gong, brassware, wood, and ironware, Fuzhou has a highly developed banking system, with paper currency in transactions in higher frequencies than that of any other Chinese cities. Fuzhou natives seemed more outgoing compared to people from northern towns. Fuzhou people bore a close resemblance to Guangzhou people in personality. It was not rare to see them eat beef or even drink milk. Fuzhou ladies were fond of wearing jasmine flower to decorate their hair. Fortune paid a visit to the tea garden of Drum Mountain just to find out that black tea and green tea consumed by British people were made from the same leaves of tree but with different processing methods. Black tea and green tea were not from different kinds of trees as most English imagined at that time. Fuzhou has been a fertile land teemed with succulent-fruits like lychee, Euphoria longan and Chinese olive. You could easily embark on an aromatic jasmine flower journey in Cangshan District. There weren't many foreigners in town at that time. However, the foreign tourists showed great interest in Fuzhou root carving and bronze art crafts. The bodiless lacquerware made by the Fuzhou native craftsmen would cost you arms and legs.

During the end of late nineteenth and early twentieth century, Fuzhou locals had become inured to foreign guns and cannons as well as imported products. New style schools and new-fangled things like tap water and telegram came in a throng. One of the most famous Fuzhou telegram schools was founded in 1875 by Ding Richang, the Fujian imperial inspector at the time. The Fuzhou native Ye Jinglv developed a strong interest in photography and took a self-portrait every year from 1907 to 1968. He was hailed as "The Emperor of Selfie" for his annual portraits which spanned 62 years. It also indicates that new-fangled things attracted attention and were prevalent in Fuzhou then.

In 1863, Lydia Trimble was born the ninth among the ten children to a devout Christian family in Canada. She followed her brother and travelled to Iowa at the age of 20 and graduated from the Iowa State Normal School at Cedar Falls, a teacher preparatory institution. On December 19, 1889, Lydia Trimble was only 26 when she arrived in Fujian, sent by the Des Moines branch of the Women's Foreign Missionary Society (WFMS). After a short period of language learning in Fuzhou, her over 50 years of career in China as an educator commenced as she began covering vast rural areas around Pingtan, Fuqing and Putian.

2009 年，我在新华南大学城新校区见到程吕底亚后人程闽岱（又译为程鲍勃）。据他自述，他是有中文名字的，发音近似"min-dai"，意思是"在福建的青色的山"，故而为"闽岱"。我曾询问过闽岱，他姑婆程吕底亚为何来到中国，他沉默未语，他儿子程高登说："这也是我很想搞明白的一个问题。"2019 年，我们到福建师范大学图书馆做真人图书馆项目时，又聊过这个话题。记得高登对我说，程吕底亚成长于美国女权运动的第一波浪潮时代，受女权主义领袖伊丽莎白·卡迪·斯坦顿和苏珊·B. 安东尼的影响。在她接受教育的时代，教材只有《圣经》。那时美国刚开始让女性接受高中至大学的教育，然而当时社会对于女性开放的职业寥寥无几。当程吕底亚了解到中国宣教的职业时，生性开放而好奇心满满的她就毅然决然地递交了申请。正如有位美国学者所表达的，在 19 世纪末 20 世纪初，美国社会为妇女所能提供的只有婚姻，以及图书馆员、教师等几个很少的职业，薪水低，几乎没有升迁机会，"……但海外差传工作为他们提供了独立、地位和事业的成就感。"（Eschbach，1993：37–38）

从 1889 年到 1901 年的 12 年间，程吕底亚一直行走在莆田、福清、平潭等地的渔村及田野乡间。她一到福州就马不停蹄地学习福州话、了解福州习俗。她遵循当时学习的惯例，把自己的姓 Trimble 向中文发音相似度上靠近，翻译成中文里的"程"姓，名字 Lydia 依照发音译为汉语"吕底亚"，故而她有了"程吕底亚"的中文名字。她家后人程闽岱传承此姓，建立"程氏基金"，以印有"程"字的信笺沟通，自费出版《程氏男孩》（程闽岱：2007）个人传记书。

In 2009, I met Cheng Min-dai (Mr. Bob Trimble, a. k. a. Cheng Baobo) in the International Faculty House of Fujian Hwa Nan Women's Voc-Tech College campus in the University Town. Later he said he had a Chinese name with the pronunciation sound similar to "min-dai", which means "green mountain in Fujian". As a child he had met and still had vivid memories of Lydia Trimble. I asked him why his grand aunt journeyed to China. He became very still, and his son Gordon after a while said: "This is also a question I'm exploring." In 2019, when we worked on a Living Library project in Fujian Normal University, we talked about this topic again. I remember what Gordon told me. He said Lydia Trimble grew up in the first wave of feminism in America and was deeply influenced by prominent feminist leaders like Elizabeth Cady Stanton and Susan B. Anthony. However, on the farm when she grew up the only book was the Bible and that was what children learned to read. At that time, the United States of America was just beginning to allow women to receive a formal education from high school to college, and there were very few careers available to women in society. When Lydia Trimble got to know about the job of missionary in China, as an open-minded woman that was full of curiosity, she resolutely submitted her application. Just as an American scholar stated, at the end of the 19th century and the beginning of the 20th century, what the American society could offer women were only marriage and a few occupations such as librarian and teacher, all with low salaries and little chance of promotion, "... However, oversea missions provided them with independence, social status and a sense of achievement in career."

For 12 years from 1889 to 1901, Lydia Trimble trekked across the fields and fishing villages of Putian, Fuqing and Pingtan. Upon her arrival in Fuzhou in 1889, she focused her efforts on learning Fuzhou dialect and understanding its customs. She followed the practice of learning at that time, and translated her surname Trimble to the Chinese surname "Cheng" with similarities in pronunciation. Her first name Lydia was translated into Chinese "Lvdiya" according to the pronunciation. Thus she had a complete Chinese name "Cheng Lvdiya". Her descendant Bob Trimble inherited this surname and set up The Trimble Foundation, where they communicate through letters with the Chinese character "Cheng" on it, and published at his own expense an autobiography *The Trimble Boys*.

程吕底亚在八闽大地行走过程中，与莆田、福清和平潭的女性深入接触。有几件事情让程吕底亚深感震撼，促使她下定决心留下。一是看到女性需要缠足，年纪大的婆婆因此走路颤颤巍巍，无法健步如飞但得操持家事；小姑娘被迫缠足，否则以后无法嫁人。虽然在中华民国建立后的 1912 年缠足被禁，但是在不少边远区域，这种做法仍然长久地存续着。二是看到负担全家生计的妇女任劳任怨，看到中国妇女们的温柔、韧性、坚毅和刚强。程吕底亚自己也是女性接受教育的受益者，自然了解教育对于女子的影响。在传教工作中，她尤其重视女子教育事业（朱峰，2002：43）。虽然彼时美国女权运动正风起云涌，但是同时期的福建乡间妇女却需要缠足。有的人家里的男人吸食鸦片，妇女根本没有受教育的机会，精神力量匮乏，情况之紧急可以想见。

程吕底亚"一朝醒来时，她竟然既不会讲英文，又不能说福建话。她的中国同工非常担心，经过一天休息后，她才恢复语言能力……"（朱峰，2002：70）。在农村与女性沟通、交流和宣教的过程中，程吕底亚历经千辛万苦，但她坚信，女子教育极其重要，她逐步创立了福清毓贞女校和平潭毓贤女校。她认为："中国妇女完全有受教育的权利。"

到 1900 年底，她已经觉得："只要有人关心中国的女孩和青年，没有什么是她们办不到的，我很愿意告诉她们五个字：'我能，且我会'。接着的问题是，为什么这些女孩不能同男孩子一样享受大学教育的权利。我萌生了建立女子大学的念头，要在福州建所女子大学。中国的女孩子应该和美国女孩一样，享有完整的大学教育。"（朱峰，2002：70）彼时美国第一所女校于 1836 年刚刚建立，距离程吕底亚在福建八闽大地宣教和建校才半个世纪。

While walking through the land of Fujian Eight Min (Eight Min means 8 administrative districts of the province), Lydia had built up deep connections with women in Putian. Fuqing and Pingtan. Several things deeply touched Lydia Trimble and made her decide to stay. First, she saw that the sisters needed to bind their feet. Old ladies walked tremblingly because of this. They were unable to walk fast, but still had to do the housework; little girls were forced to bind their feet or they would be rejected in marriage in the future. Although foot-binding was banned in 1912 after the establishment of the Republic of China, this practice persisted in more remote areas. Second, she saw the Chinese women had to bear the burden of providing livelihood for the entire family by working tirelessly without any complaint, and she could not help but feel their tenderness, tenacity, perseverance and unyieldingness. Lydia had also benefited from an early American women education, and she naturally understood the impact of education on women. In her missionary work, she paid special attention to women's education. Although the feminist movement in America was in full swing at that time, women in rural areas of Fujian still bound their feet; some men in their families smoked opium, leaving no opportunity for the women to receive education, and they lacked spiritual strength. It was a most dire situation.

Lydia felt the immensity of her task until one morning when she woke up, she could neither speak English nor Fujian dialect. Her Chinese co-workers were acutely worried, and she finally regained her language ability after a day's rest. In the process of communicating, exchanging and preaching with women in rural areas, Lydia went through untold hardships, but she firmly believed that women's education was extremely important, and she gradually established Fuqing Yuzhen Girls' School (being named "Fuqing No. 2 Middle School" now) and Pingtan Yuxian Girls' School (it developed into Pingtan Experimental Primary school and Pingtan No. 1 Middle School). She believed that "Chinese women have every right to be educated".

By the end of 1900 Lydia's direction and purpose had evolved with her success in promoting the education of women. She said, "as long as someone cares about the girls and youth in China, there is nothing they can't do. I began telling them five simple words: 'I can, and I will.' I endlessly pondered why these girls could not enjoy the same rights of university education as the boys. Chinese girls should have the same rights as American girls to receive college education." Concurrently, Wesleyan Academy, the first girls' school in the United States of America, was established in 1836 which was half a century before Lydia Trimble preached and established girls' schools in the land of Eight Min, Fujian.

走过福清的田埂稻间，越过平潭的山水农田，穿过莆田的村庄农舍，在广袤沿海附近的渔村村庄，她先后兴办了福清毓贞女塾等 6 所女子中学，这便是程吕底亚 12 年疾走的成果。

1889 年，程吕底亚抵达福州学了一些基本的福州话后，立马被安排到离福州 70 余公里的福清龙田开展工作。1890 年，她在龙田建立了第一所女子寄宿学校——毓贞女塾。在早期的岁月里，只有程吕底亚一个人，她四处找地址建学校、开班、招生、与家长谈话、与女孩子私聊、进行公共演讲。她被村里人称为程师姑，直到最后有三个新传教士到来，程师姑才得以解脱，去开创新的局面。1905—1906 年，她在靠近台湾海峡的平潭建立了一所女子学校。（朱峰王、爱菊，2005：4）进入 21 世纪，福清龙田中心小学、福清二中、平潭实验小学以及平潭一中等几所学校，在其校庆之时，均承认程师姑是其学校的创始人。正是因为这种渊源，程吕底亚的后人程高登与这几所学校发生了新的互动和连接，开启了中美民间教育和文化交流的新篇章。

1901 年 7 月，程吕底亚经上海返回美国爱荷华州晨边学院进修。她这次从中国返回美国的另一个原因是身体有恙，急需返美医治休养。在美国求学休养的程吕底亚，还密切关注与中国，特别是福州教育发展相关联的会议，并热情参与其中。1903 年秋，程吕底亚参加美以美女布道会在美国爱荷华州召开的会议，她在会上倡议在华南建立女子大学。（朱峰，2002：71；汪征鲁，2007：58）到了第二年，在福清龙田创建过女子寄宿学校的程吕底亚参加了美以美会在洛杉矶召开的总议会会议。会议达成两项决议，一是在福州建立一所女子大学，二是由程吕底亚、柏森和威尔逊三人负责办女子大学的前期准备。（朱峰、王爱菊，2005：4－5）

Stepping along the ridges on rice paddies of Fuqing, walking over the terraces in the mountains of Pingtan, passing through the village farmhouses in Putian, she had successively established six girls' middle schools including Fuqing Yuzhen School in the fishing villages near the vast coast. These were the achievements of Lydia's first 12 years of dedicated engagement.

In 1889, as soon as Lydia Trimble arrived in Fuzhou and learned some basic Fuzhou dialect, she was immediately assigned to work in Longtian, Fuqing, which was more than 70 kilometers away from Fuzhou. In 1890, she founded the first girls' boarding school in Longtian, the Yuzhen Girls' School. In the early days, Lydia was the only one that was working on the founding of schools. She went around looking for locations to build schools, starting classes, recruiting students, talking to parents, privately chatting with girls, and even giving public speeches. It was not until three new missionaries finally arrived that she was relieved and came to create a new situation. In 1905 – 1906, she founded a girls' school in Pingtan, near the Taiwan Strait. When it comes to 21st century, Fuqing Longtian Central Primary School, Fuqing No. 2 Middle School, Pingtan Experimental Primary School, and Pingtan No. 1 Middle School all recognized Lydia Trimble as the founder during their school anniversary celebrations. It is because of this close relation that Gordon Trimble, the descendant of Lydia Trimble, has initiated a new interaction and connection with these schools, opening a new chapter of educational and cultural exchanges between Chinese people and American people.

In July 1901, Lydia returned to Morningside College in the State of Iowa of the USA via Shanghai for further studies. Another reason why she left China this time was because she suffered from an illness and needed to return for medical treatment. While studying and recuperating in America, Lydia was still paying close attention to conferences related to the development of education in China, especially Fuzhou, and participated enthusiastically in these conferences. In the autumn of 1903, Lydia Trimble attended the Methodist Episcopal Church Women's Evangelism Fellowship meeting in Iowa, USA, where she initiated the founding of a women's college in southern China. The next year, Lydia Trimble, who had founded a girls' boarding school in Longtian, Fuqing, attended the General Synod Meeting of the Methodist Episcopal Church in Los Angeles. In this meeting two issues were resolved, one was to establish a women's college in Fuzhou, and the other was that Lydia, Bosen and Wilson would be responsible for the preliminary preparations for the founding of this women's college.

1904 年 10 月，曾任俄亥俄州卫斯理安大学校长多年、时任美以美会会督的柏锡福抵榕，与上述三人负责组商议后，成立了 12 人临时校董会，柏锡福任主席。正是在那一年，中国著名的宋氏三姐妹中的大姐——15 岁的宋霭龄，乘坐由上海开往美国的"高丽号"轮船，经过一个多月的航行到达美国佐治亚州的卫斯理安大学女子学院留学。可见当时中美之间的人际沟通、留学交往已然成风。只不过当时的境况是，中国只有极少数出生于富裕家庭的孩子才有可能到美国留学，而中国女子在本土受教育之希望才刚刚开始萌芽。

1907 年，董事部在福州正式成立，开设四年制的中学班和师范班，命名为南省华英女书院。同年，校董会收到首笔捐款，是来自美国洛杉矶的商人彭恩先生为纪念女儿而捐献的 15 000 美金。学校首座筹建的行政大楼——"彭氏楼"便是以彭恩先生的姓命名的。（朱峰、王爱菊，2005：6）

另外，美以美会为纪念劳拉·谷莲夫人而募捐到 10 000 美元。华南为纪念该善举，将宿舍楼命名为"谷莲楼"。（朱峰、王爱菊，2005：6）

1908 年，华南女子大学预科班开学了，程吕底亚是首任校长。但她真是个"四无"校长：无学生，无校舍，无教员，无经费。办学条件是如此艰难，程吕底亚一无所有，她不得不向"没有"借东西，校舍就是从福州毓英女校租借过来的。在女子教育不受重视的年代，华南女校的预科首批招收到 13 人实属不易。程吕底亚奔波走访，与家长族长费尽口舌，与当事人——学生们一个一个地聊，一遍一遍地说。她克服和跨越了"女子不如男""女子无才便是德"的千年传统障碍，让华南女子大学这颗种子在福州仓山的藤山之巅、闽江江畔生根发芽。后来的华南以及华南校友复办的新华南，连同把华南看作前身校之一的福建师范大学，均视 1908 年为华南的建校元年。

In October 1904, Dr. James W. Bashford, who had been the president of Ohio Wesleyan University for many years and the bishop of the Methodist Episcopal Church, arrived in Fuzhou and discussed with the preparatory team consisting of the above-mentioned three responsible persons. Later on, an interim school board with 12 members was established, and Dr. Bashford become its chairman. It was right in that year that 15-year-old Soong Ai-ling, the eldest of the famous Soong sisters in China, took the "Korea" ship bound for the USA from Shanghai, and arrived at Wesleyan College at Macon, Georgia for studying after a voyage of more than one month. This indicates that the interpersonal communication, overseas study and exchange between countries had become common at that time. However, the fact was that only a very small number of young people in China that were born to wealthy families could study in the USA, while the hope of Chinese women being educated domestically just began to emerge.

In 1907, the school board was formally established in Fuzhou. The initial name of school was the Woman's College of South China. It had a four-year middle school class and a normal class. The school board had received the first donation in the sum of $15,000 from Mr. Payne, a businessman from Los Angeles, USA, in memory of his daughter. The school's first administrative building, "Payne Hall", was named after Mr. Payne.

In addition, another gift of $10,000 was made by the Women's Foreign Missionary Society of Methodist in memory of Mrs. Laura Cranston, and the money was used for a dormitory later called the Laura Cranston Hall.

In 1908, the Preparatory of Foochow Women's College started. Lydia Trimble was the first principal, but she was really a "four no" principal with no student, no school building, no teacher, and no funds. The conditions were so difficult that Lydia had literally nothing, and she had to borrow things from "nothingness". A school building was rented from Foochow Uk Ing Girls' School. In those years when women's education was not taken seriously, it was not easy for them to enroll the first group of 13 students in the Preparatory. Lydia ran around and paid many visits. She spent considerable time talking with the parents and patriarch, as well as persuading the students one by one, over and over again. She overcame the obstacles caused by traditions of thousands of years that "women are not as good as men" and "lack of talent in a woman is a virtue". Lydia enabled the seed of Hwa Nan Women's College to take root and sprout on the top of Tengshan Mountain in Cangshan, Fuzhou, by the Minjiang River. Hwa Nan later on, as well as new Hwa Nan that was re-established by Hwa Nan alumnae, and Fujian Normal University which regarded Hwa Nan as one of its predecessors all regard 1908 as the year Hwa Nan was founded.

但是，华南校舍的建设荆棘载途，从砖瓦石墙、校内设备、装修设计、工人工钱，到教师薪资等等都急需费用。程吕底亚一边要上课教导学生，一边要负责正在建设的学校，她不得不在学校、工地两头跑，每天要解决无数问题。"当时校舍建筑了一年，因经费告乏而停顿，后来还是创办人程师姑的哥哥将他美国住宅出卖，所得的房金寄到中国来，方使校舍落成。以后不知经过多少艰难困苦，而前任校长程师姑，卒以百折不挠的精神，打破难关，至终将女子最高深教育的根基奠定在华南。"（唐尚凯，1941：7）

1911 年 12 月 12 日，学校行政楼——"彭氏楼"举行奠基仪式。如前所述，这栋楼的命名有着彭恩先生为纪念其女的故事。1914 年秋，全校师生迁入彭氏楼和谷莲楼，并开始招收两年制新生。1916 年，董事会将华英女子学堂正式改为"华南女子大学"（汪征鲁，2007：61）。表 7-1 展示了华南的名称及其沿袭变革。

表 7-1　华南女子文理学院名称及其沿袭变革

时间	学校名称	时间	学校名称
1907 年	南省华英女书院	1933 年	私立华南女子文理学院
1908 年	华英女子学堂	1951 年	福州大学（私立华南女子文理学院与私立福建协和大学合并）
1914 年	华南女子大学		
1916 年	南省华英女书院/福建华南女子学院	1953 年	福建师范学院
		1972 年至今	福建师范大学
1924 年	华南女子文理学院	1984 年至今	福建华南女子职业学院

根据汪征鲁主编的《福建师范大学校史》，1917 年，华南开始按照美国学制招收 4 年制学生，首届招到包括王世静在内的 5 名学生，以英文课程为主；1921 年，3 位学生毕业并获得大学文凭。

However, the construction of the school building in Hwa Nan still had a long way to go. From bricks and stone walls, school equipment, decoration and design, workers' payments, to teachers' salaries, there was an urgent need for funds. Lydia Trimble was responsible for both teaching the children who were studying, and overseeing the school construction. She had to run between the classes and the construction site, solving countless problems every day. "At that time the construction of the school building lasted for a year, then stopped due to lack of funds. After that, it was the elder brother of the founder Cheng Su-koo who mortgaged his farm in the USA and sent the money to China for the completion of the school building. The former principal Cheng Su-koo fought with an indomitable spirit for breaking through the barriers, and finally laid the foundation of the most advanced education for women in Hwa Nan (South China). "

On December 12, 1911, the foundation stone laying ceremony was held for the school's administrative building, "Payne Hall". As mentioned above, the story behind the name of the building was about the generous donation of Mr. Payne in memory of his daughter. In the autumn of 1914, the teachers and students of the school moved into Payne Hall and Cranston Hall, and the recruiting of two-year freshmen had begun. In 1916, the board of directors officially changed the name Huaying Women's College to "Hwa Nan Women's College". Table7 – 1 is a list of the names of Hwa Nan and how it changed over time.

Table 7 – 1　Summary of lineages and changes in the name of Hwa Nan Women's College of Arts & Sciences

Time	Name of School	Time	Name of School
1907	The Woman's College of South China	1933	Hwa Nan Women's College of Arts & Science
1908	The Preparatory of Foochow Women's College	1951	Fuzhou University (Hwa Nan Women's College of Arts & Sciences merged with Fukien Christian University)
1914	Hwa Nan College		
1916	The Woman's College of South China/Fujian Hwa Nan Women's College	1953	Fujian Normal University
		From 1972 to now	Fujian Normal University
1924	Hwa Nan Women's College of Arts & Science	From 1984 to now	Fujian Hwa Nan Women's Voc-Tech College

According to *the History of Fujian Normal University* edited by Wang Zhenglu, Hwa Nan began to recruit 4-year students based on the American academic system in 1917. In the first year, five students including Lucy Wang were recruited. The courses were taught primarily in English. In 1921, three students graduated with a college diploma.

1922 年 9 月 28 日是福建华南女大历史上第一个转折点（朱峰，2002：75）。华南获得了美国纽约州立大学临时特许证，学生毕业可同时获得纽约州立大学文凭，并且可以直升研究所进一步学习（岳峰，2018：333）。时任纽约州立大学副校长阿尔伯特·穆特在贺信上说："（该校）目前办理的情形以及教育的计划，都能使人满意。根据女士所条陈意见，和该校所设立的学科，足见主持该校教育的人，实属眼光长远，思想前进，其所栽培之中国女子将来必能应付一切问题与责任，不失为妇女领袖的地位。"（朱峰，2002：76）

这一年，深具历史纪念意义的"立雪楼"动工了，该楼是为了纪念程吕底亚建校功绩而命名的。1925 年，这座新宿舍楼大楼建成，起初被命名为"程吕底亚楼"，后称"立雪楼"。从"程吕底亚楼"到"立雪楼"之间隔了一个中国古成语"程门立雪"。"立雪楼"这一名字含蓄、有文化，富有人情味。程吕底亚在自己 Trimble 的姓氏基础上取了发音相似中国"程"的姓氏。如前所述，她家族后人的中国姓名均用这个"程"姓。

但凡在中国受过教育的人都懂得"程门立雪"这个成语是用来形容尊师重道、恭敬受教的，可见当时的人们用"立雪楼"来表达尊重爱戴程吕底亚的深情厚谊。后来华南并入福建师范大学，成为师大前身校之一后，"立雪楼"改为"和平楼"则见证了时代的境况和要求。20 年前，我从江西引进到福建时，第一次去福建师范大学行政部门报到，就是在位于和平楼（原名立雪楼-程吕底亚楼）的人事处。记得当时踏上楼梯可听到木板被踩的咚咚回音，满满的历史厚重感。当时大家称之为师大校部，因为具体教学楼在隔壁的校园里。那时的我无论如何也不会预测到，今生今世我会见证三个 Trimble Hall 的来龙去脉。

September 28, 1922 has been the first turning point in the history of Hwa Nan Women's College. Hwa Nan obtained a provisional license from the State University of New York, which is to say, students earned a diploma from the State University of New York at the same time of their graduation from Hwa Nan, and thus went directly to the graduate school of the University for further study as well. Albert Moot, Vice President of the State University of New York at that time, wrote in his congratulatory letter: "The current situation (of the college) and the education plan are satisfactory. Based on the comments made by Madame and the disciplines established by the college, the person in charge of the academic affairs of college has a long-term vision and advanced thinking. The Chinese women educated in this college will be able to cope with all problems and responsibilities in the future, they will be accepted as women leaders."

In this year, the construction of the historic "Lixue Hall" started, which was named to commemorate Lydia's achievements in founding the school. This new dormitory building, which was completed in 1925, was originally called "Lydia A. Trimble Hall" and later "Lixue Hall". From "Lydia A. Trimble Hall" to "Lixue Hall", there is an ancient Chinese idiom "Cheng Men Li Xue" (Standing in the snow before Cheng Yi's gate, from a story in the Song Dynasty). The name of "Lixue Hall" is subtle, cultural and humane. Lydia Trimble took a Chinese surname "Cheng", which is similar to Trimble in pronunciation. As mentioned above, her descendants also use this surname "Cheng" as their Chinese surname.

Those who are educated in China know that the idiom "Cheng Men Li Xue" is used to describe those who respect teachers and learn reverently. People at that time used "Lixue Hall" to express their respect and love for Lydia Trimble. After Hwa Nan was merged into Fujian Normal University and became one of its predecessor schools, the "Lixue Hall" was changed to "Heping Hall" (Heping means Peace in Chinese), which witnessed the circumstances and requirements of the times. Twenty years ago, when I transferred to Fujian from Jiangxi, the first place I went to register my attendance with the administrative department of Fujian Normal University was its personnel office in Heping Hall (formerly known as Lixue Hall—Lydia A. Trimble Hall). I remember that when I stepped on the stairs, I could hear the echoes in the wooden boards, which were full of strong senses of history. At that time, everyone called it the administration hall of the Normal University, because the teaching buildings were in the neighboring campus. I would never have predicted back then that I would witness the ins and outs of three Trimble Halls in my lifetime.

• 三个 Trimble Hall

如果你足够心细并且对于老仓山有一定的历史背景知识，是可以在师大老校区校部找到刻有 TRIMBLE HALL 字样的大楼的。在老校区上课时，我总喜欢鼓励十几位学生同时去寻觅那几个字，通常只有四分之一的学生能找到。这座建于百年前的校舍承载了太多的历史信息量，新中国成立前一直是私立华南女子文理学院的校舍。1951 年由政府接管，合并了福建协和大学等诸多的高校，先后被命名为福州大学、福建师范学院，1972 年改称福建师范大学至今。因为这座建筑的风格是中西结合，历史悠久，2008 年《福州市区优秀近现代建筑保护规划》收录了该建筑，一年后仓山区将之列为文物保护单位，2013 年被列为福建省文物保护单位。这座建筑能保留下来实属不易，20 世纪 90 年代三县洲大桥修建时为了直通，原本计划要摧毁这座楼，好在福建师大历史系教授们懂得它的历史价值，联名请求绕开此楼修桥，最终此楼得以保留完好。

: 高登父子在 Trimble Hall 合影
: The Trimbles visiting Trimble Hall

程吕底亚宿舍位于东侧楼，俗称程氏楼，源于汉语成语程门立雪的典故，一度被人们称为立雪楼，现名和平楼。20 世纪 80 年代，程闽岱和程高登父子首次见到该楼时欣喜若狂，留下了合影。这几个刻有 TRIMBLE HALL 字样的石碑是他们家先人在此耕耘工作的见证。这是与程氏家族有深交的学校必定会去拜访的地方，程吕底亚在此住过，这座楼也见证了她临终的岁月。

第二个程吕底亚楼字样位于由华南女子文理学院老校友于 1985 年复办的新华南在旗山新校区的行政楼，是为了纪念首任校长以及程氏家族对学校的长期资助。

第三个程吕底亚楼我早有耳闻，一直盼望能目睹。它位于美国普吉湾大学，在西雅图附近的塔科马市，而塔科马与福州是友好姐妹城。2011 年，福州派出 4 名技工到塔科马，花了 6 周时间，顺利在华人协和公园里建成了象征友谊的标志性建筑"福州亭"。

Scan for more
扫码了解更多

• Three Short Stories of Trimble Hall

If you are careful enough and have some historical background knowledge about old Cangshan, you can't miss the building engraved with the words TRIMBLE HALL on it in the old campus of Fujian Normal University. When giving classes on the old campus, I always liked to encourage more than a dozen students in each class to look for those words, and usually only a quarter of the students managed to spot them. This school building, constructed a hundred years ago, carries tomes of historical information with it. Before the founding of the P. R. C. , it was the school building of the private Hwa Nan Women's College of Arts & Sciences. The college was taken over by the government in 1951 and merged with Fukien Christian University and many other colleges and universities in Fuzhou. It has been given the names of Fuzhou University and Fujian Teachers College, and finally Fujian Normal University. Because this building's architecture combines Chinese and Western styles and has a long history, it was included in the "Fuzhou District Outstanding Modern Architecture Protection Plan" in 2008. A year later, Cangshan District classified the building as a cultural relics protection unit, and in 2013 it was classified as Fujian Provincial cultural relics protection unit. As a matter of fact, it was not easy to preserve this building. In the 1990s, when the Sanxianzhou Bridge nearby was to be built, the initial plan was to destroy this building for a straighter and cheaper approach. Fortunately, the professors of the History Department of Fujian Normal University were aware of its historical value and requested that the bridge bypass the building. The building was preserved well in the end.

Commonly known as Trimble Hall, Lydia A. Trimble Hall is located in the east. For a time it was called Lixue Hall, a name originated from the Chinese idiom Cheng Men Li Xue (Standing in the snow before Cheng Yi's gate). In 1989, Bob and Gordon Trimble were overjoyed when they saw Trimble Hall for the first time and took a photo of it. This stone tablet with the words Trimble Hall was the testimony of their elders' hard work here. This is a place where schools in close relationship with the Trimble family will definitely visit. Lydia Trimble lived here, and this hall also witnessed her last years.

The second Trimble Hall is the administrative building of the new Hwa Nan on its new campus in Qishan. The new Hwa Nan was re-established by the alumnae of Hwa Nan Women's College of Arts & Sciences in 1985. This name of building commemorates its namesake's first president and the Trimble family's long-term support to the college.

I had heard about the third Trimble Hall and had been looking forward to seeing it with my own eyes. It is located at the University of Puget Sound, in Tacoma near Seattle, USA. Tacoma and Fuzhou are sister cities. In 2011, Fuzhou sent four technical workers to Tacoma, and it took six weeks for them to build the landmark building "Foochow Pavilion" in the Chinese Reconciliation Park as a symbol of mutual friendship.

2020 年，我作为福建师范大学的访问学者赴塔科马，不仅有幸看到了"福州亭"，出入普吉湾大学的 Trimble Hall，而且还宿于其内之套房——Trimble Suite。为什么塔科马有 Trimble Hall 和 Trimble Suite 呢？原来程闽岱出生于福建古田，他父亲程嘉尼在南平当医生，所以闽岱在南平度过童年时期。记得 2009 年他 94 岁来福州期间，我们与他一起去南平寻根，他说记得小时候常常乘船，通过水路闽江往来于南平和福州之间。他告诉我们坐船一般要花上一周时间，他甚至记得南平的闽赣古道——三千八百坎古道；他还告诉我们，从福州到鼓岭要走六到八个小时。他会说一口流利的福州话，爱吃光饼，爱打乒乓球，12 岁的时候才回到美国，对福建有很深的故乡情怀。他们全家回到美国后，闽岱的父亲程嘉尼在塔科马的普吉湾大学担任校医，程闽岱后来毕业于普吉湾大学化学专业。作为校友，他捐资赞助了母校普吉湾大学 Trimble Hall 的建设。这座大楼的 Trimble Suite 里面，家具材质上乘，装修精美，从办公桌、五斗橱到床都是由从中国购置的上等檀香木制成。我住在里面倍感温暖亲切。

经过多年努力和探索，我终于寻访并记录下福州、塔科马两地三个 Trimble Hall，并深刻了解其中的来龙去脉，甚感欣慰。

● 程吕底亚来华 50 年纪念

由于受到封建思想的束缚，当时很多家庭不让女孩外出读书（朱峰，2002）。从 1908 年程吕底亚首任校长时华南女子大学预科班的 13 人，到 1917 年华南开始按照美国学制招收 4 年制的 5 名学生，再到 1923 年华南学生增加到 63 人，1926 年增加到 87 人，这些数字的逐步变化说明了当时工作的艰难和成效。

1925 年 1 月，程吕底亚不再是华南校长，"她从华南女子大学校长任上引退"后继续传教布道 16 年，直至 1941 年逝世于立雪楼，享年 78 岁。谢必震在 2008 年《图说华南女子学院》中提到年逾花甲的她引退了校长一职，而岳峰 2018 年的《春色任天涯》也用了"引退"字样。

In 2020, when I went to Tacoma as a visiting scholar of Fujian Normal University, it was lucky for me to not only see the "Fuzhou Pavilion", frequent the Trimble Hall of the University of Puget Sound, but also live inside a suite in the dormitory—Trimble Suite. Why are there Trimble Hall and Trimble Suite in Tacoma? It turned out that Cheng Mindai (Robert A. Trimble) was born in Gutian, Fujian, and his father—Dr. Charles Garnet Trimble was a doctor in Nanping, so Mindai spent his childhood in Nanping. I remember that when he came to Fuzhou in 2009 at the age of 94, we went to Nanping with him to rediscover his roots. He said that when he was a child, he used to take a boat to travel between Nanping and Fuzhou along the Minjiang River. He told us that it took a week to travel by boat. He even kept in memory the ancient Fujian-Jiangxi Road in Nanping—3, 800 steps Ridge Road (pronounced as "San Qian Ba Bai Kan"). He also told us that it took six to eight hours to walk from Fuzhou City to Guling. He spoke fluent Fuzhou dialect, loved to eat kompyang and stayed fit by playing table tennis. He returned to the United States of America in 1927 when he was 12 years old, so he had deep feelings for Fujian as his hometown. After his family returned to the United States, Mindai's father Dr. Charles Garnet Trimble worked as the school doctor at the University of Puget Sound, and Cheng Mindai later graduated from there with a major in chemistry. As an alumni, he donated for the construction of Trimble Hall at his alma mater, the University of Puget Sound. I lived in the Trimble Suite in the hall, which is equipped with furniture of high quality and beautifully decorated. In the suite, the desk, the chest of drawers and the bed are made of the finest sandalwood purchased from China. When I was staying in it, I felt at home.

After years of hard work and exploration, I have finally searched, visited and recorded three Trimble Halls in Fuzhou and Tacoma. Having a good grasp of the origin and development of them, I feel very gratified.

● Lydia A. Trimble's Golden Jubilee

Due to the constraints of feudal ideology, many families at that time did not allow girls to go out to study. In 1908, when Lydia Trimble was the first president, there were 13 students in the Preparatory School of Foochow Women's College. In 1917, Hwa Nan enrolled 5 students in the 4-year college according to the American academic system. The number of students in Hwa Nan increased to 63 in 1923, and 87 in 1926. The gradual growth in these numbers prove how difficult and productive the work was at that time.

In January 1925, Lydia Trimble was no longer the president of Hwa Nan, and Zhu Feng wrote that "she retired from the presidency of Hwa Nan Women's College" and continued to preach for 16 more years until she passed away in Lixue Hall in 1941 at the age of 78. Xie Bizhen mentioned that she was over sixty years old when she resigned from the position as the president in *Illustration of Hwa Nan Women's College* (2008), and Yue Feng's *International Faculty with Fujian Hwa Nan Women's College since 1908* (2018) also used the word "retire".

陈明霞在 2012 年出版的《近代福建教会学校教育研究》一书中说到程吕底亚向校董会递交辞呈。我仔细查阅后发现以上各位都是从华惠德的书《华南女子大学》里引用来的。程吕底亚辞职的原因之一是她已经 62 岁，但我认为 1925 年非基督教运动和收回教育主权运动在全国的推开才是她考虑辞职的更为重要和直接的因素。

1939 年 12 月，老华南为程吕底亚来华 50 年召开题为"欢乐五旬"庆祝会。这个庆祝会于 1939 年 12 月 26 日在福建延平（南平）一个借来的校园里举行，庆祝程吕底亚——这位传教士、教育家和组织者来华 50 年。程吕底亚满头白发、身体挺拔地听取发言。大家回忆一路走来的艰辛历程，感谢她，赞美她，令她热泪盈眶。王世静校长致开幕词，对于学校的创办者、前任送上崇高的敬意，对于程校长比众人早 20 年的先见——建立女子学校，表示无限钦佩和感谢。王世静回忆 1919 年华南学生参加全国性游行回校后，受到程校长的责备。程校长认为她自己是中国人的时间长于各位同学（即便在她自己的祖国——美国，她也声称自己是中国人），说她自己比同学们更加爱中国，告诉大家"罢课游行"无助于国家发展，号召大家做实事。华南学生周日服务社区的社会活动始于程校长的鼓励。在庆祝会上，程校长也对自己在华 50 年经历进行了回顾。她说话简洁果断、一语中的。她深感自己被爱和美包围。她说，到中国一年后很快明白一件事情：中国女性是无所不能的。她非常高兴能够了解中国这片土地，爱上这里的人民。她引用三位著名诗人的诗句表达她的心境和迎接逆境的心理准备（中国当时正处于抗日战争时期）。仔细阅读程吕底亚在百年前发表的这段讲话，她那严肃而且不苟言笑的形象跃然纸上，正如程闽岱所说，他姑婆程吕底亚非常严肃，一板一眼。更让我觉得神奇的是，她演讲中提到了三位著名诗人：德国伟大诗人歌德、与她大致同时代的美国女诗人埃莉诺·怀利和英国诗人鲁伯特·布鲁克。可是从美国传统宗教标准来看这三位诗人并不符合基督教道德人物标准，这是否可视为程吕底亚的说教非常接地气，并不完全按照宗教标准影响办学治学呢？

Chen Mingxia's book *Research on Education in the Modern Fujian Mission Schools* published in 2012 mentioned that Lydia Trimble submitted her resignation to the school board. I checked carefully, only to find that all of the references mentioned above cited the same book *Hwa Nan College: The Women's College of South China* by L. Ethel Wallace. One of the reasons for Lydia's resignation was that she was 62 years old, but I think that the spreading of the Anti-Christian Movement and the Education Right Recovery Movement in the country in 1925 were more important and direct factors for her to consider resigning.

In December 1939, Hwa Nan held a celebration entitled "Fifty Joyous Years" for Lydia's Golden Jubilee in China. The celebration with the theme of Fifty Joyous Years was held on a borrowed campus in Yanping (Nanping), Fujian on December 26, 1939, to pay tribute to Lydia A. Trimble—a missionary, educator and organizer—for her life's work in China spanning fifty years. Silver-haired Lydia listened to the speeches with her back straight. Everyone recalled the hardships along the way. They thanked her, praised her, and brought tears to her eyes. President Lucy Wang delivered the opening speech, paying high respect to the founder of the school and the predecessor, while expressing infinite admiration and gratitude to President Trimble's foresight to have founded a women's college 20 years earlier. Lucy Wang recalled that in 1919, after Hwa Nan students participated in a national march and returned to school, they were criticized by President Trimble. Lydia Trimble believed that she had been Chinese for longer years than the students (even in her own homeland, the United States of America, she also claimed to be a Chinese), Lydia said that she loved China more than anyone, telling everyone that "school strikes and marches" would not help the country to develop, and calling on everyone to do practical things. The social activities of Hwa Nan students serving the community on Sundays began with the encouragement of President Trimble. At the celebration, President Trimble also reviewed her 50 years in China. She spoke succinctly and decisively, and always came to the point. She felt that she was surrounded by love and beauty. She said that after spending a year in China, she quickly realized one thing: Chinese women were omnipotent. She was very happy to learn about this land and to fall in love with the people here. She quoted three famous poets to express her state of mind and her mental preparation for adversity (China was in the War of Resistance Against Japanese Agression). I carefully read this speech made by Lydia Trimble a hundred years ago. Her serious and unsmiling image is vivid on the paper. Just like Cheng Mindai said, his grandaunt Lydia was very serious and strict. What struck me even more was that she mentioned three famous poets in her speech: the great German poet Goethe and the American poet Elinor Wylie, who was roughly contemporary with her, and the English poet Rubert Brooke. But from the perspective of traditional American religious standards, these three poets did not meet the standard of Christian moral model of its day. Is it appropriate to think that Lydia Trimble's preaching was very humanistic and down-to-earth, and that the running of the college was becoming less dependent on religious standards?

从 1925 年 1 月程吕底亚辞职，到美以美女布道会决定由卢爱德继任，以及卢爱德 1926 年 1 月正式就职，这期间有近一年的时间．董事会决定由教务长华惠德代理校长一职（朱峰、王爱菊，2005）。正是由于华惠德，这位早期华南的教务长、代理校长、华南的参与人，将华南自创建到 1950 年 40 余年的建校史和来龙去脉进行了详细的描述，今日读者方能知晓这已经逝去的历史。华惠德也是程闽岱爸爸程嘉尼的表姐（Trimble，2007）。但是，程吕底亚从 1925 年引退到 1941 年在立雪楼逝世的这 16 年里的行踪记录，除了 1939 年程吕底亚来华五十载庆祝活动外，其他事项鲜有描述，这对后人来说是个谜。

● 教育家卢爱德博士治校时代

华南第二任校长最终花落卢爱德，是有必然性的。卢爱德成为华南第二任校长经历了华惠德教务长代理校长后的时期。卢爱德是个妥妥的"学二代"，父亲卢思义是美国爱荷华州晨边学院校长、福州美以美会会督。她本人于 1909 年获晨边学院文学学士，1919 获哥伦比亚大学教育学博士，研究的内容是"中国女子教育"。这篇 100 多年前的博士论文细致描写了中国从无到有的女性教育——当时受教育的女性少，仅为千分之几，完全是精英教育。翻阅这部百年前的博士论文，不禁感慨万千，又如同与百年前的智慧学人对话。世事沧桑，女性的教育何其艰辛困苦。她对于中国教育、中国女性教育的了解和洞察，胜过很多当代教育人。作为第二任校长，卢爱德能讲流利的中国话，对中国、中国女性、中国女性教育之了解可想而知。

From the resignation of Lydia in January 1925 to the decision by the Methodist Episcopal Church Women's Evangelical Fellowship to assign Dr. Ida B. Lewis as the successor, and the official inauguration of Dr. Ida B. Lewis in January 1926, there was a gap of almost a year, when the board of directors decided that the Provost L. Ethel Wallace should act as president. It is precisely because of Wallace, the early provost, the acting president and the participant in the development of Hwa Nan that the detailed history of Hwa Nan, and the ins and outs of Hwa Nan's establishment for more than 40 years from its founding to 1950 was recorded, and today we readers may get to know this past history. Wallace was also the cousin of Cheng Mindai's (Bob Trimble's) father, Dr. Charles Garnet Trimble. However, the records of Lydia's whereabouts in the sixteen years from her retirement in 1925 to her death in Lixue Hall in 1941, except for the celebration of Lydia Trimble's Jubilee in 1939, are rarely described, which remains a mystery to people now and in the future.

• Era of Dr. Ida Belle Lewis, the Educator

The appointment of the second president of Hwa Nan was finally determined. It turned out to be Lu Aide (Dr. Ida Belle Lewis, 1887 – 1969), which was inevitable. Dr. Lewis became the second president of Hwa Nan after being with the acting president, Provost L. Ethel Wallace. Dr. Lewis was born to a family of scholars. Her father Wilson S. Lewis (pronounced Lu Siyi in Chinese) was the second president of Morningside College in Iowa, USA, and the bishop of Fuzhou Methodist Episcopal Church. She herself was awarded a Bachelor of Arts degree by Morningside College in 1909 and a Doctor's Degree of Education by Columbia University in 1919. Her research was on "Chinese Women's Education". This doctoral dissertation written more than 100 years ago described in detail the development process of women's education in China, which was created from scratch. At that time, there were very few educated women, only several in a thousand, and the education they received was completely elite. Reading this doctoral dissertation written only a hundred years ago, I can't help but feel a lot of emotion. It is like having a dialogue with a wise scholar. The world is changing all the time, but women's education has always been extraordinarily difficult. Her remarkable understanding and insight into Chinese education and Chinese women's education are better than many contemporary educators. As the second president, Dr. Lewis spoke fluent Chinese, and her understanding of China, Chinese women and Chinese women's education was as personal as it was academic.

卢爱德的身世背景、天津教学的实践经验、教育博士的专业学术研究经历、与时俱进的教育理论等足以令她胜任华南的校长职务。她在哥伦比亚大学攻读博士学位时，就深受同校声名威震四方的杜威教授的实用主义教育理论影响，根据杜威实用主义教育理论对华南女大教育进行规划，作了较大调整；她任内为华南女大从外国传教士治校向华人治校转变作好了基础准备。

与首任校长程吕底亚相比，卢爱德具备更加专业的教育视角，教育理念更加纯粹，她具有研究中国女性教育的理论和在中国天津的教学实践，而程校长是传教宣教的信念更深更甚，故而治校方略有所不同。

卢爱德的博士论文介绍了中国古代科举制度精髓——习诵理解四书五经、撰写八股文、参加科举考试，认为这是中国传统保守式教育；而自1874年开始的美国进步教育运动和五口通商后的西式教育为新教育观；介乎新旧之间的是变化中的教育观。她详尽分析了当时中国人的教育现状、背景和原因。"在中国女性地位得到提升之前，中国极其需要考量如何为教育进步而努力抗争。"（Lewis，1919：3）

根据她的调查，当时北京地区的官员中有海外背景的占23.2%。辛亥革命期间，女性争取平等选举权的呼声日渐高涨，出现了很多女性筹办的私立学校、报刊等。红十字会和医疗界产生了一些杰出的女性。这些走出去的女性为华东、华南、华中和华北人民的健康作出了重大贡献。在高校的女性，在中国的每个省以及美国的许多高校，继续贯彻着进步教育、新教育运动的理念，这为中国的女性开辟了一个新纪元。更多的是介乎新旧教育观念之间变化的大众，吸纳新旧长短处以适应个体需求。

Dr. Lewis's background, practical experience of teaching in Tianjin, professional academic experience of doctoral research, and cutting-edge educational theory were enough to make her fully qualified for the position of president of Hwa Nan. When she was studying for her doctorate degree in Columbia University, she was deeply influenced by the pragmatic education theory of Professor John Dewey, who was legendary in the same school. According to Dewey's theory, she planned and adjusted the education of Hwa Nan Women's College. During her tenure, she had laid the foundation for the transformation of Hwa Nan Women's College from a foreign missionary school to a domestic college administered by Chinese.

Compared with the first President Lydia Trimble, Dr. Ida B. Lewis had a more professional educational perspective and purer educational philosophy. Dr. Lewis had the theory of Chinese women's education research and the teaching practice in Tianjin, while Lydia Trimble had a more profound belief in missionary education. Therefore, their management policies were different.

Dr. Lewis's doctoral dissertation introduced the essence of the ancient Chinese imperial examination system—reciting and understanding the *Four Books* and *Five Classics*, writing eight-part essays, as well as taking the imperial examinations. She considered these to be traditional Chinese conservative education. Western education beginning with the Progressive Education Movement in America since 1874 and the opening of five treaty ports was the new educational perspective. What lay between the old and the new was the changing educational concept. She analyzed in detail the current situation, background and root cause of Chinese education at that time. "Before the improvement of female status, China desperately need to figure out how to fight for educational progress."

According to her survey, 23.2% of officials in Beijing at that time had an overseas background. During the Revolution of 1911, women's voices for equal suffrage grew louder and louder. Many private schools, journals and magazines run by women appeared, and some outstanding women emerged from the Red Cross and the medical fields. These women had stepped out of their families to make significant contributions to the health of the people from east, south, central and north China. In every province of China, in many states of America, women in colleges and universities continued to implement the concepts of Progressive Education and New Education Movement, which had opened up a new century and a new era for women in China. There were quite a few people who were changing their mind between old and new educational concepts to absorb the strengths of the old and new to fit individual needs.

卢爱德的博士论文对当时中国女性接受教育的路径做了梳理，分为三类：私塾、教会和政府。通过对当时 1 000 多名学生的调查，得出入学的中国女孩比通常的 6～7 岁要大 4 岁，大龄超龄的初中、高中女生占比很高，论文呼吁政府要加强指导和管理。她发现，当时拥有上学权利的女孩属于精英阶层的孩子，占比非常小。卢爱德对当时中国女性学校学生的入学年龄、科目设置、课程设置作了详尽的描述和分析，是部 20 世纪初中国女性教育的百科全书。

朱峰（2002：78）认为，卢爱德是教育家办学，她的任期重点理念是以服务为核心的教育思想和华南女大需要调整转型的行政管理。

卢氏以服务为核心的教育理念得益于其博士学习期间的母校，她在哥伦比亚大学师范学院求学，彼时杜威教授研究的实用主义教育哲学理论风靡全球。她就利用所学知识治理当时的华南，发现并指出当时既有的女子学校已存在的忽视贫下阶层子女就读、女子教育同社会严重脱节等问题，并加以严厉批评。关于调整转型期间的成绩，可以看到，她用当时最先进的教育理念对华南女大进行教育规划的大调整，调整了院系，开设了公共卫生系和家政系两门服务于社会的实用学科专业，非常有前瞻性。她支持学校向政府注册，服务中国贫下阶层。她启用了中国教师陈叔圭作为华南女大附中代理校长，并将陈叔圭提为副教授（汪征鲁，2007：64）。此举为华南女大转为由华人治校奠定了基础。当时华南已经和美国七所"姊妹校"建立了友好合作关系，有经济上的资助往来。但她促成华南和美国七所姊妹校进一步深入地关联，让每个姊妹校和华南其中的一个系进行对接资助。具体如表 7-2 所示：

Dr. Lewis's doctoral dissertation sorted out the paths of Chinese women's education at that time, which were divided into three categories: private school, church and government. Through a survey of more than 1,000 students at that time, it concluded that the Chinese girls who entered schools were four years older than the usual 6 – 7-year age, and the proportion of older middle school and high school girls was very high. The dissertation called on the government to improve guidance and management. She found that the girls with the right to go to school at that time were of the select class, and this proportion was very small. Dr. Lewis made a detailed description and analysis on the enrollment age, subject setting and curriculum setting of Chinese women's schools, which made her dissertation an encyclopedia of Chinese women's education in the early 20th century.

Zhu Feng believed that Lewis's way was to run the college by educators, and the focus of her tenure was on the educational idea that emphasized service as the core and that the administrative management at Hwa Nan needed to adjust and transform.

Dr. Lewis's service-centered educational philosophy was derived from her alma mater during her doctoral research. She studied at the Teachers College of Columbia University. At that time, the pragmatic educational philosophy researched by Professor John Dewey of Columbia University was popular all over the world. She used the knowledge she had learned to manage Hwa Nan at that time. She found out and pointed out that the existing girls' schools at that time neglected the children of the poor and lower classes, and women's education was severely out of touch with society. She criticized these phenomena sharply. In respect to her achievements during this period of adjustment and transformation, we can see that she used the most advanced educational concepts at that time to greatly adjust the education planning of Hwa Nan Women's College. She changed the faculties and departments, and set up two practical departments that would serve the society—the Department of Public Health and the Department of Home Economics—which was very forward-looking. She supported the school's registration with the government to serve the poor and lower classes in China. She appointed Chen Shugui, a Chinese teacher, as the acting principal of the High School Affiliated to Hwa Nan Women's College, and promoted Chen Shugui to be associate professor. This move laid the foundation for Hwa Nan Women's College to be run by Chinese people. Hwa Nan had established friendly cooperative relations with seven "sister schools" in the United States, and the eight schools had exchanges in terms of financial support. However, she facilitated further associations between the seven sister schools in the United States and Hwa Nan, and encouraged each sister school to match with one of the departments in Hwa Nan. Details are shown in Table 7 – 2:

表 7-2 华南和美国七所姊妹校合作对接表

美校英文名字	美校中文名字	华南受资处	资金（美元）
Mt. Union College，Ohio	俄亥俄州高山协会（又译州联合）学院	运动体育馆	2 000
Baldwin-Wallace College，Ohio	俄亥俄州鲍德温（又译宝灵）华莱士学院	家政系	1 000
West Virginia Wesleyan College	西弗吉尼亚州韦（卫）斯里学院	物理系	1 000
Cornell College，Iowa	爱荷华州康奈尔学院	音乐系	2 000
Morningside College，Iowa	爱荷华州晨边学院	化学系	1 500
SouthWestern College，Kansas	堪萨斯州西南学院	生物系	1 500
Missouri Wesleyan College	密苏里州卫斯理学院	师范专业	300

　　华南与美国七校有姊妹校关系的影响力不容小觑，它一直为当地人、受益人以及后人所津津乐道和广为传播，在接下来的近 20 年里影响巨大，直至影响到全省。由于开放，福州很多行业需要懂得西方文化的人才来处理洋行、海关、税务、出版、教育等方面的问题，涌现了许多传统之外的新型职业，也为本地人提供了在这些行业就业的机会。如 20 世纪 40 年代，在美国哈佛大学攻读人类学并获得博士学位的福建古田人林耀华，曾在他的英文版作品《金翼》里提到教会女子学校华南学院。主人公的儿子三哥心仪一位华南女大的学生，自由恋爱娶了她，其父是牧师。书中提道："通过妻子的家庭，他与教会的关系得到强化，这使他得以实现最高求学理想。他的成功为他的家庭和……带来莫大荣耀。在乡村社会，留洋是一个莫大的机会，回国的学生构成一个特殊的特权阶层。"（林耀华，1944：115）

Table 7 - 2　Matching Table of Hwa Nan Departments versus American Sister Schools

Names of American Schools	Departments Being Supported in Hwa Nan	Fund($)
Mt. Union College, Ohio	Gym	2,000
Baldwin-Wallace College, Ohio	Department of Home Economics	1,000
West Virginia Wesleyan College	Department of Physics	1,000
Cornell College, Iowa	Department of Music	2,000
Morningside College, Iowa	Department of Chemistry	1,500
SouthWestern College, Kansas	Department of Biology	1,500
Missouri Wesleyan College	Education Discipline	300

The influence of the sister school relationship between Hwa Nan and the seven American schools cannot be underestimated. It has always been talked about and widely spread by local people, beneficiaries and future generations. In the next two decades, it even came to impact the whole province. Due to the opening up, many industries in Fuzhou needed talented individuals who understood Western culture to deal with issues in many related fields, such as foreign banks, customs, taxation, publishing and education. Many new types of occupations beyond traditional ones emerged, providing local people with employment opportunities in these industries. For example, in the 1940s, Lin Yaohua, a native of Gutian, Fujian, who studied anthropology at Harvard University in the United States and received a doctorate, once mentioned Hwa Nan College, a girls' missionary school in his work *The Golden Wing* (English version). In his book the protagonist's son, the third brother, was fond of a Hwa Nan girl. He married this student of Hwa Nan Women's College after pursuing free love, and the girl's father was a pastor. In the book he writes: "Through his wife's family, his relationship with the church was strengthened, which enabled him to achieve his highest academic ideals. His success brought great honor to his family and ... In rural society, studying abroad was a great opportunity, and returned students constituted a special privileged class. "

1925 年，全国非基督教、收回教育主权运动走向高潮。在社会政治压力下，当时的教会学校均面临办学危机。卢爱德 1926 年 1 月任职，到 1927 年 1 月国民革命军入闽，治校环境发生巨变，福州各界涌现了反文化侵略、收回教育权的运动，华南面临停办还是续办的抉择。她早几年在自己的博士论文里就指出过，华南要完成在政府注册的工作，所以她的态度是一以贯之的。她放弃了校长职务，成为学校的顾问；程吕底亚的侄女华惠德也辞了教务长一职；校董会任命当时华南中学校长陈叔圭为校长，遭到陈叔圭婉拒；于是校董会成立了包括陈叔圭、王世静在内的"五人校务委员会"（朱峰、王爱菊，2005：39）。1928 年，卢爱德生病回美国治疗。自此，华南不再有外国人当校长。1928 年 6 月，校董会在王世静和陈叔圭两位最佳校长候选人中，最终选择了王世静。她成为华南女院第一位华人校长。

　　卢爱德虽然在任不到两年，但她丰富的教育素养和资深的教育专业背景对于华南办学水平的提升是毋庸置疑的，对华南声誉的传播是深远的。华南在她治校期间走向更加专业化、教育化和国际化的道路。专业的更新调整、重用华人教师和华人管理、与美国七校结成姊妹校、重视办校注册登记等治校措施令人目不暇接；特别令世人刮目相看的一点是，她任内打下了华南由外国传教士领导向华人治校转变的各种基础，华人治校的乐章开始奏响。

In 1925, the Anti-Christian Movement and the Education Rights Recovery Movement in the country reached their peak. Under the social and political pressure of the time, the church schools were all facing a crisis. Dr. Lewis took office in January 1926; by January 1927, the National Revolutionary Army entered Fujian, and the environment for school management had undergone great changes. Movement to fight against cultural invasion and take back the rights of education emerged from all walks of life in Fuzhou, and Hwa Nan was confronted with a hard decision: to close down, or to carry on. She pointed out in her doctoral dissertation a few years earlier that Hwa Nan had to complete the work of registering with the government, so her attitude was consistent. She gave up the position of president and became the college's consultant; Lydia's niece L. Ethel Wallace also resigned her position as the provost; the school board appointed Chen Shugui, the then-principal of Hwa Nan Middle School, as the president of the college, but Chen Shugui declined; the board set up a "five-member faculty committee" including Chen Shugui and Lucy Wang Shijing. In 1928, Dr. Lewis fell ill and returned to the United States for treatment. Since then, there have been no foreigner serving as president in Hwa Nan. In June 1928, the school board finally chose Wang Shijing, one of the two best candidates for president, Wang Shijing and Chen Shugui, as president. She became the first Chinese president of Hwa Nan Women's College.

Although Dr. Lewis was in office for less than two years, there was no doubt that her rich literacy and senior professional background in education greatly improved the level of school operation in Hwa Nan, and broadened the spread of South China's reputation for quality education. During her tenure, Hwa Nan moved towards a more professional, educational and international path, including renewal and adjustment of disciplines, valuing Chinese teachers and management by Chinese, entering into sister schools with seven American schools, and attaching importance to school registration and other measures, which were riveting. What impressed other people greatly is that during her tenure, she laid various foundations for the transformation of Hwa Nan from a foreign missionary school to a Chinese-run school. The time for Chinese governance had come.

● 华人主校：王世静时代

我曾经在一张 1928—1929 年度美国密歇根大学巴伯学者合影中认出了王世静，我个人认为她是众人中最端庄美丽的一位，她优雅大方，有大家闺秀的韵味。美国密歇根大学巴伯奖学金设立于 1917 年，全称"巴伯东方女子奖学金"，是最古老、最负盛名和最独特的奖项之一。王世静于 1922—1923 年已经获得过一次巴伯奖学金资助，完成硕士学习。华惠德写道："（王世静）是第一位接受巴勃（即巴伯）奖学金赞助的中国女性。"（Wallace，1956：45；朱峰、王爱菊，2005：42）1928—1929 年，王世静以华南校长候选人的身份获得用于资助访问学者的巴伯研究员奖金，再次进入密歇根大学学习，获得学习成绩优异、工作能力突出和品德高尚的评价。从此，华南拥有每年一名教师到密歇根大学攻读博士学位的待遇（汪征鲁，2007：67）。曾任福建协和大学校长的美以美会会督高智先生说："王世静在密歇根大学的业绩是华南女子大学影响力的重要表现。从 1928 年以后，王世静使华南女子大学的老师可以到密歇根大学攻读博士学位，从而培养了一群高素质的中国教职员。在这方面，许多美国小型高等教育机构都会自叹弗如。"（朱峰、王爱菊，2005：42）

今日国人特别是闽人，大都知晓民国时期福州才女林徽因，却不知华南女院的第三任校长王世静是毫不逊色于林徽因的民国才女。请和我一起踏上寻访这位守护华南的传奇女神的旅程吧。

- ## Chinese Governance: Era of Lucy Wang (Wang Shijing)

From a group photo of 1928 – 1929 Barbour Scholars at the University of Michigan, I recognized Lucy Wang at first glance. I personally think she was the most dignified one among the crowd. She was beautiful, elegant and gracious, with a sophisticated sense of place. The Barbour Scholarships at the University of Michigan was formally established in 1917. Its full name is "The Barbour Scholarships for Oriental Women". It's one of the oldest, most unique and prestigious awards in the United States. In 1922 – 1923, Wang Shijing had already received her first Barbour Scholarship to complete her master's studies. L. Ethel Wallace wrote that "(Lucy Wang) was the first Chinese woman to be supported by Barbour Scholarships". In 1928 – 1929 she again received a Barbour Fellowship as a candidate for the presidency of Hwa Nan for further study. She was praised for her excellent academic performance, outstanding work ability and high moral character. Based upon her stellar performance, Hwa Nan gained the privilege to have one teacher study for a doctoral degree at the University of Michigan every year. Quoting from Bishop Gowdy, the former president of Fukien Christian University, "Lucy Wang's performance at the University of Michigan was an important manifestation of the influence of Hwa Nan Women's College. Starting from 1928, Lucy Wang enabled teachers from Hwa Nan Women's College to pursue doctoral degrees at the University of Michigan, thereby cultivating a group of high-quality Chinese faculty members. In this regard, many smaller American institutions of higher education were put to shame."

Most Chinese people today, especially those from Fujian, know about Lin Huiyin, a talented woman from Fuzhou in the time of the Republic of China. However, they probably don't know that Lucy Wang Shijing, the third president of the Hwa Nan Women's College, was also a talented woman in the Republic of China, and was directly comparable to Lin Huiyin. Please join me on a journey to search for this legendary goddess who guarded Hwa Nan for more than two decades.

王世静 1879 年出生于福州的官宦世家，祖父王仁堪是状元，他父亲王孝绳承父亲荫护，在武汉、北京等地任职。王世静在四个孩子中排行第三，上有哥哥世达、姐姐世秀，下有妹妹世婉，一起随父亲在武汉、北京生活长大。王世静 14 岁时因父亲病故，由母亲带着四个孩子回到原籍福州王氏家族。王氏家族在清末民初是福建一大望族。王世静的父亲虽早逝，但她的叔叔伯伯都是当时学界、政界名流。1913 年，王世静 16 岁时进入华南预科——华英女学堂学习，此乃她人生的转折点。与她同时入校的还有姐姐王世秀。两姐妹是当时就读的"官家"子女，因而成为华南现身说法的、办学成绩好的广告范例。

1919 年，王世静赴美国晨边学院学习。不难发现，华南前三任校长程吕底亚、卢爱德和王世静本科均毕业于晨边学院。1921 年，王世静获密歇根大学巴伯奖学金；1923 年，她获得该校化学硕士学位；同年回国，以副教授身份在厦门大学化学系任教，月薪百元。1924 年秋，她回到母校任教，月薪 30 元。1928 年，学院董事会任命王世静担任校长，但她因获得巴伯研究员奖金再次入学密大，推迟担任校长职务，直到 1930 年 1 月才就职。时任福建省教育厅厅长和福建协和大学校长参加了王世静的就职典礼并分别致贺词。王世静在她的答词中提到华南历经挣扎奋斗的成长历程，提到校训"受当施"，感谢前任校长和职员，牢记学院早期一无所长，从零开始，所知的一切皆源自前面的先行者，有义务将已得到的一切传给后来者，表明"为中华妇女的缘故，我不敢拒绝这一职任"。（华惠德，2005：49）

Lucy Wang Shijing was born to an aristocratic family of governmental officials in Minhou, Fuzhou in 1897. Her grandfather Wang Renkan was the Zhuangyuan (Number one scholar), her father Wang Xiaosheng benefited from his father and worked in Wuhan, Beijing and other places as an official. Wang Shijing was the third among the four children, with an older brother Shida, older sister Shixiu, and younger sister Shiwan. They grew up with their father in Wuhan and Beijing. When Wang Shijing was 14 years old, her father died of illness, and her mother returned to the Wang family in Fuzhou with her four children. The Wang family was a prominent family in Fujian at the end of the Qing Dynasty and the beginning of the Republic of China. Although Wang Shijing's father died young, her uncles were all celebrities in the academic and political circles at that time. In 1913, at the age of 16, Wang Shijing was enrolled in the Preparatory of Foochow Women's College, which was a turning point of her life. Her sister, Wang Shixiu, also went to the Preparatory at the same time so the two sisters as children of the "official family" gave, through their example, credibility to women's education as well as the school in which they were enrolled. In a sense the two girls were advertisements for Hwa Nan.

In 1919, Wang Shijing went to study at Morningside College in the United States. It is not a coincidence that the first three presidents of Hwa Nan (Lydia Trimble, Ida B. Lewis and Wang Shijing) all graduated from Morningside College in Iowa. In 1921, Wang Shijing was awarded the Barbour Scholarships at the University of Michigan; in 1923, she obtained her master's degree in chemistry. In the same year, she returned to China to teach in the Department of Chemistry of Xiamen University as an associate professor with a monthly salary of 100 yuan. In the autumn of 1924, she returned to her alma mater (Hwa Nan) to teach with a monthly salary of 30 yuan. In 1928, the school board appointed Wang Shijing as president, but she had returned to the University of Michigan on a Barbour Fellowship. Thus she deferred her acceptance as president until January 1930. The then director general of the Fujian Provincial Department of Education and the president of Fukien Christian University attended Wang Shijing's inauguration ceremony and delivered the congratulatory speeches. In her acceptance speech, Wang Shijing observed that Hwa Nan had experienced arduous times and struggled to grow. She quoted the school motto "Saved for Service" which recognizes women's special role, thanked the former president and staff, and reminded people to keep in mind that the school had nothing in its early days, that all she knew derived from her forerunners, and that she was obliged to pass on what they have acquired for the latter. She declared: "For the sake of Chinese women, I dare not turn down this position."

王世静校长开启了长达 22 年的华人治校历史，她提出了影响后人的华南精神，以"受当施"为校训；她化解了华南遭遇的多场重大危机，为华南在国内高等教育界占据一席之地立下了汗马功劳，贡献了毕生精力。

华南这所小型女子学院的物质条件完全比不上同时期的其他院校，所以王世静非常强调以"民主和谐，友爱互助以及服务牺牲"的"华南精神"（吴梓明，2001）管理教育师生（潘丽珍，2008：70）。华南精神之献身精神和团队精神内核也时常被师生提及。王世静终身未嫁，"过去，将来，我都属于华南。"（Wang，1936：5）

上任伊始，如何让华南获得政府立案是迫在眉睫，关乎华南存亡的问题。在资金不达标等不利因素之下，王世静四处奔走游说，最终使得华南于 1934 年成功获得中华民国教育部永久立案以及美国纽约大学正式证明，有其文、理学士学位授予权。王世静认为校友们的杰出表现才是大学得以成功注册的关键（谢必震，2008）。第二个重大危机是 1937 年日本入侵中国，抗日战争全面爆发。华南迁校于内陆山区南平，艰难存息。学校一部分学生被疏散回家，一部分随校内迁，还有留在福州看校舍的庶务长华惠德等。在南平办学条件极其简单困苦，教室是借来的，实验分批进行，躲过空袭再上课，住宿拥挤；1941 年、1944 年福州两度沦陷，华南在福州的校舍被日寇洗劫一空，经历了一场大火，图书馆、实验室被付诸一炬。程吕底亚安慰师生，表示这座大楼不是华南，华南精神存在全体师生心里，无法摧毁（华惠德，2005）。与此同时，王世静领导的华南坚持关注局势，宣传爱国，服务社会，积极参与抗日救亡活动。

President Lucy Wang Shijing thus began her 22-year history of Chinese governance. She came up with the Hwa Nan spirit that influenced future generations, and championed the school Motto "Saved for Service". She resolved many major crises encountered by Hwa Nan, made immense contributions and spent great effort for Hwa Nan to have a place in domestic higher education for women.

As a small women's college, the material conditions of Hwa Nan were no doubt inferior to other prestigious schools of the same period, so Lucy Wang emphasized the "Hwa Nan Spirit" of "democracy and harmony, fraternity and mutual assistance, and sacrifice of service" to manage and educate teachers and students. The dedication and team spirit of Hwa Nan are often mentioned by teachers and students. Lucy Wang never married, "In the past and in the future, I belong to Hwa Nan."

At the beginning of Wang's tenure, obtaining the government's registration was an imminent challenge. It was a matter of the survival for Hwa Nan. Under the circumstances of unfavorable factors such as substandard funds, Lucy Wang Shijing went around and lobbied, and finally in 1934, Hwa Nan successfully obtained the permanent registration by the Ministry of Education of the Republic of China and formal certification by New York University of the United States of the college's right to confer Bachelor of Arts and Bachelor of Science degrees. Wang Shijing believed that the outstanding performance of alumnae was the key to the successful registration of the college. The second major crisis was the Japanese invasion of China in 1937 and the ensuing War of Resistance. Hwa Nan moved to Nanping in the mountainous area of Fujian for survival. Some students abandoned their homes, some moved with the college, and Provost Wallace and others stayed in Fuzhou to look after the school building. The conditions for school operation in Nanping were extremely bare and difficult. Classrooms were borrowed, experiments were carried out in turn, classes were often held after hiding from air raids, and dormitories were overcrowded. Fuzhou was occupied twice in 1941 and 1944, and the school buildings of Hwa Nan in Fuzhou were looted by Japanese invaders. A fire destroyed the library and laboratory. But Lydia Trimble reassured them that this building was not Hwa Nan. The spirit of Hwa Nan existed in the hearts of all teachers and students and cannot be destroyed. At the same time, under the guidance of Wang Shijing, Hwa Nan insisted on paying close attention to the situation, promoting patriotism, serving the society, and actively participating in the anti-Japanese national salvation activities.

特别值得一提的是中华南女院师生在 1941 年 4 月福建著名的"大湖战役"中所作的贡献。时年 5 月，日寇意欲经闽侯大湖乡挺进古田，北侵南平、建瓯，逼近国民党第三战区江西上饶。黄埔军校第一期毕业生，出生于华侨家庭的国民党福建驻军副总司令李良荣请缨指挥"大湖战役"。大湖山山脉险峻，部队在交通不便的崎岖山路辗转，粮食补给困难。南平驻军决定赶制 20 万个光饼支援大湖前线官兵。躲避日寇、迁校南平的华南师生踊跃投入光饼制作的支前工作，200 多人全员齐上阵，还非常有创意地在每袋光饼串干粮里附上鼓舞士气的一纸短笺，给前线战士们以极大的精神鼓舞，为取得大湖战役胜利起到了重要的作用。李良荣高度评价了华南师生的爱国举措，并赠送 200 多本《大湖之战》纪念册（汪征鲁，2007：78）。

1945 年抗日战争结束时，王世静已任职 15 年。1946 年，华南全校回迁福州。王世静拥有对华南的绝对和最高管理权限，但她从未独揽大权。学院重大决策由校务会共同决议，行政上实施集体领导制，由王世静负责 9 人校务委员会。当她外出募款集资、为学校大事周旋于政府或赴美参加国际会议之时，学校则由以陈叔奎为首的校务会共管。自 1946 年到 1948 年，学院发展达到了鼎盛时期，这期间学生数量几乎接近 1946 年以前的总和（吴梓明，2001）。

The critical contribution made by the teachers and students of Hwa Nan Women's College particularly worth mentioning was in the famous "Dahu Campaign" in Fujian in April 1941. By May of that year, the Japanese invaders intended to advance into Gutian through Dahu Town, Minhou to invade Nanping and Jianou in the north, and approach Shangrao, Jiangxi Province, the third war zone of the Kuomintang. Li Liangrong, one of the first graduates of the Whampoa Military Academy, who was born to an overseas Chinese family, the deputy commander-in-chief of the Kuomintang Fujian garrison, requested to command the "Dahu Campaign". The Dahu Mountains are steep, so the troops were marching on rugged mountain roads, and it was difficult to supply food. The Nanping garrison decided to make 200,000 kompyangs to support the officers and soldiers on the front line of the Dahu Town. Having moved to Nanping to hide from the Japanese invaders, Hwa Nan actively participated in the preparatory work of making kompyangs. More than 200 teachers and students were involved. They also creatively attached a morale-boosting note to each bag of kompyangs. This gave great spiritual inspiration to the front-line soldiers and played an important role in the winning of the Dahu Campaign. Li Liangrong spoke highly of the patriotic deeds of the teachers and students in Hwa Nan, and present them with more than 200 commemorative books of "Dahu Campaign".

In 1945, the eight-year War of Resistance Against Japanese Aggression ended, and it was the fifteenth year of Wang Shijing's tenure. In 1946, the entire Hwa Nan moved back to Fuzhou. Lucy Wang had the absolute and highest management authority over Hwa Nan, but she never monopolized the power. The major decisions of the college were jointly made by the school council, and the collective leadership system had been implemented in respect to administration. Lucy Wang was in charge of the 9-member school council; when she went out to raise funds, deal with the government for the school's major events, or go to the United States to participate in international conferences, the school was jointly managed by the school council headed by Chen Shukui. From 1946 to 1948, the development of the college reached its peak because the number of students during this period was close to the total of all years before 1946.

1949 年 8 月 17 日福州解放了，王世静主动表示拥护中国共产党，销毁了 1949 年前国民党政府给的嘉奖证书（吴梓明，2001）。1950 年，朝鲜战争爆发，同年中央人民政府颁发《关于处理接受美国津贴的文化教育、救济机关及宗教团体的方针的决定》，接管了接受外国津贴的高校 21 所（汪征鲁，2007：84）。1951 年 5 月，王世静将华南全部十枚印章上交福建省文教部；专门单独的华南女子文理学院停办，与其他学校院系合并调整，命名为福州大学，王世静改任福州大学校务委员会副主任委员。1952 年福州大学并入福建省立师院，王世静任师院副院长，图书馆馆长。1956 年，不受重视、郁郁寡欢、经年生病的王世静离开了大学校园。从此，她鲜与人沟通交流，只能一个人独处，一直到 1983 年 9 月王世静在福州病逝，无人知晓这位教育家的精神世界。（潘丽珍，2008）

● 跨入新时代的新华南

与老华南第一任校长程吕底亚创校建校的艰辛困苦、第二任校长卢爱德的转型任务相比，第三任校长王世静任内则经历了立案更名、抗日战争迁校闽北、抗日战争胜利回迁福州、合并融入福建师范学院等 4 个过程。朱峰认为王世静是华南女大第一任校长，也是最后一位校长（朱峰，2002）。我认为是也不是。是的原因在于完全招收女生、沿袭受当施校训、由美国教会在中国办的 13 所大学之一的私立华南女子文理学院由于时代变迁、政治面貌改变而产生改变。但是，历史不能遗忘的是，1984 年 11 月 30 日，以余宝笙博士为首的华南女子文理学院暨附中校友会理事会发出《敬致校友书》，次年秋季招生，有特区实用英语、学前教育、营养与食品科学和服装设计四个专业，其中"将来准备将学生中成绩优异者选送出国深造"（陈钟英，2016）。让人印象深刻。并非所有中国高校在 20 世纪 80 年代改革开放伊始，都有这样的国际视野和先见之明。

On August 17, 1949, Fuzhou was liberated. Lucy Wang Shijing took the initiative to express her support for the Communist Party of China, and destroyed the certificates of merit given by the Kuomintang government before 1949. When the Korean War broke out in 1950, the Central People's Government issued the "Resolution on the Disposition Policy of Cultural Education Institutions, Relief Organizations and Religious Organizations Receiving American Subsidies", and took over 21 colleges and universities that received foreign subsidies. In May 1951, Wang Shijing handed over all ten stamps of Hwa Nan to the Ministry of Culture and Education of Fujian Province. The independent Hwa Nan Women's College of Arts and Sciences ceased as it was combined with other colleges and departments, and then reopened under the name of Fuzhou University. Wang Shijing was appointed as Vice Chairman of the Fuzhou University Council. In 1952, Fuzhou University was merged into the Fujian Provincial Teachers College, and Wang Shijing served as the vice president of the Teachers College and the director of the library. In 1956, Wang Shijing, who was undervalued, upset and sick for years, left the campus. From then on, she rarely communicated with others and stayed alone. In September 1983, Wang Shijing had reached the end of her life in Foochow because of illness. No one got to know about the spiritual world of this exceptional educator.

• New Hwa Nan in the New Era

Compared with the hardships during the school founding Lydia Trimble endured as the first president of Hwa Nan, and the transformation task of the second president, Dr. Ida Lewis, the third president Wang Shijing lived through the formal registration, change of name, whole scale evacuation of the school to northern Fujian during the War of Resistance Against Japanese Agression, and its return to Fuzhou after the war, as well as assimilation into Fujian Teachers College. Zhu Feng believes that Wang Shijing was the first and last president of Hwa Nan Women's College. In my opinion, the answer is both "yes and no". The reason for "yes" is that Hwa Nan Women's College of Arts & Sciences, one of the thirteen institutions of higher learning run by the American Church in China, which recruited only girls, followed the school motto of "Saved for Service", evolved due to the changing times and political environment. However, what cannot be forgotten is that on November 30, 1984, the Council of Alumnae Association of Hwa Nan Women's College of Arts and Sciences and the Affiliated High School, headed by Dr. Yu Baosheng, issued "A letter to Alumnae" and announced that the college will enroll new students in the autumn of 1985. There were four majors: SAR (special area) Practical English, Preschool Education, Nutrition and Food Science, and Fashion Design. Even more stunning was the commitment: "In the future, the students with outstanding performance will be selected to study abroad." Not all Chinese institutions of higher learning had such an international vision and foresight at the beginning of the Reform and Opening Up in the 1980s.

华南女子职业学院创办后有余宝笙、陈钟英、马秀发等 46 名毕业于华南女子文理学院的校友回校任教（陈钟英，2016：79），推举余宝笙博士为校长。所以从这个意义上看，余宝笙是第四任校长，王世静就不算是最后一位了。当然也有人简单地以老华南、新华南加以区分。但是因为华南女子职业学院确实是由老华南校友复办，所以存在一定的老华南精神和文化基因；另外一方面，仅用十余年时间，即在 20 世纪 90 年代完成与美国佛罗里达州立大学、俄勒冈大学、美国普吉湾大学、世纪学院、晨边学院、芬兰瑞典职业技术学院、韩国梨花大学、日本广岛女子大学、泰国易三仓大学、菲律宾施利蒙大学等十多所大学建立校际合作交流协定，说明华南女子文理学院在国际上的认可度，也说明新老华南文化基因有一定的沿袭传承。

因为早年就有姊妹校的关系，1984 年由余宝笙等老华南校友复办的福建华南女子职业学院开始了与国际间高校的交流来往。还是以新华南和美国晨边学院的交流为例吧！

从 2008 年美国晨边学院校长率团来访女院（谢必震，2008：202）之后，两校开始多次交流互访。岳峰（2018）的《春色任天涯》特别讲到来自晨边学院的格雷戈里·盖尔教授多次来访女院，其中 2013 年利用学术年假到女院上课一学期，躬身捡拾垃圾的故事，令人动容。每次美国晨边学院老师或者学生来访，女子学院都会邀请对方师生拜访参观仓山福建师大老校部，也是私立华南女子文理学院的校舍。他们看了都会目瞪口呆，因为师大老校部建筑与晨边学院主楼 Lewis Hall 内外非常相像，特别是内部的风格构建并无两样。何故？说来话长，老华南第一任校长程吕底亚毕业于晨边学院，她的哥哥是晨边学院建校校董之一；第二任校长卢爱德的父亲是晨边第二任院长。如前文所述，晨边与华南结为姊妹校，对接资助化学系；当初建设华南时候的彭氏楼是用了晨边学院的建筑设计师比奇先生的图纸，再加了中国式屋顶。（吴梓明，2001）

With its metamorphosis as Fujian Hwa Nan Women's Voc-Tech College, 46 alumnae who graduated from Hwa Nan Women's College of Arts & Sciences, including Yu Baosheng, Chen Zhongying and Ma Xiufa, returned to their "beloved" school to teach. Dr. Yu Baosheng was elected as the president. With this reincarnation, Yu Baosheng became the fourth president, thus Lucy Wang Shijing in reality could not be the last one. Of course, some people distinguish between the legal entity of old Hwa Nan and new Hwa Nan. However, because Fujian Hwa Nan Women's Voc-Tech College was indeed rebuilt with the vision, spirit and labors of old Hwa Nan alumnae, the culture of old Hwa Nan was simply reborn in a new form while maintaining the cultural genes of old Hwa Nan. The traditions simply evolved with new cooperation and exchange agreements reached with over ten international colleges and universities, including Florida State University, University of Oregon, University of Puget Sound, Centenary University, Morningside University in America, Svenska Tekniska Vetenskapsakademien in Finland, Ewha University in the Republic of Korea, Hiroshima Women's University in Japan, Asicang University in Thailand, and Silliman University in the Philippines. This proved the international recognition of the Hwa Nan Women's College of Arts and Sciences, and demonstrated that new Hwa Nan inherited its perspective from old Hwa Nan, and the two shared the same cultural genes, international character and passion for women's education.

Because of the relationship with sister schools in the early years, Fujian Hwa Nan Women's Voc-Tech College, which was re-established by Yu Baosheng and other old Hwa Nan alumnae in 1984, emphasized exchanges with international colleges and universities during its formative years. Let's take the exchange between new Hwa Nan and Morningside College in America as an example.

Since 2008, when the president of Morningside College led a delegation to visit the new Hwa Nan, the two schools re-established communication and exchanges with each other. Professor Gregory Guelcher visited Hwa Nan many times, including the one in 2013, when he went to Hwa Nan for a semester on his sabbatical leave, and the moral story of him picking up litter by himself is impressive. Every time a teacher or student from Morningside College visits, Hwa Nan invites them to tour the old campus building of Fujian Normal University in Cangshan District, which was the original footprint of Hwa Nan Women's College of Arts and Sciences. The interior and exterior of this building is very similar to Lewis Hall, the main building of Morningside College. Take a moment to compare the similarities of the style construction. Why is that? Well, it's a long story. Lydia Trimble, the first president of the old Hwa Nan, graduated from Morningside College, and her brother was one of the founding directors of Morningside College. The father of the second president, Dr. Ida B. Lewis, was the second president of Morningside College. As previously stated, Morningside became sister schools with Hwa Nan and supported the Department of Chemistry. When Hwa Nan was built, Payne Hall was constructed using the drawings of Mr. Beach, the architect of Morningside College, with a Chinese-style roof added to it.

福建华南女子职业学院作为全国第一所具有国家承认学历教育招生资格的女子高校，其全日制民办女子高校的唯一性、敢为人先的开创性、非营利性以及为社会培养了两万多位大学生等事实，获得了政府和社会的高度认可。1995年新华南复办十年之际，时任福州市委书记习近平同志亲临视察（谢必震，2008：185），留下"巾帼不让须眉，华南女杰辈出"的题词，一直鼓舞华南人前行。这个题词目前立在新校区进门处，中英文双语，成为学校与国际友人交流时展示的内容之一。

新华南成为福州高新区大学城唯一的一所民办非营利高校，从1984年复办之初的4个专业，发展到2022年的5个系，25个专业，实属不易。到目前为止先后获得"全国民办高校先进单位""全国五四红旗团支部""国家级示范职业资格技能鉴定站""福建省第一、第二文明校园""福建省高技能人才培训基地""第三届福建省十佳志愿者服务集体""福建省高校校园文化建设优秀成果一等奖"等20余项国家级、省级奖项和荣誉称号。有理由相信，乘着国家大力发展高等职业教育的东风，牢记习总书记嘱托的"不求最大，但求最优，但求适应社会需要"的指示，新华南必将为社会培养更多符合社会实际需求的高职人才，取得更大的办学成就。

透过撰写华南的前世今生，我发现华南是个巨大的学术宝藏。新旧华南内涵丰富，具有一定国际知名度和影响力。用华南作为主题的期刊论文、硕士论文、博士论文和图书的数量相当丰富。各位作者对于新旧华南历史的梳理、挖掘，或是基于人，或是基于教育背景，或是基于其办学理念性质，又或曾经是其中的一分子等等，不一而足。

Fujian Hwa Nan Women's Voc-Tech College is the first women's college in the country that has the qualification for enrollment of academic education approved by the government. It is the uniqueness of being a full-time private women's college, its pioneering and non-profit nature, and the fact that it has trained more than 20,000 college students for society that makes it highly recognized by government and society. In 1995, ten years after the rebuilding of new Hwa Nan, Xi Jinping, then secretary of the Fuzhou Municipal Party Committee, inspected the campus, and left the inscription "Women are not inferior to men, Hwa Nan women of distinction appear one after another". This saying has always encouraged the people of Hwa Nan to make progress. The inscription, in both Chinese and English, is currently carved at the entrance of the new campus, and has become one of the guiding beacons to be shared by the college when exchanging with friends from all over the world.

New Hwa Nan has become the only private non-profit college in Fuzhou High-tech Zone University Town. It has gone a long way from its four initial majors after its revival in 1984 to five departments and twenty-five majors in 2022. So far, it has won more than 20 provincial, national awards and honorary titles such as the "National Advanced Unit of Private Colleges and Universities" "National May 4th Red Flag Youth League Branch" "National Vocational Qualification and Skills Appraisal Station Model" "Fujian Province First and Second Civilized Campus" "Fujian Provincial High-skilled Talent Training Base" "The Third Fujian Province Top Ten Volunteer Service Groups", and "First Prize for Outstanding Achievements in Campus Culture Construction in Fujian Province". There are reasons to believe that by taking advantage of the country's vigorous facilitation of higher vocational education, and keeping in mind the instructions of Xi Jinping—"not seeking the largest, but the most optimized, to meet the needs of society", new Hwa Nan will thus cultivate more vocational talents that meet the actual needs of the society and achieve greater prosperity for its future development.

By writing about the past and present of Hwa Nan, I have discovered that Hwa Nan is a huge academic treasure. Both old and new Hwa Nan have rich connotations and a certain international reputation and influence. Hwa Nan was chosen as the topic of many journal papers, master theses, doctoral theses and books. Throughout the literature, it can be seen that these authors' sorting and excavation of the history of new and old Hwa Nan are based on people, their educational backgrounds, the nature of their school-running philosophy which contributed to making Hwa Nan the unique institution that it is today.

● 余宝笙——新华南创办带头人：仓山百年女性力量之一

余宝笙博士（1904—1996）是福建莆田人，她于1922—1924年就读于私立华南女子文理学院，曾赴美国留学，1928年硕士毕业于美国哥伦比亚大学，回母校任教，开设化学课程。1935年二度赴美求学，于1937年获得美国约翰·霍普金斯大学生物化学博士学位后回到祖国。在此后的8年，即1938—1946年间，余博士与华南同艰苦，共命运，与陈叔奎、吴芝兰、周贞英和许引明诸位博士一起，坚守母校，立誓终身不嫁，共同协助王世静校长（陈钟英，2016：25）。她经历了老华南的三位女校长时代、抗日战争内迁南平的艰苦时代、学院建筑两次被毁以及合并进入福建师范大学时代，为社会培养了一批又一批的优秀女性人才。

：余宝笙
：Yu Baosheng

• Yu Baosheng—Founding Leader of New Hwa Nan: Part of the Female Power in Cangshan in the Past 100 Years

Dr. Yu Baosheng (1904 – 1996) was a native of Putian, Fujian. She studied at Hwa Nan Women's College of Arts and Sciences from 1922 to 1924. She then went to the United States to study. She graduated from Columbia University with a master's degree of chemistry in the United States in 1928, and returned to her alma mater to teach chemistry courses. In 1935, she returned to the United States for further study. In 1937, she returned to Hwa Nan after obtaining a doctorate in biochemistry from Johns Hopkins University. During the following eight years, from 1938 to 1946, Dr. Yu and Hwa Nan shared immense challenges that shaped the school's destiny. Together with Dr. Chen Shukui, Dr. Wu Zhilan, Dr. Zhou Zhenying and Dr. Xu Yinming, she stood by her alma mater and vowed to stay single for life. They jointly assisted President Lucy Wang Shijing. She faced all manner of adversities which old Hwa Nan encountered—the era of three female presidents, evacuation to Nanping during the War of Resistance Against Japanese Aggression, the two times the college building was destroyed, and the assimilation by Fujian Teachers College. With her remarkable talents she trained a large number of outstanding female graduates for society.

1984 年 10 月，历经生活起伏跌宕、已 80 岁的余宝笙博士以华南女子文理学院暨附中校友会理事长之名，在福建师范大学信笺上向福建省高教厅并报省人民政府写出筹办华南女子学院的报告。她同时发出"敬致校友书"。46 名来自各行各业的华南校友齐聚烟台山，在 6.6 亩的土地上开始辛苦地耕耘，福建华南女子职业学院从此诞生。为了募集筹措更多的办学资金，提升学院师资水平，余宝笙不顾年事已高，借助自己在美国留学的资源，多次往返世界各地。新华南师资水平很高，一是利用国内老华南校友，二是海外校友和美国亚洲基督教高等教育联合董事会（亚联董）联络外教来授课，三是派出新华南培养的学生留学攻读硕士学位。1990 年与美国佛罗里达州立大学签订校际交流协议后，先后有 11 位新华南毕业生在佛罗里达州立大学获得硕士学位，其中有 8 位先后回母校教书服务。

1996 年 5 月，余宝笙还助力学院与美国普吉湾大学签订校际交流协议（陈钟英，2016：92），先后引来 20 余位青年教师来华南任教。没有余宝笙热爱祖国、热爱教育的一片赤诚之心，就没有今天福建华南女子职业学院的成长和壮大。从 1984 年到 1996 年，余宝笙治校 12 年。在迈向社会就业方面，新华南毕业生找工作获得"华南女儿不愁嫁"的美誉。

余宝笙的创业故事影响非常大，福州当地青年深受感动和鼓舞，2022 年将她评为仓山百年女性力量之佼佼者。在福州仓山区复园路 1-1 号的一座民国老宅"厅见"咖啡馆，斑驳的墙上悬挂着大幅布艺"寻找余宝笙"，还有特别设置的余宝笙事迹照片展览。举办者通过余宝笙重新记录福建华南女子学院的事迹，鼓励新时代女性认识余宝笙，发现自己，健康成长。

In October 1984, Dr. Yu Baosheng, who successfully faced many of life's most arduous challenges and who was 80 years old, wrote, as Chairman of the Council of Alumnae Association of Hwa Nan Women's College of Arts and Sciences and the Affiliated High School, a report to the Fujian Provincial Department of Higher Education and the Provincial People's Government on the letterhead of Fujian Normal University. She proposed in her report the establishment of new Hwa Nan Women's College. At the same time, she issued "A letter to Alumnae", and 46 Hwa Nan alumnae from all walks of life gathered on Yantai Mountain and began to work in earnest on this site of 6.6 mu. Thus Fujian Hwa Nan Women's Voc-Tech College took root. In order to raise essential funding for expanding the school and improving the level of new teachers in the college, she employed her own resources to travel internationally. Yu Baosheng traveled back and forth around the world many times in spite of her advanced age. Teachers in new Hwa Nan were very proficient and came from four sources. Firstly, there were talented old Hwa Nan alumnae in China; secondly, there were overseas alumnae; thirdly, the United Board for Christian Higher Education in Asia (UBCHEA) helped recruit foreign teachers; and finally, Hwa Nan sent its most talented graduates to study abroad for their master's degrees. After signing an inter-school exchange agreement with Florida State University in Tallahassee in 1990, 11 new Hwa Nan graduates obtained master's degrees at Florida State University, and eight of these returned to their alma mater to work and teach.

Yu Baosheng signed an inter-school exchange agreement with the University of Puget Sound in May 1996 which resulted in a score of young English instructors coming to Hwa Nan over the next quarter of a century. Without Yu Baosheng's dedication to the country and love of education, there would have been no Fujian Hwa Nan Women's Voc-Tech College. For 12 years from 1984 to 1996, Yu Baosheng managed the school. It should come as no surprise that the graduates of new Hwa Nan were welcomed into the job market and soon parents knew that "Hwa Nan daughters did not have to worry about getting hired".

The story of Yu Baosheng's rebuilding of Hwa Nan had a great impact, and local young people in Fuzhou were deeply impressed and inspired by her. In 2022, she was designated as the leader of Cangshan's female power during the past 100 years. In an old house (now "Tingjian" Café) built in the time of Republic of China at No. 1 – 1 Fuyuan Road, Cangshan District, Fuzhou, a large-scale cloth artwork "Searching for Yu Baosheng" was designed and displayed on the old wall. There is a special photo exhibition of Yu Baosheng's deeds in this restored old house. The curator encourages women of the new era to model after Yu Baosheng, find themselves and grow up robustly by demonstrating Yu Baosheng's deeds of rebuilding Hwa Nan.

• 首任校长程吕底亚后人与新华南的情缘

上文提到新华南与美国普吉湾大学 1996 年签订校际交流协议，可是，这又是如何在成百上千的美国高校里进行挑选后而结下的缘分呢？这不得不讲到程吕底亚后人与新华南的故事。

1983 年，改革开放后五年，美国普吉湾大学组织了由校长、中国史专家和校友们共 24 人的"中国行"活动团，吸引了程闽岱和夫人一同前往。当时国门开放不久，他们到了北京、洛阳、西安、上海、杭州、桂林、广州和香港旅行。普吉湾大学有亚洲研究专业。对中国历史具有相当研究、毕业于哈佛大学的白淑珍博士一同前往。可是，程闽岱和夫人却未能访问他们更感兴趣的福州。可能是靠近台湾的原因，当年福州尚未对广大外国游客完全开放（Trimble，2007：67）。那么程闽岱夫妇为何特别想前往福建福州呢？前文有述，程闽岱 1915 年出生于福建古田闽江边，到 12 岁时，才与在中国做医生的父亲和家人回到普吉湾大学所在地塔科马，而福州的华南女子学院，程氏家族一直有人参与建设。事实上，从程吕底亚开始到程闽岱，再到现在的程高登，程氏家族与福建有着百年情（林本椿，2014）。

从小在福建长大的程闽岱在阔别 56 年后，重返中国却没能回到家乡，心情可想而知。所以 6 年后的 1989 年，程闽岱和小儿子程高登、儿媳程索尼娅策划回到了从小长大的福建南平，盼望能遇上小时候一起玩乒乓球的中国小朋友。他们来到新华南，见到了时任外事处负责人的许道锋，她也同时管理特区实用英语专业（陈钟英，2016：80）。许道锋曾经是老华南华惠德的学生，而华惠德是程闽岱爸爸程嘉尼的堂妹（Trimble，2007：78）。按照中国的习俗和辈分，程闽岱应该叫程吕底亚姑婆。

• The Everlasting Friendship Between Hwa Nan and the Descendants of Her First President

As mentioned above, new Hwa Nan and the University of Puget Sound signed an agreement in 1996. One might ponder how this bond was formed with this school instead of one of the other hundreds of American universities. This brings us to the story of Lydia's descendants and how and why they determined to reconnect with Fujian, Fuzhou and the education of women at new Hwa Nan.

In 1983, China was in the fifth year of the Reform and Opening Up when Puget Sound organized a "China Discovery" tour activity group consisting of 24 people including its president, experts on Chinese history and alumnus. This trip attracted Robert A. Trimble as an alumnus and his wife Genevieve. They diligently completed the required reading and attended all the pre-tour lectures as this adventure satisfied one of their life long ambitions. They journeyed to Beijing, Luoyang, Xi'an, Shanghai, Hangzhou, Guilin, Guangzhou and Hong Kong shortly after China opened its doors to foreign tourists. The University of Puget Sound had a newly established major in Asian studies whose program was headed by Dr. Suzanne Barnett. She was fluent in Mandarin, earned her PhD at Harvard University, and her expertise was in Chinese history. Her ability to tell stories that made history come alive endeared her to the group. However, Robert and his wife's thirst was not quenched as they longed to visit Robert's historical roots in Fuzhou. Perhaps they failed to reach Fuzhou because of its proximity to Taiwan which caused Fuzhou not to be fully open to foreign tourists. So why did Robert and his wife particularly want to go to Fuzhou? Robert was born in 1915 in Gutian, Fujian in an era when the Minjiang River was the "highway" that connected Yanping to Fuzhou. His mother was a nurse and his father ran an 80-bed hospital in Yanping. The family visited Hwa Nan every time they came to Fuzhou. In fact, from Lydia Trimble to Robert, and now Gordon, the Trimble family has more than a century-old relationship with Fujian. Robert left China at the age of 12. The family settled in Tacoma not far from the campus of the University of Puget Sound.

It is not difficult to appreciate that Robert's yearning, having spent his first 12 years in Fujian and finally returning to China after an absence of 56 years, was not satisfied because he was unable to recapture the images that had been locked away in his head for so many years. Six years later in 1989, Robert's passion to return to Nanping to experience again the sights and sounds of old China so deeply etched in memory came to pass. He and his wife Genevieve traveled with his younger son Gordon and Gordon's wife Sonia, hoping to meet childhood Chinese friends with whom he had played table tennis a half-century before. They of course paid their first of many visits to new Hwa Nan and met Xu Daofeng, who was then managing the Foreign Affairs Office and the SAR Practical English program. Xu Daofeng was a student of L. Ethel Wallace from old Hwa Nan, and Wallace was the cousin of Robert's father Dr. Charles Garnet Trimble. According to Chinese customs and seniority, Lydia was Robert's grandaunt.

因为有上述渊源，福建华南女子职业学院于1996年与普吉湾大学签订了"普吉湾华南英语教师专案"，内容是普吉湾大学每隔一年派一位女性毕业生到华南担任十个月英语教师，工资、保险、机票等费用由普吉湾大学负责，华南负责安排工作、食宿等。从1996年到2016年，普吉湾大学共派出13位优秀毕业生到新华南做英语教师，程氏一家在其中起到重要作用（岳峰，2018：465）。由于程高登夫妇在华南任教多年，非常了解华南的办学目标和师资情况，因此把最初隔一年派一位，变成一年派一位普吉湾毕业生来担任英语教师。在他们夫妇的努力帮助下，从2017年到2019年，普吉湾大学更是由每年派一位变为每年派出两位优秀毕业生到华南教书。到2020年，来新华南教书的"普吉湾华南教师"达到19位。普吉湾大学之所以愿意负担费用，是因为校友程闽岱曾大力捐资捐助母校普吉湾大学，致力于母校与福建福州大力合作。这才会有前文讲的，在普吉湾大学也能找到程闽岱捐资的Trimble Hall。

身为美国夏威夷州议员的程高登与父亲程闽岱于2005年利用议会休会期来新华南教授学生英语，不收取分文工资，他们继承了家族热爱中国的传统。程闽岱于2009—2012年，从94～98岁五年间，每年独自乘坐飞机来往中美，亲赴新华南听课，设立并颁发三届程吕底亚奖学金，这种情怀令人动容（岳峰，2018）。

有感于程氏家族与福建跨越百年的友谊，多家福建电视媒体记录下90多岁高龄的程闽岱多次往返故乡，以及家族捐资捐力、助力华南教育事业的事迹。

It all comes down to the human—person to person connections with Robert Trimble that explains how Fujian Hwa Nan Women's Voc-Tech College signed the "Puget Sound—Hwa Nan English Teacher Project" with the University of Puget Sound in 1996. It provides that the University of Puget Sound will send a female graduate to Hwa Nan to teach English for ten months every other year. The salary, insurance, flights and other expenses are covered by Puget Sound, and Hwa Nan is responsible for arranging work, room and board. From 1996 to 2016, the University of Puget Sound sent a total of 13 outstanding graduates to new Hwa Nan as English teachers. The Trimble family thus played an indispensable and important role. Because Gordon and his wife have been teaching in Hwa Nan for many years, they are very familiar with the goals of school operation and the situation of recruiting native English instructors. Puget Sound changed the initial cooperation from sending one graduate every other year to sending one Puget Sound graduate every year. Later, from 2017 to 2019, the University of Puget Sound changed its previous arrangement from sending one graduate each year to sending two outstanding graduates to teach in Hwa Nan every year. By 2020, before the pandemic broke out, the number of "Puget Sound—Hwa Nan English Teachers" who came to experience Fujian and live at new Hwa Nan reached 19. The reason why Puget Sound was willing to cover the cost is that Robert made a substantial donation to his alma mater and promoted the strengthening of cooperation between his alma mater and Fuzhou. His childhood memories of life in Yanping and Fuzhou left a very deep impression on him and his affection for the people of Fujian was apparent in everything he did. This is why at Puget Sound, you can also find that Trimble Hall came to pass as a result of a donation by Cheng Mindai (Robert) to honor his father Dr. Charles Garnet Trimble who taught surgery and ran the Alden Speare Memorial Hospital in Nanping.

Gordon Trimble, a Hawaii State Senator, together with his father Robert, came to Hwa Nan to teach English in 2005 after Hawaii's regular legislative session. He offered his services without charge as a symbol of his friendship to promote better cultural understanding. Even when he was in his nineties Robert returned to China almost every year for the next five years. The family's good will and affection for the Chinese people were demonstrated on numerous occasions. In Hwa Nan he visited classes, set up and awarded three Lydia Trimble Scholarships. My eyes are filled with tears whenever hearing about such noble sentiments and such moving deeds.

I was deeply touched by the friendship between the Trimble family and Fujian that has lasted well over a hundred years. Various Fujian TV media interviewed Robert Trimble while he was in his 90s to record his remarkable life journey.

程高登 2017 年在第三届"海上丝绸之路"（福州）国际旅游节上的演讲特别值得一提，因为它详细讲到了他的家族和福建、福州以及烟台山附近华南女子学院的渊源。

尊敬的各位嘉宾，尊敬的主持人：

程高登是我的名字。我在美国圣地亚哥北部的一个农场长大，梦想着有一天能跟随马可·波罗的足迹。从孔子那里，我懂得了三人行必有我师焉。从庄子那里，我懂得了人生的多样、逍遥，无须受束缚。我第一次来福建的时候觉得气候又热又潮湿，身上的毛孔都浸满了汗水。尽管 30 年过去了，我仍清晰地记得福州的人们。当看着他们骑自行车时，我能感受到他们眼中的好奇，他们脸上的决心。他们将爱倾入对福建菜肴的烹饪中。闽菜闻起来很香，尝起来更棒。但打动我内心的是他们真诚的问候。

三年后，我敬畏地站在西安城墙门前，如此之大，能容纳一个刚穿越丝绸之路归来的千只骆驼商队。我静静地站在那里，但我的思绪已回到了泉州北部的尘土飞扬的那段路，沿路有清真寺、海事博物馆和神奇的石桥，就是在那我看到了一个 20 人的团队正在用石头手工铺路。几天后，我们再次南下，在这短短的时间内，那个团队将这条路推进了 5 公里。拿破仑是对的。雄狮已经觉醒。看看今天的福州吧！当我旅行的时候，我意识到中国人对美国的了解比美国人对中国和中国人的了解多得多。这种缺乏理解的现象对未来的发展不利。所以我在 20 世纪 90 年代初与普吉特湾大学进行了交流。虽然我知道我不会改变美国或中国，但也不妨像愚公决定移山时一样慢慢开始。然而，我该从哪里开始呢？虽然这个城市需要的是充实与国际化，但是不要太向美国化方向发展。98 年前，面对周围都是令人兴奋的美景与历史文化，一位美国的教育家兼心理学家来到了中国。本该只是两周的访问，最后他却在中国待了足足两年的时间。他对于中国的印象通过倾听人们的声音发生了转变，他解释道，当人们真心实意地尝试交流时，交流过程会把人们紧密地联系在一起。想知道他的名字吗？他叫约翰·杜威。是的，他 1919 年来过福州。

生活是美好的，充满了难以置信的福气。我们程氏家族的榕树，首先扎根在福清，然后是平潭，然后是福州，然后是塔科马，然后是夏威夷。为什么不让你的榕树传播到福建，生根扎根在福州？让福州的一些"福"也赐福于你的生活呢？我们本来是来旅游，结果却花了半辈子的时间留在福州。现在你知道我们为什么称福州为家了吧。谢谢！

A speech made by Gordon Trimble at the 3rd Maritime Silk Road (Fuzhou) International Tourism Festival in 2017 is particularly worthy to be mentioned here because this speech delineates the relationship between the Trimble family and Fujian. Let me show you as follows.

Honored guests, gracious host,

Gordon Trimble is my name. I grew up on a ranch north of San Diego dreaming that someday I would follow in the footsteps of Marco Polo. From Confucius, I knew that I would always learn from my traveling companions. From Zhuangzi I knew that life's possibilities needed to be imagined, unfettered by words. It was hot, humid—my pores were full of sweat that first time in Fujian. But the people of Fuzhou, I remember vividly even though it was three decades ago. The curiosity in their eyes, the determination on their face, their intensity—you could feel when you watched them ride their bicycles. The love they poured into the cooking of Fujian food. The smell was great. The taste was even better. But it was the sincerity of their greeting that touched my heart.

Three years later, I stood in awe in the Gatehouse of Xi'an. It was so large that it could accommodate a caravan, fresh from across the Silk Road, of a thousand camels. But even as I stood there in silence, my images went back to that dusty stretch of road north of Quanzhou with its mosque, and maritime museum and totally surreal stone bridge. It was there that I saw a crew of 20 building a road—by hand—of stone. A few days later, we headed again south and during that short period of time, the crew had advanced that road five kilometers. Napoleon was right. The lion is awake. Look at Fuzhou today! As I traveled, I realized that Chinese knew much more about America than Americans knew about China and Chinese. This lack of understanding did not bode well for the future. So I sat down with the University of Puget Sound in the early 1990s. I knew I was not going to change America or China, but why not begin much as Yu Gong had done when he decided to move his mountains. But, where would I start? The city needed to be substantial, cosmopolitan, but not too American... surrounded by places that were exciting, of beauty, of culture, of history. An American educator and psychologist came to China 98 years ago on a trip which was supposed to last two weeks. He wound up spending two years. As he started to listen to people, his image of China began to evolve, and he reasoned that when people sincerely try to communicate, the process brings them closer together. His name? John Dewey! Yes, he came to Fuzhou in 1919.

Life is wonderful! Incredible blessings! Our banyan tree first put its root down in Fuqing, then Pingtan, then Fuzhou, then Tacoma, then Hawaii. Why not let your banyan spread to Fujian, and sink a root also in Fuzhou. Let some of that Fu in Fuzhou also bless your life. We came for a visit and wound up spending half of a lifetime. And now you know why we call Fuzhou home.

Thank you!

程高登夫妇自 2009—2019 年，除了作为志愿者在新校区的新华南授课十年，赴福建师大图书馆、历史学院、外语学院等作讲座外，还多次组织美国学生来福建与中国学生一起研学交流；促成华南和美国夏威夷圣心女校交流，赞助组织了四批次美国圣心学生来福建研学，与华南学生结对子，游览福州；赞助支持华南三批次教师赴夏威夷参观学习，一批次学生赴圣心女中学习。

圣心女中来闽研学学生
（2017 年）
Students from Sacred Hearts
Academy（SHA），2017

高登夫妇与平潭实验小学代
表合影图
The Trimbles with teachers
from Pingtan

　　程氏家族在福州的时候，每年 11 月会举行"程闽岱友谊晚会"。晚会宴请与程吕底亚有关的学校的代表，到 2019 年大约有 11 次。之所以选取每年的 11 月份，是因为程闽岱 1915 年 11 月出生于福建古田，以此纪念程闽岱在福建度过的 12 个美好的岁月。一般会有华南师生代表，福清二中、福清龙田中心小学、平潭实验小学、平潭一中和福建师范大学代表一起聚会。

From 2009 to 2019, Gordon and Sonia Trimble organized American students to visit Fujian to research and communicate with Chinese students on multiple occasions. In addition to volunteering to teach at new Hwa Nan on its new campus for a decade he gave lectures at the library, College of Sociology and History, College of Foreign Languages and other colleges of Fujian Normal University. The couple facilitated the exchange between Hwa Nan and Sacred Hearts Academy in Honolulu in addition to the interaction of students and faculty between the University of Puget Sound in Tacoma and the various schools in Fujian having a connection with Lydia Trimble. They sponsored and arranged four groups of Sacred Hearts students to be immersed in Chinese culture while learning and studying in Fujian. They also supported Hwa Nan teachers on three occasions to visit and study in Hawaii and a group of Hwa Nan students to study in Hawaii networking with Sacred Hearts.

When the Trimble family was in Fuzhou, there was always at least one "Bob Friendship Dinner". The tradition began in 2005 and the banquet was held usually in November to celebrate the connection of the family with representatives from schools related to Lydia Trimble. There have been about 11 banquets before 2020. While Bob Trimble was born in Gutian, Fujian on November 15, 1915, he figured he would celebrate his birthday anytime he could get a group of friends together. Some years he celebrated his birthday more than three times. Most often attendees include representatives from Hwa Nan (teachers and students), Fuqing No. 2 Middle School, Fuqing Longtian Central Primary School, Pingtan Experimental Primary School, Pingtan No. 1 Middle School and Fujian Normal University with either a group of students from the University of Puget Sound or Sacred Hearts Academy.

为了更高效、更有序地做好中美学校之间的文化教育双向交流，2017年，程氏家族进行了中美交流项目双向互动的创新。区别于往年只是美方学校赴福建交流的做法，他们于2018年、2019年分批次资助派送华南女院师生和福清二中教师赴夏威夷研学。

夏威夷圣心女校和华南女院学生互动研学一般选择在秋季。为了让2018年秋季两校交流更有成效，当年8月，有两位中国老师赴美做前期准备，提前与即将于秋季来闽的圣心学生互动交流。两位老师将中国概况、福建、福州地理人文特色特点、茉莉花茶文化、船政文化、教育特色等内容预先做好PPT，到夏威夷圣心给同学们上课。当夏威夷学生秋季来福州研学时，就已经对于中国、福建、福州和华南有了一定了解。

：介绍福州茉莉花茶文化以及扇子文化（2018）
：Introducing Fuzhou Jasmine tea & silk fan to SHA girls（2018）

华南两位老师在8月提前完成周详的准备，等到圣心女校学生来福建研学时，华南和圣心女校的交流互动有了先期的讲课预备，就更加得心应手。2018年9月开学伊始，程高登教授在华南学生中，挑选了两批学习努力的女生与圣心女生结对子成姐妹，利用早读、晚自习加强对于她们的英语口语培训，预先探访福州，开发了几条步行福州市的研学路线，学生用英语练习如何介绍。还利用现代化融媒体手段，让双方学生自制自我介绍视频，在其见面前通过视频互相认识、熟悉。

In order to do a better job in the two-way cultural and educational communication between Chinese and American Schools, in 2017, the Trimble family introduced an innovation in this exchange project by having Chinese teachers travel to Hawaii for a 10-day period in the Summer to provide a detailed orientation for the next batch of female students from Sacred Hearts Academy. In 2019 one of the Chinese teachers who traveled to Hawaii to provide this orientation was from their sister school, Fuqing No. 2 Middle School.

Cultural immersion and interactive research of students from the Sacred Hearts Academy and Hwa Nan Women's College occurred in October following the National Holidays. In order to make the exchange between the two schools in the fall of 2018 more meaningful, in August, two Chinese teachers went to the United States with a multi-day detailed orientation program for the "China Scholars" to prepare them for their cultural immersion experience. The two teachers prepared presentations which they reviewed with the Trimbles that introduced basic facts about China, general geographical and cultural characteristics of Fuzhou and Fujian. These two Chinese teachers by their presence let the entire school know of the upcoming China trip. They motivated the "China Scholars" and their parents to prepared more diligently for the experience. Finally the students were more relaxed and receptive and their parents more relieved because they knew two people in Fuzhou that would assist with the experience. The Chinese teachers with their understanding of the culture, and educational characteristics of China could do a much better job in the pairing of American students with Chinese students. This simple innovation in the manner of orientation greatly enhanced the learning process.

The two teachers from Hwa Nan prepared and rehearsed their presentations well ahead of schedule, so when the students from Sacred Hearts Academy arrived in Fujian for their immersion, research and study, the exchanges and interactions progressed more rapidly and at a much higher level. At the beginning of school year in September 2018, Gordon selected two groups of Hwa Nan students who had participated in the FLTRP English Cup contest from the previous year. These girls after a detailed orientation process became the older sisters of Sacred Hearts girls. He made use of the time of morning reading and evening self-study to enhance their spoken English. He canvassed Fuzhou in advance to develop several walking routes, and challenged students to practice introducing culturally significant sights in English. He also utilized modern integrated media methods to let the students from both sides make self-introduction videos for each other, and become familiar with each other through their video projects before actually meeting each other in person.

华南女生到机场迎接圣心姐妹
HN welcome SHA students at Fuzhou Airport

圣心女生学做月饼，华南女生做翻译
SHA girls making mooncakes with HN girls's help of translation

华南学生通过这种研学活动，对于福州本土文化有了更深的了解。在高登的指导下，学生们对于研学旅行课程和路线进行设计、开发、行走，然后用英语学习讲解，以准备向美国来访的同学描述。

美国的圣心女生在家校电子校刊上发表了到中国的心得，她们认为中国之行带给了她们欣喜和启迪，体验了动车，了解了"一带一路"、郑和，还赴泉州等地，收获满满。

在平潭还有程氏家族关注的两所学校：平潭实验小学和平潭一中。华南女院曾多次派老师陪同高登夫妇赴平潭寻找先辈足迹。这两所学校都是从曾经是程吕底亚创办的平潭毓贤女校逐渐分离而发展壮大的。

另外一个传统固定交流活动，是高登父亲程闽岱母校美国普吉湾大学来福建研学活动。每次普吉湾大学特色研学游学项目——"PacRim（环太平洋区域）亚洲行"进行时，程氏家族都会督促 20 多位 PacRim 成员来华进行研学。一般都安排来福建，在华南食宿，与华南或者福建师大学生交流联欢，于游走福州中研学福州，学习福州文化和传统（岳峰，2018：405 - 406）。至今，项目成员分别于 2008 年、2011 年、2017 年、2019 年四次来闽交流。

The Hwa Nan students practiced their skills of presenting in English the sights and smells of Fuzhou's cultural highlights to prepare for their role as big sisters for the students from the US. Under the instruction and guidance of Gordon, several strolling routes of the Fuzhou City were designed, and Chinese students actually promenaded along the Minjiang River and public squares with the Trimbles rehearsing in English what they might say to their American buddies.

Girls from Sacred Hearts wrote what they experienced in China in the e-parentline magazine. They deemed their trip to China delightful and enlightening. They experienced the bullet train to Quanzhou and had a better understanding of the "Belt and Road Initiative" plus coming to know famous voyager Zheng He. They thought the trip extraordinarily rewarding.

The Trimble family is also involved with two other schools which are in Pingtan: Pingtan Experimental Primary School and Pingtan No. 1 Middle School. Hwa Nan Women's College has visited Pingtan with Sonia and Gordon several times to follow the footprints of their predecessor. The two schools in Pingtan gradually separated and evolved from the Pingtan Yuxian Girls' School, which was founded by Lydia Trimble. The elementary school has preserved the original well developed by its founder.

Another traditional is the periodic student research activity of University of Puget Sound (the alma mater of Gordon's father, Robert Trimble) in Fujian. Every time the University of Puget Sound's special research and study tour project—"PacRim (Pan-Pacific Region) Asia Tour" is carried out, the Trimble family will urge the more than 20 PacRim members to include Fujian in their study of China. On several occasions the group used Hwa Nan as their home base for a larger study in Fujian. This facilitated extensive personal interaction between the American students and those of Hwa Nan and Fujian Normal University. Their individual research projects required detailed personal interaction in English as they examined culture and tradition by walking around Fuzhou. So far I recall that project members visited Fujian four times: 2008, 2011, 2017, and 2019.

： 2019 年普吉湾大学学生来华研学，于华南外专楼
： Puget Sound students staying at the International Faculty House of Haw Nan

　　2020 年 1 月，笔者通过申请，获批到美国普吉湾大学做访问学者。从 2016 年开始，已经有三位美国普吉湾大学教授来福州访学；我是互派项目里中方第二位赴普吉湾大学的访问学者。笔者见到了 2019 年来华访学的那批学生，进行了项目回访。

　　访学期间，笔者拜访了与华南有关系、来过华南和福建师大的普吉湾老师。首先是联络上了玛吉，她于 2010—2012 年在华南担任两届"普吉湾华南英语教师专案"项目的教师（岳峰，2018）。她已成为西雅图附近莱文沃斯的森林护林公务员，特地驱车来到普吉湾大学见我。玛吉非常开心，时隔多年能在美国她的母校，与福州来的老朋友相见。

　　接着笔者与程高登一家人拜访了程闽岱的妹妹佩吉，她生于 1929 年，比程闽岱小 14 岁，华南百年校庆时她被邀请来福州参加庆祝活动。此时她已经 91 岁了。我们谈到她哥哥程闽岱，她说哥哥时常与她谈起福建和福州。

　　我也拜访了促成普吉湾大学校友 1983 年"中国之行"的前校长——菲利普·菲布斯和夫人，同时我还特地与普吉湾大学著名学者、资深教授白淑珍进行了多次访谈。白淑珍对于福州鳌峰书院颇有研究，我在普吉湾大学 Collins Memorial 图书馆档案室读到了她两篇关于福州鳌峰书院的论文。她先后两次来访福州，访问过华南。她是当初塔科马和福州成为姐妹城市的推动者之一（林本椿，2019：38）。退休后被授予普吉湾大学"Suzanne W. Barnett 当代中国研究讲座教授席"的荣誉。我们一起回顾了程氏家族与普吉湾大学、与中国、与福州的种种故事和百年情缘。

　　在普吉湾大学的时候，华南将《春色任天涯》赠送给了指导并带领了多次 PacRim 项目到福建多次的卡尔·菲尔德教授，他会一口地道的中文，中文名叫田立凯。卡尔是程氏家族的老朋友，一直致力于推动中美高校合作交流。同时，我也见到了高登的哥哥查尔斯。

In January 2020, I spent more than a month at the University of Puget Sound as a visiting scholar. Since 2016, three professors from the University of Puget Sound have come to Fuzhou as visiting scholars; I was the second Chinese visiting scholar to go to the University of Puget Sound under this exchange program. I met the group of students who came to study in China in 2019 and conducted a project return visit.

During this faculty exchange, I paid full visits to the professors and administrators who deal with China, paying close attention to those who were related to Hwa Nan and those who have been to Hwa Nan and Fujian Normal University. Firstly I contacted Margie. She spent two years as a "Puget Sound-Hwa Nan English Teacher" from 2010 to 2012. She is now a forest ranger in Leavenworth near Seattle, but she specially drove to Tacoma to meet me. Margie very happily reconnected with her old friend from Fuzhou at her alma mater after so many years.

Then the Trimbles and I visited Robert's younger sister Peggy (Margaret) Campbell. She was born in 1929 and was 14 years younger than Robert Trimble. She also graduated from Puget Sound and journeyed to Fuzhou to represent the Trimble family during the Centennial Celebration of Hwa Nan in 2008. At this point she was 91 years old. We talked about her older brother Robert. She said that her brother often talked to her about Fujian and Fuzhou.

I also visited Dr. Philip Phibbs, the former president of Puget Sound who crafted the school's "China Discovery" expedition in 1983 and his wife Gwen. Meanwhile I interviewed Dr. Suzanne Wilson Barnett multiple times. She is a famous scholar, living legend and a most distinguished professor emeritus at Puget Sound. Suzanne has extensively researched the Fuzhou Aofeng Academy. I had read two of her papers on Fuzhou Aofeng Academy in the archive room of Collins Memorial Library at Puget Sound. She has come to Fuzhou twice and has visited Hwa Nan. She was one of the early promoters of Tacoma and Fuzhou becoming sister cities. After her retirement, she was honored by the creation of the "Suzanne Wilson Barnett Endowed Chair in Contemporary Chinese Studies" which was made possible by a contribution from The Trimble Foundation. Together we reviewed only some of the stories and predestined love that lasted for a hundred years between the Trimble family, the University of Puget Sound, China, and Fuzhou.

When at the University of Puget Sound in 2020, I presented the book *International Faculty with Fujian Hwa Nan Women's College since 1908* to Professor Karl Fields on behalf of Hwa Nan. Dr. Fields was instrumental in guiding several PacRim projects to Fujian as well as being the director the Asian Studies program for many years. He speaks authentic Chinese. Karl is an old friend of the Trimbles and has been committed to promoting cooperation and exchanges between Chinese and American colleges and universities. At the same time, I also met Gordon's older brother Charles.

由于程高登一心一意促进中美民间交流，全身心致力于教学，他多次获得各种荣誉称号。程高登是福建华南女子职业学院名誉理事长。

2010 年，程高登获得福建省"友谊奖"。

2019 年，程高登被评为福州荣誉市民。

2021 年，程高登被聘为福州市人民对外友好协会第二届理事会理事，任期五年。

Due to Gordon Trimble's dedication to promoting non-governmental exchanges between China and the United States and his devotion to teaching, he has merited various honorary titles. Gordon Trimble is the honorary chairperson of Fujian Hwa Nan Women's Voc-Tech College.

In 2010, Gordon Trimble was the winner of the "Friendship Award" in Fujian Province.

In 2019, Gordon Trimble was named an honorary citizen of Fuzhou.

In 2021, Gordon Trimble was appointed as member of the Second Council of Fuzhou Municipal People's Association for Friendship with Foreign Countries for a term of five years.

CHAPTER
EIGHT

从福建协和大学
到福建师范大学①
From Fukien Christian University
to Fujian Normal University

第八章

㊉

① 本章所用图片，除特殊标注外，均由福建师范大学党政办公室文书档案室提供。

福建协和大学，今福建师范大学的主要前身之一，是一所创建于 1915 年的教会大学。作为福建现代高等教育的重要组成部分，福建协和大学虽然仅有 36 年的办学史，却为近现代中国培养和输送了大量人才，为祖国的建设与发展作出了巨大的贡献。1951 年 1 月，国家教育部接办福建协和大学和华南女子文理学院（1908 年创办），将两校合并，改名为福州大学（非现如今的"福州大学"）。至 1952 年 6 月，福州大学先后并入福建省立师范学院（1941—1952 年）、福建省研究院（1939—1951 年）、私立福建学院（1911—1951 年）等单位。1953 年福州大学更名为福建师范学院，1972 年更名为福建师范大学。

● 探访旧址　感悟时光

常往来于福州与马尾之间的人们，定能注意到在快安附近路边山坡的丛林中掩映着一群红砖复古式楼房，这就是位于鼓山之麓、闽江之畔的原福建协和大学魁岐校区旧址，是福州现今保存下来的最大的近代建筑群。

福建协和大学（1915—1951 年），在其短短 36 年办学期间曾三迁校址，从初立时的仓前观音井校区到经多方筹措建起的新校址魁岐校区，再因战时临时迁往福建邵武校区，最后复校魁岐。其中魁岐校区的使用时间最长，存留的记载也最多。魁岐校区建筑群位于福州市马尾区魁岐村，陆续建成于 1921—1932 年间，校舍占地面积 1000 多亩，由曾为燕京大学进行校园设计的美国著名建筑设计师亨利·墨菲设计，在当时被誉为全球十大最美校园之一。曾在协和大学执教的叶圣陶先生"在散文《客语》中描述：'向来不曾亲近江山的，到此却觉得趣味丰富极了。书室的窗外，只隔一片草场，闲闲地流着闽江。彼岸的山绵延重叠，有时露出青翠的新妆，有时披上轻薄的雾，有时不知从什么地方来了好些云，却与山通起家来，于是更见得那些山郁郁然有奇观了……卧室的窗对着山麓，望去有裸露的黑石，有矮矮的松林，有泉水冲过的涧道。间或有一两个人在山顶上樵采，形体渺小极了，看他们在那里运动着，便约略听得微茫的干草瑟瑟的声响。这仿佛是古代幽人的境界，在什么诗篇什么画幅里边遇见过的。暂时充当古代的幽人，当然有些新鲜的滋味。'"（谢必震，2005：15）

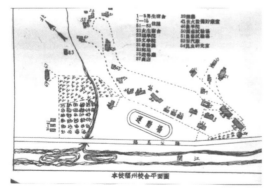

: 协大魁岐校区平面图
: Architectural plan of Kuiqi Campus

: 协大魁岐校园远景
: A distant view of Kuiqi Campus

Fukien Christian University (FCU), one of the major forerunners of today's Fujian Normal University (FNU), was a missionary university founded in 1915. As an important part of modern higher education in Fujian Province, Fukien Christian University, although only with a history of 36 years, trained and supplied a large number of talents for modern China and made great contributions to the construction and development of the country. In January 1951, the Ministry of Education took over Fukien Christian University and Hwa-Nan Women's College of Arts and Science (founded in 1908), merging them to form Fuzhou University (not today's Fuzhou University). Till June 1952, Fujian Provincial Teachers School (1941 – 1952), Fukien Academy (1939 – 1951), and Private Fujian College (1911 – 1951) had also been merged into Fuzhou University, which then was renamed Fujian Teachers College in 1953, and Fujian Normal University in 1972.

● A Visit to the Former Site

Scan for more
扫码了解更多

People who often travel between Fuzhou and Mawei must have noticed a group of red-brick retro-style buildings hidden in the jungle on the hillside near Kuai 'an. Located at the foot of the Mount Gu and on the bank of the Minjiang River, they are the buildings of Kuiqi Campus of former Fukien Christian University, the largest modern architectural complex preserved in Fuzhou today.

Fukien Christian University (1915 – 1951) moved its campus three times during its short period of 36 years, from the original Guanyinjing (Guang-ing-cang) Campus at Cangqian to the new expanse in Kuiqi, to the Shaowu Campus due to the War of Resistance Against Japanese Aggression, and finally back to Kuiqi Campus. Among them, Kuiqi campus was used for the longest time and has kept the most records. Kuiqi Campus complex, located in Kuiqi Village, Mawei District of Fuzhou City, was built from 1921 to 1932, covering an area of more than 1,000 *mu*. It was designed by H. K. Murphy, a famous American architect having designed the campus for Yenching University, and was praised as one of the top-10 most beautiful campuses in the world at that time. Mr. Ye Shengtao, once teaching in Fukien Christian University, "described the campus in his essay *Visitor's Words*: 'Never close to countryside, I feel here quite interesting though. Outside the window of my study, only a meadow apart, the Minjiang River flows idly. The mountains on the other side stretch and overlap, sometimes showing new green, sometimes covered with light fog, and sometimes with clouds and mist curling up. What lush wonders! ... The windows of my bedroom face the foothills with bare black stones, low pine forests, and spring-washed gullies. Occasionally one or two men chop and collect firewood on the mountaintop. Watching them work there, I can faintly hear the rustling of hay. It seems to be the realm of ancient recluses, which I might have come across in some poem or painting. Temporarily pretending to be an ancient recluse certainly gives a feeling of freshness.' "

百年沧桑，时光流转，这所曾经名震四方的大学在历史洪流中就这么静静地矗立一隅，见证着时代的变迁与发展。当年的琅琅读书声已远去，当年的意气风发也已成为回忆，唯有目睹晨昏变幻、风雨洗礼的一砖一瓦、一草一木、一窗一花还在静静诉说着它曾经的辉煌。如今协大魁岐村建筑群仍保存有 11 幢楼房，主要有教学楼 2 栋、宿舍楼 7 栋、办公楼 1 栋、校长楼 1 栋，都是砖石木结构，中西结合建筑风格。2013 年 1 月，福建省人民政府将福建协和大学建筑群（马尾区马尾镇魁岐村）及私立协和大学旧址（仓山区仓前街道观井路，为"烟台山近代建筑群"之一，即协大创办时在观音井租用的俄商茶行）列为第八批省级文物保护单位。

协大魁岐校区女生宿舍楼，下方即是福州三环魁岐隧道 The former dormitory for girls in Kuiqi Campus, below which is the Kuiqi Tunnel of Fuzhou Airport Highway

协大魁岐校区面向闽江，旧时的校门位置现如今已是福州海王福药制药有限公司的大门，与之相隔约 100 米处是另修建的一扇铁条拱形大门，门牌上写着"私立福建协和学院"。从新大门往里便是一片空地，穿过、拾级而上是一条较宽的路，这应是当时校区的主干道之一。路旁是两座方形斜顶的楼宇——光荣楼和光华楼，二者皆为当时的男生宿舍。道路尽头盘山而上，是又一栋男生宿舍光国楼，恰好位于光荣楼的上方。当时整个校区的男生宿舍楼有五幢，而女生宿舍楼则只有一幢，就是我们现今在福州机场快速魁岐隧道口抬头即可见到的那座红砖楼房，位于校园东北方向的山坡下。近年来因为道路交通建设的需要，它被整体平移了约 20 米。

继续沿着山路向上，便是两幢著名的教学楼——文学院和理学院，它们是该校区最具有标志性的建筑。一步一景，移步换天，不知不觉间我们来到了 2021 年翻新而成的校长楼。从 1916 年正式开学至 1951 年由人民政府接管合并，协和大学共经历了五任校长，他们分别是庄才伟、高智、林景润、陈锡恩和杨昌栋。与校长楼相邻的是教授楼和教职宿舍，这里可谓是旧时协大的"心脏"，今时今日漫步其间，似乎空气中还依旧弥漫着浓厚的学术气息。

As time goes by, after going through the vicissitudes of a hundred years, this once well-known university is standing quietly in the flood of history, witnessing the changes and development of the times. When the sound of reading has gone, when the high spirit has become memories, only its bricks, windows, trees, and flowers are still telling its once brilliance. Today, Kuiqi Campus complex still has 11 buildings, including 2 teaching buildings, 7 dormitory buildings, 1 office building and 1 President's House, all of masonry and timber structure in the combination of Chinese and Western architectural style. In January 2013, Fujian Provincial People's Government listed Fukien Christian University building complex (located in Kuiqi Village, Mawei Town, Mawei District) and the former site of Private Fukien Christian University (located at Guanyinjing Road, Cangqian Street, Cangshan District; one of the "Modern Building Complexes in Mount Yantai"; the Russian Tea Shop at Guanyinjing rented by FCU when it was firstly founded) as the 8th batch of provincial-level Cultural Relics Protection Units.

The Kuiqi campus of FCU faces the Minjiang River. Its former gate is now the gate of Fuzhou Haiwang Fuyao Pharmaceutical Co. , Ltd. About 100 meters away stands another iron arch gate, with the name "Private Fukien Christian College" on the doorplate. Entering the new gate, an open space spreads in front of us. Walking across and taking steps up, we can see a wide road, which should have been one of the main roads of the campus at that time. Along the road are two square buildings with sloping roofs, Guangrong House and Guanghua House, both of which were boys' dormitories.

：协大魁岐校区大门
：The gate of Kuiqi Campus

Winding up the road leads to another boys' dormitory, Guangguo House, located just above the Guangrong House. At that time, there were five boys' dormitory houses on the whole campus, while only one was girls'—the red brick building that can be seen at the entrance of the Quiqi Tunnel of Fuzhou Airport Highway. The girls' dormitory lies northeast of the campus at the foot of a hillside. In recent years, due to the needs of roads construction, it has been monolithically moved by about 20 meters.

Up along the main road are two famous teaching buildings, the College of Arts and the College of Science, the most iconic buildings of the campus. Touring the campus around, every step makes a difference. Soon we arrived at President's House, which was renovated in 2021. From 1916, when Fukien Christian University was officially opened, to 1951, when it was taken over and merged by people's government, it had experienced five presidents—Edwin C. Jones, John Gowdy, Lin Jingrun, Chen Xi'en, and Yang Changdong. Adjacent to President's House are Professors' House and Faculty Dormitory. Here can be regarded as the "heart" of former Fukien Christian University. Nowadays, wandering around, you can still "smell out" the strong academic atmosphere.

表 8-1　福建协和大学历任校长

姓　名	任职年份
庄才伟（1880—1924）	1915 年—1923 年
高智（1869—1963）	1923 年—1927 年
林景润（1898—1947）	1927 年—1946 年
陈锡恩（1902—1993）	1946 年—1947 年
杨昌栋（1897—1983）	1947 年—1948 年

：光荣楼①
：Guangrong House

：光华楼
：Guanghua House

：光国楼
：Guangguo House

：女生宿舍楼
：Dormitory for girls

：教职宿舍
：Faculty Dormitory

这么一所曾可比肩厦门大学的高等学府，历经风雨却依旧生动且富有灵气，它到底有着怎样的前世？让我们一起回望其灼灼其光的历史，拼凑时光碎片中当初的模样！

① 本页图片皆由作者拍摄于 2022 年春。

Table 8 - 1　Presidents of Fukien Christian University

Names	Years in Office
Edwin C. Jones (1880 - 1924)	1915 - 1923
John Gowdy (1869 - 1963)	1923 - 1927
Lin Jingrun (1898 - 1947)	1927 - 1946
Chen Xi'en (1902 - 1993)	1946 - 1947
Yang Changdong (1897 - 1983)	1947 - 1948

文学院
College of Arts

理学院
College of Science

校长楼
President's House

教授楼
Professors' House

Going through ups and downs, such an institution of higher education, once comparable to Xiamen University, still presents a vivid aura and strong vitality. What past life did it have? Let's look back at its shining history and piece together what it looked like in the fragments of time.

• 西学东渐　建校肇始

鸦片战争后，广州、福州、厦门、宁波、上海被迫开放为通商口岸，允许外国人士在这些口岸地区进行传教活动或开设学堂、医院。传教活动就越来越多地从早期的南洋地区迁至这东南沿海一带，开启了晚清西学的新阶段。鸦片战争前，许多传教士已与南洋一带的闽籍华人有较多的互动交流，有些甚至已学会了福建的方言，所以福州、厦门开埠后，熟悉两地方言民情的他们接踵而至，纷纷在福厦两地建立传教据点，发展教会，开展西学传播活动。其中，最早在福州创办教会学校的是柯林、麦利和、卢公明。这类新式学校，相比官学、私塾、书院等传统中国学堂，在教学内容、方式及管理等方面都有着很大的差异，为中国近代教育的发展起到了一定的推动作用。

1911 年 3 月 25 日，在高绰先生的邀请下，闽基督教六差会中对福建基督教会高等教育感兴趣的人士齐聚高智先生在福州的住所。六差会分别是美部会、美国美以美会、英国圣公会、美国归正教会、伦敦会和英国长老会。

美以美会的柏锡福会督认为"有必要在福建省建立一所教会联合大学，所有新教教派都可参加，开设学士、硕士及专业课程"（耶鲁大学档案 106 2375 - 6）。自此，一个漫长且波折的大学筹备历程开启了。

会议后不久，福建基督教六个差会各派一名代表加入"福建省教会联合大学筹备委员会"。1911 年 8 月，教会联合大学筹备委员会在福州鼓岭召开第一次会议，拟定："①招生条件需与伦敦大学或耶鲁大学相当；②教学以中文为主要沟通语言，但一些科目有必要用英语讲授；③大学选址应在福州；④应草拟各差会间的出资分配建议。"（耶鲁大学档案 106 2375 - 6）

1913 年 2 月，筹备委员会在厦门召开第二次会议，六大差会就具体筹办事宜进行商榷。会议当天，筹备会开始起草建校章程，初拟校名、校董事会的构成及其权利与义务、校董事会的组建、各差会的职责、校内部行政管理等。其中，校名被提议为 The Fukien University（福建大学）。会议确定学校一开学就需开设有文理科课程，开学时间可设在 1914 年秋或 1915 年春，由福州的某家差会负责暂时租借校舍，或者考虑美以美会是否可能暂时出借其楼房。

• Eastward Spread of Western Learning and the Start of FCU

After the Opium War, Guangzhou (Canton), Fuzhou (Foochow), Xiamen (Amoy), Ningbo (Ningpo) and Shanghai were forced to open as treaty ports, allowing foreigners to carry out missionary activities or set up schools and hospitals in these port areas. More and more missionary activities moved from Southeast Asia to China's southeast coastal area, starting a new stage of Western learning in the late Qing Dynasty. Before the Opium War, many missionaries had already made lots of interactions with Fujian (Fukien) people in Southeast Asia and some even had learned Fujian dialects. Therefore, after the opening of Fuzhou and Xiamen, the missionaries familiar with the two local dialects and customs flocked there, to establish missionary sites, develop churches and hold activities of Western learning. Among them, Judson Dwight Collins, Robert Samuel Maclay and Justus Doolittle were the first establishing missionary schools in Fuzhou. Compared with traditional Chinese schools such as official schools, private schools and academies, these new-style schools were quite different in terms of teaching contents, methods and management, promoting modern education in China.

On March 25th, 1911, at the invitation of John F. Goucher, a meeting was held at the residence of John Gowdy in Fuzhou for members of the six Missions at work in Fujian Province, who were interested in Fujian Christian higher education. The six Missions were ABCFM (American Board of Commissioners for Foreign Missions), MEM (American Methodist Episcopal Mission), CMS (Church Mission Society), ARCM (American Reformed Church Mission), LMS (London Missionary Society) and EPM (English Presbyterian Mission).

Bishop J. W. Bashford from MEM believed it was "essential to establish in the Province of Fukien a Christian Union University, in which all the Protestant denominations may join and which shall include Bachelor, Post-graduate, and Professional courses". Since then, a long and bumpy process of university preparation had begun.

Soon after the meeting, each of the six Missions elected one representative to serve on the Preliminary Committee on Higher Christian Education in Fujian Province. They held their first meeting on Guling (Kuliang), Fuzhou in August, 1911. The following propositions were drawn up: "(a) The standard of admission to the University should correspond to the standard of London or Yale Universities; (b) The aim shall be to make Mandarin Chinese the medium of instruction, but for some time to come it may be necessary to teach some subjects in English; (c) The location of the University should be at Foochow; (d) A series of proposals concerning the financial responsibility of the cooperating Missions was drafted."

In February, 1913, the second meeting of the Preliminary Committee was held in Xiamen, six Missions discussing specific preparations of the planned university. On the same day, the Committee proceeded to draft the Constitution, including its name, the composition of the Board of Trustees together with their rights and obligations, the formation of the Board of Trustees, the responsibilities of the Missions, executive administration, etc. The name of the university was proposed as The Fukien University. It was decided that the university should offer science and arts courses as soon as it opened, either in the autumn of 1914 or the spring of 1915. The temporary quarters could be loaned or leased by one of the Missions in Fuzhou, or if possible, MEM could temporarily lend some of their buildings.

在接下来的两年时间内，筹备会在福州鼓岭又分别召开了第三、第四次会议，全面审议建校计划，暂定校名为 The Foochow Christian University（福州协和大学）或 The Fukien Christian University（福建协和大学）。会议指出可将福州、厦门两地的以下教会学校并入筹备中的大学，如协和医学院、协和神学院、英华学院、福州书院（格致中学前身）、圣马可书院、厦门英华书院、福州三一学校（福州九中前身）、打马字学院（也称为寻源书院）、协和师范学校等。

1915 年 5 月，协和大学召开理事会首届会议。会议投票推选俾益知担任理事会主席，庄才伟先生担任首任校长。庄才伟，美国人，1880 年出生于纽约州的弗拉兴，父亲是一位美以美会的牧师。1904 年，他在卫斯理安大学取得文学学士学位。之后由美国差会派到中国学习汉语，在美以美会创办的福州英华书院（今福建师范大学附属中学）教授自然科学。在假期返美进入耶鲁大学学习化学且取得化学硕士后，又返回英华书院教授化学。1915 年被聘请为福建协和大学首任校长。（袁勇麟，2013：13）

：庄才伟
：Edwin Chester Jones

同年六七月，理事会投票通过：定于 1916 年 2 月 16 日举办第一次招生入学考试。在最后确定的建校章程中明确学校的名称为"福建协和大学校"，董事会亦相应更名为"福建协和大学校董事会"。至此，历经五年的波折与艰辛后，协大的筹建使命终于完成。

● 厚积薄发　开校仓前

在首任校长庄才伟先生带领的协大理事会的努力下，1915 年校董事会批准租借福州市仓前观音井街旧俄商茶行作为协大的临时办学地点。这一临时校址位于闽江南岸的烟台山上，从观音井往上数百步。当时的烟台山聚集了各国的领事馆、外国人住宅楼以及各差会的办事处。1920 年就读于协和大学的张圣才先生（1990：11）在《协大旧事》一文中回忆道：

In the following two years, the Preliminary Committee held the third and fourth meetings on Guling, Fuzhou, comprehensively reviewing the university construction plan. The university's tentative name was Foochow Christian University or Fukien Christian University. The meetings pointed out that the following missionary schools in Fuzhou and Xiamen could be incorporated into the planned Fukien Christian University: Union Medical College, Union Theological School, Anglo-Chinese College, Foochow College, St. Mark School, Amoy Anglo-Chinese College, Foochow Trinity College, Talmage College and Union Normal School.

In May 1915, the first meeting of the Board of Managers of Fukien Christian University was held. It voted to elect Mr. W. L. Beard as the Chairman of the Board and Mr. Edwin Chester Jones as the first president. Edwin Chester Jones, American, was born in Flushing, New York in 1880. His father was a Methodist minister. He received his B. A. from Wesleyan University in 1904, and later was sent to China by the Mission to learn Chinese and taught natural science at Foochow Anglo-Chinese College (now Affiliated High School of Fujian Normal University) founded by the MEM. When he went on holiday back to the USA, he studied chemistry at Yale University and received a Master's Degree, with which he returned to teach chemistry at Anglo-Chinese College. In 1915, he was appointed as the first president of Fukien Christian University.

In June and July, the Board of Managers voted to decide the first entrance examination would be held on February 16th, 1916. In the finalized Constitution (the Constitution of the Proposed Fukien Christian University), the name of the proposed university was decided as the Fukien Christian University (FCU), and the Board of Trustees as the Board of Trustees of the Fukien Christian University. After five years of twists and turns, the preparatory task of Fukien Christian University was finally completed.

• Opening at Cangqian with Profound Accumulation

Under the efforts of the Board of Managers led by Edwin C. Jones, who was the first president of FCU, the Board of Trustees approved of the leasing of the former Russian Tea Shop at the Guanyinjing (Guang-ing-cang) Street of Cangqian, Fuzhou as the temporary site for FCU. It was located on the Mount Yantai on the southern bank of the Minjiang River, hundreds of steps up from the Guanyinjing Street. At that time, Mount Yantai gathered many consulates of countries, residential buildings of foreigners and offices of missionary societies. Mr. Zhang Shengcai, who studied at FCU in 1920, recalled in his article *Memories about Fukien Christian University*:

1920—1922 年协大校址在仓前观音井一座有 80 级台阶的大楼。这一座楼房曾经是一家洋行，后被协大租用。前门在观音井，后门在烟台山。校园小路向外开放。石阶上有个平台栏杆可供座位。学生们喜欢在这里聊天、嗑瓜子、吃零食。教授们也经常在这里跟我们闲谈。他们像是有意识地同我们交朋友。我们无所不谈，百无禁忌，无形中把这个平台变成一个民主沙龙。

谢必震教授（2005：9 - 10）在《香飘魏歧村：福建协和大学》一书中也对此楼有较详细的记述：

那是一座两层楼洋房，在校舍左边，有一株数百年的大榕树。从这里俯瞰闽江，万寿桥和福州全景一览无遗。由观音井大街走入校门，要登上八十余级的大台阶。一楼是教室和礼堂，在楼的转弯处是教务长的办公室，仅放得下一张办公桌和一张座椅。二楼除学生宿舍外，另一边就是庄校长的住所和办公室。楼前空地有网球、篮球和排球共用的球场，在场边亦有跳远、跳高、撑竿跳的沙坑。所有的实验室和图书馆都借用毗邻的英华中学。

1916 年 2 月 16 日，几经波折筹备的福建协和大学终于在福州仓山正式开学，迎来了它的首批 86 名学生（一年级学生 54 名，二年级学生 27 名，特别生 5 名）。这些学生大多是从福州英华、格致、三一等中学的七八年级转至协和大学的一二年级就读（黄涛，2007：91）。首批教师 9 人，均是由几个差会派出的良好师资：五位专职教师分别是庄才伟先生任校长兼教授化学，倪乐善任教务长兼授社会学及英文，薛来西教授社会科学，克立鹄教授生物学，万尔西教授英国文学；四名兼职教师为何乐益、饶卫礼、卡彭特、来必翰（黄涛，2007：15）。这是当时福建省内较为规范的一所高等院校，促进了福建省近现代高等教育的发展。

From 1920 to 1922, Fukien Christian University was sited in a building boasting 80 steps along the Guang-ing-cang Street of Cangqian. The building used to be a foreign firm and was later rented by Fukien Christian University, its front door at Guang-ing-cang Street and back door to Mount Yantai. The campus paths led outwards, with a platform on stone steps providing seats for students to chat and eat melon seeds and snacks. Professors often chatted with us there as well, who seemed to be consciously making friends with us. We talked about everything, virtually turning this platform into a democratic salon.

Professor Xie Bizhen also gave a detailed account of this building in his book *Kuiqi Village with Sweet Fragrance: Fukien Christian University*:

It was a two-story Western house, to the left of which was a big banyan tree that had stood for hundreds of years. Overlooking the Minjiang River from there, we could enjoy a panoramic view of the Bridge of Ten Thousand Ages and Fuzhou City. Entering the school gate from Guang-ing-cang Street, over 80 steps led you to the first floor, where classrooms and auditorium were located. Around the corner was the office of the Dean of Studies, only with a set of desk and chair in it. On the second floor were students' dormitories on one side and President Edwin Chester Jones 's residence and office on the other. Public courts for tennis, basketball and volleyball as well as sandpits for long jump, high jump and pole vault were set in front of the house. We used the laboratories and libraries of the adjoining Anglo-Chinese College.

On February 16th, 1916, after going through difficulties and obstacles in preparation, Fukien Christian University officially opened in Cangshan District of Fuzhou, welcoming its first batch of 86 students (54 freshmen, 27 sophomores and 5 special students). Most of them were transferred from Grades 7 and 8 of Foochow Anglo-Chinese College, Foochow College, Foochow Trinity College, etc. The first 9 teachers were all experienced ones appointed by the Missions: five full-time teachers were E. C. Jones teaching Chemistry as well as holding the post of President, C. A. Neff teaching Sociology and English as well as holding the post of Dean of Studies, C. M. Lacey Sites teaching Social Science, C. R. Kellogg teaching Biology, and W. Pakenhan-Walsh teaching British Literature; four part-time teachers were Lewis Hodous, G. M. Newell, J. B. Carpenter and W. P. W. Williams. It was a rather standard institution of higher education in Fujian at that time, and promoted the development of Fujian modern higher education.

: 协和大学的第一张招生广告
: The first enrollment ad by FCU

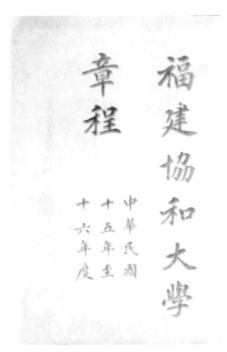

: 福建协和大学章程
: The Constitution of FCU

: 福建协和大学校歌
: The alma mater of FCU

"博爱、牺牲、服务"是协大的校训,是贯穿协大办学始终的灵魂——"以博爱的情怀,用牺牲的方式,达到服务的目的"(袁勇麟,2013:38)。为协大竭尽心力的历任校长、每一个协大师生,都在亲身践行着校训的精神,使之成为协大人的核心力量和行为印记。"博爱、牺牲、服务"亦与校歌中的"协和,协和,大德是钦"相互呼应。正是在这种教育理念的影响下,协和大学的1 000多名毕业生皆成为国家的栋梁之才,在各行各业发挥着光和热。

1916年协和大学初立时部分教职员及家属在协和大学观音井校址合影
The group photo of some of the faculty and their families at the beginning
of FCU in 1916, taken on the Guang-ing-cang campus

1916年福建协和大学教职员
The faculty of FCU in 1916

1917年福建协和大学第一届毕业生
The first graduates from FCU in 1917

"Fraternity, Sacrifice and Service" is the motto of Fukien Christian University and the soul throughout its whole process of running—"To provide service with fraternity and sacrifice". The presidents, having devoted every effort to FCU, along with its teachers and students, all practiced the spirit of the motto with words and deeds, making it their core strength and behavior mark. "Fraternity, Sacrifice and Service" also echoes its school song "While life shall last, may we faithful be, to thee, to China and to the World!" It is under the influence of this spirit that more than one thousand graduates of FCU have become the pillars of the country, exerting their efforts and talents in all walks of life.

● 精心设计　最美魁岐

　　协大位于观音井的狭小校区，其简陋的办学条件限制了它的扩大发展。故而，庄才伟校长与校董事会成员高智先生、何乐益先生积极筹措资金，穿梭于中美两地，获得捐助，购置了一片永久性的校园用地。这就是协大魁岐校区，距离福州30多公里，背倚鼓山，面瞰闽江，地势开阔，环境优美。

　　1922年春，协和大学从仓前观音井迁往马尾魁岐校区。新校区占地面积达1 000多亩，几十座校舍错落分布，甚是雄伟壮观。楼宇设计精美，雕梁画栋，极具东方古典韵味。协大的师生们还在校门前沿着江边修筑了一条大路，取名为协大路，路边沿着石阶向下即协大码头，从此处逆流向上船行一个小时可达福州城，顺流而下可达著名的罗星塔和马尾船政学堂。故而，每逢周末及节假日，协大的师生们便聚集在此排队登船，去享受美好的假日时光。漫步于协大路上，抬头即可见坐落于半山腰的文学院和理学院。文学院是机关办公室、图书馆、大礼堂和各学科教室的所在地；理学院里有各类大小实验室、仪器室、标本室等，其中还有一个可容纳200余人的演讲厅。遥想风雨飘摇的20世纪初，能在教学设施如此完备的高等学府学习，是何其有幸！

∶ 协和魁岐校区远景
∶ A distant view of Kuiqi Campus of FCU

• Elaborate Design of Kuiqi Campus

FCU's small campus at Guanyinjing and its poor conditions limited its development. Therefore, President E. C. Jones, together with the board members Mr. John Gowdy and Mr. Lewis Hodous, actively raised funds, shuttling back and forth between China and the United States, and finally obtained donations to purchase a permanent campus land. This was Kuiqi Campus, more than 30 kilometers away from Fuzhou. Facing the Minjiang River and with the Drum Mountain(Mount Gu) at its back, it boasted an open terrain and beautiful environment.

In the spring of 1922, FCU moved from Guanyinjing, Cangqian to Kuiqi Campus in Mawei. The new campus covered an area of more than 1,000 *mu*, with dozens of well-spaced and magnificent buildings. The combination of exquisite building design and rich ornaments fully displayed its oriental and classical charm. The teachers and students of FCU built a road along the Minjiang River in front of the university gate, named Xieda Road ("Xieda" is the Chinese pronunciation of Christian University). Along the road down the stone steps was Xieda Wharf, from which it took one hour upstream to get to Fuzhou City, and downstream to the famous Luoxing Tower and Mawei Ship Administration School. Therefore, at weekends and during holidays, teachers and students from FCU gathered here, queuing up to board ships and enjoy their holiday time. Strolling along Xieda Road, you could see the buildings of College of Arts and College of Science halfway up the hill. The building of College of Arts was the location of offices, a library, an auditorium and classrooms of various disciplines. And the building of College of Science boasted various laboratories, instrument rooms and specimen rooms, along with a lecture hall which could accommodate more than 200 people. What a privilege it was to study in such a well-equipped institution of higher education in the turbulent early 20th century!

关于协和大学的校园之美，最高赞誉来自卫斯理安大学历史学教授达切尔的评价，他是庄才伟先生的好朋友。他在第二次来福州期间，于 1922 年 1 月 27 日写信给何乐益说："新校址当列世界十大最佳校园之一而无愧。"（翁迈东，2016：25）

: 协大魁岐校区的江边公路
: The riverside road of Kuiqi Campus

: 魁岐校区正大门
: The front gate of Kuiqi Campus

: 魁岐校区门口的协大码头
: Xieda Wharf near the front gate of Kuiqi
: Campus

: 魁岐校区景色
: A corner of Kuiqi Campus

The highest praise for the beauty of Kuiqi Campus came from George B. Dutcher, a history professor from Wesleyan University and a good friend of Mr. E. C. Jones. During his second visit to Fuzhou, he wrote to Lewis Hodous on January 27, 1922, "The new campus deserves to be listed as one of the Top 10 campuses in the world."

教职住宅楼
Faculty Dormitory

游艺厅
Recreation Hall

光华楼（男生宿舍）
Guanghua House, the dormitory for boys

光荣楼（男生宿舍）
Guangrong House, the dormitory for boys

光国楼（男生宿舍）
Guangguo House, the dormitory for boys

游泳池
Swimming pool

● 匠心坚守　发展传承

： 高智
： John Gowdy

就在福建协和大学步入正轨之际，庄校长因积劳成疾，辞去了校长职务。之后，董事会推荐时任福州英华书院校长的高智先生担任协和大学的第二任校长。高智，出生于苏格兰，15 岁时移居美国，先后获得卫斯理安大学学士学位、德鲁神学院神学学士学位、哥伦比亚大学文学硕士学位和贝克大学神学博士学位。1902 年 9 月，他与夫人一起来到福州，在福州英华书院执教，1924 年接任福建协和大学校长之职。

高智先生接任校长之职后，面临着一个十分棘手的问题，即学校的高额债务。他多次返美筹措资金，最后成功解决了学校的财务危机，于 1924 年和 1927 年建成了文学院和理学院两座大楼，还争取到中华医学会的一笔赞助款购置所需设备。协大规模由此建立，各项教学规程日趋成熟，成果显著。1927 年，高智结束他的校长任职，此后校长由华人担任。

： 协大师生欢送高智夫妇回国
： Faculty and students of FCU bid farewell to Mr. John Gowdy and his wife

高智校长的接任者是由五人构成的校务委员会主席林景润。林景润是福建莆田人，是协大的第二届毕业生。他 1898 年 3 月 4 日出生于莆田，从莆田哲理中学毕业后，于 1916—1919 年就读于福建协和大学政治系，于 1919 年被派往美国深造，1920 年从协大获得文学学士学位，同年在奥柏林学院获文学硕士学位。之后他继续于 1920—1922 年在哈佛大学、1922—1925 年在哥伦比亚大学、1925—1927 年在耶鲁大学深造。学成回国后，他受聘于福建协和大学执教政治学与经济学，且在 1927—1946 年近 20 年间担任福建协和大学校长。

• Persistence and Inheritance

Just when Fukien Christian University stepped onto the right track, President E. C. Jones fell ill because of long-term hard work and was forced to leave his beloved job. Afterwards, the Board of Trustees recommended John Gowdy, who was the president of Foochow Anglo-Chinese College, to serve as the second president of FCU. John Gowdy was born in Scotland and moved to the USA when he was 15. He got a bachelor's degree from Wesleyan University, a bachelor's degree in Theology from Drew Theological Seminary, a master's degree from Columbia University, and a Ph. D. in Theology from Baker University. In September 1902, he came to Fuzhou with his wife to teach at Foochow Anglo-Chinese College. In 1924 he took over as the President of Fukien Christian University.

Having taken over the presidency, Mr. John Gowdy faced a rather tough problem, i. e. the high debt of the university. For this reason, he returned to the USA several times to raise funds and at last successfully solved its financial crisis. In 1924 and 1927, two buildings, the College of Arts and the College of Science, were built up. He also managed to obtain a grant from the Chinese Medical Association to purchase necessary equipment. Since then, the scale of Fukien Christian University had been established, along with the gradually matured teaching procedures and remarkable results. In 1927, Mr. John Gowdy finished his term as the president, after which the post of president was taken by Chinese.

The next president was Mr. Lin Jingrun, chairman of the five-member Board of Regents. He was from Putian, Fujian Province, and was one of the second graduates of Fukien Christian University. He was born in Putian on March 4, 1898. After graduating from Putian Zheli Middle School, he studied in the Department of Political Science of FCU from 1916 to 1919 and was sent to the United States for further study in 1919. He got his bachelor's degree from FCU in 1920 and his master's degree from Oberlin College in the same year. Then he went on to study at Harvard University from 1920 to 1922, Columbia University from 1922 to 1925, and Drew University from 1925 to 1927. After returning to China, he taught Political Science and Economics in FCU, and from 1927 to 1946 held office as its president for nearly 20 years.

林景润
Lin Jingrun

　　1931 年，福建协和大学正式在教育部立案。但由于当时的协大未达到具备三个学院的要求，故只能以"私立福建协和学院"之名注册。为提高协大的教学水平，林校长求贤若渴，诚心聘请高水平的本国教师到校任课。在他的努力下，协大的本国教师队伍不断壮大。1932 年秋季，协大开始兼收女生，真正实现了中国男女教育机会均等的理想。这不仅是协大展示对女性教育权的尊重，同时也是向外界大力宣传、扩大名声与威望的有效时机与方式。1994 年 9 月出版的《协大校友》第 9 期中，时年 94 岁高龄的校友邓碧玉撰文《我的心愿》回忆道：

　　　　福建协和大学是我的母校，校舍依山临江，环境优美宁静，是个进修学习的好地方。我于一九三二年夏考入协大，是母校第一届女生，我感到幸福，感到骄傲。我在这个严谨求实的校风熏陶下，培养成严谨求实的性格，使我在人生道路上，扎扎实实地闯过一关又一关，我深深感戴母校培育之恩。当我闭起眼睛，那雄伟壮丽的文、理两学院就呈现在我的眼前，它不仅是最具优美环境的最高学府，而且在培育高级人才方面，不论对本国对世界都作出了卓越的贡献，我常为此感到骄傲。

　　协和学院成功注册立案以来，林校长一直考虑把学院办成大学。当时教育部要求增办农学院，然后合文、理、农三学院成立大学。于是林校长一面与美国托事部沟通，一面筹备创设农学院。1936 年协和学院获得政府的补助，成功增设农学及农业经济两系，还开办了农业试验场，之后逐渐发展为农学院。最终于 1942 年 4 月，邵武时期的"私立福建协和学院"被当时的教育部准予改称"私立福建协和大学"。

: 林景润在校长办公室
: Mr. Lin Jingrun in the President's Office

In 1931, Fukien Christian University was officially registered in the Ministry of Education of that time. But because it did not meet the requirements of having three colleges, it could only be registered as Private Fukien Christian College. In order to enhance FCU's teaching level, President Lin was eager to recruit high-level Chinese teachers. Under his efforts, Chinese teaching staff of FCU had grown steadily. In the autumn of 1932, FCU began to enroll female students, truly realizing the ideal of equal educational opportunities for men and women in China. This was an opportune moment and efficient way for FCU not only to show its respect to women's rights of receiving education, but also to promote its reputation and prestige to the outside world. In the 9th issue of *Alumni of Fukien Christian University* published in September 1994, Deng Biyu, a 94-year-old alumnus, recalled in her article *My Wish* :

> Fukien Christian University is my alma mater, surrounded by the mountains and the river with picturesque and quiet environment. It was a good place for further study. I was admitted to the university in the summer of 1932 as one of its first female students. I felt happy and proud of it. It was under the influence of its rigorous and realistic spirit that I formed the meticulous and strict character, so that I could go through the hurdles in my life. I deeply appreciate the cultivation by my alma mater. Every time when I close my eyes, the magnificent College of Arts and College of Science recur to memory. I always pride myself not only on its reputation of being the most beautiful campus, but also on its outstanding contribution to the country and even to the world in the cultivation of senior talents.

Since Private Fukien Christian College was successfully registered, President Lin had been striving to turn it into a university. The Ministry of Education of that time required that the College of Agriculture be added, and that the three colleges of Arts, Science and Agriculture merge to form a university. Therefore, President Lin communicated with Board of Trustees in America on one hand, while making preparations to establish the College of Agriculture on the other. In 1936, after getting subsidies from the government of that time, the Department of Agriculture and the Department of Agricultural Economics were successfully set up, equipped with an agricultural experimental field. Then the two departments gradually developed into the College of Agriculture. Finally, in April 1942, the "Private Fukien Christian College" in Shaowu period was approved to be renamed as Private Fukien Christian University by the Ministry of Education of that time.

- **严谨办学 全面发展**

组织机构

经过多年的探索与改进，福建协和大学逐步形成完备的组织机构。与其他教会大学一样，福建协大也是采取校董事会指导下的校长负责制，下设行政、教学及教辅部门。行政部门如教务处、总务处和训导处等，承担处理学校从教学至后勤的行政事务；教学部分由各学院、系构成，负责教学课程的设置与实施；教辅部分包括校各级委员会、研究会等。随着协大办学规模的扩大，组织结构也在不断地改革调整。越来越严密、高效的组织结构推动着协大健康、稳步发展，成为当时远近闻名的教会大学。

入学程序

协大招收的学生是公立或已注册立案的私立高级中学的毕业生，也可以是各大学或学院转学而来的学生。每学年春夏开学前举行入学考试，考点分别设在厦门、漳州、泉州、莆田、广东、上海等地。针对协和大学承认学历的中学毕业生，即原毕业学校与协大历史上相关的学生，考试科目有党义、国文作文、国学常识、英文作文、英文新字、英读、智力测验、口试等8门；而对其他普通的中学毕业生，还须加试社会科学、数学和自然科学（理化生三科任选一科）。

入学时，学生要填写各种表格。例如，招生报名表，表上须填写学生的个人信息，粘贴个人照，背面是入学志愿书；学校介绍信，由学生前一段教育历程的毕业学校开具；入学保证书，多由学生的中学校长或亲属担保该生在学校的一切行为。

学费的收取情况请参看1934年度公布的收费清单（福建协和大学校友会总会，2006：30）：

• Rigorous Management and All-Round Development

Organizational Structure

Going through years of exploration and improvement, FCU had gradually formed a complete organizational structure. Like other missionary universities, it also adopted the President Responsibility System under the guidance of the Board of Trustees, with Administrative, Teaching and Auxiliary Sections. Administrative Section, including the Office of Academic Affairs, the Office of General Affairs and the Office of Discipline, was responsible for handling the school's administrative affairs from teaching to auxiliary services. The Teaching Section consisted of colleges and departments, responsible for the setting and implementation of curricula. The Auxiliary Section included school committees and research groups of all levels. In accordance with the expansion of university-running scale, FCU's organizational structure had been constantly reformed and adjusted. The increasingly strict and efficient organizational structure promoted its healthy and steady development, making it a well-known missionary university at that time.

Admission Procedures

The students FCU recruited were graduates from state senior high schools or registered private senior high schools, as well as the students transferred from other universities or colleges. Entrance examinations were held before the start of spring and summer school semesters in Xiamen, Zhangzhou, Quanzhou, Putian, Guangdong, Shanghai, etc. For the middle school graduates whose academic qualifications were recognized by FCU, or in other words, the graduates who were from the schools related to the development history of FCU, they needed to take the exams of eight subjects, including Party Doctrines, Chinese Writing, General Knowledge of Chinese Studies, English Writing, English New Words, English Reading, Intelligence Test and Oral Examination, while for other average high school graduates, exams of Social Science, Mathematics and Natural Science (choose one among Physics, Chemistry and Biology) were also demanded.

At admission, students were required to fill out various forms, such as Enrollment Application Form, which included personal information, individual photo, and a Consent Form overleaf; Introduction Letter, provided by the school of the student's previous period of education; Admission Guarantee, mostly by the student's middle school principal or relatives to guarantee his/her behavior in the university.

Please refer to the list of fees published in 1934:

表 8-2 协大学生交纳费用实例（1934 年）

项目	金额（大洋/元）	项目	金额（大洋/元）
学费	40	学生自治会费	2.75
新生入学费	10	校服费	7
膳费（4 个半月）	32	实验室费、预交损耗费	2～5
宿费	8	原料费	3～6
钥匙赔偿费	1	讲义费	1
电灯费	6	钢琴费	5
医药费	1	毕业证书费	10
体育费	1.25	过期注册费	2

随着物价的波动，协大的收费标准也有所变动，尤其是 1949—1959 年间，因粮价飞升，物价跟着飞涨。为保护群众利益，社会上通行以粮代金的交易，于是协大也采用收缴学米的办法。1949 学年度有以下记录（福建协和大学校友会总会，2006：30-31）：

【甲】学杂费

（一）学费　上等白米　二百五十斤

（二）宿舍　上等白米　十三斤

（三）电灯　上等白米　四十斤

（四）图书　上等白米　八斤

（五）试卷　上等白米　七斤

（六）体育　上等白米　七斤

（七）医药费　上等白米　十斤

【乙】实验赔偿费

（一）实验费（每实验学分）

（1）化学　上等白米　十斤

（2）物理、生物、农艺、园艺　上等白米　六斤

（二）赔偿费

凡破损仪器及一切实验用具者，应于学期结束时按市价赔偿。

【丙】特别费

（一）毕业文凭　上等白米　五斤

（二）礼服　上等白米　十斤

（三）补考费每课　上等白米　五斤

（四）转院系手续费　上等白米　十斤

（五）钢琴　上等白米　七十五斤

（六）声乐　上等白米　五十斤

Table 8 - 2　List of Fees of FCU (1934)

Items	Amount (Silver Dollar/Yuan)	Items	Amount (Silver Dollar/Yuan)
Tuition	40	Student Council Fee	2.75
Freshmen Entrance Fee	10	Uniform Fee	7
Board Expenses (four and half months)	32	Lab Fee & Prepayment for Tear and Wear	2 - 5
Accommodation Fee	8	Material Cost	3 - 6
Key Damages	1	Handouts Fee	1
Electric Charge	6	Piano Fee	5
Medical Charge	1	Diploma Fee	10
Sports Fee	1.25	Overdue Registration Fee	2

As prices fluctuated, FCU's charges were changed, especially from 1949 to 1959, when the prices of grain and others all skyrocketed. In order to protect the interests of the masses, grain took the place of silver dollar as the currency in deals and trades. FCU also adopted the method of collecting rice as tuition. The following were the records of 1949 academic year:

　　i. Tuition and Fees
　　(1) Tuition: top level white rice 125 kg
　　(2) Dormitory: top level white rice 6.5 kg
　　(3) Electric light: top level white rice 20 kg
　　(4) Books: top level white rice 4 kg
　　(5) Test paper: top level white rice 3.5 kg
　　(6) Physical education: top level white rice 3.5 kg
　　(7) Medical fee: top level white rice 5 kg
　　ii. Lab and Damages Fees
　　(1) Lab fee (every experiment credit)
　　① Chemistry: top level white rice 5 kg
　　② Physics, Biology, Agriculture and Gardening: top level white rice 3 kg
　　(2) Damages:
Any broken instruments and laboratory equipment shall be compensated at the market price at the end of the semester.
　　iii. Special Charges
　　(1) Diploma: top level white rice 2.5 kg
　　(2) Formal attire: top level white rice 5 kg
　　(3) Resit fee for each subject: top level white rice 2.5 kg
　　(4) College or department transfer: top level white rice 5 kg
　　(5) Piano: top level white rice 37.5 kg
　　(6) Vocal music: top level white rice 25 kg

（七）梵亚林　上等白米　七十五斤

【丁】迟到费（若迟到注册，以天为单位增缴）

课程设置及学分制

协和大学在课程设置上秉承有深度、有高度的原则，目的是造就一批国家社会急需的栋梁之才。学校十分注重联系实际和服务社会，同时还高度关注学生各方面的修养，故而除了各类学术学科之外，艺术课程也列入学习内容中。一个学生从入学到毕业，须完成138学分。必修课程全部修完、毕业论文评定合格者方可毕业。

校友张尊玄在《追忆母校二三事》中对协大的学分制印象深刻，且记录得尤为详细（1997：19－20）：

本校采取学分制：学制四年，规定一学期修满18学分。但各科目学分数不同，开学前由教务处公布全校各学期各院系所开设科目学分数及科目号码（便于注册，属于哪学年科目，如化学101、201、301、401。101、201、301、401分别为一、二、三、四年级所修）。注册时，学生把所修科目号码学分数填上登记单，经系主任审核后交教务处存查。发给学生每科目一张上课证，上第一课时交授课老师。

科目成绩等级分四等记录

一等　优（90—100）	成绩　优/学分	得3绩点
二等　良（81—90）	良/学分	得2绩点
三等　及格（65—80）	及格/学分	得1绩点
四等　不及格（65分以下）	无	

学年成绩优良的可获准多修学分2～4学分。除主修科外，其他科目包括4个群体虽有成绩，但不给绩点。

在课程内创立四个群体，完成四个群体才符合规定。群体的意义是在同系的科目中修满16学分即组成一个群体，或在文科中各科目修满16学分也成一个群体。很明显，不论是学文科或理科要在同一系内完成四个群体是不可能的。必须文理相互交错，文科学生必须修理科学分，理科学生必须修文科学分凑足成四个群体，课程内创立四个群体道理即在此。

绩点的计算、算式如下：科目学分数×成绩的绩点数＝该科目总绩点数。某一科目为5学分：

成绩为优　5×3＝15

成绩为良　5×2＝10

及　格　5×1＝5

学校对毕业条件的规定除主修数理系外文理各系定主修科为60学分，应得绩点为90绩点，其他选修与四群体都不计绩点。从规定可以看出对毕业生质量的要求较严格，从课程的措施及其精神，便意识到其目的在于促使科学长远发展及造就功底深厚的高等人才。

(7) Violin: top level white rice 37.5 kg

iv. Overdue Registration Fee (increase by days)

Curriculum and Credit System

FCU adhered to the principle of being in-depth and high-level in its curriculum design, with the aim of cultivating a group of talents urgently needed by the country and the society. The university attached great importance to connecting with reality and serving the society, and also focused on students' all-round development. Therefore, in addition to various academic subjects, art courses were also included in their learning contents. Since admission, a student must complete 138 credits before graduation. Only those who had completed all required courses and passed the graduation thesis assessment could graduate.

Mr. Zhang Zunxuan, an alumnus, was deeply impressed by the credit system of Fukien Christian University and recorded it in detail in his article *Recall the Alma Mater*:

Our university adopted the credit system: four school years and 18 credits to be completed in each semester. The credits for subjects were varied. Before a semester began, the Academic Affairs Office would announce the credits and serial numbers of the courses offered by colleges and departments (In order to make the registration work efficient, for example, the courses of Chemistry were numbered 101, 201, 301 and 401, indicating the year in which the subject was offered, i.e. the courses 101, 201, 301 and 401 were offered to freshmen, sophomores, juniors and seniors respectively.) At registration, students should fill in registration forms with the serial numbers and credits of the subjects they had chosen. After being reviewed by the department directors, the forms would be submitted to the Teaching Affairs Office for record. Students would be given a class certificate for each subject and hand it in to the teacher in the first class.

4-Grade Scores for Each Subject

First Class	Excellent (90 – 100)	Scores: Excellent/Grade Point: 3
Second Class	Good (81 – 90)	Good/Grade Point: 2
Third Class	Pass (65 – 80)	Pass/Grade Point: 1
Fourth Class	Fail (less than 65)	No Grade Point

Students with good academic performance would be allowed to take 2 – 4 extra credits. Besides major subjects, other subjects including 4 groups could be taken, but only giving scores, no grade point.

It was required to form and complete four "groups" within the curriculum. The meaning of "group" was that if you completed 16 credits in the subjects offered by the same department or in the subjects of liberal arts, you would form one "group". Apparently, it was impossible for students to complete four groups in the same department, whether in arts or science. Therefore, students had to take both arts and science courses so as to meet the requirement. It was the significance of the curriculum design.

奖学金制度

为激发同学们的学习热情、帮助贫困学生解决学费及生活费等，学校设立了奖学金制度，如"承认中学新生奖学金""陈滔庵先生文化奖学金""益友奖学金""学费奖学金""医学奖学金"，以及以校友会发起或以个别教师姓名命名的奖学金"克立鹄奖学金""徐光荣奖学金""倪乐善奖学金"等。其中，"承认中学新生奖学金"是指为协和大学认可的几所中学中，每年毕业考试成绩优异者、入学考试各科成绩在三等以上者提供的奖学金。此外，学校还提供助学贷款、勤工俭学等助学措施，很大程度上解决了学生的后顾之忧。

团契

团契是教会大学中特有的一种基督教组织形式，它有固定的聚会时间、具体的聚会内容（如讨论、游艺等），是学生或师生之间相互交流的一种场合，也是当时协大保持其教会大学色彩的一种方式。

学生社团组织

福建协和大学自办学以来一直注重培养学生的优良品格和组织实践能力，因此各类研究会、社团涌现，不仅丰富了学生们的校园生活，也助益创造和谐、活泼的教育气氛。学术类研究会有以下几个：

学生自治会，始创于1918年，主要工作是组织同学们开展迎新会、欢送会、游艺会、运动会等，负责编写、发行会刊《协大学生》，同时还曾在学校附近的魁岐村创办附属模范小学。

青年会，创办于1916年，下设进德部、学术部、交际部、服务部和会员部5个部门，分别负责学生思想塑造、学术进步（如会刊《协大青年》的编写、邀请名人演讲、开设图书阅览室等）、交流联谊活动、学校服务管理、发展会员等工作。

：协大青年会全体会员，1930—1931
：All members of the Youth Association of FCU, from 1930 to 1931

The calculation and formulas of grade points were as follows: credit $\times$ grade point $=$ total grade point. Suppose a subject was worth 5 credits:

Excellent: $5\times3=15$; Good: $5\times2=10$; Pass: $5\times1=5$

The university's requirement for graduation was that students of liberal arts and science, except those majoring in mathematics and physics, should get 60 credits and 90 grade points for major courses. Optional courses and Four Groups were not graded. The regulation showed its strictness on the quality of graduates, and the measures and spirit of curricula design manifested its purpose of promoting the long-term development of science and cultivating high-level talents with profound knowledge and skills.

Scholarship System

In order to stimulate students' enthusiasm for learning and help poor students with their tuition and living expenses, the university set up the scholarship system, such as the Scholarship for the Freshmen from Accredited Secondary Schools, Culture Scholarship by Chen Tao'an, Friendship Scholarship, Tuition Scholarship, Medical Science Scholarship, as well as the scholarships initiated by the Alumni Association or named after individual teachers, such as Kellogg Scholarship, Scott Scholarship, Neff Scholarship, etc. Furthermore, the university also provided student loans, work-study programs and other measures, to a large extent helping students solve their worries.

Fellowship

Fellowship was a special form of Christian organization in missionary universities. It had fixed meeting time and specific meeting contents (such as discussion, entertainment, etc.). It was an occasion for students and teachers to communicate with each other, and also a way for the university to maintain its missionary university nature.

Student Clubs

Since its establishment, FCU had always attached much attention to cultivating students' fine character and ability of organization and practice. Hence, various research institutes and clubs emerged, which not only enriched students' campus life, but helped to create a harmonious and lively educational atmosphere as well. Academic research clubs included:

Students Self-governing Council, founded in 1918, mainly burdened the tasks of holding welcome parties, farewell parties, entertainment parties, sports meetings etc. It was also responsible for compiling and publishing the journal *Students of Fukien Christian University*. Meanwhile, it had also founded an affiliated primary school in Kuiqi Village.

Youth Association, founded in 1916, had such five departments as Progressive and Moral Department, Academic Department, Communication Department, Service Department, and Members Department, respectively responsible for students' thoughts, academic progress(such as the compiling of *Youth of Fukien Christian University*, inviting celebrities to give speeches, setting up reading rooms and so on), communication activities, service management and expansion of membership, etc.

文化研究会，创办于 1930 年，主要由学校教职员和学生组成，是一个民间的学术研究团体。研究会分为语音、民族、史地、歌谣、风俗和物产 6 组，每 3 个月举行一次全体大会，交流学术研究心得，旨在促进学术进步。

　　国语研究会，由协大国文系组织，旨在提倡国语的普遍运用与统一。每学期会组织国语演说会或演出会，还组织会员代表学校参加福建大学生国语竞赛等，曾取得不俗的成绩。

　　自然科学社，成立于 1917 年，汇集了对自然科学特别感兴趣的同学们，共同致力于科学探讨与研究。

　　此外，摄影研究会、教育学会、社会科学社、化学社、农学会、生物学会、数理学社、英语研究会、哲学会、历史学会、宗教研究会、艺文社等学术活动也如火如荼地开展起来。

: 福建协和大学文化研究会
: Culture Seminar of FCU

: 福建协和大学自然科学社成员，1927
: Members of Natural Science Society of FCU，1927

: 教育学会
: Education Society

: 农学会
: Agronomy Society

: 生物学会
: Biology Society

: 数理学社
: Mathematics and Physics Society

Culture Seminar, founded in 1930, was a non-governmental academic research organization mainly composed of university's faculty and students. The seminar was divided into six groups: phonetics, nationalities, history and geography, ballads, customs and natural resources. A general meeting was held every three months to exchange academic ideas and promote academic progress.

Mandarin Chinese Seminar, organized by the Department of Chinese Language and Literature, was aimed to advocate the universal use and unity of mandarin Chinese. Every semester, Mandarin speeches or performances were held, and members were organized to enter for Fukien College Students' Mandarin Competition on behalf of FCU and had achieved remarkable results.

Natural Science Society, founded in 1917, attracted students with special interest in natural science. They were jointly committed to scientific exploration and research.

In addition, academic activities such as Photography Society, Education Society, Social Science Society, Chemistry Society, Agronomy Society, Biology Society, Mathematics and Physics Society, English Seminar, Philosophy Society, History Society, Religious Research Seminar, and Art Club were also flaring up.

：英语研究会
：English Seminar

：艺文社
：Art Club

：化学社
：Chemistry Society

文艺团体有歌咏团、民乐团、口琴社、铜管乐队、剧团、唱诗班等。

歌咏团
Chorus

民乐团
Chinese Orchestra

口琴社
Harmonica Club

体育团体有篮球队、足球队、排球队、网球队、乒乓球队、田径队、游泳队、国术队等。

男子排球队
Men's Volleyball Team

女子排球队
Women's Volleyball Team

Art societies included Chorus, Chinese Orchestra, Harmonica Club, Brass Band, Opera Troupe, Choir, etc.

: 铜管乐队
: Brass Band

: 剧团剧目《罗宾汉》
: Opera Troupe's play *Robin Hood.*

: 唱诗班
: Choir

Sports teams included Basketball Team, Football Team, Volleyball Team, Tennis Team, Table Tennis Team, Track and Field Team, Swimming Team, National Wushu Team, etc.

: 男子足球队
: Men's Football Team

: 国术队
: National Wushu Team

各类同学会或同乡会有福中同学会、兴化同学会、闽南同学会、融岚同学会等。

：福中同学会
：Student Association of Foochow Middle School

：兴化同学会
：Student Association of Xinghua

● 内迁邵武　积蓄力量

卢沟桥事变后，战争形势日益严峻。日本敌机不断来榕轰炸，日军军舰亦沿福建各口岸射击并试图登陆。为了积蓄力量，持久抗日，自 1938 年 4 月下旬，国民福建省政府的部分机构开始向山区转移，省政府也早就向各学校颁布了疏散令，协大的迁址势在必行。实际上，林景润校长早已洞察到福州这座沿海城市必会卷入战火之中，于早些时候就已开始寻找可供协大继续办学的避难校址。这就是坐落于闽北山区的邵武。

邵武，地处武夷山南麓、富屯溪畔，自古以来便是中原入闽的重要通道。因其地形险要，易守难攻，是历代兵家必争之地，故有"铁城"之称。在 1938 年初，协大就已派人前往邵武向美部会借用了十余座房屋，紧接着就是大规模的房屋修缮和部分校舍的自建工作，为迁校做好准备。随着战事紧逼，5 月中旬日军占领了厦门，且不断向闽江口逼近，协大的搬迁事宜刻不容缓。

1938 年 5 月底的一个清晨，协大首批搬迁人员在众人的质疑与叮咛声中挥别了这片魁岐山水，开启硝烟下的搬迁之旅。当时的邵武没有公路，从福州往邵武要乘船沿闽江溯富屯溪而上，经南平再往北。一路滩高流急，舟车劳顿，必是艰辛无比。全校师生分为甲乙丙丁四队。甲乙两队于 5 月 31 日启程，搭乘柴油机汽轮驶离协和大学校园的码头，3 日抵达邵武。丙丁两队 6 月 5 日启程，6 月 8 日抵达。共计迁往邵武的教职员有 37 人，学生约 145 人。为躲避战火，当时迁往邵武的还有格致中学、文山女中，以及外省迁来的东吴大学和之江大学。各个学校的"蜂拥而至"使得山城邵武一时间成了文化重镇。

Student associations were Student Association of Foochow Middle School, Student Association of Xinghua, Student Association of the South Fukien, Student Association of Ronglan, etc.

闽南同学会
Student Association of the South Fukien

• Relocation to Shaowu

After Lugou Bridge Incident (also called Marco Polo Bridge Incident), the war situation became increasingly serious. Japanese enemy planes continually bombed Fuzhou, and Japanese warships fired along Fujian ports, trying to land. In order to accumulate strength and persist in resistance against Japanese aggression, since late April of 1938, some institutions of Fujian Provincial Government of that time had begun to move to mountainous areas. As the provincial government had also issued evacuation orders to all schools, the relocation of FCU was imperative. As a matter of fact, President Lin Jingrun had already been aware that Fuzhou, a coastal city, would be caught in the flames of war, and had begun to look for a refuge site for the university to continue running. This was Shaowu, lying in the mountainous area of northern Fujian.

Shaowu, located at the southern foot of Mount Wuyi along Futun Stream, had been an important channel from central plains to Fujian since ancient times. Being strategically situated, easy to hold but hard to attack, it had always been contested for military importance, hence its name "Iron City". At the beginning of 1938, FCU had already sent people to Shaowu to borrow over ten houses from American Board of Commissioners for Foreign Missions (ABCFM), and then carried out a large scale of house repair and self-construction work so as to prepare for its relocation. As the war intensified, Japanese army occupied Xiamen in mid-May and kept approaching the mouth of the Minjiang River, which made FCU's relocation even more urgent.

In an early morning at the end of May 1938, with people's doubts and exhortations, the first team of FCU's faculty and students waved goodbye to Kuiqi and started their relocation trip under the threat of gunpowder. At that time, there was no road in Shaowu. Consequently, from Fuzhou to Shaowu people needed to take a boat up along the Minjiang River and the Futun Stream, going northward through Nanping. Swift water and stretches of shoals made it a hard journey. The teachers and students of the university were divided into four teams, A, B, C and D. Teams A and B set off from Xieda Wharf by diesel steamships on May 31 and arrived in Shaowu on May 3. Teams C and D departed on June 5th and arrived on June 8th. A total of 37 faculty members and 145 students moved to Shaowu. In order to escape the flames of war, many other schools also moved to Shaowu nearly at the same time, including Foochow College, Wenshan Girls Middle School, together with some universities from other provinces such as Soochow University and Hangchow University. Schools' and universities' "swarming" suddenly converted Shaowu, the mountainous city, to a cultural town.

"最初到邵武时，协和大学借用的是美部会汉美、乐德两所教会中学的校舍和外国传教士的住宅计有十八座楼房为校舍，后逐渐建造了图书馆（高智楼）、庄才伟楼、公洽楼、食堂、礼堂、发电厂、医院及教师住宅。"（谢必震，2005：81）校园内高楼矗立，绿树成荫，如此幽静宽敞的学习环境在战时可谓难能可贵。其中最受到师生们珍视的是已全部运到邵武的协大重要图书，可以想象在战争年代能坐拥如此丰富的藏书是多么幸运。

：邵武校区全景
：Panorama of Shaowu Campus

：邵武校区汉美楼
：Hanmei Building of Shaowu Campus

"When first located in Shaowu, Fukien Christian University borrowed from Hanmei and Lede, two missionary middle schools of ABCFM a total of 18 houses including foreign missionaries' residences as its school buildings. Later, the library (John Gowdy Building), Edwin C. Jones Building, Gongqia Building, Dining Hall, Auditorium, Power Plant, Hospital and Teachers' Residence were constructed in turn."The Shaowu Campus was filled with tall buildings and shady gloves. Such quiet and spacious learning environment was extremely precious during the wartime. What the FCU's faculty and students cherished most were all the important books that had been shipped to Shaowu. It could be imagined how lucky it was to have such a large collection of books in the war years.

: 邵武校区校门
: The Gate of Shaowu Campus

: 邵武校区高智楼
: John Gowdy Building of Shaowu
: Campus

: 邵武校区运动场
: Sports Ground of Shaowu Campus

: 邵武校区公洽楼
: Gongqia Building of Shaowu Campus

邵武的物质及办学条件不如福州，但师生员工在国难之下同仇敌忾，共同克服了诸多困难，原先衣冠楚楚的"白衣书生"都被生活磨砺成坚忍不拔的热血青年。因为物资匮乏，当时的许多教具都是协大师生自己动手制作的，如黑板、粉笔、酒精、胶水等。尽管条件困苦，但协大育人育才、办好教育的信念丝毫未减，课程设置上注重多学科教育与实际运用能力相结合。俞元桂先生（1990：6）在《邵武读书记》中详细记述了他当年上过的课程：

> 头两年，我们接受基础课教育，修读大一国文、各体文习作，一二年级英语、初中高三级英语作文，中国通史和西洋通史，哲学和经济学原理，还要必修一门自然科学，物理、化学、生物任选其一，每周六节，四节讲授，两节实验，学一年。三、四年级是专业必修课和选修课，再有十二节的副系课程。每种课程都规定阅读不少的参考书，严格要求缴交阅读笔记和作业。明显的这里进行的是大文科教育，通才教育，充实多学科知识，训练实际运用能力。基础课教师多由教授、系主任执教，因为他们才有学力统观全局。

待教学秩序步入正轨后，协大师生们又着手创办民众夜校、乡村小学、儿童图书馆和民众阅报所，经常举办科学演讲，放映科学影片等，旨在向民众传输基本知识及保家卫国的思想，受到村民们的普遍欢迎。同时协大师生还深入农村，调研当时的农村经济问题及生产改良，设立农村问题研究机构、农村服务部，建立乡村试验区。之前，福建的农业教育比较落后，没有专门的农业学校，故协大的农业系正好填补了这里的空缺，再加上天然的山区环境，使得邵武期间的协大在农学方面有了长足的发展。正是在这个时期，申报农科的学生人数大大增加，原来的农学系细分为农艺学系和园艺学系，与原来的农业经济学共同组建成农学院。有了文学院、理学院和农学院的协大终于达到了当时教育部对"大学"的标准，于1942年4月被教育部准予改称"私立福建协和大学"。

：田野实践中的协大师生
：Teachers and students of FCU doing field practice

Shaowu's material and educational conditions were certainly not so good as those in Fuzhou, but the faculty and students, sharing bitter hatred against Japanese invaders, overcame a great many difficulties. The former well-dressed scholars were hardened into firm and indomitable youths. Due to the lack of materials, lots of teaching aids, such as blackboards, chalk, alcohol, glue and so on, were made by teachers and students themselves. In spite of the tough conditions, Fukien Christian University had never lost its faith in cultivating talents and running good education. Its curricula emphasized the combination of multi-disciplinary education and practical application. Mr. Yu Yuangui gave a detailed account of the courses he took during those years in his writing *My Learning Experience in Shaowu* :

In the first two years, we took basic courses: Chinese Literature and Chinese styles writing in the freshman year, English for freshmen and sophomores, English writing of junior, intermediate and advanced levels, Chinese and Western countries' general history, philosophy and economic theories. In addition, a natural science course was also required, to be picked from physics, chemistry and biology. It was offered for one year, 6 periods each week, 4 for lectures and 2 for experiments. In the junior and senior years, professional compulsory courses and elective courses were provided, along with twelve associated courses. Each course demanded a lot of reference reading, with strict requirements on reading notes and homework. Obviously, what was carried out here was broad liberal arts and general education, aimed to enrich students' multidisciplinary knowledge and train their application capacity. Basic courses were mostly taught by professors and department heads because of their academic ability of getting the general view of the situation.

When the teaching order got on the right track, FCU's faculty and students started to set up evening schools, rural primary schools, children's libraries and public newspaper reading stations. They often held scientific lectures and played scientific films, aiming to transmit to local people some basic knowledge and the idea of protecting our country. The practice was widely welcomed by the villagers. Meanwhile, the teachers and students also went into the countryside to investigate rural economic problems and explore ways about how to improve production. They established research institutions on rural issues, rural service departments, and rural test sites. Previously, the agricultural education in Fujian had been relatively backward with no special agricultural school, so FCU's Department of Agriculture just filled the vacancy. Coupled with the natural mountainous environment, FCU during Shaowu period made great advancement in agriculture. It was during this period that the number of students applying for agricultural science increased greatly. Consequently, the Department of Agriculture was subdivided into the Department of Agronomy and the Department of Horticulture. Then together with the original Department of Agricultural Economics, they merged and formed the College of Agriculture. With the College of Arts, the College of Science and the College of Agriculture, FCU finally reached the standard of being a "university" set by the Ministry of Education of that time. In April 1942, it was approved by the Ministry to be renamed as "Private Fukien Christian University".

除了农学院之外，协大的生物系在闽北山区的发展也十分令人瞩目，野外采集、动植物展览会等教学科研工作开展得有声有色。在庆祝协和大学建校 25 周年之际，生物学系举办了"闽北经济动植物展览会"，分为脊椎动物、昆虫、寄生动物及植物 4 组。其中闽北经济作物达 600 余种，经济昆虫 950 多种，挂敦采集昆虫 5 000 多种，福建寄生动物标本 100 多种，标本片 120 片，标本挂图 10 余组，闽北脊椎动物 40 余种，鸟类 220 种。经展会后统计，参观者多达一万余人，盛况空前，为我国生物学的发展作出了巨大的贡献（谢必震，2005：89）。在《战时中国之科学》一书中，英国科学家、中国科学院外籍院士李约瑟教授对邵武协大在生物学、茶叶研究及化学物理学领域的发展赞叹不已：

> 该省北部邵武的福建协和大学……在林校长景润主持下，该校的图书馆，因有许多福建望族捐赠中国书籍，已成为全国最好的图书馆之一。生物学实验室也是非常宽广，系主任郑作新博士说：该校从福州迁来此地，对于他们确是有益的。因为这里有与福州不同的动物区系可供研习。该校有极多鸟类和爬虫类标本和一大批海产生物标本。我看到那种过去常受福建农夫崇敬的大树蟾（Rhacophorus Schlegeli）时，觉得很是有趣。新近有一次该校布置了一个通俗的展览会，市民参观者户限为穿。能干的昆虫学家赵修复（治蜻蜓）和省立昆虫局马骏超，以及专门于血吸虫研究的寄生虫学家唐仲璋，工作都很刻苦。丁汉波博士那时正用一种有趣的本地蝾螈（学名 Pachytriton Brevipes）做着并体愈合和杂交的实验。
>
> 这个大学有一个特设的茶叶研究室，它邻近以产茶著名的武夷山。我们带走好几罐该校自制负有盛誉的茶叶。农业科学别的部门，在几个康纳尔大学毕业的人员主持之下，也很活跃，有几块大的园地和一个实验农场。

生物系主任郑作新在武夷山采集标本
Mr. Zheng Zuoxin, Director of the Department of Biology, was collecting specimens in Mount Wuyi

In addition to the advancement of College of Agriculture, the development of FCU's Department of Biology in the mountainous area of northern Fujian was also very remarkable. Its teaching and research work, such as field collection and exhibitions of animals and plants, etc., was carried out outstandingly. On the occasion of celebrating FCU's 25th anniversary, the Department of Biology held "North Fujian Exhibition of Economic Animals and Plants", displaying four groups of exhibits: vertebrates, insects, parasitic animals and plants. There were more than 600 kinds of economic crops, 950 kinds of economic insects, over 5,000 kinds of insects collected from Guadun Village of Mount Wuyi Area, more than 100 kinds of Fujian parasitic animal specimens, 120 specimen pieces, over 10 groups of specimen wall charts, more than 40 kinds of vertebrates and 220 kinds of birds from northern Fujian. According to the statistics after the exhibition, it attracted unprecedentedly over 10,000 visitors and made a great contribution to the development of biology in China. In the book *The Science of China in War*, Professor Joseph Needham, a British scientist and foreign academician of the Chinese Academy of Sciences, praised FCU's development in the fields of biology, tea research and chemical physics:

Fukien Christian University lies in Shaowu, the northern part of the Province... Under the leadership of President Lin Jingrun, its library had become one of the best in China, thanks to the donations of Chinese books by many prominent families in Fukien province. The biology labs were also very spacious, and Dr. Zheng Zuoxin, the Dean, said the university's relocation from Foochow was really beneficial to them, because there was a different fauna to study there from that in Foochow. The university boasted of many specimens of birds and reptiles as well as a large number of marine specimens. I was greatly intrigued when seeing Rhacophorus Schlegeli, a tree toad that used to be revered by Fukien farmers. In recent time the university had put up a popular exhibition, attracting an endless stream of visitors. Mr. Zhao Xiufu, a talented entomologist studying dragonflies, Mr. Ma Junchao from Provincial Entomology Bureau, and Mr. Tang Zhongzhang, a parasitologist specializing in schistosomiasis, all worked whole-heartedly and enthusiastically. Dr. Ding Hanbo was conducting experiments on parabiotic healing and hybridization with an interesting native salamander called Pachytriton Brevipes.

The university had a special tea research office near Mount Wuyi, where tea production was very famous. We took several jars of the university's highly-praised self-made tea. The other branches of agricultural science were also very active under the leadership of several Cornell graduates, dealing with large gardens and an experimental farm.

这里的化学和物理学现时虽然限于教学方面，但是教学在当年所达到的水准，已可非常确实地证明了。协和大学的毕业生林一博士，从未出国求学过，已负责发展一项非常有趣而对于该省有很大价值的工业。在过去的几年中，封锁使石油的来源完全切断，该省的公共汽车和卡车，几乎全靠一项特制的石油行驶。这种石油是用废弃无用的松树根加以干蒸馏，再把所得到的像松节油样的油类裂化而制成的。闽北有河流运输网，可以把那种树根顺流而下，运到几个主要的蒸馏厂去。芳香性的松木油，裂化颇非易事，不像脂肪族的植物油如同桐油那般在中国广泛地被裂化着。裂化过程中必要的铝接触剂，是用一种本地产的酸性黏土球供给的，那种黏土与 FULLER 氏土相像，放在金属线的笼里，悬在裂化室中油的上方。这种石油，在最后应用时，辛烷数很高，约为七五。总厂有一个极好的润滑油和分析的实验室，设在一个雕刻工细的古庙里。当我们想起它大部分的设备都是用装石油的旧钢筒、竹管和福州海军造船厂所遗弃的汽锅拼凑改造而成的时候，我们对于林一博士和化学家倪松茂博士的创造力和不屈不挠的精神，就不难得到一个概念了。这项事业对该省的切合实用，令人赞叹。它是我所见到的战时灵机应变的创作中最富有启发性的例子之一；即使在太平时世，这对于木材工业副产物的利用，也有很大的经济展望。（胡善美，2006：3）

虽然战时条件简陋，但协大师生们的精神世界依然丰富多彩。除了原有的各专业研究会、青年会、团契小组、体艺社团活动之外，各类抗日主题活动也纷纷开展。协大响应国民政府"抗日战争建国"的号召，组织了"抗建五团"——抗建剧团、抗建歌咏团、抗建宣传团、抗建服务团、中乐团进行抗日主题宣传。校友江由（2006：51）在《母校难忘 恩师难忘》一文中回忆道："由协大学生组成的话剧团，先后公演了《家》《雷雨》《北京人》《金门除夕》《东北一角》《有力的出力》《汉奸的子孙》《死里求生》《胜利的前奏》等二十多部进步话剧。"学校还定期举办总理纪念周、国民月会、师生座谈会、抗日战争建国研究会等集会，组织学生分析抗日战争形势、讨论时局、树立必胜信念，无形中将学习知识与国家命运统一起来，帮助学生们树立正确的人生观、世界观。

Though chemistry and physics here were only limited to teaching at that time, the teaching standard attained had proved itself with great certainty. Dr. Lin Yi, a graduate of Fukien Christian University who had never studied abroad, had been in charge of developing a very interesting industry that was of great value to the province. In the past few years, the blockade had cut off oil supply totally, so buses and trucks in the province ran almost entirely on a specially-made oil, which was got by dry distillation of discarded pine roots and cracking of the turpentine-like oil. Northern Fukien had a network of rivers that could carry the roots downstream to the major distilleries. Aromatic pine oil was not so easily cracked as aliphatic vegetable oil, which was widely cracked in China like tung oil. The necessary aluminum contact agent in cracking was supplied by balls of indigenous acid clay, similar to FULLER's clay. It was put in a cage of wire and hung above the oil in the cracking chamber. This oil, in its final application, had a very high-octane number, about 75. The main plant had an excellent lubricating oil analysis laboratory, housed in a finely carved ancient temple. When we thought that most of its equipment was modified and scrapped together by old steel tubes containing oil, bamboo tubes and steam pots abandoned at the Foochow Naval Shipyard, it was not hard to understand how creative and perseverant Dr. Lin Yi and the chemist Dr. Ni Songmao were. The project's practical contribution to the province development was really amazing. It was one of the most illuminating examples of wartime ingenuity I had ever seen. Even in times of peace, this also had great economic prospects for the utilization of wood industry by-products.

Despite the poor wartime conditions, the spiritual world of FCU's faculty and students was still rich and varied. In addition to the original professional seminars, youth associations, fellowship groups, and sports & art society activities, a series of anti-Japanese aggression themed activities were also carried out. In response to the National Government's slogan of "Resistance and Reconstruct", the university organized "Five Resistance and Reconstruct Groups"—Resistance and Reconstruct Troupe, Resistance and Reconstruct Choir, Resistance and Reconstruct Publicity Group, Resistance and Reconstruct Service Group and Chinese Orchestra to carry out anti-Japanese aggression themed campaigns. Alumnus Mr. Jiang You recalled in the article *Unforgettable Alma Mater and Teachers*: "The drama troupe composed of students from Fukien Christian University had staged more than 20 progressive dramas, such as *Home*, *Thunderstorm*, *Peking Man*, *Golden Gate on Lunar New Year's Eve*, *A Corner of The Northeast*, *Powerful Efforts*, *Descendants of Traitors*, *Seek Life in Death* and *Prelude to Victory*." FCU also held regular meetings such as Premier's Memorial Week, National Monthly Meeting, Teacher-Student Colloquium, and Resistance and Reconstruct Seminar, etc. Students were organized to analyze the situation of the War of Resistance Against Japanese Aggression, discuss the current situation, and foster confidence in victory, which unified the knowledge learning with the destiny of the country, and helped students set up correct outlooks on the world and life.

• 抗日战争胜利　重返魁岐

　　1945 年 8 月 15 日，日本宣布无条件投降。当胜利的消息传来，在邵武山区蛰伏 7 年多的协大师生们彻夜欢腾，高呼口号，声嘶力竭。不久，他们就盼来了要搬回魁岐校园的通知。同学们喜气洋洋，打点行装，迫不及待。但校方正冥思苦想：该如何将现今的 600 多名学生及各类书籍、仪器、设备迁回福州？原有仅设计容纳 200 多名学生的魁岐校园现在该如何修建以迎合目前的办学需要？邵武校区该如何保存和利用？……为了给搬迁工作做好准备，林景润校长一边提前派人回到协大魁岐校区，组织人员修建校舍，另一边在邵武积极组织安排人员物品的交通运输问题。回迁工作大约于 1945 年 11 月开始。关于此次搬迁的水上运输，要大大归功于闽江上放木排的传统。学校雇请了一些放排的工人，将先前购买的、用于修建校园的大批木材捆绑固定，再将需运回的物资搬上木排，就此沿闽江缓缓而下，经过三天的水程后回到魁岐。

　　战后的魁岐校园已是满目疮痍。7 年间，日军洗劫校园，造成教学设备、图书资料和古物藏品的大量损失；校园树木被肆意砍伐，文学院大楼被纵火烧毁，各处校舍楼房破败不堪……面对这一切，林景润校长顶住压力，苦心经营，以坚韧不拔的意志带领协大师生在不到一年的时间内完成校园修复工作。1946 年 5 月 1 日，回迁后的福建协和大学重新开学。

　　复校的喜悦还回荡在心，一个噩耗却已传来。林景润校长病倒了！7 年半在山城的过度操劳与艰苦生活，使他的身体不堪重负，患上肝癌。1946 年 9 月，林校长被迫辞职赴美就医，1947 年 1 月在美国不幸辞世，年仅 49 岁。

：陈锡恩
：Chen Xi'en

　　此时的福建协和大学，历经庄才伟、高智和林景润三位校长，在全体教职员的团结奋斗中已然成长为当时全国著名、福建首屈一指的高等学府。但是在饱受战争摧残后，协和大学乃至整个教育界的发展都元气大伤。林校长辞职之后，临危受命的是陈锡恩先生。他出生于福建福州，1922 年毕业于协和大学教育学系，1924 年赴美留学，1939 年从南加利福尼亚大学获教育博士学位。之后他于 1946 年回到福州，出任协大代理校长和校长之职。赴任之初情绪十分高涨的他，不到一年的时间便辞职赴美。本该致力于发展壮大协大教学科研能力的陈校长在任职期间深陷各类繁琐事务中：周旋于学校的物资供给、处理各种矛盾等。迫于时局形势，有心无力的他只能黯然离开，赴美继续他的教育生涯。

• Victory of the War and Resuming of Kuiqi Campus

On August 15, 1945, Japan announced its unconditional surrender. When the news of victory came, teachers and students having hibernated in Shaowu for more than seven years exulted all night, shouting slogans hysterically. Soon they received the news that they were to move back to Kuqi Campus. Students were jubilant, packing up and being too impatient to wait. But the heads of FCU were racking their brains about how to move the 600 students and all kinds of books, instruments and equipment back to Fuzhou. How should the Kuiqi Campus, originally designed to accommodate only 200 students, be built to meet the current needs? How should Shaowu Campus be preserved and utilized?... In order to make preparations for returning, on one hand, President Lin Jingrun had sent people back to Kuiqi Campus in advance to organize workers to repair and construct buildings. On the other hand, he actively settled and arranged the transportation of personnel and belongings in Shaowu. The returning work began around November 1945, and the water transportation of this relocation drew much from the local tradition of placing wooden rafts on the Minjiang River. The university hired workers to tie and fix a large amount of wood that had been purchased for building campus, and then load the belongings and materials that should be shipped onto the raft. Afterwards, the raft began to drift down the Minjiang River to Kuiqi. The water journey took three days.

Postwar Kuiqi Campus was in a state of devastation. During the past 7 years, Japanese troops had ransacked it, causing extensive loss of teaching equipment, books and antiquities. Campus trees had been wantonly chopped down, the building of College of Arts had been set on fire, and everywhere was in ruins... Facing these, President Lin Jingrun withstood pressure, painstakingly managing to lead FCU's teachers and students to complete the Campus restoration work in less than one year. On May 1, 1946, Fukien Christian University reopened.

While the joy of resuming Kuiqi Campus still reverberated in minds, the sad news came. President Lin Jingrun fell ill. After seven and a half years of hard work and tough life in the mountainous area, his body became overwhelmed and suffered from liver cancer. In September 1946, President Lin was forced to resign and went to the United States for medical treatment. In January 1947, he died in the United States at the age of 49.

After the first three presidents, E. C. Jones, John Gowdy and Lin Jingrun, Fukien Christian University had grown into a famous leading institution of higher education. However, ravaged by war, the development of Fukien Christian University and even the whole educational circle suffered greatly. After President Lin's resignation, it was Mr. Chen Xi'en who took over. He was born in Fuzhou, graduated from the Department of Education of Fukien Christian University in 1922 and went to the United States in 1924 to pursue further study. He received his Ph. D. in Education from the University of Southern California in 1939. In 1946, he returned to Fuzhou and served as the Acting President and President of Fukien Christian University. He was in high spirits at the beginning of his appointment, but resigned and left for the United States in less than a year. President Chen, who should have been committed to developing and strengthening FCU's teaching and research capacity, was instead involved in all kinds of complicated affairs during his tenure: dealing with the university's material supply, settling complex contradictions, etc. Compelled by the situation, he had to leave for the U. S. to continue his educational career.

仓促上阵的第五任校长杨昌栋原是福建神学院的院长，经多方考虑后接受了协和教职工们要求他代理校长的请求。他是福建平潭人。1921年考入协和大学，并以优异成绩提前毕业，获得学士学位。1930年秋在耶鲁大学学习，获得社会学博士学位。但由于各种原因，上任仅一年后，杨校长亦辞职。之后的协和大学便进入了校政委员会时代。校政委员会由主席、教务长、文学院院长、理学院院长及农学院院长组成，共同管理协大各项事宜。

: 杨昌栋
: Yang Changdong

● 政府接管　三校合一

1949年8月17日，福州宣告解放。8月24日，福建人民政府宣告成立。9月，福建协和大学连同其他学校的教师代表面见人民政府的教育局长。之后，各校校长被召集开会，要求各校加强领导，执行人民政府的各项政策与法规。1950年春季开学起，协大就增加了"辩证唯物主义、青年修养与毛泽东人生观、时事学习、社会发展史、中国革命问题、政治经济学"等课程（谢必震，2005：112）。同年秋天，所有外籍教师都离开了学校。1951年4月12日，福建协和大学正式被人民政府接管，并与华南女子文理学院合并组成福州大学（非现今的福州大学），成立典礼在魁岐协和大学举行。1952年8月，福州大学又与福建省立师范学院、福建省研究院、私立福建学院等单位先后合并，仍称福州大学，校址定于仓山区后岭路，在原华南女子文理学院旧址的基础上扩建校园。魁岐协大校园则为当时的福州制药厂所用。至此，福建协和大学完成了它的历史使命，存留在人们的记忆里。它培育出来的民族栋梁融入八闽大地乃至全国各行各业中，为现代化建设贡献力量。

: 1951年，协大与其他学校合并为福州大学
: In 1951, Fukien Christian University
: merged with other colleges to form Fuzhou
: University

The fifth president, Yang Changdong, had originally been the president of Fukien Theological Seminary. After much consideration, he accepted the request of FCU's faculty to serve as the Acting President. He was born in Pingtan, Fujian Province. In 1921, he was admitted to Fukien Christian University and graduated in advance with honors with his bachelor's degree. In the fall of 1930, he studied at Yale University and received his Ph. D. in sociology. But for various reasons, President Yang resigned after only one year in office. After that, FCU entered the era of University Administrative Committee. The University Administrative Committee was composed of the Chairman, the Provost, the Dean of Arts, the Dean of Science and the Dean of Agriculture, managing all matters of the university together.

• Government's Taking Over and the Merging of Three Colleges

On August 17, 1949, Fuzhou announced its Liberation. On August 24, Fujian People's Government was established. In September, teacher representatives from Fukien Christian University and other colleges met with the Director of Education of the People's Government. Later, the Presidents of universities and colleges were summoned to a meeting and were asked to strengthen leadership and implement the policies and regulations of the People's Government. Since the spring semester of 1950, FCU added some courses such as "Dialectical Materialism, Youth Cultivation and Mao Zedong's Outlook on Life, Study on Current Affairs, History of Social Development, Chinese Revolution, Political Economics etc." In the fall of the same year, all the foreign teachers left. On April 12, 1951, Fukien Christian University was officially taken over by the People's Government and merged with Hwa Nan Women's College of Arts and Sciences to form Fuzhou University (not today's Fuzhou University). The inauguration ceremony was held on Kuiqi Campus. In August 1952, Fuzhou University merged with Fujian Provincial Teachers School, Fukien Academy, and Private Fujian College, with its name unchanged. Its campus was located at Houling Road, Cangshan District, expanded from the former site of Hwa Nan Women's College of Arts and Science. Kuiqi Campus was resettled to Fuzhou Pharmaceutical Factory of that time. Till that moment, Fukien Christian University completed its historical mission, but remained in people's memory. The national talents it cultivated have integrated into all walks of life in Fujian and even the whole country, proceeding with their contribution to the modernization of the motherland.

• 名满天下　人才荟萃

协和大学创办之初，仅有教师 9 名。历经 36 年的苦心经营，在前后任教的 100 余名中外教职员工的共同努力下，协和大学凭借其雄厚的师资力量为国家和社会培养了一批又一批的专业人才，在全国享有极大的威望。名儒陈宝琛的入室弟子陈易园，著名文学家和教育家叶圣陶、郭绍虞，著名考古学家、甲骨文专家董作宾，严复之子、著名教授严叔夏，著名黄麻遗传学者卢浩然，著名历史学家傅家麟，著名动物学家、两栖爬行动物国际委员会委员丁汉波，著名昆虫学家、博士生导师赵修复，著名微生物学家、"庆大霉素"发明者王岳，以及著名学者陈锡恩、陈文渊、陈兴乐等都曾任教于福建协和大学。培养出来的人才中成为中国"两院"院士的多达 12 位，包括中国现代鸟类学奠基人之一郑作新，中国海藻学研究奠基人之一曾呈奎，病毒学家黄祯祥，寄生虫学家唐仲璋，生物化学家王应睐，半导体物理学家林兰英，小麦专家余松烈，计算数学研究奠基人和开拓者冯康，有机氟化学奠基人之一黄维垣，病毒学、生物制品学专家俞永新，寄生虫学家康崇惕和中国生物医用高分子材料重要奠基人之一卓仁禧。

福建协和大学办学 36 年间几经动荡，却依然顽强屹立、坚持办学，它的办学模式与教育经验都为中国的高等教育发展起到一定的借鉴作用。协大的教育宗旨"博爱、牺牲、服务"始终深扎于每一个协大人的心中。这些协大人可谓是当时整个中国社会，尤其是福建地区各行各业的生力军，他们不仅是协和大学发展的亲历者与贡献者，同时也是福建乃至整个中国高等教育事业的强大助推力。在 20 世纪 50 年代初，高等院校调整后，协大人又融入福建八闽大地的各个高等学府中，继续为中国高等教育事业奉献力量。

回望协大百年历史，耳边隐约又响起了它那激昂雄壮的校歌："协和大学闽江东，世界思潮此汇通，高山苍苍，流水泱泱，灵境产英雄；萃文化，作明星，明星照四方；无远弗届，真理是超，乐群众于一堂兮，作世界大同之先声，协和，协和，大德是钦！"

• Being World-Renowned for Its Galaxy of Talents

At the beginning of its establishment, Fukien Christian University only had nine teachers. After 36 years of painstaking and joint efforts of more than 100 Chinese and foreign faculty members, it cultivated a great number of professionals and talents for the country and society, enjoying great prestige nationwide. Chen Yiyuan, a disciple of well-respected scholar Chen Baochen; Ye Shengtao and Guo Shaoyu, celebrated writers and educators; Dong Zuobing, a famous archaeologist and expert in inscriptions on oracle bones; Yan Shuxia, the son of Yan Fu and a well-known professor; Lu Haoran, a famous jute geneticist; Fu Jialin, a distinguished historian; Ding Hanbo, a well-known zoologist and a member of International Committee on Amphibians and Reptiles; Zhao Xiufu, a famous entomologist and doctoral supervisor; Wang Yue, a well-known microbiologist and the inventor of Gentamicin, together with these outstanding scholars and doctors such as Chen Xi'en, Chen Wenyuan and Chen Xingle, had all taught in Fukien Christian University. As many as 12 of the talents it had cultivated became academicians of the the Chinese Academy of Sciences and the Chinese Academy of Engineering: Zheng Zuoxin, one of the founders of modern Ornithology in China; Zeng Chengkui, one of the founders of seaweed research in China; Huang Zhenxiang, virologist; Tang Zhongzhang, parasitologist; Wang Yinglai, biochemist; Lin Lanying, semiconductor physicist; Yu Songlie, a wheat expert; Feng Kang, the founder and pioneer of computational mathematics; Huang Weiyuan, one of the founders of organic fluorine chemistry; Yu Yongxin, an expert in virology and biological products; Tang Chongxi, parasitologist, and Zhuo Renxi, one of the founders of biomedical polymer materials in China.

During the 36 years, Fukien Christian University had gone through several turbulences, but still stood firm and persisted. Its mode of running universities and educational experience played a certain reference role for the development of higher education in China. Its educational objectives and the motto of "Fraternity, Sacrifice and Service" were deeply rooted in the hearts of its faculty and students, who could be reputed as the fresh force in all walks of life in the whole Chinese society, especially in Fujian Province at that time. They had not only witnessed and contributed to the development of Fukien Christian University, but also greatly promoted the development of higher education in Fujian Province and even the whole country. In the early 1950s, after the readjustment of colleges and universities, the members of Fukien Christian University were integrated into various colleges and universities in Fujian Province, continuing to contribute to the cause of higher education in China.

Looking back at the hundred years of Fukien Christian University, its passionate and magnificent alma mater gradually drifts into our ears and falls on our heart: "Where the mountains of Fujian are lifting, their noble crests to heaven above, by the waters of Min so stately flowing, there thou art, dear Alma Mater whom we love. All hail to thee! All hail to thee, Fair college, object of our hearts' devotion, while life shall last, O may we faithful be, to thee, to China and to World!"

● 百年传承　续写华章

由福建协和大学、华南女子文理学院、福建省立师范学院、福建省研究院、私立福建学院等单位合并组成的福州大学，于1953年更名为福建师范学院，1972年更名为福建师范大学，并沿用至今。百年春秋，薪火相传。经过一代又一代师大人的创新传承与砥砺奋进，今日的福建师范大学已经成长为综合实力名列全国大学百强、师范大学十强的综合性大学。2012年，教育部与福建省人民政府共建福建师范大学，2014年福建师大被确定为福建省重点建设的高水平大学，2018年被确定为福建省全国一流大学建设高校。"知明行笃，立诚致广"的校训精神与"重教、勤学、求实、创新"的优良校风推动着学校的突破与发展。截至2021年6月，福建师范大学有旗山、仓山两个校区，占地面积约4000亩；本科专业89个（2021年全日制普通本科招生专业77个），全日制普通本科学生2.3万多人，各类研究生8千多人；拥有1839名专任教师，其中高级职称人员占63.46%，具有博士学位的教师占63.62%。福建师范大学始终牢记立德树人之初心，牢记为党育人、为国育才的神圣使命，扎根八闽大地办学，努力造就时代良师，培养时代新人，为社会先后输送了50多万名各级各类英才，为国家和福建当地的发展作出了巨大的贡献。

：福建师范大学仓山校区
：Cangshan Campus of Fujian Normal University

• Inheritance and Development

Through the merger of Fukien Christian University, Hwa Nan Women's College of Arts and Science, Fujian Provincial Teachers School, Fukien Academy and Private Fujian College, Fuzhou University was renamed Fujian Teachers College in 1953, and Fujian Normal University in 1972, which has been thus referred to since then. After generations of innovation and endeavor through the vicissitudes in its century-old history, Fujian Normal University has grown into a powerful comprehensive university ranking among the top 100 universities and top 10 normal universities in China. In 2012, the Ministry of Education and Fujian Provincial People's Government began to jointly support the development of the University. It was designated as the provincial high-level university for prioritized construction in 2014, and as the first-class university of Fujian Province in 2018. Fujian Normal University's motto—"To Know and to Act, with Devotion and with Aspiration" and its pledge—"To Teach Earnestly, Study Diligently, Seek Truth and Promote Innovation" have facilitated its breakthrough and development. Until June, 2021, it consists of two campuses: Qishan Campus and Cangshan Campus, with a total land area of about 4,000 *mu* or 266 hectares. It offers 89 undergraduate programs (77 of which enrolled students in 2021). Currently there are over 23,000 full time undergraduate students, over 8,000 graduate students of various types, and 1,839 strong teaching staff. Its faculty counts 63. 46% full or associate professors and 63. 62% doctorate degree holders. Fujian Normal University always keeps in mind the original aspiration of fostering morality and integrity, and the sacred mission of educating talents for the Party and the State. It has been taking root in Fujian Province and striving to cultivate good teachers and new talents of the times. Since its establishment, Fujian Normal University has educated over 500,000 students talented at various levels and of diversified types, making tremendous contribution to the economic and social development of the province and the State.

福建师范大学旗山校区
Qishan Campus of Fujian Normal University

2003 年，乘着全国上下公有民办二级学院快速发展的东风，福建师范大学沿用"协和"之名创办了福建师范大学协和学院，继承和发扬老协和大学的优良办学传统，依托福建师范大学的优质教育资源，积极探索办学模式，创办特色品牌专业，为社会培养新型的高素质应用人才。协和学院位于福州闽侯上街大学城学府南路，校区占地面积近千亩，背靠繁茂郁葱的旗山，溪源江从校区穿行而过，校园环境优美雅致，文化氛围浓厚，具有完善的教学、实验、文化、体育和生活设施，有"山水学村"之美称。

目前，福建师范大学协和学院设有文化产业系、外语系、国际商学系、信息技术系、经济与法学系、管理学系、马克思主义学院和国际教育学院等 8 个教学单位，共开设涵盖文、工、教、经、法、管、艺等学科门类的 32 个本科专业和 2 个国际化本科教育实验班，现有专任教师 700 多名，全日制在校生约 1.3 万人。

：福建师范大学协和学院
：Concord University College，Fujian Normal University

百年时代风雨，从福建协和大学到福建师范大学，协大精神穿过漫漫历史尘烟，植根于每一个师大人的心中，指引着师大人时刻牢记使命与责任，在新的发展征程上继续谱写荣光，再创下一个辉煌百年。

In 2003, following the development trends of affiliated private colleges run by universities, Fujian Normal University established Concord University College, adopting the homonymous name of Fukien Christian University. The Concord University College inherits and carries forward the excellent traditions of former Fukien Christian University. Relying on the quality educational resources of the century-old Fujian Normal University, it actively explores new modes of school-running and strives to set up characteristic majors, aiming to cultivate urgently needed application-oriented innovative talents. Concord University College was located in Xuefu South Road, Shangjie University Town, Minhou County, Fuzhou, covering an area of nearly 1,000 *mu* or 66 hectares. Backed by the lush Qishan Mountain and with the Xiyuan River passing through the campus, it boasts a picturesque environment and rich cultural atmosphere. Equipped with complete teaching, experimental, cultural, sports and living facilities, it is reputed as an "academic village surrounded by hills and streams".

At present, Concord University College has 8 teaching units including Department of Cultural Industry, Department of Foreign Languages, Department of International Business Studies, Department of Information Technology, Department of Economics and Law, Department of Management, School of Marxism and Institute of International Education, offering 32 undergraduate programs in such subject areas as liberal arts, engineering, education, economics, law, management and fine arts and two international undergraduate education experimental classes. It now has over 700 full-time teachers and approximately 13,000 full-time students.

From Fukien Christian University to Fujian Normal University, the spirit of Christian University has gone through the long history and taken root in the hearts of the faculty and students of Fujian Normal University, guiding them to bear in mind their mission and responsibility firmly and continue its splendid development to create another brilliant century.

福建师范大学协和学院院徽
The school badge of Concord University College, Fujian Normal University

CHAPTER
NINE

从福音精舍到
福建神学院
From Gospel House to Fujian
Theological Seminary

第九章

福

历史的脚步总是匆匆，像遥远的钟声。19 世纪初，英国第一个完成了工业革命，随后法、德、美等资本主义国家先后从农业社会转向工业社会和商业社会。欧洲资本主义需要急速向世界扩张，占领世界的市场，经济全球化开始加速。于是，他们盯上了经济自给自足的中国。对于中国这个特殊的市场而言，英国人只能用白银换茶叶，而中国人基本不需要从英国进口任何产品（仲伟民，2010：24）。为了垄断贸易、赚取白银，英国不顾道义，贩卖毒品鸦片给中国，在中国最先通过茶叶贸易拓展市场，之后通过鸦片战争强行打开中国市场。1840 年爆发的中英鸦片战争和 1842 年签订的中英《南京条约》直接改写了中国历史，中国从此进入近代的半封建半殖民地社会。宁波、上海、福州、厦门和广州成为被迫开放通商的五个口岸。《南京条约》还规定了允许外国人在这些口岸城市建立教堂、医院和学校。从此，大批的传教士接踵而来，在中国亦有了合法化身份。

　　19 世纪 50 年代，太平天国起义期间，上海被小刀会占领，欧洲商人无法从上海出口茶叶，贸易中心从上海转移到福州，越来越多的传教士和商人来到福州，或传教或经商。由于福州本土居民对外国人怀有敌视心理，称呼他们为番仔，不允许外国人住到城内的鼓楼和台江城区。因此，多数外国人只能居住在城外的仓山区，与市区隔着闽江相望。前后共有 16 个国家选择在仓山成立领事馆或代办处，基督教多个宗派在此设立教堂、医院和学校，外贸和航运也随之迅速发展。因此，仓山文化在福州本土文化中独树一帜，带有典型的西方文化特质，这点与官宦云集的鼓楼区和商贾文化突出的台江区截然不同（岳峰等，2021：327）。

The footsteps of history are always in a hurry like the distant bell. At the beginning of the 19th century, Britain was the first country to complete the Industrial Revolution. Then came France, Germany, the United States and other capitalist countries successively which changed from agricultural societies to industrial and commercial ones. So European capitalist countries needed to expand rapidly and occupy the world market, thus speeding up the economic globalization. Since then, they had targeted at the market of China, which was in the period of economic self-sufficiency. In the special market of China, the British had to pay a great deal of silver for the tea while the Chinese hardly needed to import any products from Britain. To monopolize the trade and earn silver, Britain, regardless of morality, sold opium to China. It first opened its market through the tea trade in China, and then forced its way into the Chinese market through the Opium War. The outbreak of the Opium War between China and Britain in 1840 and the signing of the *Treaty of Nanking* between China and Britain in 1842 directly rewrote the history of China. From then on, China entered the modern semi-feudal and semi-colonial society. Ningbo, Shanghai, Fuzhou, Xiamen, and Guangzhou became the five treaty ports forced to open to trade. The *Treaty of Nanking* also allowed foreigners to establish churches, hospitals, and schools in these port cities. Consequently, a large number of missionaries came one after another and obtained legal identity in China.

In the 1850s, during the Taiping Rebellion, Shanghai was occupied by the Swords Society. Tea had to be exported from Fuzhou. Consequently, the trade center was shifted from Shanghai to Fuzhou. More and more missionaries and merchants came to Cangshan, Fuzhou, to preach or to trade. The residents of Fuzhou were hostile to foreigners, calling them *Fanzai* which meant foreign child or bastard, and did not allow them to go to the walled city such as Gulou District and Taijiang District. As a result, most foreigners stayed outside the city in Cangshan District, overlooking the downtown from the Minjiang River, where sixteen countries chose to establish consulates or agencies, and many churches, hospitals and schools were set up. Foreign trade and shipping also developed rapidly. Therefore, Cangshan District was typical of the Western style for the cultural heritage, which is unique in the local culture of Fuzhou. It was completely different from Gulou District where officials gathered and Taijiang District where commercial culture was prominent.

所以，历史上福州①是最重要的基督教新教传教区之一。1846 年 1 月 2 日，美部会的第一位新教传教士杨顺牧师来到福州仓山，并很快在城外仓山区建立了第一个传教点。紧接着，卫理公会于 1847 年 9 月上旬抵达福州。圣公会也于 1850 年 5 月抵达福州。这三个新教机构一直留在福州，直到 1950 年中国有了属于自己的独立的三自教会。

福州人平时提到的基督教主要指基督教新教，进入福州仓山区的主要有三个宗派：美国公理宗海外传道部（简称美部会）、美以美会②（后称卫理公会）、英国圣公会福音派布道会，俗称三公会。从创办义塾到创办正式神学书院，属美以美公会历时最长，无论是福州协和道学院还是福建协和神学院的创建，美以美会都在其中发挥了重要作用，其雄厚的资金和自身的包容性延续了这一脉的神学传承。

仓山区拥有基督教新教三大宗派独立创建或联合建立的神学机构、中国本土教会以及中国"三自"政策下成立的福建神学院。按照地理位置和时间顺序，最早是中洲岛小规模的家庭礼拜堂、福音精舍；往南过了解放大桥向右转就到了仓前路，那里有基督徒聚会处的玉林山馆、美以美会的天安堂、圣公会的石厝教堂、卫理公会旧址；之后穿过神秘小巷就到了麦园路 52 号大院，穿越百年前的女神学院、福州协和道学院、福建协和神学院，各大宗派的教堂和学校交汇融合；沿着麦园路往南走，经过前福建协和大学，再往南约 500 米，就到了施埔路的真学书院。站在 140 多年历史的圣公会教堂，闭上眼，仿佛就能听到教堂的钟声和圣乐。历史的脚步到这里停止了。1949 年，随着新中国成立的礼炮声响起，中国开始筹办自己的神学院。福湾路的福建神学院就是在中国"三自"政策指导下建造的完全独立自主的神学院校。

---

① 在传教士的英文出版物中常见的罗马拼音为 Foochow，Fuh-Chow，Fuh-chau 或 Hockchew.
② 美以美会的英文为 the Methodist Episcopal Church，是美国的一个基督教宗派，后改称为美国卫理公会教会。美以美会差会的英文全称为 the American Methodist Episcopal Mission，缩写为 MEM，指美国基督教卫理公会海外传教的一个机构。中文按其谐音译为美以美，富有美好的寓意。在中国，尤其在福州，称为美以美差会，也常常被称为美以美会。

Therefore, Fuzhou was one of the most important Protestant mission fields in China. The first Protestant missionary, Rev. Stephen Johnson from American Board of Commissioners for Foreign Missions, entered the city on January 2, 1846, and soon set up the first missionary station there. Then followed by the Methodist Episcopal Missionary Society, who reached Fuzhou in early September 1847. Later the Church Missionary Society arrived in Fuzhou in May 1850. These three Protestant institutions remained in Fuzhou until 1950 when China started to set up its independent churches.

Christianity in China mainly refers to Protestantism. There were three main sects in the Cangshan District: American Board of Commissioners for Foreign Missions (hereinafter called ABCFM for short), American Methodist Episcopal Church (hereinafter called MEC for short), Church Missionary Society (hereinafter called CMS), which are also called Three Missionary Societies. MEC had the longest history in building elementary schools and theological colleges, ranging from Foochow Union Theological Seminary to Fukien Union Theological College. Its inclusiveness and abundant funds made it possible for MEC to keep the theological tradition.

There are theological institutes established by three major Protestant sects, one local Chinese Christian church and Fujian Theological Seminary set up under China's policy of the Three-Self Patriotic Movement. According to the geographical location and time sequence, the first theological place to be mentioned is the Gospel House, a small family chapel on Zhongzhou Island. Going straight southward along the 10,000 Ages Bridge (now the Jiefang Bridge), we will be at the Cangqian Road. To the left is the Yulin Villa, the indigenous Christian church in China, to the right not far away is the Church of Heavenly Peace, St. John's Church, former site of MEC Conference. Going through a long and mysterious lane, we will find No.52 Building Complex on Maiyuan Road where Foochow Women's Biblical Institute, Foochow Union Theological Seminary and Fukien Union Theological College were located consecutively. Churches and schools set up by different Protestant sects integrated harmoniously. Walking along Maiyuan Road southward, in 7 minutes around, we will pass former Fukien Christian University. In about 500 meters further, the Theological College is in front of us. Standing in front of the Holy Church with a history of more than 140 years with closed eyes, we could hear the bell and sacred music from the church. It seems that the time stops and history pauses here. Then guns salute celebrated the foundation of the P.R.C. who started to establish her own theological seminaries. Fujian Theological Seminary on Fuwan Road was set up under the guidance of China's "Three-Self" policy, completely independent of foreign missions.

● 中洲岛的神学机构

中洲岛是西方传教士步入福州的第一站。不论是初来乍到的美部会，还是紧随其后的美以美会，还是更迟的圣公会，在创办之初，都在中洲岛暂住过一段时间。福州是近代中国基督教传教史上的重镇。中洲岛产生了中国本土教会基督徒聚会处，中洲基督教堂是中国最大的地方教会聚会处。从三公会的教会背景来看，福州三个基督教宗派的神学启蒙滥觞应溯于"义塾"的创办年代，初因经验不足、资金短缺、教员青黄不接等问题，且未能平衡教育与传教之间的关系，发展较为波折。之后改革观念明晰，得到政策和资金支持，发展逐渐平稳起来，教学质量与教育课程设置也日渐为社会所接受，教育学段覆盖小学、中学，其后教会大学产生；与此同时，女子教育也如雨后春笋，蓬勃发展。

杨顺和第一个礼拜堂

1844年1月1日，作为中国通商口岸之一的福州开埠后，西洋传教士纷至沓来。1847年1月2日，美部会派遣的传教士杨顺乘坐鸦片船抵达福州，这是福州第一位新教传教士。经过近半年的海上漂泊，杨顺抵达福州后暂住在鸦片船船长家中。他来榕后做的第一件事，就是联系当时的英国驻福州领事若逊，试图在城里建造住所，无奈未果。杨顺只能单独一人在中洲岛租房暂住。他敏锐地预见到福州可能成为一个传教中心，于是要求美部会迅速增派牧师来福州传教。几个月后弼利民[①]夫妇来到福州与他会合，他们都曾和杨顺在暹罗（今泰国）曼谷传教多年。于是他们就在中洲"兴建两层楼的西洋房子，既是寓所又是礼拜堂，以此吸引过路的旅客，扩大基督教的影响。这是福州的第一个礼拜堂，具有特殊的意义"（林金水，1997：391）。由于中洲岛人口密集，处于交通要道，百姓相对包容，对外国人较为友好，美部会早期的宣教活动得以在这座城外的岛上进行。

---

① 弼利民（Rev. Lyman B. Peet），又译为弼栾满、弼来满、弼履仁等。

• Theological Institute on Zhongzhou Island

Zhongzhou Island was the first stop for Western missionaries to enter Fuzhou, where either the earliest ABCFM or its immediate successor MEM, or the late comer CMS stayed for a period of time. Fuzhou is an important city in modern Chinese Christian missionary history. Zhongzhou Island emerged indigenous Christian church in China named Christian Assembly. The Zhongzhou Christian Church is the largest local Christian church in China. In terms of the missionary background of the Three Missionary Societies, the origin of theological teaching of the three Christian sects in Fuzhou can be traced back to the foundation of "free private schools". At the beginning, due to lack of experience, funds, and teachers, they failed to balance the relationship between education and missionary work, so the development of missionary schools was rather bumpy. After the reform, the teaching concept was clear. The missionaries were supported by the government and raised funds. The stable development made the teaching quality and educational curriculum accepted by society. At the same time, women's education mushroomed and flourished.

The First Church by Stephen Johnson

On January 1, 1844, Fuzhou opened as one of China's treaty ports, and Western missionaries poured in. On January 2, 1847, Stephen Johnson from ABCFM, the first Protestant missionary in Fuzhou, arrived, who later got a popular Chinese name Yang Shun. After nearly half a year of sailing at sea, Stephen reached Fuzhou and stayed at the home of the opium ship's captain during the first few days. The first thing he did when he arrived was to contact the British consul (R. B. Jackson) in Fuzhou in an unsuccessful attempt to build a residence within the city wall. Stephen Johnsonhad to rent a house on Zhongzhou Island alone. He keenly foresaw that Fuzhou would become a mission center, so he asked ABCFM to quickly send more priests to Fuzhou. He was joined by Lyman Birt Peet and his wife a few months later, both of whom had spent many years preaching with Stephen Johnson in Bangkok, Siam (now Thailand). Together, they built a two-story Western house on Zhongzhou Island, which was both a residence and a chapel, to attract passing travelers and expand the influence of Christianity. This chapel was the first church in Fuzhou. Being densely populated in the traffic artery, residents on Zhongzhou Island were relatively tolerant and friendly to foreigners. The early missions and education activities of ABCFM outside the city wall were mainly held on this island.

1847 年 7 月 1 日，杨顺在中洲的后洲角建立了"圣经斋学塾"（林立强，2004），后称"福音精舍"。这是福州第一所神学课堂。卢公明牧师在日记写道：杨顺的学校成立了。学校所在的那个房间就在他的小教堂所在的那栋楼里，学校大约召集了 14 个学生。传教士弼利民的学校大约招收了 25 位学生（林立强，2005）。1850 年 11 月，卢公明夫妇抵达福州，也在中洲岛福音精舍服务。该学塾在兴办初期聘用了中国本土教师，如进士、举人等当塾师，教授中文，以《圣经》为必修课，主修科目英语由美国传教士担任教师。辅修课主要有国语、四书等，由中国籍教师讲授。当时的学校都招收穷苦学生，不但免学费，还补贴生活费，因此也称为义塾。

根据卢公明 1852 年 1 月 5 日的统计，当时仅福州美部会传教团举办的义塾"一共有 4 所。义塾中有男生 54 名，女学生 33 名。学生总人数为 87 名。学校开支是 524.89 美元。传教团图书馆共有图书 216 册……一共有校舍 4 间"（林立强，2005：89）。"福音精舍"首批培训的华人沈守真、宋玉兴、刘孟提等人毕业后均参加了传道工作，是全美基督教会在中国培育产生的第一批具备相当水平，且能胜任中国传播基督教义工作的传道人员，刘孟提先生则是史上首位华人牧师（姚午生，2000）。

卢公明与格致书院

卢公明是美部会派驻福州的最著名的传教士，于 1850 年 5 月携妻子抵达福州，最初也居住在中洲岛。他在闽传教 20 多年，著作颇丰，最有影响力的是《中国人的社会生活》，其中翔实地描述清朝时期福州的政治、经济、民间信仰、习俗、宗教、教育等方面的情形。卢公明坚决反对吸食鸦片，他说一个人可以边走边抽烟，也可以躺着抽烟，也可以边从事业务边抽烟；但是吸鸦片的人是放下所有吸食鸦片，总是躺着吸烟，把全部注意力放在吸鸦片的过程上。鸦片对中国的影响是毁灭性的（Doolittle，1865）。卢公明于 1853 年撰著的《劝戒鸦片论》力劝当时的国人戒掉鸦片，但他没有提出具体的戒烟方法，而是站在传教士的立场上，宣传只有信仰基督教才能彻底戒除鸦片烟瘾。

On July 1, 1847, Steven established a Biblical Private School at Houzhou Corner of Zhongzhou Island, later called the Gospel House. It was the first theological school in Fuzhou. Rev. Justus Doolittle wrote in his diary that Steven's school was founded, which was just within the building where his chapel was, with about fourteen students recruited. Rev. Lyman B. Peet's school enrolled about 25 students. In November 1850, Justus Doolittle and his wife arrived in Fuzhou and also served in the Gospel House on ZhongzhouIsland. The School employed local teachers, such as those who passed the highest imperial examinations, to teach Chinese. *The Bible* was the compulsory course and American missionaries taught the major subject English. Chinese teachers taught supplementary courses including Mandarin and Four Books (*The Great Learning*, *The Doctrine of the Mean*, *The Analects of Confucius* and *Mencius*). At that time, the school was called free school since it enrolled poor students, not only free of tuition but also providing subsidy.

According to Justus Doolittle's statistics, on January 5, 1852, there were "four schools organized by ABCFM in Fuzhou. The total number of students was 87, among which 54 were boys and 33 girls. School expenditure was $524. 89. There were 216 books in the library... There were 4 School houses." Shen Shouzhen, Song Yuxing and Liu Mengti, the first Chinese missionaries educated in the Gospel House, all participated in missionary work after graduation. They were the first missionary talents cultivated by the American Christian Church in China, who were qualified to spread Christianity in China. Mr. Liu Mengti was the first Chinese pastor in history.

Justus Doolittle and Foochow College

Justus Doolittle was the most famous missionary to Fuzhou appointed by the ABCFM. He arrived in Fuzhou with his wife in May 1850 and originally stayed on Zhongzhou Island. Rev. Doolittle preached in Fujian for more than 20 years and wrote quite a number of books, the most influential of which was *Social Life of the Chinese*, which described in detail the politics, economy, folk beliefs, customs, religion, education, and other aspects of Fuzhou during the Qing Dynasty. Justus was strongly against smoking opium. He said one could smoke while walking, doing business, or lying in bed, but one would give up everything to smoke opium. Opium smokers always lie down, smoking, giving their full attention to the smoking process. Opium smoking is devastating to China. In his book *Exhortation to Abandon Opium* in 1853, he persuaded the Chinese to give up opium smoking. But, rather than suggesting a specific way, he, from the point of view of a missionary, declared that only by believing in God could one quit opium completely.

卢公明在福州建立了三种教会学校：主日学校、寄宿学校和培训学校，提倡以中文课本为主，向中国人传教，培养传教士的助理及本土传道人。由于中洲岛的福音精舍校舍太小，被学生戏称为"白墨盒"（林立强，2004：64）。为改善办学条件，1853年卢公明筹资建立了一座校舍，位于南台崎顶的"婆奶山"（林立强，2004：64），将福音精舍迁于此处。"婆奶山"即保福山，今南台铺顶吉祥山，现在的铺前顶救主堂所在地，当时的行政归属福州仓山区。格致书院是西方教会在福州创设的首批教会学校之一，而后改办为中学性质的"榕城格致书院"，即现在格致中学的前身。这是西洋教会在榕建立的最初的中学教育学校，也是福州市近代最早的普通中学（边晓丽，2011）。1854年，卢公明在铺前顶的保福山创办寄宿学校保福山学院，招收平民女子，学制8年，1915年更名为文山女中，即现在福州第八中学的前身，旨在宣传教义、培养少年读书人，由福州传向全国（林金水，1997）。

最早的西医诊所

1847年，美以美会派出第一批传教士摩西·怀德夫妇和柯林赴福州。怀德是韦斯利安大学毕业生，后在耶鲁大学学神学和医学。柯林毕业于密歇根大学。他们从波士顿出发途经香港换船继续前行。到厦门时，遇到美部会的弼利民夫妇，五人同行抵榕。由于不能在福州城内居住，他们暂时到美部会杨顺在中洲岛租借的房屋落脚，并在此建起美以美会的第一个据点。同年，怀德在中洲岛设立诊所，这是福州第一个西医诊所。医药传道是外国传教士宣教的方法之一。治好中国人的病，就容易消除他们的误会和敌对心理，能吸引他们来听道，并与教会发生来往（段琦，2005：27）。1848年3月，柯林在中洲岛开办学校，为美以美会在仓山地区最早的教会学校。1851年，第二批美以美会传教士高礼夫妇、怀礼夫妇和西利小姐抵达榕城。

Justus Dolittle established three kinds of missionary schools in Fuzhou: Sunday schools, boarding schools, and training schools. He advocated preaching to the Chinese people with Chinese textbooks and training missionaries' assistants and local missionaries. The Gospel House on Zhongzhou Island was so small that it was nicknamed "White Ink Box" by students. To improve school conditions, Justus Doolittle raised funds to set up a school building at the top of "Ponashan Mountain①", Nantai② in 1853 and moved the Gospel House here. From then on, the school was renamed Foochow College, which was one of the first Christian schools set up by the Western missions. It is the predecessor of Fuzhou Gezhi Middle School nowadays. Foochow College provided the first secondary school education and started the earliest ordinary middle school in modern times in Fuzhou. Justus Doolittle founded Ponasang Girls' School to enroll civilian girls with 8 years of schooling in 1854. It was renamed Wenshan Girls' Middle School in 1915, i. e. the predecessor of Fuzhou No. 8 Middle School, aiming to evangelize and cultivate young scholars from Fuzhou to the whole country.

The First Western Clinic

In 1847, the first missionaries delegated by the American Board of Missionaries, the newly-wed Rev. & Mrs. Moses Clark White and Mr. Judson Dwight Collins, came to Fuzhou. Rev. White was a graduate of Wesleyan University and later studied theology and medicine at the Yale University. Rev. Collins graduated from the University of Michigan. They sailed from Boston to Hong Kong to transfer and continued their voyage to China. When in Xiamen, they met Rev. & Mrs. Lyman B. Peet from the ABCFM. The five missionaries accompanied each other to reach Fuzhou, the City of *Banyan*. Being unable to live in the walled city of Fuzhou, they temporarily settled in a rented house on Zhongzhou Island, where they built the first stronghold of the Methodist Episcopal Mission (MEM). In the same year, Rev. M. C. White set up a clinic on Zhongzhou Island, the first Western medicine clinic in Fuzhou. The medical missionary was one of the preaching methods of foreign missionaries. By curing the diseases of the Chinese people, it is much easier to eliminate their misunderstanding and hostility, and attract them to listen to the preaching and have contact with the church. In March 1848, Collins opened a school on Zhongzhou Island, the earliest mission school for the MEM in the Cangshan District. In 1851, a second group of Methodist missionaries, Rev. & Mrs. James Colder, Mr. and Mrs. Wylie, and Miss Seeley, arrived in Fuzhou, the City of *Banyan*.

---

① Ponashan Mountain, i. e. today's Baofu Mountain, is located in Puding, Jixiang Mountain where Dudley Memorial Church is. This area belonged to the administrative attribution of the Cangshan District in old Fuzhou City.

② From the south gate to the river, and is called Nantai, or southern suburb. (Maclay, 1861)

● 麦园路的神学机构

从百年老校福建师范大学仓山校区向北出发，步行到麦园路 52 号的女子神学院旧址，需要 20 多分钟的时间，沿途会看到多处西式建筑。从校门口往左，沿着围墙外人行道步行不到 5 分钟就能看到古色古香的胜利楼，这是 20 世纪美以美会在仓山建立的华南女子文理学院最著名的教学楼，矗立在三县洲大桥头，成为地标性建筑。沿着福海路和对湖路就能看到海军礼堂，是笔者大学时经常看电影的地方，也曾经是美以美教会的建筑之一。沿途目之所及都是一个世纪前美以美会建立的中小学以及神学机构。福州是美以美会在中国的策源地，而美以美会以福州仓山为中心，相继建立天安堂（1856），创办毓英女中（1859）、美华书局（1862）、鹤龄英华书院（1881）、马高爱医院（1877），俗称岭后妇孺医院，即福建协和医院的前身之一。会治病的传教士医生更容易宣教。

麦园路 52 号大院分为前院和后院，前院现为福州仓山区人民政府仓前街道办事处。对面隔着马路就是红砖楼的十六中，即原来的毓英女中。每天上下学高峰期，这里是车水马龙，好不拥挤。前院是政府大楼，楼前"真抓实干，马上就办"八个字十分醒目。后院就是福州市基督教协会和三自运动爱国会，简称"市两会"。副会长林雪英牧师热情地接待我们这些到访的女教师们，并提供了珍贵的资料。据林牧师介绍，52 号大院共有 6 座楼，最早是 1879 年卫理公会创立的女子神学院及其教职员住宅地，经历多次变迁，几易其主。1912 年由三公会联合成立的福州协和道学院也曾在这里办学，其前身是美以美会的保灵福音书院。

• Theological Institutes on Maiyuan Road

It takes more than 20 minutes to walk northward from the century-old Cangshan Campus of Fujian Normal University, its predecessor Fukien Christian University built by the Methodist Episcopal Church, to No. 52 Building Complex on Maiyuan Road, the former Foochow Women's Biblical Institute. Quite a few Western architectures built by churches can be easily recognized on this short trip. Walking for 5 minutes from the gate of the University to the left along the footpath outside the wall, we will see the antique Victory Hall, which was the most famous teaching building of Hwa Nan Women's College of Arts and Sciences established by the Methodist Episcopal Mission last century in Cangshan. The Victory Hall, known as Malian Payne Hall, stands at the bridgehead of Sanxianzhou Bridge, becoming a monument nearby. Along the Fuhai Road and Duihu Road, we can see the Naval Auditorium, also a building by MEM, where the author used to watch movies when she was studying in Fujian Normal University. As far as one's eye can see, primary schools, middle schools and theological institutions established by MEM more than a century ago stand all the way. Fuzhou was the origin of the Methodist Episcopal Mission in China, and the Cangshan District was the center of its missionary activities. MEC successively set up the Church of Heavenly Peace (1856), Uk Ing Girls' School (1859), Methodist Publishing House (1862), Hok-Ling Anglo-Chinese College (1881), Magaw Memorial Hospital (1877), commonly known as Liang Au Women's and Children's Hospital, is one of the predecessors of Fujian Union Hospital. Doctors who could cure diseases were easier to preach.

No. 52 Compound on Maiyuan Road is composed of front yard and back yard. The front yard contains Cangqian Subdistrict Office, the People's Government of Cangshan District, Fuzhou City. Just opposite the road is the red-bricked No. 16 Middle School, i. e. the former Uk Ing Girls' School. This is a busy and crowded road, especially in the peak hour of the school. In front of the government building, eight Chinese characters in red are quite eye-catching, saying "Do solid work and do it right away". On the rear portion of the compound is the Three-Self Patriotic Movement Committee of Christian Churches in Fuzhou and the Fuzhou Christian Council (abbreviated as Fuzhou TSPM/Fuzhou CC). Rev. Lin Xueying, Vice President of the Three-Self Patriotic Movement Committee of Christian Churches in Fuzhou, warmly received us, the visiting women teachers and provided valuable information. According to Rev. Lin, No. 52 Compound has a total of 6 buildings. The earliest buildings were for Foochow Women's Biblical Institute by the MEM founded in 1879 and the staff residence. The Compound has undergone many changes and different owners. In 1912, the Three Missionary Societies jointly established Foochow Union Theological Seminary whose predecessor was called Baldwin School of Theology by Methodist Episcopal Church.

保灵福音书院

　　仓山的保灵福音书院曾是福州知名的神学校。其前身是创于 1852 年的美以美会的教会学校，也称美会学塾，负责人是教士基顺。美会学塾于 1856 年 11 月 26 日开办，有男生 4 名，之后增加到 12 名（林显芳，1936：21）。据麦利和牧师回忆，学校地址位于买下来的旗昌洋行。房子很宽敞，木质结构，是由不熟悉西方建筑风格的中国工匠建造的西式房屋之一（Maclay，1861）。据基顺牧师记录，咸丰九年（1859），这个寄宿学校建立新校舍，耗资 500 美元，包括厨房、饭厅、教室和 16 间睡房。每间睡房住 2 个男生（林键，2012：238）。民国之前男女授受不亲，男女生分别在不同的学校，道学院专门招收男生，妇女学校或者女神学院则专门招收女生。

First Premises for Boys' Academy

：美会学塾（来源：Maclay，1861：232）
：Boys' Academy（Source：Maclay，1861:232）

　　直至 1872 年，美会学塾才改名为保灵福音书院，是为了纪念教士保灵，他对建会立有大功。同年，美以美福州年议会根据武林吉牧师的建议，将美会学塾分设"福州培元书院"与"保灵福音书院"。1879 年，保灵福音书院与英华书院合为大书院，"其时校长为武林吉牧师，故为总主理、正主理之分。1892 年，分设福州、兴化两所学校。福州母校人数更多"（林显芳，1936：25）。保灵福音书院的主要目的是培养华人神职人员。1904 年，高智出任英华校长，与保灵福音书院重新分开。1905 年保灵福音书院校长沈雅各逝世，由萌为廉继任院长。1912 年，与美部会的圣学书院合办，成立福州协和道学院。保灵福音书院结束了长达 60 年的历史（林显芳，1936）。

Baldwin School of Theology

Baldwin School of Theology in the Cangshan District was a famous Bible school in Fuzhou whose predecessor was MEC Boys' Academy founded in 1852 when Rev. Otis Gibson was in charge. Boys' Academy opened on November 26, 1856, with 4 boys and later on 12 boys. As Rev. Maclay recalled, the school was located at Russell & Co. that he had bought. The house was spacious and wood-structured, one of the Western houses built by Chinese craftsmen unfamiliar with Western architectural styles. Rev. Otis Gibson recorded that in 1859, the boarding school built a new school building at a cost of $500, including a kitchen, a dining room, classrooms and 16 bedrooms with 2 boys per bedroom. Before the Republic of China, male and female students were separated from each other in different schools, with boys' schools for male students while girls' schools or women's biblical institutes for female students.

It was not until 1872 that the Boys' Academy was renamed Baldwin School of Theology, in honor of the Rev. Stephen Livingston Baldwin, who was instrumental in founding the school. In the same year, at the suggestion of the Rev. Franklin Ohlinger, the MEM Annual Conference divided the Boys' Academy into Boys' Boarding School and Baldwin School of Theology. In 1879, Baldwin School of Theology and Anglo-Chinese College merged to form the Great College, with the Rev. Franklin Ohlinger as its principal at that time, so there were General Principal and Principal Proper. In 1892, the Great College had a branch school in Hing Hwa (Xinghua) as well. The mother school in Fuzhou had more students. The main purpose of Baldwin School of Theology was to train Chinese local missionaries. In 1904, Rev. John Gowdy became principal of Anglo-Chinese College and it was separated from Baldwin School of Theology. In 1905, Baldwin School of Theology was succeeded by the Rev. William A. Main after the death of its former principal, Jacob Shen. In 1912, Baldwin School of Theology merged with the Theological Academy of ABCFM and founded Foochow Union Theological Seminary. Baldwin School of Theology ended its 60-year history.

福州女子神学院

美以美会开办女学之鼻祖是麦利和牧师的夫人。1851 年 1 月 1 日，麦利和夫人主持开办了女日学，地址设于仓前麦利和牧师住宅后院，是个当时仅耗资 55 美元建造的框架结构房屋（Maclay，1861）。美以美会在仓山兴建第一个寓所，地点在镜山（天安堂附近，现已不复存在），供柯林与麦利和牧师居住。根据麦利和牧师的描述："教堂就在我居住的地方前面，紧靠新马路，从街道可以通向山上的外国人住宅。"（Maclay，1861：209）麦利和的房子是简易的木框架房子，有板条、石灰墙和隔墙。倒不是因为非常缺乏经费，而是因为不知道能在福州待多久，也不了解福州的天气，常规是要为住宅、教堂等建造坚固的砖砌建筑。

First Dwelling-House built by the Mission.

：美以美会建造的第一个寓所（来源：Maclay，1861：280）
：The first dwelling-house by MEC（Source：Maclay，1861:280）

咸丰九年（1859）2 月 19 日，美以美会女布道会派遣女传教士娲标礼、娲西利、蒲缇师姑以及保灵牧师夫妇抵达福州。同年 11 月 28 日在福州仓山创办一所女塾，即后来的毓英女子初级中学。毓英女中即现今福州第十六中学的前身。初办女塾时，教会每天给学生家长 10 吊钱，以弥补上学的女孩不能干活造成的经济损失。这个女塾的经费就来自保灵夫人家乡的主日学校的资助。10 个月的招生宣传才录得 15 名小女孩，肄业 8 人；10 年之久，学生人数才达到 28 名。（陈忠钦、谢东楼，2003）

Foochow Women's Biblical Institute

It was under the care of Mrs. Maclay that the first day school for Chinese girls was commenced, which was located in the backyard of Rev. Robert Maclay in the Cangqian area. The cost of the frame-structure house was fifty-five dollars. The Mission built its first residence in the Cangshan District on Mirror Hill (near Church of Heavenly Peace, now defunct) to house Collins and Maclay. In his book, Maclay wrote, "The church was in front of the place where I live, close to the new road, which led from the street to the foreigners' residence on the Hill." Maclay's dwelling house was a light frame structure, with lath and plaster walls and partitions. It was not due to lack of money, but that they were not sure how long they could stay in Fuzhou, nor did they know about the weather in Fuzhou. The conventional practice was to build solid brick buildings for houses, churches, etc.

In Feb. 1859, the Women's Foreign Missionary Society of Methodist Episcopal Church designated the female missionaries Miss Beulah Woolston, Miss Sallie Woolston, Miss Phoebe E. Potter, and Rev. Stephen Livingston Baldwin to come to Fuzhou. On November 28 of the same year, a girls' school was set up in Cangshan, Fuzhou, which was later called Uk Ing Girls' School while Uk Ing Girls' School was the predecessor of today's Fuzhou No. 16 Middle School. At the beginning of the girls' school, the church gave 10 cents a day to the parents of the students to make up for the economic losses caused by the absence of the girls to work. The girls' school was funded by Mrs. Baldwin's Sunday school in her hometown. After ten months of recruiting, only 15 girls were enrolled, and eight finished the schooling. It took 10 years for the number of students to increase to 28.

First House for Girls' School

1851 年建成的第一座女日学校舍（来源：Maclay，1861：422）
The first house for Girls' School by MEC in 1851 (Source: Maclay, 1861: 422)

1879 年，美以美会的福州女布道会设立了两年制的学校，取名"妇女学校"，地点就设在福州仓前山，与毓英女中毗连（林键，2012：243）。由于这些妇女多数为文盲，主要授以罗马拼音写成的福州话圣经，后改为四年制，课程设置也比之前多。福州以外的县城愿意做女布道的信徒也都在这里学习布道方法，这是福州基督教女子神学院（俗称女神学校）的前身。福州史志网记录：1916 年，美以美会女传教士韦师姑，即韦嘉德，在仓山区仓前山土地庙（现在的麦园路 52 号）创办成立懿德道学校。后校址迁往聚和里（现在福建师范大学位于进步路的教工宿舍）。

1921 年，在仓前山毓英女中对面建校舍一座，其规模较之前大许多，迁校新址。1928 年，韦师姑提议升级学校程度，经美乐安师姑之赞助以及各教区女布道的同意，遂改组为福州女子神学院。美乐安师姑出任女子神学院校长，继任者有耐弼师姑。学校改名为女子神学院后，分设神学科，招收高中毕业生；道学科，招收初中毕业生入学。从以下这张老照片可以看出原来妇女学校和懿德道学校同时出现在现在的麦园路 52 号大院里。

：懿德道学校和"妇女学校"两所神学校（来源：洪伟）
：Yide Theological School and Women's Bible School（Source: Hong Wei）

In 1879, the Women's Foreign Missionary Society of Methodist Episcopal Church in Fuzhou established a two-year school named Women's Bible School located in the Cangqian area, adjacent to Uk Ing Girls' School. Since most of these women were illiterate, they were mainly taught *the Bible* written in the Romanized Fuzhou dialect. The schooling was later changed to four years. More courses were provided than before. Followers outside Fuzhou who were willing to serve as female evangelists must learn preaching methods here, which was the predecessor of the theological school. According to the website of the Fuzhou Chronicle, in 1916, the missionary from MEC, Miss Phobo G. Wells established Yide Theological School in Cangqian, Cangshan District (now No. 52 Maiyuan Road). Soon afterward, the campus was moved to Juheli (now the faculty dormitory of Fujian Normal University located on Jinbu Road).

In 1921, the school was moved into the newly built site just opposite Uk Ing Girls' School, which was much larger than before. In 1928, Miss Phobo G. Wells proposed to upgrade the school. Under the auspices of Miss E. D. Miner and with the consent of the women evangelists of the parishes, it was renamed the Foochow Women's Biblical Institute. Miss E. D. Miner was appointed as the first principal of the Women's Biblical Institute and Miss Jane Eden Nevitt the second. The new Institute set up a theological department to recruit senior high school graduates and an evangelistic department to recruit junior high school graduates. From this old picture, we can see the former Women's Bible School and Yide Theological School coexisted within No. 52 Building Complex on Maiyuan Road almost at the same time!

恢复原样的福州女子神学院校舍之一（2022）
One of the restored buildings of Foochow Women's Biblical
Institute（2022）

可惜到了 1936 年，女子神学院神学科并未成功招到学生，所有学生多为道学科。高中毕业生在当时的福州比较少。通常，未曾接受中等教育的青年妇女，但担任过教会执事，又能胜任传道工作的，要入校学习《圣经》及其他课程。因此，女子神学院准备与福州协和道学院合作。1935 年两个学校正式合作，学制 4 年。

福州基督教女子神学院的建筑呈现为中西合璧风格，因为拆迁现在已经无法见到全貌，根据《福州美以美年会史》的老照片可以看出教学楼呈"H"字形，古老的红砖加上中式的青瓦。建筑中间 3 层，两边各 4 层。

By 1936, unfortunately, the Women's Biblical Institute had failed to recruit students for its theological department, since most students came for evangelism. There were few senior high school graduates in Fuzhou at that time. Those young women, who had not received secondary education yet served as church deacons and were competent to be missionaries, may go to the Institute to study *The Bible* and other subjects. Thus, the Women's Biblical Institute prepared to cooperate with Foochow Union Theological Seminary. Consequently, the two schools merged, turning into a four-year college in 1935.

The architecture of Fuzhou Women's Biblical Institute combines Chinese and Western styles. Due to the demolition, it is impossible to see the whole building complex now. According to the old photo from of *Historical Records of Foochow Methodist Annual Conference*, the school buildings were in the shape of "H", with ancient red bricks and Chinese green tiles. The buildings had three floors in the middle and four on both sides.

1915 年美以美会建造的福州女子神学院（来源：《福州美以美年会史》）
Fuzhou Women's Biblical Institute built by MEC in 1915 (Source: *Historical Records of Foochow Methodist Annual Conference*)

现在麦园路 52 号大院里，面向麦园路的是前院，即仓山区政府仓前街道办事处大楼，后面的一栋是福州市两会的办公场所，这些建筑物都是原来福州基督教女子神学院院址。1951 年 9 月的卫理公会房屋土地及外国差会财产呈报表里清晰地写着："地点：麦园路 11 号（即现在的 52 号），神学院院址，神学院教职员住宅；购买人：美以美会；使用经过：前为福州女子神学院校址（1915 年建造）；费用来源：美女布道会，全部建筑为院址。"大院里目前有 6 栋楼。1951 年为福州协和神学院院址，一度租借给中共福建省党校。根据以上资料，麦园路 52 号大院最早是美以美会女布道会于 1951 年所建的福州基督教女子神学院院址，之后福州协和神学院和福建协和神学院借用该院址办学，并非之前有些文章所述是协和神学院的财产。

• 仓前山的神学机构

天安堂及其聚会点

美以美会在仓前山建有多个教堂，其中天安堂最具知名度。

天安堂位于仓前路，面向闽江，现在是烟台山著名景点之一，这里风景独美。据天安堂主任陈安俤牧师介绍，天安堂正门右侧三块重叠着的石碑见证了天安堂的落成、扩建与重建的日子，分别刻着"1856、天安堂 1897、天安堂史略 1999"，诉说着天安堂 160 多年（1856 年建）的历史。早在 1847 年 3 月 26 日，美以美总会就决定向福州派遣传教士开辟新区，福州遂为该会在远东地区的第一个传教站。

年仅 22 岁的柯林斯教士受美以美布道部派遣，偕同新婚的怀德教士夫妇从波士顿乘坐帆船，绕道非洲好望角，横渡重洋，历时 145 天，于 1847 年 9 月 6 日抵达福州口岸。第二年，富有远见卓识的麦利和牧师抵榕，在仓前山购地建住屋，协助柯林斯、怀德工作。1856 年 8 月 3 日购地茶亭，建"真神堂"；同年 10 月，又于仓前天安山购地建"天安堂"；供中西人合用，成为主堂。麦利和身兼两堂主理，成为天安堂第一任主理。

At present, No. 52 Building Complex on the Maiyuan Road faces Maiyuan Road in the front where the Cangqian Subdistrict office of the People's Government of Cangshan District is located. Behind the yard is the building of the Three-Self Patriotic Movement Committee of Christian Churches in Fuzhou and the Fuzhou Christian Council. These buildings are where the former Fuzhou Women's Biblical Institute stood. The Methodist Housing Land and Property Declaration of Foreign Missionary Societies in September 1951 clearly stated the location: "11 of Maiyuan Road (now 52), the site of Fuzhou Women's Biblical Institute, the residence of the Seminary staff; the purchaser: MEC; usage: the former site of the Fuzhou Women's Biblical Institute (built in 1915); fund source: Women's Foreign Missionary Society of Methodist Episcopal Church, all buildings for the Institute." There are currently 6 buildings in the compound. In 1951, the compound was leased to Foochow Union Theological College, and was once rent to Fujian Provincial Party School of the Communist Party of China. According to the above information, No. 52 Building Complex was originally Women's Biblical Institute built in 1951 by Women's Foreign Missionary Society of Methodist Episcopal Church. Fuzhou Union Theological College and Fukien Theological Seminary rented the site for teaching afterwards, not the owners of the compound. Some documents misinterpreted that the Courtyard was the property of Fukien Union Theological College.

● Theological Institutes in Cangqianshan Area

Church of Heavenly Peace and Its Assembly Places

Tian'an Church, originally called Church of Heavenly Peace, is located on Cangqian Road, facing the Minjiang River. It is now one of the famous scenic spots of the Yantai Mountain. According to Rev. Andy Chen, director of Tian'an Church, three overlapping stone tablets in front of the entrance respectively inscribed "1856, 1897 and 1999" represent the inauguration, expansion, and reconstruction of Church of Heavenly Peace, telling its story of more than 160 years. As early as March 26, 1847, the headquarters of Methodist Episcopal Church decided to dispatch missionaries to Fuzhou to open up a new area, thus Fuzhou became its first station in the Far East.

At the age of 22, Judson Dwight Collins, with Rev. & Mrs. Moses Clark White, a newlywed couple, was appointed by MEC to sail from Boston to Fuzhou via Africa's Cape of Good Hope. The voyage across vast oceans lasted 145 days before they arrived at Port of Fuzhou on September 6, 1847. The next year, in 1848, the visionary Rev. Robert Samuel Maclay arrived at the City of Banyan to buy land and build dwelling houses in the Cangqianshan area and assist Mr. Collins and Mr. White. A land lot was purchased on August 3, 1856 in Cha Ting (the tea pavilion) for the Church of True God. In October of the same year, he bought a land lot on Tian'an Mountain in the Cangqian area to build the Church of Heavenly Peace which became the main Church for the Chinese and Western followers. Rev. Maclay served as the first director of Tian'an Church.

咸丰六年（1856年）10月18日，麦利和牧师亲自主持天安堂落成献堂仪式。当时，由于民风闭塞，语言隔阂，再加上西方在对中国的殖民过程中犯下的罪行，当地居民反教仇洋，布道工作困难重重。从1847年到1857年，历时十年，才有一人信教受洗，此人正是长乐来榕开染坊的商人陈安，时年47岁。刚开始他在美以美会建立的第一所教堂茶亭真神堂慕道。之后麦利和夫妇亲自到陈安家中访问观察，吸收其入教。同年10月，陈安的妻子和两个孩子也受洗入教（Maclay，1861）；继而又有许金訇女士受洗。他们成为美以美会在中国第一批受洗的男女信徒。

江滨远眺，夜幕下的天安堂（2022）
Church of Heavenly Peace from the river view at night
（2022）

Scan for more
扫码了解更多

On October 18, 1856, Rev. Robert Maclay personally presided over the inauguration ceremony of the Church of Heavenly Peace. At that time, due to the conservative folk customs, language barriers and crimes committed by the Westerners when colonizing China, the local residents were anti-religious and anti-foreigners, so it was a tough job to evangelize the Fuzhou people. During the ten years from 1847 to 1857, only one believer was baptized. That first baptized follower was named Ting Ang, aged 47, a businessman from Changle running a dye shop in Fuzhou. In the beginning, he was a catechumen in the Church of True God①, the first church established by MEC. Rev. & Mrs. Maclay visited Ting Ang's home in person, and they admit Ting Ang as a member of the church. In October of the same year,

天安堂版画（来源：Maclay，1861：209）

Tian'an Church (Source: Maclay, 1861:209)

Chen's wife and two children were also baptized; Miss Hü King-eng was subsequently baptized. They became the first men and women to be baptized in China.

麦利和牧师
（来源：《福州美以美年会史》）
Rev. Maclay (Source: *Historical Records of Foochow Methodist Annual Conference*)

现在的天安堂讲台（2022）
Altar of Tian'an Church now（2022）

① Other versions are Tea Pavilion Church, the Ching Sing Tong, Chen-shent'ang.

天安堂为了实现宣教工作本土化，入闽布道之初就注意从本地人中物色愿献身布道业者予以精心栽培。1869年，在天安堂举行林振珍、谢锡恩、许播美、许承美、许扬美、李有美、叶英官等首批"七执事"按立典礼，由此产生闽省首批传道人，被誉为"七金灯台"。他们也是第一批华人传道者。1872年，闽清人黄乃裳（后成为著名马来西亚侨领）被保灵教士聘任为天安堂文案，并与武林吉教士共同创办福建省第一份教会刊物《郇山使者》。1884年，《郇山使者》改为《闽省会报》，前后总共延续了20多年。

1897年，天安堂主理黄治基牧师鉴于原建殿屋狭窄、难以容纳更多崇拜者，经努力筹集银币九千元，将原堂扩建为一座可容千人以上的巍峨新宇。从此，天安堂知名度甚高，成为全省乃至全国美以美会重要会议的会场。

据陈安悌牧师回忆，天安堂闻名遐迩。曾接待过美国前总统克林顿的北京基督教会崇文门堂可以说是天安堂的子堂，其建立于1870年。1911年11月9日，福州辛亥革命爆发，天安堂有信徒积极参加。1912年4月21日，孙中山先生在天安堂进行爱国演讲。会上，爱国志士群情激昂，踊跃签名，投身革命。1988年，天安堂被定为区级文物保护单位。

1996年，百年旧堂因年久失修，濒临坍塌，遂按原貌重建新堂。1999年10月30日新堂正式落成，举行盛大的献堂典礼。新建后的教堂一次能容纳1000人，总面积达2300平方米，造价300万元。

美以美会另有一座百年教堂小岭堂，1893年成立牧区。1914年拓建成三进院落的新教堂：一进为阅报所和钟楼；二进为礼拜堂；三进为牧师楼和小学，在当时的福州也很有名气。1995年作为天安堂的附属聚会点重新开放。1999年获准重建。新小岭堂属钢筋混凝土结构，共三层（不含地下室），建筑面积700平方米，一次能容纳800人，耗资150万元。2000年12月，位于仓山下渡十锦祠的新教堂落成，供举行青年团契、少年团契、主日学、查经祷告会、主日崇拜等活动，成为天安堂教会所属第一聚会点。

At the very start of their missionary work in Fujian, the Church of Heavenly Peace managed to select and train local followers who were willing to devote themselves to preaching. In 1869, Lin Zhenzhen, Xie Xin-en, Hü Bo-mi, Hü Sing-mi, Hü Yong-mi, Li You-mei and Iek Ing-Guan were the first deacons in Fujian Province, also honored as the "seven golden lamp stands". They were also the first Chinese evangelists. In 1872, Wong Nai Siong (1849 – 1924), a native of Minqing, who later became a famous overseas Chinese leader in Malaysia, was appointed as a copywriter of the Church of Heavenly Peace by Rev. Baldwin. He co-founded *Zion Herald*, the first church publication in Fujian Province, with the Reverend Ohlinger. In 1884, the publication was renamed *Fukien Church Advocate*, which lasted for more than 20 years.

Since the original church was too small, Rev. Uong De Gi raised 9,000 silver dollars to rebuild and expand the former temple into a lofty new building that could accommodate more than 1,000 worshippers in 1897. From then on, the Church of Heavenly Peace has become a well-known venue for important meetings of the Methodist Episcopal Mission in Fujian Province and even the whole nation.

As Rev. Andy Chen recalls, the Church of Heavenly Peace is widely reputed. The famous Chongwenmen Christian Church in Beijing, originally named Asbury Church, having hosted former US President Bill Clinton was founded in 1870 as a branch of the Church of Heavenly Peace. Some adherents of the Church of Heavenly Peace participated actively in the Revolution of 1911 uprising in Fuzhou on November 9, 1911. Dr. Sun Yat-sen gave a patriotic speech in Church of Heavenly Peace on April 21, 1912. At the meeting, patriots were enthusiastic to sign up in the revolution. In 1988, the Church of Heavenly Peace was designated as a cultural site under district protection. In 1996, the century-old Church was on the verge of collapse, so it was rebuilt as it was. A grand inauguration ceremony was held on 30 October 1999. The new church cost 3 million yuan, which can seat 1,000 people at a time and has a gross area of 2,300 square meters.

Another century-old church, Sieu Liang Dong (now also called Xiaoling Church), was established in the pastoral area in 1893. It was expanded in 1914 with three courtyards: the first yard for the newspaper office and the bell tower; the second for the chapel; the third for the pastor building and primary school, which made it a famous church in Fuzhou at that time. Sieu Liang Dong reopened in 1995 as an assembly place attached to Tian'an Church. It was approved for reconstruction in 1999. The new Sieu Liang Dong, located at Shijinci, Xiadu, is a reinforced concrete structure, with a total of three floors (excluding the basement), and a construction area of 700 square meters, which can accommodate 800 people at a time, and cost RMB 1.5 million yuan. Completed in December 2000, it is the first assembly place of Tian'an Church for the teenagers and youth fellowship, Sunday school, prayer meeting, *Bible* study, and Sunday worship.

1855 年建造的基督教小岭堂（来源：
《福州美以美年会史》）
Sieu Liang Dong in 1855（Source:
*Historical Records of Foochow Methodist
Annual Conference*)

小岭堂新堂（2022）
New Sieu Liang Dong（2022）

福州协和道学院

1912 年，闽北三公会（中华基督教会、中华圣公会和中华卫理公会）决定将圣公会的真学书院、美部会的圣学书院和美以美会的保灵福音书院合并，成立"福州协和道学院"，借用仓前山原美以美会保灵福音书院旧址①。有三种学制：两年的特科、四年的正科（相当于本科）和两年的附科或称简易科。1925 年进行学制改革，神学科学制三年，学成属于高中毕业，或者程度相当的肄业。圣经科三年，学成即为初中毕业或肄业。三公会所选任的教职员皆为美国教士。首任院长是萌为廉牧师，第二任（1914—1917）为美国汉学家何乐益牧师，第三任为葛树棠牧师。多位华人牧师担任监学，如陈文畴牧师是首任监学，第二任是高哲善牧师。陈芝美牧师则教授英语。三公会各派西牧师 1 名，中国籍牧师 1 名，国文教员 1 名，担任该学院教师（林键，2012：86）。

---

① 烟台山改造后，原鹤龄路和爱国路只剩部分路段，目前这些建筑亦难觅踪迹。

Foochow Union Theological Seminary

In 1912, Three Missionary Societies in northern Fujian (the Church of Christ in China, the Anglican-Episcopal Church in China and the Methodist Church of China) decided to merge the Theological College of Church Missionary Society, the Theological Academy of ABCFM and MEC's Baldwin School of Theology into the Union Theological Seminary in Fuzhou. The new Theological Seminary borrowed the former site of MEC's Baldwin School of Theology in Cangqianshan area. [1] There are three types of schooling: two years for special subjects, four years for full subjects (equivalent to undergraduate courses) and two years for supplementary subjects or easy subjects. In 1925, the academic system was reformed, and the theological science lasted three years, which was equal to high school graduation or equivalent study. Three years of *Bible* study, which was equivalent to junior high school graduation or similar study. The faculty members of the Three Missionary Societies were all American priests. The first dean was Rev. William A. Main, the second (1914 – 1917) Rev. Lewis Hodous, an American Sinologist, and the third Rev. J. B. Eystone. A number of Chinese priests served as overseers, such as Pastor Chen Wenshou as the first overseer and Pastor Gao Zheshan as the second. Rev. James L. Ding taught English. The Three Missions dispatched one foreign pastor, one Chinese pastor, and one Chinese teacher to teach Chinese respectively.

[1] Due to reconstruction of the Yantai Mountain, only some sections of the former Heling Road and Aiguo Road remain. These buildings no longer exist.

福州协和道学院学生众多，全盛时期达到百余人，前后毕业 200 多人。1914 年，学校进行扩建，建筑面积达到 2 447.89 平方米，校园占地面积达到 4.56 亩（林键，2012：98）。在旧校址的右边盖了一座五层楼的建筑，上层为宿舍，中间层为教室，下层是餐厅和厨房。又在学校北面新建造监学堂一座。宿舍共有百余间，教室有五间。新校舍有藏书房、阅报室。校外则为体育场。校园周边筑起高高的围墙，牢不可摧（林显芳等，1936：25）。来自美以美会和美部会的学生寄宿在保灵福音书院，圣公会的学生则寄宿在施埔路的真学书院。上午全体师生举行早祷后上课。特科学生下午在真学书院上课，正科学生上下午都在保灵福音书院上课（黄仰英，1972）。1917 年，福建协和大学成立的第二年，就与福州协和道学院合作，合办神科。学生分别在协和大学和道学院上课。

贝嘉德主教时任福州协和道学院的总理，书记是公理会裨益知牧师，圣公会牧师木约翰为在职教师。全校师生近百名，各教派齐心协力办学。1927 年，福州协和道学院停办，最后一位校长华惠成回国，学生由三公会本地教职工维持直到毕业。这样福州协和道学院暂告一段落（林显芳等，1936：26）。

：福建协和道学院（来源：《福州美以美年会史》）
：Fukien Union Theological Seminary（Source: *Historical Records of Foochow Methodist Annual Conference*）

Foochow Union Theological Seminary had more than 100 students in its heyday, altogether more than 200 graduates. In 1914, the school was expanded and the building area reached 2,447.89 square meters. The campus covered an area of about 4.56 *mu*. To the right of the old campus, a five-story building was built, with dormitory rooms on the upper floor, classrooms in the middle, and a dining hall and a kitchen on the lower floors. A new supervising building was built to the north of the school. There were more than 100 dormitory rooms and five classrooms. The new school building had a library and a reading room. Outside the campus is the playground. High walls were built around the campus to make it safe. According to documents, students from the Methodist Episcopal Church and ABCFM were housed at Baldwin School of Theology, while Anglican students are housed at the Theological College at Shipu Road. The class began after the morning pray. Special-subject students had classes in the afternoon at the Theological College, while full-subject students had morning and afternoon classes at Baldwin School of Theology. In 1917, the second year after its establishment, Fukien Christian University cooperated with Foochow Union Theological Seminary for a joint department of theology. Students took classes both at Union Theological Seminary and Fukien Christian University.

Rev. H. Mc C. E. Price was then the director of Foochow Union Theological Seminary, Rev. W. L. Beard was the secretary, and Rev. John Carpenter served as a teacher. There were nearly 100 teachers and students in the Seminary. The various sects worked together to run the school. Foochow Union Theological Seminary suspended its teaching in 1927. The last Principal Rev. H. W. Worley returned to the United States while the students were kept by the local staff of the Three Societies until their graduation. Thus, Foochow Union Theological Seminary came to an end temporarily.

据司徒雷登的有关记录：1920 年全国共有 13 所提供与圣经学校不同的神学教育的神学院校，此 13 所神学院校有三级入学资格：（甲）大学肄业两年以上或大学毕业；（乙）大学预科毕业；（丙）中学毕业。规定甲级入学资格的有 4 所，共有学生 26 人，全部用英语教学，分别是燕京大学神科（12 人）、金陵神学院（1 人）、圣约翰大学神科（5 人）、文华大学神道科（8 人）。规定乙级入学资格的有 4 所，学生 55 人，分别是广州神科学校（13 人）、沪江大学神科（22 人）、金陵神学院（1 人）、齐鲁大学神科（19 人）。规定丙级入学资格的有 7 所（司徒雷登，1923：92）。福州协和道学院应属于丙级。

福建协和道学院

在反帝国主义运动以及抗日战争时期，全国各地的神学院校均经历了一些变化。福州协和道学院为躲避战乱迁址到闽清，甚至到闽北顺昌办学，教会办学十分艰辛。1941 年，道学院附近的懿德女子神学院在抗日战争时期只能与福州协和道学院合并。福州协和道学院停办后，圣公会认为需要继续办学，就在真学书院原址复校。1928 年福州美以美会决定独立在福音书院旧址重新设立道学院，学制四年，招收的学生均是初中毕业或相当程度的学生，经过考试合格方可录取。学费依旧由学校补贴，毕业后就要担任传道人，享有薪俸。1929 年春，华惠成牧师从美国回到福州，招收学生 18 人，第二年 14 人。当时来自延平和兴化年议会的学生加入，有毕业生 25 人，这样道学院成为美以美会在福州、延平和兴化三个年议会的"福建美以美会道学院"。1935 年，中华基督教会闽中协会亦正式加入道学院，于是学校改名为福建协和道学院，学生实际人数 32 名。但是每天早晨的崇拜及课堂教学，与美以美会女子神学院各年级学生和圣公会真学书院一年级生联合，让学院看起来颇有规模了（林显芳等，1936：25）。

John Leighton Stuart recorded: in 1920, there were 13 theological schools in China that offered theology education different from Bible schools. These 13 theological schools had three levels of admission: (A Level) undergraduate students having finished two or more years of education or undergraduates having four year education; (B Level) students having accomplished university preparatory courses; (C Level) those who graduated from secondary schools. There were four A Level universities, with a total of 26 students, and all courses were taught in English. They were: Theological Department of Yenching University (12 students), Nanjing Union Theological Seminary (1 student), St. John's University (5 students), and Theological Department of Boone University (8 students). There are four schools with 55 students for B Level admission. The four schools were Guangzhou Theological School (13 students), Theological Department of St. John's University (22 students), Nanjing Union Theological Seminary (1 student) and Theological Department of Shantung Christian University (Cheeloo) (19 students). Seven schools prescribed the admission qualification for C Level. Foochow Union Theological Seminary might be one of the C Level.

Fukien Union Theological Seminary

During the anti-imperialist movement and the War of Resistance Against Japanese Aggression, theological schools all over China experienced some changes, including Foochow Union Theological Seminary. It moved to Minqing and even Shunchang in northern Fujian so as to escape from the war. In 1941, the nearby Yide Women's Theological School had to be merged with Fuzhou Union Theological Seminary during the War of Resistence Against Japanese Agression. After Foochow Union Theological Seminary was closed, the Church Missionary Society decided that it was necessary to continue running the school, so it resumed the school at the original site of Theological College. In 1928, the Methodist Episcopal Mission decided to re-establish their theological school at the former site of Baldwin School of Theology, with a four-year schooling system. The students enrolled were all junior high school graduates or equivalents who could only be admitted after passing the entrance examination. Tuition was still subsidized by the Seminary, and after graduation they were paid to serve as missionaries. In the spring of 1929, Rev. H. W. Worley returned to Fuzhou from the United States and enrolled 18 students, and 14 in the next year. At that time, students from Yen Ping and Hing Hwa Annual Conference joined the Seminary with 25 graduates in total, which became Fukien Methodist Theological Seminary for Annual Councils in Fuzhou, Yen Ping and Hing Hwa. In the spring of 1935, the Mid-Fuchien Synod of the Church of Christ in China formally joined the Seminary. From then on, the school was renamed as Fukien Union Theological Seminary with 32 students. But the Seminary showed a certain scale in the morning worship and classroom teaching when including students from the Women's Biblical College and the first-year students from the Theological College.

福建协和神学院

　　1943 年，福建神学教育研究会在福建协和道学院召开。福州基督教三公会领袖及真学书院、福建协和道学院、华南女子文理学院和福州协和大学的代表均极力主张福建协和道学院与华南女子文理学院、福州协和大学合作，兴办具有大学水准的高级神学院，并组成董事部，以促成此事（福建省志・宗教志编委会，2014）。1945 年 9 月 4 日，抗日战争胜利，日本宣布无条件投降后，道学院从闽清迁回福州。真学书院参与联合，于是三公会合作创办的福建协和神学院宣告成立，圣公会主教张光旭为董事长。院址设在福州仓前山麦园路（即现在的麦园路 52 号大院），当时的毓英女子中学对面（陈振华，1987：70）。福建协和神学院借用福州基督教女子神学院的旧址上课。根据史料，1951 年学院的整个建筑面积 3 531 平方米，校园面积 6 亩多。男生宿舍则设于原福州协和道学院教学楼之内（林键，2012）。因为时局动荡，加上教会学校为非官方办学机构，固时有动荡，常常经历创办、停办和再办的曲折过程。

曾位于麦园路 52 号的福建协和神学院教学楼，拍摄时间不明。该图和《福州美以美会史》里的基督教女子神学院的基本相同。（来源：池志海）
Fukien Union Theological College located once within No. 52 Building Complex, The shooting date is unknown. It is almost the same as that of Women's Biblical Institute from *History of M. E. C. in Fuzhou*. (Source: Chi Zhihai)

Fukien Union Theological College

In 1943, Fukien Theological Education Research Conference was held in Fukien Union Theological College. Leaders from Three Missionary Societies in Fuzhou, Theological College, Fukien Union Theological College, Hwa Nan Women's College of Arts and Sciences and Fuzhou Christian College urged that Fukien Union Theological College should cooperate with Hwa Nan Women's College of Arts and Sciences and Fuzhou Christian College to establish a high-end seminary. A board of directors should be formed to make it happen. The Theological Seminary moved back to Fuzhou from Minqing on September 4, 1945, after the victory of the War of Resistance Against Japanese Aggression. Theological College joined the merger, thus announcing that Fukien Union Theological College was set up jointly by the Three Missionary Societies with Chinese Bishop Michael Chang (Kwang Hsu) selected as the president. The college was located on Maiyuan Road, Cangqianshan area, Fuzhou (the current No. 52 Building Complex, on Maiyuan Road), right opposite the then Uk Ing Girls' School. Fukien Union Theological College employed the old site of Foochow Women's Biblical Institute for classes. According to historical data, the building area of the College was 3,531 square meters in 1951. The campus covered an area of more than 6 *mu*. The boys' dormitory was located in the teaching building of the former Foochow Union Theological Seminary. Due to the turbulent situation and not being officially supported by the government, missionary schools were often unstable, undergoing ups and downs of establishment, closure and re-establishment.

1945 年 10 月，真学书院与福建协和道学院合并，华南女子文理学院、福州协和大学参与，正式组建福建协和神学院，首任院长为平潭人杨昌栋牧师。英国差会的裴大卫牧师曾在 1948—1951 年任教务长。

1945 年，福建协和神学院升级为 4 年制本科，招收高中毕业生或具有同等学力者，由各公会选送，经过考试择优录取学生。学制分为道学士科 4 年、大学专科 2 年和进修科 1 年。道学士科招收高中毕业生或具有同等学力的学生，考生由各宗派教会选送，统一参加福州协和大学或华南女子文理学院入学考试，合格者即被录取（福建省地方志编纂委员会，2014：585）。最初课程只有四科：道学科（4 年制）；神学科（5 年制）；专修科（2 年制）；进修科（1 年制）。与现在的神学院大为不同的是，当时的协和神学院学生可以取得双重学籍，神学院与福建协和大学和华南女子文理学院共建，互认学籍。学生入学后，第一学年在神学院修神学课程，第二、三年男女生分别到福建协和大学或华南女子文理学院读文科，第四年回到神学院修完神学课程，期满毕业时，既取得神学学士学位，又取得协和大学或华南女子文理学院的文学学士学位（陈振华，1987）。

大学专科的入学资格和考试办法与道学士科相同，学生毕业时成绩优秀者，可再报考道学士科；高中毕业或具有同等学力并曾在教会工作几年者可以报考进修科。协和神学院附设圣经学校，学制 2 年，招收有教会工作经验的初中毕业生或具有同等学力者，年龄不限。专科读完两年后，到南京金陵神学院再读两年，相当于本科毕业（姚午生，2000：205）。

In October 1945, Theological College merged with Foochow Union Theological Seminary. Soon after, Hwa Nan Women's College of Arts and Sciences and Fuzhou Christian College joined the merger. Fukien Union Theological College was formally established. Rev. Yang Changdong, a native of Pingtan, Fuzhou, was the first president. Rev. David MacDonald Paton of Church Missionary Society (CMS) served as provost from 1948 to 1951.

In 1945, Fukien Union Theological College was upgraded to a four-year undergraduate college. It enlisted high school graduates or those with equivalent educational experience, recommended by various churches and recruited by examination. The length of schooling was divided into four years for Bachelor of Divinity, two years for junior college and one year for further education. The bachelor's degree program recruited high school graduates or students with the same educational background. Candidates were selected by various churches and denominations. All candidates attended the entrance examination of Foochow Christian College or Hwa Nan Women's College of Arts and Sciences. Those who passed the examination would be admitted. The initial curriculum consisted of only four kinds: preaching (4-year program); theology (5-year program); junior college (2-year program); further education (1-year program). Different from today's seminary, students at that time could obtain two bachelor's degrees. The College was the partner of Fukien Christian University and Hwa Nan Women's College of Arts and Sciences and acknowledged each other's academic status. After admission, students spend their first year in the Theological College. In the second and third years, male and female students studied liberal arts at Fukien Christian University or Hwa Nan Women's College of Arts and Sciences respectively. In the fourth year, all of them returned to the Theological College to complete theological courses. Upon graduation, they obtained a bachelor's degree in Theology and a bachelor's degree in Arts from Fukien Christian University or Hwa Nan Women's College of Arts and Sciences.

The admission and examination method of junior college was the same as that of the bachelor's degree program. Students graduating with honor could apply for the Bachelor's program again. High school graduates or equivalents who had worked in the church for several years were eligible to apply for further education. The Bible School attached to Union Theological Seminary had a two-year schooling system. It recruited junior high school graduates with church service experience or those with the same educational background, regardless of age. After two years of junior college education, they would study in Nanjing Union Theological Seminary for another two years, which was equivalent to a bachelor's degree.

中华人民共和国成立以后，西方传教士陆续撤出中国，各宗派教会与外国差会逐渐失去联系。1950年7月28日，吴耀宗带领福建基督教教育协会会长陈芝美、福州华南文理学院首任华人女院长王世静等40位知名基督教代表人物发表了《中国基督教在新中国建设中努力的途径》的宣言（简称《革新宣言》），指出了中国基督教反帝、爱国、爱教的道路，号召全国教会和基督徒割断与帝国主义的关系，肃清帝国主义的影响，彻底实行中国教会的自治、自养、自传的"三自原则"，建立自办的教会（福建省地方志编纂委员会，2014）。而要办好教会，就需要成立中国自己的神学院。1950年底，福建协和神学院宣布割断与外国差会的关系，在经济上拒绝接受差会津贴，教学任务全部由福建教会中的中国教师承担。

1951年上学期，福建协和神学院还有学生约90人，其中神学科学生有50人，专修科学生约20人，圣经科和进修班学生约20人（陈振华，1987：73）。当时国务院决定对全国大专院系进行调整，将宗教与教育进行区分，神学院要与大学分离。在这一背景下，多数学生选择了大学。1951年夏，神学院仅剩7位学生，于是迁到施埔路原真学书院内上课，维持了一年，而陈振华是最后一届学生（陈振华，1987：71）。他之后成为牧师，担任过苍霞洲基督堂、施埔堂以及小岭堂的堂主任。

1991年12月，陈振华牧师在天安堂为一对新人主持婚礼
Rev. Chen Zhenhua was presiding over a wedding for a couple at Church of Heavenly Peace in Dec. 1991

1952年，华东神学教育会议在上海召开，由全国基督教三自革新委员会召集相关教会成员。会议决定成立"金陵协和神学院"。当时有11所院校先后并入金陵协和神学院，它们是南京金陵神学院暨金陵女子神学院、上海圣公会中央神学院、上海浸会神学院、济南齐鲁神学院、漳州闽南神学院、福建协和神学院、杭州中国神学院、无锡华北神学院、宁波三一圣经学院、镇江浸会圣经学院、济南明道圣经学院。1961年，第12所机构燕京协和神学院也并入金陵协和神学院（徐以骅，1999：59–60）。

After the founding of the People's Republic of China, Western missionaries left China one after another, and the churches of various denominations gradually lost contact with their foreign missions. On July 28, 1950, Wu Yaozong led 40 well-known Christian figures such as Rev. James L. Ding, the head of Fujian Christian Education Association, and Rev. Lucy Wang, the first Chinese President of Hwa Nan Women's College issued the Declaration—How to Construct Christianity in China (hereinafter referred to as the Declaration of Reformation). It suggested the way of China's anti-imperialism, patriotism and Christianity that called on churches and Christians across the nation to cut off relationship with imperialists, to eliminate the influence of imperialism, to thoroughly implement the "Three-Self Principles" of self-government, self-support and self-propagation, and to establish independent churches. Only by setting up its own seminaries, can China run good churches. At the end of 1950, Fukien Union Theological Seminary announced that it would cut off its relations with foreign missions and declined mission subsidies economically. The Chinese teachers accomplished all teaching tasks in Fujian churches.

In the first semester of 1951, Fukien Union Theological College still had about 90 students, with 50 from theological department, 20 from specialism department and 20 from the Bible department and further education. At that time, the State Council of the People's Republic of China decided to adjust the national colleges and universities, separating religion from education, and separating divinity schools from general universities. In this context, most students chose universities. In the summer of 1951 when there were only seven students left, Fukien Union Theological College moved to Theological College on Shipu Road for one year and Mr. Chen Zhenhua was the last student of Fukien Union Theological College, who became a reverend and served as Director in Christ Cathedral, Shipu Christian Church and Sieu Liang Dong.

In 1952, East China Theological Education Conference was held in Shanghai, and members of related churches were convened by the National Christian Three-Self Reform Committee. The Conference decided to establish Nanjing Union Theological Seminary. By that time, 11 colleges and universities had been merged into Nanjing Union Theological Seminary successively. They were Nanjing Union Theological Seminary & Nanjing Bible Teachers Training School for Women, Central Theological Seminary, Shanghai, Baptist Theological Seminary, Shanghai, Cheloo Theological Seminary, Jinan, Minnan Theological Seminary, Changzhou, Fujian Union Seminary, Fuzhou, China Theological Seminary, Hangzhou, North China Theological Seminary, Wuxi, Trinity Theological Seminary, Ningbo, Jiangsu Baptist Bible College, Zhenjiang, Ming Dao Bible Seminary, Jinan. In 1961, the twelfth institution joined the Union, i. e. Yenching Union Theological Seminary, Beijing.

金陵协和神学院由当时华东 12 所基督教神学院院校联合组成，成为中国基督教目前唯一一所全国性神学院。福建协和神学院的创办始末是中国近代教会教育进程的一个典型缩影。

洋墓亭

福建协和神学院后，新中国开启了基督教中国化的进程，进入了中国基督教完全独立的"三自"时代。为了梳理仓山神学机构和神学人物，有必要了解洋墓亭的故事。

洋墓亭是一个基督教新教墓地，此前的一些西洋传教士安葬于此。它曾经位于仓山区麦园路，在福建师大附中和原市橡胶厂一带，始建于 1848 年。据力宣德牧师说，这个公墓有不同的名称，有人叫它"外国公墓"，有人叫它"国际公墓"，因为有一些中国人、法国人和日本人葬在那里。但最古老的、也许也是最准确的说法是"美国公墓"。它一直由卫理公会和美国传教会拥有和维护，但对其他人开放。

美以美会摩西·怀德牧师的第一任太太简·伊莎贝拉·怀德是第一位病逝于福州的基督教新教传教士。自此之后才有了洋墓亭，美国人称之为福州的美国公墓。福州宣教团墓地占地约 2 平方公里，自 1847 年宣教团成立以来，用于安葬死在福州的西方新教传教士、医生和领事。直到 1949 年，共有 400 多个墓葬，所有的墓葬尺寸都是 2 米乘 1 米，排列整齐。现在一切似乎都消失殆尽，但有两根特殊花纹的石柱后来被发现，一根竖着嵌入福建师大附中的一面砖墙上，另一根横着作为奠基石静卧于墙角。

洋墓亭现存的两根石柱位于福州仓山进步路 22 号附近，间隔 200 多米
The two existing stone columns of the Foochow Mission Cemetery located at No. 22 of Jinbu Road, Cangshan District

Thus, Nanjing Union Theological Seminary comprises 12 Christian theological colleges and universities in East China at that time, making it the only national theological seminary in China. The beginning and the end of Fukien Union Theological College is a typical epitome of modern Christian education in China.

Foochow Mission Cemetery

After Fukien Union Theological College was closed, the People's Republic of China started the process of Christianity with Chinese characteristics and entered the "Three-Self" era of complete independent Chinese Christianity. If we want to sort out theological institutions in Cangshan District and some theological figures, it is necessary for us to read the story of Foochow Mission Cemetery.

Foochow Mission Cemetery was a Protestant cemetery where Western missionaries were buried. It was once located on Maiyuan Road, Cangshan District, near the Affiliated High School of Fujian Normal University and the former Rubber Factory. The Cemetery was built in 1848. The former site of Mission Cemetery is now a corner of the Affiliated High School of Fujian Normal University. According to Rev. George Lacy, there were different titles for the cemetery; some called it Foreign Cemetery; some called it International Cemetery, since some Chinese, French and Japanese were buried there. The oldest, and most nearly correct perhaps, is the "American Cemetery" since it had always been owned and maintained by the Methodist and American Board Missions, but open to others.

Jane Isabel White, the first wife of Rev. Moses White, was the first Protestant missionary who died in Fuzhou. After that the Cemetery was built, which the Americans call the American Cemetery in Foochow. Foochow Mission Cemetery covered about 2 square kilometers and had been used for the burial of Western Protestant missionaries, doctors and consuls who died in Fuzhou since the mission was founded in 1847. Up to 1949, there were more than 400 burials, with each tomb the size of 2 by 1 meter and arranged in neat rows. All seems to have disappeared now, but two distinctly-patterned stone columns were later found to be remains of the Cemetery, one inserted vertically into the brick wall of the Affiliated High School of Fujian Normal University and the other one resting horizontally in a corner as a cornerstone.

现在发现的两根石柱就是洋墓亭的大门柱子（来源：Lacy, 1951: 2）

The two stone columns were found to be part of the gate of the cemetery (Source: Lacy, 1951:2)

1947 年中国卫理公会（即美以美会）百年纪念有一篇题为《见证》的文章，纪念埋葬在洋墓亭的怀德太太。文中说摩西·怀德夫人，卫理公会的三位传教士之一，于 1847 年来到中国，在亚洲大陆开设了美国卫理公会教会的第一个宣教团。墓碑铭文简述了她的信仰、来华事宜及去世原因。她和她的丈夫在满清道光二十七年的 7 月 27 日来到福州，没过几个月，她就染上了肺结核，于 1848 年 5 月 25 日去世，年仅 26 岁。（耶鲁大学神学院档案馆 R8b221f10）

　　由于水土不服再加上医疗条件差，传教士常常面临疾病和死亡的威胁，有些人因健康原因不得不离开中国。怀德太太到福州不到九个月就去世了，是第一位在福州去世的宣教士。他们买下了现在福州的美国公墓核心的两块茉莉花田，作为她的安息之所。

　　从 1847 年开始，四年间来榕的传教士连同家属共有 27 人，到 1853 年底，只有差不多一半留下来。1853 年，高礼夫妇和怀德牧师离榕返美。怀礼太太 1853 年 11 月 3 日病逝后，怀礼也于 1854 年初回国。1855 年，美以美会又派万为夫妇和基顺夫妇来福州，充实美以美会，但不幸的是半年后万为太太也病逝（林金水，1997）。著名的美以美会主教怀礼牧师（1825—1884），福建英国圣公会之父胡约翰（1832—1915），生于福州、死于福州的中国大陆最后一任卫理公会会督力宣德（1888—1951），美以美会女传教士华南女子文理学院的创始人程吕底亚牧师（1863—1941），亦安葬于洋墓亭。

：1858 年美国传教士万为绘画的福州洋墓亭（来源：Wiley，1958：2）
：Illustration of the Mission Cemetery at Fuh Chau，by Erastus Wentworth（Source：Wiley，1958：2）

One article titled "A Testimony" in the Centennial of Chinese Methodist Church (i. e. Methodist Episcopal Church) in 1947 commemorated Mrs. Moses White who was buried in Foochow Mission Cemetery. The paper said Mrs. Moses White, one of the three Methodist missionaries, came to China in 1847 to open the first mission for American Methodist Church on the Continent of Asia. The inscription on the tombstone introduced her belief and mission in China and the cause of her death. She and her husband arrived in Fuzhou on July 27, 1847. Just a few months later, she contracted tuberculosis and died on May 25, 1848 at the age of 26. (Yale Divinity School Archive R8b221f1)

Due to acclimatization and poor medical care, missionaries often faced the threat of disease and death, and some had to leave China for health reasons. Mrs. White died less than nine months after she arrived in Fuzhou, the first missionary to die here. Two pieces of jasmine field were bought at the heart of the American Cemetery in Foochow as her final resting place.

During the four years from 1847 to 1853, there were 27 missionaries and their families who came to Fuzhou. By the end of 1853, only about half of them remained. In 1853, Mr. & Mrs. James Colder and Rev. Moses White left Fuzhou to return to the US When his wife passed away on November 3, 1853, Mr. Wiley returned to his motherland in 1854. In 1855, American Methodist Episcopal Church sent Mr. & Mrs. Erastus Wentworth and Mr. & Mrs. Otis Gibson to Fuzhou to revive the mission. But unfortunately six months later, Mrs. Wentworth died of illness. Rev. Isaac William Wiley (1825 – 1884), the Father of Fujian Anglican Church, John Richard Wolfe (1832 – 1915), George Carleton Lacy (1888 – 1951) who was born and died in Fuzhou, the last bishop of Chinese Methodist Church, and Rev. Lydia Trimble (1863 – 1941), the founder of Hua Nan Women's College of Arts and Sciences, were also buried in Foochow Mission Cemetery.

● 施埔路的神学机构

拥有140多年历史的真学书院（现在基督教施埔堂的前身）坐落在仓山施埔路34号，位于最热闹的学生街。它独居一隅，静观熙熙攘攘的人世间。附近的福建师范大学、福建省邮电学校、福建警察学院、福建船政交通职业学院等高校的学生常常在这里用餐、购物，偶尔闲逛放松心情。

笔者1985年就读福建师范大学，居然毕业30多年后才认识这座与母校仅一墙之隔、饱经沧桑、拥有丰厚底蕴的圣公会书院！尤其在采访在教堂服务10年的陈传道并阅读相关书籍之后，才深刻感受到其历史的厚重，影响的深远，以及英伦风格的优雅。一眼百年，从残垣断壁中依稀可见往日的盛况。

：真学书院旧址
：Theological College premises

：施埔堂
：Shipu Christian Church

据陈传道介绍，真学书院可以追溯至1867年胡约翰于福州乌山创立的"道学校"。史荦伯到福州后，于1877年在此基础上创立了真学书院。1878年"乌山教案"事发，当地民众认为西人破坏当地风水，群起捣毁新盖楼屋。最终圣公会被要求离开福州城区，得到一定的赔偿金后，退往仓山发展教务。于是真学书院迁至仓山施埔（原名蛇埔），这里是原外国人居住的地区。

• Theological Institute on Shipu Road

With a history of more than 140 years, the Theological College (predecessor of the current Shipu Christian Church) is located at No. 34 of Shipu Road, Cangshan District. It stands at a quiet corner in the busiest and youngest Student Street in Fuzhou, watching the bustle and hustle of the dusty world. Students from neighboring universities such as Fujian Normal University, Fujian Posts and Telecommunications School, Fujian Police College and Fujian Chuanzheng Communications College often go dining, shopping and hanging out there in their spare time.

I started my studies in Fujian Normal University in 1985. Regretfully I visited this Anglican Theological College more than 30 years later. The College experienced vicissitudes of life with rich heritage. The author is impressed with its profound history, far-reaching influence and elegance of British style especially after interviewing the evangelist Mr. Chen, who has served in the church for ten years. Visitors can feel the magnificence of the past even from the ruins of the walls built one hundred years ago.

According to Chen, a catechist, Theological College can be traced back to the Theological School founded by Rev. J. R. Wolfe in Wushan, Fuzhou in 1867. Divinity College was founded in 1877 by Rev. R. W. Stewart upon his arrival in Fuzhou. In 1878, the Wushan Religious Persecution broke out. The local people insisted that the Westerners had damaged the local geomantic omen, and a group of citizens destroyed the newly built buildings. Eventually, the Christian Mission Church was requested to leave the downtown of Fuzhou for the outside of the city, i. e. Cangshan District to develop its educational affairs with a certain amount of compensation. It moved to Shipu Road (formerly Shepu Road) of the foreign settlement in the Cangshan District.

Scan for more
扫码了解更多

整个真学书院建筑群始建于 1881 年，占地约 14 亩，由一道围墙将之与外隔绝。至今尚存七栋（甲、乙、丙、丁、戊、己和戊座附属楼），建筑风格为中西合璧，保留了清代至民国中西元素相融的建筑风格。立面采用西方古典主义构架，但立面色彩上则运用了白墙灰瓦中式元素（陈孝杰，2019）。甲座原为教区职工住宅，为红砖洋楼。据说当年新四军曾租用该楼开办门诊，现在是一家酒店所在地；丙座为教堂，即现施埔堂的地标性核心建筑，建筑呈 L 型平面，为英式殖民地柱廊式砖木结构；戊座是主教住宅，胡约翰、恒约翰、张光旭主教等曾居住于此。建筑群的坡屋顶平缓、舒展，适合福州的气候，具有中式传统韵味（陈孝杰，2019）。

：真学书院全图（池志海绘制）
：A panoramic view of the Theological College（Source: Chi Zhihai）

：真学书院全景（伯明翰大学图书馆藏）
：A panoramic view of the Theological College（Source: University of Birmingham Library）

The entire Theological College complex was built in 1881, covering an area of about 14 *mu*, isolated from the outside by a wall. There are still seven buildings left, i. e. A, B, C, D, E, F and G, which is the affiliated building of E. The architectural style is the combination of the Chinese and Western elements, keeping the elements of the Qing Dynasty and the Republic of China. The facade adopts the Western classical framework, but the Chinese elements of white walls and grey tiles are manifested in the color of the facade. Building A, a red brick mansion, used to be the residence of parish staff. It is said that the New Fourth Army had rented the building to offer outpatient service, where now a hotel is located. Building C is the core mansion, the landmark building of Shipu Christian Church with an L-shaped layout plan. It is of British colonnaded brick and wood structure. Building E is for the bishop's residence, where Rev. John Wolfe, John Hind and Bishop Michael Chang (Kwang Hsu) once lived. All the pitched roofs of the compound are gentle and stretched, which are suitable for Fuzhou's climate and with a traditional Chinese style.

清代的真学书院（伯明翰大学图书馆藏）
A panoramic view of the Theological College in the Qing Dynasty（Source: University of Birmingham Library）

福建圣公会与胡约翰

现在的施埔堂会客厅里挂着一张有着精致相框手绘的胡约翰头像。陈传道说没有胡约翰牧师就没有福建圣公会，也就没有真学书院。此话毫不夸张。胡约翰扎根中国福建传教50多年，在1906年福建成立教区之前，一直是福建安立甘会的总负责人，被称为福建的圣公会之父（张金红，2007）。

英国安立甘会是新教传入福州的第三大公会，其英文为Anglicanism，故也音译为安立间会、英国圣公会或英国布道会，属于英国安立甘宗，但英国差会统称为Church Missionary Society，简称CMS。在中华圣公会未成立之前，各教会对此的中文称呼不统一。从福建差会的会议记录来看，当时福建也称其为安立甘会。19世纪传入中国的安立甘宗差会除了英国布道会，还有加拿大和美国安立甘宗所组织的差会。1912年，该宗在中国各差会决定联合，成立统一的中华圣公会。

1956年5月，中华圣公会主教院在中国举行最后一次会议。前排左二为张光旭主教，后排左一为薛平西主教，二排右一为刘玉苍主教。这三位主教都住过圣公会创建的施埔堂主教楼。（来源：陈安偀牧师）
The last conference in the Cathedral College of the Anglican-Episcopal Church in China was held in May, 1956. The second from the left in the front row was Bishop Michael Chang; the first from the left in the second row was Bishop Moses Hsieh; the first from the right in the second row was Bishop Liu Yucang. (Source: Rev. Andy Chen)

CMS in Fuzhou Mission & the Rev. John Richard Wolfe

An elaborate wooden frame of free hand sketching of Rev. John Richard Wolfe hangs on the wall of the reception lounge in Shipu Christian Church. Missionary Chen is not exaggerating when he says that without Rev. John Richard Wolfe, there would be neither CMS in Fuzhou Mission nor the Theological College. Wolfe had been preaching in Fujian, China for more than 50 years. Before the establishment of the Diocese of Fujian in 1906, he was always the general director of Anglican Church in Fujian, and was known as Father of CMS in Fuzhou Mission.

Anglicanism is the third major association of Protestants introduced to Fuzhou, from which it is also transliterated as Anglicanism or the Church Missionary Society. It is part of the Anglican School, England. However, the English Mission is generally called the Church Missionary Society, or CMS for short. Before the establishment of the Anglican-Episcopal Church in China, different churches were inconsistent in its Chinese name. According to the conference minutes of CMS in Fujian Mission, it was also called Anglican Mission. In the 19th century, the Anglican missionary society was introduced to China. Besides the CMS in Britain, there were also CMS in Canada and CMS in the United States. In 1912, all the Anglican missions in China decided to unite to establish a unified Anglican-Episcopal Church in China, and they did it.

胡约翰牧师（来源：Wolfe，1904：10）
Rev. John Richard Wolfe（Source：Wolfe，1904：10）

札成和温敦（亦译温顿）是最早进入福州的英国圣公会传教士，温敦更是圣公会第一位医生传教士。他们于 1850 年 5 月 31 日到达福州，与美部会的卢公明同船抵达。1851 年温敦在乌石山英国领事馆边上的神光寺开了诊所，边行医边传教，各个阶层的中国人都挤到小诊所看病。由于劳累过度，年仅 40 岁的温敦于 1856 年退休回英国，第二年病死于伦敦。1855 年 6 月 15 日，安立甘传教士方理和麦考夫妇来到福州。1858 年，密牧师来福州，独自一人负责传道工作。历经 10 年之久仍未有一人受洗入教。圣公会打算放弃福州。但是密牧师坚持留下来传道，第二年就有两人受洗礼。1863 年密牧师在福州去世时，有 13 人受洗，外加 5 位慕道友。

1862 年，胡约翰受命来榕，圣公会获得转机。胡约翰入闽以来，至其 1915 年去世，在长达 53 年的时间里，除了几次因健康原因回国休假之外，其余时间全部生活在福建。他是圣公会第一位进行福州以外县市巡游布道的传教士，连江、兴化、建瓯、邵武等几乎所有的传教点都是他最先访问和创建的（张金红，2007：4）。

福建圣公会在仓山设立的学校主要有真学书院、寻珍女子初中（曾位于福建师大附中校）、岭后的陶淑女校（1864 年位于福建师范大学旧校区的音乐学院）和仓山公园路的三一中学；在仓山设立的医院有福州地方医馆及药房、1866 年续办的塔亭医馆（现在的福州市第二医院）；在仓山建立的主要教堂有仓山麦园顶塔亭路明道堂（1866）、岭后陶淑女中的圣保罗堂、公园路三一中学的圣马可礼拜堂。

Rev. Robert David Jackson and William Welton (1809 – 1858) were the first Anglican missionaries to enter Fuzhou, while Welton was the first medical missionary of CMS in China. They arrived on May 31, 1850, on the same ship with Justus Doolittle, a member of the ABCFM Mr. Welton opened a dispensary in Shen-kuang-szu (or Shenguang Temple) near the British Consul in Wu-shi-shan (or Black Stone Hill), to which Chinese of all classes thronged. Being overloaded with work, Mr. Welton had to retire to England in 1856 and died in London the following year. A second group of missionaries, Mr. & Mrs. Matthew Fearnley and Mr. & Mrs. Francis McCaw were appointed to join CMS in Fuzhou on June 15, 1855. Due to harsh environment and difficult work, Mr. McCaw died in Fuzhou. But holy jobs continued without stop. In 1858, Rev. G. Smith arrived to be in sole charge of the mission. However, ten years passed by with no fruit. In 1860, CMS proposed to close the Mission in Fuzhou. Thanks to Mr. Smith who insisted to stay. Two Chinese were baptized in the following year. Rev. G. Smith passed away in Fuzhou in 1863, leaving thirteen baptized Christians and five catechumens. Wolfe complained later in 1868 that there were only four inquirers "in this obdurate city". It was said that Foochow seemed least willing to receive the message of salvation compared with other places.

In 1862, CMS took a turn for the better when Rev. John Richard Wolfe[1] came to the City of *Banyan*. From his entry into Fujian to his death in 1915, Rev. John Richard Wolfe lived in Fujian for 53 years except when he returned to Britain a few times for sick leave. He was the first Anglican missionary to carry out outstation tour and preach in counties and cities outside Fuzhou, and the first to pioneer and establish almost all outstations such as Lianjiang, Xinghua, Jian'ou and Shaowu.

The Christian schools set up by CMS in Cangshan mainly include the Theological College, Sing Ding Girls' School (which used to be located in the High School Affiliated to Fujian Normal University), Do-seuk Girls' School at Liang Au (located on the old campus of Fujian Normal University in 1864) and Trinity College of Foochow 1907 on Cangshan Park Road. The hospitals established in Cangshan are Foochow Native Hospital and Dispensary (later became the Takding Hospital in 1866, now Fuzhou No. 2 Hospital). The main churches built in Cangshan are Anglican Church of CMS (1866 on Tating Road, Maiyuanding), St. Paul's Chapel in the Do-seuk Girls' School at Liang Au and St. Mark Chapel in the Trinity College of Foochow.

---

① Wolfe got a Chinese name Hu Yueh-han.

乌石山教案

1850 年 5 月 31 日，英国圣公会差会到福州的传教士札成和医生传教士温敦在中洲岛居住几个月后，得到侯官县知县兴廉批准租赁，到南门内乌石山神光寺两间房屋居住。当时的闽浙总督规定只有外国领事馆才能设在城内，其他外国侨民只能居住在城外。这时，退休总督林则徐联合福州地方士绅，写信质问兴廉和英国领事，要求将城内的传教士驱逐到城外。1851 年初，札成和温敦迁出神光寺民房，搬至乌石山道山观英国翻译官住地，事件暂告平息。1864 年，英国圣公会在福州乌石山办女学堂。1866 年，胡约翰主持福州圣公会教务后，增租乌石山的文昌宫，续租道山观的房子，并进行翻新改造。1867 年，胡约翰在乌石山创办道学校。1877 年，史荦伯在此基础上创建真学书院。再加上在此前后几年，福州火灾水灾频仍，民众认为是洋人破坏风水，强烈反对洋教。1878 年，传教士在私筑围墙内兴建真学书院，当地乡绅率领众人抗议。传教士非但没有停工，还派兵驻守，导致民愤极大。官府再次勘查，确认真学书院属侵占公地，但是胡约翰不服，还挥手驱赶围观群众。民众情绪失控，拆毁新建的真学书院并放火焚烧院内书籍、衣物等，边上的两间旧洋楼也因火势蔓延被烧毁。1879 年，时任福建船政大臣的丁日昌亲自调查、协调，聘请英国律师出庭，与领事威妥玛和星查理协商。最终要求传教士退出福州城区乌石山道山观，福建官府以仓山施埔的洋楼花园出租给教会，租期 20 年，赔偿教会财产损失 5 000 美金。乌石山女学堂迁至南台下渡电线局（后来的陶淑女子中学）。1880 年 3 月，史荦伯也迁出乌石山道山观，迁往仓山施埔。至此，乌石山教案才了结。（福建省地方志编纂委员会，2014：478）

The Wu-shih-shan Incident[①]

On May 31, 1850, R. D. Jackson, a missionary from the Anglican Mission to Fuzhou, and Welton, a medical missionary, got approval from Hsing Lian, the governor of Houguan County, to rent two houses in Shenguang Temple on Wushishan, South Gate, after staying on the Zhongzhou Island for a few months. According to the regulations of the governor of Fujian and Zhejiang at that time, only foreign consulates could stay within the city wall, and other foreigners could only stay in the outer city. The then retired Governor-General Lin Zexu together with the local gentry of Fuzhou, wrote a letter to Hsing Lian and the British consul, demanding that the missionaries in the city be expelled from the city. At the beginning of 1851, Rev. Robert David Jackson and Rev. William Welton had to move out of the Shenguang Temple and stayed in the residence of the British interpreter in Tao-shan-kuan Temple. In 1864, the Anglican Church established a girls' school in Wushishan Hill (now, Wushan Mountain), Fuzhou. After Rev. John Richard Wolfe presided over the missionary affairs of the Church Missionary Society in 1866, he rented Wenchang Temple in Wushishan Hill, renewed the rent of the house of Tao-shan-kuan (Daoshan Temple), and rennovated them. In 1867, Wolfe established the "Theological School" in Wushan Mountain, which was developed into the Theological College by Rev. R. W. Stewart in 1877. Since calamities such as fires and floods were frequent in Fuzhou during these ten years, residents thought it was foreigners who had destroyed *Feng-shui*. Consequently they strongly resisted foreign religions. In 1878 when the missionaries built the Theological College within the private wall, the local gentry led the people to protest against it. Instead of stopping the project, the missionaries stationed their troops to protect it, causing great anger among the people. The government again made another investigation and confirmed the results that Theological College indeed occupied the public land, but Wolfe refused to accept the truth. Furthermore, he wanted to drive away the onlookers. The gentry and people were irritated. They demolished Theological College and set fire to books, clothing, etc., causing two nearby old buildings to burn down. In 1879, the then Fujian Shipping Minister Ding Richang investigated, coordinated, and communicated with Sir Thomas Wade and Consul Sinclair in person, inviting British lawyers to appear in court. In the end, the missionaries were requested to withdraw from Tao-shan-kuan on Wushishan Hill in the walled city. The Fujian Government rented the Foreign Settlement in Shipu, Cangshan District to the church for a lease of 20 years, and compensated the church $5,000 for the loss. The girls' school moved to Telegram House, which it had acquired from the Great Northern Telegraph Company, later named Do-seuk Girls' School. In March 1880, Stewart also moved out of Tao-shan-kuan, Wushishan Hill to Shipu, Cangshan District. Thus, the Wu-shih-shan missionary case was closed.

---

① Ellsworth C. Carlson, *The Foochow Missionaries, 1847 - 1880* 一书里的英文用词，教案也译为 missionary cases（chiao-an）。

施埔的真学书院

1880年3月30日，圣公会从福州乌石山迁出。乌石山道学校也一同迁往仓山蛇浦（今施埔），胡约翰等人购地14多亩，筹建新的真学书院。根据麦利和牧师记载，1883年，包尔腾主教在南台岛的外国人居住地蛇埔开办新的神学院，经费主要来自中国政府对拆毁的道学院的赔偿，建起了可以容纳50名学生的宿舍以及可以容纳200人的小教堂（Maclay，1904），也就是现在施埔堂的标志性建筑（原来的丙座）。真学书院第一任主理（校长）是史荦伯会长（1877—1883年在任），继而是班为兰会长（1883—1885年在任），同时黄求德牧师和陈信基牧师先后担任副校长。1898年，马丁会长任主理，同时陈永恩牧师为副主理，1927年被任命为首位华籍副主教（黄仰英，1927）。

: 基督教施埔堂
: Shipu Christian Church

真学书院一直办学到1912年，该书院与美以美会保灵福音书院及美部会圣学书院联合成立福州协和道学院。上课地点仍在福音书院，分为特科（两年）与正科（三年），但圣公会学生寄宿在真学书院，卫理公会和公理会的学生住宿在福音书院，全体学生近百名（黄仰英，1927：58）。

Theological College in Shipu

On March 30, 1880, the C. M. S. moved out of Wushishan Hill, so did the Boarding School. Wolfe purchased more than 14 acres of land to build a new Theological College in Shepu (now Shipu), Cangshan District. According to Rev. Maclay, Bishop John Shaw Burdon established a new seminary at Shepo, a foreign settlement on Nantai Island, financed largely by the Chinese government's compensation for the demolition of the Boarding School in 1883. A dormitory building for 50 students and a chapel for 200 were built, which is now the landmark building of Shipu Christian Church (the original Building C of the Theological College). The first president of the Theological College was Rev. R. W. Stewart (1877 – 1883), followed by Rev. W. Banister (1883 – 1885). At the same time, Rev. Huang Ch'iu-te and Rev. Ch'en Hsin-chi served as vice presidents successively. In 1898, Rev. J. Martin assumed the presidency, while Rev. Chen Yoog-eng (1873 – 1851) was appointed vice president who was ordained as the first Chinese archdeacon in 1927.

The Theological College kept running till 1912 when the College merged with Baldwin School of Theology of The Methodist Episcopal Church and the Bible School of the American Board of Commissioners for Foreign Missions (ABCFM) and established Foochow Union Theological Seminary. Classes were still held at Baldwin School of Theology. There were two kinds of schoolings, two years schooling for special subjects, three years for full subjects. But Anglican students still lived at the Theology College while students from Methodist Church and ABCFM stayed at the School of Theology, with a total of nearly 100 students.

20 世纪初中国基督教发展迅速。1913 年，全国基督教会成立中华续行委办会，开始对中国基督教的各项事业进行全面调查。1918—1922年，时任委办会执行干事的罗炳生牧师认为要在中国信徒中树立对教会的主人翁感，使教会成为真正的中国的教会。当时中国教牧人员占比增加，民族意识也得到提升，国外传教士开始正视这一现实。在入华传教百周年纪念大会上，就有不少传教士肯定中国的教会可以用"中国的教会"，而不是"在中国的教会"。中国的基督教徒意识到必须走中国化道路，才能使基督教得到较快发展（段琦，2005：125）。

在对中国基督教进行了大规模调查后，1922 年出版了中英文调查报告《中华归主》，也译为《基督教占领中国》。这本调查资料显示基督教"由 20 世纪初的 8 万人到 20 年代发展到 36 万人"，还表明了基督教的最终野心是要"占领全中国"。恰逢 1922 年 4 月世界基督教学生同盟准备在北京清华大学召开第十一届大会。这引起了非基督徒学生的强烈反对，上海学生成立非基督教学生同盟，在 3 月 9 日发布《非基督教学生同盟宣言》。北京学生成立"反宗教大同盟"，得到新文化运动领袖陈独秀、李大钊、蔡元培等人的支持。他们也发表宣言，反对宗教，重点反对基督教。在他们看来，基督教代表了资本主义列强对中国的文化侵略（段琦，2005）。此后，全国上下掀起"反基督教同盟运动"。1927 年，蒋介石在南京建立国民政府，开始收回教育权，很多教会学校深受影响。

1927 年，福州协和道学院在反基督教运动中被迫解散，圣公会回到真学书院原址复校。1928 年，美以美会建立了自己的道学院，之后，更名为福建美以美道学院。1941 年，日本占领福州，圣公会福州三一中学迁往古田县，真学书院学生寄宿于福州三一学校内，由高凌霄牧师亲自管理。1941 年，真学书院和三一中学迁往崇安，由伟牧师领导（黄仰英，1927）。1945 年，真学书院再次并入三公会联合创办的"福建协和神学院"。

Christianity in China developed rapidly in the early 20th century. In 1913, churches of Christ in China established the China Continuation Committee, which began to carry out a comprehensive investigation of geographical distributions and various causes of Christianity in China. Rev. E. C. Lobenstine, who served as executive director of the Committee from 1918 to 1922, believed that the church should foster a sense of ownership of the church among Chinese believers and make the church become a real Chinese church. At that time, the proportion of Chinese priests increased, and the national consciousness was also improved. Foreign missionaries began to face up to this reality. At the centenary conference of missionary work in China, quite a few missionaries affirmed that the term "Churches in China" could be translated as "Chinese Church" instead of "Churches in China". Chinese Christians have realized that they must take the road of Chinization to achieve the rapid development of Christianity.

After a large-scale survey of Christianity in China, a survey report in both English and Chinese, *The Christian Occupation of China*, was published in 1922. This survey showed that Christianity "grew from 80,000 people in the early 20th century to 360,000 people in the 1920s", and that the ultimate ambition of Christianity was to "occupy the whole of China". It so happened that the World Christian Student League prepared to hold its 11th congress at Tsinghua University in Beijing in April 1922, which aroused strong opposition from non-Christian students. Shanghai students formed a Non-Christian Student Alliance and issued the Declaration of the Non-Christian Student Alliance on March 9. Beijing students formed an "anti-religion alliance", which was supported by Chen Duxiu, Li Dazhao, Cai Yuanpei and other leaders of the May Fourth New Culture Movement. They also issued declarations against religion, with emphasis against Christianity, which in their view represented the cultural invasion of China by capitalist powers. Since then the Anti-Christian Alliance Movement had been launched across the country. In 1927, Chiang Kai-shek established the Nationalist Government in Nanjing and began to reclaim the educational rights, which greatly affected many missionary schools.

In 1927, Fuzhou Union College was dissolved in the Anti-Christian Movement, and Anglican Church returned to the original site of Theological College. In 1928, The Methodist Episcopal Church established its theological college, later renamed Fujian MEC Theological College. When the Japanese occupied Fuzhou in 1941, the Anglican Trinity Fuzhou High School was moved to Gutian County, and the students of Theological College were housed in Fuzhou Trinity School, which was managed personally by Rev. Edward M. Norton. In 1941, the Trinity Middle School and Theological College were moved to Chong An under the leadership of Rev. T. R. Wilkinson. In 1945, Theological College was once again incorporated into Fukien Union Theological College established jointly by the Three Missionary Societies.

岭后的"陶淑女校"

　　教会学校的建立是为了给当地的传教事业配备人才，服务于教务。传教士来福州后，他们的女眷家属对成立女校很有兴趣，因为清代男女学生不同校，而且女校屈指可数。于是，各差会开始兴办女校。陶淑女中就是在这样的背景下产生的。陶淑女校以胡约翰的妻子为校长，黄求德的妻子梁氏为监学。通过学生深入家庭，带动邻居到教堂礼拜。

　　由于清朝时期男女授受不亲，传教士不方便对中国女性宣教，因此他们的太太对福音在女性中的传播起到了非常重要的作用。1864 年，英国圣公会在英国领事协助下，租用乌石山弥陀寺房间创办女子小学校，最初名为"安立间会女学堂"。1878 年，由于受"乌石山教案"影响，校舍尽毁，只好迁往他处，租电报局楼房为临时场所。1903 年，迁到仓山岭后鳌头凤岭新校舍，遂定名为陶淑女子学校，并从小学扩充为中学，学制为 9 年。据收藏家池志海先生介绍，在 1910—1920 年期间，学校的全称是中华圣公会福州陶淑女学堂，如下图的毕业印章所示。

福州陶淑女学堂印章（来源：池志海）
Stamp of CMS Do-seuk Girls' School (Source: Chi Zhihai)

陶淑女中的圣保罗堂，摄于 2022 年 3 月
St. Paul's Chapel in Do-seuk Girls' Middle School (March 2022)

　　1927 年，陶淑女校经国民政府批准立案，正式定名为陶淑女子中学，并由华人黄求恩女士担任校长。1951 年，陶淑女子中学与英华中学、华南女子文理学院附中合并为福州大学附属中学，后改为福建师大附属中学。

　　陶淑女子中学的旧校址为造型精致、环境优美的西洋近代建筑群，现归属福建师大音乐学院，因年久失修，定为危房，等待维修，是仓山区不可移动文物登记点。

Do-seuk Girls' School at Liang Au

Missionary schools were established to provide the local mission with talents to serve in missionary affairs. After the missionaries came to Fuzhou, their female family members showed great interest in establishing a girls' school. Because in the Qing Dynasty, male and female students could not study in the same school, and there were few female schools. Thus, the different missions began to set up girls' schools. Do-seuk Girls' School came into being under such a background. Wolfe's wife was its first principal and Liang, Wife of Rev. Huang Ch'iu-te served as its superintendent. The Gospel was passed to parents through students, reaching families, bringing neighbors to church.

In the Qing Dynasty, it was not convenient for missionaries to preach to Chinese women because any physical contact between men and women in public was regarded improper at that period. So the wives played a very important role in spreading the Gospel among women. In 1864, the Anglican Church, with the assistance of the British consul, rented a room in Wushishan Hill to establish a girls' primary school, which was originally called "Anglican Girls' School". In 1878, due to the influence of the "Wu-shi-shan Incident", the school building was destroyed, so they had to move to another place and rent Telegram House as a temporary place. In 1903, it moved to a new school building in Liang Au, Cangshan District. The school was renamed as Do-seuk Girls' School. It was expanded from a primary school to a middle school with a schooling system of nine years. According to Mr. Chi Zhihai, a collector, the full name of the school was CMS Do-seuk Girls' School during 1910 – 1920, as shown in the graduation stamp.

In 1927, the school was registered with the approval of the Nationalist Government and officially named as Do-seuk Girls' Middle School. Ms. Uong Ch'iu-eng (Huang Qiu-en) was appointed as the first Chinese principal. In 1951, Do-seuk Girls' Middle School was merged with Anglo-Chinese High School and the Affiliated High School of Hwa Nan Women's College of Arts and Sciences to establish the Affiliated High School of Fuzhou University (later renamed the Affiliated High school of Fujian Normal College).

Located on the old campus of Fujian Normal University in 1864, the former site of Do-seuk Girls' Middle School is a modern Western architectural complex with exquisite shape and a beautiful environment. It now belongs to the College of Music, Fujian Normal University. Due to its long disrepair, it is classified as a dangerous building waiting for repair and is an immovable cultural site of historical heritage under protection registered in Cangshan District.

GIRLS' BOARDING-SCHOOL, FUH-CHOW.

陶淑女中（来源：Wolfe，1904：28）
Do-seuk Girls' School (Source: Wolfe, 1904:28)

圣公会的阿福女校

圣公会早期的一个女校鲜为人知，那就是福州女性自己发起的阿福女校。

福州的阿福夫人是一个传奇人物，是福宁教区第一位访问英国的女性。1889 年，她前往英格兰和爱尔兰，带着女佣同行，期间由英国人邵小姐照顾，经由 1876 年就到福州传教的史荦伯牧师夫人介绍到各地参加会议。她通过翻译在许多会议上做了发言，呼吁传教士到中国传教，引起了人们的极大兴趣。阿福夫人也请求英国圣公会女布道会来闽服务（黄仰英，1972）。

阿福夫人最大的愿望是专门任命一位传教士在中国的上层阶级的妇女中工作。之前，教会主要关注普通阶层或者底层的女性。1890 年，英国的米德小姐陪同阿福夫人回到福州。米德小姐一学会汉语就开始拜访城里的中国妇女。米德小姐教她们《圣经》及简单的家庭英语。1897 年底，在南台的阿福夫人家里开办了上流社会女子学校，她接受了校监的职位。两年后，学校搬到福州城内，在海军上将懿先生的帮助下，找到了在圣公会房产附近的地方，最多时候录得 200 多名女生（《中国基督教年鉴》编委会，2012）。

石厝教堂

石厝教堂原名圣约翰堂，位于福州市仓山区乐群路，建于 1860 年，是英国圣公会在福州建造的第一座教堂，由圣公会在福州的英国侨民集资创办，主要供英国人使用。与周边砖木结构的建筑不同，石厝教堂是石砌木构，外立面由青石砌成，故福州人称之为石厝教堂，体现了英国乡村小教堂的风格。之前，教堂占地很大，但院子外面都是墓地，现在占地 600 平方米，仿哥特式建筑（谢承平等，2012）。据当地老前辈说，参加礼拜的人社会地位都很高，有领事馆的官员，有欧美等国的基督教信徒，因此有国际教堂之称。1950 年秋，福州最后一批外籍传教士离榕，中华圣公会福建教区的薛平西主教接管圣约翰堂。"文革"期间，教堂被挪作他用。石厝教堂曾作为福州高级中学的校办工厂，后为海军闽海印刷厂使用，立面装饰遭受破坏，屋顶原有一钟楼及十字架，现已毁。1992 年，福州市政府公布其为三级文物保护单位（谢承平等，2012）。

Madame Ahok & Her Girls' School

Little is known about an early Anglican girls' school initiated by Madame Ahok, a lady from Fuzhou.

Madame Ahok of Fuzhou was a legendary figure, the first woman from the Diocese of Funing to visit England. She went to England and Ireland, accompanied by her maid in 1889. An English lady Miss C. Bradshaw took good care of her and the Reverend Louisa Kathleen Stewart (wife of Rev. Robert Stewart who had been preaching in China since 1876) introduced her to different conferences. She delivered speeches at many meetings through an interpreter, appealing for missionaries to go to China, which aroused great interest. Madame Ahok also called for CEZMS to evangelize in Fukien.

It was Madame Ahok's great desire that a missionary should be specially appointed to work among the women of the upper classes in China. Previously, the church focused mainly on women of the ordinary or lower classes. Miss Mead accompanied Madame Ahok on her return to Fuzhou in 1890. As soon as she learned some Chinese, Miss Mead began visiting Chinese women in the walled city, teaching them *The Bible* and simple daily English. At the end of 1897, an upper-class girls' school opened in the home of Madame Ahok in Nantai, who accepted the post of matron. Two years later, the school moved to downtown Fuzhou, with the help of Navy Commander Yih who found a house near the CEZMS property. At its height, the school obtained more than 200 girls.

St. John's Church

St. John's Church is located in Lequn Road, Cangshan District, Fuzhou city. Built in 1860, it was the first church built by CMS in Fuzhou, which was founded by the Anglican British in Fuzhou mainly at the service of the British Christians. Different from the surrounding half-timbered buildings, St. John's Church is made of stone, and its facade is made of bluestone, so the Fuzhou people call it Stone Church. It reflects the style of British village chapel. The church used to cover a large area surrounded by graveyards, now it covers an area of 600 square meters with somewhat Gothic style. According to local old-timers, those worshippers enjoyed high social status. Some were consular officers. Some were Christians from Europe, the United States and other countries, so it got the name of the International Church. In the autumn of 1950, the last group of foreign missionaries left Fuzhou for their homelands. Bishop Moses Hsieh of CMS in Fujian took over St. John's Church. During the Cultural Revolution, the Church, like other church properties, was used for other purposes. St. John's Church was once used as a factory of Fuzhou Senior High School, and later as Minhai Printing Factory of the Navy. The facade decoration was damaged, and the original bell tower and the cross on the roof were destroyed. In 1992, Fuzhou Municipal Government announced it as a tertiary cultural heritage under protection.

目前教堂没有对外开放，好奇的游客从围着的栅栏往里看，希望透过门缝揭开里面的神秘面纱，但只能看到外面大院以及斑驳红漆的大门。门前有一棵老银杏树，左侧边有两棵樟树。这棵百年银杏树和教堂交相辉映，成为目前烟台山的打卡景点。每年圣诞节前后，银杏飘黄之时，落叶缤纷。在阳光的照耀下，金黄色的叶子洒落一地，满园金色醉人，与百年教堂交映成趣，犹如一幅色彩缤纷的油画。许多当地媒体自然不会错失宣传机会，对石厝教堂做了大量报道。仓山区委区政府于 2022 年 1 月 4 日举行第二届烟台山银杏旅游节，烟台山的小确"杏"，吸引了不少游客。

晚清时期石厝教堂老照片（来源：池志海）
An old picture of Stone House Church in the late Qing Dynasty（Source: Chi Zhihai)

The church is currently closed to the public. Some curious visitors peek through the fence, hoping to uncover the mystery of the inside through the door crack, but can only see the courtyard and the red painted door. There is an old ginkgo tree in front of the door, and two camphor trees on the left. This century-old ginkgo tree is now a clock-in tourist attraction in the Yantai Mountain. Every year around Christmas when the ginkgo tree turns yellow, the fallen leaves are colorful. Under the sunshine, the golden leaves all over the ground together with the century-old church make the garden intoxicating, presenting a beautiful oil painting. Local media will never miss such a golden chance to promote local tourism, giving the Church plenty of coverage. The People's Government of Cangshan District held the second Yantai Ginkgo Tourism Festival on January 4, 2022. The homophone of ginkgo tree is "for sure and happiness" in Chinese, attracting many tourists.

：彼此守望的石厝教堂及其门前的百年杏树图（2021）
：St. John's Church and the century-old ginkgo tree accompanying each other（2021）

明道堂

座落在麦园顶塔亭路的明道堂建于 1866 年，建筑面积约 600 平方米，与圣公会的塔亭医院同时建成，拥有 150 多年的历史。1928 年第二次修造，2022 年第三次修造。曾经是英国圣公会在福州建造的一座重要教堂，现在是美以美会天安堂的一个聚会点。

追溯历史，该堂有段时间是灵光盲童学校（招男童）和明道女童盲校所在地。1893 年，澳大利亚的岳爱美女士来华创办，至 1900 年共收养盲童 17 人。1894 年，向澳大利亚友人募得善款，乃建校舍于北门，称灵光学校（只收男童）。1901 年，岳爱美再次来到福州仓前梅坞创办女盲校。

盲校的学生不但精于各种竹、草编手艺，且擅于唱诗、演奏等。在 1915 年国际巴拿马博览会上，盲人所制工艺品获得金奖。1922 年，盲校铜管乐队前往英国皇宫演奏，在王宫贵族前演出中西经典曲目，受到高度评价（姚午生，2000：208）。他们原计划在英巡回演出 3 个月，因为受到英国女王接见，英国人民又热情挽留，行程延长至 22 个月才回国。

据统计，1928 年明道盲童女校有 80 多名学生，从 3 岁多的幼童到40 多岁的成人。由于当时女性地位卑微，盲校女生大多不愿出嫁，更多选择留校任教或辅助传教士工作。这给盲校带来较大的财政负担。学校另外雇用了 10 多位视力正常的女工协助校务工作。到民国中后期，女童盲校无法完全对外招生，需要经人引荐才能入学。后来明道女童盲校继任校长的有胡约翰的女儿胡师姑、兰师姑等。盲校的校长虽然是外国人，但学校具体事务由中国人管理。

The Anglican Church Mingdao Church

The Anglican Church Mingdao Church, located between Tating Road and Maiyuanding, was built in 1866 with a construction area of about 600 square meters. It was built at the same time with Takding Hospital of Anglican Church and has a history of more than 150 years, which was renewed the second time in 1928 and the third time in 2022. Though being once an important church of CMS in Fuzhou, it is now one of the meeting places of Church of Heavenly Peace of MEC.

The Church can be traced back to CMS Boys' Blind School and CMS Girls' Blind School built by Amy Oxley Wilkinson from Australia in 1893. By 1900, it had adopted 17 blind children. In 1894 when her Australian friends raised a large sum of fund, Amy Oxley Wilkinson built a new school in the North Gate, known as the CMS Boys' Blind School (only enrolling boys). Amy Oxley came to Meiwu, Cangqian area again to establish a school for blind girls in 1901.

Boys and girls in the blind school were not only good at bamboo and straw weaving but also good at singing and playing. During the International Panama Exposition in 1915, handicrafts made by the blind won the Gold Medal. In 1922, their performance of Chinese and Western classical songs given by the Brass Band at the presence of the royal nobles in the British Royal Palace was highly praised. The original plan of 3 months to tour Britain was extended to 22 months, having the honor of being received by the Queen of England and being held up by the enthusiastic British.

According to statistics, in 1928, there were more than 80 students in the Blind Girls' School, with students ranging from 3 years old to 40 years old. Because of the low social status of women at that time, most girls in blind schools were reluctant to get married. Instead, they chose to stay in schools to teach or assist missionaries, which loaded a great financial burden to the blind school. The school also employed more than 10 female assistants with normal vision. In the middle and late periods of the Republic of China, the Blind Girls' School did not open completely to the public applicants who were admitted through recommendation. Rev. Wolfe's daughter Miss A. M. Wolfe and Miss Lamb became the principal of the school successively. The principal of the Blind Girls' School was a foreigner, but the school was managed by the Chinese.

1922 年，明道盲童女校在施浦建红砖楼校舍，学校分为幼儿园、初级小学。教授科目主要以《圣经》为文本，学习福州方言盲文、珠算、唱歌、旗语、弹琴等。1944 年 9 月，兰师姑回国，中国人李孟雄身兼灵光、明道两校校长之职。1951 年，"灵光"和"明道"两所盲校合并为"福州市盲人学校"。1995 年 8 月，福州市盲校的新校舍在仓山区首山路110 号建成。至今常常有福建师范大学的学生到盲校当志愿者。该校一直是福建省首屈一指的盲人学校。盲校校歌的一句歌词"'灵光明道'是我的骄傲"就表明了历史的传承。

2020 年初，修复工程的人员发现一块刻有"明道堂"三个字的石碑，正是这座教堂百年历史的见证。随后工程队将石碑重新装饰在教堂大门的正中央。据天安堂陈安俤牧师表示，堂内设备添置后就对外开放礼拜，百年老堂将焕发出新的生命。

2001 年刚刚恢复的明道堂（来源：天安堂）
The Anglican Church of CMS reopened in 2001 （Source: Tian'an Church)

In 1922, the Blind Girls' School built a red brick school building in Shipu. The school was divided into kindergarten, and primary school. *The Bible* was the main textbook. Students learned Fuzhou dialect Braille, abacus, singing, flag language, piano, etc. In September 1944, Miss Lamb went back to the US, so Li Mengxiong, a Chinese, became the principal of the Boys' Blind School and the Girls' Blind Schools. 1951 witnessed the merging of the two blind schools into Fuzhou Blind School. In August 1995, the new school building of Fuzhou Blind School was built at No. 110 Shoushan Road, Cangshan District. Up to now, students from Fujian Normal University often volunteer at the school. The school has long been the leading blind school in Fujian Province. One line of the school song goes: "Boys' Blind School and Girl's Blind School are our pride", which shows the inheritance of the history of Fuzhou Blind School.

At the beginning of 2020, workers of the restoration project found a stone tablet inscribed with three Chinese characters "Ming Dao Tang", which is evidence of the hundred-year history of the church! The Restoration team then redecorated the stone at the center of the church gate. Director Chen of Tian'an Church said that after setting proper facilities, the church would open to the public for services. The century-old church is expected to shine again.

修缮中的明道堂(笔者摄于 2022 年 2 月)
Anglican Church of CMS under renovation
(Taken in February 2022)

• 倪柝声与神学机构之缘

倪柝声原名倪述祖，1903 年 11 月 4 日出生于广东汕头，祖籍福建福州，其祖父倪玉成是卢公明创办的福音精舍最早的 14 名学生之一（边晓丽，2011：18）。父亲倪文修毕业于福州美以美会所办的著名学府鹤龄英华书院，在当时就是中学性质的书院。倪柝声毕业于英国圣公会于 1907 年在仓山创办的三一书院，该校 1952 年改为福州市第九中学，1993 年更名为现在的福州外国语学校。

1920 年，倪柝声因为在美以美会的天安堂聆听当时中国著名女布道家余慈度的布道会而信仰基督，从此成为热心追求的信徒。经由余慈度介绍，认识了英国独立传教士和受恩。在她的影响下，倪柝声发起了影响全球的地方教会运动，是中国近代史上最为成功的基督教本土化实践之一（林金水、郭荣刚，2014）。

倪柝声是拥有最多传记图书版本的中国基督徒领袖（郭荣刚，2014：2），主要有《倪柝声文集》《正常的基督徒生活》等。《属灵人》是倪柝声最重要的一本属灵经典著作。笔者拜访了一位 1993 年在中洲岛基督教堂接受洗礼的基督徒聚会处的姐妹。她讲述了一些倪柝声与福州基督徒聚会处的往事。1896 年，和受恩作为英国圣公会传教士第一次抵达福州，在陶淑女中任教 7 年，因为受排挤而离开陶淑女中。之后，成为独立传教人，没有任何差会经济支持，全凭信心生活，不接受固定的薪资给予、不借贷、不题捐。和受恩能讲一口流利的福州话，融入当地白牙谭的百姓生活。难以想象，1911—1930 年，和受恩在长乐白牙潭山坡上的出租小屋里，度过了 20 年卑微、隐士般的生活。1930 年 2 月，和受恩去世时身上仅有 100 多元，办完丧事仅遗留几十元。临终前遗言赠予倪柝声一袋物品，1930 年 5 月才送到他上海的住处，其中唯一值钱的就是一本大字的《圣经》，有一页的空白处写着一句话："为己我无所求，为主我求一切！"，正贴切地描绘了她的一生。这句话也成为倪柝声的座右铭。

• Watchman Nee and His Christian Assembly

Watchman Nee (original name Henry Nee) was born in Shantou, Guangdong Province on November 4, 1903. His ancestral home was in Fuzhou, Fujian Province. His grandfather, Nee Yucheng, was one of the first 14 students of "Gospel House" founded by the Rev. Justus Doolittle. His father, Ni Weng-Sioe, graduated from the famous Anglo-Chinese School in Fuzhou, which was a middle school at that time. Watchman Nee graduated from Trinity College in Cangshan, now Fuzhou Foreign Languages School.

In 1920, Watchman Nee became a Christian after listening to a sermon by Dora Yu, a famous female evangelist in China, at the Church of Heavenly Peace. Through the introduction of Dora Yu, Watchman Nee met Margaret E. Barber, the British independent missionary. Under her influence, Nee launched a local church movement, which is one of the most successful Christian localization practices in modern Chinese history and became influential in the world.

Watchman Nee was the Christian leader in China who wrote the most biographical books. His main works include *Watchman Nee Collection*, *Normal Christian Life*, etc. *Spiritual Man* is Watchman Nee's most important spiritual classic. I visited a sister who was baptized at a Christian church on Zhongzhou Island in 1993. She shared some memories of Watchman Nee and Fuzhou Christian Assembly. Margaret E. Barber first arrived in Fuzhou in 1896 as an Anglican missionary and taught at Do-seuk Girls' School for seven years. The reason for her quitting Do-seuk Girls' School was that she was marginalized and later became an independent missionary without any financial support from any mission. She "lived by faith", with no salary, no loans, no donations. Margaret E. Barber could speak fluent Fuzhou dialect and integrated into the life of the local people in Baiyatan, Fuzhou. It is hard to imagine that she lived a humble, hidden life for 20 years (1911 – 1930) in a rented hut on the hillside of Baiyatang, Changle. She died in February 1930, leaving only one hundred yuan for her own funeral. Watchman Nee received a bag of remains, which was delivered to his residence in Shanghai in May 1930. The only valuable belonging was a *Bible* in large font, with a single blank page that read: "I want nothing for myself. I want everything for the Lord", which was an apt description of her life. This also became Watchman Nee's motto.

仓山的基督徒聚会处

1922年，倪柝声与前海军军官王载连同王连俊、陆忠信等人，脱离原宗派教会（比如三公会的教会），共同成立了福州教会。这是中国第一个完全脱离宗派公会管理的地方教会，标志着我国基督徒中主要宗派之一的基督徒聚会处开始建立，形成了"走出宗派，回归圣经"的潮流（郭荣刚，2014：25）。倪柝声是第一位对西方基督徒产生影响力的中国基督徒，他有关教会真理及信仰的中外文著作也十分丰富，对中外教会影响深远（查时杰，1983：306）。倪柝声凭借其神学的丰富性和经验性，得到广大传统教会的认可，也为许多新兴教会的反传统斗争提供了理论支撑。

基督徒聚会处是中国本土基督教会，教会不设牧师，提倡脱离宗派，强调教会的地方性。由于各聚会处之间没有组织隶属关系，彼此独立，但相互支持，形成团契，因而也被称为小群会（福建省地方志编纂委员会，2014：496）。1923年初，聚会处租用仓山12间排屋聚会，是基督徒聚会处的第一个固定聚会场所（或是教堂）。目前为福州市历史建筑，是受保护的不动产。

最早聚会的光景是家徒四壁，来参加聚会的人要自带板凳。有位何氏（何肃朝）信徒愿意以较低的价钱租房子给教会，每间房月租9元，但要先缴3个月房租。教会没经费支付房租，只能先租12间排中的一间，取名为"基督徒会堂"。第一次的27元租金是和受恩牧师赞助的。后因来聚会的越来越多，就续租第二间、第三间。

十二间排屋（摄于2022年2月）
Twelve-row Houses (Taken in Feb. 2022)

1922年开始的非基督教同盟运动蔓延至全中国。1925年，在南京发生的"五卅运动"使福州的学生中出现新的爱国主义浪潮，反宣教士暴动时有发生。到了1928年，基督教各差会的复兴时期似已结束，为本土教会的发展提供了一个良好的机遇（郭荣刚，2014）。

Christian Assembly in Cangshan District

In 1922, Nee and former naval officer Wang Zai, together with Wang Lian-jun, Lu Zhong-shin and others, broke away from the original denominational church (such as the Churches of the Three Missionary Societies) and founded the Christian Assembly in Fuzhou, the first local church in China to completely break away from the management of all missions. The Christian Assembly, which marked one of the major denominations of Christians in China, began to form a trend of "going out of denominations and returning to *The Bible*". Watchman Nee was the first Chinese Christian to have influence on Western Christians. His works on church truth and faith in both Chinese and foreign languages are abundant and have a profound influence on churches both at home and abroad. With his theological richness and experience, Watchman Nee was accepted by the majority of traditional churches, and also provided theoretical support for the anti-tradition struggle in many emerging churches.

The Christian Assembly is a local Christian church in China where there is no pastor, no sects, or organizational affiliation between churches. All churches are independent of each other, yet they support each other, forming a kind of fellowship. So it is also called a small gathering. At the beginning of 1923, the church rented Twelve-row Houses in Cangshan District for the Assembly, which was the first fixed gathering place for the Christian Assembly (or church). At present, it is a historical building of Fuzhou City under protection.

The earliest assembly was held in an utterly destitute house where attendees had to bring benches by themselves. One believer He Suchao was willing to rent a room to the church at a lower price, 9 yuan per room per month but with rents of three months to be paid in advance. Being short of money, the church could only afford one room of the Twelve-row Houses, calling it the "Christian Assembly". The rent of twenty-seven yuan for the first three months was sponsored by Margaret E. Barber. Later, as more and more people came to the party, they renewed the lease of two rooms and then the third one.

The Non-Christian Alliance Movement that started in 1922 spread throughout China. The May 30th Movement in Nanjing in 1925 led to a new wave of patriotism among students in Fuzhou, and anti-missionary riots were frequent. By 1928, the revival of the foreign Christian churches seemed coming to an end, thus providing a good opportunity for the development of local churches.

倪氏祖上在福州的家产主要是中洲、海关巷的房产及玉林山馆 3 处,后来倪柝声在鼓岭购买的 13 处及自建 2 处房产,基本上奉献给教会使用(郭荣刚,2014)。

1948 年,倪柝声的母亲将位于中东巷 24 号的祖宅捐出,供基督徒聚会使用,这是砖木结构的教堂,占地面积 800 多平方米,可容纳 1 400 人聚会。世界各地的信徒会认为该堂是基督徒聚会处的发源地,时常有人到此追根溯源(福建省志·宗教志编委会,2014:569)。在"文革"期间,聚会处停止聚会。1990 年落实政策后,才收回聚会处,但聚会所内仍住着 32 户船民。1992 年 3 月,宗教局依法落实宗教政策,32 家住户顺利迁出。聚会处有了完整的空间。1993 年,中洲岛全面拆迁,改建公园,800 多户居民迁出,只保留聚会处。1995 年教堂改造结束,扩建成能容纳 600 人的聚会场所,外观是仿欧式古典建筑,黄色外墙,在当时十分抢眼,也吸引了不少游客。1996 年春,聚会所临江一侧的墙倾斜,同时内部木屋为白蚁蛀空,二楼房子摇摇欲坠,已成危房,直接威胁到信徒和游客的安全,教会决定彻底修造会所。1996 年 10 月 1 日,正式修建完毕。下方左图是刚刚改造完毕的教堂。由于种种原因,教堂 2000 年彻底拆迁到中洲岛西侧。教堂共有 5 层(含负一层),砖木结构,内设电梯。建筑整体呈西式风格,以白色、棕色色调为主。

1996 年 9 月拆迁前的中洲聚会处
The Zhongzhou Christian Church before the demolition in September 1996

中洲基督教堂(2022)
The Zhongzhou Christian Church (2022)

据统计,国外有近 3 000 处基督徒聚会处教堂,均将倪柝声作为他们在属灵和神学上的主要奠基人之一,这是倪氏执事本土化和全球化的表现(林金水、郭荣刚,2014:462)。

玉林山馆与鼓岭执事之家

清末至民国初期,曾在汕头海关就职的倪柝声之父倪文修在福州仓山梅坞路 16 号创建了玉林山馆,占地面积约 300 平方米。这是一座双层红砖四坡顶的西式建筑,后由倪柝声捐出,作传教之用。该建筑是倪柝声在福州的 3 处房产之一,现在是烟台山保护建筑。

Watchman Nee's ancestral property in Fuzhou mainly included two houses located on Zhongzhou Island and Haiguan Lane as well as the Yulin Mountain Villa. Nee later bought 13 villas and built 2 houses in Kuliang, mostly dedicated to the church.

In 1948, Nee's mother donated her ancestral home at No. 24 of Zhongdong Lane for Christian gatherings. The brick-and-wood church, covering an area of more than 800 square meters, could accommodate 1,400 people. The church is considered by believers around the world to be the birthplace of the Christian Assembly, who often come and trace its roots there. During the Cultural Revolution, gatherings stopped. After the policy was carried out to restore the Christian Assembly in 1990, 32 households of the boat residents still lived in it. In March 1992, the Department of Ethnic and Religious Affairs implemented the religious policy by the law, and 32 families moved out. Finally, the Christian Assembly owned the whole space. In 1993, Zhongzhou Island was completely demolished and rebuilt into a park. More than 800 households were moved out, keeping only the Christian Assembly. In 1995, the church was renovated and expanded into a gathering place that could accommodate 600 people. The church was a kind of European classical architecture with a yellow wall, which was very eye-catching at that time, attracting many visitors. In the spring of 1996, the wall along the riverside tilted while the internal wooden house was hollowed by termites. The house on the second floor was crumbling and became a dangerous house, which was a threat to the safety of believers and tourists. Therefore, the church decided to completely renew the house. On October 1, 1996, the construction project was completed. The postcard below shows the Christian Assembly on Zhongzhou Island after renovation. It was completely demolished and moved to the west of the Island in 2000 for some reason or other. The church has a total of five floors (including one basement), a brick and wood structure, with an elevator. The whole building is in Western style, a half-timbered structure with white and brown colors.

According to statistics, there are nearly 3,000 Christian Assembly churches abroad that regard Watchman Nee as one of their main spiritual and theological founders, which is a manifestation of the localization and globalization of Deacon Nee.

Yulin Mountain Villa and Deancons' Home in Kuliang Mountain

Yulin Mountain Villa, located at No. 16 of Meiwu Road, Cangshan, Fuzhou, covering an area of about 300 square meters, was built by Nee Weng-Sioe, the father of Watchman Nee, who once worked in Shantou Customs from the end of the Qing Dynasty to the beginning of the Republic of China. This is a two-story red-brick Western-style building with an Italian roof, once donated by Watchman Nee for missionary purposes. The building is one of Nee's three houses in Fuzhou and is now a scenic building under protection in Yantai Mountain.

梅坞路修缮中的玉林山馆（2022）
Yulin Mountain Villa under renovation（2022）

修缮前的玉林山馆东、西楼（来源：池志海）
The East Building and the West Building of Yulin Mountain
Villa before renovation (Source: Chi Zhihai)

  因为没有国外差会的经济支持，教会非常缺乏资金。倪柝声在上海创办中国最大的药业公司之一，用于牧养教会，这是实业自养的体现，其中部分盈余用来在家乡福州鼓岭购买别墅，捐给教会。作为福州的文化名片之一，鼓岭在远东基督徒中颇具名气。许多传教士在福州市区工作，选择在鼓岭别墅度假，尤其在炎炎夏日之时。美部会的麻安德牧师在 2012 年 6 月 22 日中央电视台《走遍中国》节目的专题片《鼓岭往事》中提到外国人在鼓岭的别墅有 300 多座。

倪柝声在鼓岭购买的基督徒聚会处之一
One of the villas Watchman Nee bought for Christ Assembly at Kuliang

Without any financial support from foreign missions, Chinese churches were short of funds. But Watchman Nee's local church was sponsored by one of the largest pharmaceutical companies set up by Nee in Shanghai, which was a reflection of the self-support of the local church. Some of his income went towards buying villas in his hometown of Kuliang, Fuzhou, most of which were donated to the church. As one of the cultural cards of Fuzhou, Kuliang is well known among Christians in the Far East. Many missionaries worked in downtown Fuzhou and spent their holidays in their villas located in Kuliang, especially during the hot summer season. Alden E. Wattews, a pastor of ABCFM, mentioned that there were more than 300 foreigners' villas in Kuliang in the feature film "Old Time in Kuliang" in the Program "Travel around China" by CCTV on June 22, 2012.

1945 年抗日战争胜利后，倪柝声买下日本人和德国人在鼓岭的 10 多座别墅（福州市政协文史资料委员会，2012），主要捐献给教会使用。1948 年至翌年夏季，倪柝声成立基督教"执事之家"，举办了两期影响深远的全国性"同工长老训练"，历时 4 个月，共有 200 多位负责人参加。训练内容主要涉及对教会事务的管理、权柄问题、对初信者的培养、怎样读经、如何传教等，参训者多是中国各地区教会的负责人（郑怡玲，2020）。鼓岭的"执事之家"成为全国各地聚会处的联络中心。倪柝声也被称为中国 20 世纪的马丁·路德。经鼓岭培训后，中国国内各地教会大复兴，如今，鼓岭的许多村民依然都还是基督徒。

倪柝声真正开启了"中国的基督教时代"，西方基督教开始退出中国历史舞台，取而代之的是中国化的自立、自养、自传的基督教。倪柝声渴望做个"属灵人"，将具有中国特色的家庭价值、伦理道德的文化融入中国教会的建构中，让西方学术界接受中国化的基督教，对推进我国文化战略、建立本土神学很有意义（郭荣刚，2014）。

江滨远眺现在的中洲基督教堂（2022）
The Christ Assembly on Zhongzhou Island
from the river view（2022）

After the victory of the War of Resistence Against Japanese Agression in 1945, Watchman Nee bought more than 10 villas owned by Japanese and Germans in Kuliang and mainly donated them to the church. From 1948 to the summer of the following year, Nee established a Christian "Deacon's Home" and held two far-reaching nationwide "training sessions for fellow workers and presbyters" that lasted four months and attracted more than 200 directors. The training mainly involved the management of church affairs, authority issues, the cultivation of new believers, how to read the Scriptures and how to preach, etc. The participants were mostly the heads of churches in various regions of China. The "Deacon's Home" in Kuliang became a liaison center for Christ Assembly across the country. He was also known as China's Martin Luther of the 20th century. The training in Kulaing led to a revival of churches across China, and many villagers at Kuliang are still Christians today.

It is Watchman Nee who started the "Chinese Christian era", in which Western Christianity began to withdraw from the stage of Chinese history and was replaced by the self-governance, self-support and self-propagation policy. Watchman Nee aspired to be a "spiritual man", integrating family values and ethics with Chinese characteristics into the construction of Chinese churches, and making Western academia accept Chinese Christianity, which is significant for promoting China's cultural strategy and establishing local theology in China.

● 福建神学院

党的十一届三中全会以来，宗教自由政策得以重新贯彻执行，各项宗教事业百废待兴，亟需推进国内外的交流。由于福建协和神学院、闽南神学院等华东地区所有的神学院全部并入南京金陵协和神学院，福建的教牧人员长期得不到及时培养和补充。于是，1981年元旦成立的福建省基督教协会开始积极培养和造就年轻一代爱国教牧人员，举办神学培训班，开办神学院。从1981年5月至1982年3月，连续举办3期义工培训班，对各地教会选送的149名学员分别进行了为期2～3个月的神学培训。1982年9月，将短期义工进修班改办成一年制神学专修科，办学地点设在福州鼓楼区东街口花巷基督教堂。花巷堂原属美以美会，是福州市著名的石厝教堂之一。1914年，美国知名布道家、美国青年会干事艾迪博士到福州后，建议创立一特别教堂以吸引社会名流加入基督教，该堂因此而兴建，于1915年落成。该堂取名为尚友堂，意即社交会堂，1979年后改名为花巷堂（福建省志·宗教志编委会，2014）。1982年，46名初中毕业以上文化程度的学员在此参加学习，第一学期为15周，第二学期为25周。在义工进修班课程的基础上，增加了"语文""神学""中国教会史"，以及选修课"风琴""钢琴""英语"等课程。当时的任课教师有薛平西副主教、郑玉桂牧师、刘扬芬牧师、郑证光长老、潘镜高牧师等。

花巷堂办学时期（1983—1986）

1983年6月3日，福建省人民政府批准福建省基督教两会关于开办福建神学院的申请。

Scan for more
扫码了解更多

• Fujian Theological Seminary

Since the Third Plenary Session of the 11th CPC Central Committee in 1978, the policy of religious freedom has been implemented well. Various religious undertakings are still in ruins and need promoting exchanges at home and abroad. Because all seminaries in East China such as Fujian Union Theological Seminary, Minnan Theological Seminary were merged into Nanjing Union Theological Seminary, ministers in Fujian churches have not been timely trained and supplemented for a long time. Founded on New Year's Day of 1981, the Fujian Christian Council began to actively train and cultivate the young generation of ministers, to organize theological training courses and to set up theological schools. From May 1981 to March 1982, three co-worker training courses were held, and 149 students selected from various churches were trained in theology for 2 – 3 months respectively. In September 1982, the short-term co-worker program was transformed into a one-year theological specialism, located in Fuzhou Flower Lane Christian Church (also called Huaxiang Christian Church, Fuzhou). Huaxiang Church is located in Flower Lane (in Chinese Pinyin: Huaxiang), Dongjiekou, Gulou District, Fuzhou City. It is one of the famous granite chapels in Fuzhou City. In 1914, Dr. George S. Eddy, a well-known American preacher and secretary of the American YMCA, came to Fuzhou and suggested building a special church to attract celebrities to join Christianity. The church was built and completed in 1915. Its English name was originally Institutional Church or Central Institutional Church, which means church for social activities, in Romanized Fuzhou dialect: Siong Iu Dong. After 1979, it was renamed as Flower Lane Christian Church or Huaxiang Christian Church. 46 graduates of junior middle schools studied here in 1982. The first semester lasted 15 weeks and the second semester 25 weeks. New courses such as "Chinese language" "Theology" "History of the Church in China", as well as elective courses like "Organ" "Piano" and "English" were supplemented on the basis of the co-worker courses. At that time, the teachers were Archdeacon Moses Hsieh, Rev. Zheng Yugui, Rev. Liu Yangfen, Presbyter Zheng Zhengguang, Rev. Pan Jinggao, etc.

School Period in Huaxiang Christian Church(1983 – 1986)

On June 3, 1983, the People's Government of Fujian Province approved the application of Fujian Christian Council (abbreviated as Fujian CC) and National Committee of Three-Self Patriotic Movement of the Protestant Churches in Fujian, China (abbreviated as Fujian TSPM) to establish Fujian Theological Seminary (abbreviated as FJTS).

同年9月，福建神学院在福州基督教花巷堂正式开办。9月13日，福建省基督教两会在花巷堂举行福建神学院成立暨福建神学院1983级开学典礼。参加的学生共46名。典礼由福建省基督教两会主席兼会长、福建神学院院长薛平西副主教主持，省基督教两会副主席兼副会长、神学院副院长郑玉桂牧师报告筹备经过，并宣读省政府批文。福建省宗教事务局郭钢局长、福州市宗教事务处周伟庄处长等省市政府领导以及福建省天主教爱国会主任林泉主教应邀到会祝贺（岳清华，2013：59）。这是"文革"后中国成立的第一所超宗派的省级神学院，师生不分宗派背景，求大同，存小异，致力于培养和造就政治上热爱祖国、拥护中国共产党的领导和社会主义制度，坚持中国基督教"三自"办教方针，具有相当基督教学识，在"灵、德、智、体、群"各方面全面发展的年轻教牧人员队伍。

　　由于办学场地等条件限制，学院只能招收一个班。第一届录取的学员共46人，其中女生20人，男生26人，年龄最大的40岁，最小的20岁，平均年龄25岁。次年，增加专修科结业的插班生，该班到毕业时学生人数达到64人。在花巷堂培养的神学生有82级专修科、83级专科和85级专科第一学年（共73位学生，第二学年搬到福州基督教青年会旧址内），后又增加原来专修科毕业的9位插班生，是学院办学以来最大的一个班级。从1983年9月开办至1989年7月，福建神学院共有3届2年制学生196人毕业，其中95%在省内各教会组织效力。

　　当时神学院属中等专业学校性质，面向全省招生，招收初中以上学历的学生入学，学制2年（姚午生，2000）。课程设置按宗教课占70%，政治、文化课占30%的比例安排，其办学经费由省基督教两会筹措。学生在学期间免收学费和住宿费，每月生活费均由本人或由推荐教会支付费用。福建神学院开办之初，附设于福州花巷基督教堂内附属房屋。随后于1986年迁至苍霞福州基督教青年会旧址。

：1982年9月开办为期一年的专修科班在花巷堂的毕业留影（福建省基督教协会）
：Graduates of one-year training program in Sept. 1982（Source: Fujian Christian Council）

In September of the same year, Fujian Theological Seminary was formally opened in Fuzhou Flower Lane Christian Church. On September 13, Fujian CC and TSPM held the grand ceremony to celebrate the establishment of Fujian Theological Seminary and the opening of 1983 class of FJTS in Huaxiang Church. The ceremony was presided over by Archdeacon Moses Hsieh, Chairman of Fujian CC/TSPM and Rev. Zheng Yugui, President of Fujian Theological Seminary, reported the preparatory process and read the approval document by the People's Government of Fujian Province. Guo Gang, Director General of Fujian Religious Affairs Bureau, Zhou Weizhuang, Director of Fuzhou Religious Affairs Bureau and other provincial and municipal government leaders, as well as Bishop Lin Quan, Director of Fujian Catholic Patriotic Association, were invited to the ceremony. This is the first non-denominational provincial seminary established after the Cultural Revolution in China. The teachers and students, regardless of denominational background, seek great common ground while setting aside minor differences. The Seminary is devoted to comprehensively cultivating young ministers in spiritual, moral, intellectual, physical and social domains, who love their motherland, support the leadership of the Communist Party of China and the socialist system, adhere to the Principle of "Three Self Education" of Chinese Christianity, and possess considerable Christian knowledge.

Due to the limitations of school grounds, the Seminary could only enroll one class at the beginning. There were 46 students enrolled in the first class, including 20 girls and 26 boys. The oldest was 40 years old, the youngest 20, and the average age 25. In the following year came the transferred students who had finished the theological specialism courses, so the number of graduates reached 64, which were the first graduates after the establishment of the Seminary. There were 73 students including Class 1982, Class 1983 and Class 1985 in the Seminary held in Huaxiang Church. Later they moved to the former site of the YMCA in Fuzhou in the second school year. Then another 9 transferred students, who had finished the former specialism courses, joined the class, making it the largest class since the establishment of the Seminary. 196 students graduated from Fujian Theological Seminary within 3 years, referring to those who completed two-year specialism courses, 95% of whom are serving in various church institutions in Fujian Province.

At that time, the Seminary was a secondary professional school, which recruited students from all over the province with a two-year schooling system. The curriculum was arranged according to the proportion of 70% religious courses and 30% political and cultural courses, and the funds for running the school were raised by the Fujian Christian Council and TSPM. Students were exempt from tuition and accommodation fees during their studies. Monthly living expenses were to be paid by students or the recommended church. At the beginning of the establishment of Fujian Theological Seminary, it was held in the affiliated house of Fuzhou Huaxiang Christian Church. Then in 1986, the Seminary moved to the former site of YMCA on Cangxia Road.

苍霞洲办学时期（1986—1990）

因神学院招生人数增加，花巷堂的校舍显得拥挤不堪。经省、市基督教两会的努力，将福州市第十三中学退还的福州基督教青年会旧址（苍霞洲71-1号）底层的15%左右和面积极小的一层楼作为神学院校舍。1986年夏，神学院迁至福州苍霞洲原基督教青年会旧址继续办学。

青年会旧址的教室仍只有一间。一楼有两间女生宿舍、医务室、会议室等；地下室是图书馆、总务室、餐厅、男生宿舍和教师宿舍，极其阴暗潮湿。由于空间有限且与十三中和菜市场毗邻，教室和宿舍异常嘈杂，学院师生常常利用课余时间到江边公园读书、散步、交谈、健身等，而琴房、地区交通会和重大活动均借用附近的苍霞州基督堂。1989年，郑玉桂牧师任院长，学院各项工作有序开展。

据统计，1986年至1989年间，学院共培养两年制专科神学生184名，其中毕业的学生有八七级81人，八九级55人。八九级48位学生在那里度过一个学年，1990年7月搬到仓山区乐群路。

神学院在基督教青年会旧址，1985届专科班福州籍的同学留念（来源：吴育楠）
Fujian Theological Seminary at the former site of the YMCA; A group photo of students from the city of Fuzhou, Class of 1985 of FJTS (Source: Wu Yunan)

School Period in Cangxia (1986 - 1990)

Because of the increase in enrollment, the Seminary at Flower Lane Church was overcrowded. Through the efforts of Fujian and Fuzhou CC and TSPM, FJTS was granted a new small campus, including 15% of the ground floor and part of the first floor of the former site of Fuzhou YMCA (No. 71 - 1 of Cangxia Road) that were returned by Fuzhou No. 13 Middle School.

There was only one classroom in the former site of Fuzhou YMC. There were two female dormitories, a dispensary, and a meeting room on the first floor while the library, the general office, the cafeteria, male dormitories, and teachers' dormitories were located in the basement that was extremely dark and wet. Due to the limited space and proximity to No. 13 Middle School and a food market, classrooms and dormitories were extremely noisy. Teachers and students of the college often went to riverside parks for spiritual reading, walking, talking, workout, etc., in their spare time. Furthermore, the piano room, regional fellowship, and major activities were held in the nearby Christ Cathedral on Cangxia Road. In 1989, Rev. Cheng Yugui became President of FJTS, who took the lead in the orderly management of FJTS.

According to statistics from 1986 to 1989, FJTS trained a total of 184 two-year college students, among which 81 graduates from Class 1987, 55 from Class 1988, and 48 students enrolled in 1989 who studied there for one year. In July 1990, FJTS moved to Lequn Road, Cangshan District.

∶ 青年会旧址上的青年会广场(2022)
∶ The YMCA Square on the former site of the YMCA(2022)

乐群路办学时期（1990—2014）

为办好福建神学院，1988年，省基督教两会决定改善办学条件，在福州仓前山原福州卫理公会年议会办事处旧址兴建一座神学院大楼。1990年7月，一座四层半的综合大楼落成，学院从福州基督教青年会旧址迁至乐群路7号（现为16号）。1994年夏，加盖一层半，弥补办学场所之不足。新建神学院为6层大楼，占地面积3 500平方米，可容纳120名学生学习和住宿。该楼有16间学生宿舍，6间教室，还有小礼堂、祷告室、办公室、招待所等，由省基督教两会和学院共同使用。大楼右前方另建一座集办公、会议、膳食诸功用为一体的三层综合楼。至此，福建神学院的整体环境得到较大改善，教室、宿舍等硬件设施基本上可以满足办学需求。

中华基督教卫理公会旧址
The former site of the Methodist Church in China

乐群路16号的神学院旧址，现为福建省基督教三自爱国运动委员会、福建省基督教协会和福建省基督教培训中心3个单位联署办公场地，也成为福州烟台山景点之一
The former site of the seminary, No. 16 of Lequn Road is now the joint office of Fujian CC and TSPM, which has also become one of the scenic spots of Yantai Mountain

School Period in Lequn Road(1990 – 2014)

In 1988, the Fujian CC and TSPM decided to build a new building for the Theological Seminary, right next to the former site of Fuzhou Annual Conference of the Methodist Church in China, to improve the conditions of the Seminary. A four-and-a-half-story complex was built. Completed in July 1990, the Seminary moved from the former site of Fuzhou YMCA to No. 7 (now No. 16) Lequn Road. In the summer of 1994, one and a half floors were added to make up for the lack of school space. The new complex is now of six-story high, with an area of more than 3,500 square meters and can accommodate 120 students. On the right front of the building, another three-story complex building was built for the office, conference rooms and catering. Then, the overall environment of the Fujian Theological Seminary had been greatly improved, and the hardware facilities such as classrooms and dormitories could meet the requirements of students and teachers.

除院长薛平西副主教和副院长郑玉桂牧师外，学院还有 7 位专职教师，8 位兼职教师。从 1990 年起，学院各项事务逐步得到完善。学院调整了招生政策，将每两年招生改为每年招生，在校学生人数增加。各班设立班主任和辅导员，负责班务及学生工作。学生管理工作更加规范，规定每年 10 月份民主选举产生学生会，分组分工更加细化，起到沟通学院和学生之间的桥梁作用。

尽管学院加大招生力度，仍无法满足基层堂会对教牧人员的需求。为此，学院从 1991 年开设一年制圣经班，从 1991 年至 1993 年、1998 年至 2002 年共 8 届结业生，2003 年后停止招生。

2002 年 4 月，省民族与宗教事务厅（闽民宗［2002］6 号文）批准学院升格为 3 年制大专院校，2008 年，学制被国家宗教事务局确认。从 2003 年起，学院开始招收大专插班生（教牧班），招生对象是学院历届两年制专科毕业生。他们当中不少人已在省、市、县基督教两会或堂会担任要职，教牧班的开办使他们有进修的机会，从而得到充实和提升。此外，根据福建教会的实际情况，为满足农村和偏远山区教会的需求，学院自 2008 年开始增设两年制中专班，每两年招生一次。

福湾路新校区（2014 年至今）

由于教牧与管理人才的需求与日俱增，而福建神学院乐群路校区最多只能容纳 120 名学生，"一楼一舍一餐厅"的布局就显得十分简陋与拥挤，且现有教学及附属设施较为陈旧，因此急需建设新校舍。2006 年，在福建省政协九届四次会议上，林志华副院长等基督教界省政协委员申请新校区征地的提案被列为"重点提案"。时任省政协副主席邹哲开、福州市市长郑松岩召开专题调研会议，组织省基督教两会选址小组实地勘察，现场解决新校区基建用地问题。最终，福州市政府以划拨价提供 23.29 亩土地给学院作为新校区建设用地。

Besides the President, Archdeacon Moses Hsieh, and the Vice President, Rev. Cheng Yugui, FJTS had seven full-time teachers, eight part-time teachers. Since 1990, FJTS had gradually improved in various teaching affairs. The Seminary changed its admissions policy from every two years to every year, and the number of students on campus increased. Each class had a head teacher and a counselor in charge of class affairs and student work. Student management is more standardized. It was stipulated that the student union was elected democratically in October every year, and the division of labor was more detailed. The student union acted as a bridge between the Seminary and students.

Although the Seminary increased its enrollment, it still could not meet the demand for ministries from remote areas. To this end, the FJTS opened a one-year Bible training program in 1991, which nurtured eight classes of students from 1991 to 1993 and 1998 to 2002, but stopped enrolling students after 2003.

In April 2002, Fujian Provincial Department of Ethnic and Religious Affairs (Doc. No. 6 of Minminzong [2002]) approved the upgrading of the Seminary to a three-year college. In 2008, the academic system was confirmed by the State Bureau of Religious Affairs. Ever since 2003, FJTS had started to recruit transferred secondary college graduates of ministers' classes. They were two-year graduates, many of whom had already played leading roles in the local CC/TSPMs and churches of Fujian Province. Through this program, these ministers were provided with the opportunities for further study, refreshment and progress. Besides, in response to the needs of the actual situation of Fujian Christian churches in rural areas and remote mountainous areas, FJTS started to add a two-year secondary school class in 2008, recruiting students every two years.

New Campus at Fuwan Road (From 2014 to Present)

With the increasing demand for pastoral and administrative talents, the status quo ante of "one complex, one dormitory and one dining hall" in the Lequn Campus of FJTS, which could accommodate 120 students at most, and the timeworn facilities made it difficult for FJTS to meet the increasing requirement. So it is urgent to build a new campus. In 2006, on the 4th session of the 9th CPPCC of Fujian Province, Lin Zhihua and other members of the CPPCC of Fujian Province made a proposal for a landlot for the new campus, which was listed as the "key proposal". Zou Zhekai, Vice Chairman of the Provincial CPPCC at that time, and Zheng Songyan, Mayor of Fuzhou, held a special meeting, led Fujian CC and TSPM to conduct a field investigation and solved the land lot problem of the new campus on the spot. Finally, the Fuzhou Municipal Government provided 23. 29 *mu* of land to the Seminary as the allocated land for the new campus at the allocation price. And it was so.

2010 年 5 月 11 日，学院在福湾路举行新校区奠基典礼，省人民政府、省政协、省委统战部、省民族宗教事务厅等领导出席。2015 年 3 月 16 日，国家宗教事务局正式批准学院升格为本科高等基督教院校，学制 4 年，全日制规模 200 人。2015 年 9 月，位于福州市仓山区福湾路 121 号的新校区正式投入使用，校园占地面积 15 525.1 平方米，总建筑面积 17 981.4 平方米，建筑群主要包括崇拜区、教学区和生活区三大部分。崇拜区有礼拜堂、钟楼、副堂、琴房等；教学区有教室 15 间，图书馆、学术演讲厅、多功能会议厅、办公室 16 间；生活区有食堂、学生标准宿舍 75 间，专家楼 15 间，健身房、运动场等配套设施。新校区环境优美、功能完备、设施现代，为学生提供了空间宽敞、安全舒适的学习、灵修和牧会训练环境。

福建神学院全景图（来源：福建神学院）
A panoramic view of Fujian Theological Seminary
(Source: Fujian Theological Seminary)

福建神学院走过风雨 40 年，截至 2022 年为全省教会输送了 2006 位教职人员，他们当中的绝大多数都已成为基层爱国宗教团体、基督教活动场所的骨干。目前在校生 150 位，延伸部学员 565 人；专职教师 19 人，兼职教师 29 人。根据教学需要，学院先后引进了 13 位具有博士、硕士学位的教师；图书馆现有藏书 8 万余种，11 万余册。

神学院的福堂，每周天举行礼拜（来源：福建神学院）
The Gospel Hall provides worship service each Sunday (Source: Fujian Theological Seminary)

神学院的福堂，学生在这里学习崇拜仪式（摄于 2022 年 2 月）
The Gospel Hall of Fujian Theological Seminary where students are learning worship service (Taken in Feb. 2022)

On May 11, 2010, FJTS held a groundbreaking ceremony for the new campus on Fuwan Road and leaders from the People's Government of Fujian Province, FPPCC, the United Front Work Department of Fujian Province, and Fujian Provincial Department of Ethnic and Religious Affairs were invited. On March 16, 2015, the State Administration of Religious Affairs officially approved FJTS' upgrade to an undergraduate higher Christian university with a 4-year schooling system and 200 full-time students. In September 2015, the new campus, located at No. 121 Fuwan Road, Cangshan District, Fuzhou City, was officially put into use. The campus covers an area of 15,525.1 square meters and has a total construction area of 17,981.4 square meters. The architectural complex is mainly comprised of three parts: the place of worship, the teaching area and the living area. The place of worship has a chapel, bell tower, secondary hall, piano room and so on; there are 15 classrooms, a library, an academic lecture hall, a multi-functional conference hall and 16 offices in the teaching area; the living area has a dining hall, 75 standard dormitories for students, 15 guest rooms, one gym and one playground. The new campus boasts of beautiful environment with modern facilities, providing a spacious, safe and comfortable learning, spiritual and pastoral training environment for students.

Fujian Theological Seminary has gone through 40 years. By 2022, it had nurtured 2,006 ministers for Fujian Christian churches, most of whom have become the backbone of patriotic religious groups and Christian activity venues at grassroots level. There are 150 students on campus and 565 students for further education. There are 19 full-time teachers and 29 part-time teachers. Due to teaching requirements, FJTS has recruited 13 teachers with doctor's and master's degrees. The library has a collection of more than 80,000 varieties of books and 110,000 volumes.

福建神学院优秀校友

笔者有幸采访了福州基督教协会会长黄玉官牧师，收集到神学院前期办学的第一手资料。黄会长是 1982—1983 年福建神学院圣经专修科学生，之后插班在 1985—1987 大专班，本科和研究生均就读于南京金陵神学院，是福建神学院开班的第一届学生，也是 1992 年第一批在天安堂接受薛平西主教按立的牧师。黄牧师回忆因为当时教室有限，神学院隔年才招生一次，因此前三届只有 83 级、85 级和 87 级学生，之后就每年都招生。

黄会长首先介绍目前福州的基督教教会有六大教派，分别是中华基督教会闽中协会、中华圣公会、中华卫理公会、基督徒聚会处、基督复临安息日会和真耶稣会。以上各教会代表性教堂分别是铺前堂、天安堂和花巷堂、苍霞堂、中洲基督堂、城守前基督教堂和大墙根教堂。其中前三者关系比较密切，通常称为三公会，因此历史上多次相互合作办学。中华基督教会主要是 1916 年美部会与中华基督教长老会合并的"中华基督教大会"；福州地区原美部会称为"中华基督教会闽中协会"；闽南地区信徒较多，称为"中华基督教会闽南大会"；闽北邵武地区为"中华基督教会闽北大会"。1941 年，福州美以美基督教会改称卫理公会，卫理公会总部旧址位于乐群路 14 号，是三层红砖西式楼房。年议会是卫理公会的最高权力机关，全国设 10 个年议会，而福建有 3 个：福州、兴化、延平。1990 年，福建神学院搬迁至此，与福建省两会共同使用办公楼。乐群路上门牌号码变化比较大，福建神学院曾经所在的乐群路 16 号，而 20 年前是乐群路 7 号。六大教会中，福州的基督复临安息日会是小众教会，于 1911 年传入福州，信徒较少，总部在鼓楼区城守前路 37 号，原名大根路福音堂，设有礼拜堂、办公室和教牧人员宿舍，是福建省安息日会最大的教堂（福建省地方志编纂委员会，2014）。20 世纪初，基督复临安息日会创办了三育学校，包含一至十年级的中学 1 所，小学 5 所。几乎同一时期，美以美会创办了英华中学，英国圣公会创办了陶淑女中。

Outstanding Alumnus of FJTS

The author had the honor to interview the Rev. Huang Yuguan, Director of Fuzhou CC and collected first-hand information about the early stage of FJTS. Rev. Huang Yuguan was in a one-year theological specialism class in FJTS in 1982 – 1983 and later transferred to Class 1985 – 1987. He attended Nanjing Union Theological Seminary as both an undergraduate and a graduate student. He was one of the first graduates of FJTS and meanwhile one of the first priests ordained by Bishop Moses Hsieh at the Church of Heavenly Peace in 1992. Rev. Huang Yuguan recalled that FJTS recruited students every two years due to a shortage of classrooms, thus having the first three classes of 1983, 1985, and 1987 at the beginning years of the Seminary. Since 1999, it enrolls students every year.

Director Huang first mentioned that there are currently six major denominations in Fuzhou, namely Church of Christ in China, Mid-Fuchien Synod, the Anglican-Episcopal Church in China, Methodist Church of China, the Christian Assembly, the Seventh-day Adventist Church and the True Jesuit Church. The representative churches of these denominations are Puqian Christian Church, Tian'an Church, Huaxiang Christian Church, Christ Cathedral, Zhongzhou Christian Church, Chengshouqian Adventist Church and Daqianggen Christian Church. Among them, the first Three Missionary Societies are relatively closely related, and are usually called the Three Missionary Societies, so they have cooperated with each other in establishing schools for many times in history. The Church of Christ in China was mainly formed in 1916 between the ABCFM and the Chinese Presbyterian Mission known as "Church of Christ in China Conference"; the original ABCFM in Fuzhou was named "Church of Christ in China, Mid-Fuchien Synod"; believers in southern Fujian are known as the "Southern Fujian Conference"; Shaowu prefecture in northern Fujian Province is the Northern Fujian Conference. In 1941, the Methodist Episcopal Church was renamed the Methodist Church. The former headquarters of the Methodist Church is located at No. 14, Lequn Road, a three-story red-brick building. The Annual Conference is the highest authority of the Methodist Church, with 10 annual councils nationwide, and three in Fujian: Foochow Conference, Hsinghua Conference, and Yenping Conference. Fujian Theological Seminary moved here in 1990 and shared the office building with the Fujian CC and TSPM. The house numbers along Lequn Road have changed a lot. No. 16 of Lequn Road, where Fujian Theological Seminary was formerly located, was No. 7 20 years before. Among the six churches, the Seventh-day Adventist Church in Fuzhou is a small congregation, which was introduced to Fuzhou in 1911 and has relatively fewer followers. Its headquarters is located at No. 37 of Chengshouqian Road, Gulou District, formerly known as Dageng Road Gospel Church, with a chapel, an office and a pastoral dormitory. It is the largest Seventh-day Adventist Church in Fujian Province. In the early 1900s, the Seventh-day Adventist Church established the Adventist School, including one middle school from grade one to ten and five primary schools. Almost at the same time, the Methodist Episcopal Church established Anglo-Chinese School and the Anglican Church established Do-seuk Girls' School.

1981 年，成立福建省基督教协会，管理宗教业务，促进各宗派在信仰观点和礼仪上互相尊重。由于 1979 年开始落实的归还教会的房产还未完全到位，教堂场所有限，三公会共同使用花巷堂，按照各宗派的仪式，在星期天上午、下午聚会；基督徒聚会处在晚上礼拜；基督复临安息日会和真耶稣会在星期六上午、下午轮流礼拜。

黄会长说这是后宗派时期的特点，中国基督教自 1958 年以来结束宗派林立局面，各原教派参加三自爱国运动委员会，不再在组织上自成体系，不再单独以原宗派的名号活动，不再独自进行宗派性的海外联系。

福州市基督教协会的副会长林雪英牧师是神学院 98 届校友。她介绍道，中国政府在 1980 年发布了 188 号文件，宗教团体房产政策得到落实，产权归各宗教团体所有。在福州，所有教会房产产权统一归福州市三自爱国会所有，教会自主牧养，主要是根据地理位置和需要来使用教堂。这也解释了为何原来属于圣公会的明道堂现改为美以美会天安堂的一个聚会地点。"文化大革命"之后，福建各地重新开放的基督教堂全部取消了原各宗派教会名称，统一以教堂所在的地理位置所属地区命名，如坐落市中心的福州花巷基督教堂原名为福州卫理公会尚友堂（福建省地方志编纂委员会，2014：559）。

福建神学院 85 级开学典礼（来源：吴育楠长老）
The opening ceremony of the Grade 1985 of Fujian Theological Seminary on September 12, 1985
(Source: Presbyter Wu Yunan)

In 1981, the Fujian Christian Council was established to administrate evangelism, which promoted all denominations to show more respect to each other in their beliefs, views and rituals. Due to the limited places of worship, the Three Missionary Societies shared Huaxiang Christian Church, worshipping on Sunday morning and afternoon according to their denominational ritual. Christian Assembly worshiped in the evening, while the Seventh-day Adventists and the True Jesuits on Saturday morning and afternoon respectively.

Director Huang said that this is a feature of the post-sectarian period. Since 1958, Chinese Christianity has ended the situation of numerous sects, and all original sects have participated in the Three-Self Patriotic Movement Committee of Christian Churches in China. They are no longer organized independently by themselves, nor carry out activities in the name of original sects, nor make sectarian overseas contacts on their own.

Rev. Lin Xueying, Vice Director of Fuzhou CC, graduated from FJTS in 1998. She said that according to Document No. 188 issued by the Chinese Government in 1980, the policy concerning religious group property was carried out, i.e. property would be returned to various religious groups. In Fuzhou, the property of all churches is uniformly owned by the Three-Self Patriotic Movement Committee of Christian Churches in Fuzhou, meanwhile, the churches implement self-government, self-support and self-propagation. This also explains why the Anglican Church of CMS is now used by Tian'an Church of the Episcopal Methodist Church, which demonstrates church unity. The venues can be employed according to its geographic location. After the Cultural Revolution, the Christian churches reopened all over Fujian, where churches are renamed after the geographic location without keeping the original denominations. For example, Huaxiang Christian Church, located in the city center, was originally named as Central Institutional Church set up by the Episcopal Methodist Mission.

无独有偶，黄会长的同学吴育楠长老来自基督复临安息日会，是福建神学院85级87届的毕业生。她1981年就在神学院预备班里接受过短期培训，可谓元老级学生。当初由基督复临安息会选派，参加了圣经知识、语文、数学、历史等科目考试，成绩合格才被神学院录取。87届有80多名学员，都在各地教会负责传道，大多已经成为牧师，成为教会或各地两会的负责人。值得一提的是方牧师和高牧师，夫妇二人同心为基督复临安息日会服务。吴长老说她的同学来自不同的信仰背景，有中华基督教会、卫理公会、圣公会、基督徒聚会处、基督复临安息日会和真耶稣会，来自八闽大地的福州、永泰、连江、平潭等27个地市。85级第一学年还在花巷堂上课，第二学年，即1986年便迁到十三中上课，即台江区苍霞洲基督教青年会旧址。因为青年会旧址场地很小，借用苍霞基督堂举行毕业典礼。苍霞基督堂的前身是1882年圣公会创建的教堂，1927年建成主教座堂，即福州基督堂。圣公会福建教区历届会议均在此堂举行，并按立了不少牧师。苍霞基督堂是圣公会教堂，曾有三任华人主教坐堂，他们是张光旭主教、薛平西主教和刘玉苍主教。这三位主教都住过仓山的施埔真学堂。

　　神学院培养了很多人才，89级学生陈安俤牧师就是其中一位。1991年，陈安俤神学院毕业后回霞浦任三沙镇教会传道、霞浦县三自爱国会副秘书长。1992年去金陵协和神学院本科班深造，1994年本科毕业后任福州天安堂传道、牧师。1996年与1999年分别筹划、组织天安堂和小岭堂的重建工作。2000年以来，陈安俤牧师担任天安堂主任，目前也是明道堂聚会点的负责人。

Coincidentally, Director Huang's classmate Presbyter Wu Yunan is from the Seventh-day Adventist Church who was a graduate of FJTS, Class 1985 - 1987 and received short-term training in the preparatory class of the Seminary in 1981, making her a veteran student of FJTS. She was recommended by the Seventh-day Adventist Church and was admitted to the Seminary after passing exams in Biblical knowledge, Chinese, mathematics and history. There were more than 80 students for Class 1987, most of whom have been ordained as reverends, or in charge of various churches, or CCC/TSPMs. It is worth mentioning that Mr. & Mrs. Fong and Gao serve the Seventh-day Adventist Church together.

Presbyter Wu said her classmates are from Church of Christ in China, Mid-Fuchien Synod, the Anglican-Episcopal Church in China, Methodist Church of China, the Christian Assembly, the Seventh-day Adventist Church and the True Jesuit Church. They are from 27 cities and counties of Fujian Province such as Fuzhou, Yongtai, Lianjiang, Pingtan. The Grade 1985 had classes in Flower Lane Hall in the first year, and moved to the former site of YMCA in Cangxia Road of Taijiang District next to No. 13 Middle School in the second year, i. e. 1986. Because the former site of the YMCA was very small, they held graduation ceremony in Christ Church Cathedral, Foochow (also known as Cangxia Church). The predecessor of Christ Church Cathedral was the Anglican Church founded in 1882. In 1927, it was rebuilt into a church cathedral. All previous conferences of the Diocese of Fujian were held in this church and many priests were ordained there. Christ Cathedral is an Anglican church with three Chinese bishops in charge consecutively. They were Bishops Michael Chang, Moses Hsien and Liu Yucang whose residences were once in Shipu Christian Church, i. e. the Theological College in Cangshan District.

The Seminary has nurtured many talents, including Rev. Andy Chen from Grade 1989 of FJTS. In 1991, he graduated from FJTS and returned to Xiapu, where he served as an evangelist of Sansha Church and Deputy Secretary of Xiapu TSPM. In 1992, he went to Nanjing Union Theological Seminary for further study. After graduation in 1994, he served as a preacher and Director of Tian'an Church in Fuzhou. In 1996 and 1999, he planned and organized the reconstruction of Tian'an Church and Xiaoling Church respectively. Rev. Andy Chen has been Director of Tian'an Church since 2000 and is currently responsible for Mingdao Church (the former Anglican Church of CMS).

基督教中国化之路

神学院的组织管理机制是董事会领导下的院长负责制。董事会由省基督教两会班子全体成员组成。院务会议为最高行政机构，内设办公室、教务处、学工处、财务部等职能部门（岳清华、陈立福，2013：1）。福建神学院的第一任院长是薛平西主教（1983—1994 年在任），第二任是郑玉桂牧师（1997—2011 年在任），现任院长是岳清华牧师（2013 年至今）。岳院长认为神学院不但要建好，更要办好，要有全球化的视野，一定要坚持走基督教中国化的道路，创全国一流的神学院校，要"培养具有爱国素养、生命素养、管理素养、神学素养的人才"。

在课程设置方面，神学院以神学为核心课程，注重全科教育。第一学年侧重基础，第二学年侧重提高，第三学年侧重实践和扩宽视野。学院专业课程设圣经神学、历史神学、系统神学、实践神学等，约占全部课程的 70%。公共课程设政治、法律、语文、历史、哲学、心理学、逻辑学、外语等，约占全部课程的 30%（岳清华、陈立福，2013：1）。学生要参加语文、英语、政治、历史和圣经知识的考试。招生对象是教会推荐的人选，高中毕业、40 岁以下均有资格报考。

教学课程方面最具特色的当属圣乐系。基督教是音乐的宗教，福建神学院在圣乐方面找到基督教中国化的一条实践之路，把信仰的思想和感情进行有效表达（林超群，2018）。福建神学院圣乐系成立于 2016 年，长期聘请全国资深的音乐专家授课，其中有厦门大学音乐学院的客座教授，有福建师范大学音乐学院的兼职教授，从演唱到钢琴弹奏，无不体现其专业水平。在神学院的福神堂最能体验到喜乐的圣乐之旅。值得一提的是，由福建省两会和神学院组织的福建省基督教联合圣歌团于 2013 年代表中国基督教参加两年一届的塞尔维亚埃迪茨特国际音乐节，表现出色，获得好评。

The Chinization of Christianity

FJTS adopts the system of presidential responsibility under the leadership of the board of directors which consists of all members of Fujian CC/TSPM. The Seminary Affairs Council is the top administrative body, consisting of the Administration Office, Academic Affairs Office, President's Office, Student Affairs Office, and Finance Department. The first president of Fujian Theological Seminary was Bishop Moses Hsieh (1983 – 1994), the second was the Reverend Zheng Yugui (1997 – 2011), and the current president is the Reverend Yue Qinghua (2013 – present). President Yue insists that they will not only build FJTS well but also run it well. FJTS aims to be a first-class seminary in China with a global vision under the guidance of the Chinization of Christianity. It is to cultivate talents with strong patriotism, Christian spirits, managerial ability and theological knowledge.

As far as the curriculum is concerned, FJTS takes theology as its core curriculum, yet pays attention to comprehensive education. The curriculum of the first academic year is focused on foundation subjects, the second year on improvement, and the third year on practice and broadening of horizons. The specialized courses include biblical theology, historical theology, systematic theology, practical theology and so on, which cover 70% of the total courses, while the general courses are politics, law, Chinese, history, philosophy, psychology, foreign languages, covering 30% of the total courses. Students take entrance exams in Chinese, English, politics, history, and biblical knowledge. Applicants with a high-school education and under 40 years old can be recommended by the church.

The most distinctive curriculum is the establishment of the Sacred Music Department. Christianity is a religion of music. Fujian Theological Seminary has found a way to practice the Chinization of Christianity in sacred music and effectively express the thoughts and feelings of faith. The Department of Sacred Music of FJTS was established in 2016 and has employed senior music experts on long tenure, including visiting professors from Xiamen University and part-time professors from Fujian Normal University, who demonstrate their professionalism from singing to piano playing. We can experience the most joyful journey of holy music in the Gospel Hall of FJTS. It is worth mentioning that the Fujian Christian Chorus organized by Fujian CC/TSPM and the Seminary participated in the Serbian Edizite International Music Festival held every two years on behalf of Chinese Christianity in 2013, whose excellent performance won high praise.

福建神学院历经 40 载办学，三次易址，栉风沐雨，走过花巷堂、苍霞洲、乐群路的峥嵘岁月，到今天的福湾路新校区，学院规模不断扩大，逐渐提升为高等神学院校。

习近平主席在 2021 年 12 月全国宗教工作会议上指出，"宗教工作在党和国家工作全局中具有特殊重要性"，强调"要全面贯彻新时代党的宗教工作理论，全面贯彻党的宗教工作基本方针，全面贯彻党的宗教信仰自由政策"，强调"坚持我国宗教中国化方向，积极引导宗教与社会主义社会相适应"①。

仓山是福州著名的文化区，也是中西文化多维碰撞、荟萃之地。2005 年，仓山区共有基督教堂 9 所，神职人员共有 22 人。分别是仓前天安堂、中洲基督教堂（原为中洲基督教徒聚会处）、义序基督教堂（原称"宣道堂"）、浦下基督教堂（原名"天道堂"）、施埔基督教堂（原名"真学堂"）、胪下基督教堂（原称"福音堂"）、上渡基督教堂、马厂街基督堂（前身为基督徒聚会所）、城门教堂等。截至 2005 年，仓山区信徒约 10 300 人（福州市仓山区地方志编纂委员会，2017：637）。截至 2021 年，根据教会的统计，福州的信徒人数达到 60 万，不在册的暂未计数。根据仓山民族与宗教事务局的统计，仓山区登记在册的基督教信徒大约为 1 万多人。

---

① 习近平出席全国宗教工作会议并发表重要讲话. 新华社. 2021 - 12 - 04.

FJTS has 40 years of history, staying true to its mission. The four locations from Flower Lane, Cangxia Road to Lequn Road, and now the new campus of Fuwan Road witness the eventful years of FJTS, developing from a two-year secondary professional college to a four-year university.

In December 2021, President Xi Jinping pointed out that religious work is of special importance to the overall work of the Party and the State, emphasizing the full implementation of the Party's religious theory in the new era, the full implementation of the Party's basic religious policy, and the full implementation of the Party's religious freedom policy. Xi also emphasized the importance of insisting on the direction of Chinization of Christianity, and actively guiding the adaptation between religion and socialist society.

Cangshan is a famous cultural district in Fuzhou with a multi-dimensional collision and integration of the Chinese and Western cultures. In 2005, there were 9 Christian churches in Cangshan District with 22 clergies. They are Tian'an Church, Zhongzhou Christian Church (formerly known as the Christian Assembly on Zhongzhou Island), Yixu Christian Church (originally named Christian and Missionary Church), Puxia Christian Church (originally named Tiandao Church), Shipu Christian Church (formerly known as Theological College), Luxia Christian Church (originally called the Gospel Church), Shangdu Christian Church, Machangjie Christian Church (formerly known as the Christian Assembly), Chengmen Christian Church, etc. By 2005, about 10,300 believers were registered in Cangshan District. According to the statistics of the churches, the number of believers in Fuzhou has reached 600,000 by 2021, without including non-registered believers. The Cangshan Bureau of the Ethnic and Religious Affairs reports that there are about 10,000 registered Christians in Cangshan District.

CHAPTER
TEN

仓山出版业

Publishing Industry in Cangshan

第十章

福

福建出版业历史悠久，始于五代初期的福建刻书业到两宋时期已十分发达，刻书机构遍布全省，刻书数量居全国之首，以寺院刻书驰名的福州与以典籍经史刊刻著称的建阳并称福建两大刻书中心。然而，福州图书出版的千年辉煌大多集中于中心城区，而位置相对偏远的仓山，其出版业勃发与繁荣是在第二次鸦片战争硝烟散去之后。

● 仓山：福建近代出版业的发源地

自 1723 年清政府颁布禁教令开始，西方在华持续数百年的传教活动受到严格限制，传教士们不得不转至马六甲、新加坡等南洋地区。鸦片战争后随着禁教令的废止和福州、厦门等沿海通商口岸的开放，传教士获得了在华居留与宣教的权利，很快再次蜂拥而至。由于不少传教士此前在南洋地区时已掌握了当地通行的闽方言，同时也由于巨大的商业潜力和人口规模，福州成为当时西方教会来华传教的重要目标。1844 年，福州开埠后，美部会、美以美会率先派遣传教士来到福州，数年之后福州发展成为这两大差会的在华传教中心。英国圣公会等其他差会也在 1850 年后陆续抵榕。

与此前来华的天主教传教士不同，这些以新教为主的传教力量尤为重视文字宣传的效果。他们秉持"文牍救世"的观点，认为一般的办法可使千人改变想法，文字能影响的人则可数以百万计（方汉奇，1981）。因此，即便是刚刚抵达中国、语言不通的传教士，也能借助出版物的力量达到理想的宣传效果。

19 世纪西方传教士在福州出版的部分早期书籍（来源：哈佛燕京图书馆）
Some early works published by missionaries in Fuzhou in the 19th century (Source: Harvard-Yenching Library)

最初，传教士们使用的宣教材料都是不远万里从母国或南洋运送而来，但随着传教范围的扩大，这些材料越来越难以满足现实需求。一方面，当时对新教感兴趣的多是身处社会中下阶层的民众，他们没有受过教育，既不具备识字能力，也不会说官话，因此要让他们阅读《圣经》，首先要根据其方言发音的特点创造出土白罗马语言，继而将《圣经》翻译成这种民众易学会用的语言。这些都以出版相关的识字读本和宗教读物为前提。

Fujian's publishing industry boasts a long and lustrous history. Its xylography, the art of printing from wood carving, started in the early Five Dynasties (907 – 960 CE), and prospered during the Song Dynasty (960 – 1296 CE), when publishers were found in almost every city and town, with the printing volume topping the national list. Fuzhou and Jianyang were once the twin centers of Fujian's printing industry, renowned for Buddhist canon printing and Confucian classic printing respectively. Such a glorious past, however, was mostly confined to the city proper, and the out-of-town Cangshan had to wait until the end of the Second Opium War (1856 – 1860) before the booming of its own publishing industry.

• Cangshan: The Birthplace of Fujian Modern Publishing Industry

After the Qing Government issued the ban on Christianity in 1723, the centuries-old missionary work in China ground to a sudden halt, forcing the missionaries to Malacca, Singapore and other parts of Southeast Asia. When the ban was lifted and ports like Fuzhou and Xiamen were made open to international trade after the First Opium War (1840 – 1842), missionaries soon returned to China with the granted right to stay and preach. For them, Fuzhou was an optimal choice with huge commercial potential and an impressive population size, not to mention that its dialect was already familiar to them during their stay in Southeast Asia. It was for these reasons that the American Board of Commission for Foreign Mission (ABCFM) and the Methodist Episcopal Church promptly dispatched missionaries to this city soon after it was forced to open in 1844. Within a few years, they made it the center of missionary work in China. They were followed by more churches after 1850, including the Anglican Church.

Different from their Catholic predecessors, these Protestant missionaries emphasized the power of written word. For them, written word can save the world by influencing millions of people, compared with merely thousands by ordinary means. Aided by publications, even newcomers could throw themselves into work despite speaking no local language.

Protestant missionaries had their first batches of books and other materials shipped to Fuzhou thousands of miles from their home countries or Southeast Asia. But these prints soon fell short of demand when the mission work expanded. Most of the Chinese interested in Christianity were the lowest rung of society, usually uneducated and illiterate. If they were to read *The Bible*, Romanized languages must be first created based on the pronunciation of local dialects, followed by the translation of *The Bible*. This made the publication of primers and Christian texts an absolute necessity.

另一方面，基督教要在中国落地生根，就必须和本土文化相结合，必须根据中国社会状况和中国民众的特点编写内容更新颖、更具针对性和说服力的宣教材料。此外，在华传教士也须以书面报告、报刊、书籍等形式定期或经常向母国教会组织、其他传教士及在华商人等提供关于中国的情况。

以上因素促使传教士寻找就地印刷出版的途径。福州是当时中国南方重要的刻书和文化中心，当时洋人聚集的仓山仓前一带也自然成为近代发展出版业的首选之地。传教士们创造了巨大的出版需求，也带来了当时世界上较先进的出版技术和理念，仓山因此成为福建近代出版业的发源地。

● 卢公明：19世纪后半叶以文传教的典型

1850年5月31日，一位年仅26岁的美国传教士携新婚妻子，经过6个多月的漫长旅程，终于抵达了他们此行的目的地——福州。这位年轻人的英文名是Justus Doolittle，他是美部会派遣来榕的第二批传教士之一。和当时其他许多传教士一样，他也替自己取了一个中文名字——卢公明，以便更好地融入这个他虽向往已久但仍十分陌生的社会。

卢公明抵达的这座东方古城，当时已拥有约25万人口，规模远超宁波、上海、厦门等其他港口城市，在通商五口中仅次于广州，同时还是福建茶叶远销海外的重要门户通道，因此西方各国教会都把福州视为理想的传教点，纷纷派遣传教士前来布道。当然，作为一位虔诚而充满热情的传教士，卢公明此行的主要目的是潜心传教而非谋求经济利益。早在1848年，当卢公明还在纽约州澳本神学院学习期间，就曾致函教会，表达毕业后到偏远地区传教的愿望。1849年临近毕业时，他正式将中国确定为自己传教的目的地，并发表了题为"基督教在中国传播的主要障碍"的毕业演说，认为语言不通是布道的首要障碍，学习当地方言则是布道的重要前提（林立强，2005：219-220）。正因如此，他抵达福州后立刻投入汉语和福州方言的学习中，不仅聘请了专门的家庭教师，还利用各种机会学习中国语言。他原本就具有出色的语言天赋，加上后天的刻苦努力，仅4个多月后就能用福州话进行传教，6个月后就能为中国人做家庭祷告，两年之后出版了用福州平话写的第一本宣教册子《劝戒鸦片论》。

Besides, Christianity had to integrate itself into the local culture if it was to survive and develop in new situations. Such an integration would entail newer, more targeted and persuasive literature adapted specifically to this country and its people. Finally, missionaries stationed in China also needed to regularly communicate information about China with churches in their home countries, their fellow missionaries and businessmen in China in the form of written reports, papers and books.

It was crucial, therefore, for the churches to find ways to print and publish locally in China. For them, Fuzhou proved an ideal choice, since it had long been a center of woodblock carving and culture in southern China. With the huge demand created by the missionaries as well as their up-to-date technology and management, Cangshan became the cradle of Fujian modern publishing industry.

• Justus Doolittle: An Exemplary Missionary Aided by Printing in the Second Half of the 19th Century

On May 31, 1850, a 26-year-old American missionary and his newlywed wife arrived at their destination, Fuzhou, after a voyage of more than six months. This young man, named Justus Doolittle, was among the second wave of ABCFM missionaries sent to this city. Like many of his colleagues, he gave himself a Chinese name—卢公明 (Lu Gongming) in order to better fit in this new place, the one he had long yearned for yet still found strange.

What Doolittle saw was a bustling city harboring about 250,000 people, far exceeding Ningbo, Shanghai, and Xiamen. With such a population and booming trade, it was deemed ideal for missionary work. The devout and zealous Doolittle, of course, came to dedicate himself to the cause of Christ instead of seeking personal gains. Back in 1848, while attending Auburn Theological Seminary in New York, he wrote to the ABCFM to apply for missionary work in the most remote corners after graduation. Such a desire took a clearer shape when, in 1849, he decided upon graduation that China would be his destination. In his graduation speech entitled "Peculiar Obstacles to the Evangelization of China", he claimed that the primary obstacle to evangelization was language barriers, and that learning the local dialect was the prerequisite for any missionary work. Because of this, he devoted himself to learning Mandarin and the Fuzhou dialect right after his arrival. He not only learned from his tutor, but also availed himself of all opportunities that arose. With extraordinary linguistic talent and strenuous effort, Doolittle was able to preach in the Fuzhou dialect just over four months after his arrival, and to pray for Chinese families in just six months. Only two years later, he completed the first book written in the dialect for missionary purposes: *Exhortation to Abandon Opium*.

卢公明尤为重视文字出版的作用，将其作为传教工作的重中之重。在入闽传教的第一年内，他就印刷了总数多达 25 万张的《圣经》、宣教小册子和宣传单（林立强，2005：39），在 1853—1858 年这短短 5 年内，他共编写、翻译、出版了 25 种书籍和传教小册子，这些书籍绝大部分都是宣扬基督教教义，不少采用了当地方言，还有一些则将传播福音与中国社会问题的解决结合起来。例如，《劝戒鸦片论》一书列举了吸食鸦片的六大罪状，指出戒除鸦片的根本办法是信奉耶稣，以宗教信仰抵抗鸦片；1856 年出版的《赌博明论》一书，揭露了赌博的九大危害，劝人皈依基督教，依靠上帝的力量戒除赌瘾。

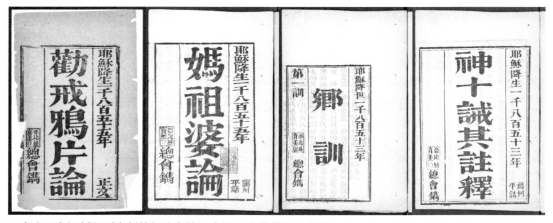

：卢公明在福州印刷出版的部分书籍（来源：哈佛燕京图书馆）
：Justus Doolittle's other works published in Fuzhou（Source: Harvard-Yenching Library）

这些批判封建陋习、恶习的小册子，语言通俗易懂，内容贴近民众生活，在当时颇受欢迎，因此产生了不小的社会影响。这些宣教小册子带有明确的宗教目的，但也为不少原先目不识丁的底层人民提供了接触书籍、学习阅读的机会。此外，卢公明还著有介绍西学的《中外问答》《生意人事广益法》等书籍，为长期处于闭关锁国状态的中国打开了一扇通往外界的窗户。一些像卢公明这样受过高等教育的知识分子，反对鸦片和封建陋习，并积极发展教育（卢公明和他的妻子先后创办了福音精舍和保福山学院，分别是今天的福州第五中学和福州第八中学的前身），对推进社会蒙昧的开化起到了积极作用。

卢公明在福州十余载的传教生活也是他日后其他作品的灵感来源。1867 年，他返回美国养病期间整理出版了《中国人的社会生活》一书。在这部两卷本、近千页的著作中，他用十分平实的语言，以福州为例对 19 世纪中叶的中国政治、经济、教育、宗教、科举、艺术、民俗、医疗、慈善等方面进行了细致的描述，并配有 150 幅插图，堪称一部晚清中国的百科全书。该书出版后广受西方各界关注，成为外国人，尤其是传教士了解中国的必备案头参考书，也代表了当时西方对中国社会研究的最高水平，被后世奉为西方汉学研究之经典。它同时也是第一部关于中国民俗的民俗志，为中国现代民俗学的萌发创造了有利条件。

For Doolittle, publishing was the top priority of his missionary work. Within the first year of his stay in Fujian, he printed a total of 250,000 pages of *The Bible* and other religious texts. Within just 5 years (1853 – 1858), he wrote, translated or published a total of 25 books and pamphlets. Most of these extolled Christian virtues, many were in the local dialect, and some incorporated evangelism into the solution of Chinese social problems. For example, in *Exhortation to Abandon Opium*, he listed six baneful effects of opium, then argued that to abstain from opium, one had to believe in Jesus and rely on the religious belief; similarly, in *Discourse on Gambling*, he elaborated on the nine vices of gambling, and believed that to overcome the addiction, one had to convert to Christianity.

Such works proved very popular and influential, as they were written in plain language and touched on everyday topics. Although unmistakably religious in nature, Doolittle's works provided the illiterate at the bottom with rare opportunities to be exposed to and learn to read books. His other works, such as *Dialogue between a Native and a Foreigner* and *Laws of Trade*, introduced Western learning into China, a country self-isolated for centuries. Doolittle, like many fellow intellectuals who had received higher education, were also keen on promoting Chinese education while attacking opium and bad habits. He set up the Gospel House (which later became Fuzhou No.5 Middle School), while his wife started Ponashan College (which later became Fuzhou No.8 Middle School).

The decade-long missionary life in Fuzhou inspired Doolittle's later works. In 1867, after returning to the US due to poor health, he published *Social Life of the Chinese: With Some Account of the Religious, Governmental, Educational, and Business Customs and Opinions*. This two-volume, nearly 1,000-page book, written in very plain language with 150 illustrations, touched upon almost every aspect of the mid-19th century China, ranging from politics, economy, education, religion, imperial examinations, to art, folklore, medical care and charity. Hence, it could be considered an encyclopedia of late imperial China. Since publication, it soon garnered wide attention in the West and was praised as a crucial reference for anyone who wanted to know about China, especially missionaries. As the first book on Chinese folklore, it also heralded the birth of modern Chinese folklore studies.

表 10 - 1　卢公明在榕期间出版著作一览表

序号	出版时间（年）	中文书名	序号	出版时间（年）	中文书名
1	1853；1855	《劝戒鸦片论》	13	1856	《中外问答》
2	1853	《乡训》	14	1856	《耶稣教小引》
3	1853	《神十诫其注释》	15	1857	《生意人事广益法》
4	1854	《悔罪信耶稣论》	16	1857	《西洋中华通书》
5	1854	《天文问答》	17	1858	《辩鬼神论》
6	1854	《约翰福音》	18	1858	《辩性论》
7	1855	《妈祖婆论》	19	1858	《辩毁谤》
8	1855	《守礼拜日论》	20	1858	《华人贫苦之故》
9	1855	《天律明说》	21	1858	《祈祷式文》
10	1855	《寒食清明论》	22	1858	《弃主临死畏刑》
11	1855	《钟表匠论》	23	1858	《辩孝论》
12	1855；1856	《赌博明论》	24	1858	《异端辩论》

作为一名十分注重语言学习尤其是方言学习的传教士，卢公明在与福州各阶层民众接触的过程中搜集了大量福州方言素材，结合其他传教士的中文资料，于 1872 年编辑出版了英汉词典《英华萃林韵府》。作者原计划在福州出版此书，但由于种种原因一再推迟，在上卷前 480 页由福州仓前美华书局出版后，剩余部分改由上海华美书馆出版。全书分两卷，共计 1 243 页，收录约 66 000 个词组、175 000 个单词和大量关于历史、民俗、律例、西学的资料，包括对偶句、格言警句、计量单位、中国历史年表、姓名实例、茶业术语、航海术语、地理术语等，体现了这一时期"中学西传"和"西学东渐"的交汇（林金水、吴巍巍，2008）。

Table 10 - 1　Justus Doolittle's publications during his stay in Fuzhou

N	Year	Title	N	Year	Title
1	1853; 1855	*Exhortation to Abandon Opium*	13	1856	*Dialogue between a Native and a Foreigner*
2	1853	*Village Sermons*	14	1856	*Introduction to Christianity*
3	1853	*Commentary on the Ten Commandments*	15	1857	*Laws of Trade*
4	1854	*Repentance and Faith*	16	1857	*European Chinese Almanac*
5	1854	*Catechism of Astronomy*	17	1858	*Disquisition on Heathen Gods*
6	1854	*John's Gospel*	18	1858	*Disquisition on Human Nature*
7	1855	*Discourse on Ma-tsoo-po*	19	1858	*Disquisition on Slander*
8	1855	*Discourse on Keeping the Sabbath*	20	1858	*Causes of Poverty among the Chinese*
9	1855	*Exposition of the Decalogue*	21	1858	*Forms of Prayer*
10	1855	*Discourse on the Feast of the Tombs*	22	1858	*Fear of the Wicked on the Approach of Death*
11	1855	*Story of a Watchmaker*	23	1858	*Disquisition on Filial Piety*
12	1855; 1856	*Discourse on Gambling*	24	1858	*Discussion of False Doctrines*

During his stay in Fuzhou, Doolittle collected abundant materials on Chinese language and dialects which he himself was keen on. Based on his findings and those of his fellow missionaries, he completed in 1872 *Vocabulary and Handbook of the Chinese Language: Romanized in the Mandarin Dialect*. Originally it was to be published in Fuzhou, but after the first 480 pages were printed by Methodist Episcopal Mission Press, the remaining part had to be turned over to the Methodist Publishing House in Shanghai. This two-volume book has 1, 243 pages, with entries of 66, 000 phrases and 175, 000 words, covering Chinese history, folklore, laws, and Western learning. The appendices include couplets, aphorisms, units of measurement, chronology of Chinese history, Chinese names, tea terms, navigation and geographical terms, etc. It manifests the confluence of Eastern and Western learning.

卢公明是 19 世纪 50 年代福州出版界最活跃、成就最高的一位传教士，当时像他这样白日游走街巷乡野、夜晚挑灯夜书的传教士并不少见。事实上，各差会抵华后为配合口头传教、培育并扩大中国识字民众群体，都积极从事文字事业，尤其重视《圣经》的方言翻译出版（主要是便于散发的圣经单章、单节的小册译本）。

从各传教士所属差会分布和出版著述数量来看，美部会和美以美会作为最早进入福建的两大差会，在推动传教所需的文字事业方面做了较多的努力，其中又以美以美会最为突出。在内容上虽以基督教为主，但同时也关注中国社会问题和西学介绍。

在卢公明来榕宣教的前十年间，福建一直没有专门的教会出版机构（张雪峰，2005），各类宣教材料大多委托福州本土书坊代为印制。受印刷速度、质量和价格等因素影响，难以满足实际宣教需求。这一局面在美以美会创办美华书局后迅速改观。

● 美华书局：19 世纪中国出版业的翘楚

穿过城市的喧嚣，沿着仓前山天安里拾级而上，抬头便可望见半山的尖顶与十字架，那是美以美会在中国最早修建的教堂之一——天安堂。教堂的西南侧是一座带有浓郁古典主义建筑风格的四层洋楼，这里就是近代福建最大的图书印刷出版机构——福州美华书局。据陈兆奋先生的博文记载，该楼底层当年为书局职工家属宿舍，二、三层为印刷、装订工场、洋纸文具储存室和负责邮寄和收费的办公室，顶层则是总经理和正副编辑的办公室。

Scan for more
扫码了解更多

Doolittle might be the most devoted and accomplished missionary in terms of publications during the 1850s in Fuzhou, but he was by no means the only one working so hard. To improve preaching and promote literacy, many missionaries emphasized literature work, especially the translation and publication of *The Bible* in dialects (mostly in the form of booklets, containing one or two biblical chapters and convenient for distribution).

Most of these works focused on Christianity, but some also dwelt on Chinese social problems and introduced Western learning. ABCFM and the Methodist Episcopal Church, the first two churches to arrive in Fujian, had been especially committed to publishing, with the former being arguably the most prominent.

During the first ten years since Doolittle came to Fuzhou, there was no Christian publisher within Fujian. Most missionary literature, therefore, was printed by local publishing houses, whose printing speed, quality and price often fell short of the expectations. Things changed after the Methodist Episcopal Church established its own press.

• **Methodist Episcopal Mission Press: A Pioneer of the 19th-Century Publishing Industry**

Visitors to Cangqian Mountain will find themselves away from the hustle and bustle of the city when walking along the Tian'an Alley. Looking up, they can easily spot on the hillside the spire and the cross of the Heavenly Peace Church, one of the earliest churches of the Methodist Episcopal Church in Asia. On its southwest side is a four-story Western-style building with a distinctly classical style. It used to house the largest press in modern Fujian: Foochow Methodist Episcopal Mission Press. According to Mr. Chen Zhaofen, its ground floor was the residential quarters for the staff and their families; on the second and third floors were the printing and binding workshop, the storage for imported stationery, and the office responsible for mailing service and rate collection; on the top floor were the offices of the general manager and the editors.

这栋洋楼的历史可以追溯到1859年。是年得到美国圣经出版协会5 000美元首期资助的福州美以美会，开始筹划建设一座应用新设备新技术、专门印刷《圣经》等宣教材料的现代书局。由于在华开展传教活动需要大量宣教材料，而此前的传统木活字印刷的印数和速度都很有限，印刷质量一般，费用却居高不下（陈林，2006：32），因此创办新式书局势在必行。1859年，在美以美会传教士怀德、麦利和、保灵和万为的筹建下，美华书局大楼开始动工兴建，1862年初落成并投入使用，麦利和出任第一任书局主理。

美华书局成立之后在福建创下了多个第一：1861年，万为亲往粤港采购美国印刷机和活字雕刻石盘，不仅在香港印书局学习了石印技术，还聘请了一位广东印刷工，在福州第一次引入了近代印刷技术；1862年，第一次使用活字印刷，开创了福建印刷史的新时期；1884年，首次引入滚筒印刷机、华英活字模等先进设备……

美华书局：历史与现在（左图来源：UMC Digital Galleries；右图来源：池志海）
Foochow Methodist Episcopal Mission Press: Past and present [Sources: UMC Digital Galleries(left)；Chi Zhihai (right)]

美华书局率先引入的西方现代印刷术推动了福建印刷技术的更新，木雕印刷和石印印刷逐渐淘汰。在成立后的第一年，该书局就印刷了10 000本小册子，包括《马太福音》和《约翰福音》各5 000本，并很快实现了盈利。在此后的20余年，美华书局技术设备一直保持全国领先，不仅拥有先进的进口印刷机和中英文铅字，还购置了铸字、铸版设备和订书机、穿孔机、切角机等设备。在印刷速度、排版正确率、字迹美观等方面均居全国前列，年均《圣经》印刷量达数十万册，年印刷总量达千万张，是当时中国最重要的出版中心之一，带动了福州乃至整个福建出版印刷业的迅猛发展：20世纪初福州报刊发行量和福建出版印刷行业均跃居全国第四（林金水，1997：437）。

This building can be traced back to 1859, when the growth of missionary work in China necessitated printing in bulk, a need barely met with the traditional movable type printing in terms of volume, speed, quality or cost. So, when the Methodist Episcopal Church in Fuzhou received an initial funding of US $5,000 from the American Bible Society in 1859, Rev. M. C. White, Rev. R. S. Maclay, Rev. S. L. Baldwin, and Rev. E. Wenworth promptly started planning for a modern press with up-to-date equipment and technologies for printing *The Bible* and other religious materials. The construction of this building started soon, but it was not completed and put into use until early 1862. Rev. R. S. Maclay was made its first superintendent.

The Mission Press set one record after another in Fujian: It was the first to introduce lithography when in 1861, Rev. E. Wenworth purchased from Canton and Hong Kong an American printing press and movable stone tablets, bringing back a Cantonese printing worker as well; it was the first to use, in 1862, movable types, ushering in a new era of printing in Fujian; it was again the first to introduce, in 1884, cylinder printing presses and movable types of Chinese and English.

These accelerated the upgrading of printing technology in Fujian, pushing woodblock printing and lithography gradually out of market. In its first year, the Press printed 10,000 copies of booklets, including 5,000 copies of *The Gospel of Matthew* and another 5,000 of *The Gospel of John*. Such a huge volume soon yielded profits, and in the following decades, the press maintained a leading position nationwide in terms of equipment and technology. It not only imported up-to-date printing machines and types of both Chinese characters and English letters, but also purchased machines for type and plate casting, bookbinding, perforation, corner cutting, etc. Not surprisingly, it soon became one of the top presses in China in terms of printing speed, typesetting accuracy and printing clarity. As one of the most important and busiest publishing centers in China of its time, it had an annual print volume of 10 million pages, including hundreds of thousands of copies of *The Bible*. It fueled the rapid development of publishing industry in Fuzhou and even the entire Fujian: At the beginning of the 20th century, newspaper circulation in Fuzhou, and publishing in Fujian both ranked the fourth nationwide.

美华书局发行的书籍报刊主要为各类宗教书刊，服务对象不仅包括福州本地教会，还包括北京、上海、台湾、香港等其他地区的教会，甚至远及海外。福建是近代中国传教的主要教区，作为教会出版发行机构的福州美华书局跟全国各地其他出版机构形成网络，因此其出版物能很方便迅速地销往全国甚至全球各地。此外，美华书局还专门设有"美华书坊"（初设在观音井，后移至书局楼上），除售卖本书局所印书籍报刊之外，还代售本地其他教会出版社和上海、广东等地书籍，兼营西式文具纸张等。由此可见，美华书局的业务范围较传统书局更广，覆盖了出版、印刷、发行和销售等多个环节，体现了近代西方出版业的新理念。

早期的美华书局主要出版中英文的宗教类书刊，但传教士们很快发现介绍西方的科技文化等世俗知识更能引起中国人的兴趣，于是他们在出版宣教材料之余，也翻译出版了不少西学图书和语言学习用书，如《天演学正诠》《天文图说》《地球全图》《卫生浅说》《大美国史略》等，涉及天文、地理、历史、医学、语言等各门类知识，极大地拓宽了福建了解西方的渠道，促进了西学东渐。传教士们译介西学一方面是为了更好地传播宗教，但他们同时也为面临内忧外患、探索救亡图存的晚清爱国知识分子提供了了解世界的窗口，打开了他们的视野。美华书局的副主编多由华人担任，黄乃裳、谢锡恩等均曾任职于此，他们掌握了近代印刷技术和先进的出版理念，逐渐成为中国近代出版业的先行者和中坚力量（张雪峰，2005）。

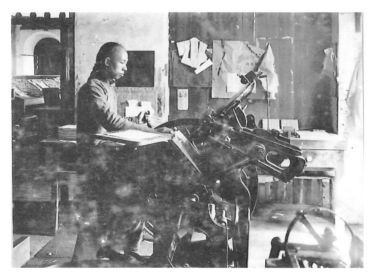

福州美华书局从事印刷的中国工人（来源：UMC Digital Galleries）
A Chinese worker at a printing press in the Foochow Methodist Episcopal Mission Press（Source: UMC Digital Galleries）

Foochow Methodist Episcopal Mission Press published mostly Christian books and periodicals, serving both the local churches and those in Beijing, Shanghai, Taiwan, Hong Kong, even outside China. Located in the heart of Fujian diocese, it was part of a national printing and publishing network, thus distributing and selling its own publications was made easy and swift both at home and abroad. The Press also especially set up a bookstore (initially located in Guang-ing-cang, and later moved to the upper floor of the main building) for its own books and periodicals, as well as a large assortment of books published by other local Christian presses or shipped from Shanghai, Guangdong and other places. Also available in this bookstore was Western-style stationery. The Press, compared with its Chinese counterparts, handled multiple tasks such as publishing, printing, distribution and sales. They embodied the new ideal of modern Western publishing industry.

In its early days, the press published mostly religious books in Chinese and English, but it was soon found that secular knowledge such as Western technology and culture generated more interest among Chinese readers. This encouraged more translation and publication about Western science and language learning. Books of this kind included *A Commentary on the Theory of Evolution, Illustrated Astronomy, World Atlas, An Introduction to Hygiene and Sanitation, Brief Geographical History of the United States of America,* to name just a few. They covered a wide range of topics from astronomy, geography, history to medicine, language and others, greatly promoting the eastward spread of Western learning. Such translations were mostly for a religious purpose, yet for those patriotic intellectuals in late imperial China desperate for solutions to China's domestic strife and foreign aggression, these books provided a rare opportunity to get to know and learn from the outside world. The press also helped to train local talents in publishing: Chinese were employed as its associate editors, among which were Wong Nai Siong and Sia Sek Ong. With modern printing technology and advanced publishing ideals acquired during their terms, these Chinese employees gradually grew into forerunners and backbones of modern Chinese publishing industry.

1903年，美以美会和监理会联合创办了上海华美书局，福州美华书局为其所属分局，改称美华书馆。此前长期担任福州美华书局主理的传教士力为廉，次年出任上海华美书馆总经理，兼管福州美华书馆。此次合并降级对福州美华书局来说不仅意味着出版管理人员和部分设备的流失，也意味着它作为中国基督教出版中心的辉煌历史已经过去。再加上新崛起的中国民族印刷业的竞争，美华书馆的业务逐渐减少，日益衰微。1915年，因经营困难宣告停业，自此退出历史舞台。然而，福州美华书馆原来的四层洋楼还继续发挥作用，供卫理公会举行年议会之用，顶层的原总经理和正副编辑办公室曾改作学生宿舍，先后借给培元书院、鹤龄英华书院和福音书院。福建神学院院长、福建协和大学校长杨昌栋也曾在此居住。20世纪50年代土改（房改）运动中，该楼被分配给居民居住后遭改造损毁。2015年，列为仓山区文物登记点，目前已修缮完毕并对外开放。

在美华书局成立30年后即1892年，另一个重要出版机构——闽北圣书会在仓山成立。它隶属伦敦圣书公会，是一个宗教书籍出版机构，主要服务地方教会组织，出版物主要包括《圣经》、《福音全书》、小学阶段的宗教教材和主日课程教材等，曾印行由弼履仁创办并主编的《榕城报》、榕腔注音字母月刊《快字》（赵广军，2005），后也代印协和大学的部分刊物。以美华书局和闽北圣书会为代表的基督教出版机构的兴起，标志着福建出版事业走上了近代化道路。

: 闽北圣书会印刷出版的部分书籍（来源：哈佛燕京图书馆）
: Some books published by North Fukien Religious Tract Society in Fuzhou (Source: Harvard-Yenching
: Library)

Things took a different turn when, in 1903, the Methodist Episcopal Church and the Methodist Episcopal Church South jointly established the Methodist Publishing House in Shanghai, and Foochow Methodist Episcopal Mission Press was reduced to one of its branches. Rev. W. H. Lacy, the superintendent of Foochow Methodist Episcopal Mission Press, was appointed General Manager of this new institution the following year, still in charge of its Fuzhou branch. For Foochow Methodist Episcopal Mission Press, this merger and downgrade meant not only the loss of management staff and equipment, but also the end of its glorious history as a Chinese Christian publishing center. Things further deteriorated during the ensuing years, when Chinese own emerging printing industry took away much of its market share. In 1915, it was finally closed down due to business difficulties, but its four-story building continued to be used as the venue for annual Methodist Church meetings. The former offices of the general manager and editors on the top floor were converted into student dormitories for Foochow Boy's Boarding School, Anglo-Chinese College and the Gospel House. This building was also once the residence of Yang Chang-tung, Dean of Fukien Theological Seminary and President of Fukien Christian University. Unfortunately, during the land and housing reform in the 1950s, the building suffered serious damage after being allocated for private residence. It was listed in 2015 as a cultural and historic relic in Cangshan District, and is now open to public after restoration was completed.

In 1892, thirty years after Foochow Methodist Episcopal Mission Press was founded, another important publishing organization, North Fukien Religious Tract Society, was also established in Cangshan. It was affiliated to Religious Tract Society in London and mainly served local churches in Fuzhou. Among its publications were *The Bible, The Gospels*, religious primers, day-school coursebooks, newspaper *Banyan City News* started and edited by Rev. L. P. Peet, and the monthly *Quick Word* in the Romanized Fuzhou dialect. Later it also printed journals of Fukien Christian University. With Foochow Methodist Episcopal Mission Press and North Fukien Religious Tract Society, Fujian's publishing industry embarked on the journey of modernization.

• 最早的福州方言英汉、汉英词典与教材

福州方言历史悠久，表达丰富，语流音变复杂，这些都给外来传教士们带来了巨大困难。面对普遍不懂官话的下层民众，传教士们首先需要克服语言障碍，学习当地方言，因为"只有使用当地方言传教，才能让民众明白教义真理"（Carlson，1974：15）。为提高自身的语言学习效率，同时也使传教地群众能读懂罗马拼音字母、理解和接受基督教教义，传教士们在日常积累的方言词语基础上编纂了英汉、汉英的福州方言词典，其中成就最大的当属麦利和与摩怜。

这两位传教士在福州 20 余年，堪称福州通，他们将福州方言音韵拼读法和罗马字母相结合，于 1870 年编纂出版了第一部供西方人学习福州方言的工具书——《福州方言拼音字典》（即《榕腔注音词典》）。这部现存最早的英文福州方言词典由福州美华书局印刷发行，全书共 1 130 页，分序言、导论、正文和附录四部分，收录近 1 万个字词和 3 万多个短语，其中绝大多数是日常用语，具有很强的实用性，易学易用，一经推出就大受欢迎，是传教士学习福州方言的必备工具书，也是许多文盲教友阅读宗教书籍的辅助参考书。该书分别于 1897 年和 1929 年修订再版，至今仍是研究福州方言最权威的参考工具（郑辉，2005）。

1871 年，由摩怜编纂[①]、美华书局出版的第二部福州方言词典——《榕腔初学撮要》问世。全书分为①语法，②短语，③商业词汇，④宗教、文学、政府用语，⑤数词、度量衡单位、地名、省府县名、朝代顺序、亲属称谓等，后附汉英和英汉词汇总表，共收录近 9 000 词条，不仅有助于西方人学习福州方言，同时也有助于他们了解中国，认识福州。

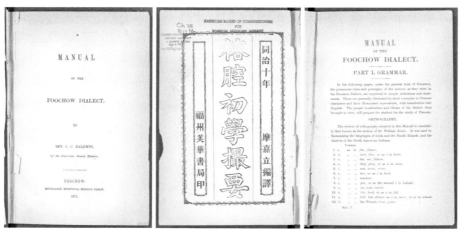

▪ 摩怜编纂的《榕腔初学撮要》英文扉页、封面与正文（来源：哈佛燕京图书馆）
▪ *A Manual of the Foochow Dialect* by Rev. C.C. Baldwin (Source: Harvard-Yenching Library)

---

① 该书中文扉页上标明编纂者为摩嘉立，即摩怜。

- ## The Earliest English-Chinese, Chinese-English Dictionaries and Textbooks on the Fuzhou Dialect

For the missionaries new in Fuzhou, the local dialect posed great difficulties with its long history, rich expressions, complicated pronunciation and intonation. Yet most Chinese at the social bottom understood nothing but the local dialect, so the missionaries in China had to learn this language first, for "if they were to make Christianity known to the people of Fuzhou, they would have to do so in the local dialect". To improve their own language learning efficiency as well as to help local people read Roman alphabet and understand the Gospel, missionaries soon set to compiling dictionaries and handbooks.

The most notable one was *An Alphabetic Dictionary of the Chinese Language in the Foochow Dialect*, co-authored by Rev. R. S. Maclay and the Rev. C. C. Baldwin. Having both stayed in Fuzhou for more than two decades, they understood and spoke the local dialect almost perfectly. Their knowledge and experience were put into this first reference book for Westerners in the Romanized dialect. First printed and distributed by Foochow Methodist Episcopal Mission Press in 1870, this dictionary has a total of 1,130 pages and consisted of a preface, an introduction, the main body and appendices. Nearly 10,000 words and more than 30,000 phrases are included, all taken from daily conversations, hence easy to learn and use. This dictionary was an immediate success, praised as both a must for missionaries learning the Fuzhou dialect, and a valuable reference for illiterate Chinese trying to read Christian books. Revised and republished in 1897 and 1929, it has remained the most authoritative reference book for studies of this dialect.

In 1871, Rev. C. C. Baldwin's *A Manual of the Foochow Dialect* was published. This is the second dictionary of the Fuzhou dialect published by Foochow Methodist Episcopal Mission Press. It includes parts on ① grammar; ② phrases; ③ commercial terms; ④religion, literature, and government terms; ⑤ miscellany (including numerals and ordinals, units of measurement, geographical names, provincial capitals and county names, Chinese chronology and dynasties, family relations, etc.) Appended to the book is a Chinese and English glossary of nearly 9,000 entries, helpful for learning the Fuzhou dialect as well as understanding China and Fuzhou in general.

1872 年，由卢公明编纂的英汉词典兼百科全书《英华萃林韵府》出版。1891 年，由传教士亚当编写的《英华福州方言词典》由美华书局出版，该书收录近万英语单词，每一英文词条后列出对应的福州方言词语（采用罗马注音方式，无对应汉字），为西方人学习福州方言提供了检索上的极大便利，该书分别于 1905 年和 1923 年修订再版。

1908 年，传教士钱尼斯夫妇编写的《福州话学习手册》出版，该书分 20 讲依次分类介绍福州方言中最常用的 1 000 个词汇，每讲后配有朗读练习、英语与福州方言句子互译练习，书末附有练习答案，适合作为西方人初学福州话的自学教材，前言部分还就如何学习福州方言、如何用福州方言宣教等提出建议。

这些方言书籍虽主要是为了方便来华传教士学习中国语言、提高传教效果，但客观上也将福州的政治、经济、文化、教育、宗教等介绍给了世界，促进了闽文化的西传。同时，这些书籍采用了西方当时最新的语言学理念，将其用于对福建方言的描述分析上，总结出福州方言的发音规律，为福州方言研究作出了贡献，也推动了汉语语言科学的发展。传教士们在翻译和写作实践中逐渐形成了欧化的白话文（如冠词、量词、被动句的增加，人称代词的分化、句子主语的添加），丰富了汉语的表达，促使汉语从文言文向现代白话文转变。

●《教务杂志》与《郇山使者》：中国近代报刊史上最成熟的杂志

西方各国差会传教士长途跋涉来到中国，在传教中常因语言文化障碍而遭遇重重困难。他们身处陌生的国度，渴望收到母国亲友的消息，也希冀能拥有一个沟通在华传教讯息、分享工作经验的平台。正是出于方便在华传教士沟通讯息的目的，1867 年 3 月，福州美以美会在仓山创办了面向全球发行的英文报刊《教务杂志》。

In 1872, Foochow Methodist Episcopal Mission Press published the aforementioned English-Chinese dictionary-cum-encyclopedia by Justus Doolittle—*A Vocabulary and Handbook of the Chinese Language: Romanized in the Mandarin Dialect*. In 1891, the Rev. T. B. Adam's *An English-Chinese Dictionary of the Foochow Dialect* came out, which listed nearly 10,000 English words with corresponding words in the Romanized dialect. Providing great convenience for Westerners learning the Fuzhou dialect, it was revised and republished in 1905 and 1923.

In 1908, Rev. C. E. Champness and his wife completed *Manual of the Foochow Dialect*. The book consists of 20 lectures introducing 1,000 commonly used words in the dialect. After each lecture, there are reading exercises, sentence translation exercises between English and the Fuzhou dialect. The answers to the exercises were provided at the end. Such a layout made it an ideal handbook for Westerners who tried to teach themselves the dialect.

Although mainly designed to help with language learning and missionary work, these books also introduced Fuzhou's politics, economy, culture, education and religion to the world. They, in the meanwhile, promoted studies of Chinese language (especially the Fuzhou dialect) by describing and analyzing Fujian dialects in modern linguistic terms and by working out their pronunciation rules. Along with the translation and writing, a Europeanized vernacular emerged, which distinguished itself with increased use of articles, quantifiers and passive sentences, differentiated personal pronouns, and added sentence subjects. These diversified expressions in Chinese were a catalyst in transforming classical Chinese into the modern vernacular version.

- ### *The Missionary Recorder* and *Zion Herald*: The Most Mature and Enduring Journals in Modern China

In March 1867, ABCFM launched in Cangshan the famed English-language journal: *The Missionary Recorder: A Repository of Intelligence from Eastern Missions, and Medium of General Information* (hereinafter referred to as *The Missionary Recorder* for brevity, though renamed differently later on). It was to facilitate the communication among missionaries who, after trekking thousands of miles to China, encountered language and cultural barriers in their missionary work. Stationed in a strange country, they were always eager for words from their families and friends. They also needed a platform for communicating missionary information in China and sharing work experience. It was to this very goal that *The Missionary Recorder* was conceived and created.

福州美华书局 1872 年出版的《教务杂志》第 4 卷封面与目录（来源：www. babel. hathitrust. org）

The cover page and table of contents in Volume 4 of *The Chinese Recorder and Missionary Journal* published by Foochow Methodist Episcopal Mission Press in 1872（Source：www. babel. hathitrust. org）

　　在中国发行的诸多英文刊物中，《教务杂志》不仅以其权威性广受赞誉，更以 74 年的出刊历史独占鳌头。正如陶飞亚（2007）所言："如果单从报刊的出版持续时间来看，19 世纪传教士在华出版的刊物中，无论是享有较高声誉的中文报刊《万国公报》（1889—1907）、《中西教会报》（1891—1917），抑或英文的《中国丛报》（1832—1851），均不及《教务杂志》。"该刊发行量最多达到单期 3 000 册，出版后分别邮寄给国内外各地订户。

　　在总计七十几卷、五万多页的《教务杂志》中，不仅有基督教福音内容和各种传教讯息，还包含在华传教士的语言学习、生活习惯、中国儒释道思想、中国典籍翻译、当地风土人情，以及教育、经济、医疗、社会服务等，甚至还涉及日本、朝鲜、东南亚等地的教会情况。更为难得的是，它还附有许多内部统计数据和约 1 500 张图片，记录了当时的历史事件、人物、少数民族、建筑等，是研究基督教在华发展及中国近现代史的重要史料。

　　该刊创刊号采取 1 至 3 期连刊的形式，共刊登五篇文章。次月即 1867 年 4 月起，改为月刊形式。1868 年 1 月，曾因经费不稳一度停刊。同年 5 月复刊并将名称由 *The Missionary Recorder：A Repository of Intelligence from Eastern Missions，and Medium of General Information* 改为 *The Chinese Recorder and Missionary Journal*，由保灵接任编辑。在复刊号中，保灵明确重申办刊的主要目的是为在华传教士提供沟通传教事务的平台，而不同主题的文章均可服务于这一目的，包括中国的语言文字、风俗习惯、法律法规、政府机构、宗教信仰、文明特征、自然资源等，并不局限于直接宣教（Baldwin，1868）。

The Missionary Recorder overshadowed other contemporary English journals in China with its authoritativeness and the unparalleled 74-year history. As Tao Feiya (2007) put it: "... of all the missionary journals in the 19th-century China, *The Missionary Recorder* is the longest-running, exceeding the highly-reputed Chinese-language *A Review of the Times* (1889 – 1907) and *Missionary Review* (1891 – 1917), and the English-language *Chinese Repository* (1832 – 1851)." Its popularity was obvious: With circulation peaking at over 3,000 copies per issue, it could reach a wide readership at home and abroad.

Spanning over seven decades, the journal totaled in more than 70 volumes, over 50,000 pages. Readers would find articles on not just the Gospel and missionary work, but also missionaries' learning of Chinese language and their life habits, Confucianism, Buddhism and Taoism, local customs, as well as Chinese education, economy, medical care and social services. This journal was also concerned with missionary work in Japan, Korea, and Southeast Asia. Especially valuable about this journal is the internal statistical data and about 1,500 illustrations about Chinese historical events, figures, ethnic minorities and buildings at that time, making it an important source for studies of Christianity development in China and Chinese modern history.

The first three issues were published as a single booklet, carrying a total of five articles. Starting with the fourth issue in April, 1867, this journal came out on a monthly basis. However, it was suspended in January, 1868 due to financial difficulty. When it was resumed four months later and renamed as *The Chinese Recorder* and *Missionary Journal*, the Rev. S. L. Baldwin, its new editor, stated that the primary goal of this journal is to "give the Protestant missionaries in China a medium of communication on all matters appertaining to their work, and that it would not be limited to articles explicitly about missionary work, but would welcome articles on all subjects including Chinese language, customs and habits, laws and regulations, government agencies, religious views and worship, characteristics of Chinese civilization, as well as Chinese geography, history and natural resources".

保灵为《教务杂志》奠定了此后的标准，该刊以其不拘一格的选材和简洁明了的文字与排版，赢得了大批包括传教士在内的读者的支持，也拥有较为稳定的撰稿人和发行渠道，声誉渐隆。然而1872年5月，随着时任编辑卢公明辞去编辑一职、离开福州前往上海治疗失音症，《教务杂志》第二次停刊。同1868年一样，这次停刊引发了传教士们强烈的复刊呼声，两年后在上海复刊①，由美国长老会美华书局出版。上海得天独厚的航运和邮政优势为《教务杂志》的复刊提供了有利的条件。读者范围也从创刊之初的偏重福州一隅，逐渐发展成为面向包括中国在内的亚洲各国以及欧美教会机构，此后稳定出刊直至1941年太平洋战争爆发、日本占领上海为止。

虽然《教务杂志》的历任编辑来自不同差会，但他们的办报宗旨始终如一，即便观点有所不同，也能自由交流，各抒己见，避免出现某个差会独大、一言堂的情况。该刊不仅时刻关注各地传教士面临的新情况新问题，同时也密切关注中国政治生活，具有较为明显的言论自由倾向，这一点深刻影响了后来的中国近代报刊，为清末报业的"政论时代"埋下了伏笔。

英文月刊《教务杂志》在包括海内外传教士和教徒在内的广大读者中影响深远，而稍晚出现的《郇山使者》（该刊多次更名易址，为行文方便，本书统称《郇山使者》），在中国本土读者中获得的巨大成功也同样令人瞩目。1874年末，诞生于福州仓山的这份中文月刊由美国传教士武林吉和李承恩（亦译为普洛姆）共同创办，由黄乃裳担任主笔。这是福建省最早的教会报刊，其英文刊名 Zion Herald 中的 Zion 即位于耶路撒冷南边的锡安山，是传说中耶稣和门徒们"最后的晚餐"之处，是基督教的圣山，"郇山使者"意即基督教徒。顾名思义，该报创办之初带有浓厚的基督教色彩，但很快就出现了世俗化的趋势。

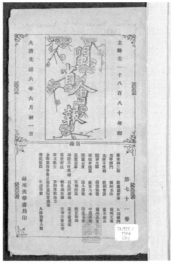

1875年、1888年出版的《闽省会报》（来源：哈佛燕京图书馆）
Fuhkien Church Advocate published by M. E. Mission Press, Foochow（1875/1880）（Source: Harvard-Yenching Library）

---

① 该刊1874年迁至上海后曾数度更名：1915年更名为 *The Chinese Recorder* 并增加中文刊名《教务杂志》，故后来的国内史学界通俗地称其为《教务杂志》；1924在原刊名基础上增加副标题，即 *Missionary Journal: Journal of the Christian Movement in China*；1938年与 *Education Review* 合并为 *The Chinese Recorder and Education Review*。

The standards Rev. S. L. Baldwin set for this journal, together with its wide range of topics, lucid language and clear layout, helped to win over a large readership both within and beyond Protestant churches. It also attracted a galaxy of contributors and maintained stable means of distribution. However, when the then editor Justus Doolittle resigned and left for Shanghai seeking treatment of aphonia in May 1872, the journal was suspended for the second time. Again, this was met with vehement calls from missionaries, and two years later it was resumed in Shanghai, where it was published by American Presbyterian Mission Press. This new city was deemed ideal for its unparalleled shipping and postal services, and the relocation turned the local journal into an international one, servicing missionaries in Asia, Europe and the US. Since then, it was published and distributed regularly until 1941, when the Pacific War broke out and the Japanese occupied Shanghai.

The journal's success could also be attributed to its editors. Despite their coming from different churches, the editors adhered to the same tenet of providing missionaries with a forum for free exchange of opinions. Hence no one particular church group would predominate. It also secured a large readership with close attention to not just the new situation and emerging problems faced by missionaries, but also the political life in China. Its inclination towards freedom of speech was to shape Chinese modern newspapers in the years to come, heralding "the era of political comments" for Chinese journalism during the late Qing Dynasty.

If *The Chinese Recorder and Missionary Journal* exerted a far-reaching influence on missionaries and Christian believers both in and outside China, the Chinese journal *Zion Herald* and its successors could be said to have achieved equal success among Chinese readers. *Zion Herald,* the first missionary journal in Fujian, was started in Cangshan in late 1874 by Rev. F. Ohlinger and Rev. N. J. Plumb, with Wong Nai Siong serving as the chief editor. "Zion" in its English name referred to Mount Zion in the south of Jerusalem. As the name suggested, the journal was started with strong Christian overtones, but soon it took a secular turn.

1875 年底，《郇山使者》更名为《闽省会报》，每月初一出版，内容从基督福音扩大到国内外时事要闻、社会民生、文学、科学等众多非宗教内容，是福建当时容量最大、内容最丰富的报纸。其中大部分涉外内容从外文报刊直接编译而来，这对当时偏于东南一隅、资讯匮乏的闽人而言无疑是了解国内外大事的重要途径，因此除信徒外还吸引了士大夫、政府官员、学校师生、各国领事馆职员等大批稳定读者（徐斌，2008），在传播西学新知、开启民智方面发挥了重要作用。1895 年时，该刊每月发行已达 3 500 本，数量位居当时全国月报之首。它还与上海的《万国公报》《申报》等重要报刊保持密切联系，通过互相转载的方式将自己的影响范围扩大到全国（方汉奇，1992：371）。

由于《闽省会报》的巨大成功，1898 年，中华美以美会将其与《中华教保报》合并为《华美报》，定为全国美以美会的公报，总揽美以美会的在华会务，内容也相应进行了调整，减少了福建本土的新闻评论，更为关注全国性的问题。该刊仍由福州美华书局印刷发行，但发行量剧增，读者遍布全国，远及海外。和《闽省会报》一样，《华美报》除宗教类文章外，亦刊登时闻和自然科学方面的文章，因此在教徒之外还拥有较为庞大和稳定的世俗读者群，并承接商业广告。1904 年，《华美报》与上海监理会的《教保》合并为《华美教保》，改为上海发行。1910 年，《华美教保》更名为《兴华报》，从月刊改为周刊，1938 年左右停刊。

1900 年由福州美华书局出版的《华美报》（第 27 册）（来源：哈佛燕京图书馆）
Chinese Christian Advocate （Issue 27）published by Foochow M. E. Mission Press in 1900（Source: Harvard-Yenching Library）

在《郇山使者》之前，仓山已有其他传教士所办的报纸：诞生于 1858 年的福建近代第一份报纸——《福州府差报》（亦译为《福州信使报》），同期创办的《福州捷报》《福州每日回声报》《福州广告报》《福州每日广告与航运报》等。但这些均为英文报纸，出刊时间较短，影响也相对有限。相比之下，《郇山使者》虽经历多次更名、合并和迁址，但仍长盛不衰，前后存续时间长达 60 余年，堪称中国报刊史上的特例（赵晓兰、吴潮，2011：241）。

In late 1875, *Zion Herald* was renamed as *Fuhkien Church Advocate* and came out on the first day of every month. Apart from the Gospel, it now covered a wide range of non-religious topics like domestic and international news, social development, literature and science, making it the most informative journal at that time. Most of the articles about foreign countries were directly adapted and translated from Western periodicals. For the people in Fujian, who had very limited access to crucial information due to its geographical location, this journal was a rare chance to keep themselves informed of important domestic and international events. It was, therefore, no surprise that this journal soon garnered appreciation from a large and stable readership consisting of not just Christian believers, but also scholars, government officials, school teachers and students, and staff of consulates. Such a readership, in turn, helped spread Western learning and enlighten Chinese people. By 1895, it had become the most popular journal in China with a monthly circulation of 3,500 copies. Close communication had also been maintained with other quality journals like *Wan Kwoh Kung Pao* and *Shun Pao* (or *Shen-pao*), extending its influence beyond provincial borders by way of reciprocal reprints.

Fuhkien Church Advocate's phenomenal success soon led to its upgrade in 1898 when it was merged with *The Central Christian Advocate* into *Chinese Christian Advocate*. It was now designated as the national journal serving all Methodist Episcopal Churches in China. Accordingly, it reduced local news and comments about Fujian and increased national events and issues. Though still printed and distributed by Foochow Methodist Episcopal Mission Press, its readership now extended all over the country and even abroad, pushing the circulation to a new height. Like *Fuhkien Church Advocate*, it published articles on Christianity as well as current news and natural sciences, which helped to maintain a large, stable readership. This, in turn, attracted commercial advertisements. In 1904, *Chinese Christian Advocate* was merged with *The Chinese Advocate* of Shanghai Methodist Episcopal Church South into *Christian Advocate*. In 1910, *Christian Advocate* was renamed *Chinese Christian Advocate*, published on a weekly instead of monthly basis. It was ceased around 1938.

Zion Herald was not the first missionary journal to appear in Cangshan. *The Foochow Courier*, the first journal in modern Fujian, appeared in 1858, and its contemporaries included *The Foochow Herald*, *Foochow Daily Echo*, *The Foochow Advertiser*, *Foochow Daily Advertiser* and *Shipping Gazettte*. These English journals were short-lived and exerted little impact. *Zion Herald*, on the other hand, though renamed, merged and relocated, remained popular for over six decades. It is an exceptional case in the history of Chinese periodicals.

传教士们坚持办报，显然是因为他们相信报刊与传统的书籍相比，更新速度更快，内容更新颖，成本也更低廉，易于传播，能吸引更多的读者，产生的社会影响也更为明显和直接。随着罗马化福州方言的传播和识字群体的扩大，创办面向中文读者的报刊时机成熟，《郇山使者》等于是应运而生。不仅如此，传教士们还将蒙童列入目标读者，为低龄儿童创办专门的期刊。1874年，传教士李承恩的夫人在福州创办了《小孩月报》。这是中国最早的儿童刊物之一，内容包括圣经故事、箴言、童话、小说等，采用福州方言编写，语言浅显易读，附有插图，每期发行量维持在500份左右。1895年该刊物被传教士孟存慈选为义塾识字教材后，月发行量一度增至2500份。

报刊突破了传统文学媒介的形式，创造了新的阅读形式和阅读群体，为中国后来的语言变革做好了准备。尽管传教士们在华办报主要是为了灌输西方基督教思想和西方文化，但这些报纸对西方自然科学、实用科技、地理历史、政治经济等的介绍客观上也促进了中西文化的交流。受雇于这些报纸的中国员工在参与办报过程中掌握了新闻的采访、编辑、发行、广告、印刷等技术，积累了较为先进的办报经验，成为中国近代民族报业的先行者和中坚力量，其中就包括长期在华美书局任职并担任《郇山使者》报主笔的黄乃裳。

● 黄乃裳：福建近代民族报业第一人

黄乃裳（1849—1924），福建闽清人，曾参与公车上书、百日维新、辛亥革命等活动，是一位卓越的民主革命家和华侨领袖，也是我国近代出版史上的风云人物。他在17岁时受洗入教，后长期在教会中供职。由于具有极强的中英文功底而倍受教会信任和重视，常协助传教士们解决翻译中的问题，他曾与美国牧师薛承恩、保灵、武林吉等人合译了《圣经图说》《天文图说》《大美国史略》《卫斯理传》《美以美会纲例》《依经问答喻解》等多达上百册书籍，还独立将《旧约全书》翻译成福州方言读本。

黄乃裳（来源：池志海）
Wong Nai Siong（Source: Chi Zhihai）

The missionaries' zeal for running newspapers and journals came from the conviction that, compared with traditional books, periodicals were characterized by faster update, up-to-date contents, lower cost, easier distribution, as well as wider readership, hence stronger social impact. With the spread of the Romanized Fuzhou dialect and the growth of the literate community, the time had come for newspapers and journals to target at locals, even preschoolers. In 1874, Mrs. Plumb started *Child's Paper* in the colloquial language. This monthly was one of the earliest papers for children in China, featuring Bible stories, proverbs, fairy tales and novels with well-designed illustrations. Its circulation had remained stable at around 500 copies per issue, but after the Rev. G. S. Miner introduced it into his day-schools, the circulation increased to 2,500.

Periodicals broke with traditional literary forms, created novel reading experiences, built new readerships, and paved the way for the subsequent language reform in China. Though mainly for instilling Christian values and Western culture, missionary periodicals also promoted exchanges of Chinese and Western cultures by introducing Western science and technology, geography, history, politics and economy. Moreover, the periodicals were also an incubator of Chinese talents for publishing. With experience and expertise in interviewing, editing, printing, distribution and advertising, these Chinese would soon rise to be the forerunners and backbone of Chinese modern national newspapers. One of them was Wong Nai Siong, who had long served in Methodist Episcopal Mission Press in addition to being the editor-in-chief of *Zion Herald*.

• Wong Nai Siong: The Pioneer of Chinese Modern National Journalism in Fujian

Wong Nai Siong (1849 – 1924), an outstanding revolutionary and a leader of overseas Chinese, was born in Minqing County west of Fuzhou. He was an activist in the 1895 Petition of Chinese Scholars and Intellectuals, the 1898 Hundred Days of Reform, and the 1911 Revolution. Equally noticeable was his achievement in Chinese modern publishing industry. Baptized at the age of 17, he served in the church for years and was highly praised for his fluency in both Chinese and English. His bilingualism came in handy when helping the missionaries sort out translation difficulties. His collaboration with the Rev. N. Sites, Rev. C. C. Baldwin and Rev. F. Ohlinger yielded nearly one hundred translation works, among which were *The Bible Picture Book*, *Illustrated Astronomy*, *Brief Geographical History of the United States of America, The Life of the Rev. John Wesley*, *The Constitutional Practice and Discipline of the Methodist Church, Catechism*. There was also his solo translation of the *Old Testament* into the Fuzhou dialect.

黄乃裳认为当时中国羸弱的根本原因在于"民智不开"，而要开启民智，非"办学办报"不可。于是，他在创办学校或任教的同时，将大量精力投入现代报刊的创办和经营之中。1875年，黄乃裳在担任主笔的《郇山使者》上发表了《劝种牛痘文》《戒缠足论》等针砭时弊、揭露陋习的文章，后者除登报外还另印了3万余份分发全省各地（王植伦，1997：7），足见其受欢迎程度。在《郇山使者》更名为《闽省会报》后，黄乃裳继续担任该报主撰长达数十年。

翻译西学著作和编辑出版报刊的经历使黄乃裳认识到出版业在广开民智、传播信息和改变思想方面的巨大力量，也掌握了现代报刊的创办经营之道。1896年4月，他自筹资金在仓前山创办了福建首份国人自办的报纸——《福报》。报馆设在美华书局之内，由美华书局印刷发行，并在全省各市县以及上海、台湾等地设售报处。

该报不依附于任何党派，也不受教会控制，因而更具独立性和自由。内容主要分新闻和评论两类，其中评论文章每期一篇，主要宣传维新变法的思想，为该报之精华。除极少数明确署名的外稿，均出自黄乃裳之手（林其锬，1987），分别阐述维新变法、开办学堂、发展实业、革除陋习、富国强兵等观点，每篇长逾千字，个别长文则分期连载，其中连载于1、2期的《福州宜设报馆说》，宣称西方最值得效仿的就是其大力发展的新闻业，只有报刊出版才能增长人们的见识，促进新思想的诞生和传播，进而增强国力（黄乃裳，1896），首次将报刊提高至关乎国家兴衰存亡的高度。这篇文章浓缩了黄乃裳的新闻思想和多年办报经验，堪称我国现代报刊史上的丰碑。

《福报》宣传维新变法思想和民主精神，立场鲜明，说理透彻，令当时的福建知识界为之一振，很快脱颖而出成为国内介绍维新变法思想的重要刊物，和《万国公报》《强学报》等遥相呼应。然而和当时其他许多民报一样，《福报》销售数量有限，亏损严重，至1897年4月已亏损2800元，债台高筑的黄乃裳不得不停办此刊，之后转让给日本人并更名为《闽报》。这是日本在华办的第一份报纸，后因消息灵通且常披露中国地方军政内幕而备受欢迎，发行量一度高达3000份，是当时福建首屈一指的大报，抗日战争爆发后停刊。

Wong believed that the root cause of China's weakness was benightedness among its people, and that enlightenment would not happen without schools and journals. In 1875, *Zion Herald* published his serial articles attacking social malaise and vile habits, among which were his much-acclaimed pieces like "A Case for Vaccination against Smallpox" and "Against Foot-binding". Of the latter, over 30,000 extra copies were printed and distributed throughout Fujian Province, a sure sign of its popularity. After *Zion Herald* was renamed *Fuhkien Church Advocate*, Wong continued to serve in the same position for decades.

While translating Western works and publishing periodicals, Wong came to realize the formidable power of the publishing in enlightening people, communicating information and shaping thoughts. In April 1896, with expertise in publishing honed during his working years and the fund raised independently, he started on Cangqian Mountain *Fu Pao* (or *Fortune Newspaper*), the first one in Fujian started by Chinese. It was printed and distributed by the Methodist Episcopal Mission Press, in whose main building its office was also located. This paper was available in newstands within Fujian as well as in Shanghai and Taiwan.

Unaffiliated to any party nor controlled by the church, it managed to maintain independence and freedom by carrying news reports and editorials. Each issue usually contained one editorial, which, unless specified, was assumed to be penned by Wong himself. These editorials were often over 1,000 words long, focusing on social reforms, starting schools, promoting industry, eradicating vile habits, building national power and military strength. Occasionally, when too long to fit in one single issue, they would appear in series. One such example was "A Case for Setting up Newspaper Offices in Foochow", which appeared on the first two issues. In this seminal essay (1896), Wong claimed that the first thing China was to learn from the West was the highly developed journalism. He was convinced that periodicals were the only route to a broadened horizon, the generation and dissemination of new thoughts, and ultimately the strengthening of national power. Wong was the first to give periodicals a pivotal role in China's survival and prosperity, and his views on journalism were epitomized in this landmark essay in Chinese modern journalism.

Fu Pao soon became one of the most influential papers touting social reform and revolution, the others being *The Wan Kwoh Kung Pao* and *Chi'ang Hüeh Pao*. Its incisive analysis and unmistakable stance in popularizing reform and democracy helped Fujian intellectuals to shake off the lethargy that had plagued them. But like most other civilian newspapers at that time, *Fu Pao* could barely make both ends meet with only limited subscription. When its debts increased in April 1897 to 2,800 yuan, Wong was compelled to suspend before selling it to some Japanese. Renamed *Min Pao* thereafter, it became the first paper run by Japanese in China. With informed sources, especially about Chinese military and political insider stories, it turned out to be so popular as to become *de facto* the leading newspaper in Fujian then, selling over 3,000 copies per issue. However, it was discontinued when the War of Resistence Against Japanese Agression broke out in 1937.

1905 年 1 月，黄乃裳在厦门接任《福建日日新闻》（后更名为《福建日报》）的主笔，因支持该报进行反美宣传和揭露官员贪腐等遭当局罚款和压制，次年被迫停刊。1910 年，黄乃裳出任教会报刊《左海公道报》主编，此时他早已投身民主革命。在他的影响下，该报刊登了大量充满革命思想、介绍革命形势和时局的文章。1916 年，黄乃裳应福建同盟会的要求创办了《伸报》，广受社会欢迎，但因抨击时弊也很快遭封禁。此外，他还在新加坡参与创办了《星洲日新报》和《图南日报》（王植伦，1997：362），宣传资产阶级革命思想。

从逾弱冠到古稀，黄乃裳怀抱启蒙救国的信念，七次参与办报，对福建近代报业的贡献难以估量。以《福报》为代表的近代报纸发行量大，出版周期短，传播速度快，读者范围广，是新兴资产阶级实现"立言"参政的重要途径；对于普通百姓而言，这些报纸唤起了他们的求知欲和参政议政的热情，推动了中国民主化的发展进程。

● 辛亥革命烽火中的仓山报刊

在仓山区梅坞路 57 号，有一栋占地约 100 平方米、坐东朝西、双层抹灰的洋楼。1905 年郑祖荫、林斯琛等人在此组织了"桥南公益社"，以查禁鸦片、消防救火、发展体育等为掩护，秘密宣传革命，发展组织。1912 年 4 月，孙中山先生曾在此发表演说，并题写了"独立厅"三字，这是因为它自 1906 年以来就是中国同盟会福建支部的所在地，仓山则是福建辛亥革命的大本营。据不完全统计，1906 年至 1911 年福建同盟会在福州创立的 9 个团体中仓山占了 6 个，而创办的 3 种报刊——《警醒报》《建言报》《民心》——全部在仓山。

1910 年，福州警醒社创办月刊《警醒报》，以"警醒国民""生爱国思想"为目的，在政治上赞成君主立宪，但也表现出浓厚的爱国主义色彩。该报由美华书局印刷，销往福州周边以及省内大部分地区，甚至远至南洋，影响较大。

Scan for more
扫码了解更多

In January 1905, Wong worked as the editor-in-chief of *Fukien Daily News* (later renamed *Fukien Daily*) in Xiamen. Unfortunately, he was later fined and penalized by the authorities for supporting the newspaper's anti-American coverage and exposing government corruption. This led to the closure of the paper the following year. A few years later, in 1910, Wong became the editor-in-chief of the Christian newspaper *Cau Hai Kung Dao Pao*. Already a devoted revolutionary, Wong transformed the paper into one which touted revolution and informed the public of the current situation. In 1916, Wong started the popular *Shen Pao* at the request of Fujian Branch of the United League of China. This newspaper, though highly popular, was again closed down for critiquing domestic events. Apart from these, Wong helped run another two reformers' papers in Singapore: *Jit Shin Pau* and *Thoe Lam Jit Poh*.

Wong's contribution to Fujian's modern journalism is immeasurable. Convinced of their power in enlightening and saving the country, he started or helped start seven periodicals. With large circulations, short publication cycles, fast dissemination and wide readership, they facilitated the debut of Chinese bourgeoisie on the political arena. For ordinary Chinese, they aroused a desire for knowledge and enthusiasm for participating in politics. They sped up China's democratization.

• Cangshan's Periodicals during the 1911 Revolution

At No. 57 on Meiwu Road in Cangshan, stands a two-story Western-style building. Facing west, it covers an area of about 100 square meters. This was a historic building where Qiaonan Public Welfare Society was set up in 1905 by Zheng Zuyin, Lin Sichen and a few other revolutionary-minded locals. They aimed to spread the revolutionary thoughts and recruit new members under the cover of cracking down on opium, fighting fires, and promoting sports. It was also the headquarters of the Fujian Branch of the United League of China when Cangshan became the stronghold of the 1911 Revolution in Fujian. Here Dr. Sun Yat-sen, on a tour in Fujian in April 1912, delivered a speech and wrote in calligraphy "Independence Hall". From 1906 to 1911, six out of the nine organizations founded by the League were located in Cangshan, and its three periodicals—*Ching Hsing Pao*, *Chien Yen Pao* and *Min Hsin*— were all in Cangshan.

The monthly *Ching Hsing Pao* (or *Awakening*) was the earliest of the three. Launched in 1910 by Fuzhou Ching Hsing Society, it aimed to awaken patriotism. It was printed by Foochow Methodist Episcopal Mission Press and distributed throughout Fujian and even in south Asian areas. Though favoring constitutional monarchy (hence considered only partly revolutionary), it was nevertheless overflowing with patriotism and exerted a considerable influence.

1911 年 1 月，福建同盟会会员和其他一些革命志士，在原"桥南公益社"内刊《调查录》的基础上，创办了《建言报》，由同盟会会员、福州琅岐人刘通担任主编。该报社址位于仓前梅坞，每周二、四、六出版，宣传资产阶级革命思想，后来成为福建同盟会总部机关报。虽然人手缺乏（专职与兼职员工合计不足 10 人，甚至总编也需身兼采访、撰稿、编辑、校对等职），经费困难（仅 1000 块大洋），但《建言报》仍在内容选择、编排印刷方面取得了不俗的成绩，深受民众喜爱，发行量高达六七百份。辛亥革命福建起义之后不久，该报认为反清宣传的历史使命已完成，由副刊编辑接手原报纸编务和财产等事务，并更名为《共和》报，自此与同盟会脱离了关系。

1911 年 3 月，福州警醒社创办发行宣传资产阶级革命思想的《民心》月报（第 6 期改为"福建民心社"），该报反对君主立宪，坚持革命推翻清朝政府，坚持民主共和，尤为推崇美国的资产阶级共和制，曾全文刊载美国独立宣言与宪法的译文。同年 8 月停刊。

这些报刊诞生于革命烽火中，虽延续时间短暂，但却在人们心中播下了"民主"和"革命"的种子，推动了中国现代化进程。

• 百花齐放的福建协和大学出版物

福建协和大学（下文简称"协大"）是 1916 年美国教会创办的一所著名高等学府，最初校址位于仓前观音井，虽不久即迁址魁岐，但在相当长的时间里仍保持与仓山的密切关系。仓山深厚的宗教文化底蕴和中西交汇的特殊氛围赋予这所学府以独特的气质和魅力。而仓山作为福建近代出版中心和出版业现代化的引领者，不仅拥有美华书局和闽北圣书会这样的现代出版机构，更是福建近代报刊业的发源地和中心，培育了大批出版业人才。这些都为在此办学的协大提供了得天独厚的优势，为其出版活动的开展铺平了道路。

In January, 1911, *Chien Yen Pao* came into being when the insider journal of Qiaonan Public Welfare Society was adapted by, among other revolutionaries, members of the Fujian Branch of the United League of China. Liu Tong, a member of the League and a native of Langqi, Fuzhou, served as the editor-in-chief. Its office was located on Meiwu Road in Cangqian and the paper was published every Tuesday, Thursday and Saturday. It promoted bourgeois revolutionary ideas, and later became a mouthpiece of the League in Fujian. Despite understaffing (with fewer than 10 full-time and part-time employees, the editor-in-chief had to assume multiple roles of interviewing, writing, editing, and proofreading) and inadequate funding of only 1,000 yuan, *Chien Yen Pao* managed to win over a considerable readership (about 700 subscriptions) with excellent content selection, layout design and high-quality printing. Shortly after the 1911 Revolution in Fujian, however, it was believed that the paper had accomplished its mission of mobilizing people in anti-imperial China. The paper then severed its relations to the League when it was handed over to its assistant editor and renamed as *Kung He*.

In March 1911, Fuzhou Ching Hsing Society started another monthly, *Min Hsin* (renamed as *Fukien Min Hsin She* since the 6th issue). Unlike *Ching Hsing Pao*, this new journal was against constitutional monarchy and insisted on overturning the Qing Government by revolution and establishing a democratic republic. Embracing the American ideal of republic, it published the translation of the American *Declaration of Independence* and *the Constitution* in full text. However, it was closed in August of the same year.

These journals, though all short-lived, were seminal in introducing to China the concepts of democracy and revolution. They accelerated China's modernization.

• Publications by Fukien Christian University

The prestigious Fukien Christian University (hereinafter referred to as FCU) was founded in 1916 near Guang-ing-cang on Cangqian Mountain. Though soon relocated to Kueichi (or Kuiqi) Village (about 5 miles south of Fuzhou), it maintained for decades close relationships with Cangshan, which, thanks to its rich religious and cultural heritage resulting from confluence of China and the West, endowed this institution with a unique charm. Cangshan also provided FCU with unrivaled publishing amenities: It boasted of not just pioneering modern publishing institutions like the Mission Press and North Fukien Religious Tract Society, not just the first modern newspapers in Fujian, but also many a talent of publishing. All these expedited the booming publications of FCU.

作为一所教会学校，协大秉持"博爱、牺牲、服务精神"（罗德里克·斯科特，1999：48），竭力为中国青年提供高水平的大学教育。在创立之初，协大的教育目标是培养基督教人才、传播基督福音，但在中国的土壤中萌芽和成长起来的协大，不可避免地走上了本土化和世俗化的道路，不仅允许传授世俗知识，从事科学研究，协大师生作为中华民族的一分子还直接组织和参与了反帝反封建的示威游行，办报办刊，著书立说，有力推动了革命斗争的发展。

协大的第一份重要刊物是1925年10月由协大学生会创办的《闽潮》，办刊的目的在于"介绍新潮（思想），促省闽人猛进"，这表明协大学生正式加入全国革命报刊的行列，投身如火如荼的学生运动当中。该刊物通过邮政发行，在福州市内各校设有代销处和通讯员（吴国安、钟健英，1990），很快成为当时福州各大学校进步学生的阵地，并获不少外地进步学生的关注和投稿。《闽潮》自创办至次年停刊的这两年正是福州革命斗争迈向高潮的时期，该刊物所刊登的关于收回教育权、中国青年、教会学校、国际形势等问题的文章，分析鞭辟入里，回应了人们关注的重大问题，推动了反帝爱国运动的开展。

或许出于对冲破旧世界之革命浪潮的期待，1927年，协大学生会又创办了同样以"潮"为名的《协大新潮》。这份诞生于北伐胜利之后的刊物，怀抱在制度、政治和思想上顺应世界潮流的信念，刊登探讨社会主义、中日关系等话题的文章，同时还设有短评、社论、文艺、科学等栏目，密切关注和介入当时的社会发展，在福建文化发展史上占据重要的一席之地。

在前两份刊物的经验基础上，1931年，协大学生会创办了《协大学生》，刊登大批学术论文，推动抗日救亡运动。同年，协大教师成立"福建文化研究会"并创办了《福建文化》，旨在发扬民族精神，鞭策世人，造福民众。由于拥有一支高质量的创作队伍，该刊物很快崭露头角，成为全省最富盛名的学术期刊，在福建文化史研究领域影响深远。

协大在抗日战争爆发前创办的其他期刊还有：1921年左右创办的英文刊物《闽星》，1928年由协大校刊编辑部创办，主要报道校内新闻的《协大半月刊》（后更名为《协大消息》）；1929年10月协大学生会创办的综合性刊物《协大月刊》；1930年协大学生自治会创办的《协大季刊》；1930年6月创办的学术研究类刊物《协大学术》；1931年5月协大学生自治会创办的时政新闻类期刊《协大青年》；1933年协大国文系创办的学术类刊物《国学杂志》；1935年协大国文系创办、以文学作品和文学研究为主的《协大艺文》；1935年1月协大英语俱乐部创办的英文期刊《闽声》……（陈林：2006）

As a missionary school, FCU upheld the spirit of fraternity, sacrifice, and service, and strove to provide high-level university education for Chinese youth, to cultivate Christian talents and to spread the Gospel. But embedded in China, it was gradually but inevitably localized and secularized. Not only was secular knowledge taught, scientific researches were conducted, but the staff and students organized or participated in anti-imperialist and anti-feudal demonstrations. They vigorously promoted the development of Chinese revolution by running newspapers and journals, writing books and articles.

The first important journal to emerge out of FCU was *Currents in Fukien* by its Student Republic in October 1925. As the name suggests, this journal aimed to introduce new thoughts and provide impetus for social change. It marked the beginning of FCU's revolutionary journals as well as its participation in the raging national student movements. Distributed with postal service, it set up sales agencies and correspondents in almost all schools and colleges in Fuzhou. It soon attracted progressive students both in and outside Fujian, many of whom even became its regular contributors. Though lasting less than two years, it witnessed the climax of Fuzhou revolution, and provided a significant boost to the anti-imperialist movement. Major social concerns were addressed here, such as regaining education rights, Chinese youths, church schools and international situations.

Probably with the same hope of bringing in revolutionary tides to wash away the old world, FCU Student Republic started in 1927 another periodical *New Currents*. Coming out after the victory of the Northern Expedition, this journal embraced the ideal of merging with the world mainstream in terms of system, politics and values. Concerned about and intent on promoting social development, it carried articles on socialism and Sino-Japanese relations. It featured prominently in the history of Fujian cultural development with columns like short reviews, editorials, literature, art and science.

With experience of the two periodicals, FCU Students Republic started in 1931 *FCU Students*, a journal devoted to academic researches and movements against Japanese agression. In the same year, FCU faculty established Fujian Culture Research Center and *Fukien Culture*, a journal aiming to carry forward the national spirit, to spur and benefit the citizens. Thanks to its outstanding contributors, it soon rose to be the most prominent academic journal in Fujian and exerted far-reaching influence on the studies of cultural history of Fujian.

Other FCU journals before the War of Resistance Against Japanese Aggression included the English journal *Fukien Star* in around 1921, and *FCU Bimonthly* (later renamed *FCU News*) in 1928, comprehensive journal *FCU Monthly* started by the Student Union in October 1929, *FCU Students Quarterly* by the Student Republic in 1930 for school events, the academic journal *Hsieh Ta Hsio Shu* in June 1930, *FCU Youths* on current affairs by the Student Republic in May, 1931, the academic journal *Chinese Studies* by the Department of Chinese Literature in 1933, *FCU Arts and Literature* in January 1935 by the Department of Chinese Literature 1935 for literary works and literary theories, the English-language *The Fukien Voice* by its English Club ...

抗日战争爆发后，协大为避战乱于 1938 年 5 月迁往闽北山城邵武。虽然邵武的出版条件远远不如福州，但协大师生的热情和决心不减，在不到一个月的时间内就筹办出版了《协大周刊》。该刊主要介绍指导抗日战争的正确理论，揭露日寇罪恶，报告战区生活，后增设学术、时事、校闻、文学、科学等栏目。在近 8 年的办刊历程中，该刊始终紧扣全民抗日战争这一时代主题，积极探索抗日战争途径，同时积极参与当地经济文化建设，表现出协大师生与国家民族同呼吸共命运的决心。在创刊号"协大学生在邵武"一文中，协大学子陈长城（1938）呼吁同学们走出象牙塔，"跨过那重横在社会与学校间的高墙"，将所学理论付诸实践，积极投身闽北抗日救亡运动和社会建设。协大青年们意识到，日寇入侵使邵武等地民众陷于困惑无助，他们急需帮助，重建生活，协大对此责无旁贷。

针对当时中国最紧迫的乡村建设问题，协大急当地民众之所急，一方面进行农业试验（如水稻选种、鸡品种改良、土壤检测、害虫治理等），同时主动下乡提供服务（如开展健康运动、扫盲、开办成人和儿童学校、举办科学讲座等），并且组织合作银行和商店，帮助农民获得销售农产品所需资金。正是怀抱这样炽热的爱国爱民之心，该刊广受国内外协大校友和国内文化教育机构的欢迎，发行数持续增加直至上千。

协大在邵武创办的其他刊物包括 1938 年 1 月协大学生青年会创办的基督教刊物《协大青年》，1938 年 5 月"协大救亡剧团"创办，以"励我民众、宏我社会、大我国家"为目标的戏剧刊物《协大剧团舞台人》，1939 年 4 月协大数理学社创办的《数理》，1940 年 11 月创办、沟通校友的《协大校友》半月刊，以及《科学年刊》（英文版）《协大生物学报》《协大农报》《协大教育季刊》等高水平学术期刊。

抗日战争胜利后，协大于 1946 年迁回福州，办刊条件大为改善。同年 6 月创办了《协大校刊》，作为此前《协大周刊》延续，除继续报道校内活动外，也刊发讨论社会问题的文章。福州解放后，随着协和大学和华南女子学院合并入新成立的福州大学，协大的辉煌办刊历史也随之落下帷幕。

In May 1938, the threat of Japanese invasion compelled FCU to flee its Fuzhou campus and resettle in Shaowu, about 250 miles inland. The unfavorable publishing conditions, however, did not dent the enthusiasm and determination of the staff and students. Just a month later, they started *FCU Weekly*, which explored theories of the war, revealed the atrocities of the invaders, and reported on life in the war zone. The journal, in its 8-year history, had shown the determination of FCU faculty and students to share the nation's destiny by focusing on national resistance against Japanese agression, and by actively participating in the local economic and cultural construction. Just as Chen Changcheng announced in his essay "FCU Students in Shaowu" in the first issue, students should step out of the ivory tower, cross the high wall separating schools from society, put the theories learned into practice, and actively participate in the local anti-agression efforts and social construction. Chen was one of the many students who realized that the Japanese invasion had left people in Shaowu and other places confused and helpless, and that they needed help urgently to rebuild their lives. To this FCU was committed.

To help people in a targeted way, FCU conducted agricultural experiments (such as rice breeding, chicken breed improvement, soil testing, and pest control), provided door-to-door services in the countryside (such as rolling out health campaigns and literacy campaigns, setting up schools for adults and children, and giving science lectures), and secured for the farmers the funds needed to sell the produce by organizing cooperative banks and shops. It is precisely because of such ardent patriotism and love for the people that the journal was widely welcomed by its alumni and educational institutions, driving its circulation to over 1,000.

Other FCU publications produced in Shaowu included: the Christian journal *FCU Youth* started in January 1938 by its YMCA, the Drama Club's *Stage Man* to spur and strengthen the nation, *Mathematics and Physics* by the Mathematics & Physics Society in April 1939, *FCU Alumni*, a bimonthly in November 1940, as well as high-quality academic journals like the *Science Annual* in English, *Biological Bulletin of Fukien Christian University, Fukien Agricultural Journal, FCU Education Quarterly,* etc.

When FCU moved back to Fuzhou in 1946 after the victory of the War of Resistence Against Japanese Agression, publishing and printing were much easier. In June of the same year, *FCU Journal* was started as a continuation of the previous *FCU Weekly*. Apart from the usual campus news, it was also concerned about social issues. All FCU journals were halted when, after the liberation of Fuzhou, FCU and Hwa Nan College merged into Fuzhou University.

协大虽然只走过了短短的半个世纪，但却先后创办了近50种期刊，囊括了综合性刊物、学术类刊物、时事类刊物、校友通讯类刊物、宗教类刊物等诸多类型，包括了周刊、半月刊、月刊、季刊、年刊等各种形式，主办方既有学校、系，也有学生团体，绝大部分采用中文（多附有英文目录），但也不乏中英文并用和专门使用英文的期刊。除了精彩纷呈的各类期刊，协大还出版了约50本图书（陈林，2006），包括学术专著、调查报告、教材教参、字典、学校章程等，其中学术专著占六成以上，涉及生物、历史、文学、农业、经济、哲学、教育等诸多领域，反映了协大的学术水平。

协大之所以能够取得如此辉煌的出版成就，首先得益于其雄厚的资金保障。协大创办之初曾获美国基金会的支持和福建省国民政府的拨款，得以聘请大批优秀人才，他们在研究和教学之余亦可在出版方面有所突破。其次，协大对非宗教的刊物和书籍给予了宽容与支持。作为一个教会学校，协大没有强制学生学习宗教神学思想，也没有禁止世俗知识传播。许多教师虽具有教会背景，但仍心系国家民族之命运，独立追求知识和真理。例如代表当时国内生物学研究最高水平、著述等身的郑作新教授，深感原版美国生物教材的局限性，于是亲自编写适合中国国情的新教材。他仅用一年就完成了《大学生物学实验教程》的编写。该书1933年由上海商务印书馆出版，是第一部中国人自己编写的大学生物教材（谢必震，2004：50）。

协大对出版活动的支持还体现在机构设置和交流体制上。协大在1944年成立了自己的印刷所，并委派熟悉印刷事务的弼敏霖教授主理，印刷所拥有各类印刷、装订设备和独立的印刷场所，大大改进了当时的办刊条件。协大的教务处下设管理学校出版事务的"出版课"，在教授会下设处理学术专著出版的"出版委员会"，在校园设有出售书籍和文化用品的"协大书店"（后改为协大书局）（陈林，2006）。协大出版的不少期刊都通过交换和捐赠的方式传播到国外，目前在美国哈佛、耶鲁等大学档案馆中仍存有当年交换的协大出版物。协大以其出版物数量之巨、种类之多、影响之广，在福建教育史和出版史上写下了气势恢宏的篇章。

In its short history of less than five decades, FCU created about 50 journals in dazzling variety. In terms of contents, they could be categorized as comprehensive, academic, religious journals as well as current affairs journals, alumni newsletters, etc. In terms of publication cycle, there were weekly, semi-monthly, monthly, quarterly, annual or irregular ones. They were started by FCU, its departments or student groups, and the language used was Chinese (usu. with English content pages), English, or both. Besides, FCU had also published about 50 books, including monographs, research reports, textbooks and reference books, dictionaries, FCU Constitution, etc. Among them, the monographs, as an index of academic achievement, accounted for more than 60% of the total, covering biology, history, literature, agriculture, economics, philosophy, education, etc.

FCU's achievements in publishing was first attributed to generous funds. With grants from the Board of Directors of the Rockefeller Foundation and the Fujian Provincial Government, FCU was able to secure scholars capable of producing written works in addition to research and teaching. Secondly, FCU was supportive of non-religious publications. Though a missionary school, it imposed no theological thoughts, nor did it prohibit the dissemination of secular knowledge. Many Christian staff members were deeply concerned about the country's destiny and pursued knowledge and truth courageously. Prof. Zheng Zuoxin, a top biologist of his time, for example, was pained to see the limitations of American biology textbooks and in just one year completed *Biology Experiment for College Students* (published in 1933 by the Commercial Press in Shanghai). It was the first college biology textbook produced by Chinese scholars.

The booming of FCU's publications was also due to its support system. It set up its own print shop in 1944, and put Prof. Bi Minlin, who was familiar with printing and publishing, in charge. Within the Office of Academic Affairs there was a Publishing Section. In the same vein, there was a Publishing Committee within the Faculty Board handling the publication of monographs. Publications were always available in FCU Bookstore (later renamed as FCU Bookroom) that sold stationery as well. Last but not least, many FCU journals were mailed abroad by way of exchange and donation, some still archived in Harvard, Yale and other universities. The number, variety and influence of its publications earned FCU a prominent position in Fujian's history of education and publishing.

新中国成立后，国内形势逐渐稳定和全面好转，大学师生无须再将抵御外敌入侵或解决国计民生当作头等大事，而是能将更多精力投入教学与学术研究中。与此同时，我国出版业也逐渐走上由政府主导和管理的规范化发展道路。因此，大学出版更多地集中在学术期刊和著作上。承继协大优秀传统的福建师范大学，于1956年创办的《福建师范学院学报》（后更名为《福建师范大学学报》），入选"全国中文核心期刊""RCCSE中国核心学术期刊""中文社会科学引文索引来源期刊（CSSCI）""中国科学引文数据库（CSCD）来源期刊""中国人文社会科学核心期刊"等。同样由协大发展而来的福建农林大学，于1953年创办的《福建农林大学学报（自然科学版）》入选"中国自然科学核心期刊"，于1998年创办的《福建农林大学学报（哲学社会科学版）》入选"RCCSE中国核心学术期刊"。协大的优秀出版传统，正以新的方式延续和发展。

● 倪柝声：著述等身、名扬四海的基督教神学家

1903年出生的倪柝声，自幼在私塾接受传统的中国文化教育，诗词歌赋、四书五经无所不通，打下了深厚的中国传统文化基础。1916年，他进入英国圣公会办的三一书院接受西式教育，熟练掌握了英文和希腊文，为后来广泛阅读西方宗教原著、在欧美各国用流利英文讲道以及用英文写作与翻译奠定了基础。

1922年暑假期间，倪柝声和另一位教徒王载决定效仿《使徒行传》中初期教会的做法，在仓山毓英女校的王载住所举行擘饼聚会。虽仅王载夫妇和倪柝声三人参加，却标志着中国基督教本土教会的萌芽。随着参加人数的增加，中国第一个脱离宗派公会的地方教会——"基督徒聚会处"成立了。聚会处日常活动场所选择在离三一书院和毓英女校仅百米之遥的陶园十二间排，参加者以青年为主，他们身穿写有福音标语的背心，拿着福音旗子，摇铃唱诗，游行各处，一时轰动全城。

和当时国内其他的复兴布道家不同，倪柝声尤为重视文字布道的力量，他先后分别在福州仓山和马尾创办了《复兴》和《基督徒》这两大宗教报刊。前者创办于1923年1月，主要刊载倪柝声研究英国属灵作家和阅读《圣经》的心得，大多讨论较为深奥的神学问题，而"各种的问题、普通的教训、经文的意义"都不在这份报纸的讨论范围之内（倪柝声，1993：7）。第一期发行1 400份，很快售罄。1928年，移沪出版后每期印刷2 000份也仍供不应求，短短两年内寄出近三万份（倪柝声，1993：53），送出的福音单张数十万份。倪柝声的新神学思想在当时中国教徒中的影响可见一斑。

The founding of the P. R. C. in 1949 was a watershed in China's publishing industry. With things gradually stabilized and improved, fending off foreign invasion and meeting basic needs of survival were no longer the top priority for university faculty and students. They could now channel more energy to teaching and academic research. In the meanwhile, the publishing industry started to be standardized and regulated by the government. Universities accordingly narrowed their publications to academic journals and monographs. FCU was no exception. One of its successors, Fujian Normal University, started in 1956 *Journal of Fujian Normal College* (later renamed *Journal of Fujian Normal University*); another inheritor, Fujian Agriculture and Forestry University, started in 1953 *Journal of Fujian Agriculture and Forestry University*. These journals were highly credited within Chinese academia. FCU's fine tradition has remained and is still developing vigorously in new ways.

• Watchman Nee: A Prolific and Renowned Christian Theologian

Watchman Nee spent his early years receiving traditional Chinese education in a private school, where he was taught Confucian classical works and well-versed in Chinese poetry. In 1916, he attended the Anglican Trinity College in Fuzhou, where he learnt both English and Greek. These two languages prepared him in his later years to read theological works extensively, to preach in fluent English when touring European countries and the US, as well as to write and translate in English.

During the summer vacation of 1922, Watchman Nee and Leland Wang (or Wang Zai), another Christian, decided to follow the practice of the early church described in *Acts* and held Holy Communion with the Wangs at their residence near Uk Ing Girls' School in Cangshan. It marked the budding of the indigenous mission movement in China. When the number of participants increased, they established "the Little Flock", the first independent Chinese local church. The venue for its daily activities was Taoyuan Row House, only a stone's throw from both Trinity College and Uk Ing Girls' School. The participants, mainly young people clad in vests painted with gospel slogans, held flags, rang the bells and chanted chorus as they paraded through the streets, causing a sensation in the whole city.

Unlike other revivalists in China at that time, Nee attached great importance to the power of language and publication. Two of his major Christian magazines were *The Present Testimony* and *The Christian*, started in Cangshan and Mawei respectively. The former, set up in January 1923, was about Nee's studies of *The Bible* and British spiritual works. It was mostly concerned with abstruse theological issues, ignoring ordinary teachings, the interpretation of the Scriptures and other common topics. For the first issue, a dazzling total of 1,400 copies were distributed. Yet it still fell short of the demand, even with a circulation of 2,000 copies per issue when it was relocated to Shanghai in 1928. In just two years, nearly 30,000 copies and hundreds of thousands of Gospel brochures were mailed. Nee was undoubtedly a great influence for Chinese believers then.

1924 年夏，倪柝声从三一书院毕业，他拒绝遵从父亲的安排前往美国留学，选择来到水运交通发达、邮件往来方便的福州马尾，设立"福音书局"，继续发行《复兴》报，并新创《基督徒》。《基督徒》报所刊载的文章不似《复兴》报般深奥，更易为一般读者所接受。和《复兴》报一样，《基督徒》报面对的读者多是具有较高文化水平和一定基督教神学造诣的教徒，是各教会的精英，具有较强社会影响力。

随着活动的开展，倪柝声参与创办的地方教会很快遍及全中国，并进一步传播到马来西亚、印度尼西亚、新加坡等地。在这一过程中，办报著书发挥了重要作用。继《复兴》报和《基督徒》报之后，倪柝声又创办了近十种宗教报刊，通过邮局送达全国乃至海外的读者手中。由于订阅价格大多远低于成本，不少甚至免费赠送，因此不少刊物供不应求。在这些密集出版、读者遍及全国甚至海外的刊物中，倪柝声重塑了华人基督徒的思想观点，逐渐形成了具有中国本土特色的基督教思想体系。

除讲道、带领聚会、训练同工外，倪柝声将毕生心血都倾注于著书办报之中。在他看来，送好书能"叫人接受主""帮助人明白真理""离弃异端"（倪柝声，1993：179）。他所著的不少书对信徒来说正是具有这样的力量。他被称为中国最具影响力的基督教作者之一，全球许多基督教出版机构（如中国台湾福音书房、美国加州的水流职事站、美国纽约的基督教团契出版社、中国香港教会书室）至今仍大量再版他的著作（其中三卷本《属灵人》和《正常的基督徒生活》销量均超百万册），为全世界数以百万计的教徒提供源源不断的宗教指导。

表 10-2　倪柝声在华创办刊物一览表

序号	刊名	创办时间	创办地点	出刊总数
1	《复兴》	1923 年 1 月	福州仓山	36 期
2	《基督徒》	1925 年	福州马尾	41 期
3	《讲经记录》	1930 年 4 月	上海	50 期
4	《通问汇刊》	1933 年 11 月	上海	12 期
5	《佳音》	1934 年 7 月	上海	3 期
6	《敞开的门》	1937 年 9 月	汉口	24 期
7	《信徒消息》	不详	上海	8 期
8	《执事》	1948 年 7 月	上海	4 期
9	《见证》	1948 年	上海	不详
10	《道路》	1948 年	上海	不详
11	《福音》	1948 年	上海	不详

Upon graduation from Trinity College in the summer of 1924, Nee decided not to attend an American university as hoped by his father, but to come to Mawei, Fuzhou, where water transportation and mail service were convenient. Here he founded a publishing house called Gospel Bookroom, where he continued to publish *The Present Testimony* and the newly-started *The Christian*. Both journals targeted at the well-educated Christians, who were also the church elites with considerable social influence. But compared with *The Present Testimony*, *The Christian* was not as abstruse, hence more accessible to ordinary readers.

As Nee's work unfolded and evolved, the local churches he helped to found quickly spread all over China, to Malaysia, Indonesia, Singapore and many other countries. This was made possible by his running journals and writing books: He started over 10 Christian periodicals which were distributed across the country and even overseas. They, to a large extent, reshaped the views of Chinese Christians and brought into being a Christian theology with Chinese characteristics. Since most of them were priced much lower than the actual cost (many were even free), the demand often far outstripped supply.

For Nee, writing books and running journals were no less important than preaching, holding meetings and training co-workers. He believed giving out good books could bring people to Christ, accept the Truth, and reject heresy. Such a magical power was manifested in Nee's own works — regarded as one of the most influential Christian authors in China, his works are now still republished in large numbers by Christian publishing houses around the world (including Taiwan Gospel Book Room, Living Stream Ministry in California, Christian Fellowship Publishers, Inc. New York and Hong Kong Church Book Room). Over 1 million copies of both the 3-volume *The Spiritual Man* and *The Normal Christian Church Life* have been sold. Nee's legacy has continued to provide guidance to millions of his believers around the world.

Table 10 - 2　Journals started by Watchman Nee in China

N	Names	Time	Place of establishment	Number of issues
1	*The Present Testimony*	Jan. 1923	Cangshan, Fuzhou	36
2	*The Christian*	1925	Mawei, Fuzhou	41
3	*Notes of Scriptural Messages*	Apr. 1930	Shanghai	50
4	*Questions and Answers on the Gospel*	Nov. 1933	Shanghai	12
5	*The Good News*	July, 1934	Shanghai	3
6	*The Open Door*	Sept. 1937	Hankou	24
7	*Disciples' News*	unknown	Shanghai	8
8	*The Ministers*	July, 1948	Shanghai	4
9	*The Testimonies*	1948	Shanghai	unknown
10	*The Path*	1948	Shanghai	unknown
11	*The Gospel*	1948	Shanghai	unknown

● 结语

　　仓山近现代出版业的兴盛虽缘起于西方传教士印刷出版宗教书报的需求，但其实际影响却大大超过了传教本身，它深刻地改变了福州甚至中国的社会历史面貌：识字群体的扩大，西方科学与技术的引入，革命思想的传播，无不受益于出版业的发展。书籍报刊构筑了近代中国独一无二的"想象的共同体"（Anderson，1983），其历史意义有待学界进一步挖掘。

　　新中国成立后不久，我国成立了出版事业的领导机构——中央人民政府出版总署，加强对全国出版业的统一领导与集中管理。1956年，随着私营出版业的社会主义改造基本完成，国有经济成为我国出版体系的主导力量。出版业采取集中统一的管理模式，书刊印刷和流通环节均主要由国有企业负责，这标志着我国出版业近代以来公私合营、私营为主局面的结束，新的出版业制度开始建立。在这一新历史背景下，私营出版机构的生存发展空间受到明显压缩，原先位于仓山的各私营出版机构多数收编国有或改行关闭，逐步退出历史舞台。同时受城市布局规划的影响，鼓楼区成为福州城市发展的核心区，聚集了政治、经济、文化、教育、金融、体育、医疗等多个行业领域的资源，这里也自然成为新中国成立后福建发展出版业的首选。

• Concluding Remarks

Cangshan's modern publishing industry thrived in response to missionary needs for religious publications, but it also profoundly changed the social and historical landscape of Fuzhou and even China: It expanded the literate community, introduced Western science and technology into China, and disseminated revolutionary thoughts. Books and periodicals constructed a unique "imagined community" in modern China, and their historical significance remains to be further explored.

The founding of the People's Republic of China in 1949 marked a turning point for Cangshan's publishing industry. A regulating body—the Central Government's General Administration of Publishing—was set up to manage national publishing industry. In 1956, when the socialist transformation of the private sectors in publishing industry was completed, the state-owned enterprises assumed the leading role. The publishing industry started to be highly centralized, with publishing and distribution of all books and periodicals reserved for state-owned publishing houses only. When coexistence of private and public sectors gave way to the new publishing system, those private publishing houses in Cangshan were either turned over to the state, or closed down for good. Urban planning is another contributing factor to the decline of Cangshan's publishing industry. Since 1949, Gulou District, where both the provincial and municipal governments were located, has become the city center with concentrated resources in politics, economy, finance, culture, education, sports and health-care. Thus, Gulou District became the first choice when Fujian publishing industry entered the new era.

专名术语英汉对照表

68 Playground 六八运动场

A-hok Hall 鹤龄楼

A Hundred Years of China Methodism 《美以美百年中国布道史》

Alumni Clock Tower 校友钟楼

Alumni Science Hall 校友楼

Ambition Pavilion 立志亭

American Board of Commissioners for Foreign Missions（ABCFM） 美国公理宗海外传道部，简称美部会

American Methodist Episcopal Church（AMEC） 美国美以美教会（常称为美以美教会，也有人简称为美以美会）

American Methodist Episcopal Mission（MEM） 美国美以美差会（俗称美以美会）

American Mission Cemetery 美国传教公墓

American Reformed Church Mission（ARCM） 美国归正教会

American World Exposition 美国万国博览会

Amoy Anglo-Chinese College 厦门英华书院

An English-Chinese Dictionary of the Foochow Dialect 《福州方言英汉词典》

An Epic of the East 《东方史诗》

Anglo-Chinese Building 英华楼

Anglo-Chinese College 鹤龄英华中学/鹤龄英华书院/英华书院/英华学院

Anglo-Chinese High School 英华中学/鹤龄英华中学/鹤龄英华中学校

Anti-Aircraft Artillery College（nowadays The Airborne Troops College of Air Force）高射炮兵学校

Anti-Christian Movement 非基督教运动

Apollo Moon-landing Program 阿波罗登月计划

Baldwin School of Theology 保灵福音书院

Baldwin-Wallace College，Ohio 俄亥俄州鲍德温（又译宝灵）华莱士学院

Baltimore Female Academy 巴尔的摩女子中学

Banyan City Institute 榕城格致书院

Barbour Scholarship of the University of Michigan 密歇根大学巴伯学者奖

Beulah Woolston 娲标礼

Bing Tang，Fukien 福建平潭

Birdwood van Someren Taylor 雷腾

Bishop Beverly Waugh 贝弗利·沃主教

Bishop Edward Thompson 爱德华·汤姆森主教

Bishop John Hind 恒约翰主教

Bishop J. W. Bashford 柏锡福会督

Bishop Kingsley 金斯理会督

Board of Education of the Methodist Episcopal Church 美以美教育部

Board of Trustees 董事会

Boise Hall 保志楼

Boy Scouts Organization 童子军组织

Brand & Co., H. S. 兴豫洋行

Bridge of Ten Thousand Ages 万寿桥

British Medical Journal 《英国医学报刊》

C. A. Neff 倪乐善

Cangqian Mountain 仓前山

Cangshan District 仓山区/仓山

Cantonese 粤语

Capital Normal University 首都师范大学

Carrie Jewell 凯莉·朱维尔（朱师姑）

C. C. Baldwin 摩怜

Ceng Daik (Girls' School) 进德女校

Cha-Chang Christ's Hospital 柴井基督医院（简称柴井医院）

Charlie Trimble 程查理

Cheeloo College of Medicine, Shandong University 山东大学齐鲁医学院

Cheeloo University in Shandong 山东齐鲁大学

Chemical Society of British Royal Society 英国皇家学会化工学会

Chen Ancestral Hall 陈氏祠堂

Chen's Theorem 陈氏定理

China Export Import & Bank Co., Ltd. 谦信洋行

Chinese Christian Advocate 《华美报》

Chinese education section 中教科

Chinese Medical Association 中国博医会

Chinese Medical Journal 《中华医学杂志》

Chinese Nurses Association 中华护士会

Chinese Nursing Association (CNA) 中华护理学会

Chinese Nursing Federation 中国看护组织联合会

Chinese Postal Service 中华邮政局

Ching Sing Dong (Church of the True God) 真神堂

Christ Cathedral 苍霞基督堂

Church of Christ in China, Mid-Fuchien Synod 中华基督教会闽中协会

Chu Xue Jie Ti （*The Premier of Christianity*） 《初学阶梯》

City Work Department　城工部

Cleveland Hall　克廉楼

Cliff Stone Carvings　摩崖石刻

C. M. Lacey Sites　薛来西

Collection of Hong Ye's Theories　《洪业论学集》

College of Foreign Languages，FJNU　福建师大外国语学院

Commission of Science，Technology and Industry for National Defence of the People's Republic of China　国家国防科工委

Committee of Regaining Education Rights Movement　收回教育权运动委员会

Communist Party of China（CPC）中国共产党

Communist Youth League of China（CYLC）中国共产主义青年团

Compilation of Cultural and Historical Data on Fujian　《福建文史资料选编》

Comprehensive Interpretation on the Body　《全体阐微》

Concord University College，Fujian Normal University　福建师范大学协和学院

Cora Simpson（C. E. Simpson）信宝珠

Cornell College，Iowa　爱荷华州康内（奈）尔学院

Cranson Hall　谷莲楼（民主楼）

C. R. Kellogg　克立鹄

Dahu Campaign in the War of Resistance Against Japanese Agression in 1941　1941 年抗日"大湖之战"

Dang Hie Pek　郑惠碧

day school　日学

D. B. McCartee　麦嘉谛

Deacons' Home in Kuliang（Guling Mountain）鼓岭执事之家

Ding Buoi Daik　陈佩德

Diongloh　长乐

Domestic Science Building　家政楼

Dongsheng Printing Plant　东升印刷厂

Do-seuk Girls' School　陶淑女子学校/陶淑女中

Dr. Charles Garnet Trimble　程嘉尼医生

Dr. Dauphin William Osgood　多芬·威廉·奥斯古德（医生，博士）

Dr. George B. Smyth　施美志博士

Dr. Ida Belle Lewis　卢爱德博士

Dr. James L. Ding　陈芝美博士

Dr. James Simester　沈雅各博士

Dr. John Gowdy　高智博士

Dr. Laura G Dyer（Dai Yuzhao）戴毓昭博士

Dr. Lyon　莱昂医生

Dr. Sigourney Trask　西格尼·特拉斯克（医学博士）

Dr. Thomas H. Coole　邱永康博士

Dudley Memorial Church　救主堂

Durham High School　达拉姆中学

D. W. Chandler　曾大辟

E. A. Barron　留师姑

Eastern Extension Telegraph Company　向东电话公司

Edinburgh Conferene　爱丁堡传教士会议

Educational Records in Chronicles of Fujian Province　《福建省志·教育志》

Edwin C. Jones　庄才伟

Elizabeth Fisher (Mrs. E. M. Brewster)　伊丽莎白·费雪（婚后称蒲师母）

Elsie Mawfung Chung　钟茂芳

English Presbyterian Mission　英国长老会（简称 EPM）

Essays　《文萃》

Exhortation to Abandon Opium　《劝戒鸦片论》

Florence Nightingale Training School for Nurses and Midwives　佛罗伦斯·南丁格尔护士和助产
　士培训学校

Florence Nightingale　佛罗伦斯·南丁格尔

Foochow Boys' Boarding School　（福州）培元中学

Foochow Christian Union Hospital Senior Nursing Vocational School　福州基督教协和医院高级
　护士职业学校

Foochow Christian Union Hospital　福州基督教协和医院

Foochow College　格致中学/格致书院/福州书院

Foochow Custom House　福州海关

Foochow Girls' Boarding School　福州女子寄宿学校

Foochow Guild Hall　福州会馆

Foochow Massacre　台江事件

Foochow Methodist Episcopal Mission Press　福州美华书局

Foochow Missionary Hospital　圣教医院

Foochow Mission Cemetery　洋墓亭

Foochow Native Hospital and Dispensary　福州地方医馆及药房

Foochow Union Theological Seminary　福州协和道学院

Foochow Women's Biblical Institute　女子神学院

For Christ in Fuh-Kien　《英国布道会》

former site of MEC Conference　卫理公会旧址

Foundling Asylum　保生堂

Four Books　《四书》

Franklin Ohlinger　武林吉

fringe tree　流苏树

Fuhkien Church Advocate　《闽省会报》

Fujian Advanced Academy　福建高等学堂

Fujian Christian Council（Fujian C. C.）福建省基督教协会

Fujian College of Traditional Chinese Medicine　福建中医学院

Fujian Daily　《福建日报》

Fujian Health College　福建省卫生职业技术学院

Fujian Medical University Union Hospital　福建医科大学附属协和医院

Fujian Normal University（FNU）福建师范大学

Fujian Provincial Department of Culture and Education　福建省文教厅

Fujian Provincial Department of Education　国民政府福建省教育厅

Fujian Provincial People's Hospital　福建省立人民医院

Fujian Provincial Secondary School Survey Table　《福建省中等学校概况调查表》

Fujian Provincial Teachers School　福建省立师范学院

Fujian Teachers College　福建师范学院

Fujian Theological Seminary/Fukien Theological Seminar　福建神学院

Fujian Union Theological Seminary　福建协和神学院

Fukien Academy　福建省研究院

Fukien Christian University（FCU）福建协和大学

Fukien Construction Bureau（FCB）福建建设局

Fukien Methodist Theological Seminary　福建美以美会道学院

Fukien Union Theological Seminary　福建协和道学院

Fu Pao（*Fortune Newspaper*）《福报》

Futsing　福清

Fuzhou Cangshan Primary School　福州仓山小学

Fuzhou Cholera Hospital　时疫医院

Fuzhou Communist Party History Newsletter　《福州党史通讯》

Fuzhou Evening News　《福州晚报》

Fuzhou Foreign Languages School（FFLS）福州外国语学校

Fuzhou Instrumentation Manufacturer　福州仪器仪表成套设备厂

Fuzhou Joint Hospital of Cholera　福州合组时疫医院

Fuzhou Maiyuan Primary School　福州麦园小学

Fuzhou Medical Doctor Union　福州市医师公会

Fuzhou No. 16 Junior High School　福州第十六中学

Fuzhou No. 27 Middle School　福州第二十七中学

Fuzhou No. 9 Middle School　福州第九中学

Fuzhou No. 2 Girls' Middle School　福州第二女子中学

Fuzhou No. 2 Middle School　福州第二中学

Fuzhou Private Post and Telecommunications School　福州私立邮电学校

Fuzhou Second Hospital　福州市第二医院

Fuzhou Takding Private Advanced Vocational Nursing School　福州私立塔亭高级护士职业学校

Fuzhou Tourism Vocational School　福州旅游职业学校

Fuzhou Union Hospital of China　福州中国协和医院

Fuzhou University　福州大学

Fuzhou Workers Hospital　福州市工人医院

Fuzhou Yingcai Middle School　福州英才中学

G. M. Newell　饶卫礼

Goldbach Conjecture　哥德巴赫猜想

Gordon Trimble　程高登

Gospel Bookroom　（马尾）福音书局

Goucher College　古彻学院

G. Siemssen　G. 禅臣

Guang-ing-cang　观音井

Guangxue Academy　广学书院

Guangzhou Theological School　广州神科学校

Gulou District　鼓楼区/鼓楼

Gutien　古田

Hakka　客家话

Harold N. Brewster　蒲天寿

Harrison Park，Dublin　都柏林李逊公园

Harvard-Yenching Institute　哈佛燕京学社

Hü Bo-mi　许播美

Heber　赫伯尔号邮轮

Helen W. Osgood　海伦·W·奥斯古德

Henry V. Lacy　亨利·维·勒希

Heroes Wall　英雄墙

historical materialism　历史唯物主义

Historical Records of Foochow Methodist Annual Conference　《福州美以美年会史》

Hü King-eng　许金訇

H. Krüger　居茄

Hokkien　闽南语

Hong Kong & Shanghai Banking Corporation（HSBC），Foochow Branch　汇丰银行福州支行

Hong William　洪煨莲/洪业

Horace MacCartie Eyre Price　贝嘉德

Hou Process　侯氏制碱法

H. Philips　菲利普斯

Hü Seuk Eng　许淑旬

Hü Sing-mi　许承美

Huang Jiasi　黄家驷

Lucy Wang　王世静

Lugou Bridge Incident　卢沟桥事变

Lu Hall　卢宿室

Lungtien, Fukien　福建福清龙田（亦称垄田）

Lydia A. Trimble　程吕底亚

Lyman B. Peet and Rebecca C. Peet　弼利民（也译作弼履仁或弼来满）夫妇

M. A. F. C. Harighorse　夏平和

Magaw Memorial Hospital（also known as Liang Au Woman's Hospital, Foochow Woman's Hospital）马高爱医院/岭后妇孺医院/岭后妇幼医院

Maiding Primary School　麦顶小学

Maiyuan Road　麦园路

Malian Payne Hall　彭氏楼（又称马莲彭楼、胜利楼）

Martha R. Barr　巴师姑

Mary E. Carleton　兰玛利亚

Mary Sing-Gieu Carleton　兰醒球

May Fourth Movement　五四运动

May Fourth Teaching Building　五四教学楼

Medical Labor Union of Fuzhou City　福州市医务工会

Mencius　《孟子》

Methodist Church of China　中华卫理公会

Methodist United Middle School　卫理联中

Ministry of Education of the Nationalist Government　国民政府教育部

Mintsing County　闽清县

Miss Edith W. Simester　沈师姑

Miss Gu　顾师姑

missionary David Abeel　传教士雅裨理

missionary schools　教会学校

Miss Jacobs　杰克女士

Missouri Wesleyan College　密苏里州卫斯理安学院

Miss Seeley　西利小姐

Miss Worley　华师姑

Morningside College, Iowa　爱荷华州晨边学院

Movement of Regaining the Education Rights　收回教育权运动

Mr. and Mrs. M. C. White　怀德夫妇

Mr. and Mrs. Wylie　怀礼夫妇

Mr. Colin Pears　悉尼大学李科林教授

Mr. Donald E. MacInnis　穆蔼仁先生

Mr. John A. Pilley　毕理先生

Mr. John Hegarty, the then provost of TCD　都柏林三一学校原校长海格蒂先生

Mr. John Leighton Stuart　司徒雷登先生

Mrs. Maclay　麦利和夫人

Mrs. Murvel C. Pilley　毕理夫人

Mrs. Nathan Plumb　李承恩夫人

Mrs. Nathan Sites　薛承恩夫人

Mr. Sydney Arthur Davidson Jr.　德辟孙先生

Mt. Union College, Ohio　俄亥俄州高山协会（又译州联合）学院

Nanchang Uprising　南昌起义

Nanjing Union Theological Seminary　金陵神学院

Nanping San Qian Ba Bai Kan（3,800 steps Ridge Road）南平三千八百坎闽赣古道

Nantai　南台

National Administration of Traditional Chinese Medicine（NATCM）国家中医药管理局

National Founders　《开国将士》

Nebraska Methodist Medical College　内布拉斯加卫理公会医学院

Neixue（Boarding School, or higher-level primary school）内学（圣教高等小学校）

New Observation　《新观察》

Ngu Cie Lang　吴芝兰

Nind-Lacy Memorial Chapel　力礼堂

Ni Weng-Sioe　倪文修

N. J. Plumb　李承恩

No. 52 Building Complex on the Maiyuan Road　麦园路 52 号大院

North Fukien Religious Tract Society　闽北圣书会

Number Theory　数论

Nursing Federation of Central China　中国中部看护联合会

Nursing School Affiliated to Fuzhou Magaw Memorial Hospital　福州马高爱医院附设看护学校

Nursing School at Hodge Memorial Hospital in Hankou　汉口普爱医院护士学校

N ü Xue San Zi Jing（*Girls' Three Character Classic*）《女学三字经》

Ode to the Chinese　《中华颂》

Office Director of the New Fourth Army in Fuzhou　新四军驻榕办事处主任

On Battle of the Liberated Areas　《论解放区战场》

On New Democracy　《新民主主义论》

On Protracted War　《论持久战》

On the United Government　《论联合政府》

Opening Monument　开启碑

Orchid Garden　兰花圃

Otis Gibson　基顺

Paul Prince Wiant　范哲明

Peking Union Medical College　北京协和医学院

People's War of Resistance　《全民抗日战争》

Phebe Potter　宝姑娘

pneumonic plague　肺鼠疫

Pogada Anchorage　罗星塔

Pok Oi Hospital　博爱医院

Ponasang Girls' School（Ponashan College）保福山学院

Ponasang Hospital　保福山医院

Popular Philosophy　《大众哲学》

president　主理

Private Foochow Christian Union Hospital Senior Nursing Vocational School　私立福州基督教协
　和医院高级护士职业学校

Private Fujian College　私立福建学院

private schools（charging no tuition）义塾

Private Tongren School　私立桐仁学校

Protestantism　新教

P. Walsham　乐善

Qiaonan Public Welfare Society　桥南公益社

Qigong Temple　戚公庙

Qilu Medical College　齐鲁医学院

R. B. Jackson　若逊

R. D. Jackson　札成

Records of Fuzhou Local Organisation of Community Party of China　《中国共产党福州地方组
　织志》

Red Star Over China　《西行漫记》

resident bishop of the Methodist Episcopal Church　美以美会会督

Rev. & Mrs. James Colder　传教士高礼夫妇

Rev. Erastus Wentworth　万为牧师

Rev. Justus Doolittle　卢公明牧师

Rev. Nathan Sites　薛承恩牧师

Rev. William A. Main　萌为廉牧师

Rev. W. P. W. Williams　来必翰牧师

Robert A. Trimble　程闽岱

Robert Samuel Maclay　麦利和

Robert Warren Stewart　史荦伯

Rongnan Primary School　榕南两等小学

R. S. Maclay　麦利和

Runde Building　润德楼

Russell & Co.　旗昌洋行

Russian Consulate　俄国领事馆

Ryukyu Kingdom　琉球王国

Sallie H. Woolston　娲西利

School of Medicine of West China Union University in Chengdu　成都华西协和大学医学院

semi-feudal and semi-colonial society　半封建半殖民地社会

Shanghai Renji Hospital　上海仁济医院

Shanghai Tongren Hospital　上海同仁医院

Sharp Peak Island（Jianfeng Island）（闽江河口附近的）尖峰岛

Sheng Xue Wen Da（*Colloquial Catechism*）《圣学问答》

Sia Sek Ong　谢锡恩

Siemssen & Krohn　禅臣洋行

Simester Hall　沈宿室

Simmons College（Boston）（波斯顿）西蒙斯学院

Sing Ding Girls' School　寻珍女校/寻珍女中

Sino-French Majiang Sea Battle　中法马江海战

Sir Harry Parkes　夏巴礼

Sites Hall　薛宿室

S. L. Baldwin　保灵

Social Life of the Chinese　《中国人的社会生活》

Soda Manufacturing Industry　《制碱工业》

Solvay Alkali Proces　索尔维制碱法

Solvay Group　苏尔维集团

Soong sisters　宋氏三姐妹

Southwestern College，Kansas　堪萨斯州西南学院

Soviet Surgery Conference　全苏外科会议

State and Revolution　《国家与革命》

St. Bede's Catholic High School　圣贝德斯中学

Stephen Johnson　杨顺

St. John's Church　圣约翰堂

St. John's University　圣约翰大学

St. Luke's Hospital in Xinghua，Putian　莆田兴化圣路加圣教医院

St. Mark's College　圣马可书院

Strategies of the Warring States　《战国策》

Student Work Commission of Minjiang Working Committee　闽江工委学委

Sun Yat-sen　孙中山

Suzanne Wilson Barnett　白淑珍

Swiss International Commodities Fair　瑞士国际商品展览会

Symth Hall　施教室

Taiguping　太古坪

Tai Maiu & Co.　太茂茶行

Tai Maiu（Girls' School）太茂女斋

Takding (or Tahding) Hospital　塔亭医院

Takding (or Tahding) Nursing School　塔亭护士学校

Ta Kung Pao　《大公报》

Talmage College　打马字学院（也称为寻源书院）

Taoist school　道学校

Taoyuan Community　陶园

Taoyuan Row House　陶园十二间排

TCF Chapel　三一礼拜堂

Ten Commandments　《十诫》

Tengshan Annals　《藤山志》

the 10,000 Ages Bridge (now the Jiefang Bridge)　解放大桥

the Affiliated High School of Fujian Normal University　福建师范大学附属中学

the Affiliated Middle School of Fujian Teachers' College　福建师范学院附属中学

the Affiliated Middle School of Fuzhou University　福州大学附属中学

The Analects of Confucius　《论语》

the Anglican Church　圣公会

the Anglican-Episcopal Church in China　中华圣公会

the Bank of Taiwan Ltd.　台湾银行

The Book of Songs　《诗经》

the Boys' Academy　美会学塾

the British Chamber of Commerce in Shanghai　上海英国商会

the Chartered Mercantile Bank　有利洋行

the China Missionary Society of Baltimore　巴尔的摩中国布道会

The Chinese Revolution and the Chinese Communist Party　《中国革命和中国共产党》

the Christian Assembly　基督徒聚会处

The Chronicle of Zuo　《左传》

the Church Mission Society (CMS)　英国圣公会差会（简称英国圣公会）/安立甘会

the Church of England Zenana Missionary Society (CEZMS)　英国圣公会女差会

the collegiate department　书院班

the Commission of Inquiry of Minjiang Working Committee　闽江工委调委

The Communist Manifesto　《共产党宣言》

The Constitution of Anglo-Chinese College　《鹤龄英华书院章程》

The Doctrine of the Mean　《中庸》

the Dublin Mission　都柏林布道会

the Eight-year-and-four-month System　"八年四"学制

the Event of "Wall of Democracy"　"民主墙"事件

the Foochow College Preparatory of Foochow Woman's College　福州女子大学预科班

the Foreign Community/European Community of Foochow　福州西侨团体

the former German Consulate in Fuzhou　前德国驻福州领事馆

the former Provincial Federation of Trade Unions　原省总工会

the Gospel House　福音精舍

The Great Learning　《大学》

the International Academic Olympiad　国际奥林匹克学科竞赛

The Mencius　《孟子》

the Methodist Church　美国基督教卫理公会

the Methodist Episcopal Conference（The MEC）美以美年会

the Methodist Publishing House in Shanghai　上海华美书馆

the Middle School of Workers and Peasants　工农速成中学

the Ministry of Education of the East China Military Commission　华东军委会教育部

the Minjiang River　闽江

The Missionary Recorder　《教务杂志》

the National Tsing Hua University　国立清华大学

the New Culture Movement　新文化运动

the Northern Expedition　北伐战争

Theological College　真学书院

Theological School　真学堂

The Opium War　鸦片战争

the People's Liberation War　人民解放战争

the Political Department of the Provincial Revolutionary Committee　省革委会政治部

the preparatory department　侯进班

the Private Anglo-Chinese High School　私立英华中学

the Prix Stanislas Julien　茹理安（儒莲）奖金

the Publicity and Education Group of the Municipal Revolutionary Committee　市革委会宣教组

the Quest Monument　求索碑

the Republic of China　中华民国

the Revolution of 1911　辛亥革命

the Sacred Hearts Academy of Hawaii　夏威夷圣心女中

the Seven Golden Candlesticks (also known as the Seven Golden Lampstands)　七金灯台

the Seventh-day Adventist Church　基督复临安息日会

the Society for Missions to Africa and the East　英国海外传道会

the Taiping Rebellion　太平天国起义

the Theological Academy　圣学书院

the Theological Seminary of the MEM　美以美会道学院

The Treaty of Nanking　《南京条约》

The Trilogy of the Exiles　《流亡三部曲》

the True Jesuit Church　真耶稣会

the United League of China (also known as Chinese Revolutionary Alliance)　中国同盟会

the University of Aberdeen, Scotland　阿伯丁大学

the War of Resistance Against Japanese Agression　抗日战争

the Xi'an Incident　西安事变

The Yellow River Cantata　《黄河大合唱》

the Young Men's Christian Association（YMCA）基督教男青年会

Thomas Rennie　连尼/任尼

Three Character Classic　《三字经》

Three Lanes and Seven Alleys　三坊七巷

Three Mountains（Yushan Mountain，Wushan Mountain，Pingshan Mountain　三山（于山、乌山、屏山）

Three Self Patriotic Movement，Fujian（or Fujian TSPM）福建省基督教三自爱国运动委员会

Tian'an Alley　天安里

Tianjin Yongli Soda Co.，Ltd.　天津永利制碱公司

Tien Ang Dong（Tian'an Church，or the Church of Heavenly Peace）天安堂

Tien Ju Middle School　天儒中学

Times Teaching Building　时代教学楼

Tiong A-hok　张鹤龄

Trimble Hall　立雪楼（程氏楼，和平楼）

Trinity College Dublin of Ireland（TCD）爱尔兰都柏林圣三一大学

Trinity College Foochow（TCF）三一中学/三一学校

Trinity Primary School affiliated to Private Fuzhou Trinity College　私立福州三一中学附属三一小学

Trinity-Taoshu Joint Middle School（San-Tao Lianzhong）三陶联中

T. Seth Lin　林缉西

Tu-Di-Miao Street　土地庙街

Uk Cing（Girls' School）毓真女校

Uk Ing（Girls' School）毓英女校

Union Architectural Service　协和建筑部

Union Medical College　协和医学院

Union Normal School　协和师范学校

Union Theological School　协和神学院

University of Puget Sound　美国普吉湾大学

Waixue（lower-level primary school）外学（初等小学校）

Watchman Nee　倪柝声

Waugh Female Seminary　沃女子学校

Wenru Lane　文儒坊

Wesleyan Female College　卫斯理安女子学院

Wesleyan University　卫斯理安大学

West Virginia Wesleyan College　西弗吉尼亚州韦（卫）斯里安学院

White Tower　白塔

参考文献

- 第一章

［1］ 百年塔亭［Z］. 福州市第二医院 150 周年院庆册，2016. 未出版.

［2］ 仓山区志编写组. 仓山区志［M］. 福州：福建教育出版社，1994.

［3］ 陈平原，夏晓红. 点石斋画报图像晚清［M］. 上海：东方出版社，2014.

［4］ 点石斋画报［M］. 广州：广东人民出版社，1983.

［5］ 何小莲. 西医东渐与文化调试［M］. 上海：上海古籍出版社，2006.

［6］ 李文巍. 晚清闽海关医员研究［D］. 福州：福建师范大学，2014.

［7］ 廖乐柏. 中国通商口岸［M］. 上海：东方出版社，2010.

［8］ 林恩燕. 行走烟台山［M］. 福州：鹭江出版社，2016.

［9］ 刘燕萍. 中国护理史上的男护士［J］. 当代护士，2004（2）：13 - 16.

［10］ 孟丰敏. 流翠烟台山［M］. 福州：海峡书局，2016.

［11］ 福州市政协文史资料委员会. 烟台山史话［M］. 福州：海峡书局，2014.

［12］ 郑芳. 看不见的烟台山［M］. 福州：福建人民出版社，2020.

［13］ 周典恩. 近代福建基督教教会医院述略［J］. 厦门广播电视大学学报，2010（1）：84 - 88 + 96.

［14］ 周典恩. 福建新教教会之研究［D］. 福州：福建师范大学，2004.

［15］ 翟昕，罗宝珍. 福州塔亭医院记略［J］. 福建史志，2015（4）：53 - 55.

［16］ 朱永春. 从中国建筑看 1932—1937 年中国建筑思潮及主要趋势［C］.《中国近代建筑研究与保护（二）2000 年中国近代建筑史国际研讨会论文集》，北京：清华大学出版社，2001.

［17］ 董黎. 从折衷主义到复古主义——近代中国教会大学建筑形态的演变［C］.《中国近代建筑研究与保护（二）2000 年中国近代建筑史国际研讨会论文集》，北京：清华大学出版社，2001.

［18］ 陈丹. 太牛了，为了大家这事，福州真拼［EB/OL］.［2022 - 04 - 03］. https://www. 163. com/dy/article/H2RICJ4K0550IMZX. html.

［19］ 陈兆奋，陈建中. 福州版"辛德勒"传奇鼓岭塔亭医院与红十字旗帜下的白衣战士［EB/OL］.［2022 - 02 - 20］. https://www. gospeltimes. cn/index. php/portal/article/index/id/29402.

［20］ 陈兆奋. 百年福州红十字会［EB/OL］.［2022 - 02 - 20］http://blog. sina. com. cn/s/blog _ 71ea653e0101efq5. html.

［21］《福建抗日战争故事 2：塔亭医院》（福建电视台，2011 年 8 月 15 日播出）.

［22］ 福州老建筑百科：塔亭路［EB/OL］．［2022 – 02 – 20］http://www. fzcuo. com/index. php?doc-innerlink –塔亭路．

［23］ 福州老建筑百科：塔亭医院旧址［EB/OL］．［2022 – 02 – 20］http://www. fzcuo. com/index. php?doc-view-1493．

［24］ 福州老建筑百科：马高爱医院［EB/OL］．［2022 – 02 – 20］http://www. fzcuo. com/index. php?doc-view-215. html♯3．

［25］ 福州老建筑百科：林步瀛故居［EB/OL］．［2022 – 02 – 20］http://www. fzcuo. com/index. php?doc-view-78. html．

［26］ Doyle G. Wright: Shanghai Faithful［EB/OL］．［2022 – 03 – 02］https://www. globalchinacenter. org/analysis/shanghai-faithful．

［27］ Guling-Kuliang［EB/OL］．［2022 – 03 – 02］http://www. guling-kuliang. com/．

［28］ Hwa Nan News［EB/OL］．［2022 – 03 – 02］https://divinity-adhoc. library. yale. edu/UnitedBoard/Hwa _ Nan _ College/Box%20177/RG011-177-3212. pdf．

［29］ 潘亮. 发生在福州塔亭医院的沦陷记忆［J］. 闽都文化，2015（5）：76 – 79．

［30］ 王小虎，游庆辉. 刺刀下的白衣天使［N］．［EB/OL］．［2022 – 02 – 20］http://news. sohu. com/20050729/n226491021. shtml．

［31］ 原创：踏着历史的足迹，追寻我国近现代护理的发展历程［EB/OL］．［2022 – 02 – 20］http://med. china. com. cn/content/pid/176942/tid/1026．

［32］ 中西医学发展历史比较［EB/OL］．［2022 – 03 – 25］http://www. cntcm. com. cn/zhuanti/node _ 1580. htm．

［33］ King, A. Hospital Planning: Revised Thoughts on the Origin of the Pavilion Principle in England［J］. *Medical History*，1966，10(4):360 – 373．

［34］ Carlson, E. C. *The Foochow Missionaries, 1847 – 1880*［M］. Cambridge: Harvard University Press, 1974．

［35］ Slate, F. *The Wolfe Sisters of Foochow, China: Born to Evangelise*［M］. // Angela W and Patricia（eds）. Christian Women in Chinese Society: The Anglican Story. Hong Kong: Hong Kong University Press, 2018．

［36］ Lin, B. *The Buildings and Practices of Fukien Construction Bureau* 1916 – 1949：*A Study of Western Missionary Architecture in China and the Preservation of Its Contemporary Legacy*［D］. New York: Columbia University, 2020．

［37］ Medical Reports (for the half-year ended 30th September 1887)［R］. Shanghai: Statistical Department of the Inspectorate General of Customs, 1890(34):3 – 6．

［38］ Pakehham-Walsh, W. S. *Twenty Years in China*［M］. Cambridge: W. Heffer & Sons, Ltd., 1935．

［39］ The Anti-Cobweb Club, Foochow. *Fukien, A Study of a Province in China*［M］. Shanghai: Presbyterian Mission Press, 1925．

［40］ The Foochow Native Hospital and Dispensary Report 1921［R］. Foochow, 1921．

［41］ Thomas Rennie, M. D. *British Medical Journal*［J］. 1912，1（2678）：983．

［42］ Whitney, H. T. Medical Missionary Work in Foochow ［J］. *The China Missionary Medical Journal*, 1889, 3(3):85-90.

● 第二章

［1］ 陈美者. 创我护史，归尔士光——记"中华护士会之母"信宝珠 ［J］. 闽都文化，2016（2）：79-81.

［2］ 牛桂晓. 近代中国基督教会公共卫生运动研究（1901—1937）［D］. 长沙：南师范大学，2019.

［3］ 施德芬. 护病历史大纲 ［M］. 上海：上海广协书局，1946：116-117.

［4］ 洪常青，王屏，伍丽萍，等. 福建现代护理教育的起源与发展 ［J］. 福建教育学院学报，2012，13（4）：75-78.

［5］ Carlson, E. C. *The Foochow Missionaries, 1847-1880* ［M］. Massachusetts: Harvard University Press, 1974.

［6］ Wheeler, M. S. *First Decade of the Woman's Foreign Missionary Society of the Methodist Episcopal Church* ［M］. London: Forgotten Books, 2018.

［7］ Wen, X. Hü King-eng, Chinese Female Doctor in the First Batch of Overseas Returnees ［EB/OL］. ［2021-12-1］ http://chinachristiandaily.com/news/china/2021-05-21/h%C3%BC-king-eng-chinese-female-doctor-in-the-first-batch-of-overseas-returnees_10153.

● 第三章

［1］ 卞军凯，何柏华. 南昌起义战地玫瑰 ［N］. 福建日报，2017-07-31（1）.

［2］ 陈美者. 一代风华——何柏华小记 ［J］. 闽都文化，2015（5）：53-57.

［3］ 福建省地方志编纂委员会. 福建省志·教育志 ［M］. 北京：方志出版社，1998.

［4］ 福建省政协文史资料委员会. 福建文史资料选编. 第五卷. 基督教天主教编 ［M］. 福州：福建人民出版社，2003.

［5］ 林显芳. 福州美以美年会史 ［M］. 福州：美以美会宗教教育部事务所，1936.

［6］ 沈艾娣. 传教士的诅咒：一个华北村庄的全球史（1640—2000）［M］. 郭伟全，译. 香港：香港大学出版社，2021.

［7］ 石建国. 中国共产党福州地方组织志 ［M］. 北京：中国大百科全书出版社，1998.

［8］ 十六中. 麦园里的故事：福州第十六中学建校158周年 ［M］. 2017. 未出版.

［9］ 王尊旺，李颖. 医疗、慈善与明清福建社会 ［M］. 天津：天津古籍出版社，2010.

［10］ 吴巍巍. 近代西方传教士关于中英双语教育的个案——以福州英华书院为个案 ［J］. 福建论坛（社科教育版），2007（12）：46-51.

[11] 杨天宏. 基督教与民国知识分子：1922 年—1927 年中国非基督教运动研究 [M].
北京：人民出版社.

[12] 中共南平市委党史办公室. 南平党史通讯 [G]. 1985，7.

[13] 赵梅. 架起爱与友谊的桥梁——美国家庭收养中国儿童问题研究 [J]. 美国研究，
2019（2）：1-21.

[14] Burton, M. E. *Notable Women of Modern China* [M]. New York: Chicago
Fleming H. Revell Company, 1912.

[15] Carleton, M. S. *My Task* [C]. Forty-Seventh Annual Report of the Foochow
Woman's Conference of the Methodist Episcopal Church for 1931, Foochow,
China, 1931:50-52.

[16] Dunch, R. *Fuzhou Protestants and the Making of Modern China 1857-1927*
[M]. New Haven, Conn.: Yale University Press, 2001.

[17] Ford, E. L. *The History of the Educational Work of the Methodist Episcopal
Church in China: A Study of Its Development and Present Trends* [D]. Evanston,
Illinois: NorthWestern University, 1936.

[18] Lacy, W. N. *A Hundred Years of China Methodism* [M]. Nashville: Abingdon-
Cokesbury Press, 1948.

[19] Maclay, R. S. *Life among the Chinese: With Characteristic Sketches and
Incidents of Missionary Operations and Prospects in China* [M]. New York:
Carlton & Porter, 1861.

[20] McCoy, J. R. *Through the Missionary's Lens: One Woman's Rhetorical Strategies
to Promote China* [D]. Ohio: Graduate College of Bowling Green State
University, 2004.

[21] Methodist Episcopal Church. Woman's Foreign Missionary Society. Fourteenth
Annual Meeting of the Executive Committee of the Woman's Foreign Missionary
Society [J]. *Heathen Woman's Friend*, Dec. 1883:128.

[22] Moran, H. A. *Physical Training in China* [C]. The China Mission Year Book,
Shanghai: Christian Literature Society for China, 1912:356-362.

[23] Robert, D. L. The Methodist Struggle over Higher Education in Fuzhou,
China, 1877-1883 [J]. *Methodist History*, 1996,34(3):173-189.

[24] Sites, S. M. *Nathan Sites: An Epic of the East* [M]. New York: Fleming H.
Revell Company, 1912.

[25] Uberoi, P. Chinese Woman in the Construction of Feminism [J]. *Alternatives:
Global, Local, Political*, 1991,16(4):387-405.

[26] Uk Ing: The Pioneer [C]. Foochow: Christian Herald Missionary Press, 1939.

[27] Wilson, E. W. Foochow Girls' School [C]. Minutes of Foochow Woman
Conference, Foochow, China, 1926:23-24.

[28] Ye, W. Nü Liuxuesheng: The Story of American-Educated Chinese Women,

1880s – 1920s ［J］. *Modern China*，1994，20(3)：315 – 346.

［29］ Board of Missions of the Methodist Episcopal Church，"Mission Photograph Album—China ♯2 page 21，" UMC Digital Galleries［DB/OL］.［2022 – 07 – 05］ https://catalog. gcah. org/omeka/items/show/3359.

［30］ Board of Missions of the Methodist Episcopal Church，"Mission Photograph Album—China ♯11 page 13，" UMC Digital Galleries［DB/OL］.［2022 – 07 – 05］ https://catalog. gcah. org/omeka/items/show/3018.

［31］ Board of Missions of the Methodist Episcopal Church，"Mission Photograph Album—China ♯13 page 42，" UMC Digital Galleries［DB/OL］.［2022 – 07 – 05］ https://catalog. gcah. org/omeka/items/show/5855.

● 第四章

［1］ 林殷. 福州三一学校与民国福建社会［D］. 福州：福建师范大学，2006.

［2］ 葛桂录. 福州烟台山：文化翡翠［M］. 福州：福建人民出版社，2021.

［3］ 史晓洪. 世纪弦歌［Z］. 福州：福外建校100周年纪念册，2007. 未出版.

［4］ 庄才水. 在黄鸿恩艺术与教育研讨会上的发言［Z］. 福州：2021. 未出版.

［5］ 庄才水. 在追梦、铸魂的路上——福州外国语学校初创历程［Z］. 福州：2017. 未出版.

［6］ 刘海峰，庄明水. 福建教育史［M］. 福州：福建教育出版社，1996.

［7］ 施宝霖，秦人. 福建省志·教育志［M］. 北京：方志出版社，1998.

［8］ 陈孝杰. 福州施埔堂（真学书院）市两会资料［Z］. 福州：2019. 未出版.

［9］ 江中美. 记我在三一学校读书时的几件事［M］. 福州：福建人民出版社，2003.

［10］ 福州新闻网. "三一"足球队百岁了 几代校友同场竞技［EB/OL］.［2022 – 07 – 20］http://www. taihainet. com/news/fujian/szjj/2017-10-30/2068549. html.

［11］ 柏涂. 烟台山，竟藏了这么多美好［EB/OL］.［2022 – 03 – 18］http://www. 360doc. com/content/19/1205/16/60762743 _ 877643330. shtml.

［12］ 小鱼网. 朝九晚五上班苦？快来看看百年前的福州白领生活［EB/OL］.［2022 – 04 – 02］https://m. sohu. com/a/251461200 _ 254088.

［13］ 东南网. 各式风貌老洋房若保护好福州烟台山堪比鼓浪屿［EB/OL］.［2022 – 03 – 15］https://www. chinanews. com. cn/house/2013/10-21/5405423. shtml.

［14］ 陈兆奋. 鼓岭上有座其貌不扬的老厝［EB/OL］.［2022 – 03 – 13］http://blog. sina. com. cn/s/blog _ 71ea653e01018lyi. html.

［15］ 盛观熙. 近代来华基督教传教士略传（41）：贝嘉德［EB/OL］.［2022 – 03 – 11］ http://blog. sina. com. cn/s/blog _ 78117d5a0102vuya. html.

［16］ 菖蒲泛舟. 老福州的记忆之陶淑女子学校［EB/OL］.［2022 – 03 – 20］http:// www. 360doc. com/content/19/0724/16/13919421 _ 850766137. shtml.

［17］ 海峡教育报. 文明风·最美校园竞晒｜福州外国语学校：百年福外，献礼祖国

［EB/OL］．［2022－03－08］https://www.sohu.com/a/344263488_673362.

［18］ 福州城事 V. 我骄傲，我们都是福外人！110 个春秋，她是三一学校、是九中……是我们的母校！［EB/OL］．［2022－03－03］https://www.sohu.com/a/200810188_372387.

［19］ 桂杰．谢冕：我一辈子只做文学，文学只做了诗歌［EB/OL］．［2022－03－10］http://news.cyol.com/yuanchuang/2018-10/17/content_17695230.htm.

［20］ 孟繁华．谢冕和他的文学时代［EB/OL］．［2022－03－01］http://www.zuojiawang.com/xinwenkuaibao/49065.html.

［21］ Gemini. 纪念陈景润先生诞辰 85 周年：陈景润妻子、独子的往事回忆［EB/OL］．［2022－03－01］https://www.sohu.com/a/232663615_701814.

［22］ 丁雅诵．中国科学院数学所原研究员陈景润——力摘数论皇冠上的明珠［EB/OL］．［2022－02－01］http://www.xinhuanet.com/politics/2019-09/23/c_1125026367.htm.

［23］ 三明日报．三明印记：《陈景润学籍档案》背后的故事［EB/OL］．［2022－03－06］http://fj.sina.com.cn/news/city/sanming/information/s/2014-04-11/16165687.html.

［24］ 老朱．迎世遗系列·福州古厝——俄国驻福州领事馆官邸［EB/OL］．［2022－03－02］http://www.360doc6.net/wxarticlenew/971699280.html.

［25］ 林春茵．福州外国语学校迎 110 周年校庆［EB/OL］．［2022－02－26］http://mip.news.wmxa.cn/gundong/201710/515257.html.

［26］ 蓝胖子吃．南派足球名将录（七十六）：福建籍国脚，原中国队主力中场李国宁［EB/OL］．［2022－02－06］https://3g.163.com/dy/article/FGMPNNHQ0522L827.html.

［27］ 安梓．特色班揭牌！福州这所学校厉害了！［EB/OL］．［2022－02－03］https://3g.163.com/dy/article/G9MG1RSG0550IMZX.html.

［28］ 福州老建筑百科：三一弄［EB/OL］．［2022－02－20］https://www.fzcuo.com/index.php?doc-view-1095.html.

［29］ 张英英．陈哲人对世界科技的贡献到底是什么［EB/OL］．［2022－02－13］http://www.jmxrgl.com/lwbk/44143753.htm.

［30］ Pakenham-Walsh，W. S. *Twenty Years in China*［M］. Cambridge：W. Heffer & Sons Ltd，1935.

• 第五章

［1］ 仓山区地方志编纂委员会．仓山区志［Z］．福州：福建教育出版社，1994.
［2］ 陈明霞．近代中国教会学校教育研究［M］．北京：人民出版社，2012.
［3］ 陈世明．把天堂建在人间［M］．内部资料，2014.
［4］ 陈毓贤．洪业传［M］．北京：商务印书馆，2013.

［5］ 福建省地方志编纂委员会．福建省志・教育志［Z］．北京：方志出版社，1998．

［6］ 福建省顺昌县委文史资料委员会．英华在洋口（1938—1945）［Z］．未出版．

［7］ 福建省政协文史资料研究会．福建文史资料选编（第五卷）［Z］．福州：福建人民出版社，2003．未出版．

［8］ 福建师范大学附属中学．福建师大附中（1881—1986）［Z］．未出版．

［9］ 福建师大附中校志编委会．八闽之光：福建师范大学附属中学校志［Z］．2001．未出版．

［10］ 福建师范大学附属中学．福建师范大学附属中学名师谱［Z］．未出版．

［11］ 福建师范大学附属中学校友会．校友风采（第一、二、三册）［Z］．未出版．

［12］ 福建师范大学附属中学，福建师大附中校友会．福建师大附中通讯［J］．2021（56）．

［13］ 福建师范大学附属中学校史编写组．福建师范大学附属中学校史［Z］．未出版．

［14］ 福州市英华校友会．尔乃世之光：福州鹤龄英华中学校史［Z］．未出版．

［15］ 福州市英华校友会．陈芝美校长在英华［Z］．未出版．

［16］ 福州市英华中学1943惊涛级友联谊会．双庆专刊［J］．

［17］ 福州市英华校友会．陈景汉先生纪念册［Z］．未出版．

［18］ 李青藻．暮年回首话圆梦［M］．未出版．

［19］ 李挺章（口述），宋葵（撰文）．“英华老校友——李挺章的英华情结”［N］．福建侨报．

［20］ 林金水．福建对外文化交流史［M］．福州：福建教育出版社，1997．

［21］ 林耀华．金翼——一个中国家族的史记［M］．庄孔韶，方静文，译．北京：生活・读书・新知三联书店，2015．

［22］ 刘海峰，庄明水．《福建教育史》［M］．福州：福建教育出版社，1996．

［23］ 英华中学福州校友会．我与英华［Z］．1992．未出版．

［24］ 英华中学一九四五届校友会．《荟蔚通讯》第十三、十五、十八、十九期［J］．

［25］ 游莲．美以美会传教士武林吉研究［D］．福建：福建师范大学，2006．

［26］ Yale Divinity Library Archive，hr167‐1［Z］．1939．

［27］ Yale Divinity Library Archive，hr167‐2［Z］．1899．

［28］ Christian Education in China．1922［Z］．Committee of Reference and Counsel of the Foreign Missions Conference of North America，Inc．

［29］ Dunk，R．F．1996．Piety，Patriotism，Progress：Chinese Protestants in Fuzhou Society and the Making of a Modern China，1857‐1927［D］．Yale University．

［30］ 福建师范大学附属中学官网 https：//sdfz．fjnu．edu．cn/．

［31］ 福州高级中学官网 http：//www．fzgjzx．cn/．

［32］ 福州英华职业学院官网 http：//www．fzacc．com/．

［33］ 王亮．中国式“反叛”：鹤龄英华书院对早年林森的影响——以鹤龄英华书院的课程教育特点为视角［EB/OL］．［2021‐01‐23］．https：//ishare．iask．sina．com．cn/f/1jFMIyqEsX．html．

［34］　鹤龄英华书院［EB/OL］．福州老建筑百科［2021－12－21］．http://www.
　　　　fzcuo. com/index. php?doc-view-2222.

［35］　佚名．寻梦追忆鼓岭行——外国友人走访英华（师大附中）［EB/OL］．中国教育
　　　　在线［2021－01－20］．https://fujian. eol. cn/fujian/201709/t20170925 _
　　　　1556786. shtml.

● 第六章

［1］　仓山区地方志编纂委员会．仓山区志［M］．福州：福建教育出版社，1994.

［2］　陈国华．习近平、洪永世等市领导会见陈景润一行［N］．福州晚报．1991－10－
　　　05（1）．

［3］　福建师范大学附属中学140周年图史编委会．福建师范大学附属中学140年图史
　　　［Z］．2021．未出版．

［4］　福建师范大学附属中学校史编写组．福建师范大学附属中学校史（含原英华中
　　　学，华南女中，陶淑女中）［Z］．2021.

［5］　练仁福．福建师大附中130年校庆院士忙着和"自己"合影［N］．东南网．
　　　2011－10－03

［6］　王永利．人生因追求而壮丽：记张钹院士［J］．中国科技月报，2000（9）：36－
　　　38.

［7］　福建师大附中校志编委会．八闽之光：福建师范大学附属中学校志［Z］．2001.
　　　未出版．

［8］　叶青，叶蓓．回首九十五载漫漫人生路——特级教师陈荫慈访谈录［J］．教育史
　　　研究，2019，1（04）：183－188.

［9］　中国工程院科学道德建设委员会．工程科技的实践者——院士的人生与情怀
　　　［M］．北京：高等教育出版社出版，2010.

［10］　陈荫慈（口述），叶青、叶蓓（整理）．记忆里的陈景润——专访陈景润的中学老
　　　　师陈荫慈老先生［EB/OL］．（2020－09－08）［2022－01－05］．http://www.
　　　　jyb. cn/rmtzcg/xwy/wzxw/202009/t20200908 _ 356827. html.

［11］　福州的东走西看．［2022－03－22］http://blog. sina. com. cn/s/blog _ 6b85a816
　　　　0102y73o. html♯commonComment.

［12］　福州老建筑百科．寻珍女子初级中学教学楼［EB/OL］．［2022－01－05］
　　　　https://www. fzcuo. com/index. php?doc-view-219. html.

［13］　葛帮宁，郭孔辉．汽车动力学开拓者［J/OL］．中国汽车报．（2020－05－05）
　　　　［2022－03－22］．https://www. sohu. com/a/393151086 _ 216791.

［14］　郝静，佟静．追求完美精益求精——专访：中国科学院院士张钹［EB/OL］．胶
　　　　东在线．（2005－11－02）［2022－03－22］http://www. jiaodong. net/2005/11/
　　　　287025. htm.

［15］　何佳媛．同学少年今安在，北峰分校走一回［EB/OL］．福州晚报．（2019－12－

03）［2022 - 03 - 22］https://new. qq. com/omn/20191204/20191204A0AVJ900. html.

［16］ 黄启权. 沈元陈景润师生情［EB/OL］.（2009 - 06）［2022 - 01 - 05］http://www. fjlib. net/zt/fxmr/mrwy/ywys/202010/t20201015 _ 442840. htm.

［17］ 黄松生. 雪泥鸿爪——我在福建师院附中的班主任生涯［EB/OL］. 2010 - 09 - 08［2022 - 01 - 05］https://sdfz. fjnu. edu. cn/7a/53/c14387a293459/page. htm.

［18］ 金青. "桃山成蹊"是我们心中尊师爱校的歌——有关感恩石的说不完的话［EB/OL］. 2012 - 10 - 16［2022 - 01 - 05］https://sdfz. fjnu. edu. cn/79/f4/c14387a293364/page. htm.

［19］ 李青藻. 谈谈我这一辈子——一位老共产党员的人生轨迹［EB/OL］.（2021 - 11 - 29）［2022 - 01 - 05］https://sdfz. fjnu. edu. cn/b6/38/c15180a308792/page. htm.

［20］ 林涛. 记我敬重的两位附中老师［EB/OL］.（2021 - 04 - 15）［2022 - 01 - 05］. https://sdfz. fjnu. edu. cn/79/fc/c14387a293372/page. htm.

［21］ 林正德. 原福建师院竹篷礼堂的记忆［EB/OL］.（2021 - 03 - 01）［2022 - 01 - 05］. https://www. meipian. cn/3fzqpmw0.

［22］ 施焕军. 他还是陈景润的中学数学老师：其实陈景润是特别细心的学生［EB/OL］. 东南快报.（2007 - 07 - 18）［2022 - 03 - 02］. https://news. sina. com. cn/s/2007-07-18/002112221914s. shtml.

［23］ 王锦燧. 我的附中故事——桃花山上的简易阶梯教室［EB/OL］.（2021 - 04 - 08）［2022 - 01 - 05］https://sdfz. fjnu. edu. cn/79/fa/c14387a293370/page. htm.

［24］ 叶令炀. 离开母校五十多年了，你还怀恋母校吗？还记得母校的梯形教室吗？——一个海外游子的乡愁与校愁［EB/OL］.（2021 - 12 - 14）［2022 - 05 - 01］https://sdfz. fjnu. edu. cn/bd/29/c14387a310569/page. htm.

［25］ 原北峰古山里分校将要重建［EB/OL］.（2010 - 10 - 13）［2022 - 05 - 02］https://sdfz. fjnu. edu. cn/4a/a2/c14766a281250/page. htm.

● 第七章

［1］ 彼得·海斯勒. 江城［M］. 上海：上海译文出版社，2012.

［2］ 陈明霞. 近代福建教会学校教育研究［M］. 北京：人民出版社，2012.

［3］ 陈钟英. 余宝笙百年画传［M］. 福州：福建教育出版社，2016.

［4］ 福建省地方志编纂委员会. 福建省志：宗教志［M］. 福州：厦门大学出版社，2014.

［5］ 葛桂录. 福州烟台山：文化翡翠［M］. 福州：福建人民出版社，2021.

［6］ 郭银土. 爱国华侨领袖黄乃裳——中国近代杰出的教育家［N］. 福建日报，2006.

［7］ 华惠德. 华南女子大学［M］. 朱峰，王爱菊，译. 珠海：珠海出版社，2005.

［8］ 黄乃裳. 绂丞七十自序［Z］. 1918. 未出版.

［9］　林耀华. 金翼. 一个中国家族的史记［M］. 北京：生活·读书·新知三联书店，2015.

［10］　林本椿. 一个美国家族的百年福建情［J］. 福建乡土，2014（6）：54-56.

［11］　林本椿. 塔科马访问记［J］. 闽都文化，2019（3）：37-40.

［12］　卢公明. 中国人的社会生活：一个美国传教士的晚清福州见闻录［M］. 陈泽平，译. 福州：福建人民出版社，2009.

［13］　罗伯特·福琼. 两访中国茶乡［M］. 敖雪岗，译. 南京：江苏人民出版社，2015.

［14］　齐上志. "百年风华赤子侨心"气作山河留忠骨——记大湖战役华侨抗日英雄群体［EB/OL］.（2021-03-11）［2022-03-29］https://www.youzikankan.com/index/index/newinfo/id/42164.html.

［15］　马克·克莫雷，温迪科尔. 哈佛非虚构写作课怎样讲好一个故事［M］. 王宇光，译. 北京：中国文史出版社，2015.

［16］　潘丽珍. 伊人宛在——守护精神［D］. 福州：福建师范大学，2008.

［17］　史景迁. 改变中国——在中国的西方顾问［M］. 温洽溢，译. 桂林：广西师范大学出版社，2014.

［18］　史景迁. 康熙与曹寅：一个皇帝宠臣的生涯揭秘［M］. 温洽溢，译. 桂林：广西师范大学出版社，2014.

［19］　唐尚凯. 我意念中的华南. 华南学院校刊：三十五周校庆纪念专号［C］. 南平：华南女子学院，1941.

［20］　汪征鲁. 福建师范大学校史（上篇）［M］. 北京：中国大百科全书出版社，2007.

［21］　威廉·亨特. 天朝拾遗录［M］. 景欣悦，译. 北京：电子工业出版社，2015.

［22］　吴梓明. 基督教大学华人校长研究［M］. 福州：福建教育出版社，2001.

［23］　谢必震. 图说华南女子学院（1908—2008）［M］. 福州：福建教育出版社，2008.

［24］　杨习超. 近代中国教会大学中籍校长角色冲突研究［D］. 苏州：苏州大学，2016.

［25］　岳峰. 春色任天涯［M］. 厦门：厦门大学出版社，2018.

［26］　朱峰. 基督教与近代中国女子高等教育——金陵女大与华南女大比较研究［M］. 福州：福建教育出版社，2002.

［27］　Eschbach, E. S. *The Higher Education of Women in England and America 1862-1920*［M］. New York: Garland Publishing INC, 1993.

［28］　Lewis, I. B. The Education of Girls in China by Teacher College［D］. New York City: Columbia University, 1919.

［29］　Lin, Y. *The Golden Wing—A Sociological Study of Chinese Familism*［M］. London: Kegan Paul, Trench, Trubner & Co., Ltd, 1947.

［30］　Wang, L. *My Call*［C］. Shanghai: Methodist Episcopal Church, 1936.

［31］　Trimble, L. *The Fiftieth Milestone in Retrospect*［Z］. Miss Lydia A. Trimble YDSL（Yale Divinity School Library），UB Archives, Box177, Folder 3217.

[32] Wallace, L. E. *Hwa Nan College: The Women's College of South China* ［M］. New York: United Board for Christian Colleges in Asia, 1956.

[33] Glassburner, M. *Pentecost and Jubilee* ［C］. Lydia Trimble Archives of United Board For Christian Higher Education in Asia, Box177, Folder 3217.

[34] Hessler, P. *River Town* ［M］. Harper Collins e-books, 2001.

[35] Trimble, R. A. *Trimble Boys* ［M］. 2007.

[36] Fortune, R. *Two Visits to the Countries of China and the British Tea Plantations in the Himalaya* ［M］. London: John Murra, Albemarle Street, 1853.

● 第八章

［1］ 耶鲁大学档案（Yale Divinity Library Archive），编号：106 2375 - 6.

［2］ 熊月之. 西学东渐与晚清社会修订版 ［M］. 北京：中国人民大学出版社，2010.

［3］ 翁迈东主编/福建协和大学校友汇编. 福建协和大学史料汇编 ［G］. 福州：福建人民出版社，2016.

［4］ 袁勇麟. 百年协和 ［M］. 福州：福建人民出版社，2013.

［5］ 谢必震. 香飘魏歧村：福建协和大学 ［M］. 石家庄：河北教育出版社，2005.

［6］ 林金水，谢必震. 福建对外文化交流史 ［G］. 福州：福建教育出版社，1997.

［7］ 刘海峰，庄明水. 福建教育史 ［M］. 福州：福建教育出版社，1996.

［8］ 陈明霞. 近代福建教会学校教育研究 ［M］. 北京：人民出版社，2012.

［9］ 黄涛. 大德是钦：记忆深处的福建协和大学 ［D］. 福州：福建师范大学专门史，2007.

［10］ 陈新. 教会大学与近代福建社会 ［D］. 福州：福建师范大学专门史，2008.

［11］ Rodericle Scott. 林景润与福建协和大学 ［J］. 游捷，陈德琼，译. 教育评论，1991（3）.

［12］ 张圣才. 协大旧事 ［J］. 协大校友，1990（4）：11.

［13］ 俞元桂. 邵武读书记 ［J］. 协大校友，1990（4）：6.

［14］ 邓碧玉. 我的心愿 ［J］. 协大校友，1994（9）：12.

［15］ 张尊玄. 追忆母校二三事 ［J］. 协大校友，1997（12）：19 - 20.

［16］ 胡善美. 1944 年李约瑟在邵武协和大学考察 ［J］. 协大校友，2006（25）：3.

［17］ 江由. 母校难忘　恩师难忘 ［J］. 协大校友，2006（26）：51.

［18］ 福建协和大学校友会总会. 学生交纳费用实例 ［J］. 协大校友，2006（26）：30 - 31.

［19］ 福建省人民政府关于公布第八批省级文物保护单位名单和保护范围的通知 ［EB/OL］.（2013 - 01 - 28）［2022 - 03 - 16］http：//zfgb. fujian. gov. cn/3390.

［20］ 福建师范大学校友会. 学校简史——世纪回眸 1 ［G/OL］.（2021 - 10 - 14）［2022 - 03 - 20］https://xyzh. fjnu. edu. cn/9e/62/c13936a302690/page. htm.

［21］ 福建师范大学校友会. 学校简史——世纪回眸 2 ［G/OL］.（2021 - 10 - 14）

［2022－03－20］https://xyzh.fjnu.edu.cn/9e/61/c13936a302689/page.htm.

● 第九章

［1］ 边晓丽．福州早期教会学校研究（1847—1900）［D］．福州：福建师范大学，2011．

［2］ 陈孝杰．福州施埔堂［Z］．2019．

［3］ 陈振华．福建协和神学院始末［M］．//福州基督教三自爱国运动委员会文史资料工作组福州基督教文史资料选辑第一辑，1987：70．

［4］ 陈忠钦，谢东楼．美以美会福州义塾史略［M］．//福建省政协文史资料委员会文史资料选编（第五卷）．福州：福建人民出版社，2003：530．

［5］ 段琦．中国基督教本色化史稿［M］．台北：宇宙光全人关怀机构，2005．

［6］ 福建神学院建院30周年纪念册编委会．福建神学院建院30周年纪念册［Z］．2013．未出版．

［7］ 福建省地方志编纂委员会．福建省志·宗教志下册［M］．厦门：厦门大学出版社，2014．

［8］ 福建省政协文史资料委员会．文史资料选编第五卷"基督教天主教篇"［M］．福州：福建人民出版社，2003．

［9］ 福州市仓山区地方志编纂委员会．仓山区志：1990—2005［M］．北京：方志出版社，2017．

［10］ 福州市政协文史资料委员会．鼓岭史话［M］．福州：海峡出版发行集团，2012．

［11］ 福州市宗教志编纂委员会．福州市宗教志［M］．福州：福建人民出版社，2000．

［12］ 郭荣刚．西方倪柝声之研究（1972—2006）［D］．福州：福建师范大学，2014．

［13］ 何绵山．福建宗教文化［M］．天津：天津社会科学院出版社，2004．

［14］ 黄仰英．饮水思源［M］．新加坡：新马出版印刷（彩印）公司，1972．

［15］ 柯乐益，林有书．福州协和道学院［M］．//中华续行委办会中华基督教会年鉴，上海：商务印书馆，1916．

［16］ 李少明．近代福建基督教宣教活动特点［J］．世界宗教文化，2006（4）：25－28．

［17］ 林超群．思考与实践并行努力推进基督教中国化进程基督教中国化研讨交流会暨基督教中国化原创圣乐优秀作品专辑首发式侧记［J］．中国宗教，2018（6）：58－59．

［18］ 林键．近代福州基督教神学教育事工的创始与发展［J］．金陵神学志，2012（Z1）：228－244．

［19］ 林金水．福建对外文化交流史［M］．福州：福建教育出版社，1997．

［20］ 林金水，郭荣刚．基督教中国化研究初探［M］．台北：以琳出版社，2014．

［21］ 林立强．美国传教士卢公明与晚清福建社会［D］．福州：福建师范大学，2004．

［22］ 林显芳，等．福州美以美年会史［M］．福州：美以美会宗教教育部事务所，1936．

［23］ 司徒雷登．中国教牧，载自中国差会年鉴［M］．1923．

［24］ 图片编辑委员会．难忘的历程［M］．福建省基督教三自爱国运动委员会，福建省基督教协会：2001．

［25］ 谢承平，关瑞明．福州圣约翰堂的建筑特征及其文物价值［J］．先锋论坛，2012：5－9．

［26］ 徐以骅．教会大学与神学教育［M］．福州：福建教育出版社，1999．

［27］ 杨洁．倪柝声神学人论研究［D］．济南：山东大学，2017．

［28］ 岳峰，兰春寿，李启辉．福州烟台山：文化翡翠［M］．福州：福建人民出版社，2021．

［29］ 岳清华．荣神益人创建和谐花巷堂［J］．中国宗教，2011（4）：70－72．

［30］ 张金红．胡约翰与福建安立甘会研究1862—191［D］．福州：福建师范大学，2007．

［31］ 查时杰．中国基督教人物小传（上）［M］．台北：中华福音神学院出版社，1983．

［32］ 张永广．改革开放以来中国基督教会对外交流活动述评［J］．世界宗教研究，2015（2）：173－181．

［33］ 郑瑞荣．榕城格致书院：福州私立格致中学简史［M］．福州：榕城格致书院出版社，1995．

［34］ 郑怡玲．倪柝声的重生观研究［D］．上海：上海师范大学，2020．

［35］ 《中国基督教年鉴》编委会．中国基督教年鉴第5卷［M］．北京：国家图书馆出版社，2013．

［36］ 《中国基督教年鉴》编委会．中国基督教年鉴［M］．北京：国家图书馆出版社，2012．

［37］ 仲伟民．茶叶与鸦片：十九世纪经济全球化中的中国［M］．北京：生活・读书・新知三联书店，2010．

［38］ Carlson，E. C. *The Foochow Missionaries，1847 － 1880*［M］．Cambridge：Harvard University Press，1974．

［39］ Lacy，G. C. *The Story of the Foochow Foreign Cemeteries*［Z］．1951．

［40］ Doolittle，J. *Social Life of the Chinese，Volume II*［M］．New York：Harper & Brothers，1865．

［41］ Doolittle，J. *The Diary of Justus Doolittle*［Z］．Hamilton College 转引自林立强．卢公明与福州基督教教育的发端［J］．教育评论，2005（6）：89．

［42］ Maclay，R. S. *Life among the Chinese: With Characteristic Sketches and Incidents of Missionary Operations and Prospects in China*［M］．New York：Carlton & Porter，1861．

［43］ Nanjing Theological Review［金陵神学志］．南京：2012年Z1期．

［44］ Salisbury Square，K. C. *For Christ in Fuh-Kien*［M］．4th ed. London：The Church Missionary Society，1904．

［45］ Geil，W. E. *Eighteen Capitals of China*［M］．Philadelphia & London：J. B.

Lippincott Company，1911.

[46] Wiley，J. W. *The Mission Cemetery and the Fallen Missionaries of Fuh Chau，China* [M]. New York：Carlton & Porter，1958.

[47] Wolfe，J. R. 给 Henry Wright 的信件 [L]. CMS/B/0MS/CCH/092/44，1873. 转引自张金红. 胡约翰与福建安立甘会研究 1862—1915 [D]. 福州：福建师范大学，2007.

[48] Wolf，J. R. For Christ in Fuh-Kien [M]. Wertheimer，LRA&CO.，1904.

[49] Yale Divinity School Archive，R8b221f1 [Z]. 1947.

[50] 玉林山馆 [DB/OL]. [2022 - 07 - 03] http://www.fzcuo.com/index.php?docview-829.html = .

• 第十章

[1] 陈长城. 协大学生在邵武 [J]. 协大周刊，1938，1（4）：7 - 8.

[2] 陈林. 近代基督教图书出版事业之研究（1842—1849）[D]. 福州：福建师范大学，2006.

[3] 陈林. 福建教会大学出版活动探析——以福建协和大学为例 [J]. 福建师范大学校报，2006（6）：190 - 196.

[4] 方汉奇. 中国近代报刊史（上）[M]. 太原：山西人民出版社，1981.

[5] 方汉奇. 中国新闻事业通史（第 1 卷）[M]. 北京：中国人民大学出版社，1992.

[6] 福州老建筑百科. 美华书局旧址 [EB/OL]. [2022 - 04 - 05] http://www.fzcuo.com/index.php?edition-view-2330-8.html.

[7] 黄乃裳. 福州宜设报馆说 [N]. 福报，1896 - 04 - 28，1896 - 05 - 01.

[8] 教务杂志 [DB/OL]. [2022 - 05 - 04] https://hdl.handle.net/2027/uc1.b3079816.

[9] 林金水. 福建对外文化交流史 [M]. 福州：福建教育出版社，1997.

[10] 林金水，吴巍巍. 传教士工具书文化传播——从《英华萃林韵府》看晚清"西学东渐"与"中学西传"的交汇 [J]. 福建师范大学学报，2008（3）：126 - 132.

[11] 林立强. 美国传教士卢公明与晚清福州社会 [M]. 福州：福建教育出版社，2005.

[12] 林其锬. 黄乃裳和他创办的《福报》[J]. 文献，1987（1）：112 - 125.

[13] 罗德里克·斯科特. 福建协和大学 [M]. 陈建明，姜源，译. 珠海：珠海出版社，1999.

[14] 倪柝声. 倪柝声文集（第一辑）[M]. 台北：台湾福音书房，1993.

[15] 陶飞亚. 传教运动的圈内"声音"：The Chinese Recorder（1867—1941）初论 [A]. 张先清（编）. 史料与视界：中文文献与中国基督教史研究. 上海：上海人民出版社，2007：244 - 262.

[16] 王植伦. 福州新闻志·报业志 [M]. 福州：福建人民出版社，1997.

［17］　吴国安，钟健英．近代福建协和大学的报刊活动及其文化贡献［J］．党史研究与教学，1990（4）：49－58.

［18］　谢必震．香飘魁岐村——福建协和大学［M］．石家庄：河北教育出版社，2004.

［19］　徐斌．从《闽省会报》的报道看刘铭传台湾建省［A］．福建师范大学闽台区域研究中心．闽台区域研究论丛（第六辑）．北京：中国环境科学出版社，2008.

［20］　张雪峰．福建近代出版业的兴衰［D］．福州：福建师范大学，2004.

［21］　张雪峰．晚清时期传教士在福建的出版活动［J］．出版史料，2005（1）：113－119.

［22］　赵广军．近代闽方言罗马字母字出版与基督教会扫盲运动之研究［J］．基督宗教研究，2005（17）：329－361.

［23］　赵晓兰，吴潮．传教士中文报刊史［M］．上海：复旦大学出版社，2011.

［24］　政协福州市仓山区文史资料委员会．仓山文史（第六辑）［Z］．1991.

［25］　ANDERSON, B. *Imagined Communities: Reflections on the Origin and Spread of Nationalism*［M］. London：Verso，1983.

［26］　BALDWIN, S. L. ed. The Chinese Recorder and Missionary Journal［DB/OL］. Vol. 1，May，1868［2022－05－13］. https://babel. hathitrust. org/cgi/pt?id = uc1. b3079816&view = 1up&seq = 7&skin = 2021.

［27］　Official Minutes of the Nineteenth Session of the Methodist Episcopal Church［C］. Foochow：Methodist Episcopal Mission Press，1895.

［28］　Baldwin, C. C. Manual of the Foochow Dialect. Foochow：Methodist Episcopal Mission Press，1871. seq. 7，8，15［2022－05－20］. https://nrs. lib. harvard. edu/urn-3：fhcl：32423456.

［29］　Board of Missions of the Methodist Episcopal Church, "Mission Photograph Album—China ♯4 page 0102," UMC Digital Galleries［DB/OL］.［2022－06－13］. https://catalog. gcah. org/omeka/items/show/3874.

［30］　Board of Missions of the Methodist Episcopal Church, "Mission Photograph Album—China ♯1 page 0126," UMC Digital Galleries［DB/OL］.［2022－06－07］. https://catalog. gcah. org/omeka/items/show/3257.

［31］　Carlson, E. C. The Foochow Missionaries, 1847－1880［M］. Cambridge：Harvard University Press，1974.

［32］　Doolittle, J. Quan shan liang yan Fuzhou ping hua［DB/OL］. Fuzhou：Yabisi xi mei zong hui juan，1856. seq. 5，27，43，157［2022－05－19］. https://nrs. lib. harvard. edu/urn-3：fhcl：32823941.

［33］　Doolittle, J. Xing shi liang gui［DB/OL］. Fuzhou：Yabisi xi mei zong hui juan，1856. seq. 22，23［2022－05－20］. https://nrs. lib. harvard. edu/urn-3：fhcl：30885370.

［34］　Fuzhou Mei Hua Shu Ju. Min sheng hui bao［DB/OL］. Fuzhou：Mei hua shu ju，1875，seq. 3［2022－05－19］. https://nrs. lib. harvard. edu/urn-3：fhcl：

32304518.

[35] Fuzhou Mei Hua Shu Ju. Min sheng hui bao [DB/OL]. Fuzhou: Mei hua shu ju, 1880，seq. 3 [2022 - 05 - 19]. https://nrs. lib. harvard. edu/urn-3: fhcl: 32304583.

[36] Hartwell, C. San zi jing [DB/OL]. Fuzhou: Min bei sheng shu hui yin fa, 1913. seq. 5 [2022 - 05 - 19]. https://nrs. lib. harvard. edu/urn-3: fhcl: 30888227.

[37] Jie yan xing shi tu [DB/OL]. Fuzhou: Min bei sheng shu hui yin fa, 1900, seq. 2 [2022 - 05 - 20]. https://nrs. lib. harvard. edu/urn-3: fhcl: 32079551.

[38] Matai fu yin [DB/OL]. Fuzhou，1851 [2022 - 05 - 20]. https://nrs. lib. harvard. edu/urn-3: fhcl: 32722959.

[39] Meyer，F. B. 牧长诗歌：榕腔 [DB/OL]. 福州：闽北圣书会，1900，seq. 5 [2022 - 05 - 20]. https://nrs. lib. harvard. edu/urn-3: fhcl: 30431993.

[40] Milne，W. You xue qian jie wen da [DB/OL]. Fuzhou: Yu suo, 1848. seq. 1 [2022 - 05 - 19]. https://nrs. lib. harvard. edu/urn-3: fhcl: 32814547.

[41] Whitney，H. T. Xing shen qian shuo [DB/OL]. Minbei: Sheng shu hui, 1905, seq. 1 [2022 - 05 - 20]. https://nrs. lib. harvard. edu/urn-3: fhcl: 32090632.

[42] Wilcox，M. C. Hua mei bao [DB/OL]. Fuzhou: Mei hua shu ju kan fa, 1897, seq. 1 [2022 - 05 - 20]. https://nrs. lib. harvard. edu/urn-3: fhcl: 32305660.

后 记

　　本书是福建师范大学外国语学院师生集体创作的结晶。分工如下：岳峰设计、编排、审读全书，提供耶鲁大学档案。章琳为本课题负责人，参与策划、审读与思政检查。葛桂录是福建历史文化外译丛书总主编，为本书撰写总序。编委会从不同的角度促成了本书的完成。

　　第一章由洪梅完成。第二章由福建技术师范学院徐勤良完成。第三章由李巧兰完成。第四章由陈琳完成。第五章由廖秋玲完成。第六章由林斌完成。第七章由赖黎群完成。第八章由黄丹青完成。第九章由林丽玲完成。第十章由李秀香完成。陈榕烽翻译序言。

　　仓山区委宣传部倪美飞副部长三改书稿，为意识形态把关。福建师范大学林金水教授指导了本书的宗教研究方面的问题，戴显群教授指导了地方史方面的问题。协助翻译、编排、摄像的师生还有协和学院周秦超，香港大学叶张鹏，福州外语外贸学院林风博士，福建师范大学陈泽予、梁书尧、何宇喆、刘可欣、黄婉玲、刘枫等。

　　本书的编写得到福建省财政厅与中共福州市仓山区委宣传部的资助，特此致谢！